Ganzha · Mayr · Vorozhtsov (Eds.)
Computer Algebra in Scientific Computing

Springer
Berlin
Heidelberg
New York
Barcelona
Hong Kong
London
Milan
Paris
Singapore
Tokyo

Victor G. Ganzha   Ernst W. Mayr
Evgenii V. Vorozhtsov (Eds.)

Computer Algebra in Scientific Computing

CASC '99

Proceedings of the Second Workshop on
Computer Algebra in Scientific Computing,
Munich, May 31 – June 4, 1999

 Springer

Editors

Victor G. Ganzha
Ernst W. Mayr
Institut für Informatik
Technische Universität
D-80290 München, Germany

Evgenii V. Vorozhtsov
Institute of Theoretical and Applied Mathematics
Russian Academy of Sciences
Novosibirsk 630090, Russia

Mathematics Subject Classification (1991): 68Q40, 65M06, 13P10, 12Y05, 34A25, 20C40, 34D20, 68T35

Cataloging-in-Publication Data applied for
Die Deutsche Bibliothek – CIP-Einheitsaufnahme

Computer algebra in scientific computing / CASC '99, Proceedings of the Second Workshop on Computer Algebra
in Scientific Computing, Munich, May 31 – June 4, 1999. V. G. Ganzha... (ed.). – Berlin; Heidelberg; New York; Barcelona;
Hong Kong; London; Paris; Singapore; Tokyo: Springer, 1999
ISBN-13:978-3-642-64309-5

ISBN-13:978-3-642-64309-5   e-ISBN-13:978-3-642-60218-4
DOI: 10.1007/978-3-642-60218-4

ISBN-13:978-3-642-64309-5

© Springer-Verlag Berlin Heidelberg 1999
Softcover reprint of the hardcover 1st edition 1999

The use of general descriptive names, registered names, trademarks, etc. in this publication does not
imply, even in the absence of a specific statement, that such names are exempt from the relevant protec-
tive laws and regulations and therefore free for general use.

Typesetting by the authors using a Springer TEX Macro Package
Computer to film: Weihert-Druck, Darmstadt
Cover design: *design & production* GmbH, Heidelberg

SPIN 10731807   46/3143 – 5 4 3 2 1 0 – Printed on acid-free paper

Preface

The development of powerful computer algebra systems has considerably extended the scope of problems of scientific computing which can now be solved successfully with the aid of computers. However, as the field of applications of computer algebra in scientific computing becomes broader and more complex, there is a danger of separation between theory, systems, and applications. For this reason, we felt the need to bring together the researchers who now apply the tools of computer algebra for the solution of problems in scientific computing, in order to foster new and closer interactions.

CASC'99 is the second conference devoted to applications of computer algebra in scientific computing. The first conference in this sequence, CASC'98, was held 20–24 April 1998 in St. Petersburg, Russia.

This volume contains revised versions of the papers submitted by the participants and accepted by the program committee after a thorough reviewing process. The collection of papers included in the proceedings covers various topics of computer algebra methods, algorithms and software applied to scientific computing: symbolic-numeric analysis and solving differential equations, efficient computations with polynomials, groups, matrices and other related objects, special purpose programming environments, application to physics, mechanics, optics and to other areas.

In particular, a significant group of papers deals with applications of computer algebra methods for the solution of current problems in group theory, which mostly arise in mathematical physics.

Another important trend which may be seen from the present collection of papers, is the application of computer algebra methods to the development of new efficient analytic and numerical solvers, both for ordinary and partial differential equations.

A number of papers deals with algorithmic and software aspects associated with the implementation of computer algebra methods. Other papers study the stability of satellite and mechanical systems, or the application of computer algebra to the solution of problems in technology (e.g., aerodynamics).

In addition to the accepted submissions, this proceedings volume also includes two invited papers. In the paper by W. Seiler (University of Mannheim) various indices used for numerical analysis of differential algebraic equations are studied and geometrically interpreted within the framework of the formal theory of differential equations. This provides, in particular, the theoretical estimation of the indices in view of completion of differential systems to involution which is the key concept of the formal theory.

The paper by G. Gonnet (ETH Zürich) deals with the problem how to generate many fix-point iterators of the form $x_{i+1} = F(x_i)$ in order to solve a given non-linear equation. Such methods are suitable only for computer algebra systems where the equations to be solved can be manipulated in symbolic form.

The CASC'99 workshop was supported financially by a generous grant from the Deutsche Forschungsgemeinschaft (DFG) and ADDITIVE GmbH. We are grateful to M. Mnuk for his technical help in the preparation of the camera ready manuscript for this volume. We also thank the people at Springer Verlag for their support in preparing these proceedings, and the Bildungsstätte des Bayerischen Bauernverbandes in Herrsching for hosting the workshop.

Munich, April 1999

V.G. Ganzha
E.W. Mayr
E.V. Vorozhtsov

Workshop Organization

Workshop Chairs

Vladimir Gerdt, JINR, Dubna, Russia
Ernst W. Mayr, TU München, Germany

Program Committee Chairs

Victor Ganzha, TU München, Germany
Evgenii Vorozhtsov, ITAM, Novosibirsk, Russia

Program Committee

Victor Edneral, Moscow State University, Moscow, Russia
Marc Gaetano, INRIA, Sophia, France
Richard Liska, Czech Technical University in Prague, Czech Republic
Roman Maeder, MathConsult, Wollerau, Switzerland
Yuri Matiyasevich, EIMI, St. Petersburg, Russia
Stanly Steinberg, University of New Mexico, Albuquerque, USA
Nikolay Vassiliev, EIMI, St. Petersburg, Russia
Paul Wang, Kent State University, Kent, USA
Volker Weispfenning, Universität Passau, Passau, Germany
Christoph Zenger, TU München, Germany

Local Organizing Committee

Victor Ganzha, TU München, Germany
Herbert Fischer, TU München, Germany
Ernst W. Mayr, TU München, Germany - chair
Michal Mnuk, TU München, Germany - secretary

Table of Contents

x

Solution of Ordinary Differential Equations with *MathLie*

Method of Canonical Variables

Gerd Baumann

Department of Mathematical Physics
University of Ulm
D-89069 Ulm,
Germany
e-mail: Gerd.Baumann@physik.uni-ulm.de

Abstract. This article discusses Lie's method of canonical variables to solve ordinary differential equations. The method of canonical variables is based on point symmetries and allows to construct transformations which simplify the equation prior to its solution. The method of canonical variables is closely related to the methods of first integrals and the method of first order partial differential equations. We discuss the necessary tools, the skeleton and the class of solution, providing the solution in connection with computer algebra. The procedure of canonical variables is algorithmic and implemented in *MathLie*. We demonstrate the application of the method on first- and second-order ordinary differential equations.

1 Introduction

Lie pointed out that the introduction of suitable variables will drastically simplify the representation of a group. This paper discusses how these transformations follow from the symmetries of the equation. Especially, we discuss canonical transformations allowing us to simplify the representation of an ordinary differential equation (ODE). Given a symmetry group, one can calculate canonical transformations. Allowing us to integrate first order ODEs or reducing the order of higher order ODEs. Moreover if a second-order equation admits a two-dimensional symmetry group, then instead of consecutive reduction of order, we can directly make a change of variables in which the equation is integrable. Lie called this change of variables the method of canonical variables.

Our aim here is to present a method to integrate ODEs extending the method of first integrals [1]. However both methods are based on symmetries of an ODE. The symmetries of the ODE allow to derive solutions from the equation in an algorithmic way. The basis of the present method is the change of independent and dependent variables in such a way that the symmetries of the equation remain the same. We discuss a procedure how these transformations are derived from the symmetries if the infinitesimals are known. Knowing the symmetry transformations of the ODE, we are able to simplify the original ODE in such a way that the solution follows by a quadrature.

The procedure of canonical variables is well known in literature [2,3,4]. However, it is rarely used in computer algebra programs. The reason for this refusal is the necessity to know the symmetries prior to the application of the method. Up to the present day there are only few programs allowing the automatic determination of symmetries [5,6,7]. A recent review of these programs is contained in [4]. Among the programs in Maple, Reduce, Axiom, and *Mathematica, MathLie* is capable to find completely automatic the symmetries of an ODE independent of the order of the equation. *MathLie* is the first program applying Lie's theory of canonical variables to any kind of ODEs to uncover solutions. Contrary to the program of Cheb-Terrab et al [8], we do not use an ansatz or heuristics to integrate ODEs. The routines of *MathLie* use the algorithmic steps introduced by Lie. We will demonstrate that a suited combination of these steps yield analytic solutions. However, if the single steps are applied independently from each other an integration may fail.

The paper is organized as follows: In section 2 we describe the theoretical background of the method. Section 3 introduces some basic terms for ODEs and applies these definitions to first-order equations. In section 4, we discuss an algorithm for second order equations based on canonical variables. The last section gives a summary of the results.

2 Canonical Variables

Let us first define the term canonical variables. Today the term canonical variables is used in different connections. We know from classical mechanics that canonical variables are variables which naturally describe a system in a simple and logic way. This kind of definition is also the basis of the definition given by Lie [2,3]. Lie denotes a set of variables as canonical if the equation simplify and allow an integration by quadrature. To be more specific let us examine a set of transformations consisting of two generators v_1 and v_2.

Two infinitesimal transformations v_1 and v_2 are independent from each other if the following relations do not exist

$$v_1 = cv_2 \tag{1}$$

where c is a constant, and

$$(v_1, v_2) = c_1 v_1 + c_2 v_2 \tag{2}$$

where c_1 and c_2 are also constants. The second relation can be simplified by assuming that the two independent transformations can be used to represent the product in a different way. If we assume that c_1 and c_2 are equal to zero, we find

$$(v_1, v_2) = 0. \tag{3}$$

On the other hand, we can assume that the infinitesimal transformations are given by a linear combination of v_1 and v_2 which changes (3) to

$$(a_1 v_1 + a_2 v_2, b_1 v_1 + b_2 v_2) = 0 \tag{4}$$

where a_i and b_i, $i = 1, 2$ are constants. In the cases above the group is represented by commuting infinitesimal transformations. If for example $c_1 \neq 0$, we represent the two infinitesimal transformations by

$$\bar{v}_1 = v_1 + \frac{c_2}{c_1} v_2 \tag{5}$$

and

$$\bar{v}_2 = \frac{1}{c_1} v_2. \tag{6}$$

Using relation (6), we can rewrite the above condition by

$$(\bar{v}_1, \bar{v}_2) = \frac{1}{c_1}(v_1, v_2) + \frac{c_2}{c_1}(v_1, v_2) = \frac{1}{c_1}(c_1 v_1 + c_2 v_2) = \bar{v}_1. \tag{7}$$

From (1)-(7) the following theorem follows

Theorem 1. (Canonical variables) *Each two-dimensional group of infinitesimal transformations v_1 and v_2 can be used to represent the product of the two transformations in each of the following forms*

$$(v_1, v_2) = 0 \tag{8}$$

or

$$(v_1, v_2) = v_1. \tag{9}$$

Each of the two results is independent from the other.

This theorem divides the two dimensional groups in two classes. Each of these two classes can be divided into two subclasses. Knowing the basic properties of two-dimensional algebras [1] allows us to define canonical variables.

Definition 2. (Canonical variable) Every one-parameter group of transformations reduces to the group of translations $\bar{t} = t + \epsilon$, $W = w$, with the vector field

$$v = \partial_t \tag{10}$$

by a suitable change of variables $t = t(x, u)$, $w = w(x, u)$. The variables t and w are canonical variables.

The motivation of this definition follows from the fact that the tangent vector field in the original variables transforms according to

$$v = vt\partial_t + vw\partial_w. \tag{11}$$

In other words canonical variables follow from the solution of linear partial differential equations.

$canonical Equations = \{\xi[x, u]\ \partial_x t[x, u]+$
$\phi[x, u]\ \partial_u t[x, u] == 1,$
$\xi[x, u]\ \partial_x w[x, u] + \phi[x, u]\ \partial_u w[x, u] == 0\};$
canonicalEquations // LTF

$$-1 + \phi\ t_u + \xi\ t_x == 0$$
$$\phi\ w_u + \xi\ w_x == 0$$

These equations follow from the definition of canonical variables by applying the tangent vector $\bar{v}$ to the canonical variables t and w

$$vt = 1 \tag{12}$$
$$vw = 0. \tag{13}$$

To be more specific let us discuss some examples showing the application of the definition.

Example 1. The first example considers the important scaling symmetry. A scaling symmetry is represented by the following infinitesimal symmetry

$veccan = \{\xi \rightarrow \text{Function}[\{x, u\}, x],$
$\phi \rightarrow \text{Function}[\{x, u\}, -u]\}; veccan\ // \text{LTF}$

$$\xi == x$$
$$\phi == -u$$

where ξ and ϕ denote the infinitesimals of the symmetry. The scaling symmetry stretches the x -coordinate by a factor 1 and the u -coordinate by a factor -1. Inserting the infinitesimals into the defining equations (12) and (13), we can reduce them to

$caneq = canonical Equations/.veccan;\ caneq\ // \text{LTF}$

$$-1 - u\ t_u + x\ t_x == 0$$
$$-u\ w_u + x\ w_x == 0$$

These two linear partial differential equations of first order are potential candidates for the partial differential solver DSolve[] of *Mathematica.* DSolve[]

in its extended form is capable to handle first order equations. The solution for t follows by

$$solc1 = \text{DSolve}[caneq[[1]], t[x, u], \{x, u\}]$$

$$\{\{t[x, u] \to \log[x] + C[1][u\ x]\}\}$$

representing one solution of the PDEs. We note that the solution contains an arbitrary function C[1] depending on the product of the two variables x and u. The second solution for w follows if we solve

$$solc2 = \text{DSolve}[caneq[[2]], w[x, u], \{x, u\}]$$

$$\{\{w[x, u] \to C[1][u\ x]\}\}$$

The second solution again contains an arbitrary function C[1] which is different from the first solution, however depending on the product $x\ u$. The result is that t depends logarithmically on x and allows an arbitrary function C[1] combining the two variables x and u by a product. The second canonical variable w is also given by a second arbitrary function combining x and u by a product. Lie pointed out that it is sufficient to know only a special solution of the first order PDEs. Thus we are free to choose the arbitrary function in the simplest way. In the solution for t, we set C[1] equal to zero. For w we use the argument $x\ u$ to represent the solution and thus omit trivial cases.

$$r1 = C[1][u\ x] \to x\ u$$

$$C[1][u\ x] \to u\ x$$

The general solutions derived by DSolve[] reduces thus to

$$csol = \textbf{Flatten}[\{solc1/.\ \textbf{C}[1][x\ u] \to 0,$$
$$solc2/.r1\}]$$

$$\{t[x, u] \to \log[x], w[x, u] \to u\ x\}$$

In fact these two rules contain a representation of the canonical variables for scaling symmetries. A little manipulation in *Mathematica* creating pure functions allows a proper application of the rules.

$$r2 = \textbf{Thread}[\{t, w\} \to$$
$$(\textbf{Function}[\{x, u\}, \#1]\&)/@(\{t[x, u],$$
$$w[x, u]\}/.csol)]$$

$$\{t \to \text{Function}[\{x, u\}, \log[x]], w \to \text{Function}[\{x, u\}, u\ x]\}$$

Example 2. A second example is concerned with the group of rotation. For this symmetry group the infinitesimals are

$$veccan = \{\xi \rightarrow \text{Function}[\{x, u\}, -u],$$
$$\phi \rightarrow \text{Function}[\{x, u\}, x]\}; veccan \,//\, \text{LTF}$$

$$\xi == -u$$
$$\phi == x$$

The equations determining the canonical variables read

$$caneq = canonicalEquations /.veccan; caneq \,//\, \text{LTF}$$

$$-1 + x\, t_u - u\, t_x == 0$$
$$x\, w_u - u\, w_x == 0$$

The solution for the canonical variable t is calculated by

$$solct = \text{DSolve}[caneq[[1]], t[x, u], \{x, u\}]$$

$$\left\{\left\{t[x, u] \rightarrow -\arctan\left[\tfrac{x}{\sqrt{u^2}}\right] + C[1]\left[\tfrac{1}{2}\left(-u^2 - x^2\right)\right]\right\},\right.$$
$$\left.\left\{t[x, u] \rightarrow \arctan\left[\tfrac{x}{\sqrt{u^2}}\right] + C[1]\left[\tfrac{1}{2}\left(-u^2 - x^2\right)\right]\right\}\right\}$$

The dependent canonical variable w is determined by

$$solcw = \text{DSolve}[caneq[[2]], w[x, u], \{x, u\}]$$

$$\left\{\left\{w[x, u] \rightarrow C[1]\left[-\frac{u^2}{2} - \frac{x^2}{2}\right]\right\}\right\}$$

Again we are only interested in a special solution of the first-order PDEs. However, DSolve[] delivers the most general solution. So we have to reduce the general solutions in an appropriate way. We set the arbitrary function in the solution for t equal to zero

$$solct = \text{PowerExpand}[solct[[2]] /. C[1][\_] \rightarrow 0]$$

$$\left\{t[x, u] \rightarrow \arctan\left[\frac{x}{u}\right]\right\}$$

The nontrivial solution for w is extracted by the rule

$$solcw = \text{Flatten}[solcw /. C[1][x\_] \rightarrow x]$$

$$\left\{w[x, u] \rightarrow -\frac{u^2}{2} - \frac{x^2}{2}\right\}$$

The complete solution of the canonical variables are thus

$$r3 = \textbf{Thread}[\{t, w\} \rightarrow$$
$$(\textbf{Function}[\{x, u\}, \#1]\&)/@(\{t[x, u],$$
$$w[x, u]\}/.\{solct[[1]], solcw[[1]]\})]$$

$$\{t \rightarrow \text{Function}\left[\{x, u\}, \arctan\left[\tfrac{x}{u}\right]\right],$$
$$w \rightarrow \text{Function}\left[\{x, u\}, -\tfrac{u^2}{2} - \tfrac{x^2}{2}\right]\}$$

The canonical variables of the group of rotation are given by the *ArcTan* and a circle. We note that the second variable w is an invariant of the symmetry.

The calculations so far carried out interactively are algorithmic and thus can be collected in a function, called CanonicalVariables[]. This function needs as input the dependent and independent variables of the original co-ordinates. The function also needs the infinitesimals of the related ODE. The last two arguments contain lists of the target variables. The function CanonicalVariables[] calculates the general transformation using the first order partial differential equations defining the determining equations of the canonical variables. The function is designed in such a way to incorporate the general case of an arbitrary number of variables. The result of the function CanonicalVariables[] is a list of canonical transformations represented in a pure function form.

The examples below demonstrate the application of the function Canon-icalVariables[] to different symmetry groups. Let us examine an inhomogeneous scaling group with scaling factors b and a for the two variables u and x, respectively. The names of the target variables are w and t.

$$\textbf{CanonicalVariables}[\{u\}, \{x\}, \{a\ x\},$$
$$\{b\ u\}, \{w\}, \{t\}]$$

$$\{w \rightarrow \text{Function}\left[\{x, u\}, u\ x^{-\frac{b}{a}}\right], t \rightarrow \text{Function}\left[\{x, u\}, \frac{\log[x]}{a}\right]\}$$

The result is a generalization of the result stated above for the special scaling symmetry $(\xi, \phi) = (x, -u)$. The transformation now is given by a logarithm for t and a fraction of u and $x^{b/a}$. Another example is related to the special projective group $\xi = x^2 u$ and $\phi = 1$. The canonical variables follow by

$$\textbf{CanonicalVariables}\ [\{u\}, \{x\}, \{x^2\ u\}, \{1\},$$
$$\{w\}, \{t\}]$$

$$\{w \rightarrow \text{Function}\left[\{x, u\}, \frac{u^2}{2} + \frac{1}{x}\right], t \rightarrow \text{Function}[\{x, u\}, -u]\}$$

An example incorporating more than two variables in the transformation is given by the special scaling $\xi_1 = x, \xi_2 = t, \phi_1 = x,$ and $\phi_2 = u$.

$$\textbf{CanonicalVariables}[\{u, v\}, \{x, t\}, \{x, t\},$$
$$\{x, u\}, \{un, vn\}, \{xn, tn\}]$$

$\{un \rightarrow \text{Function}[\{x, t, u, v\}, u - x], vn \rightarrow \text{Function}\left[\{x, t, u, v\}, \frac{t}{x}\right],$

$xn \rightarrow \text{Function}[\{x, t, u, v\}, v - x - u \ \log[x] + x \ \log[x]],$

$tn \rightarrow \text{Function}[\{x, t, u, v\}, \log[x]]\}$

The examples demonstrate that the function CanonicalVariables[] is general enough to handle standard as well as nonstandard situations. The following sections will use the notations introduced in this section to solve first-order ODEs.

3   First-Order ODE

Before we are dealing with the solution of first-order ODEs let us introduce two general notions of the theory of differential equations. These terms are the skeleton and the class of solution. We will show that both properties are instrumental in the geometric examination of an ODE and allow a straight forward simplification by means of canonical variables. Introducing these basic concepts it is easy to understand the geometrical meaning of a canonical transformation. Let us discuss these two properties in case of first order ODEs given in general by

$$F(x, u(x), u') \ = \ 0 \tag{14}$$

where $u' = \frac{du}{dx} = p$ is the first derivative. In the following, we will discuss the two terms and give their definitions.

Definition 1. (The Skeleton) The skeleton of a first order ordinary differential equation is defined as the surface

$$F(x, u, p) \ = 0 \tag{15}$$

in the space of the three independent variables x, u, p. The corresponding differential equation is gained from the skeleton with the replacement p = u'.

This definition can be generalized to higher-order ODEs if the corresponding derivatives are replaced by new variables independent of each other. The definition of the skeleton introduces nothing more than an extension of the manifold $\mathcal{M} = \{x, u\}$ by the variable p. This once extended manifold is very useful in the discussion of first order ordinary differential equations. Another term we will shortly define is the class of solutions.

Definition 2. (The Class of Solutions) A class of solutions is a smooth solution which is a continuously differentiable function $h(x)$ such that the curve $u = h(x)$, $u' = \frac{dh(x)}{dx}$ belongs to the skeleton, that is, $F\left(x, h(x), \frac{dh(x)}{dx}\right)$ $= 0$ identically in x for some interval.

Thus the class of solutions is defined in accordance with certain natural mathematical assumptions or chosen from a physical significance of differential equations under discussion.

However, the crucial step in integrating differential equations is the simplification of the skeleton by a suitable change of the variables x and u. The change of variables is governed by the symmetries of the ODE. Meaning that the skeleton is invariant under the group transformation and its prolongations. The term invariance of an ODE is discussed in [7]. Provided that a symmetry group is known, a simplification of the skeleton is accomplished by introducing the canonical variables discussed above. Integration of the ODE in a canonical representation is simplified in such a way that the solution follows by a quadrature. To demonstrate the contents of these remarks let us examine two examples.

Example 1. As a first example let us inspect the Riccati equation discussed by Ibragimov [9]

$$riccati = \partial_x u[x] + u[x]^2 - \frac{2}{x^2} == 0$$

$$-\frac{2}{x^2} + u[x]^2 + u'[x] == 0$$

The skeleton of this Riccati equation is defined by the algebraic equation

$$p + u^2 - \frac{2}{x^2} == 0$$

$$p + u^2 - \frac{2}{x^2} == 0$$

The surface of this relation represents a so-called hyperbolic paraboloid. The three-dimensional visualization of this geometrical object is simplified if we define the function

$$f[x_-, u_-] := -u^2 + \frac{2}{x^2}$$

The corresponding surface of the skeleton in three-dimensions is shown in Fig. 1.

Figure 1 shows that the skeleton in original coordinates x, u, and p has a singularity if $x \to 0$. Also the figure clearly shows the parabolic shape of the surface for larger x-values. Thus the surface is bent in two directions which complicates the uncovering of the solution. Our goal is to find a transformation which reduces the parabolic shape to a simpler and smoother representation. For the Riccati equation, a one-parameter symmetry group is provided by the following scaling transformations known as non-homogeneous dilations.

$$transformation = \{x \to r \ \exp[-a],$$
$$u \to \mathbf{Function}[x, w[x \ \exp[a]] \ \exp[a]]\}$$

From In[108]:=

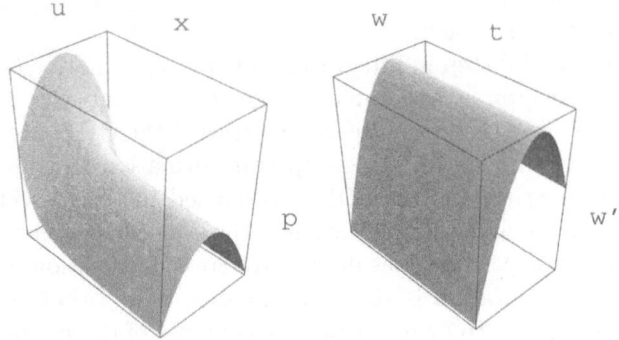

Fig. 1. Skeleton of the Riccati equation in the original (left) and the target coordinates (right).

$$\{x \to e^{-a}\, r, u \to \text{Function}[x, w[x\ \exp[a]]\ \exp[a]]\}$$

The invariance of the Riccati equation is checked by taking into account that the derivatives also need to be transformed by the rule

$$dtrafo = \mathbf{v}\_^{(n\_)}[a\_.\ x\_] :> a^{-n}\, v^{(n)}[a\, x]$$

$$\mathbf{v}\_^{(n\_)}[a\_.\ x\_] :> a^{-n}\, v^{(n)}[a\, x]$$

The rule *dtrafo* reflects the fact that the nth derivative of a function under a scaling is replaced by the nth derivative divided by the scaling factor a^n. The application of *transformation* and *dtrafo* to the Riccati equation gives us

$$triccati = riccati/.transformation/.dtrafo; triccati \mathbin{//} \text{LTF}$$

$$-\frac{2\, e^{2\, a}}{r^2} + e^{2\, a}\, w^2 + e^{2\, a}\, w_r == 0$$

We note that the original equation *riccati* is reproduced up to a common factor $e^{2\, a}$. In the definition of the transformation in *Mathematica* it is essential that we use the target variables in the representation for the original variables. x is simply replaced by the target r multiplied by the scaling factor e^{-a}. The dependent variable u is replaced by $w\, e^a$. Since w depends on the target r, we have to represent r in *Mathematica* by $x\, e^a$. We also have to take into account that the derivative needs a special treatment which is realized in the rule *dtrafo*. Applying both rules to the original equation, we end up with the equation given in *triccati*. The discussed replacements of variables are actually the steps needed in a pencil and paper calculation.

The application of *transformation* to a first derivative shows that first order derivatives transform like

$$\partial_x u[x]/.transformation/.dtrafo$$

$$e^{2\,a}\,w'[r]$$

which in conventional notation reads $w' \rightarrow u'\, e^{-2a}$. Thus we observe that the equation's skeleton is invariant under the inhomogeneous scaling $r \rightarrow x\, e^a$, $w \rightarrow ue^{-a}$, $w' \rightarrow u'e^{-2a}$ obtained by extending the transformations of the group to the first derivative u'. We also can check the invariance of the skeleton by applying the extended vector field to the skeleton. The related vector field of the scaling transformation is defined by

$$\text{Vect}[f\_] := x\,\partial_x f - u\,\partial_u f - 2\,p\,\partial_p f$$

The skeleton of the Riccati equation is

$$skeleton = riccati/.\{\partial_x u[x] \rightarrow p, u[x] \rightarrow u\}$$

$$p + u^2 - \frac{2}{x^2} == 0$$

The application of the vector field to the skeleton reveals

$$Vect/@skeleton$$

$$-2\,p - 2\,u^2 + \frac{4}{x^2} == 0$$

the invariance. If we compare both expressions in more detail we recognize that the original and the transformed skeleton is reproduced up to a factor -2. Thus, if the skeleton vanishes the application of the vector field to the skeleton also vanishes.

Example 2. Another example of a first order ordinary differential equation is the equation

$$example2 = -\frac{\partial_x u[x]}{x^2} + \left(\frac{u[x]^2}{x^2} + \frac{u[x]^3}{x}\right) == 0$$

$$\frac{u[x]^2}{x^2} + \frac{u[x]^3}{x} - \frac{u'[x]}{x^2} == 0$$

This example is also invariant with respect to an inhomogeneous scaling transformation. We define this sort of transformation by a transformation rule like

$$scalingtrafo = \{x \to \exp[-a]\ r,$$
$$u \to \text{Function}[x, w[x\ \exp[a]]\ \exp[a]]\};$$
$$dtrafo = \mathbf{v}_-^{(n_-)}[a_-.\ x_-] :> a^{-n}\ v^{(n)}[a\ x];$$

$$scaling[x_-] := x/.scalingtrafo/.dtrafo$$

The application of the function scaling[] to the second example demonstrates again the invariance of the equation up to a common factor $e^{4\ a}$

$$scaling[example2]$$

$$\frac{e^{4\ a}\ w[r]^2}{r^2} + \frac{e^{4\ a}\ w[r]^3}{r} - \frac{e^{4\ a}\ w'[r]}{r^2} == 0$$

The graphical representation of the skeleton for this equation is given in Fig. 2.

From In[83]:=

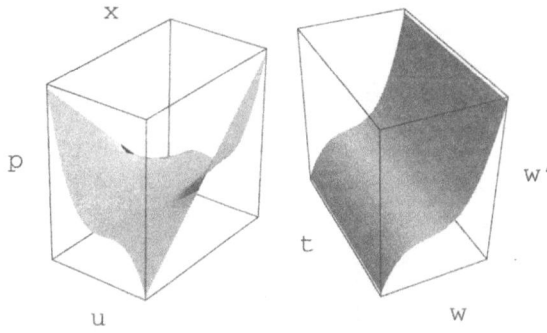

Fig. 2. On the left the skeleton of the equation $-(\partial_x u(x))/x + u^2/x^2 + u^3/x = 0$. The surface has some resemblance of a stingray missing the tail. The right part shows the canonical transformation of the left.

The structure of this surface is simplified if we apply the following canonical transformation to the skeleton.

$$canonical = \left\{x \to \exp[t], u \to \text{Function}\left[x, \frac{w[\log[x]]}{x}\right]\right\};$$

$$\textbf{canonicaltransform}[x_-] := \textbf{Simplify}[\textbf{Power Expand}[$$
$$x/.canonical]]$$

The transformation is carried out by

$$canonicaltransform[\text{Thread}[example2\ \exp[4\ t], Equal]]$$

$$w[t] + w[t]^2 + w[t]^3 - w'[t] == 0$$

The related skeleton simplifies to a third order parabola translated along the x-axis, see Fig. 2 right. This example demonstrates that canonical coordinates dramatically simplify the shape of the skeleton and thus allows access to the solution in a simpler way.

The two examples demonstrate that canonical transformations simplify the skeleton. Knowing this fact, we approach the second term, the solution. The question is how can we use the information of the symmetries to find solutions of any first order equation possessing symmetries. The idea is to use canonical variables allowing a transformation to a simpler representation of the equation.

Let us start our examination with the Riccati equation of the first example. We know that the canonical variables for a nonhomogeneous dilation is given by

$$\boldsymbol{trafo1} = \left\{\boldsymbol{x} \rightarrow \exp[t], \boldsymbol{u} \rightarrow \textbf{Function}\left[\boldsymbol{x}, \frac{w[\log[x]]}{x}\right]\right\}$$

$$\left\{x \rightarrow e^t, u \rightarrow \text{Function}\left[x, \frac{w[\log[x]]}{x}\right]\right\}$$

This type of transformations was derived in section 2 by solving the defining equations for t and w. The application of this transformation to the Riccati equation gives us the following result

$$\boldsymbol{riccati1} = \textbf{Simplify}[\boldsymbol{Thread}[$$
$$\textbf{PowerExpand}[\boldsymbol{riccati}/.\boldsymbol{trafo1}] \;\; \textbf{exp}[2\;\boldsymbol{t}], \boldsymbol{Equal}]]$$

$$-2 - w[t] + w[t]^2 + w'[t] == 0$$

Thus it straightens out the skeleton of the original Riccati equation, taking it to a parabolic cylinder, see Fig.1 right. This geometrical simplification is the reason why the Riccati equation takes on an integrable form when written in canonical variables.

Actually the scaling of the original Riccati equation is replaced by a group of translations $\bar{t} = t + \epsilon$, $w = u$, and $w' = u'$. The calculations so far executed by hand can be collected in a *Mathematica* function. The information we need for this kind of calculation are the original equation, and the dependent and independent variables. We also need the canonical transformations which are derived by our function CanonicalVariables[]. This function also has to know the names of the target coordinates.

We demonstrate the use of this function by applying it to the Riccati equation. We know that the Riccati equation is invariant with respect to an inhomogeneous scaling transformation. The related canonical variables are given by

$$ccoord = \textbf{CanonicalVariables}[\{u\}, \{x\}, \{x\}, \{-u\},$$
$$\{w\}, \{t\}]$$

$$\{w \rightarrow \text{Function}[\{x, u\}, u\ x], t \rightarrow \text{Function}[\{x, u\}, \log[x]]\}$$

Using this transformations, we can reduce the Riccati equation to

$$cricc = \textbf{CanonicalRepresentation}[riccati, u, x,$$
$$\{w \rightarrow x\ u, t \rightarrow \log[x]\}, w, t]$$

$$-2\ e^{-2\ t} - e^{-2\ t}\ w[t] + e^{-2\ t}\ w[t]^2 + e^{-2\ t}\ w'[t] == 0$$

The resulting equation has the same structure as the equation derived by hand. The common factor e^{-2t} is a non vanishing term which can be eliminated by multiplying with the inverse.

$$cricc = \text{Simplify}[\text{Thread}[cricc\ \exp[2\ t], Equal]]$$

$$-2 - w[t] + w[t]^2 + w'[t] == 0$$

This equation can be solved by quadrature or by separating variables. We use here the *Mathematica* function DSolve[] to integrate the equation.

$$sricc = \text{DSolve}[cricc, w, t]$$

$$\left\{\left\{w \rightarrow \left(\frac{2\ e^{3\ \#1} + e^{3\ C[1]}}{e^{3\ \#1} - e^{3\ C[1]}}\&\right)\right\}\right\}$$

The solution in original variables follows by applying the canonical transformation a second time

$$solricc = \textbf{Simplify}[w[x, u] == (w[t]/.sricc)[[1]]/.$$
$$t \rightarrow t[x, u]/.ccoord]$$

$$u\ x == \frac{e^{3\ C[1]} + 2\ x^3}{-e^{3\ C[1]} + x^3}$$

Solving this implicit solution with respect to u delivers

$$\text{Solve}[solricc, u]$$

$$\left\{\left\{u \rightarrow \frac{e^{3\ C[1]} + 2\ x^3}{x\ (-e^{3\ C[1]} + x^3)}\right\}\right\}$$

which is just the solution found by Ibragimov. The second example discussed above allows the same scaling symmetries as the Riccati equation. The target equation follows by

$$cex2 = \textbf{CanonicalRepresentation}[example2, u, x,$$
$$\{w \rightarrow x\ u, t \rightarrow \log[x]\}, w, t]$$

$$e^{-4\ t}\ w[t] + e^{-4\ t}\ w[t]^2 + e^{-4\ t}\ w[t]^3 - e^{-4\ t}\ w'[t] == 0$$

The common factor is eliminated by

$$cex2 = \text{Simplify}[\text{Thread}[cex2\ \exp[4\ t], Equal]]$$

$$w[t] + w[t]^2 + w[t]^3 - w'[t] == 0$$

The solution w follows by separation of variables and by integrating the left hand side and the right hand side

$$sex2 = \textbf{Simplify}\ \Big[\int \frac{1}{w + w^2 + w^3} dw == \int 1 dt + c\Big]$$

$$-\frac{\arctan\left[\frac{1+2\ w}{\sqrt{3}}\right]}{\sqrt{3}} + \log[w] - \frac{1}{2}\ \log\left[1 + w + w^2\right] == c + t$$

Since the solution contains transcendental functions it is hard to get an explicit solution for the stingray equation. The inversion of the canonical transformation does not resolve this problem.

$$iex2 = sex2/.\{w \rightarrow w[x, u], t \rightarrow t[x, u]\}/.ccoord$$

$$-\frac{\arctan\left[\frac{1+2\ u\ x}{\sqrt{3}}\right]}{\sqrt{3}} + \log[u\ x] - \frac{1}{2}\ \log\left[1 + u\ x + u^2\ x^2\right] == c + \log[x]$$

However, we can solve this problem by a graphical representation of the solution in a two dimensional plot. We create a contour plot in Fig. 3.

We observe that u increases if x increases. For small values of u there exist a linear relation between u and x.

So far we discussed two examples of first-order ODEs to show how the use of canonical variables can simplify the integration. The method of canonical variables is useful not only in the integration process of first-order ODEs but also in the integration of higher order ODEs.

16   Gerd Baumann

From In[90]:=

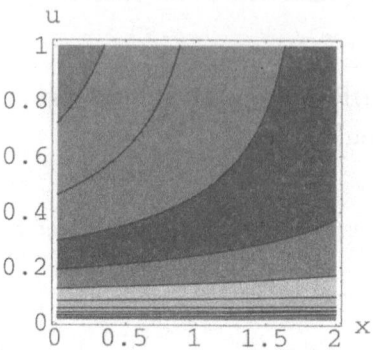

Fig. 3. Contour plot of the solution for the stingray equation.

4   Second-Order ODE

This section discusses for a second order ODE the term skeleton. The combination of canonical variables and the method of first integrals [1] serves to derive an explicit solution for an ODE for which only an implicit solution is known [9].

Example 1. The second-order ODE serves to demonstrate how canonical variables simplify the skeleton in higher order equations. We also show that the solution steps reduce to a few operations. The specific example we discuss is given by the equation

$$firstExample \; = \; \partial_{x,x}u[x] \; - \; \frac{(\partial_x u[x])}{u[x]^2} \; + \; \frac{1}{x\,u[x]}$$

$$\frac{1}{x\,u[x]} \; - \; \frac{u'[x]}{u[x]^2} + u''[x]$$

This second order equation admits the symmetries

infinites = Infinitesimals[
    firstExample, u, x, SubstitutionRules → {∂_{x,x}u[x]}];
infinites // LTF

$$\phi_1 \; == \; \tfrac{1}{2}\,u\,(k1 + 2\,k2\,x)$$
$$\xi_1 \; == \; x\,(k1 + k2\,x)$$

representing a two-dimensional group of scalings and projections. The skeleton of the second order ODE is given by a four-dimensional manifold $\mathcal{M} = \{x, u, u' = p, u'' = q\}$. Since the dimension of the manifold $\mathcal{M}$ is larger than three, we cannot plot the skeleton as a surface. However, *Mathematica* offers the cabability to represent the fourth dimension in a sequence of plots. The combination of these figures in an animation allows to graphically represent the manifold. This kind of graphical representation of the manifold is created if one of the coordinates of $\mathcal{M}$ is smoothly changed. The resulting animation generates an evolution of the manifold while we moves along a distinguished coordinate. For the above second-order ODE we define the skeleton by

$$\text{skeleton}[u_-, x_-, p_-] := \frac{p}{u^2} - \frac{1}{x\,u}$$

representing the surface for $u'' = q$. For the animation, we select the x-axis as the distinguished coordinate. The three-dimensional surface represents the submanifold $\mathcal{M}_s = \{u, u' = p, u'' = q\}$ for certain values of x, see Fig. 4.

In the discussion of first order ODEs we observed that the method of canonical variables allows a simplification of the skeleton. The same behavior happens for second order ODEs. This becomes obvious if we calculate canonical coordinates related to the subgroups *k1* and *k2*. Let us first choose the subgroup with *k1* representing a scaling

$$cck1 = \textbf{CanonicalVariables}\left[\{u\}, \{x\}, \{x\}, \left\{\tfrac{u}{2}\right\},\right.$$
$$\left.\{w\}, \{t\}\right]$$

$$\left\{w \to \text{Function}\left[\{x, u\}, \frac{u}{\sqrt{x}}\right], t \to \text{Function}[\{x, u\}, \log[x]]\right\}$$

From In[113]:=

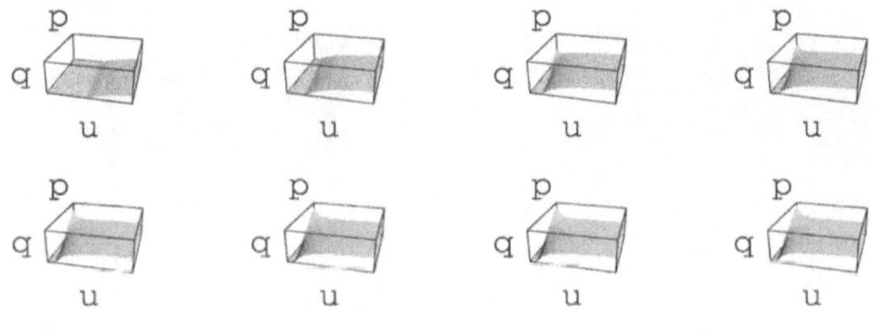

Fig. 4. The figure shows a sequence of plots for $x \in [0.01, 0.08]$ in steps of 0.01 from left to right and top to bottom. The graphs show that the manifold along the x-axis changes rapidly for small x values. For greater values of x there are no dramatic changes in M .

A second set of canonical variables follows by the choice $k1 = 0$ and $k2 = 1$ from

$$cck2 = \textbf{CanonicalVariables}\left[\{u\}, \{x\}, \{x^2\}, \{x\,u\},\right.$$
$$\left.\{w\}, \{t\}\right]$$

$$\left\{w \to \text{Function}\left[\{x, u\}, \frac{u}{x}\right], t \to \text{Function}\left[\{x, u\}, -\frac{1}{x}\right]\right\}$$

Thus for each set of canonical variables there exists a substitute of the original ODE. The target equation for the first case reads

ceqk1 = CanonicalRepresentation[$firstExample, u, x$, cck1, w, t]

$$2\, w[t] - w[t]^3 - 4\, w'[t] + 4\, w[t]^2\, w''[t] == 0$$

The second double is

ceqk2 = CanonicalRepresentation[$firstExample, u, x$, cck2, w, t]

$$t^3 \left(\frac{w'[t]}{w[t]^2} - w''[t]\right) == 0$$

Both equations are embedded in a reduced manifold $\mathcal{M}_c = \{w, w', w''\}$. This manifold is free of the target variable t. A graphical representation of the two manifolds is given in Fig. 5. We observe that the two graphics look very similar. However the skeletons in their analytical representations are different from one another.

From In[41]:=

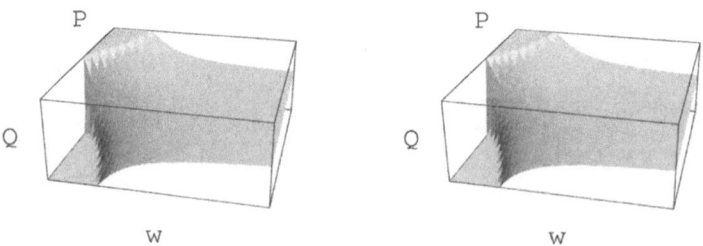

Fig. 5. The two figures show the skeleton of the equation $\partial_{x,x}u(x) - \partial_x u/u^2 + 1/(x\, u) = 0$ in the two canonical representations. Left: skeleton of the equation $2w - w^3 - 4w' + 4w^2 w'' = 0$. Right: skeleton of $w'/w^2 - w'' = 0$. The variables P and Q denote the first and second derivative of the canonical variable w.

The question arises do different solutions correspond to the nearly equal skeletons or are the solutions the same. We will examine this question by solving the two canonical representations. First let us try to solve the original equation by DSolve[]

$$\text{DSolve}[firstExample == 0, u, x]$$

$$\text{DSolve}\left[\frac{1}{x\ u[x]} - \frac{u'[x]}{u[x]^2} + u''[x] == 0, u, x\right]$$

The result shows that *Mathematica* is unable to solve the second order equation. Calculating the solution of the first canonical reduction shows

$$sol1\ =\ \text{DSolve}[ceqk1, w, t]$$

$$\text{DSolve}\left[2\ w[t] - w[t]^3 - 4\ w'[t] + 4\ w[t]^2\ w''[t] == 0, w, t\right]$$

that again *Mathematica* is unable to solve the equation. The following idea might solve this problem. We know that a given equation admits a certain type of symmetries. This is also true for the first canonical reduction. The symmetries of the first target equation follow by

$$infceqk1\ =\ \text{Infinitesimals}[ceqk1, w, t]; \text{infceqk1}\ //\ \text{LTF}$$

$$\phi_1 == e^t\ k1\ w$$
$$\xi_1 == 2\ e^t\ k1 + k2$$

representing a two-dimensional symmetry group with an exponential dependence in t. $k2$ is responsible for translations in t. Since we are looking for symmetries different from translations, we choose $k1=1/2$ and $k2=0$. The second-stage canonical variables for this subgroup follow by

$$ccceqk11\ =\ \text{CanonicalVariables}\left[\{w\}, \{t\}, \{e^t\}, \left\{\frac{e^t\ w}{2}\right\},\right.$$
$$\left.\{v\}, \{s\}\right]$$

$$\left\{v \to \text{Function}\left[\{t, w\}, e^{-t/2}\ w\right], s \to \text{Function}\left[\{t, w\}, -e^{-t}\right]\right\}$$

Inserting the second target coordinates into the first-stage canonical reduction, we gain the representation

$$ceqk11\ =\ \text{CanonicalRepresentation}[ceqk1, w, t,$$
$$ccceqk11, v, s]$$

$$-4\ i\ \sqrt{s}\ \left(v'[s] - v[s]^2\ v''[s]\right) == 0$$

The result shows that the two canonical representations of the first-stage are connected. They are identical if we choose the proper subgroup on the second-stage of the symmetry analysis.

$$eqh\ =\ \text{Thread}\left[ceqk11/(-4\ i\ \sqrt{s}), Equal\right]$$

$$v'[s] - v[s]^2\ v''[s] == 0$$

The symmetry analysis of the second-stage equation shows that it admits a second-order group. We know that a second-order group is sufficient to solve second order ODEs [1].

$$infh \; = \; \text{Infinitesimals}[eqh, v, s]; \text{infh} \; // \, \text{LTF}$$

$$\phi_1 == \frac{k2 \; v}{2}$$
$$\xi_1 == k1 + k2 \; s$$

We apply the method of first integrals to *eqh* to determine the solution [1,2]. First let us calculate the Lie matrix by extracting the infinitesimals

$$inf1 \; =$$
$$\{\{\xi[1][s,v]\}, \{\phi[1][s,v]\}\} \; /.infh/.\{k1 \rightarrow 1, k2 \rightarrow 0\} \; /.$$
$$v \rightarrow v[s];$$

$$inf2 \; =$$
$$\{\{\xi[1][s,v]\}, \{\phi[1][s,v]\}\} \; /.infh/.\{k1 \rightarrow 0, k2 \rightarrow 1\} \; /.$$
$$v \rightarrow v[s];$$

The related Lie matrix follows with

$$\boldsymbol{Dmatrix} = \textbf{DeltaMatrix}\left[s, v, \frac{v'[s]}{v[s]^2}, 2, \{inf1, inf2\}\right];$$

$$\textbf{TableForm}[\boldsymbol{Dmatrix}]$$

$$\begin{array}{ccc} 1 & 0 & 0 \\[4pt] s & \dfrac{v[s]}{2} & -\dfrac{1}{2} \, v'[s] \\[8pt] 1 & v'[s] & \dfrac{v'[s]}{v[s]^2} \end{array}$$

Whose determinant is a non-vanishing quantity

$$\det[\boldsymbol{Dmatrix}]$$

$$\frac{v'[s]}{2 \, v[s]} + \frac{1}{2} \, v'[s]^2$$

One of the two first integrals follows by applying the function FirstIntegral[] of *MathLie*

$$integral2 \; = \; \text{FirstIntegral}[s, v, \boldsymbol{Dmatrix}, 2] \; == \; c2$$

$$2 \; \log[v[s]] - 2 \; \log[1 + v[s] \; v'[s]] == c2$$

The second integral is not accessible by a direct integration

$$integral1 \; = \; \text{FirstIntegral}[s, v, Dmatrix, 1] \; == \; c1$$

$$\int \left(v[s]'[t] \left(-\tfrac{1}{2} \, v'[s][t] - \tfrac{s[t] \; v'[s][t]}{v[s][t]^2} \right) + \right.$$

$$s'[t] \left(\tfrac{v'[s][t]}{2 \; v[s][t]} + \tfrac{1}{2} \, v'[s][t]^2 \right) +$$

$$\left. \left(-\tfrac{1}{2} \, v[s][t] + s[t] \; v'[s][t] \right) v''[s][t] \right) \Big/$$

$$\left(\tfrac{v'[s][t]}{2 \; v[s][t]} + \tfrac{1}{2} \, v'[s][t]^2 \right) dt \; ==$$

$$c1$$

However, the solution of the equation *eqh* is gained if we take the first integral as defining equation for v. Thus another integration by DSolve[] delivers the solution

$$csolex2 \; = \; \text{DSolve}[integral2, v, s]$$

$\text{InverseFunction} :: \text{"}ifun\text{"} : \text{"}Warning: Inverse functions are being used. Values may be lost for multivalued inverses.\text{"}$

$$\left\{ \left\{ v \rightarrow \left(e^{c2/2} \left(1 + \text{ProductLog}[e^{-1+e^{-c2} \left(\#1 - C[1] \right)}] \right) \& \right) \right\} \right\}$$

The solution of the original equation in variables x and u follows by inversion of the canonical transformations

$$csol \; = \; ((v[s] \; /. \; csolex2)[[1]] \; == \; v \; /.$$
$$\{v \rightarrow v[t, w], s \rightarrow s[t, w]\} \; /.ccceqk11) \; /.$$
$$\{w \rightarrow w[x, u], t \rightarrow t[x, u]\} \; /.$$
$$cck1$$

$$e^{c2/2} \left(1 + \text{ProductLog}[e^{-1+e^{-c2} \left(-\tfrac{1}{x} - C[1] \right)}] \right) \; == \; \frac{u}{x}$$

The explicit solution in original coordinates reads

$$sol \; = \; \text{Solve}[csol, u] // \text{Simplify}$$

$$\left\{ \left\{ u \rightarrow e^{c2/2} \, x \left(1 + \text{ProductLog}[e^{-1 - \frac{e^{-c2} \left(1 + x \; C[1] \right)}{x}}] \right) \right\} \right\}$$

where the constants $c2$ and $C[1]$ are constants of integration. This example demonstrates that solutions of differential equations are gained if a hybrid algorithm combining the method of first integrals, the method of canonical variables, and the solution procedure of *Mathematica* are combined. The application of each single method to the original equation fails. The explicit solution in the above representation is new. A graphical representation of the solution for fixed constants $c2$ and $C[1]$ is shown in Fig. 6.

From In[59]:=

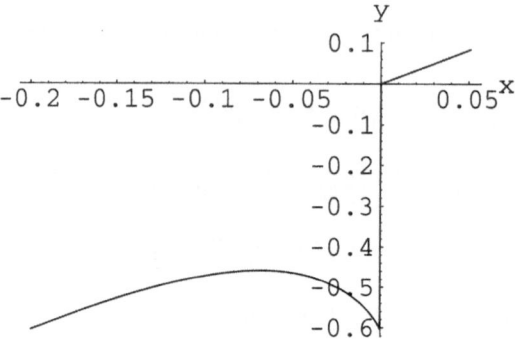

Fig. 6. Solution of the equation $\partial_{x,x} u(x) - \partial_x u / u^2 + 1/(x\, u) = 0$ under the condition $c2 = 1$ and $C[1] = 1/2$.

5 Conclusions

We demonstrated that the knowledge of symmetries is instrumental to determine canonical transformations. The derivation of the symmetries of an ODE is governed by Lie's theory of point transformations [2,3]. This theory is implemented in *MathLie* [7]. *MathLie* is capable to automatically derive the symmetries for any ODE or PDE. This package also allows the calculation of canonical variables. Knowing the canonical variables of an ODE, we are able to simplify the original equation. This simplification is directly connected with a compaction of the skeleton. The reduced ODE in canonical variables allows us the application of quadratures [1]. The result of a quadrature is at least an implicit solution in canonical variables. Inversion of the canonical transformation and the solution for the unknown function delivers an explicit solution of the equation. Thus the worst case is an implicit solution in canonical coordinates. However, experience with the package *MathLie* shows that a great number of equations [10] allows an explicit solution.

References

[1]   G. Baumann, If Lie Had Known About Mathematica, Math. Edu. Res. 7, 15-28, (1998)

[2]   S. Lie, Theorie der Transformationsgruppen, Vol. I-II, Leipzig, (1888, 1890, 1893), reprinted by Chelsea Publ. Comp., New York, 1970

[3]   S. Lie and G. Scheffers, Vorlesungen über Differentialgleichungen mit bekannten infinitesimalen Transformationen, B.G. Teubner, Leipzig, 1891

[4]   N.H. Ibragimov, CRC Handbook of Lie Group Analysis of Differential Equations, Vol. 3, CRC Press, Boca Raton, 1996

[5]   T. Wolf and A. Brand, Investigating DEs with CRACK and related Programs, SIGSAM Bulletin, Special Issue, June, 1-8, (1995)

[6]   D.W. Albrecht, E.L. Mansfield, and A.E. Milne, Algorithms for special integrals of ordinary differential equations, J. Phys. A: Math. Gen., 29, 973-991, (1996)

[7]   G. Baumann, Symmetry Analysis of Differential Equations using Mathematica, Springer-Verlag, New York, 1999

[8]   E.S. Cheb-Terab, L.G.S. Duarte, and L.A.C.P. da Mota, Computer algebra solving of first order ODEs using symmetry methods, Comp. Phys. Comm. 101, 254-268, (1997)

[9]   N.H. Ibragimov, Sophus Lie and Harmony in Mathematical Physics, on the 150th Anniversary of His Birth, The Math. Intel. 16, 20-28, (1994)

[10]   E. Kamke, Differentialgleichungen, G.B. Teubner, Stuttgart, 1977

Analysis of Stability of Rational Approximations through Computer Algebra

Massimo Cafaro[1] and Beatrice Paternoster[2]

[1] Faculty of Engineering, University of Lecce, Palazzo Stecca, Via per Monteroni, 73100 Lecce, Italy, e-mail: cafaro@sara.unile.it

[2] Dipartimento di Matematica e Informatica, Universitá di Salerno, Via S.Allende, 840841 Baronissi (SA), Italy, e-mail: beapat@dia.unisa.it

Abstract. We present a Mathematica package to compute the interval of stability of one or more rational approximations for mathematical functions. This analysis has a strong connection with the linear stability theory of numerical methods for Ordinary Differential Equations. As an example of the application of this package, we analyze the periodicity properties of Padé approximations for the cosine function. Moreover, we show its usefulness in the derivation of new numerical methods, by applying it to maximize the periodicity interval of collocation–based methods for second order initial value problems.

Keywords: Symbolic Computation, Rational approximations, Ordinary Differential Equations, Collocation methods, P–stability.

Subject Code Classification: 65L06–65L07.

1 Introduction.

Symbolic computation is a powerful instrument in the context of the analysis and construction of new numerical methods for Ordinary Differential Equations (ODEs) when we must take into account many properties at the same time (order of convergence of the method, stability properties, magnitude of error constants and so on). Through symbolic manipulation we can compute expressions leaving some free parameters which can be used to maximize the properties which we consider meaningful. Examples of usage of symbolic computation in the context of ODEs can be found in [9,10].

In this paper we present the Mathematica package StabInt.m, which computes the intervals of stability of one or more rational functions $R_1(z)$, $R_2(z), \ldots, R_m(z)$, i.e. the union of the intervals on the positive real z–axis in which: $|R_1(z)| < k_1$, $|R_2(z)| < k_2$, $\ldots, |R_m(z)| < k_m$, where $k_1, k_2, \ldots, k_m$ are constants defined by the problem. This investigation has a strong connection with the theory of numerical methods for ODEs: indeed the linear stability analysis of implicit one–step methods leads to rational approximations of the exponential and cosine function (see for example [2–5,11]).

To make this connection evident, let us consider, for example, how the linear stability analysis of a Runge–Kutta (RK) method is performed [6]. The method is applied to the scalar test equation

$$y' = \lambda y, \quad \lambda \in \mathcal{C}, \quad Re(\lambda) < 0, \tag{1}$$

obtaining the one–step difference equation

$$y_{n+1} = R(z)y_n, \quad z = h\lambda \tag{2}$$

where h is the stepsize, $R(z)$ is the *stability function* of the RK method and, if the RK method is implicit, it is a rational function. The aim of this analysis is to establish whether or not the numerical solution produced by the RK tends to zero as n tends to infinity. It happens that $y_n \to 0$ as $n \to \infty$ if and only if

$$|R(z)| < 1. \tag{3}$$

The region of *absolute stability* of the method is the region $\mathcal{R}_A$ of the complex z–plane for which (3) holds. The *interval* or *intervals* of stability are given by the intersection of $\mathcal{R}_A$ with the negative – in this case – real z–axis. The possibility to regard the *stability function* $R(z)$ as a rational approximation to the exponential function arises in a natural way, by considering that the exact solution of the test equation (1) is $y(x) = k \exp(\lambda x)$, with k an arbitrary constant. It should now be clear that the linear stability properties of a one–step implicit method which produces the difference equation (2) depend on the behaviour of its *stability function* $R(z)$ when it is regarded as a rational approximation for $\exp(z)$ [6].

In an analogous way, to investigate stability and dispersive order of a one–step numerical method for second order ODEs

$$y'' = f(x, y), \tag{4}$$

we consider the test equation

$$y'' = -\omega^2 y. \tag{5}$$

The numerical solution satisfies the recursion

$$y_{n+1} - 2R(\nu^2)y_n + P(\nu^2)y_{n-1} = 0, \tag{6}$$

with $\nu = \omega^2$ [2,4,11]. Its solution satisfies

$$y(x_{n+1}) - 2\cos\nu \; y(x_n) + y(x_{n-1}) = 0, \tag{7}$$

with $\nu = \omega h$, $z = \nu^2$ [2,4,11]. The behaviour of the numerical solution and the stability properties of the numerical method depend on the rational functions $R(\nu^2)$ and $P(\nu^2)$. In particular, if $|P(\nu^2)| \equiv 1$, then there is no numerical dissipation [4,11], as happens, for example, for *zero–dissipative* Runge–Kutta–Nyström methods: the interval of *stability* becomes an interval of *periodicity*, and the rational function $R(\nu^2)$ is regarded as a rational approximation of the cosine [2], so that the requisite is that $|R(\nu^2)| < 1$ (see [2,10–12] for details). Both in the case of existence of *stability* intervals and of *periodicity* intervals, our analysis comes down to a set of inequalities which are to be satisfied along the positive real axis.

We speak about *interval* or *intervals of stability* of one or more rational functions, referring to the intervals on the positive real z–axis on which the inequalities hold, which are meaningful in the context under analysis. The knowledge of the interval of stability of a numerical method for ODEs has a practical relevance in the choice of the stepsize h, when *stiff systems* are integrated. For most systems of ODEs (4) having oscillating solutions, it is sufficient to check the behaviour of the stability functions along the real axis, and not on the whole complex z–plane when, for example, the spectrum of the Jacobian varies mostly along the real axis.

In [10] we computed the interval of stability of a Runge–Kutta–Nyström method through computer algebra. The aim of our present analysis is to provide a flexible instrument for the computation of stability intervals of a large variety of one–step and multistep numerical methods for ODEs. Indeed our investigation ignores the form of the numerical method under analysis, and considers directly the rational function (or functions) which are associated with it, and the inequalities which have to be satisfied by a point on the real z–axis so long as it belongs to the interval of stability. In this way we can draw conclusions from stability functions rather than from the associated numerical methods.

The package StabInt.m which we present here determines the intervals on the real positive z–axis on which the inequalities hold, also taking into account the case of multiple roots and the desired accuracy. The user can also choose to determine the whole stability region on the complex plane.

In Section 2 we describe the package and its features and give indications about its usage. As an example of application, in Section 3 we analyze Padé approximations for the cosine function. In Section 4 we consider collocation methods for second order ODEs. In the Appendix we list the package.

2   Description of the package StabInt.

The Mathematica package StabInt takes the rational function or functions under analysis as input. It consists of a set of procedures which are called by the **StabIntervals** command. It returns the intervals on the positive real z–axis on which the rational functions result less than proper constants. The functions, the constants and the input parameters have been saved in *filename*, as shown below. The *filename* cannot contain spaces.

```
(******* EXAMPLE OF INPUT FILE **********)

pairs = 2;

prec = 20;

eps = 10^(-16);

rf[1] =  rational function n. 1;

rf[2] =  rational function n. 2;

cv[1] =  constant n. 1;

cv[2] =  constant n. 2;

printing = 1;

height = 3;

stepx = 0.4;

stepy = 0.4;
```

   pairs is the number of rational functions under analysis. **prec** is the precision which the user chooses in the computation; we suggest repeating the computation by using different values of **prec** when the user suspects that an ill–conditioned situation occurrs. **rf** is an array containing the rational functions; it ALWAYS starts from index 1. **cv** is an array containing the constants to be used in the inequalities; it ALWAYS starts from index 1. If **cv** contains one zero in location i, then the corresponding inequality is $rf[i] < 0$. The parameter **printing** enables the stability region on the complex plane to be plotted, if it is set to 1, with height given by the homonym parameter; if it is equal to 0, then only the intervals of stability are printed. If the computation produces an unlimited interval of stability, the stability region is not plotted for any value of **printing**. **stepx** and **stepy** are the stepsizes which are used during scanning the region on the complex z–plane along the real and imaginary axis respectively. By using the parameter **eps** the user decides to be informed about the existence of double roots in the characteristic equation which is associated to (6) when the numerical method is zero–dissipative. We decided to introduce the **eps** parameter, to allow the user to follow the weaker definition of P–stability which is stated in Definition 1 of Section 3, and is discussed in [2]. Practically, a list of *secondary intervals of stability* (γ^2, δ^2), (ϵ^2, ζ^2),... will be printed only if $|\delta^2 - \epsilon^2| < eps$, otherwise the output will be (γ^2, ζ^2).

The package starts reading the user's input. This task is accomplished by the `ReadRationalFunction` function.

`BuildExpr` builds the expressions involved in the solution of the inequality $|rf[i]| < cv[i]$, $i = 1, \ldots$,`pairs`, that are $exp[i] > 0$ and $exp[i + 1] > 0$.

Then `StabInt` computes the interval for any rational function in the following way: `MakeRoots` computes all the positive distinct real roots of $exp[i]$ and $exp[i+1]$, removing the roots which are very close to each other according to the input parameter `eps`.

By using the list of roots constructed by MakeRoots, `Bound` determines the list of intervals of stability, taking into account the change of sign of the expression under analysis. If the list of roots is empty, `Bound` calls `EmptyList` which decides whether the interval of stability is empty or unlimited, by evaluating the expression at the positive abscissa $z = 10$. If the list of roots is not empty, then the `NotEmptyList` function determines the positive roots in which the expression changes its sign, by evaluating the expression at the middle point between a couple of different roots. Moreover, it also evaluates $exp[i]$ in a point to the right of the last interval, to take into account the case of an unlimited secondary interval of periodicity. Then `Bound` computes the intersection of the intervals in which $exp[i] > 0$ and $exp[i+1] > 0$ respectively, by using the function `IntersectIntervals`.

At this point the `StabIntervals` command determines now the list of intervals of stability, by intersecting the intervals computed by `Bound` for any rational functions.

If the printing parameter is set to 1, the package plots the region of stability on the complex plane, by using a classical *scanning technique*, described for example in [8].

3   Periodicity intervals of Padé approximations for the cosine function.

In this example we consider even diagonal entries of Padé table of $\cos z$ [1]; their existence was proved in Lemma 3.6 in [4]. These approximants can be used to derive *associated* numerical methods for (4), as described in details in [2,4,5], having the maximum dispersive order and the stability properties of these Padé approximants.

For implicit Runge–Kutta–Nyström (RKN) methods [4,11], $R(\nu^2)$ and $P(\nu^2)$ in (6) are related to the *stability matrix* of the RKN method, on which the dispersive order of the method and its stability properties depend. A high dispersive order ensures that the true solution is in phase with the numerical one [4,11]. For *zero–dissipative* RKN methods the maximum dispersive order is achieved when $R(\nu^2)$ is the $[2n, 2n]$ Padé approximant for $\cos \nu$ (Theorem 1 of [2]).

To make this paper self–explanatory , we recall the following definition [2]:

Definition 1. The *primary interval of periodicity* of a method satisfying (6) with with $P(\nu^2) \equiv 1$ is the largest interval $(0, \beta^2)$ such that $|R(\nu^2)| < 1$ for $0 < \nu^2 < \beta^2$. Usually this is simply called *the interval of periodicity*. If $|R(\nu^2)| < 1 \, \forall \nu^2 > 0$, the method is P–stable. If, when β is finite, $|R(\nu^2)| < 1$ also for $\gamma^2 < \nu^2 < \delta^2$, where $\gamma^2 > \beta^2$, then the interval (γ^2, δ^2) is a *secondary interval of periodicity*.

RKN methods which are associated with Padé approximants for the cosine function have the maximum dispersive order, but cannot result P–stable (see Theorem 4 of [3]).

We present the Mathematica session of the computation of the *primary* and *secondary intervals of periodicity* of the [12/12] Padé approximant for $\cos \nu$. We obtained this approximation by applying the Mathematica command `Pade` to $\cos \nu$; the resulting function only exhibits even power of ν. The package `StabInt` requires a rational function in $z = \nu^2$, to suit Definition 1. Our function `BuildPade` performs this necessary change of variable.

```
In[1]:= << BuildRF.m
```

```
In[2]:= BuildPade[Simplify[Pade[Cos[nu],
          {nu,0,12,12}]]];
```

After saving this result in the file *pade1212*, `StabInt` computes the sequences of intervals of stability, which are really intervals of periodicity.

```
In[3]:= <<StabInt.m
```

```
In[4]:= StabIntervals[pade1212]
Intervals of stability =
>    Interval[{0, 39.469565377941},
>       {39.487294532568, 140.85398395396214}]
```

In Table 1 we list the intervals of periodicity of part of the diagonal of the Padé table for $\cos \nu$, together with the sequence of secondary intervals of periodicity. This problem is extremely ill-conditioned, because of the presence of *almost* double roots of the polynomials involved in the computation. The user can detect this situation, by performing the same computation with different values of the input parameter `prec`.

This is the function `BuildPade`:

```
BuildPade[rf_]:=Module[{n,d,cn,cd,ln,ld},
```

Table 1. Intervals of periodicity of diagonal of Padé table for cosine

Padè approximants	Primary interval	Secondary intervals
[2, 2]	(0, 6)	
[4, 4]	(0, 25.2)	
[6, 6]	(0, 9.795404440487079)	
		(9.947923222504878, 55.60620298305996)
[8, 8]	(0, 38.181080951232289)	
		(41.240267276137912, 92.9677998328157766)
[10, 10]	(0, 9.869548741396)	
		(9.869660064292, 82.770520148634116)
		(109.1739061910719, 119.41755686125643)
[12, 12]	(0, 9.86960440105883)	
		(9.86960440111902, 39.4695653779410)
		(39.4872945325676, 140.85398395396214)
[14, 14]	(0, 9.86960439)	
		(9.86960441, 88.682746726851)
		(88.973310395111, 209.65649796945982)
[16, 16]	(0, 9.86960439)	
		(9.86960441, 39.4784040969)
		(39.4784311119, 156.942454292576)
		(158.977741131784, 285.9388998537093)
[18, 18]	(0, 9.8696044)	
		(9.8696044, 39.47841761)
		(39.47841803, 88.8256949051)
		(88.8271844258, 242.682256474427)
		(252.131445440247, 364.5165001998430)
[20, 20]	(0, 9.8696044)	
		(9.8696044, 39.478418)
		(39.478418, 88.82640685)
		(88.82647236, 157.9021389866)
		(157.9252176997, 343.050857230456)
		(386.81540652350, 424.47620300929)
[22, 22]	(0, 9.8696044)	
		(9.8696044, 39.47841633)
		(39.47841887, 88.8264381)
		(88.8264411, 246.6475586166)
		(246.8333485237, 454.46285672925)
[24, 24]	(0, 9.8696044)	
		(9.8696044, 39.4784175)
		(39.4784177, 88.82644032)
		(88.82643889, 157.91365977)
		(157.91368106, 354.8079640887)
		(355.8181996545, 573.38043266510)

```
n=Numerator[rf]; d= Denominator[rf];
cn = CoefficientList[n,x];
cd= CoefficientList[d,x]; ln = Length[cn];
ld= Length[cd]; nu=cn[[1]]; de=cd[[1]];
For[i=2,i<ln,i+=2,nu+= cn[[i+1]]* x^(i/2)];
For[i=2,i<ld,i+=2,de+= cd[[i+1]]* x^(i/2)];
nrf = nu/de; Print[nrf];];
```

4   Collocation methods for second order ODEs

Let us now consider Runge–Kutta–Nyström methods for (4), based on direct collocation with symmetric points (see [7,12] for details of the properties of collocation–based methods). Kramarz showed that each symmetric collocation method, that is, the one based on collocation nodes symmetrically placed within each interval, possesses an interval of periodicity [7]. From this result, it follows that these methods exhibit the property of nondissipativity, which is of primary interest in celestial mechanics (for example, where it is desired that the numerical orbits do not spiral inwards or outwards).

As a further example of application of StabInt.m, let us consider the three-staged, collocation-based RKN method with symmetric points:

$$
\begin{array}{c|ccc}
c & \dfrac{(c-1)^2 c^2}{2(2c-1)^2} & \dfrac{c^3(5c-4)}{3(2c-1)^2} & \dfrac{(2-c)c^3}{6(2c-1)^2} \\[3ex]
\dfrac{1}{2} & \dfrac{7-8c}{96(2c-1)^2} & \dfrac{1-8c+8c^2}{16(2c-1)^2} & \dfrac{8c-1}{96(2c-1)^2} \\[3ex]
1-c & \dfrac{(1-c)^3(1+c)}{6(2c-1)^2} & \dfrac{(c-1)^3(5c-1)}{3(2c-1)^2} & \dfrac{(c-1)^2 c^2}{2(2c-1)^2} \\[3ex]
\hline
& \dfrac{1-c}{6(2c-1)^2} & \dfrac{1-6c+6c^2}{3(2c-1)^2} & \dfrac{c}{6(2c-1)^2} \\[3ex]
& \dfrac{1}{6(2c-1)^2} & \dfrac{2(1-6c+6c^2)}{3(2c-1)^2} & \dfrac{1}{6(2c-1)^2}
\end{array}
\qquad (8)
$$

For any value of the free parameter c, the RKN method represented by the Butcher array (8) has order of convergence 3 and dispersive order 4. Moreover, Theorem 4 in [3] states that there are no P–stable symmetric one–step collocation methods, so that for no value of c in (8) the method can be P–stable.

Firstly , we can use the free parameter c in (8) to heighten the dispersive order of the method [3,11]. When $c = \dfrac{5 \pm \sqrt{15}}{10}$ in (8), then the RKN method represented by the Butcher array (8) has order of convergence 3, dispersive order 6 and interval of periodicity $(0, 3.03 \ldots)$. Its periodicity interval can be computed by the symbolic package, RknStabInt.m, which is described in [10] and available at the URL http://www.netlib.org/ode/symbolic.

Let us now find the value of c which maximizes the *primary periodicity* interval, through the usage of the package StabInt.m. The file *colloc3* contains the expression of the stability function of RKN method (8), which is dependent on the free parameter $c \neq 1/2$.

```
In[3]:= Do[Print["c",c];
        Print[StabIntervals[colloc3]],
        {c,0,1/2-1/100,1/100}]
```

We suppress the output for brevity. Our aim is obtained if c is *near* $\dfrac{9}{40}$, which gives the primary interval of periodicity $(0, 3.85 \ldots)$.

We have described two applications of our package in the context of analysis of stability properties of numerical methods for ODEs, and we feel sure that it could be used in many other fields.

References

1. G.A.Baker, Essentials of Padé approximants, (1975) New York: Academic Press.
2. J.P. Coleman, Numerical methods for y"=f(x,y) via rational approximation for the cosine, *IMA J. Num. Anal.* **10** (1989) 145–165.
3. J.P.Coleman, Rational approximations for the cosine function; P–acceptability and order, *Numerical Algorithms* (1992) 143–158.
4. M.R.Crisci, B.Paternoster, E.Russo, Fully parallel Runge–Kutta Nyström methods for ODEs with oscillating solutions, *Appl. Numer. Math.* **11** (1993) 143–158.
5. M.R.Crisci, B.Paternoster, Parallel Runge–Kutta Nyström methods, *Ricerche di Matematica*, V. XLVII (1998) 125–147.
6. E. Hairer and G. Wanner, Solving Ordinary Differential Equations II: Stiff and Differential–Algebraic Problems, Springer, Berlin, 1991.
7. L.Kramarz, Stability of collocation methods for the numerical solution of $y'' = f(t, y)$, *BIT* **20** (1980) 215–222.
8. J.D.Lambert J.D. Numerical methods for ordinary differential systems, – The Initial Value Problem, John Wiley & Sons, 1991.
9. B.Paternoster, Order bound for a family of parallel Runge–Kutta–Nyström methods through computer algebra, *Computers & Mathematics with applications* 35(9) (1998) 107–119.
10. B.Paternoster, M.Cafaro, Computation of the interval of stability of Runge–Kutta–Nyström methods, *J. Symbolic Computation* **25**(3) (1998) 383–394.
11. P.J.van der Houwen, B.P.Sommeijer, Diagonally implicit Runge–Kutta Nyström methods for oscillatory problems, *SIAM J. Num. Anal.* **26** (1989) 414–429.

12. P.J.van der Houwen, B.P.Sommeijer, Nguyen Huu Cong, Stability of collocation–based Runge–Kutta–Nyström methods, *BIT* **31** (1991) 469–481.

5   Appendix

The package StabInt runs with version 3.0 of Mathematica. It is available through e–mail from the authors.

```
(*:Name: 'StabInt' *)

(*:Authors: Massimo Cafaro, Univ. Lecce, Italy,

     Beatrice Paternoster, Univ. Salerno, Italy *)

(*:Warnings: filenames can't contain spaces*)

(*:Sources: Version 1.0   *)

BeginPackage["'StabInt'"]

ReadRationalFunction[filename_]:=Module[{},
            Get[ToString[filename]]];

BuildExpr[f_,c_]:=Module[{},
        For[i=0,i<pairs,i++,
        If[c[i+1]!=0,
        exp[1+2*i]=Together[f[i+1]+c[i+1]];
        exp[2+2*i]=Together[c[i+1]-f[i+1]],
        exp[1+2*i]=Together[c[i+1]-f[i+1]];
        exp[2+2*i]=Together[c[i+1]-f[i+1]]]]];

MakeRoots[eqn_]:=Module[{zero,root,t,u},
    zero=Flatten[z /.
      NSolve[Numerator[eqn]==0,z,prec]];
    If[!NumberQ[Denominator[eqn]],
    root=Flatten[z /.
      NSolve[Denominator[eqn]==0,z,prec]],
    root=List[]];
    t=N[Select[N[Map[Chop,
       N[Union[zero,root],prec]],prec],
          Positive],prec];
    u=N[RotateLeft[t],prec];
    If[u!=t,rl=N[Sort[Delete[u,
       Position[Abs[#-#2]& @ Sequence[u,t],
       k_/; k <eps]]],prec],
    If[Length[u]>=1,rl=N[List[First[u]],prec],rl=
```

```
            N[u,prec]]]];

Bound[expr_,roots_List]:=Module[{},
    If[Length[roots]==0,
        EmptyList[expr],NotEmptyList[expr,roots]]];

EmptyList[ex_,int_]:=Module[{},Clear[z];
  If[Sign[N[ex /. {z->10}]] == 1 &&
  OddQ[int] == True,
  intlist1=Append[intlist1,Interval[{0,Infinity}]],
  intlist1=Append[intlist1,Interval[{0,0}]]];
  If[Sign[N[ex /. {z->10}]] == 1 &&
      OddQ[int] == False,
  intlist2=Append[intlist2,Interval[{0,Infinity}]],
  intlist2=Append[intlist2,Interval[{0,0}]]]];

NotEmptyList[ex_,roots_List]:=
   Module[{p,t,u,points,values,intervals},
      t=N[Prepend[roots,0],prec];
      u=N[RotateLeft[t],prec];
      points=N[Drop[t+u,-1] / 2,prec];
      values=N[Table[Clear[z];
      N[ex /. z->points[[i]],prec] ,
              {i,Length[points]}],prec];
      p=Position[Map[Sign,values],1];
      intervals=List[];
      For[i=1,i<=Length[p],i++,
          intervals=Append[intervals,
      N[Interval[{t[[p[[i,1]]]],
        t[[p[[i,1]]+1]]}],prec]]];
      If[Sign[N[ex /.
        z->Last[t]+10,prec]] == 1,
      Clear[z];
      intervals=Append[intervals,Interval[
            {Last[t],Infinity}]]];
      If[Length[intervals]==0,
          intervals={Interval[{0,0}]}];
      If[OddQ[int] == True,
          intlist1=intervals,
          intlist2=intervals]];

IntersectIntervals[a_,b_]:=
  Module[{l1,l2,f,s,},
  l1=Length[a]; l2=Length[b]; result=List[];
  Do[r=IntervalIntersection[a[[i]],b[[j]]];
```

```
   f=Min[r];s=Max[r];
   If[MemberQ[result,r]==False && f!= s
     && f!=Infinity && s!= -Infinity,
   result=Append[result,r]],{i,l1},{j,l2}];
   result=Sort[result]];

StabIntervals[filename_]:=Module[{stability},
   ReadRationalFunction[filename];
   BuildExpr[rf,cv];
   For[x = 1, x < pairs, x++,intcomp[x]=List[]];
   For[k = 1, k < 2*pairs, k+=2,
     intlist1=List[]; intlist2=List[];
     Do[MakeRoots[exp[i]];
     Bound[exp[i],rl],{i,k,k+1}];
     IntersectIntervals[intlist1,intlist2];
     intcomp[Floor[k/2]+1]=result];
     temp=intcomp[1];
     For[x = 1, x < pairs, x++,
     IntersectIntervals[temp,intcomp[x+1]];
     temp=result]; stability=temp;
       Print[StringForm[
         "Intervals of stability = ''",stability]];
     If[printing == 1,
     points=List[];
     If[Last[stability][[2]]!=0 &&
         Last[stability][[2]]!=Infinity,
     For[x=0,x<Last[stability][[2]],x+=stepx,
     For[y=0,y < height, y+=stepy,
     k=x+ I y;
     include=True;
     Do[Clear[z];If[(Abs[rf[i]] /. {z->k}) < cv[i],
     include=include && True,
       include=include && False],{i,pairs}];
     If[include == True,
         points=Append[points,{x,y}]]]]];
     ListPlot[points]]];

   ClearAll[prec,pairs,eps,rf,cv,rl,stability,
     intlist1,intlist2,printing,height];
   ClearAll[stepx,stepy,temp,result,points,
     include,z,x,k]];

End[]
Protect[StabIntervals]
EndPackage[]
```

An Automatic Symbolic-Numeric Taylor Series ODE Solver*

Brian J. Dupée and James H. Davenport

Department of Mathematical Sciences, University of Bath, Claverton Down, Bath.
BA2 7AY. UK
email: {bjd,jhd}@maths.bath.ac.uk

Abstract. One of the basic techniques in every mathematician's toolkit is the Taylor series representation of functions. It is of such fundamental importance and it is so well understood that its use is often a first choice in numerical analysis. This faith has not, unfortunately, been transferred to the design of computer algorithms.

Approximation by use of Taylor series methods is inherently partly a symbolic process and partly numeric. This aspect has often, with reason, been regarded as a major hindrance in algorithm design. Whilst attempts have been made in the past to build a consistent set of programs for the symbolic and numeric paradigms, these have been necessarily multi-stage processes.

Using current technology it has at last become possible to integrate these two concepts and build an automatic adaptive symbolic-numeric algorithm within a uniform framework which can hide the internal workings behind a modern interface.

1 Introduction

This paper introduces a symbolic-numeric implementation of Taylor series methods for the solution of initial value ODE problems. Hitherto, the only implementations have been wholly numeric, wholly symbolic or obviously a multi-stage process (one where the symbolic and numeric calculations are carried out separately with at least one other stage between them). Such methods present a variety of computational problems, some of which are better solved symbolically, others numerically. This paper identifies the characteristics of such methods and presents an algorithm for better evaluation.

The techniques of approximating an ODE by a Taylor series has been known for many years and has been implemented, for example, by a group led by A. C. Norman in Cambridge, UK, in the package "TAYLOR" [11–13,2] using the analysis by Barton, Willers and Zahar [3]. An alternative package, 'ATSMCC' (Automatic Taylor Series by Morris, Chang and Corliss) [5], was also made available a few years later. In operation, these packages generate appropriate Fortran code to define the Taylor series and the evaluation process, given the ODE and initial conditions, for further compilation and operation. So they are at least a three-stage process. In [5], Corliss and Chang freely admit that:

---

* The project "Composite Computing Methods Integrating Symbolic, Numeric and Graphical Packages for Research Engineers" is funded by the UK Govt. Joint Information Systems Committee under their Technology Applications Programme JTAP 5/11

When all the computer time for preprocessing, compiling, linking and execution was included, the relatively high system-dependent cost of linking
with the library routines overwhelmed most other differences in CPU times.

The user-time performing the intervening stages (compilation, linking etc.) only
added to the overall cost.

Some Computer Algebra Systems (CASs), such as Maple [8], Axiom [9] and
Mathematica [15], have the necessary algorithms built-in to calculate the Taylor
series symbolically. After all, this is a purely symbolic process. The evaluation stage
is performed separately, usually symbolically even though this is computationally
expensive.

The implementation in this paper, written for the CAS Axiom, is a single composite process which takes the ODE and initial conditions, creates the Taylor series,
automatically generates the Fortran evaluation code which it then compiles, links
and runs before returning the required result.

The trade-off for the speed of the evaluation process using Fortran is in the
cost of the Fortran generation and compilation[1]. It therefore makes sense to limit
the size of the generated Fortran code as much as is reasonable. The speed-up over
purely symbolic code is thus optimised. The better ease of use when compared to
the purely numerical methods and applications like 'TAYLOR' and 'ATSMCC' is
self-evident.

The paper includes comparisons between the new implementation, Taylor series
methods using purely symbolic code and using alternative symbolic-numeric code.

2 Taylor Series Methods

The two papers by Barton, Willers and Zahar [2,3] provide a succinct and as complete a description and analysis of the method as are available. However, we will
give a summary.

The method is described in [3] as an application of the process of analytic
continuation. So, given a system of differential equations

$$F(t, y, y', y'', ..., y^{(n)}) = 0 \qquad (1)$$

linear in $y^{(n)}$ and initial conditions

$$y_1 = y(t_0)$$
$$y_2 = y'(t_0)$$
$$y_3 = y''(t_0)$$
$$\vdots$$
$$y_n = y^{(n-1)}(t_0)$$

all specified, the Taylor series expansion about $t = t_0$ for y is given as

$$y_i(t) = \sum_{j=0}^{\infty} \frac{y_i^{(j)}(t_0)}{j!}(t - t_0)^j \qquad (2)$$

---

[1] The Fortran generation process in Axiom is the costliest in practice although the
compilation itself is at least of the order n^2 on the size of the code.

The general idea is that this, or rather its approximation

$$y_i(t) = \sum_{j=0}^{N} \frac{y_i^{(j)}(t_0)h^j}{j!} \tag{2'}$$

is evaluated at $t = t_1 = t_0 + h$, the series is then expanded about this point and the process continued. The calculation of the Taylor series expansion is described in [2].

The analysis of the method in [3] shows that the method is extremely accurate and that, given a step-length $h = t - t_r$, the local error $E(h)$ will be small if

- the error involved in the truncation of the Taylor series is at least as small as the tolerance ϵ and
- the step-length chosen minimises $E(h)/h$.

The ideal truncation N is assumed to be the equal to the number of significant digits of the platform and is found to be only slightly dependent on the tolerance. However, since N was not found to be particularly sensitive to the equations integrated, this value must only be considered as an arbitrary ideal.

In the "TAYLOR" package, given the example

$$y''(t) - (1 - y(t)^2)y'(t) + y(t) = 0 \tag{3}$$

(van der Pol's equation with $\mu = 1$) [16] and initial values

$$y(0) = 2$$
$$y'(0) = 0,$$

the Fortran code is generated using the commands (in a file)

```
INDEP T
DOUBLE
INIT SETUP
Y(0) = 2
Y'(0) = 0
EQNS
Y"=(1-Y**2)*Y' - Y
ADV VAL(Y,Y',T)
```

which will cause the program to create a number of Fortran subroutines for describing and evaluating the Taylor series. The user must then create a main program (in Fortran or C) to utilise these subroutines (enter parameters, print results etc.), compile, link and run the binary.

The main differences in 'ATSMCC' is in the calculation of the truncation value N and the appropriate step-size. Even though it requires less user control, the complete program has, in general, five stages:

1. create and edit the input,
2. preprocess to translate the input into object code,
3. compile the Fortran object code,

4. link with the ATSMCC subroutine library, and

5. execute the resulting load module to solve the problem.

Some of these steps may be combined and others may only need to be performed once if a single problem is to be solved repeatedly. However, this program structure does not lend itself towards a flexible and natural user-friendly interface.

The code supplied with some of the CASs use purely symbolic techniques. The main problems occur during the evaluation process since the number of substitutions (evaluations) of the parameters at each step is very large. Since substitutions are time-consuming, this part of the process is very inefficient. If the Taylor series evaluation process is compiled, there is some improvement, but not sufficient to boost the efficiency enough to be considered anything more than an exercise.

3   Composite Methods

Symbolic-numeric methods as implemented, for example, in ANNA [7] use symbolic analysis to identify sufficient parameters to be able to select and implement numeric procedures, usually from the NAG Fortran Library. The results are then returned for further symbolic processing. Underlying this is the ability within Axiom to create, compile and link Fortran evaluation procedures, named ASPs (Argument Sub-Programs), at run-time [4,10].

The technology to perform such processes, Nagman and nagd, is described in [6]. In essence, the Nagman local agent manages the data-transfer between the different computing protocols, using RPC (remote procedure call) to pass the data to the Nag daemon (nagd), which may be running on a remote system. The nagd incorporates a main program (stub), the Fortran library routine with appropriate C header files and the Axiom-generated ASP, performs the compilation and runs the resulting binary. The results are fed back through the Nagman to the current Axiom session.

The Fortran generation utilities included with recent implementations of Axiom are used to both create the Fortran code and also to verify that the full ANSI 1978 standards are adhered to with respect to variable names, types and constructs. The verification is necessary since the code may need to be compiled on a remote machine of indeterminate operating system and with any compiler.

All pre- and post-processing are performed within Axiom packages or the interactive session. The use of these packages, which may involve the use of the Axiom Category and Domain structures, allows for the automation of the complex processes and can thus become part of an intricate user interface.

In this implementation, since we are generating the algorithm, as opposed to the sub-programs, at runtime, the Fortran subroutine corresponding to the algorithm has to be compiled (using the same Fortran compiler as recognised by the nagd) and placed in a library to be accessed in a similar way to the access of the NAG Fortran Library's algorithms. The C header file is placed alongside the other C source files in the nagd directory structure and the Axiom code (the ASP Domain and the Taylor series method Package) is compiled as usual.

Algorithm 1: ODESolveTaylorSeries

% pre-processing
    calculate N from size of system

% symbolic-processing
    compute formal (lazy) Taylor series
    truncate Taylor series to order N

% Code creation, compilation and linking
    calculate Workspace requirements
    create ASP
    initiate Nagman
    compile Fortran code
    run Fortran code

% post-processing
    return result
    remove unwanted workspace
    print result

---

4 The Integrated Algorithm

The Taylor series representation is calculated symbolically within the Axiom Package `ExpressionSpaceODESolver` (written by Manuel Bronstein) which returns a lazy Taylor series in $n + 2$ variables where n is the order of the ODE. For this implementation this is truncated to form a polynomial in t of order $N = n + a$ where a is an integer ≥ 2 which can be estimated in the pre-processing stage (depending on the required accuracy and estimate of stiffness) and where the other variables may be of arbitrary order. So, for example, (3) could be approximated by (in the case where $a = 2$):

$$\left(-\frac{1}{12}y_3^3 + \left(\frac{1}{3}y_2^3 - \frac{1}{3}y_2\right)y_3^2\right.$$

$$\left. + \left(-\frac{1}{24}y_2^6 + \frac{1}{8}y_2^4 + \frac{5}{24}y_2^2 - \frac{1}{24}\right)y_3 - \frac{1}{24}y_2^5 + \frac{1}{12}y_2^3\right)t^4$$

$$+ \left(\frac{1}{3}y_1y_3^3 + \left(-\frac{4}{3}y_1y_2^3 + \left(\frac{4}{3}y_1 - \frac{1}{3}\right)y_2\right)y_3^2\right.$$

$$+ \left(\frac{1}{6}y_1y_2^6 + \left(-\frac{1}{2}y_1 + \frac{1}{6}\right)y_2^4 + \left(-\frac{5}{6}y_1 - \frac{1}{3}\right)y_2^2 + \frac{1}{6}y_1\right)y_3$$

$$\left. + \frac{1}{6}y_1y_2^5 + \left(-\frac{1}{3}y_1 + \frac{1}{6}\right)y_2^3 - \frac{1}{6}y_2\right)t^3$$

$$+ \left(-\frac{1}{2}y_1^2 y_3^3 + (2y_1^2 y_2^3 + (-2y_1^2 + y_1)\, y_2)\, y_3^2 + \left(-\frac{1}{4}y_1^2 y_2^6 \right.\right.$$

$$+ \left(\frac{3}{4}y_1^2 - \frac{1}{2}y_1 \right) y_2^4 + \left(\frac{5}{4}y_1^2 + y_1 - \frac{1}{2} \right) y_2^2 - \frac{1}{4}y_1^2 + \frac{1}{2} \right) y_3$$

$$\left. \left. - \frac{1}{4}y_1^2 y_2^5 + \left(\frac{1}{2}y_1^2 - \frac{1}{2}y_1 \right) y_2^3 + \left(\frac{1}{2}y_1 - \frac{1}{2} \right) y_2 \right) t^2 \right.$$

$$+ \left(\frac{1}{3}y_1^3 y_3^3 + \left(-\frac{4}{3}y_1^3 y_2^3 + \left(\frac{4}{3}y_1^3 - y_1^2 \right) y_2 \right) y_3^2 + \left(\frac{1}{6}y_1^3 y_2^6 \right.\right.$$

$$+ \left(-\frac{1}{2}y_1^3 + \frac{1}{2}y_1^2 \right) y_2^4 + \left(-\frac{5}{6}y_1^3 - y_1^2 + y_1 \right) y_2^2 + \frac{1}{6}y_1^3 - y_1 + 1 \right) y_3$$

$$\left. \left. + \frac{1}{6}y_1^3 y_2^5 + \left(-\frac{1}{3}y_1^3 + \frac{1}{2}y_1^2 \right) y_2^3 + \left(-\frac{1}{2}y_1^2 + y_1 \right) y_2 \right) t \right.$$

$$- \frac{1}{12}y_1^4 y_3^3 + \left(\frac{1}{3}y_1^4 y_2^3 + \left(-\frac{1}{3}y_1^4 + \frac{1}{3}y_1^3 \right) y_2 \right) y_3^2$$

$$+ \left(-\frac{1}{24}y_1^4 y_2^6 + \left(\frac{1}{8}y_1^4 - \frac{1}{6}y_1^3 \right) y_2^4 + \left(\frac{5}{24}y_1^4 + \frac{1}{3}y_1^3 - \frac{1}{2}y_1^2 \right) y_2^2 \right.$$

$$\left. - \frac{1}{24}y_1^4 + \frac{1}{2}y_1^2 - y_1 \right) y_3 - \frac{1}{24}y_1^4 y_2^5 + \left(\frac{1}{12}y_1^4 - \frac{1}{6}y_1^3 \right) y_2^3 +$$

$$\left(\frac{1}{6}y_1^3 - \frac{1}{2}y_1^2 + 1 \right) y_2 \quad (4)$$

The calculation of the optimum value of the truncation parameter N is critical. This is since the prime costs in this algorithm are in the Fortran generation, compilation and linking stages, as opposed to the evaluation stages of a fully symbolic system or the purely numeric stages of "TAYLOR". We can therefore consider, if necessary, using smaller step-sizes than those recommended in [3] rather than a larger polynomial system to cut down this cost but we then leave ourselves open to problems with any ODE showing more than the mildest of stiffness (since in a stiff system, there will be more information contained in the coefficients of the higher exponents of the Taylor series)[2]. We must, though, ensure that all appropriate y^i are calculated.

It must be noted that the step-sizes mentioned above are, or can be, much larger than the step-sizes used in other ODE solvers such as Runge-Kutta. The initial 'test evaluation' can use a step-size of as much as $\frac{1}{10}$ of the complete range of integration. So the usual number of steps is often much less than other methods.

The polynomial is then coded into a Fortran ASP. Each monomial becomes one line of Fortran code to better facilitate the calculation of the return values y, y' ... y^n (see Appendix A.1). This is then passed to the nagd for compilation and linking.

---

[2] An alternative Taylor series algorithm for stiff equations is described in [1] but this is much more expensive computationally and it is not apparent that there would likely be any major cost or accuracy benefits over other stiff methods.

Whilst Horner's rule should normally be preferred for evaluation, it is not, as yet, available in Axiom. There are other considerations though. Since the most costly part of the algorithm is in the ASP generation and not the evaluation, the use of Horner's rule would not make a significant difference. Indeed, the size of the code *may* be larger and thus less efficient overall.

Other pre-processing stages include the estimation of the amount of workspace required for the calculation stages and the setting up of the appropriate matrices. For this, a reasonable estimate must be made of the number of iterations that may be required in the calculation. This is not an easy task since the algorithm is designed to be adaptive i.e. alter the step-length according to the changes in the values of y, y' etc. Obviously a 'quick and dirty' method of estimating the workspace requirements may be inaccurate but sufficient. A reasonable overestimate is all that is required. This is calculated as a function of the truncation parameter, N, the order of the ODE, n, and the required tolerance.

The Fortran library program (see Appendix A.2), after checking input values for consistency, calculates a weight function (a function of the input values) and evaluates its first step. On the result of this evaluation it re-calculates the weight function to get a good basic estimate for the step-size before recalculating the first step. It then goes through the evaluation process modifying the step-size as appropriate. All of the calculated values for y, y' ... y^n are returned.

In order to present the information in as consistent a way as possible, the post-processing stages remove some of the excess workspace and re-order those that are left. It does, however, one other important job. If the numerical process was unable to get a sufficient answer, it may re-calculate the initial step-size or increase the amount of workspace before re-initiating the calculation.

5 Examples

Example 1: Using the system, (3) is solved with the commands:

```
y := operator 'y;
eq := D(y(t),t,2) - (1 - y(t)^2)*D(y(t),t) + y(t) = 0
solve(eq,y,t=0..20,[2,0],0.01)$TaylorSeriesODENumPackage
```

which calculates the values of y and y' from $t = 0$ to $t = 20$ and gives the result:[3]

---

[3] The returned fields in the result are:

ifail : The return status — a non-zero value indicates a failure
y : The values of y, y' ... y^n at the end point
result : The values of y, y' ... y^n at all iteration points corresponding to xout (for display etc.)
xout : The iteration points and the end point (for display etc.)
yin : the values of y, y' ... y^n at the last iteration point
count : the number of iterations.

```
(4)
[ifail: Integer, result: Matrix(DoubleFloat),
 y: Matrix(DoubleFloat), xout: Matrix(DoubleFloat),
 yin: Matrix(DoubleFloat), count: Integer]
                                      Type: Result
```

(5) -> %.'y

```
(5)   [2.00897152959078   - 0.0370573647342098]
```
                                 Type: Matrix DoubleFloat

in 214 iterations. The field y here contains the values of y and y' at the end point.

If the value of μ is set in the van der Pol equation to increase the stiffness i.e. (3) is changed to:

$$y''(t) - 5(1 - y(t)^2)y'(t) + y(t) = 0 \qquad (5)$$

then this is mildly stiff and 4 d.p. accuracy can be achieved without increasing the truncation parameter, N, at the cost of increasing the number of iterations to 647. Any further increase in stiffness would require an increase in N.

Example 2: The ODE

$$y'(t) + y(t) = \sin t \qquad (6)$$

with initial conditions

$$y(0) = 1$$

is calculated from $t = 0$ to $t = 20$ using the commands:

```
eq2 := D(y(t),t) + y(t) = sin(t)
solve(eq2,y,t=0..20,[1],0.1)$TaylorSeriesODENumPackage
```

and this produces:

```
(6)
[ifail: Integer, result: Matrix(DoubleFloat),
 y: Matrix(DoubleFloat), xout: Matrix(DoubleFloat),
 yin: Matrix(DoubleFloat), count: Integer]
                                      Type: Result
```

(7) -> %.'y

```
(7)   [0.252446658993222]
```
                              Type: Matrix DoubleFloat

in 176 iterations.

The same examples were solved using the Taylor series method incorporated within Maple and using Runge-Kutta or Adams methods as appropriate within

ANNA both as the result only and with 200 intermediate results. The new algorithm and the Maple symbolic algorithm were also timed including plotting the resulting graph. The timings are as follows[4]:

Table 1. Sample test timings

	Example 1	Example 2
Maple (Taylor)	197s	14s
including plot	795s	153s
ANNA (result only)	37s	7s
intermediate results	65s	56s
New Algorithm	66s	14s
including plot	72s	16s

Commentary: The above results require some explanation. The increase in time needed for 200 intermediate results using ANNA is due to the smaller step-size required. The Maple results are affected by the difficulty to tailor results to a given precision but similar results are obtained with a purely symbolic algorithm written in Axiom.

A simple display function provided with the package can then produce:

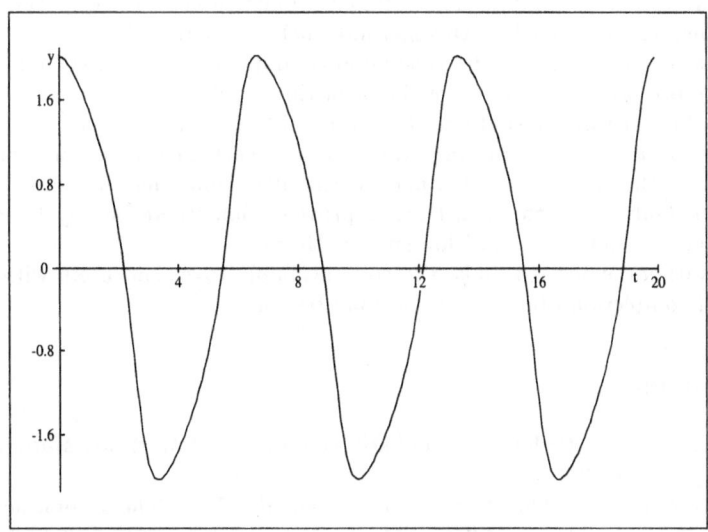

Fig. 1. van der Pol's equation with $\mu = 1$, $y(0) = 2$ and $y'(0) = 0$.

---

[4] All tests were carried out on a SUN Sparc Classic named 'dictum' under Solaris 2.5.1 at the University of Bath using Axiom 2.2 and Maple V release 4.00f to 4 d.p.

6 Conclusion

Tests show considerable speed-up over purely symbolic processing, except for the smallest of systems, but actual figures differ due to different platform/platform combinations. However, the single most immediate effect is of the simple interface and the amount of information returned. This extra information is achieved at little extra cost.

With a non-stiff system, as (3), the accuracy of the system is remarkable. If a variable loading is applied to affect the stiffness, the accuracy drops dramatically unless the order of polynomial approximation is increased. But this affects the time involved in the Fortran generation stages. This means that for anything more than mild stiffness, the algorithm is not optimal.

For simple systems, the cost can be comparable to other symbolic-numeric methods as implemented within ANNA, although the main benefits are in terms of the achieved accuracy and whether intermediate results are required for, say, display. However, this method is not appropriate to those ODEs for which the CAS cannot find the recurrence relation.

Further work will eventually include the incorporation of this method into ANNA. For this, a measure function will be created which calculates the system size, stiffness and stability of the ODE and returns a value which corresponds to the ability of this particular method to solve the ODE efficiently. It is clear from the above that increasing stiffness will warrant a larger polynomial approximation and therefore reduce the measure, up to a point where a different method (such as BDF) would be more appropriate. Similarly a larger system and decreasing stability would have the same effect.

It will also be possible under certain circumstances to increase the range of ODEs which can be solved by this method, such as where in (1) F is not linear in $y^{(n)}$ but a linear system can be calculated by differentiation. This could be done within the pre-processing stages of the algorithm.

The other area which would need attention if this method is to be widely useful, especially for *real-world problems*, would be the Fortran generation tools within Axiom. It is the slowness of this part of the algorithm which is dominating the evaluation. Only when this has been improved would there be any benefit from using a better evaluation algorithm such as Horner.

The authors expect to make the code available to Axiom users within a few months of completion (July 1999) and final testing.

References

1. BARTON, D. On taylor series and stiff equations. *ACM Trans. Math. Softw. 6*, 3 (Sept. 1980), 281–294.
2. BARTON, D., WILLERS, I. M., AND ZAHAR, R. M. V. The automatic solution of systems of ordinary differential equations by the method of taylor series. *Computer Journal 14*, 3 (1971).
3. BARTON, D., WILLERS, I. M., AND ZAHAR, R. M. V. Taylor series methods for ordinary differential equations — an evaluation. In Rice [14], pp. 369–390.
4. BROUGHAN, K. A., KEADY, G., ROBB, T., RICHARDSON, M. G., AND DEWAR, M. C. Some symbolic computing links to the NAG numeric library. *SIGSAM Bulletin 25* (July 1991), 28–37.

5. CORLISS, G. F., AND CHANG, Y. F. Solving ordinary differential equations using taylor series. *ACM Trans. Math. Softw. 8*, 2 (June 1982), 114–144.

6. DEWAR, M. C. Manipulating fortran code in AXIOM and the AXIOM-NAG link. In *Workshop on Symbolic and Numeric Computation (1993)* (Helsinki, 1994), H. Apiola, M. Laine, and E. Valkeila, Eds., pp. 1–12. Research Report B10, Rolf Nevanlinna Institute, Helsinki.

7. DUPÉE, B. J., AND DAVENPORT, J. H. An intelligent interface to numerical routines. In *DISCO'96: Design and Implementation of Symbolic Computation Systems* (Karlsrühe, 1996), J. Calmet and J. Limongelli, Eds., vol. 1128 of *Lecture Notes in Computer Science*, Springer Verlag, Berlin, pp. 252–262.

8. HECK, A. *Introduction to Maple*, 2nd ed. Springer Verlag, New York, 1996.

9. JENKS, R. D., AND SUTOR, R. S. *AXIOM: The Scientific Computation System*. Springer-Verlag, New York, 1992.

10. KEADY, G., AND NOLAN, G. Production of argument subprograms in the AXIOM-NAG link: examples involving nonlinear systems. In *Workshop on Symbolic and Numeric Computation, May 1993* (Helsinki, 1994), H. Apiola, M. Laine, and E. Valkeila, Eds., pp. 13–32. Research Report B10, Rolf Nevanlinna Institute, Helsinki.

11. NORMAN, A. C. *TAYLOR Users Manual*. Computing Laboratory, University of Cambridge, UK, 1973.

12. NORMAN, A. C. Computing with formal power series. *ACM Trans. Math. Softw. 1* (1975), 346–356.

13. NORMAN, A. C. Expanding the solutions of implicit sets of ordinary differential equations. *Comp. J 19* (1976), 63–68.

14. RICE, J. R., Ed. *Mathematical Software*. Academic Press, New York, 1971.

15. WOLFRAM, S. *The Mathematica Book*, 3rd ed. CUP, Cambridge, 1996.

16. ZWILLINGER, D. *Handbook of Differential Equations*, 2nd ed. Academic Press, San Diego, CA, 1989.

A Fortran Code

A.1 ASP

```
SUBROUTINE EVAL(N,PREC,XT,YIN,YVAL,YOUT)
INTEGER PREC,N
DOUBLE PRECISION XT,YIN(N)
DOUBLE PRECISION YOUT(N),YVAL(PREC)
YVAL(1)=(-0.08333333333333333 D0*YIN(1)**4*YIN(3)**3)+(0.3333333
&333333333 D0*YIN(1)**4*YIN(2)**3+((-0.3333333333333333 D0*YIN(1)
&**4)+0.3333333333333333 D0*YIN(1)**3)*YIN(2))*YIN(3)**2+((-0.041
&66666666666666 D0*YIN(1)**4*YIN(2)**6)+(0.125D0*YIN(1)**4+(-0.16
&66666666666667 D0*YIN(1)**3))*YIN(2)**4+(0.2083333333333333 D0*Y
&IN(1)**4+0.3333333333333333 D0*YIN(1)**3+(-0.5D0*YIN(1)**2))*YIN
&(2)**2+(-0.04166666666666666 D0*YIN(1)**4)+0.5D0*YIN(1)**2+(-1.0
&D0*YIN(1)))*YIN(3)+(-0.04166666666666666 D0*YIN(1)**4*YIN(2)**5)
&+(0.08333333333333333 D0*YIN(1)**4+(-0.1666666666666667 D0*YIN(1
&)**3))*YIN(2)**3+(0.1666666666666667 D0*YIN(1)**3+(-0.5D0*YIN(1)
&**2)+1.0D0)*YIN(2)
YVAL(2)=0.3333333333333333 D0*YIN(1)**3*YIN(3)**3+((-1.333333333
&333333 D0*YIN(1)**3*YIN(2)**3)+(1.333333333333333 D0*YIN(1)**3+(
&-1.0D0*YIN(1)**2))*YIN(2))*YIN(3)**2+(0.1666666666666667 D0*YIN(
&1)**3*YIN(2)**6+((-0.5D0*YIN(1)**3)+0.5D0*YIN(1)**2)*YIN(2)**4+(
&(-0.8333333333333334 D0*YIN(1)**3)+(-1.0D0*YIN(1)**2)+YIN(1))*YI
&N(2)**2+0.1666666666666667 D0*YIN(1)**3+(-1.0D0*YIN(1))+1.0D0)*Y
&IN(3)+0.1666666666666667 D0*YIN(1)**3*YIN(2)**5+((-0.33333333333
&33333 D0*YIN(1)**3)+0.5D0*YIN(1)**2)*YIN(2)**3+((-0.5D0*YIN(1)**
&2)+YIN(1))*YIN(2)
YVAL(3)=(-0.5D0*YIN(1)**2*YIN(3)**3)+(2.0D0*YIN(1)**2*YIN(2)**3+
&((-2.0D0*YIN(1)**2)+YIN(1))*YIN(2))*YIN(3)**2+((-0.25D0*YIN(1)**
&2*YIN(2)**6)+(0.75D0*YIN(1)**2+(-0.5D0*YIN(1)))*YIN(2)**4+(1.25D
&0*YIN(1)**2+YIN(1)-0.5D0)*YIN(2)**2+(-0.25D0*YIN(1)**2)+0.5D0)*Y
&IN(3)+(-0.25D0*YIN(1)**2*YIN(2)**5)+(0.5D0*YIN(1)**2+(-0.5D0*YIN
&(1)))*YIN(2)**3+(0.5D0*YIN(1)-0.5D0)*YIN(2)
YVAL(4)=0.3333333333333333 D0*YIN(1)*YIN(3)**3+((-1.333333333333
&333 D0*YIN(1)*YIN(2)**3)+(1.333333333333333 D0*YIN(1)-0.33333333
&33333333 D0)*YIN(2))*YIN(3)**2+(0.1666666666666667 D0*YIN(1)*YIN
&(2)**6+((-0.5D0*YIN(1))+0.1666666666666667 D0)*YIN(2)**4+((-0.83
&33333333333334 D0*YIN(1))-0.3333333333333333 D0)*YIN(2)**2+0.166
&6666666666667 D0*YIN(1))*YIN(3)+0.1666666666666667 D0*YIN(1)*YIN
&(2)**5+((-0.3333333333333333 D0*YIN(1))+0.1666666666666667 D0)*Y
&IN(2)**3+(-0.1666666666666667 D0*YIN(2))
YVAL(5)=(-0.08333333333333333 D0*YIN(3)**3)+(0.3333333333333333
&D0*YIN(2)**3+(-0.3333333333333333 D0*YIN(2)))*YIN(3)**2+((-0.041
&66666666666666 D0*YIN(2)**6)+0.125D0*YIN(2)**4+0.2083333333333333
&3 D0*YIN(2)**2-0.04166666666666666 D0)*YIN(3)+(-0.04166666666666
&666 D0*YIN(2)**5)+0.08333333333333333 D0*YIN(2)**3
YOUT(1)=YVAL(5)*XT**4+YVAL(4)*XT**3+YVAL(3)*XT*XT+YVAL(2)*XT+YVA
&L(1)
YOUT(2)=4.0D0*YVAL(5)*XT**3+3.0D0*YVAL(4)*XT*XT+2.0D0*YVAL(3)*XT
&+YVAL(2)
RETURN
END
```

A.2   Library Subroutine

```
      SUBROUTINE TAYLOR(M,N,PREC,COUNT,XO,XEND,XOUT,YIN,
     &                  WORK,EVAL,EVALOUT,YOUT,TOL,IFAIL)

      INTEGER M,N,COUNT,PREC,IFAIL
      DOUBLE PRECISION XO,XEND,TOL
      DOUBLE PRECISION XOUT(M),YIN(N),WORK(PREC)
      DOUBLE PRECISION YOUT(N,M),EVALOUT(PREC)
C     Local variables
      INTEGER I
      DOUBLE PRECISION H,W,NEXT,STEP
      LOGICAL BACKWARD, FORWARD

      EXTERNAL EVAL
      INTRINSIC ABS

C     Check values of input variables for consistency
      IF ((TOL.LE.0).OR.(XEND.EQ.XO).OR.(PREC.LE.N))
      THEN
        IFAIL = 1
        GOTO 202
      ENDIF
      YIN(1)=XO

C     Put initial value in output
      COUNT=1
      DO 49 I=1,N-1
        YOUT(I,1)=YIN(I+1)
49    CONTINUE
      XOUT(COUNT)=XO

C     First try of stepsize is 1/10th of distance
      H=(XEND-XO)/10.0
C     Divided by a weight function
      W=0.0D0
      DO 50 I=1,N
        W=W+2.0D0*ABS(YIN(I))
50    CONTINUE
      STEP=H/(1.0D0+W/N)
      NEXT=XO+STEP

C     Call the evaluate subroutine
      CALL EVAL(N,PREC,NEXT,YIN,WORK,EVALOUT)
100   IF (ABS(EVALOUT(1)-YIN(2)).GT.TOL) THEN
C        Recalculate H to get a better stepsize
         H=H/2.0
         STEP=H/(1.0D0+W/N)
         NEXT=XO+STEP
         CALL EVAL(N,PREC,NEXT,YIN,WORK,EVALOUT)
         GOTO 100
      ENDIF

C     Increment
      COUNT=COUNT+1
```

```
C     Put result in output
      DO 51 I=1,N
        YOUT(I,COUNT)=EVALOUT(I)
51    CONTINUE
      XOUT(COUNT)=NEXT

      BACKWARD=(XEND.LT.X0)
      FORWARD=.NOT.BACKWARD
C     While not finished
200   IF ((FORWARD.AND.(NEXT.LT.XEND)).OR.
     &         (BACKWARD.AND.(NEXT.GT.XEND))) THEN
C       Increment
        IF (COUNT.GE.M) THEN
          IFAIL=2
          GOTO 202
        ENDIF
        COUNT=COUNT+1
C       Result of last evaluation is input for the next
        YIN(1)=NEXT
        DO 52 I=2,N
          YIN(I)=EVALOUT(I-1)
52      CONTINUE
C       Calculate new weight from all taylor precision
        W=0.0D0
        DO 53 I=1,N-1
          W=W+ABS(EVALOUT(I))
53      CONTINUE
C       Calculate new step
        STEP=H/(1.0D0+W/(N*N))
        IF (STEP.EQ.0) THEN
          IFAIL=3
          GOTO 202
        ENDIF
        NEXT=NEXT+STEP
C       If we've got to the end then make it the end
        IF ((FORWARD.AND.(NEXT.GT.XEND)).OR.
     &         (BACKWARD.AND.(NEXT.LE.XEND))) THEN
          NEXT=XEND
        ENDIF
C       Call then new evaluation
        CALL EVAL(N,PREC,NEXT,YIN,WORK,EVALOUT)
C       Put in output
        DO 54 I=1,N
          YOUT(I,COUNT)=EVALOUT(I)
54      CONTINUE
        XOUT(COUNT)=NEXT
        GOTO 200
C       End while loop
      ENDIF
      IFAIL=0
201   CONTINUE
202   RETURN
      END
```

About Normal Form Method

Victor F. Edneral

Institute for Nuclear Physics of Moscow State University,
Vorobievy Gory, Moscow, 119899, Russia
e-mail: edneral@theory.npi.msu.su

Abstract. The paper describes usage of a normal form method for building an approximation of families of periodic solutions of nonlinear autonomous ordinary differential equations (ODEs). For illustration a center case and a limit circle are chosen.

Keywords: Resonant normal form; Dynamical systems; Computer algebra

1 Introduction

The normal form method is based on a transformation of an ODEs system to a simpler set called the normal form. The importance of this method for an investigation of ODEs near stationary point has been recognized for a long time. For the history of this subject see, for instance, (Arnold, Anosov, 1988) or (Guckenheimer, Holmes, 1986). Definitions of normal form and normalizing transformation can be formulated in different ways for general and special cases. So there are very developed approaches for Hamiltonian systems, see, for example, (Deprit, 1969), (Hori, 1966), (Bruno, 1972), (Bruno, 1990, chapters 1,2). There are also many algorithms (and their implementations) for creating normal forms and corresponding transformations. For the Hamiltonian case see an improved algorithm of Deprit and Hori in (Mersman, 1970) and its symbolic algebra realization under REDUCE system in (Shevchenko, Sokolsky, 1993), a matter of a numerical creation of normal forms of Hamiltonians is described in (Godziewski, Maciejewski, 1990). Questions of integrability and convergence of the normalizing transformation in Hamiltonian case are discussed in (Bruno, 1972, 1990), (Ito, 1989, 1992). Concerning algorithms for the creation of normal form in a general case we mention here (in an addition to Bruno's books) papers (Walcher 91,93, Vallier, 1993).

    In this paper we will use the algorithm based on the approach which was developed by A.D. Bruno (Bruno, 1971, 1972, 1989) for resonant normal form. The important advantage of this approach is a possibility to investigate a wide class of autonomous systems in united, easily algorithmized frame. In particular it provides a constructive way for obtaining the approximations of local families of periodic and conditionally periodic solutions in the form of power/Fourier series for real families and in a form of power series in time dependent exponents for complex ones. For this paper it is especially important that the problem of convergence of used transformations is investigated.

This circumstance allows us to hope that approximations of frequencies and corresponding periodic solutions families near stationary points by finite formulas can be done with acceptable precision. Except solutions themselves we can find also approximations of origin conditions, which initiate such periodic solutions. I.e. we can produce some elements of a phase analyses.

Another advantage of the used approach is an algorithmic simplicity of the creation of the normal form and the corresponding transformations. We have a direct recurrence formula for this procedure. The usage does not demand keeping of some large intermediate results as it is in other algorithms. The approach is free from a necessity to solve intermediate systems of linear equations and from any restrictions on low resonance cases.

It is also possible to approximate by the proposed method the nonperiodic families of solutions ("crude" case). The results are close to the results of the Carleman linearization method. For periodic and conditionally periodic cases the method is a generalization of the Poincare-Lindstedt approach.

Below we describe the creation of the normal form and the application for building of periodic solutions of well known second-order equations. Also we will talk briefly about higher order systems.

2   Problem Formulation

Consider the system of autonomous ordinary differential equations:

$$\dot{\mathbf{x}} = \varPhi(\mathbf{x}), \tag{1}$$

where $\mathbf{x} = (x_1, \dots, x_n)$ is a vector function of time, $\dot{\mathbf{x}} \overset{\text{def}}{=} d\mathbf{x}/dt$ is the time derivative, $\varPhi = (\varPhi_1, \dots, \varPhi_n)$ is a vector which is a function of $\mathbf{x}$ and probably of some parameters.

Such a type of equations originates from many scientific and engineering problems where oscillations, vibrations or wave processes take place. The standard way of an investigation of such systems is:

1. Bifurcation analysis, i.e. the investigation of a picture of behavior of system solutions in dependence on parameters. It is especially important if this behavior is changed sharply at some parameters values.
2. Phase portrait, i.e. an investigation of a behavior of system solutions depending on initial conditions.
3. Calculation of system solutions.

If we have solutions of a system in an analytical form, we have a clear picture of the system behavior, but we can have such solutions very rarely. As a rule we have numerical solutions, but a numerical investigation of above items 1 and 2 is sometimes a complex problem. It is also not simple to obtain numerical solutions in unstable cases. As a consequence of this, we may be interested in some "intermediate" approach, which would be between analytical and numerical methods.

The normal form method is widely used for bifurcation analysis. About methods of such an investigation see, for example, (Hassard, Kazarinoff, Wan, 1981) and (Guckenheimer, Holmes, 1986). You can see in these books that the numerical bifurcation analysis is indeed based on the normal form method. The main idea here is in replacing system (1) with some "model" system having finite order polynomial right-hand sides and transforming them to the canonical (normal) form. We can make from the lowest nonvanishing coefficients of the normal form the qualitative conclusions about the behavior of the original system. It is sufficient to know only lowest orders of the normal form for such an analysis. Sometimes this job can be done by hand, sometimes by computer algebra systems, see, for example, (Rand, Armbruster, 1987).

Here we try to demonstrate that the calculation of high orders of the normal form can be useful also for targets 2 and 3 mentioned above. We restrict our consideration here mainly to the construction of approximations to periodic solutions but we have a material for using this approach in a "crude" case and in the case of conditionally periodic solutions.

The study of systems of type (1) in the neighborhood of *stationary* point $\mathbf{x}^0$, where $\Phi(\mathbf{x}^0) = \mathbf{0}$, typically includes three preliminary steps. Firstly $\mathbf{x}$ is shifted by $-\mathbf{x}^0$ so that $\Phi(\mathbf{0}) = \mathbf{0}$, i.e. $\mathbf{0}$ is the stationary point to be studied. Each stationary point of the system is considered separately.

The second step is a reduction of the system to a model form where the vector $\Phi(\mathbf{x})$ is approximated by a vector of polynomials. If in some neighborhood of the stationary point Φ is an analytic function of $\mathbf{x}$ then its power series can be used to get a smooth approximation with desired precision. Often this step is made simultaneously with a reduction of the system to its central manifold. In any case, the right-hand sides of the model system will be polynomials without constant terms.

The third step is the transformation of the linear parts matrix to Jordan's form by a complex linear change of $\mathbf{x}$ variables.

After these steps, system (1) has the form:

$$\dot{y}_i = \lambda_i y_i + \sigma_i y_{i-1} + \tilde{\Phi}_i(\mathbf{y}), \qquad \sigma_1 = 0, \qquad i = 1, \ldots, n, \qquad (2)$$

where $\Lambda = (\lambda_1, \ldots, \lambda_n)$ is the vector of eigenvalues of the matrix of the linear part of the system and $\tilde{\Phi} = (\tilde{\Phi}_1, \ldots, \tilde{\Phi}_n)$ is a vector of polynomials of finite degree without constant and linear terms.

For this paper, we assume that system (2) satisfies the following assumptions:

- the system is autonomous and has polynomial nonlinearities;
- $\mathbf{0}$ is a stationary point and the system will be studied near $\mathbf{y} = \mathbf{0}$;
- the linear part of the right hand side is diagonal and not all eigenvalues are zero, i.e. $\Lambda \neq \mathbf{0}$.

It is not assumed that neither the system is Hamiltonian, nor that it preserves the phase volume with that it has any internal symmetries.

3   The Normal Form Method

Equations (2) can be written in the form:

$$\dot{y}_i = \lambda_i y_i + y_i \sum_{\mathbf{q} \in \mathcal{N}_i} f_{i,\mathbf{q}} \mathbf{y}^{\mathbf{q}}, \quad i = 1, \ldots, n, \tag{3}$$

where we use the multi-index notation:

$$\mathbf{y}^{\mathbf{q}} = \prod_{j=1}^{n} y_j^{q_j},$$

with the power exponent vector $\mathbf{q} = (q_1, \ldots, q_n)$ and the sets:

$$\mathcal{N}_i = \{\mathbf{q} \in \mathbb{Z}^n : q_i \geq -1 \text{ and } q_j \geq 0, \text{ if } j \neq i, \quad j = 1, \ldots, n\},$$

because the factor y_i has been moved out of the sum in (3).

The normalization is done with a near-identity transformation:

$$y_i = z_i + z_i \sum_{\mathbf{q} \in \mathcal{N}_i} h_{i,\mathbf{q}} \mathbf{z}^{\mathbf{q}}, \quad i = 1, \ldots, n \tag{4}$$

and then we will have equation (3) in the normal form:

$$\dot{z}_i = \psi_i(\mathbf{z}) \overset{\text{def}}{=} \lambda_i z_i + z_i \sum_{\substack{\langle \mathbf{q}, \Lambda \rangle = 0 \\ \mathbf{q} \in \mathcal{N}_i}} g_{i,\mathbf{q}} \mathbf{z}^{\mathbf{q}}, \quad i = 1, \ldots, n. \tag{5}$$

The important difference between (3) and (5) is a restriction on the range of the summation, which is defined by the equation:

$$\langle \mathbf{q}, \Lambda \rangle \overset{\text{def}}{=} \sum_{j=1}^{n} q_j \lambda_j = 0. \tag{6}$$

The h and g coefficients in (4) and (5) are found by using the recurrence formula:

$$g_{i,\mathbf{q}} + \langle \mathbf{q}, \Lambda \rangle \cdot h_{i,\mathbf{q}} = - \sum_{j=1}^{n} \sum_{\substack{\mathbf{p} + \mathbf{r} = \mathbf{q} \\ \mathbf{q} \in \mathcal{N}_i}} (p_j + \delta_{ij}) \cdot h_{i,\mathbf{p}} \cdot g_{j,\mathbf{r}} + \tilde{\Phi}_{i,\mathbf{q}}, \tag{7}$$

where the second summation in the right-hand side is over all integer vectors satisfying the constraint $\mathbf{p} + \mathbf{r} = \mathbf{q}$, and $\tilde{\Phi}_{i,\mathbf{q}}$ is a coefficient of the factor $z_i \mathbf{z}^{\mathbf{q}}$

in the polynomial $\tilde{\Phi}_i$ in (2), arguments of which have been transformed by (4). Here $||\mathbf{p}||$ and $||\mathbf{r}|| < ||\mathbf{q}||$, where $||\mathbf{q}|| \overset{\text{def}}{=} q_1 + \ldots + q_n$.

The ambiguity in (7) is usually fixed by the conventions:

$$\begin{aligned} h_{i,\mathbf{q}} &= 0, && \text{if} \quad \langle \mathbf{q}, \Lambda \rangle = 0, \\ g_{i,\mathbf{q}} &= 0, && \text{if} \quad \langle \mathbf{q}, \Lambda \rangle \neq 0 \end{aligned} \tag{8}$$

and then the normalizing transformation is called a "basic" one.

3.1   Local Families of Periodic Solutions

Firstly note that the sums in (4) and (5) typically include infinitely many terms even though the sum in (3) may have only finite number of ones. The convergence properties of these series were investigated in (Bruno, 1971, 1972, 1989) and, in general, these series diverge. However, using these divergent series, one can find some solutions of the initial system (3).

Let

$$\xi_1(\mathbf{z}), \ldots, \xi_s(\mathbf{z}) \tag{9}$$

be power series in $\mathbf{z}$ without constant terms. If they converge in some neighborhood of the origin $\mathbf{z} = \mathbf{0}$ then solutions of the system:

$$\xi_j(\mathbf{z}) = 0, \quad j = 1, \ldots, s \tag{10}$$

make up the *local analytic set*. If series (9) are formal (i.e. can diverge in any neighborhood of the origin), then system (10) defines the *local formal set*. In the ring of power series there is an ideal generated by series (9). If the ideal has a convergent basis then the formal set is analytic.

In (Bruno, 1989) it was shown that local analytic sets of periodic solutions of system (3) can be found by means of its normal form (5). Namely, for the normal form (5), define the formal set $\mathcal{A}$ to be:

$$\mathcal{A} = \{ \mathbf{z} : \psi_i = \lambda_i z_i \omega, \quad \text{if} \quad \mathrm{Re}\,\lambda_i = 0; \\ z_i = 0, \qquad \text{if} \quad \mathrm{Re}\,\lambda_i \neq 0; \quad i = 1, \ldots, n \}, \tag{11}$$

where ω is a free parameter and it is independent on number i. Power series ψ_i are the same as in (5).

If *all* imaginary eigenvalues of system (2) are rationally dependent numbers (i.e. in the maximal resonant case) and $\Lambda \neq \mathbf{0}$, the local formal set $\mathcal{A}$ is analytic and contains periodic solutions only. Since the ideal generated by this set has a convergent basis, corresponding system (11) has a sense as a system of equations in power series. Each connected branch of set $\mathcal{A}$ is a local analytic family of periodic solutions.

From this point of view, in the above resonant case the normal form is adequate to the original system, at least along the set $\mathcal{A}$, and this set includes all local families of periodic solutions. From the practical point of view, such system that has been normalized to some finite order can be used to approximate all families of periodic solutions near the stationary point and the precision of approximation can be increased arbitrarily.

If not all eigenvalues are rational dependent we need to split the set $\mathcal{A}$ into such subsets that in each of them all coordinates with corresponding rational independent eigenvalues would be zero. Each of these subsets is an analytic set. So in the phase space the set $\mathcal{A}$ can have several components. Each such component can have its own frequency ω.

The general case of non purely-imaginary eigenvalues and a definition of analytic sets which contain local families of conditionally periodic solutions are given in (Bruno, 1989).

3.2   Main Algorithm

The algorithm of the calculation of g and h in (4), (5) is based on (7) and (8). It is convenient to choose the representation of sets of coefficients $g_{i,\mathbf{q}}$ and $h_{i,\mathbf{q}}$ in such a way that they would be combined in homogeneous subgroups where each subgroup has the same order n, i.e. contains only terms with such vector-indexes $\mathbf{q} = \{q_j\}$ that $||\mathbf{q}|| = n$ for each i. You can calculate the sets g and h of the next order by using sets of g and h with smaller order only, i.e. (7) is a recurrence formula.

The algorithm:

Let n be a dimension of the system. For its normalization till order m we are to do:

(i). for $i = 1, 2, \ldots, n$ do:
Calculate all squared in $\mathbf{y}$ elements in the right-hand side nonlinearity $\tilde{\Phi}_i(\mathbf{y})$ in (2), i.e. calculate the subgroup of the first order ($||\mathbf{q}|| = 1$) elements of the set $f_{i,\mathbf{q}}$ in (3) and sort it into two subsets depending on the value of scalar product (6). The first set where this product is zero will be the first order subgroup of g_i and the second set after a division by the value of the corresponding scalar product will be the first order subgroup of h_i

(ii). for $k = 2, 3, \ldots, m$ do:
(a) for $i = 1, 2, \ldots, n$ do:
calculate the subgroup of order k of the nonlinear terms $\tilde{\Phi}_i(\mathbf{y})$ in (2) for which the substitution $\mathbf{y}$ is evaluated by (4) till order $k - 1$ and define coefficients at monomials $z_i\mathbf{z}^\mathbf{q}$ as $f_{i,\mathbf{q}}$;
(b) for $i = 1, 2, \ldots, n$ do:
Calculate the subgroups of g_i and h_i of order k by a subdivision of set $f_{i,\mathbf{q}}$ into two subsets as in step (i). After that you can supplement the set g_i till full order k and a part of the set h_i without a contribution from the first term of the right-hand side in (7).

(c) for $i = 1, 2, \ldots, n$ do:

for $j = 1, 2, \ldots, n$ do:

supplement the preliminary set of order k of h_i with properly sorted multiplications of *all* elements of such subgroups of $h_{i,\mathbf{p}}$ and $g_{j,\mathbf{r}}$ that their total order, i.e. $||\mathbf{p}+\mathbf{r}|| = k$. Not all these multiplications should be really calculated, because the factor $(p_j + \delta_{i,j})$ is zero at some values of j index. Before the supplement all elements above are to be divided by the corresponding scalar products too.

A cost of the algorithm above is low in comparison with a cost of evaluation of the right-hand side of the nonlinear system. Under such circumstances it is very important to calculate the right-hand sides very economically, using so much as possible the fact that we need to calculate at each step of (ii) the homogeneous terms of $\tilde{\Phi}_i$ of order k only and all terms of lower orders are not changed during the later operations. The problem of optimization of this evaluation is one of the main limitations for an automatization of generating codes for the right-hand side calculation.

3.3   NORT Package

The calculation of the coefficients of the normal form (5) and corresponding transformation (4) with respect of (7) and (8) was implemented as the NORT package. Earlier attempts of the author to compute sufficiently high orders of the normal form using high level of the REDUCE language (Hearn, 1987) were not very successful. Because of this, the NORT package (Edneral, Khrustalev , 1985, 1992) was created. NORT is written in Standard LISP and contains now about 2000 operators. NORT is a package of procedures to treat truncated multivariate power series in arbitrary dimensions. In addition to procedures for arithmetic operations with series, there are special procedures for the creation of normal forms and procedures for substitutions, for calculations of roots (when it is possible), for differentiating, for printing and for inverting

multivariate power series, etc. It contains also special procedures for a calculation of Lyapunov's values. NORT can be used as a separate program or as a REDUCE package.

Besides series, expressions in NORT can contain non-negligible variables (parameters). So there is implemented multivariate series-polynomial arithmetic. The complex-valued numerical coefficients of the truncated power series-polynomials may be treated in three different arithmetics: rational, modular, floating point and approximate rational. There are also several options for the output form of these numbers, the output is in a REDUCE readable form. The program uses an internal recurrence representation for its objects. Remark that a garbage collection time for examples below was smaller than 3% of evaluation time. This can characterize the NORT package as a program with a good enough internal organization.

Unfortunately at this moment the package has no friendly user interface yet. The main reason is that nonlinear systems of ODEs have a so wide variety that we have no clear ideas about a proper classification of properties as it was possible for second-order systems (pay your attention to the nice package ALKAHEST III (Fitch, Norman, Moore, 1986)).

4   Application of the Normal Form Method for an Approximation of Periodic Families of ODEs Solutions

4.1   The General Scheme of the ODEs Investigation

The general scheme of the investigation of a nonlinear ODEs system by the normal form method near each stationary point is as follows:

1. Recasting the system in a model (free of constants polynomial) form.
2. The linear normalization of the system, i.e. the reduction of a linear part of the right-hand sides of the system to Jordan's or to a diagonal form and an investigation of the corresponding eigenvalues.
3. Searching for "resonant" values of parameters, i.e. such values at which groups of rational dependent pure imaginary eigenvalues appear. The system should be investigated in the neighborhood of each such values of parameters.
4. The non-linear normalization of the system, i.e. the creation of the normal form and the corresponding normalizing transformation; (sometimes it is called as recasting the system in a "resonance form").
5. The bifurcation analysis of the system in parameters by observing the lowest nonvanishing orders of the normal form.
6. Building the periodic and conditionally periodic approximations of solution families which include the stationary point, i.e. *local* solutions.
7. Reducing the order of the normalized system if it is necessary, and a repetition of the investigation above in the neighborhood of each stationary point of the newest system.

4.2   Second-Order Systems as a Transparent Example

All questions of convergence and integrability of normal forms for any second-order systems of type (2) near stationary point have been investigated by (Bruno, 1971, 1989) for the case where the stationary point is an elementary singular point, i.e. both eigenvalues of the system are not equal zero simultaneously. The result of this investigation stated briefly is as follows: the normal forms for such equations are integrable. For each case there are written integrals of the normalized system. The result regarding the convergence is as follows. Let $\lambda_2 \neq 0$ and $\lambda \overset{\text{def}}{=} \lambda_1/\lambda_2$. If $Im(\lambda) \neq 0$ or if $\lambda > 0$ then the transformation is convergent, and we can produce an approximate solution of the original system from known integrals of the normal form by transformation (4) with any desirable precision. In other words, cases of "focus" and "node" can be treated without any additional demands. At a negative irrational λ the convergence will take place if for all non-zero vectors $\mathbf{q}$ with integer elements there exist positive ε, ν such that $|(\mathbf{q}, \varLambda)| > \varepsilon(|q_1| + |q_2|)^{-\nu}$. This condition can be checked before creation of the normal form. This case is a particular case of a saddle point. But at real non-positive rational $\lambda = -m/n \leq 0$ we will have convergence under some additional requirements on the normal form. This is an interesting case. It includes the cases of a center and a limit circle. Let us look at a couple of examples.

4.3   Duffing's Equation

This is an equation of the second order, which origins from a problem of a mathematical pendulum:

$$\frac{d^2\phi}{dt^2} + \omega_0^2 \sin(\phi) = 0, \tag{12}$$

where ϕ is an angle of deviation of the pendulum and it can be approximated by the series (units below have been chosen so that $\omega_0 = 1$) with the change $\phi = \sqrt{6}x$. We get the Duffing's equation:

$$\frac{d^2x}{dt^2} = -x + x^3. \tag{13}$$

This is a Hamiltonian equation with the full energy H:

$$H = \frac{1}{2}(\frac{dx}{dt})^2 + \frac{1}{2}x^2 - \frac{1}{4}x^4 \tag{14}$$

By linear complex change of variables:

$$x = y_1 + y_2, \qquad \frac{dx}{dt} = i\,(y_1 - y_2) \tag{15}$$

we can rewrite it in the diagonalized form:

$$\frac{dy_1}{dt} = iy_1 - \frac{i}{2}\,(y_1 + y_2)^3, \qquad \frac{dy_2}{dt} = -iy_2 + \frac{i}{2}\,(y_1 + y_2)^3 \tag{16}$$

Note that the above couple of equations have complex conjugate coefficients at terms with exchange $y_1 \leftrightarrow y_2$. It will take place always if the original equation has real coefficients.

The vector of eigenvalues of a linear part of the system is $\varLambda = \{i, -i\}$. In accordance with the definition of the normal form (5) we will have at sums of this form only terms, where $(\Lambda, \mathbf{p}) = i\,(p_1 - p_2) = 0$, i.e. only terms where $p_1 = p_2$:

$$
\begin{aligned}
\frac{dz_1}{dt} &= iz_1 + z_1 \left(g_{1,1,1} \cdot z_1 \cdot z_2 + g_{1,2,2} \cdot z_1^2 \cdot z_2^2 + \dots\right) \\
\frac{dz_2}{dt} &= -iz_2 + z_2 \left(g_{2,1,1} \cdot z_1 \cdot z_2 + g_{2,2,2} \cdot z_1^2 \cdot z_2^2 + \dots\right)
\end{aligned}
\tag{17}
$$

Condition (11) for the analytic set $\mathcal{A}$ of the second-order equation with eigenvalues $\lambda_1 = -\lambda_2$ has the form:

$$
\sum_{k=1,\dots} g_{1,k,k} \cdot (z_1 \cdot z_2)^k = -\sum_{k=1,\dots} g_{2,k,k} \cdot (z_1 \cdot z_2)^k
$$

As for any second-order (originally) real equation the equalities $g_{1,i,i} = \bar{g}_{2,i,i}$, $h_{1,i,j} = \bar{h}_{2,j,i}$ take place, this condition has the form:

$$
\sum_{k=1,\dots} Re(g_{1,k,k}) \cdot (z_1 \cdot z_2)^k = 0
\tag{18}
$$

After the calculation of the normal form for Duffing's equation, it can be revealed that (18) is fulfilled identically because all $g_{1,i,i}$ and $g_{2,i,i}$ are pure imaginary here. It means that for Duffing's equation we have the case, which is usually called the "center", when periodic solutions exist for any (small enough) initial conditions.

Indeed, by multiplying the first of equations (17) by z_2 and the second one by z_1 we will have $\frac{d(z_1 z_2)}{dt} = 0$ after their addition and (17) has a family of solutions:

$$
z_1(t) = c_1 e^{+i\omega(c_1 \cdot c_2)t}, \quad z_2(t) = c_2 e^{-i\omega(c_1 \cdot c_2)t}
$$

where $\omega(z_1 \cdot z_2) \stackrel{\text{def}}{=} 1 + g_{1,1,1}/i + g_{1,2,2}/i + \dots$ is a real constant and c_1, c_2 are integration constants.

Now we can obtain the approximation to original equation (13) by substitution of the found z_i into y_i with (4) and after that into x. If we choose complex conjugate values for $c_1 = \bar{c}_2$ we will have an approximation of a real family of a periodic solution in the form of truncated Fourier series.

We have obtained these series as series in the $c = c_1$ variable. It is not convenient, and for the final representation we calculated H as a series in c by substituting the found x and $\frac{dx}{dt}$ in (14). By inverting this series and substituting c as a series of H into expressions for ω and x we will have the final result as series in H. To save space we show this result here till the fifth order only:

$$\omega = 1 - \tfrac{3}{4}H - \tfrac{69}{64}H^2 - \tfrac{633}{256}H^3 - \tfrac{110421}{16384}H^4 - \tfrac{1318329}{65536}H^5 + \dots$$

$$x = \sqrt{2H}\times$$
$$\begin{aligned}
[\ &\cos(\omega t)(1 + \tfrac{9}{16}H + \tfrac{271}{256}H^2 + \tfrac{10779}{4096}H^3 + \tfrac{243613}{32768}H^4 + \tfrac{2963587}{131072}H^5) \\
&- \cos(3\omega t)H(\tfrac{1}{16} + \tfrac{3}{16}H + \tfrac{1209}{2048}H^2 + \tfrac{127233}{65536}H^3 + \tfrac{6907221}{1048576}H^4) \\
&+ \cos(5\omega t)H^2(\tfrac{1}{256} + \tfrac{11}{512}H + \tfrac{3107}{32768}H^2 + \tfrac{25567}{65536}H^3) \\
&- \cos(7\omega t)H^3(\tfrac{1}{4096} + \tfrac{1}{512}H + \tfrac{5805}{524288}H^2) \\
&+ \cos(9\omega t)H^4(\tfrac{1}{65536} + \tfrac{21}{131072}H) \\
&- \cos(11\omega t)H^5(\tfrac{1}{1048576}) + \dots]
\end{aligned}$$
(19)

The result of this calculation was verified in two ways. The first one was a direct substitution of series (19) in the original equation (13). After that we had only terms with negligible orders of H. The second way was a comparison of the numerical solutions of Duffing's equation by Runge–Kutta method (by NAG's d02baf procedure) with the values of the series tabulated at different values of H.

In view of (14) we have $H = H(x = \phi/\sqrt{6}, \tfrac{dx}{dt} = \tfrac{d\phi}{dt}/\sqrt{6})$. On the other hand, H is physically not small when at a zero velocity a maximum deviation of a pendulum takes place, i.e. when $\phi = \pi/2$ and $\tfrac{d\phi}{dt} = 0$. In this case we have $H_{max} \simeq 0.163$. Let us now introduce a function of a maximum relative error during one period $f_{err}(H)$:

$$f_{err} = \sup_{t \in [0, 2\pi/\omega]} \sqrt{\frac{(x_{series} - x_{num})^2 + (dx_{series}/dt - dx_{num}/dt)^2}{x_{num}^2 + (dx_{num}/dt)^2}}$$
(20)

This function indicates a maximum relative deviation in phase space between series (19) x_{series} and its symbolically evaluated derivation on the one hand and numerical solutions of (13) $x_{num}, dx_{num}/dt$ on the other hand as a function of full energy H. We have:

$$\begin{aligned}
f_{err}(H = 0.1) &\simeq 1.8 \times 10^{-8} \\
f_{err}(H = 0.125) &\simeq 7.4 \times 10^{-7} \\
f_{err}(H_{max} = 0.163) &\simeq 7.4 \times 10^{-5}
\end{aligned}$$

You can see that achieved precision can be used for practical goals in a physical range of energies. The use of a ready closed formula can be sometimes more preferable at real-time calculations than the numerical solution of differential equations. Form (19) must of course be improved for real usage by standard methods of preparing series for numerical tabulation.

4.4   Van der Pol Equation

This equation stems from a problem of vibrations in electronic circuits:

$$\frac{d^2x}{dt^2} = -x + (\varepsilon^2 - x^2)\frac{dx}{dt} \tag{21}$$

By linear complex change of variables (15) it can be rewritten in the diagonalized form:

$$\begin{aligned}
\frac{dy_1}{dt} &= iy_1 + \tfrac{1}{2}(y_1 - y_2)\left[\varepsilon^2 - (y_1 + y_2)^2\right]\\
\frac{dy_2}{dt} &= -iy_2 + \tfrac{1}{2}(y_2 - y_1)\left[\varepsilon^2 - (y_1 + y_2)^2\right]\\
\frac{d\varepsilon}{dt} &= 0
\end{aligned}$$

As for Duffings' case these equations have complex conjugate coefficients at terms with exchange $y_1 \leftrightarrow y_2$.

Note that the value $\varepsilon = 0$ is "resonant" here, i.e. only at this value we have a couple of purely imaginary conjugate eigenvalues. In accordance with our common receipt we should consider ε as a small perturbation. We have redefined above the parameter ε as a new variable. Such a trick allows us in practice to free eigenvalues from a parameter dependence.

And as for Duffing's equation the sums on the right-hand sides of the normal form will include only terms where $p_1 = p_2$. The third "additional" equation will be not changed. So a difference between (17) and the system presented below is only in polynomial dependence of the right sides on ε:

$$\begin{aligned}
\frac{dz_1}{dt} &= iz_1 + z_1 \sum_{k=0,1,\ldots} \left(g_{1,1,1,2k} \cdot (z_1 \cdot z_2)\varepsilon^{2k} + g_{1,2,2,2k} \cdot (z_1 \cdot z_2)^2 \varepsilon^{2k} + \ldots\right)\\
\frac{dz_2}{dt} &= -iz_2 + z_2 \sum_{k=0,1,\ldots} \left(g_{2,1,1,2k} \cdot (z_1 \cdot z_2)\varepsilon^{2k} + g_{2,2,2,2k} \cdot (z_1 \cdot z_2)^2 \varepsilon^{2k} + \ldots\right)\\
\frac{d\varepsilon}{dt} &= 0.
\end{aligned} \tag{22}$$

For the analytic set (convergent) condition (18) we now have the form:

$$Re\left[\sum_{j,k=0,1,\ldots} g_{1,j,j,2k}\,\varepsilon^{2k}\,(z_1 \cdot z_2)^j\right] = 0, \qquad g_{1,0,0,0} \overset{\text{def}}{=} 0. \tag{23}$$

Contrary to Duffing's equation the above is not satisfied automatically, but because of the implicit function theorem it may be solved in the form:

$$z_1 \cdot z_2 = \sum_{k=1,2,\ldots} q_k \varepsilon^{2k}.$$

It is easy to see that if the above is satisfied then $z_1 \cdot z_2$ is a constant in time. So we can continue the evaluations as for Duffing's case, but now the constants of integration c_1, c_2 are not free. This is the case of a "limit circle", and this restriction defines the limit circle trajectory:

$$z_1(t) = c_1 e^{+i\omega(c_1 \cdot c_2)t}, \quad z_2(t) = c_2 e^{-i\omega(c_1 \cdot c_2)t}, \quad c_1 \cdot c_2 = \sum_{k=1,2,\ldots} q_k \varepsilon^{2k}.$$

After that we obtain the approximation to the original equation (21) by substituting the found above z_i into y_i by (4) and then into x. If we choose complex conjugate values for $c_1 = \bar{c}_2$ we will have also for Duffing's equation an approximation of the real solution in the form of truncated Fourier series. It is a limit circle trajectory:

$$\omega = 1 - \tfrac{1}{16}\varepsilon^4 + \tfrac{17}{3072}\varepsilon^8 + \tfrac{35}{884736}\varepsilon^{12} - \tfrac{678899}{5096079360}\varepsilon^{16} + \cdots$$

$$
\begin{aligned}
x = \varepsilon \cdot \Big(\\
\cos(\omega t)(2 + \tfrac{1}{64}\varepsilon^4 - \tfrac{23}{49152}\varepsilon^8 - \tfrac{51619}{169869312}\varepsilon^{12} + \tfrac{948555443}{19568944742400}\varepsilon^{16}) \\
+ \cos(3\omega t)\varepsilon^4(-\tfrac{3}{32} + \tfrac{101}{12288}\varepsilon^4 + \tfrac{24061}{28311552}\varepsilon^8 - \tfrac{279818087}{815372697600}\varepsilon^{12}) \\
+ \cos(5\omega t)\varepsilon^4(-\tfrac{5}{96} + \tfrac{1865}{110592}\varepsilon^4 - \tfrac{328835}{254803968}\varepsilon^8 - \tfrac{111998015}{293534171136}\varepsilon^{12}) \\
+ \cos(7\omega t)\varepsilon^8(\tfrac{1379}{110592} - \tfrac{10923199}{3185049600}\varepsilon^4 + \tfrac{21049213549}{183458856960000}\varepsilon^8) \\
+ \cos(9\omega t)\varepsilon^8(\tfrac{61}{20480} - \tfrac{1769369}{589824000}\varepsilon^4 + \tfrac{161113663733}{237817036800000}\varepsilon^8) \\
+ \cos(11\omega t)\varepsilon^{12}(-\tfrac{409871}{331776000} + \tfrac{1359229760383}{1872809164800000}\varepsilon^4) \\
+ \cos(13\omega t)\varepsilon^{12}(-\tfrac{715247}{3715891200} + \tfrac{2076538440769}{5243865661440000}\varepsilon^4) \\
+ \cos(15\omega t)\varepsilon^{16}(\tfrac{526426361}{4661213921280}) \\
+ \cos(17\omega t)\varepsilon^{16}(\tfrac{392636471}{29964946636800}) \\
+ \sin(3\omega t)\varepsilon^2(-\tfrac{1}{4} + \tfrac{15}{512}\varepsilon^4 - \tfrac{779}{1179648}\varepsilon^8 - \tfrac{4538017}{6794772480}\varepsilon^{12}) \\
+ \sin(5\omega t)\varepsilon^6(\tfrac{85}{2304} - \tfrac{8095}{1327104}\varepsilon^4 - \tfrac{1252495}{6115295232}\varepsilon^8) \\
+ \sin(7\omega t)\varepsilon^6(\tfrac{7}{576} - \tfrac{99967}{13271040}\varepsilon^4 + \tfrac{415949513}{382205952000}\varepsilon^8) \\
+ \sin(9\omega t)\varepsilon^{10}(-\tfrac{9791}{2457600} + \tfrac{117258703}{70778880000}\varepsilon^4) \\
+ \sin(11\omega t)\varepsilon^{10}(-\tfrac{5533}{7372800} + \tfrac{1657839733}{1486356480000}\varepsilon^4) \\
+ \sin(13\omega t)\varepsilon^{14}(\tfrac{21731177}{57802752000}) \\
+ \sin(15\omega t)\varepsilon^{14}(\tfrac{138697}{2774532096}) + \cdots \Big).
\end{aligned}
$$

(24)

The calculation by the NORT package till 32nd order in ε took 1.5 minutes on the PentiumPro-200 computer. We had 145 terms for each sum in the normal form (22) and 1773 terms for the normalizing transformation from z_i to y_i. The calculated expression for frequency has 9 terms. Note that the power series for the frequency of van der Pol's equation itself has been calculated till 164th order in ε in (Andersen, Geer, 1983).

The comparison of this result with a numerical one in terms of (20) gives:

$$
\begin{aligned}
f_{err}(\varepsilon^2 = 0.5) &\simeq 8 \times 10^{-10} \\
f_{err}(\varepsilon^2 = 0.75) &\simeq 4 \times 10^{-8} \\
f_{err}(\varepsilon^2 = 1.0) &\simeq 1 \times 10^{-5}.
\end{aligned}
$$

Besides the solution of equation we can obtain also the expressions for the original conditions, which lie in the limit circle trajectory of (21) as series in

ε by inversion of series (4):

$$x = 0$$
$$\frac{dx}{dt} = \varepsilon \cdot ($$
$$2 + \frac{17}{96}\varepsilon^4 - \frac{1577}{552960}\varepsilon^8 - \frac{102956839}{55738368000}\varepsilon^{12} + \frac{48722480822161}{157315969843200000}\varepsilon^{16} + \ldots)$$

and

$$x = \varepsilon \cdot ($$
$$2 + \frac{1}{96}\varepsilon^4 - \frac{1033}{552960}\varepsilon^8 + \frac{1019689}{55738368000}\varepsilon^{12} + \frac{9835512276689}{157315969843200000}\varepsilon^{16} + \ldots)$$
$$\frac{dx}{dt} = 0$$

4.5 Examples of the Fourth-Order ODEs

Paper (Edneral, 1998) describes an application of the normal form method for building analytic approximations for all (including complex) local families of periodic solutions in the neighborhood of the stationary points of the Henon–Heiles system. The families of solutions are represented as truncated Fourier series in approximated frequencies, and the corresponding trajectories are described by intersections of hypersurfaces, which are defined by pieces of multivariate power series in phase variables of the system. A comparison of the numerical values obtained by a tabulation of the approximate solutions above with results of numerical integration of the Henon-Heiles system displays a good agreement, which is enough for the usage of these approximate solutions for engineering applications.

All local families of periodic solutions of the Henon–Heiles system are in the neighborhood of the origin. Near this stationary point, the system has 10 local families of periodic solutions. There are 8 one parameter (energy) local families of real periodic solutions, one of which lies in the Surface of Section (SOS), and each of them crosses the SOS once for each period. The SOS is defined by conditions: $x = 0$, $\dot{x} \geq 0$. The remaining two families are essentially-complex one-parameter families of periodic solutions with a zero energy and a frequency equal to ± 1.

We treated in the same way the Contopoulos system as a case of a parametric system of fourth order. Some families of its periodic solutions exist only at fixed values of a system parameter, and other families exist in an interval of its value. This is an example of bifurcation analysis by the normal form method. It is remarkable that the system has an additional nontrivial complex family of periodic solutions at one fixed value of the parameter. The results are in printing now.

5 Conclusion

Here we can conclude that the obtaining of high order normal forms enables us to produce closed formulas for a quantitative approximation of periodic solutions of autonomous nonlinear ODEs. The normal form method can be applied to a phase portrait investigation and to bifurcation analysis.

References

1. Andersen, G.M., Geer, J.F. (1983). Power series expansions for the frequency and period of the limit cycle of the van der Pol equation. *SIAM J. Appl. Math.* **42**, 678–693.
2. Arnold, V.I., Anosov, D.V. (Eds.) (1988). Dynamical Systems, I. *Encyclopaedia of Mathematical Sciences.* Springer–Verlag, N.Y.
3. Boege, W., Gebauer, R., Kredel, H. (1986). Some Examples for Solving Systems of Algebraic Equations by Calculating Groebner Bases. *J. Symbolic Computation* **1**, 83–98.
4. Bruno(Brjuno), A.D. (1971) *Analytical form of differential equations. I.* Trans. Mosc. Mat. Soc., **25**, 131–288.
5. Bruno(Brjuno), A.D. (1972) *Analytical form of differential equations. II.* Trans. Mosc. Mat. Soc. **26**, 199–239.
6. Bruno, A.D. (1989) *Local Method in Nonlinear Differential Equations. Part I - The Local Method of Nonlinear Analyses of Differential Equations, Part II - The Sets of Analyticity of a Normalizing Transformation.* Springer Series in Soviet Mathematics. ISBN 3-540-18926-2, 370 pages.
7. Bruno, A.D. (1990) *The Restricted Three-Body Problem: Plane Periodic Orbits.* Moscow, Nauka. ISBN 5-02-000683-1, 295 pages. (in Russian).
8. Bruno, A.D. (1993) Bifurcation of the periodic solutions in the case of a multiple pair of imaginary eigenvalues. *Selecta Mathematica* formerly *Sovietica* **12**, # 1, 1–12.
9. Deprit, A. (1969) Canonical transformation depending on a small parameter. *Celestial Mechanics* **1**, # 1, 12–30.
10. Godziewski, K., Maciejewski,A.J. (1990) *Celest. Mech. Dyn. Astron.* **49**, 1.
11. Ito, H. (1989) Convergence of Birkhoff normal forms for integrable systems. *Comment. Math. Helv.* **64**, 412–461.
12. Ito, H. (1992) Integrability of Hamiltonian systems and Birkhoff normal forms in the simple resonance case. *Mth. Ann.* **292**, 411–444.
13. Edneral, V.F., Khrustalev, O.A. (1985). The normalizing transformation for nonlinear systems of ODEs. The realization of the algorithm. *Proceedings of International Conference on Computer Algebra and its Application in Theoretical Physics (USSR, Dubna, September 1985).* Dubna: JINR publ., 219–224. In Russian.
14. Edneral, V.F., Khrustalev, O.A. (1992). Program for recasting ODE systems in normal form. *Sov. J. Programmirovanie,* # 5, 73–80. In Russian.
15. Edneral, V.F. (1993). Computer generation of normalizing transformation for systems of nonlinear ODE. *Proceedings of the 1993 International Symposium on Symbolic and Algebraic Computation (Kiev, Ukraine, July 1993).* New York: ACM Press, edited by M.Bronstein, 14–19.
16. Edneral, V.F. (1998) A symbolic approximation of periodic solutions of the Henon–Heiles system by the normal form method; *J.Mathematics and Computers in Simulation,* Elsevier, v. **45**, 445–463. Edited by A.Bruno, V.Edneral, S.Steinberg.
17. Fitch, J.P., Norman, A.C., Moore, P.M.A. (1986). ALKAHEST III: Automatic analysis of periodic weakly nonlinear ODEs. *Proceedings of SYMSAC 86.* Waterloo, 34—38.
18. Guckenheimer, J., Holmes, P. (1986) *Nonlinear Oscillations, Dynamical Systems and Bifurcations of Vector Fields.* Springer-Verlag, N.Y.

19. Hassard, B.D., Kazarinoff, N.D., Wan, Y.-H. (1981) *Theory and Applications of Hopf Bifurcation.* Cambridge Univ. Press. 280 pages.
20. Hearn, A.C. (1987). REDUCE. User's manual. *Rand Publication* CP78.
21. Hori, G.I. (1966).Theory of general perturbations with unspecified canonical variables. *J. Japan Astron. Soc.* **18**, # 4, 287–296.
22. Mersman, W.A. (1970) A new algorithm for Lie transformation. *Celestial Mechanics* **3**, # 1, 81–89.
23. Rand, R., Armbruster D. (1987) *Perturbation Methods, Bifurcation Theory and Computer Algebra.* Springer–Verlag, N.Y.
24. Shevchenko, I.I., Sokolsky, A.G. (1993) Algorithms for normalization of Hamiltonian systems by means of computer algebra. *Comp. Phys. Comm.* **77**, 11—18.
25. Vallier, L. (1993) An Algorithm for the Computation of Normal Forms and Invariant Manifolds. *Proceedings of the 1993 International Symposium on Symbolic and Algebraic Computation (Kiev, Ukraine, July 1993).* New York: ACM Press, edited by M.Bronstein, 225—233.
26. Walcher, S. (1991) On differential equations in normal form. *Math. Ann.* **291**, 293—314.
27. Walcher, S. (1993) On Transformations into Normal Form. *J. Math. Analysis and Appl.* **180**, 617—632.

Computer Algebra Investigation of Equivalence in 4-node Plane Stress/Strain Finite Elements

Anders Eriksson, Yunhua Luo and Costin Pacoste

Structural Mechanics group, Dept. Structural Engineering
Royal Institute of Technology
S-100 44 Stockholm, Sweden

Abstract. In this investigation, with the aid of computer algebra, a diagram showing equivalences between finite element formulations or techniques, among which including two newly formulated hybrid mixed field principles, in a 4-node plane stress/strain element was obtained. In the investigation, some known equivalence relations were confirmed; some new equivalence relations, mainly between the hybrid mixed field formulations and the others, were detected. The investigation shows that with computer algebra it is much easier to conduct parameter study in simple elements and it might provide a powerful tool for exploring more complex equivalence relations in higher order elements. It is observed from the investigation that if a finite element technique is hard to fit in a conventional variational principle, it might have a counterpart in a properly modified variational principle. The obtained equivalence diagram might provide information for establishing a more generally valid mathematical principle or theorem.

1 Introduction

Investigation of equivalence between finite elements is inducive to understand finite element techniques and to efficiently apply them in improving element performance. The topic has been dealt with in lots of publications, e. g. Refs. [1–11] among many others. In simple and lower order elements, expressions of finite element formulas are simple enough to handle manually and equivalence relations between finite elements might be obvious. But in higher order elements, equivalence relations may be not so clear, there might be several possible equivalences to confirm. Large expressions make manual derivation error-prone and tedious. Furthermore, even in a simple element, it is difficult by manual derivation to study the effects of a factor such as element shape, material parameter and so on, on an equivalence relation.

Symbolic computational techniques, e. g. *Maple* [12] and *Mathematica* [13], are capable of dealing with large symbolic expressions. This advantage could be utilized in studying finite element relations and might provide an intermediate way between analytical mathematics and approximate numerical methods. With a symbolic computational software, it is much easier to study the effects of a factor. Nevertheless, symbolic softwares are only tools. Only after an investigator somehow spot a possible equivalence relation, a symbolic computational software can be used to verify or to check such a relation. The conclusions obtained from a symbolic derivation are not as general as a mathematical theorem, but much more convincing than those drawn from even a large number of numerical examples. The obtained equivalence diagram might provide information for establishing a more generally valid mathematical principle or theorem.

There are quite several formulations or techniques, including some newly formulated mixed field principles [22,23], which are applicable in a 4-node plane stress/strain element. Their equivalences in the element were not systematically investigated. Although some conclusions about their equivalence are known, e. g. in [1,2], the hybrid stress model by Pian is demonstrated to be equivalent to the incompatible displacement model by Wilson [18] in a rectangle; reduced integration is found in [3] to be nearly equivalent to the hybrid stress model; some new equivalence relations were detected in [24], and so on, these pieces of diagrams need be sorted to get a whole picture. Furthermore, some alternative formulated elements are added in this study, their relations with the others need be explored.

2   Involved finite element formulations or techniques

According to their applicability in a 4-node plane stress/strain element, the following finite element techniques or formulations are selected in the investigation: reduced integration (including uniform and selective versions) [14–17], incompatible displacement model [18], mixed field formulations [19–22] and hybrid mixed field formulations [23]. Detailed descriptions of these formulations can be found in the cited references. Listed in Table 1 are brief descriptions and identifiers for elements based on these formulations.

Table 1: Plane stress/strain elements involved in equivalence investigation

Element Identifier	Symbol in *Maple* code	Brief description
		— plane stress/strain theory — 4 nodes, 8 degrees of freedom — bilinear isoparametric interpolations $$h_i = \frac{1}{4}(1 + r_i\, r)(1 + s_i\, s),$$ $$r_i,\, s_i = \pm 1, \quad i = 1, 2, 3, 4$$
QUAD4$_{\mathrm{uri}}$	K_uri	— a (1×1) scheme for integrating both normal- and shear-related stiffness matrices. — hourglassing
QUAD4$_{\mathrm{sri}}$	K_sri	— a (2×2) scheme for integrating normal-related stiffness matrix and a (1×1) scheme for integrating shear-related stiffness matrices
QUAD4$^0_{\mathrm{hr}}$	K_hr0	— the Hellinger-Reissner formulation with assumed stress resultants $N_x = a_1$, $N_y = a_2$, $N_{xy} = a_3$. — hourglassing
QUAD4$^0_{\mathrm{hw}}$	K_hw0	— the Hu-Washizu formulation with assumed strains $\varepsilon_x = b_1$, $\varepsilon_y = b_2$, $\gamma_{xy} = b_3$ — hourglassing
QUAD4$_{\mathrm{hr}}$	K_hr1	— the Hellinger-Reissner formulation with assumed stress resultants $N_x = a_1 + a_2\, s$, $N_y = a_3 + a_4\, r$, $N_{xy} = a_5$

continued on next page

continued from previous page

Element identifier	Symbol in *Maple* code	Brief description
QUAD4$_{hw}$	K_hw1	– the Hu-Washizu formulation with assumed strains, $$\begin{bmatrix} \varepsilon_x \\ \varepsilon_y \\ \gamma_{xy} \end{bmatrix} = d \begin{bmatrix} N_x \\ N_y \\ N_{xy} \end{bmatrix}$$ N_x, N_y, N_{xy} as in the above row, d is the flexibility matrix.
QUAD4$_{hhr}$	K_hhr	– the hybrid Hellinger-Reissner formulation with assumed shear stress resultant $N_{xy} = a_1$
QUAD4$_{hhw}$	K_hhw	– the hybrid Hu-Washizu formulation with assumed shear strain $\gamma_{xy} = b_1$
QUAD4$_{inc}$	K_inc	– the incompatible displacement model with incompatible modes $h_5 = 4(1 - r^2)$, $h_6 = 4(1 - s^2)$

3   Investigation strategy and equivalence diagram

As defined in the references, it is supposed that two finite element formulations or techniques are equivalent if they yield identical element stiffness matrices. With this definition, a possible strategy for the investigation is: first, to explicitly derive out element stiffness matrices based on the formulations or techniques, and second to compare these stiffness matrices to figure out equivalence relationships between corresponding formulations. Sample *Maple* codes are given in Appendix. In the code, the following lines are used to define and to change element shape and/or material parameter.

```
nu:=0:   # Poisson ratio
 p:=0:
x1:=-a:    y1:=-b:  # These 4 lines define a rectangle (p=0)
x2:= a:    y2:=-b:  # or a parallelogram (p~=0). If they
x3:= a+p:  y3:= b:  # are deleted, the element will be
x4:=-a+p:  y4:= b:  # an arbitrary quadrilateral
```

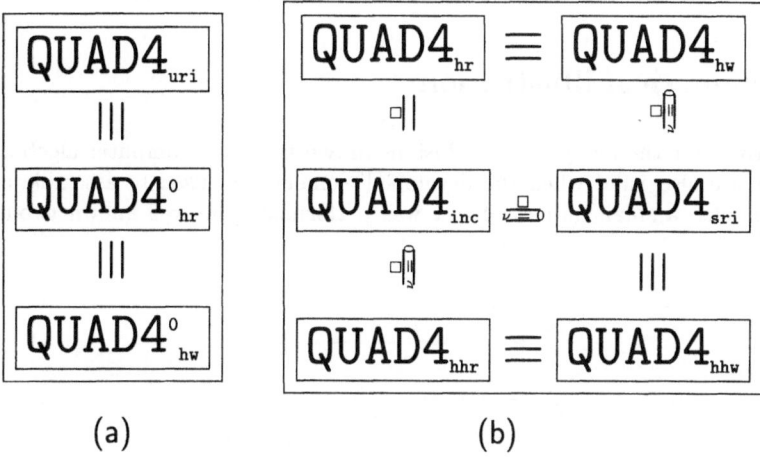

(a)   (b)

Fig. 1. Equivalence relations in a 4-node plane stress/strain element

To find out the effects of a factor on equivalence relations, only very small modifications are needed in the code. For example, supposing that one has known that some finite elements are equivalent in a rectangle with zero Poisson's ratio, he or she wants to know if these equivalences are still true in a parallelogram or in an arbitrary quadrilateral or when Poisson ratio is non-zero, what he or she needs to do is to put a '#' at the beginning of some or all the lines, re-run the code and check if the differences between element stiffness matrices are still zero. With manual derivation, it is easy to get the element stiffness matrices for a rectangle or even a parallelogram, but it takes much more effort for an arbitrary quadrilateral.

Based on the investigation, a diagram describing equivalences between the elements listed in Table 1 is obtained, cf. Fig. 1. In the figure, symbol '≡' represents an equivalence relation which is valid for an arbitrary quadrilateral and for any value of Poisson's ratio. '=' indicates that an equivalence relation is conditionally true with symbols under or over it describing the conditions satisfied. '□' stands for a rectangular shape. '$\nu = 0$' means that Poisson ratio is zero. It should be noted that elements $QUAD4^0_{hr}$ and $QUAD4_{hr}$ ($QUAD4^0_{hw}$ and $QUAD4_{hw}$) have different assumed stress resultants (or strains).

In Fig. 1, the chain of equivalence labeled (a) is simple and obvious. Some equivalences in (b) are also well-known. But with these simple cases, it is confirmed that a symbolic computational software like *Maple* is reliable in investigating finite element relations. Its advantage in efficiency might not be so obvious in dealing with such simple cases. Worthy of noticing in the figure is that the selective reduced integration is equivalent to the conventional hybrid stress model only in a rectangle and with zero Poisson's ratio, but 'unconditionally' equivalent to the two hybrid mixed field formulations with a constant assumed stress/strain, which imply that if a finite element technique is hard to fit in conventional variational principle, it might have a counterpart in a properly modified variational principle.

4   Numerical illustration

To verify that the analytical conclusions drawn from the computer algebra calculations are also valid when the developed elements are used to assemble a structural model, a small numerical test was performed. The well-known two-element

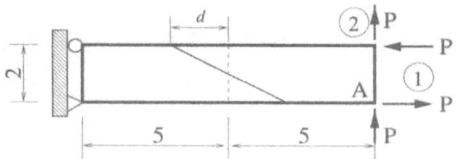

Fig. 2. Cantilever beam simulated by two plane stress elements

cantilever beam was simulated by plane stress elements. Geometric parameters describing the structure and the elements are given in Fig. 2. The parameter d was used to determine element distortion from a rectangular configuration. The structural material has $E = 15000$. Two load cases were considered. One was pure bending, the other was shear-bending.

First the structure was analyzed with $d = 0$ and Poisson ratios $0. \leq \nu \leq 0.495$. The variations of normalized vertical deflection at Point A with Poisson's ratio (ν) are given in Fig. 3. From the results, two sets of equivalence relations in Fig. 1 were verified, i. e. QUAD4$_{inc}$ = QUAD4$_{hr}$ = QUAD4$_{hw}$ and QUAD4$_{sri}$ = QUAD4$_{hhr}$ = QUAD4$_{hhw}$. Then, the structure was re-analyzed with Poisson's ratio fixed at $\nu = 0$ and the skewness parameters $0 \leq d \leq 5$. The obtained curves are displayed in Fig. 4. When elements were distorted from rectangular shapes, it is obvious that the curve from QUAD4$_{inc}$ is different from the others, but the differences between the rest curves are unreadable for a poor scale.

5   Conclusions

In this investigation, with the aid of computer algebra and based on some existing work, a whole diagram showing equivalences between finite element formulations or techniques applicable in a 4-node plane stress/strain element was obtained. The involved formulations or techniques include: uniform/selective reduced integration, incompatible displacement model, mixed field formulations and two newly formulated hybrid mixed field formulations. In the investigation, a comparison strategy was used.

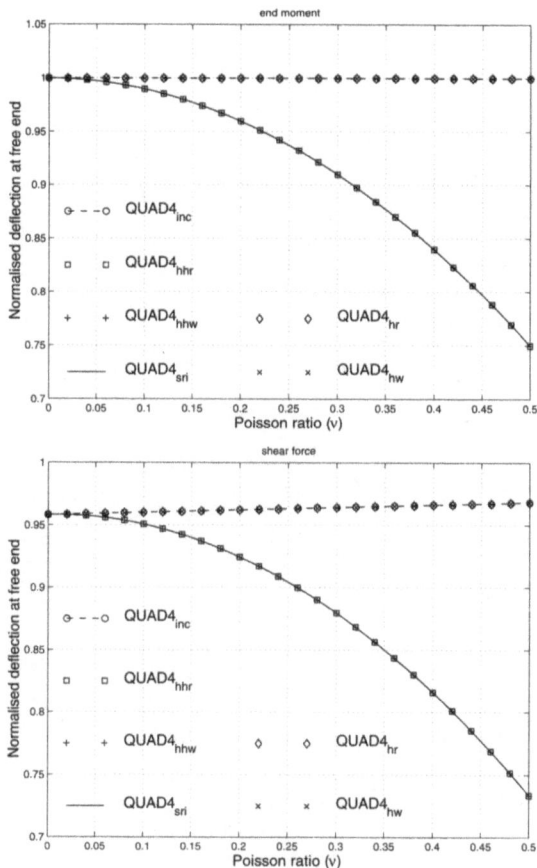

Fig. 3. Variation of deflection at free end with Poisson's ratio

The investigation shows that the computer algebra is reliable in such an investigation and could provide a powerful tool in exploring more complex equivalence relations in higher order elements. From the investigation, the selective reduced integration is equivalent to the conventional hybrid stress model only in a rectangle and with zero Poisson's ratio, but 'unconditionally' equivalent to the two hybrid mixed formulations with a constant assumed shear stress/strain, which imply that if a finite element technique is hard to put in a conventional variational principle, it might have a counterpart in a properly modified variational principle.

It must be emphasized that some equivalence relations in Fig. 1 may be untrue in other type of elements, say a 4-node Mindlin plate element, for different geometric assumptions being adopted, [26]. Studying equivalence diagrams from different element classes might be helpful for establish a generally valid mathematical principle or theorem.

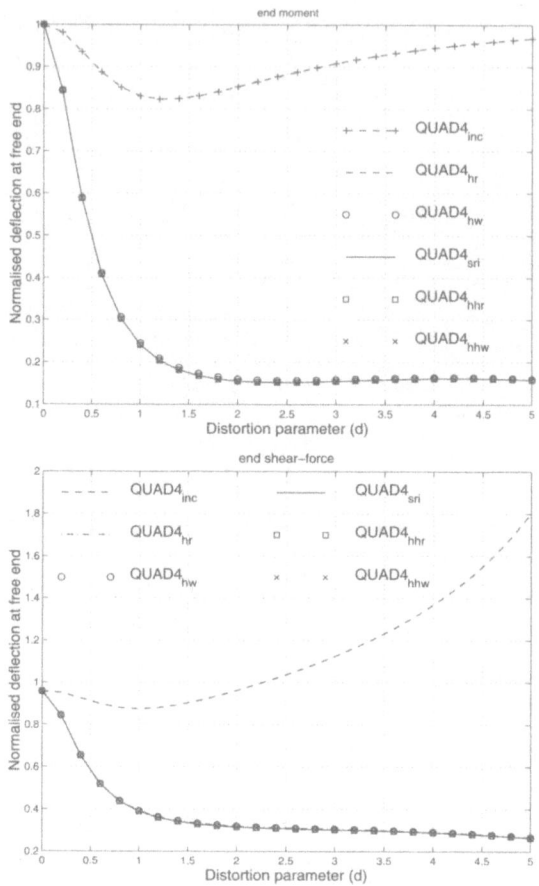

Fig. 4. Variation of deflection at free end with distortion parameter (d)

Appendix

The following *Maple* code is used to define or calculate quantities which are common for the formulations in a 4-node plane stress element. These include: isoparametric interpolations (h1, h2, h3, h4) in a 4-node plane element, Jacobian and its inverse (JJ, IJ), shape functions (X, Y), displacements (u, v), strains (ex, ey, exy), B matrix (B, Bb, Bs), material matrices (DD, DDb, DDs) and their inverse (dd, dds).

```
restart:
with(linalg):
readlib(unassign):

nu:=0:    # Poisson ratio
 p:=0:
x1:=-a:     y1:=-b:  # These 4 lines define a rectangle (p=0)
```

```
x2:= a:      y2:=-b:   #  or a parallelogram (p~=0). If they
x3:= a+p:    y3:= b:   #  are deleted, the element will be
x4:=-a+p:    y4:= b:   #  an arbitrary quadrilateral


h1:=1/4*(1-r)*(1-s):
h2:=1/4*(1+r)*(1-s):
h3:=1/4*(1+r)*(1+s):
h4:=1/4*(1-r)*(1+s):


X:=h1*x1+h2*x2+h3*x3+h4*x4:
Y:=h1*y1+h2*y2+h3*y3+h4*y4:


JJ:=matrix([[diff(X,r),diff(Y,r)],[diff(X,s),diff(Y,s)]]):
jj:=det(JJ):
IJ:=inverse(JJ):
I11:=IJ[1,1]: I12:=IJ[1,2]:
I21:=IJ[2,1]: I22:=IJ[2,2]:


u:=h1*u1+h2*u2+h3*u3+h4*u4:
v:=h1*v1+h2*v2+h3*v3+h4*v4:


dudx:=I11*diff(u,r)+I12*diff(u,s):
dudy:=I21*diff(u,r)+I22*diff(u,s):
dvdx:=I11*diff(v,r)+I12*diff(v,s):
dvdy:=I21*diff(v,r)+I22*diff(v,s):


ex:=dudx:
ey:=dvdy:
exy:=dudy+dvdx:


DOF:=vector([u1,v1,u2,v2,u3,v3,u4,v4]):


B:=matrix([grad(ex,DOF),grad(ey,DOF),grad(exy,DOF)]):
Bb:=matrix([grad(ex,DOF),grad(ey,DOF)]):
Bs:=matrix([grad(exy,DOF)]):


MODEL:=1:

if MODEL=1 then
   D1:=Ee*t/(1-nu^2):              #
   D2:=nu*D1:                      #  plane stress model
   D3:=Ee*t/2/(1+nu):              #
else
   D1:=(1-nu)*Ee/(1+nu)/(1-2*nu):  #
   D2:=nu*Ee/(1+nu)/(1-2*nu):      #  plane strain model
   D3:=D1/2:                       #
fi:


DDb:=matrix([[D1,D2],[D2,D1]]):
```

```
DDs:=matrix([[D3]]):
DD:=matrix([[D1,D2,0],[D2,D1,0],[0,0,D3]]):

dd:=inverse(DD):
dds:=inverse(DDs):
```

With the above defined or calculated quantities, element stiffness matrices based on different formulations are explicitly derived and stored with different identifiers. The following code is used to calculate element stiffness matrices from the two hybrid mixed field formulations. The element stiffness matrices from the rest formulations or techniques can be calculated by following their corresponding formulas. The full *Maple* code can be found in [26].

```
#----------------------------------------------#
#    The hybrid Hellinger-Reissner formulation  #
#    with  constant  assumed  shear  stresses    #
#----------------------------------------------#

unassign('Nxy','PP','mm'):
Nxy:=a1:
PP:=vector([a1]):
Hs2:=matrix([grad(Nxy,PP)]):

DGss2:=multiply(transpose(Hs2),dds,Hs2):
DGsu2:=multiply(transpose(Hs2),Bs):

mm:=coldim(Hs2):

Gss2:=matrix(mm,mm,0):
Gsu2:=matrix(mm,8,0):

for i to mm do
for j to mm do
    Gss2[i,j]:=int(int(simplify(DGss2[i,j]*jj),
                    r=-1..1),s=-1..1):
od: od:

for i to mm do
for j to 8 do
    Gsu2[i,j]:=int(int(simplify(DGsu2[i,j]*jj),
                    r=-1..1),s=-1..1):
od: od:

gss2:=inverse(Gss2):
KS_hhr:=multiply(transpose(Gsu2),gss2,Gsu2):
K_hhr:=add(KB_fi,KS_hhr):
```

```
#------------------------------------------#
#   The hybrid Hu-Washizu formulation with  #
#   constant    assumed    shear    strains #
#------------------------------------------#

unassign('Exy','PP','mm'):
Exy:=a1:

PP:=vector([a1]):
He2:=matrix([grad(Exy,PP)]):

DFee2:=multiply(transpose(He2),DDs,He2):
DFsu2:=multiply(transpose(He2),DDs,Bs):

mm:=coldim(He2):

Fee2:=matrix(mm,mm,0):
Fsu2:=matrix(mm,8,0):

for i to mm do
for j to mm do
    Fee2[i,j]:=int(int(simplify(DFee2[i,j]*jj),
                    r=-1..1),s=-1..1):
od: od:

for i to mm do
for j to 8 do
    Fsu2[i,j]:=int(int(simplify(DFsu2[i,j]*jj),
                    r=-1..1),s=-1..1):
od: od:

fee2:=inverse(Fee2):
KS_hhw:=multiply(transpose(Fsu2),fee2,Fsu2):
K_hhw:=add(KB_fi,KS_hhw):
```

References

1. M. Fröier; L. Nilsson and A. Samuelsson. The rectangular plane stress element by Turner, Pian and Wilson. *Int. J. Numer. Meth. Engng.*, **8**, 433-437,1974.
2. T. H. H. Pian and T. Pin. Relations between incompatible displacement model and hybrid stress model. *Int. J. Numer. Meth. Engng.*, **22**, 173-181, 1986.
3. G. A. Mohr and P. L. Cook, On near equivalence of assumed stress and reduced integration formulations of the bilinear plane stress finite element, *Computers & Structures*, **21**, 475-478, 1985.
4. H. Shimodaira, Equivalence between mixed models and displacement models using reduced integration, *Int. J. Numer. Meth. Engng.*, **21**, 89-104, 1985.

5. J. C. Simo and M. S. Rifai, A class of mixed assumed strain methods and the method of incompatible modes, *Int. J. Numer. Meth. Engng.*, **29**, 1595-1638, 1990.

6. H. Stolarski and T. Belytschko, On the equivalence of mode decomposition and mixed finite elements based on the Hellinger-Reissner principle. PART I: Theory, *Comput. Methods Appl. Mech. Engrg.*, **58**, 249-263, 1986.

7. H. Stolarski and T. Belytschko, On the equivalence of mode decomposition and mixed finite elements based on the Hellinger-Reissner principle. PART II: Application, *Comput. Methods Appl. Mech. Engrg.*, **58**, 265-284, 1986.

8. H. Stolarski and T. Belytschko, Limitation principles for mixed finite elements based on the Hu-Washizu variational formulation, *Comput. Methods Appl. Mech. Engrg.*, **60**, 195-216, 1987.

9. S. T. Yeo and B. C. Lee, Equivalence between enhanced assumed strain method and assumed stress hybrid method based on the Hellinger-Reissner principle, *Int. J. Numer. Meth. Engng.*, **39**, 3083-3099, 1996.

10. W. Zhang. Further study of the identity of incompatible displacement element and generalized hybrid element. *Acta Mechanica Sinica*, **23**, 564-570, 1991.

11. P. J. Zhao; T. H. H. Pian and Y. Sheng. A new formulation of isoparametric finite elements and the relationship between hybrid stress element and incompatible element. *Int. J. Numer. Meth. Engng.*, **40**, 15-27, 1997.

12. B. W. Char; K. O. Geddes; G. H. Gonnet; B. L. Leong; M. B. Monagan and S. M. Watt. *Maple V language reference manual.* Springer-Verlag, 1991.

13. S. Wolfram. *The Mathematica Book*, 3rd edition. Wolfram Media, Inc., Cambridge, 1996.

14. E. D. L. Pugh; E. Hinton and O. C. Zienkiewicz. A study of quadrilateral plate bending elements with 'reduced' integration. *Int. J. Numer. Meth. Engng.*, **12**, 1059-1079, 1978.

15. T. J. R. Hughes; R. L. Taylor and W. Kanoknukulchai. A simple and efficient finite element for plate bending. *Int. J. Numer. Meth. Engng.*, **11**, 1529-1543, 1977.

16. R. D. Cook. More reduced integration and isoparametric elements. *Int. J. Numer. Meth. Engng.*, **5**, 141-142, 1972.

17. H. Stolarski and T. Belytschko. Membrane locking and reduced integration for curved elements. *Transactions of the ASME. J. Appl. Mech.*, **49**, 172-176, 1982.

18. E. L. Wilson; R. L. Taylor; W. P. Doherty and J. Ghaboussi. Incompatible displacement modes. In *Numerical and Computers Models in Structural Mechanics*, ed. by S. J. Fenves *et al..* Academic Press, New York, 1973.

19. T. H. H. Pian. Derivation of element of stiffness matrices by assumed stress distribution. *AIAA J.*, **2**, 1333-1336, 1964.

20. T. H. H. Pian and C. C. Wu. A rational approach for choosing stress terms for hybrid finite element formulations. *Int. J. Numer. Meth. Engng.*, **26**, 2331-2343, 1988.

21. Y. H. Luo and A. Eriksson. Extension of field consistence approach into developing plane stress elements. *Comput. Methods Appl. Mech. Engrg.*, 1998. Accepted.

22. Y. H. Luo and A. Eriksson. An alternative assumed strain method. *Comput. Methods Appl. Mech. Engrg.*, 1998. Accepted.

23. Y. H. Luo. Two hybrid mixed variational principles for developing high performance finite elements. *Int. J. Numer. Meth. Eng.*, 1998. Submitted.

24. Y. H. Luo and A. Eriksson. Investigation of equivalence between mixed field formulation and reduced integration with symbolic computation software. *Int. J. Numer. Meth. Engng.*, 1998. Submitted.
25. *MATLAB Reference Guide*, Math Works Inc., Natick, 1993.
26. Y. H. Luo. *On Some Finite Element Formulations in Structural Mechanics.* Doctoral Thesis, Stockholm, 1998.

Symmetry Theorems for the Newtonian 4- and 5-body Problems with Equal Masses

Jean-Charles Faugère[1] and Ilias Kotsireas[2]

[1] LIP6, CNRS - Université Paris 6, 4, place Jussieu F-75252 Paris cedex 05
[2] LIP6, Université Paris 6, 4, place Jussieu F-75252 Paris cedex 05
    e-mail: {Jean-Charles.Faugere,Ilias.Kotsireas}@lip6.fr

Abstract. We present a new proof of the algebraic part of a symmetry theorem for the central configurations of the newtonian planar 4-body problem with equal masses, using Gröbner bases. This approach is used to obtain a new symmetry theorem for the central configurations of the newtonian spatial 5-body problem with equal masses in the convex case. In fact we prove a more general statement of the theorem, valid for a class of potentials defined by functions with increasing and concave derivatives.

1   Introduction

The N-body problem is one of the most widely studied problems of Celestial mechanics. We are interested in a conceptually simple but important class of solutions, called central configurations. They are the only solutions of the N-body problem that can be computed analytically. As usual the study of a dynamical system begins with the study of its singularities. Central configurations are the singularities of the N-body problem and this is one of the reasons that justifies their significance. We are interested in the central configurations of the planar newtonian 4-body problem with equal masses and the central configurations of the spatial newtonian 5-body problem with equal masses.

A symmetry theorem for the planar newtonian 4-body problem with equal masses has been proved by A. Albouy. We give a simplified proof of the algebraic part of this theorem using Computer Algebra techniques. The most important fact about our proof is that it can be used to prove a new symmetry theorem for the spatial newtonian 5-body problem with equal masses, in the convex case. Indeed, we prove that every central configuration of the spatial newtonian 5-body problem with equal masses in the convex case, has at least one plane of symmetry. The proof uses several identities involving determinants and geometric properties of concave functions. These determinental identities have been obtained by Gröbner bases computations.

This result is of great importance for completing the classification of central configurations in the spatial newtonian 5-body problem with equal masses, that has been undertaken in [10].

2   Newtonian N-body problem with equal masses

In this section we will describe the general setting of the newtonian N-body problem with equal masses and we will give the equations of central configurations.

2.1   Notations

Consider n particles of masses $m_i, i = 1, \ldots, n$ moving under their mutual gravitational attraction. Choose a point as the origin and denote by $r_i, i = 1, \ldots, n$ the
position vector of the i-th particle. Define the newtonian potential energy function
as :

$$U = \sum_{1 \le i < j \le n} \frac{m_i m_j}{\| r_i - r_j \|}$$

where $\| \cdot \|$ is the euclidean norm.

More generally, one can define

$$U = \sum_{1 \le i < j \le n} m_i m_j \psi(\| r_i - r_j \|^2)$$

where ψ is a real-valued function. The newtonian case corresponds to $\psi(x) = x^{-1/2}$.
The case of the logarithmic potential $\psi(x) = -\log x$ describes the central configurations of the vortex problem (see [2] and [11]).

The equations of motion (in the newtonian formulation) are :

$$m_i \, \ddot{r}_i \; = \; \frac{\partial U}{\partial r_i}, \quad i = 1, \ldots, n. \tag{1}$$

Note that on the left-hand side we take the second derivative of the position vector
w.r.t. time, that is the acceleration of the i-th particle, and that the right-hand side
represents the total force exercised on the i-th particle by the other $n - 1$.

The center of mass of the system is defined as :

$$r_c = \frac{m_1 r_1 + \cdots + m_n r_n}{m_1 + \cdots + m_n} \; .$$

The symmetry of the function U implies that $\ddot{r}_c = 0$, which means that r_c is a linear
function of time. This is the principle of the conservation of linear momentum,
which says that the center of mass moves in a straight line with uniform velocity.
This allows us to shift the center of mass at the origin, without loss of generality
and thus it remains to determine the motion relative to the center of mass. Using
this and other similar considerations, like the conservation of energy and angular
momentum, the order of the system is considerably reduced, but it is still quite
difficult to study it.

2.2   Central Configurations

It is well-known that the equations of the N-body problem are in general not integrable. There exists a special important class of solutions which can be computed
analytically. From the point of view of dynamical systems these are the singularities
of the dynamical system in question. We give the mathematical definition of central
configurations.

Let the center of mass of the system be at the origin of the coordinate axes.
This means that we have $r_c = 0$. In this case, we have the following definition:

Definition 1. A configuration of the n particles is called a central configuration
when the acceleration vector of each particle is a common scalar multiple of his
position vector. In mathematical terms this means that there exists a scalar λ such
that we have $\ddot{r}_i = \lambda r_i$ for $i = 1, \ldots, n$.

2.3   The equations of central configurations

In this paragraph we will give a characterization of central configurations by two groups of algebraic equations. The formulation of the equations of central configurations that we are going to present, is valid only for the (newtonian) N-body problem with equal masses in a euclidean space of dimension N-2. Due to homogeneity, the common value of the masses can be taken to be equal to one. The innovative idea of Dziobek (see [6]) was to use the mutual distances of the bodies as the coordinates to write the equations of central configurations. The resulting algebraic system is tractable by symbolic computation techniques after some preprocessing using linear algebra.

Let $r_{ij} = \| r_i - r_j \|$ for $1 \leq i < j \leq n$ and $s_{ij} = r_{ij}^2$. So s_{ij} is the square of the euclidean distance of the i-th particle from the j-th particle. There are $n(n-1)/2$ such mutual distances. Let $\psi(x)$ be a real function defining the potential. Following [1], we require that the function ψ' is strictly increasing ($\psi'' > 0$ and strictly concave ($\psi''' < 0$). These two hypotheses are satisfied for the newtonian potential ($\psi(x) = x^{-1/2}$) and for the logarithmic potential ($\psi(x) = -\log x$). Finally, let $\Delta_1, \ldots, \Delta_n$ be the oriented volumes of the n simplexes formed by the n bodies. These verify the relation:

$$\sum_{i=1}^{n} \Delta_i = 0. \tag{2}$$

Central configurations are then characterized by the following two groups of equations:

(A)	$\sum_{j \neq i} \Delta_j s_{ij} = X$, for some X independent of i
(B)	there are two real numbers x and y such that $$\psi'(s_{ij}) = x + y\, \Delta_i \Delta_j$$

The group (A) equations are due to Albouy (see [1]). The group (B) equations for the central configurations of the planar newtonian 4-body problem (with arbitrary masses) appears in [6], where it is stated that the proof is based on Analytic Geometry considerations.

The general principles developed in [3] for the N-body problem in general, allow to prove both groups of equations using a construction in Linear Algebra.

3   Newtonian planar 4-body problem with equal masses

In this section we study the central configurations of the newtonian planar 4-body problem with equal masses.

3.1   The initial equations

In order to keep up with standard notation we put:

$$a = s_{12}, \quad b = s_{13}, \quad c = s_{14}, \quad d = s_{23}, \quad e = s_{24}, \quad f = s_{34} \tag{3}$$

and

$$A = \psi'(s_{12}), \quad B = \psi'(s_{13}), \quad C = \psi'(s_{14}),$$
$$D = \psi'(s_{23}), \quad E = \psi'(s_{24}), \quad F = \psi'(s_{34}). \tag{4}$$

Finally, let $\Delta_1, \Delta_2, \Delta_3, \Delta_4$ be the oriented areas of the triangles $(2, 3, 4)$, $(4, 3, 1)$, $(1, 2, 4)$ and $(3, 2, 1)$ which verify

$$\Delta_1 + \Delta_2 + \Delta_3 + \Delta_4 = 0. \tag{5}$$

The group (A) gives the following equalities:

$$t_1 = t_2 = t_3 = t_4 \tag{6}$$

where

$$\begin{cases} t_1 = \Delta_2 \, a + \Delta_3 \, b + \Delta_4 \, c \\ t_2 = \Delta_1 \, a + \Delta_3 \, d + \Delta_4 \, e \\ t_3 = \Delta_1 \, b + \Delta_2 \, d + \Delta_4 \, f \\ t_4 = \Delta_1 \, c + \Delta_2 \, e + \Delta_3 \, f \end{cases}$$

The group (B) gives the following equations:

$$\begin{cases} A = x + y \, \Delta_1 \, \Delta_2, \quad B = x + y \, \Delta_1 \, \Delta_3, \quad C = x + y \, \Delta_1 \, \Delta_4, \\ D = x + y \, \Delta_2 \, \Delta_3, \quad E = x + y \, \Delta_2 \, \Delta_4, \quad F = x + y \, \Delta_3 \, \Delta_4 \end{cases} \tag{7}$$

3.2   Albouy's Symmetry theorem

The following theorem has been proved by A. Albouy in [1].

Theorem 2. *Every central configuration of the (newtonian) planar 4-body problem with equal masses has at least one symmetry.*

The proof of theorem (2) is done by contradiction and has two parts:

1. *The algebraic part* :
   where are obtained 4 equations of degree 2 as algebraic consequences of the initial equations.
2. *The geometric part* :
   where it is shown by geometric considerations and using the concavity of the derivative of the function ψ, that these 4 equations cannot be satisfied.

The algebraic part of the proof of theorem (2) is actually a way to eliminate the unknowns $x, y, \Delta_1, \Delta_2, \Delta_3, \Delta_4$. This is done in an elegant manner, in the following theorem:

Theorem 3. *The equations (5), (6) and (7) imply :*

$$\begin{vmatrix} 1 & 1 & 1 \\ a & b & c \\ A & B & C \end{vmatrix} + \begin{vmatrix} 1 & 1 & 1 \\ f & e & d \\ A & B & C \end{vmatrix} = 2 \begin{vmatrix} 1 & 1 & 1 \\ f & e & d \\ F & E & D \end{vmatrix} \tag{8}$$

$$\begin{vmatrix} 1 & 1 & 1 \\ a & e & d \\ A & E & D \end{vmatrix} + \begin{vmatrix} 1 & 1 & 1 \\ f & b & c \\ A & E & D \end{vmatrix} = 2 \begin{vmatrix} 1 & 1 & 1 \\ f & b & c \\ F & B & C \end{vmatrix} \tag{9}$$

$$\begin{vmatrix} 1 & 1 & 1 \\ f & b & d \\ F & B & D \end{vmatrix} + \begin{vmatrix} 1 & 1 & 1 \\ a & e & c \\ F & B & D \end{vmatrix} = 2 \begin{vmatrix} 1 & 1 & 1 \\ a & e & c \\ A & E & C \end{vmatrix} \tag{10}$$

$$\begin{vmatrix} 1 & 1 & 1 \\ f & e & c \\ F & E & C \end{vmatrix} + \begin{vmatrix} 1 & 1 & 1 \\ a & b & d \\ F & E & C \end{vmatrix} = 2 \begin{vmatrix} 1 & 1 & 1 \\ a & b & d \\ A & B & D \end{vmatrix} \tag{11}$$

We give now a new proof of theorem (3) using notions from Elimination theory and Gröbner bases theory.

Algebraic preliminaries In this paragraph we mention briefly some elements from Elimination theory and Gröbner bases theory which are needed in our proof of theorem (3). For a more detailed exposition and proofs of the theorems one can consult [4] and [5].

Let K be a field and consider the polynomial ring $K[x_1, \ldots, x_n]$ of polynomials in n variables over K. Let $f_1, \ldots, f_m$ be m polynomials in $K[x_1, \ldots, x_n]$ and consider the ideal $I = \langle f_1, \ldots, f_m \rangle$ generated by these polynomials.

Definition 4. An admissible order $>$ on $K[x_1, \ldots, x_n]$ is called a k−elimination order if

$$x_1^{a_1} \ldots x_n^{a_n} > x_{k+1}^{b_{k+1}} \ldots x_n^{b_n}$$

when $a_{i_0} > 0$ for some $i_0 \in \{1, \ldots, k\}$.

Remark 5. A lexicographical order is a k−elimination order for all k. A block order is defined using two admissible orders (see [4], p. 168). It is also a k−elimination order.

Definition 6. The kth elimination ideal I_k is the ideal of $K[x_{k+1}, \ldots, x_n]$ defined by

$$I_k = I \cap K[x_{k+1}, \ldots, x_n].$$

The fact that I_k is actually an ideal of $K[x_{k+1}, \ldots, x_n]$ can be easily verified. The 0th elimination ideal is the ideal I himself. In more intuitive terms, the elements of I_k are all the consequences of the equations $f_1 = 0, \ldots, f_m = 0$, which do not contain the variables $x_1, \ldots, x_k$. In this terminology, eliminating $x_1, \ldots, x_k$ is equivalent to finding polynomials that belong to the kth elimination ideal I_k.

Gröbner bases provide a systematic way of finding elements of I_k using suitable orders on the variables. The following theorem shows how to use Gröbner bases to effectively compute a Gröbner basis of the kth elimination ideal I_k.

Theorem 7. *Let I be an ideal of $K[x_1, \ldots, x_n]$ and let G be a Gröbner basis of I with respect to a k−elimination order for k such that $0 \le k \le n$. Then the set*

$$G_k = G \cap K[x_{k+1}, \ldots, x_n]$$

is a Gröbner basis of the kth elimination ideal I_k.

Symbolic proof of theorem (3) In order to prove theorem (3), we compute the Gröbner bases of equations (5), (6) and (7) with respect to three elimination orders that eliminate the variables $x, y, \Delta_1, \Delta_2, \Delta_3, \Delta_4$. Here are these three orders:

$$\mathcal{O}_1 = [x > y > \Delta_1 > \Delta_2 > \Delta_3 > \Delta_4 > A > B > C > D > E > F > a > b > c > d > e > f]$$

$$\mathcal{O}_2 = [x > y > \Delta_1 > \Delta_2 > \Delta_3 > \Delta_4 > A > B > C > D > E > F > d > e > f > a > b > c]$$

$$\mathcal{O}_3 = [x > y > \Delta_1 > \Delta_2 > \Delta_3 > \Delta_4 > A > B > C > D > E > F > f > e > d > c > b > a]$$

The Gröbner basis for the order $\mathcal{O}_1$ contains 44 elements. The following element has the smallest coefficients among the elements of degree two.

$$
\begin{aligned}
aD - aE + bA + 2\,bC - bD - 2\,bF - cA - 2\,cB + cE+ \\
+2\,cF - dA + dE + eA - eD + 2\,fB - 2\,fC + fD - fE.
\end{aligned}
\tag{12}
$$

The Gröbner basis for the order $\mathcal{O}_2$ contains 40 elements. The following element has the smallest coefficients among the elements of degree two.

$$
\begin{aligned}
-aB - 2\,aC + aD + 2\,aE - bD + bF + 2\,cA + cB - 2\,cE \\
-cF + dB - dF - 2\,eA + 2\,eC - eD + eF - fB + fD.
\end{aligned}
\tag{13}
$$

The Gröbner basis for the order $\mathcal{O}_3$ contains 40 elements. The following element has the smallest coefficients among the elements of degree two.

$$
\begin{aligned}
2\,aB + aC - 2\,aD - aE - 2\,bA - bC + 2\,bD + bF + cE \\
-cF + 2\,dA - 2\,dB + dE - dF - eC + eF + fC - fE
\end{aligned}
\tag{14}
$$

These computations have been performed using the Gb program ([7]). The total computation time was less than a second.

A small program in MAPLE to detect linear combinations of equations (12), (13) and (14) with small coefficients, establishes that it suffices to add them to obtain such an equation:

$$
\begin{aligned}
aB - aC - bA + bC + cA - cB + dA - dB + 2\,dE \\
-2\,dF - eA + eC - 2\,eD + 2\,eF + fB - fC + 2\,fD - 2\,fE
\end{aligned}
\tag{15}
$$

We remark that in each of the equations (12), (13), (14) and (15) there are three monomials with a coefficient of 2 and three monomials with a coefficient of -2. Starting from these monomials we can easily construct the determinants appearing on the right-hand side of relations (8), (9), (10) and (11). The remaining 12 monomials can be easily shown to be the sums of determinants appearing on the left-hand side.

4   Newtonian spatial 5-body problem with equal masses

In this section we study the central configurations of the newtonian spatial 5-body problem with equal masses.

4.1   The initial equations

In this paragraph we maintain the notations introduced in section 2.3. Moreover we put $S_{ij} = \psi'(s_{ij})$. Let $\varDelta_1, \varDelta_2, \varDelta_3, \varDelta_4, \varDelta_5$ be the oriented volumes of the five tetrahedra formed by the five bodies. They verify the equation

$$\varDelta_1 + \varDelta_2 + \varDelta_3 + \varDelta_4 + \varDelta_5 = 0. \tag{16}$$

The group (A) gives the following equalities:

$$t_1 = t_2 = t_3 = t_4 = t_5 \tag{17}$$

where

$$\begin{cases} t_1 = \varDelta_2\ s_{12} + \varDelta_3\ s_{13} + \varDelta_4\ s_{14} + \varDelta_5\ s_{15} \\ t_2 = \varDelta_1\ s_{12} + \varDelta_3\ s_{23} + \varDelta_4\ s_{24} + \varDelta_5\ s_{25} \\ t_3 = \varDelta_1\ s_{13} + \varDelta_2\ s_{23} + \varDelta_4\ s_{34} + \varDelta_5\ s_{45} \\ t_4 = \varDelta_1\ s_{14} + \varDelta_2\ s_{24} + \varDelta_3\ s_{34} + \varDelta_5\ s_{45} \\ t_5 = \varDelta_1\ s_{15} + \varDelta_2\ s_{25} + \varDelta_3\ s_{35} + \varDelta_4\ s_{45} \end{cases} .$$

The group (B) gives the following equations:

$$S_{ij} = x + y\ \varDelta_i\ \varDelta_j \tag{18}$$

where

$$(i,j) \ \in \ \{(1,2), (1,3), (1,4), (1,5), (2,3), (2,4), (2,5), (3,4), (3,5), (4,5)\}.$$

4.2   The determinental equations

Let $S = \{1, \ldots 5\}$. For integer indices i, j, k in S, let $l = \min(S\backslash\{i,j,k\})$ and $m = \max(S\backslash\{i,j,k\})$. (The indices l and m are uniquely determined by the indices i, j, k). Finally we note by E_{ijk} the equation:

$$\begin{vmatrix} 1 & 1 & 1 \\ s_{ij} & s_{ik} & s_{jk} \\ S_{lk} & S_{lj} & S_{li} \end{vmatrix} + \begin{vmatrix} 1 & 1 & 1 \\ s_{ij} & s_{ik} & s_{jk} \\ S_{mk} & S_{mj} & S_{mi} \end{vmatrix} = \begin{vmatrix} 1 & 1 & 1 \\ s_{li} & s_{lj} & s_{lk} \\ S_{li} & S_{lj} & S_{lk} \end{vmatrix} + \begin{vmatrix} 1 & 1 & 1 \\ s_{mi} & s_{mj} & s_{mk} \\ S_{mi} & S_{mj} & S_{mk} \end{vmatrix} + 2 \begin{vmatrix} 1 & 1 & 1 \\ s_{ij} & s_{ik} & s_{jk} \\ S_{ij} & S_{ik} & S_{jk} \end{vmatrix}$$

Theorem 8. *The equations (16), (17) and (18) imply the equations:*

$$E_{ijk} \quad for \ \ 1 \le i < j < k \le 5. \tag{19}$$

Proof. Following the technique used in the 4-body problem we compute the Gröbner basis of equations (16), (17) and (18). We used a (DRL,DRL) block order, that is to say a DRL order on the 7 variables $x, y, \varDelta_1, \varDelta_2, \varDelta_3, \varDelta_4, \varDelta_5$ and a DRL order on the 20 variables s_{ij}, S_{ij}. The computation has been performed with FGb ([7]) in less than 1 second. The Gröbner basis contains 6 equations of degree 2, $(e_1, \ldots, e_6)$ in the variables s_{ij}, S_{ij}. We then use a small program in MAPLE to generate the 11^6 linear combinations $\sum_{i=1}^{6} \lambda_i\, e_i$ with $\mid \lambda_i \mid \leq 5$. Keeping only the linear combinations with coefficients belonging to the set $\{-2, -1, 1, 2\}$, we obtain 716 homogeneous equations of degree two in s_{ij}, S_{ij}. By removing multiple elements we are left with 259 equations, of which only 20, have 30 monomials. A closer look to these 20 equations reveals that it suffices to keep only 10 of them, since the other 10 are just their opposites.

These 10 equations can be expressed in determinental form, just as in the case of the 4-body problem. $\qquad\qquad\qquad\qquad\qquad\qquad\qquad\qquad\qquad\qquad\qquad\qquad\square$

Remark 9. The number of triplets of indices that appear in equations (19), is the number of ways of choosing 3 distinct elements form 5. Indeed, the binomial coefficient $\binom{5}{3}$ is equal to 10.

Remark 10. The ten equations E_{ijk} in theorem (8) appear in [2] where they are derived from more general considerations. We have established these equations independently and using exclusively equations (16), (17) and (18).

Remark 11. Equations (19) are not algebraically independent since there are only 6 equations of degree 2 in the Gröbner basis. This fact agrees with the theoretical prediction in [2].

Using equations (19), we will prove that in the convex case there are no central configurations without symmetry in the newtonian spatial 5-body problem with equal masses.

4.3   The symmetry theorem in the convex case

We call *convex configuration* every spatial configuration of the 5 bodies such that:

$$\Delta_1 \leq \Delta_2 \leq 0 \leq \Delta_3 \leq \Delta_4 \leq \Delta_5. \tag{20}$$

Using equations (19), we will prove that there is no solution of the initial system of equations that does not have symmetries.

Remark 12. In the rest of the paper we will assume that all the Δ_i are different than zero, because a zero Δ_i gives rise to a symmetric solution (see [10]).

We need a lemma on concave functions.

Lemma 13. *Let ϕ be a (strictly) concave function on $\mathbb{R}$ and $x > y > z$. Then we have*

$$\begin{vmatrix} 1 & 1 & 1 \\ x & y & z \\ \phi(x) & \phi(y) & \phi(z) \end{vmatrix} > 0.$$

Proof. We put $\lambda = \dfrac{y - z}{x - z}$. According to the hypothesis $x > y > z$, we have that $\lambda \in (0, 1)$. Moreover, we have that $y = z + \lambda(x - z) = \lambda x + (1 - \lambda)z$. Since ϕ is a (strictly) concave function we have:

$$\phi(y) = \phi(\lambda x + (1 - \lambda)z) > \lambda\phi(x) + (1 - \lambda)\phi(z) = \lambda\phi(x) + \phi(z) - \lambda\phi(z)$$

and so we have

$$\phi(y) - \phi(z) > \lambda(\phi(x) - \phi(z))$$

which means that

$$\frac{\phi(y) - \phi(z)}{y - z} > \frac{\phi(x) - \phi(z)}{x - z}. \tag{21}$$

By developing the determinant in the statement of the theorem we have:

$$\begin{vmatrix} 1 & 1 & 1 \\ x & y & z \\ \phi(x) & \phi(y) & \phi(z) \end{vmatrix} = \begin{vmatrix} x - z & y - z \\ \phi(x) - \phi(z) & \phi(y) - \phi(z) \end{vmatrix} > 0.$$

□

Remark 14. Geometrically, the determinant appearing in the statement of lemma (13) can be interpreted as the oriented area of the triangle formed by the three points $(x, \phi(x)), (y, \phi(y)), (z, \phi(z))$ on the graph of ϕ.

We now state and prove the symmetry theorem in the convex case.

Theorem 15. *Every central spatial convex configuration of five equal masses is symmetric.*

Proof. Suppose that the configuration is non symmetric, which implies that all inequalities in (20) are strict:

$$\Delta_1 < \Delta_2 < 0 < \Delta_3 < \Delta_4 < \Delta_5. \tag{22}$$

Without loss of generality we may assume that $y > 0$ (if $y < 0$ we obtain opposite inequalities).

Using (22) and equations (18) we can order the S_{ij}. For instance $S_{14} - S_{15} = y\Delta_1(\Delta_4 - \Delta_5)$ so that $S_{14} - S_{15} > 0$. In the same way we obtain:

$$\begin{aligned} S_{15} &< S_{14} < S_{13} < S_{23} < S_{12}, \\ S_{14} &< S_{24} < S_{34} < S_{35} < S_{45}, \\ S_{15} &< S_{25} < S_{24} < S_{23} < S_{12}, \\ S_{25} &< S_{35} \end{aligned} \tag{23}$$

We cannot compare directly S_{25} and S_{34}.

Since ψ' is a strictly increasing function ($\psi'' > 0$) and $S_{ij} = \psi'(s_{ij})$, we have the corresponding relations for s_{ij} :

$$\begin{aligned} s_{15} &< s_{14} < s_{13} < s_{23} < s_{12}, \\ s_{14} &< s_{24} < s_{34} < s_{35} < s_{45}, \\ s_{15} &< s_{25} < s_{24} < s_{23} < s_{12}, \\ s_{25} &< s_{35} \end{aligned} \tag{24}$$

We cannot compare directly s_{25} and s_{34}.

Relations (24) and (23) and lemma (13) can be used to decide the sign of the determinants appearing in equations (19).

In particular we will prove that equation E_{123} is impossible.

Indeed the two determinants on the left-hand side of E_{123} are strictly positive, because we have:

$$\begin{vmatrix} 1 & 1 & 1 \\ s_{12} & s_{13} & s_{23} \\ S_{34} & S_{24} & S_{14} \end{vmatrix} = \underbrace{(s_{12} - s_{23})}_{>0} \underbrace{(S_{24} - S_{14})}_{>0} + \underbrace{(s_{23} - s_{13})}_{>0} \underbrace{(S_{34} - S_{14})}_{>0} > 0$$

and

$$\begin{vmatrix} 1 & 1 & 1 \\ s_{12} & s_{13} & s_{23} \\ S_{35} & S_{25} & S_{15} \end{vmatrix} = \underbrace{(s_{12} - s_{23})}_{>0} \underbrace{(S_{25} - S_{15})}_{>0} + \underbrace{(s_{23} - s_{13})}_{>0} \underbrace{(S_{35} - S_{25})}_{>0} > 0.$$

Moreover, the three determinants on the right-hand side of E_{123} are strictly negative, because the function ψ' is (strictly) concave ($\psi''' < 0$) and by applying lemma (13) we have:

$$\begin{vmatrix} 1 & 1 & 1 \\ s_{14} & s_{24} & s_{34} \\ S_{14} & S_{24} & S_{34} \end{vmatrix} = - \begin{vmatrix} 1 & 1 & 1 \\ s_{34} & s_{24} & s_{14} \\ S_{34} & S_{24} & S_{14} \end{vmatrix} < 0 \text{ because } s_{34} > s_{24} > s_{14},$$

$$\begin{vmatrix} 1 & 1 & 1 \\ s_{15} & s_{25} & s_{35} \\ S_{15} & S_{25} & S_{35} \end{vmatrix} = - \begin{vmatrix} 1 & 1 & 1 \\ s_{35} & s_{25} & s_{15} \\ S_{35} & S_{25} & S_{15} \end{vmatrix} < 0 \text{ because } s_{35} > s_{25} > s_{15},$$

$$\begin{vmatrix} 1 & 1 & 1 \\ s_{12} & s_{13} & s_{23} \\ S_{12} & S_{13} & S_{23} \end{vmatrix} = - \begin{vmatrix} 1 & 1 & 1 \\ s_{12} & s_{23} & s_{13} \\ S_{12} & S_{23} & S_{13} \end{vmatrix} < 0 \text{ because } s_{12} > s_{23} > s_{13}.$$

Consequently, equation E_{123} is impossible and there is a contradiction. The hypothesis that the configuration is non symmetric is false.   □

Corollary 16. *Every central spatial convex configuration of the newtonian 5-body problem with equal masses is symmetric.*

Theorem (15) can be proved under a weaker hypothesis than (22).

Proposition 17. *There is no central configuration such that $\Delta_1 < \Delta_2 < 0 < \Delta_3 \leq \Delta_4 \leq \Delta_5$.*

Proof. Using the hypothesis and equations (18) we see that between inequalities (23), some of them are no longer strict:

$$S_{15} \leq S_{14} \leq S_{13} < S_{23} < S_{12},$$
$$S_{14} < S_{24} < S_{34} \leq S_{35} \leq S_{45},$$
$$S_{15} < S_{25} \leq S_{24} \leq S_{23} < S_{12},$$
$$S_{25} < S_{35}$$

Using the fact that ψ' is a strictly increasing function, we have the corresponding inequalities for the s_{ij}:

$$s_{15} \leq s_{14} \leq s_{13} < s_{23} < s_{12},$$
$$s_{14} < s_{24} < s_{34} \leq s_{35} \leq s_{45},$$
$$s_{15} < s_{25} \leq s_{24} \leq s_{23} < s_{12},$$
$$s_{25} < s_{35}$$

The first 3×3 determinant of E_{123} remains strictly positive and there is still a contradiction.

Remark 18. It has been verified by direct Gröbner bases computations (using FGb) that the hypothesis

$$\Delta_1 = \Delta_2 \text{ and } \prod_{1 < i < j < 6} \Delta_i(\Delta_i - \Delta_j) \neq 0$$

gives rise to a contradiction, in the case of a logarithmic potential.

Theorem (15) is useful in the classification of central configuration types in the spatial newtonian 5-body problem with equal masses. In [10] and [9] one can find a detailed account of several symmetric central configuration types.

5   Conclusion

We used Symbolic Computation techniques to prove symmetry theorems for the newtonian planar 4-body problem with equal masses and the newtonian spatial 5-body problem with equal masses in the convex case. In the 4-body problem case, the symmetry theorem is enough to complete the classification of central configurations. In the 5-body problem case, the symmetry theorem needs to be extended for the non convex case, in order to complete the classification of central configurations. This will be done in a forthcoming paper.

6   Acknowledgments

The authors would like to thank Daniel Lazard for indicating a more general statement for the symmetry theorem as well as for many insightful suggestions and Alain Albouy for many stimulating discussions and useful remarks.

References

1. Albouy, A.: Symétrie des Configurations Centrales de Quatre Corps. C. R. Acad. Sci. Paris **320** (1995) 217–220
2. Albouy, A.: Recherches sur le problème des N corps. Habilitation, Bureau des Longitudes, Paris.
3. Albouy, A., Chenciner, A.: Le problème des n corps et les distances mutuelles. Invent. Math. **131** (1998) 151–184
4. Becker, T., Weispfenning, V.: Gröbner Bases. A Computational Approach to Commutative Algebra (In cooperation with H. Kredel). Springer Verlag, (1993)
5. Cox, D., Little, J., O'Shea, D.: Ideals, Varieties, and Algorithms. Springer-Verlag, (1991)
6. Dziobek, O.: Ueber einen merkwürdigen Fall des Vielkörperproblems. Astron. Nach. **152** (1900) 33–46
7. Faugère, J.-C.: http://posso.lip6.fr/~jcf/ Hypertext documentation on Gb and FGb.
8. Faugère, J.-C.: A new efficient algorithm for computing Gröbner bases (F4). Journal of Pure and Applied Algebra, (to appear) (1999)
9. Kotsireas, I.: Algorithms for solving systems of polynomial equations: Application to central configurations of the N-body problem in Celestial Mechanics. Ph. D. Thesis, (in french with extended english abstract) Université Paris 6, 1998.
10. Kotsireas, I., Lazard, D.: Central Configurations of the 5-body problem with equal masses in three-dimensional space. Proceedings of CASC'98, Saint-Petersburg.
11. Meyer, K.R., Schmidt, D.S.: Bifurcations of relative equilibria in the N-body and Kirchhoff problems. SIAM J. Math. Anal. **19** (1988) 1295–1313

Symbolic Derivation of Different Class of High-order Compact Schemes for Partial Differential Equations

Michel Fournié

CNRS UMR M.I.P. 5640, Université Paul Sabatier,
118 route de Narbonne, 31062 Toulouse Cedex 04, France.

Abstract. A symbolic procedure for deriving finite difference approximations for partial differential equations is described. We restrict our study to high-order compact schemes in conservative and non-conservative form.

1   Introduction

This work deals with automation of the discretization of partial differential equations (PDE). One of the most frequent methods used for solving PDE is the finite difference method, in which derivatives are replaced by divided differences. In general, on a structured grid, a derivative of order p can be approximated up to order m (see truncation error analysis [3]) with $p + m - 1$ points if p is even and $p + m$ points if p is odd. Such high-order methods (i.e. of order > 2, generally of order 4) always require non-compact stencils. Their use near boundaries are intricated, the matrix bandwidth of associated linear systems and the communication requirements for implementation on parallel computer architecture are increased in comparison with a compact discretization which only utilizes grid points immediately neighbor of the point where the derivatives are approximated (a 1D compact stencil uses 3 points, a 2D uses 3×3 points and a 3D uses $3 \times 3 \times 3$ points). The objective is to develop a class of schemes that are both high-order and compact (HOC schemes). This paper concerns this type of schemes in which the lowest-order terms of the truncation error are approximated using the differential equation in an analogous way to the Lax-Wendroff idea. These schemes may be viewed as an extension of the classical central difference scheme and present the advantage of suppressing or reducing numerical oscillations [1,2], and the problems which previously required fine grids can be solved on coarse grids. We restrict our presentation to HOC conservative and non-conservative schemes. The derivation of such schemes requires very tedious algebraic manipulations which are time consuming with the risk of bugs. In the process, several stages can be made using computer algebra [5] so as to define the discretization and to generate numerical programs (FORTRAN language). In this paper we mainly focus on 2D problem since the generalization to 3D (or restriction to 1D) problems is straightforward. The nature of the scheme (in conservative and non-conservative form) and the complexity of the scheme which increases CPU time (due to the automation of the process) are particularly considered. We present symbolic computations for the discretization of the 2D drift-diffusion system extensively used in industrial applications for the simulation of semiconductor devices. This example is representative of non-linear elliptic PDE. All manipulations are realized using the algebra system AXIOM [5].

2   The Drift-Diffusion model

To introduce the main ideas, we consider the simplified 2D drift-diffusion model in dimensionless form given in [4]. The dependent variables (ψ, n) satisfy mixed Neumann and Dirichlet boundary conditions (their treatments are described in [6]). The problem is defined on a bounded domain Ω in $\mathbb{R}^2$ by,

$$\begin{cases} \lambda^2 \Delta\psi - n + C(x,y) = 0, & \text{Poisson's equation,} \\ \operatorname{div} J_n = 0, & \text{continuity equation,} \\ J_n = -D_n \nabla n + \mu_n n \nabla\psi, & \text{current density.} \end{cases} \tag{1}$$

ψ represents the electrostatic potential, n the electron density, μ_n, D_n are the mobility and diffusivity coefficients respectively, $C(x,y)$ is the doping profile and we note $J_n = (J_{nx}, J_{ny})$. From a numerical point of view, difficulties arise in the discretization of advection-dominated current equations (due to the large size of $\nabla\psi$ in a significant part of the domain) and fine numerical results are based on an accurate computation of the current. HOC schemes are good candidates for this approximation. Considering a uniform grid where h and k are the grid size in x and y directions, we number the points $(i-1,j-1)$, $(i,j-1)$, $(i+1,j-1)$, $(i-1,j)$, (i,j), $(i+1,j)$, $(i-1,j+1)$, $(i,j+1)$, $(i+1,j+1)$, as 1, 2, 3, 4, 5, 6, 7, 8, 9, respectively (see Fig. 1) and denote by u_l the value of u at the grid point numbered l.

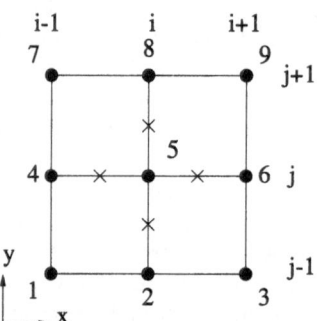

Fig 1. Computational stencil.

3   Construction of non-conservative HOC schemes

The discretization of (1) using high-order compact schemes (of order 4), is based on central difference formulas :

$$\left(\frac{\partial^2 u}{\partial x^2}\right)_5 = \frac{u_6 - 2u_5 + u_4}{h^2} - \frac{h^2}{12}\left(\frac{\partial^4 u}{\partial x^4}\right)_5 + O(h^4), \tag{2}$$

$$\left(\frac{\partial u}{\partial x}\right)_5 = \frac{u_6 - u_4}{2h} - \frac{h^2}{6}\left(\frac{\partial^3 u}{\partial x^3}\right)_5 + O(h^4), \tag{3}$$

$$(u)_5 = \frac{u_6 + u_4}{2} - \frac{h^2}{2}\left(\frac{\partial^2 u}{\partial x^2}\right)_5 + O(h^4). \tag{4}$$

Considering (1) at the grid point 5, each term can be approximated using (2-4) in x and y directions. Thus a fourth-order truncation error is obtained by using a second-order approximation of the derivatives of order 2, 3 and 4 which must call for stencil $S = \{1, 2, 3, 4, 5, 6, 7, 8, 9\}$ to preserve the compactness of the scheme. The derivatives of order > 2 can not be discretized upon S. To overcome this difficulty, algebraic manipulations on differential equations (1) and equations deduced from differentiation are required. Equivalent expressions of derivatives of ψ are deduced from Poisson's equation while derivatives of n are deduced from continuity equation (after substituting J_n by its value).

For example, we write,

$$\frac{\partial}{\partial x}\left(\lambda^2 \Delta \psi - n + C(x, y)\right) = 0, \tag{5}$$

and we deduce an exact expression of $\left(\frac{\partial^3 \psi}{\partial x^3}\right)$,

$$\frac{\partial^3 \psi}{\partial x^3} = \frac{1}{\lambda^2}\left(\frac{\partial n}{\partial x} - \frac{\partial C}{\partial x}\right) - \frac{\partial^3 \psi}{\partial x \partial y^2}. \tag{6}$$

These manipulations introduce cross derivatives $\frac{\partial^{l_1 + l_2} u}{\partial x^{l_1} \partial y^{l_2}}$, $l_1 \leq 2$ and $l_2 \leq 2$ which can be approximated with classical centered approximations (of order 2) on the compact stencil S to give HOC scheme. A similar treatment is used to discretize the continuity equation and obtain the global scheme for (1).

4 Construction of conservative HOC schemes

4.1 Recursive algorithm :

The previous technique to construct HOC schemes is attractive, however, the conservation property of the continuous problem ($\text{div}(J_n) = 0$) is not preserved. To look for a conservative discretization of the continuity equation (considered at grid point 5), we propose to discretize the continuity equation by,

$$\frac{(J_{nx})_{i+\frac{1}{2},j} - (J_{nx})_{i-\frac{1}{2},j}}{h} + \frac{(J_{ny})_{i,j+\frac{1}{2}} - (J_{ny})_{i,j-\frac{1}{2}}}{k} = 0,$$

and compute the current on restricted stencil $S_x^- = \{1, 2, 4, 5, 7, 8\}$ for $(J_{nx})_{i-\frac{1}{2},j}$, $S_x^+ = \{2, 3, 5, 6, 8, 9\}$ for $(J_{nx})_{i+\frac{1}{2},j}$, $S_y^- = \{1, 2, 3, 4, 5, 6\}$ for $(J_{ny})_{i,j-\frac{1}{2}}$, and $S_y^+ = \{4, 5, 6, 7, 8, 9\}$ for $(J_{ny})_{i,j+\frac{1}{2}}$. In view of $S = S_x^- \cup S_x^+ \cup S_y^- \cup S_y^+$, the final scheme is compact. In the following we describe the symbolic manipulations allowing to define fourth-order approximation of (J_{nx}) at the grid point $(i - \frac{1}{2}, j)$ (Fig. 1, $\times$ marks),

$$J_{nx} = -D_n \frac{\partial n}{\partial x} + \mu_n n \frac{\partial \psi}{\partial x}. \tag{7}$$

Here, we use analogous relations to (3-4),

$$\left(\frac{\partial u}{\partial x}\right)_{i-\frac{1}{2},j} = \frac{u_5 - u_4}{h} - \frac{h^2}{24}\left(\frac{\partial^3 u}{\partial x^3}\right)_{i-\frac{1}{2},j} + O(h^4), \tag{8}$$

$$(u)_{i-\frac{1}{2},j} = \frac{u_5 + u_4}{2} - \frac{h^2}{8}\left(\frac{\partial^2 u}{\partial x^2}\right)_{i-\frac{1}{2},j} + O(h^4), \tag{9}$$

which introduce derivatives of order 2 and 3 of ψ and n. Contrary to the non-conservative scheme, the second derivative (introduced by (9) and by the treatment of the third derivative in (8)) must be substituted using (1). Like in (5), we can treat each derivative and define final HOC scheme.

4.2   Alternative :

The recursive algorithm, is very interesting with regard to automation of the symbolic manipulations, however, the complexity of the scheme grows with substitutions of high-order derivatives. So we present an alternative based on particular interpolation formulas in relation with continuous problem to approximate some derivatives.

For example, we can reduce the number of substitutions without using (9) to approximate n in (7) at the grid point $(i - \frac{1}{2}, j)$. After symbolic manipulations (recursive approach to treat $(\frac{\partial^3 n}{\partial x^3})$), it appears,

$$\left(n + \frac{h^2}{24} \frac{\partial^2 n}{\partial x^2} \right)_{i-\frac{1}{2},j}, \tag{10}$$

that must be approximated at the order 4 to obtain the final scheme.

The set grid points S_x^- is too restricted to interpolate the density n at the order 4, so we add two terms to the interpolation in such a way that (10) introduces a best term. By symbolic Taylor developments and after identification in,

$$n_{i-\frac{1}{2},j} = \sum_{i \in S_x^-} \alpha_i n_i + h^2 A \left(\frac{\partial^2 n}{\partial x^2} \right)_{i-\frac{1}{2},j} + k^2 B \left(\frac{\partial^2 n}{\partial y^2} \right)_{i-\frac{1}{2},j} + O(h^4 + k^4).$$

we find an unique solution,

$$n_{i-\frac{1}{2},j} = \frac{h^2}{24k^2} (n_1 + n_2 + n_7 + n_8) + \frac{6k^2 - h^2}{12k^2} (n_4 + n_5)$$

$$- \frac{h^2}{24} \left(3 \frac{\partial^2 n}{\partial x^2} + 2 \frac{\partial^2 n}{\partial y^2} \right)_{i-\frac{1}{2},j} + O(h^4 + k^4), \tag{11}$$

and the computation of (10) introduces the term $\frac{h^2}{12} (\frac{\partial^2 n}{\partial x^2} + \frac{\partial^2 n}{\partial y^2})$ which can be directly extracted from continuity equation and it is not necessary to approximate $(\frac{\partial^2 n}{\partial x^2})$.

5   Algorithms and realization

To realize all algebraic manipulations, we used computer algebra system AXIOM [5]. Here, we describe the discretization of Poisson's equation, continuity equation is similarly approximated. Several examples of manipulations are given. They correspond to some parts of a global algorithm which takes in input the PDE and gives in output the final HOC scheme of order 4. The main difficulties are the analysis of formal expressions so as to extract terms which require a particular treatment (derivatives of high-order) and to automatically construct the substitution from the continuous problem. Using the commands already implemented in the system AXIOM, it is easy to split an expression, extract all derivatives and analyse them (What is the order of the derivation ? What is the name of the function ?), so we do not describe some procedures which include these analysis tools. During the implementation, the derivatives of the PDE are substituted using (2-4) (or (8) and (9) for the current). These substitutions are defined by the function **makeFdsOrdre4** and the resulting derivatives $(\frac{\partial^l u}{\partial x^l})$ and $(\frac{\partial^l u}{\partial y^l})$ must be approximated using the continuous equation since $l > 3$ to construct non-conservative HOC scheme (or conservative scheme since $l > 2$). Analysing their order, we deduce the nature of the derivation that must be applied to the PDE so as to define new exact relations with **highOrderDerivatives** function. Finally, the substitutions of resulting derivatives are realized (after verification of the possible compact discretization $\frac{\partial^{l_1+l_2} u}{\partial x^{l_1} \partial y^{l_2}}$, $l_1 \leq 2$ and $l_2 \leq 2$) with the function **makeFdsOrdre2** which defines compact finite difference operators of order 2.

Input to the AXIOM system is denoted by (1)-> and output by (1) where 1 is the computation step number.

```
------ We define all operators with the identification \psi = q.
```

```
(1) -> opq := operator("q"::Symbol,2); q := opq(x,y)
    (1)   q(x,y)                          Type: Expression Integer
```

```
(2) -> opn := operator("n"::Symbol,2); n := opn(x,y);
                                         Type: Expression Integer
```

```
(3) -> opC := operator("C"::Symbol,2); C := opC(x,y);
                                         Type: Expression Integer
```

```
(4) -> poisson := a*(D(q,x,2)+D(q,y,2)) - n + C = 0
    (4)   aq      (x,y) + aq      (x,y) - n(x,y) + C(x,y)= 0
            ,2,2             ,1,1

                         Type: Equation Expression Integer
------ We define Finite Difference Schemes of order 4 (see (2-4)).
```

```
(5) -> leqFdsOrder4 := makeFdsOrdre4(poisson)
    (5)
                        4
                 - h q          (x,y) + 12q6 - 24q5 + 12q4
                      ,1,1,1,1
     [q      (x,y)= ------------------------------------- ,
       ,1,1                            2
                                    12h
                      4
                 - k q          (x,y) + 12q8 - 24q5 + 12q2
                      ,2,2,2,2
     q      (x,y)= ------------------------------------- , q(x,y)= q5,
      ,2,2                            2
                                   12k
     n(x,y)= n5, C(x,y)= C5]    Type: List Equation Expression Integer
```

(6) -> poisson1 := eval(poisson,leqFdsOrder4)
   (6)

$$- a\, h\, k\, q_{,2,2,2,2}^{2\ 4}(x,y) - a\, h\, k\, q_{,1,1,1,1}^{4\ 2}(x,y) + 12a\, h^{2}\, q8$$
   +
$$12a\, k^{2}\, q6 +(- 24a\, k^{2} - 24a\, h^{2})q5 + 12a\, k^{2}\, q4 + 12a\, h^{2}\, q2 - 12h^{2}\, k^{2}\, n5$$
   +
$$12C5\, h^{2}\, k^{2}$$
 /
$$12h^{2}\, k^{2} = 0$$ Type: Equation Expression Integer

------ We define exact relations from Poisson's equation.
(7) -> hocDer := highOrderDerivative(poisson1)
   (7)

$$[q_{,1,1,1,1}(x,y) = \frac{- a q_{,2,2,1,1}(x,y) + n_{,1,1}(x,y) - C_{,1,1}(x,y)}{a},$$

$$q_{,2,2,2,2}(x,y) = \frac{- a q_{,1,1,2,2}(x,y) + n_{,2,2}(x,y) - C_{,2,2}(x,y)}{a}]$$
                    Type: List Equation Expression Integer

(8) -> poisson2 := eval(poisson1,hocDer);
                    Type: List Equation Expression Integer

------ We define Finite Difference Schemes of order 2.
(9) -> leqFdsOrder2 := makeFdsOrdre2(poisson2)
   (9)

$$[q_{,1,1,2,2}(x,y) = \frac{q9 - 2q8 + q7 - 2q6 + 4q5 - 2q4 + q3 - 2q2 + q1}{h^{2}\, k^{2}},$$

$$q_{,2,2,1,1}(x,y) = \frac{q9 - 2q8 + q7 - 2q6 + 4q5 - 2q4 + q3 - 2q2 + q1}{h^{2}\, k^{2}},$$

$$n_{,2,2}(x,y) = \frac{n8 - 2n5 + n2}{k^{2}}, \quad n_{,1,1}(x,y) = \frac{n6 - 2n5 + n4}{h^{2}},$$

$$C_{,2,2}(x,y) = \frac{C8 - 2C5 + C2}{k^2}, \quad C_{,1,1}(x,y) = \frac{C6 - 2C5 + C4}{h^2}]$$

Type: List Equation Expression Integer

------- We obtain final HOC scheme (of order 4).
(10) -> poisson3 := eval(poisson2,leqFdsOrder2);
   (10)

$$\frac{\begin{array}{l}(a\,k^2 + a\,h^2)q9 + (-2a\,k^2 + 10a\,h^2)q8 + (a\,k^2 + a\,h^2)q7 \\ + (10a\,k^2 - 2a\,h^2)q6 + (-20a\,k^2 - 20a\,h^2)q5 + (10a\,k^2 - 2a\,h^2)q4 \\ + (a\,k^2 + a\,h^2)q3 + (-2a\,k^2 + 10a\,h^2)q2 + (a\,k^2 + a\,h^2)q1 - h^2k^2 n8 \\ + -h^2k^2 n6 - 8h^2k^2 n5 - h^2k^2 n4 - h^2k^2 n2 + (C8 + C6 + 8C5 + C4 + C2)h^2 k^2 \end{array}}{12h^2 k^2}$$

= 0

Type: Equation Expression Integer

After the construction of the whole discretization, we generate FORTRAN codes necessary to obtain numerical results. In particular we compute the Jacobian matrix associated to the final discret system used in the Newton method to linearize the problem.

Remark : The robustness of the scheme is proved in various numerical tests in the case of uniform or non-uniform meshes [6] and compared with classical scheme [7] (analyse of the convergence rate).

6   Conclusion

The symbolic implementations with AXIOM for the construction of high-order compact finite difference schemes have been detailed on an interesting physical model. The main advantage is the speeding up of all the process of discretization (definition and generation of optimized numerical code) with high fiabilty. Similar techniques can be used on non-uniform grids or for more tedious model like Energy-Transport model. Fine results were found after analytic manipulations insurmountable by hand.

Acknowledgments. The author thanks D. Pinchon and A. Rigal for their assistance and discussions.

References

1. W.F. Spotz and G.F. Carey, High-order compact scheme for steady stream-function vorticity equations. *Int. J. Numer. Methods Eng.* **38**: 3497–3512, (1995).
2. R.S. Hirsh, High-order difference solution of fluid mechanics problems by a compact differencing technique. *J. of Comp. Phys.* **9**: 90–109, (1975).
3. V.G. Ganzha and M.Y. Shashkov, Local approximation sudy of difference operators by means of reduce system. *Proceedings* ISSAC *'90*.
4. W.V. Van Roosbroeck, Theory of flow electrons and holes in Germanium and other semiconductors. *Bell Syst. Tech. J.* **29**: 650–607, (1950).
5. R.D. Jenks and R.S. Sutor, Axiom - The scientific computation system. *Springer Verlag.* (1992).
6. M. Fournié, High-order conservative difference methods for 2D drift-diffusion model on non-uniform grid. *Presented at* ICOSAHOM *'98 conference and submitted in Appl. Numer. Math.*
7. M. Fournié and P. Pietra, Numerical simulation of 2D semiconductor devices using high-order conservative finite difference methods. *In preparation.*

Implementation of Aerodynamic Computations with Mathematica*

Victor G. Ganzha[1] and Evgenii V. Vorozhtsov[2]

[1] Institute of Informatics, Technical University of Munich, Munich 80290, Arcisstr. 21, Germany; e-mail: ganzha@informatik.tu-muenchen.de
[2] Institute of Theoretical and Applied Mechanics, Russian Academy of Sciences, Novosibirsk 630090, Russia; e-mail: vorozh@itam.nsc.ru

Abstract. We present a new symbolic-numerical method for stability investigation of complex finite difference or finite volume schemes for the Euler equations on curvilinear grids. We apply the method to investigation of a three-stage Runge-Kutta finite volume scheme augmented by artificial dissipator and obtain the stability condition, which is then incorporated in the Mathematica 3.0 code for aerodynamic computations. These computations for a wide range of freestream Mach numbers confirm the validity of the obtained stability condition. Results of aerodynamic numerical computations are presented.

1   Introduction

The development of efficient computer codes for the numerical modeling of various fluid flow problems is the central problem of computational fluid dynamics (CFD). These codes are usually written in such languages of numerical computation as FORTRAN or C. However, the corresponding software packages have some shortcomings: the complex procedures of code debugging; the absence of built-in PostScript computer graphics subroutines.

On the other hand, the advanced computer algebra system (CAS) *Mathematica 3.0* has many features, which are very attractive for computational fluid dynamicists: a very convenient way, in which the user interacts with the system; powerful built-in computer graphics functions, the means for any desired style of documentation of the method implemented in a *Mathematica* notebook. In addition, one can study with the aid of *Mathematica* such basic properties of numerical methods as approximation and stability [1].

The present research represents the first attempt at using the CAS *Mathematica 3.0* for the development of a computer code for the numerical solution of two-dimensional gas dynamics problems on curvilinear grids. Similar computer codes written in FORTRAN or C are used in aerospace industry for the investigation of flow processes in external and internal aerodynamics problems.

---

* This work was supported in part by Russian Foundation for Basic Research, grant No. 99-01-00573.

In order to increase the efficiency of using the computer codes it is desirable to incorporate the exact stability criteria in these codes. Then one can advance to the stationary limit by the largest time steps allowed by stability of a pseudo-unsteady difference method.

The governing equations in our case are the 2D Euler equations for compressible inviscid, non-heat-conducting fluids. These equations are discretized on a curvilinear spatial grid with the aid of a three-stage Runge-Kutta finite volume time stepping scheme with artificial dissipator [2]. The consideration of curvilinear grids in the Fourier stability analyses of difference schemes enhances considerably the complexity of arising algebraic expressions. As a result of this, until now only a few comparatively simple difference schemes on curvilinear grids have been analyzed; a review of these studies may be found in [3]. In the present work we briefly present the results of stability investigation of the above mentioned complex numerical method with the aid of our new symbolic/numerical method implemented with *Mathematica 3.0*. These results are represented by a very nontrivial inequality involving both the artificial dissipation coefficients and a number of further nondimensional similarity parameters. To our knowledge, this is the first attempt at elucidating the effect of artificial dissipators on the stability of Runge-Kutta finite volume time stepping schemes.

This paper is organized as follows. In Section 2, we describe the three-stage Runge-Kutta scheme for numerical integration of two-dimensional Euler equations on curvilinear grids. In Section 3 we briefly present our new symbolic-numerical method for stability investigation of complex finite difference or finite volume methods and describe the peculiarities of the computer implementation of our method with *Mathematica 3.0*. We apply our symbolic-numerical method to a specific finite volume time stepping scheme and derive the stability condition for this scheme. The peculiarities of the implementation of aerodynamic computations with *Mathematica 3.0* are discussed in Section 4. The results of aerodynamic computations are presented. In Section 5 we summarize the results obtained and give an overview of extensions and further research.

2   Explicit Runge-Kutta Algorithm

The governing Euler equations for two-dimensional inviscid gas flow are cast in the following conservation form:

$$\frac{\partial w}{\partial t} + \frac{\partial f(w)}{\partial x} + \frac{\partial f(w)}{\partial y} = 0, \tag{1}$$

where x and y are Cartesian coordinates and

$$w = \begin{pmatrix} \rho \\ \rho u \\ \rho v \\ \rho E \end{pmatrix}, \ f(w) = \begin{pmatrix} \rho u \\ \rho u^2 + p \\ \rho u v \\ \rho u H \end{pmatrix}, \ g(w) = \begin{pmatrix} \rho v \\ \rho v u \\ \rho v^2 + p \\ \rho v H \end{pmatrix}. \tag{2}$$

Here p, ρ, u, v, E and H denote the pressure, density, Cartesian velocity components, total energy and total enthalpy. For a perfect gas

$$E = \frac{p}{(\gamma - 1)\rho} + \frac{1}{2}(u^2 + v^2), \quad H = E + \frac{p}{\rho}, \tag{3}$$

where γ is the ratio of specific heats.

Let us take an arbitrary cell of curvilinear grid. Let the values of w at the cell center be denoted by w_{jk}, and let Γ_{jk} and V_{jk} be the cell contour and the control volume bounded by contour Γ_{jk}. The Euler equations (1) can be written in integral form for the region V_{jk} with boundary Γ_{jk} as

$$\frac{\partial}{\partial t} \iint_{V_{jk}} w \, dx \, dy + \oint_{\Gamma_{jk}} (f \, dy - g \, dx) = 0. \tag{4}$$

In the result of discretization of (4) we can obtain the semi-discrete equation [2]

$$\frac{d}{dt}(A_{jk} w) + Qw = 0, \tag{5}$$

where $A_{j,k}$ is the cell area, and the operator Q represents an approximation to the boundary integral defined by the second term of (4). For example, the flux balance for the x momentum component is represented in (5) as

$$\frac{\partial}{\partial t}(A_{j,k}\rho u) + \sum_{k=1}^{4}(Q_k \rho u_k + \Delta y_k p_k) = 0, \tag{6}$$

where the flux velocity

$$Q_k = \Delta y_k u_k - \Delta x_k v_k \tag{7}$$

and the sum in (6) is over four sides of the cell, see Fig. 1. The values Δx_k and Δy_k in (6) and (7) are the increments of x and y along side k of the cell, with appropriate signs. Each quantity in (6) and (7) such as u_2 or $(\rho u)_2$ is evaluated as the average of the values in the cells on the two sides of the face,

$$(\rho u)_2 = \frac{1}{2}[(\rho u)_{jk} + (\rho u)_{j+1,k}]. \tag{8}$$

The scheme (6)–(8) reduces to a central difference scheme on a Cartesian grid, therefore, it is second order accurate in space. As is known, the second-order schemes produce spurious oscillations of the numerical solution at the shock wave fronts and in their vicinity. In this connection it was proposed in [2] to introduce the artificial dissipation terms in the finite volume scheme in order to damp the spurious oscillations. These terms are added to equation (5) as follows:

$$\frac{dw}{dt} + (Qw/A_{j,k}) - Dw = 0, \tag{9}$$

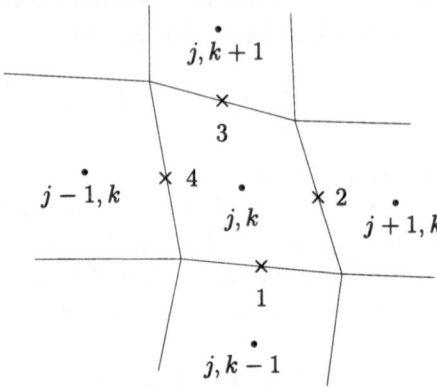

Fig. 1. The centered scheme.

where D is a dissipative operator the structure of which is similar for each of the four dependent variables:

$$Dw_{j,k} = D_x w_{j,k} + D_y w_{j,k}, \tag{10}$$

where

$$D_x w_{j,k} = (1/A_{j,k})(d_{j+1/2,k} - d_{j-1/2,k}), \tag{11}$$

$$D_y w_{j,k} = (1/A_{j,k})(d_{j,k+1/2} - d_{j,k-1/2}) \tag{12}$$

and

$$d_{j+1/2,k} = (A_{j+1/2,k}/\tau)[\varepsilon^{(2)}_{j+1/2,k}(w_{j+1,k} - w_{j,k})$$
$$- \varepsilon^{(4)}_{j+1/2,k}(w_{j+2,k} - 3w_{j+1,k} + 3w_{j,k} - w_{j-1,k})], \tag{13}$$

$$A_{j+1/2,k} = \frac{1}{2}(A_{j,k} + A_{j+1,k}).$$

The quantity τ in formula (13) is the time step of the numerical method. The coefficients $\varepsilon^{(2)}$ and $\varepsilon^{(4)}$ are variable, they are adapted to the flow. Define

$$\nu_{j,k} = |p_{j+1,k} - 2p_{j,k} + p_{j-1,k}|/(|p_{j+1,k}| + 2|p_{j,k}| + |p_{j-1,k}|). \tag{14}$$

Then

$$\varepsilon^{(2)}_{j+1/2,k} = \kappa^{(2)} \max(|\nu_{j+1,k}|, |\nu_{j,k}|), \quad \varepsilon^{(4)}_{j+1/2,k} = \max(0, (\kappa^{(4)} - \varepsilon^{(2)}_{j+1/2,k})). \tag{15}$$

Typical values of the constants $\kappa^{(2)}$ and $\kappa^{(4)}$ are [2] $\kappa^{(2)} = 1/4$, $\kappa^{(4)} = 1/256$. The values $d_{j,k\pm 1/2}$ in (12) are computed similarly to (13)–(15); for example, $A_{j,k+1/2} = (1/2)(A_{j,k} + A_{j,k+1})$.

The time stepping scheme approximating equation (9) is constructed as an explicit three-stage scheme of the Runge-Kutta type [4]:

$$w^{(0)} = w^n; \quad w^{(1)} = w^{(0)} - \alpha_1 \tau (P_h w^{(0)} - D w^{(0)});$$

$$w^{(2)} = w^{(0)} - \alpha_2 \tau (P_h w^{(1)} - D w^{(0)}); \quad w^{(3)} = w^{(0)} - \tau (P_h w^{(2)} - D w^{(0)}), (16)$$

where $w^n = w(x, y, t_n)$, $t_n = t_{n-1} + \tau_n$, $n = 1, 2, \ldots$, $t_0 = 0$, $\tau_n = \tau$; $P_h w = (1/A_{j,k}) Q w_{j,k}$, and α_1, α_2 are the nondimensional weight parameters.

3 Symbolic-Numerical Method for Stability Investigation

In the case of difference schemes on curvilinear grids the difference equation coefficients also contain the coordinates of the curvilinear grid nodes. If we "freeze" the components of the solution vector w in the difference scheme coefficients then we obtain the linearized difference scheme

$$w^{n+1} = S(x, y, w_0) w^n, \tag{17}$$

where w_0 is the "frozen" solution vector. The difference operator $S(x, y, w_0)$ in (17) is called the step operator, and its structure determines to a large extent the stability properties of difference method.

In what follows we investigate the stability of the difference initial-value problem

$$w^{n+1} = S(x, y, w_0) w^n, \ n = 0, 1, 2, \ldots; \quad w^0 = U_0(x, y), \ -\infty < x, y < \infty, \tag{18}$$

where $U_0(x, y)$ is the given initial condition at $t = 0$. We apply the von Neumann stability analysis procedure [1] for obtaining the necessary stability condition of difference problem (18). In this procedure, at first the Fourier symbol $G = \mathcal{F}(S)$ of the step operator S is obtained. After that the characteristic equation

$$\det(\lambda I - G) = \sum_{j=0}^{m} c_j \lambda^{m-j} = 0 \tag{19}$$

is computed, where $m = 4$ in the case of the Euler system of equations (1), (2), and I is the $m \times m$ identity matrix. The von Neumann necessary stability conditions then read

$$|\lambda_\alpha| \leq 1 + O(\tau), \quad \alpha = 1, \ldots, m. \tag{20}$$

These conditions are also sufficient for stability of the difference Cauchy problem (18) in the case of a normal or diagonalizable amplification matrix G [5].

One can show that the step operator S of the linearized finite volume scheme corresponding to three-stage Runge-Kutta scheme (16) has the form

$$S = I - \tau \bar{P}_h + \alpha_2 (\tau \bar{P}_h)^2 - \alpha_1 \alpha_2 (\tau \bar{P}_h)^3$$
$$- \alpha_1 \alpha_2 \tau^3 \bar{P}_h^2 \bar{D} + \alpha_2 \tau^2 \bar{P}_h \bar{D} - \tau \bar{D}, \qquad (21)$$

where $\bar{P}_h$ and $\bar{D}$ are the linear difference operators obtained as a result of the linearization of operators P_h and D in (16). The amplification matrix G obtained by the Fourier transformation of operator S (21) has the form

$$G = I + (d_1 A + d_2 B) + \alpha_2 (d_1 A + d_2 B)^2$$
$$+ \alpha_1 \alpha_2 (d_1 A + d_2 B)^3 + \alpha_1 \alpha_2 \tau^3 d_3 (d_1 A + d_2 B)^2$$
$$+ \alpha_2 \tau^2 d_3 (d_1 A + d_2 B) + d_3 I, \qquad (22)$$

where $\mathcal{F}(-\tau \bar{P}_h) = d_1 A + d_2 B$, $\mathcal{F}(-\tau \bar{D}) = d_3 I$,

$$
\begin{aligned}
d_1 = \frac{-\tau}{2A_{j,k}} [& (y_{j+1,k} - y_{j,k})(\cos \xi_2 - i \sin \xi_2) \\
& + (y_{j+1,k+1} - y_{j+1,k})(\cos \xi_1 + i \sin \xi_1) \\
& + (y_{j,k+1} - y_{j+1,k+1})(\cos \xi_2 + i \sin \xi_2) \\
& + (y_{j,k} - y_{j,k+1})(\cos \xi_1 - i \sin \xi_1)], \\
d_2 = \frac{-\tau}{2A_{j,k}} [& (x_{j,k} - x_{j+1,k})(\cos \xi_2 - i \sin \xi_2) \qquad (23) \\
& + (x_{j+1,k} - x_{j+1,k+1})(\cos \xi_1 + i \sin \xi_1) \\
& + (x_{j+1,k+1} - x_{j,k+1})(\cos \xi_2 + i \sin \xi_2) \\
& + (x_{j,k+1} - x_{j,k})(\cos \xi_1 - i \sin \xi_1)], \\
d_3 = \varepsilon_{2x} & (2 \cos \xi_1 - 2) - 4\varepsilon_{4x}(\cos \xi_1 - 1)^2 \\
& + \varepsilon_{2y}(2 \cos \xi_2 - 2) - 4\varepsilon_{4y}(\cos \xi_2 - 1)^2.
\end{aligned}
$$

The variables ξ_1 and ξ_2 in (23) represent the real wavenumbers in the Fourier particular solution $w_{jk}^n = W_0 \lambda^n e^{i(j\xi_1 + k\xi_2)}$, $i = \sqrt{-1}$, $W_0 = \text{const}$. A and B are the Jacobi matrices obtained from formulas (2):

$$A = \frac{\partial f(w)}{\partial w}, \quad B = \frac{\partial g(w)}{\partial w}. \qquad (24)$$

The coefficients $\varepsilon_{2x}, \varepsilon_{4x}, \varepsilon_{2y}, \varepsilon_{4y}$ in (23) are obtained by freezing the coefficients $\varepsilon_{j\pm1/2,k}^{(2)}, \varepsilon_{j\pm1/2,k}^{(4)}, \varepsilon_{j,k\pm1/2}^{(2)}, \varepsilon_{j,k\pm1/2}^{(4)}$ in the formulas of artificial dissipator:

$$\varepsilon_{2x} = \varepsilon_{j\pm1/2,k}^{(2)} = \text{const}, \quad \varepsilon_{4x} = \varepsilon_{j\pm1/2,k}^{(4)} = \text{const},$$
$$\varepsilon_{2y} = \varepsilon_{j,k\pm1/2}^{(2)} = \text{const}, \quad \varepsilon_{4y} = \varepsilon_{j,k\pm1/2}^{(4)} = \text{const}. \qquad (25)$$

Let us now describe some peculiarities of the symbolic computations of the entries of the amplification matrix G (22) with *Mathematica 3.0*. To save the needed memory at this stage we at first substitute the entries of matrices A and B as a21= a_{21}, b43= b_{43}, etc., where we have denoted by $a_{j,k}, b_{j,k}, j, k = 1, \dots, 4$ the entries of matrices A and B, respectively. We find thereafter the expressions for the first row of G by replacing ajk and bjk with their specific entries corresponding to the gasdynamic Jacobi matrices A and B (the expressions for these matrices may be found in [3]).

The first row elements prove to be the functions of the components of the solution vector w in (2), the nondimensional parameters (25), and the dimensional quantities

$$A_{j,k}, \quad x_{j,k+1} - x_{j,k}, \quad y_{j,k+1} - y_{j,k}, \quad x_{j+1,k} - x_{j,k}, \quad y_{j+1,k} - y_{j,k}.$$

In order to make the results of stability analysis independent both of a specific curvilinear grid and of the time step τ it is extremely important to express the entries of the amplification matrix G in terms of the nondimensional similarity parameters $\kappa_1, \dots, \kappa_M$ ($M \geq 1$). It turns out that in the case of the Runge-Kutta finite volume method defined by equations (10)–(16) it is sufficient to introduce along with the parameters (25) the following six nondimensional variables:

$$\kappa_1 = \frac{\tau c \cdot (y_{j,k+1} - y_{j,k})}{A_{j,k}}, \quad \kappa_2 = \frac{\tau u \cdot (y_{j,k+1} - y_{j,k})}{A_{j,k}},$$

$$\kappa_3 = \frac{\tau v \cdot (y_{j,k+1} - y_{j,k})}{A_{j,k}}, \quad \kappa_4 = \frac{y_{j+1,k} - y_{j,k}}{y_{j,k+1} - y_{j,k}}, \qquad (26)$$

$$\kappa_5 = \frac{x_{j+1,k} - x_{j,k}}{y_{j,k+1} - y_{j,k}}, \quad \kappa_6 = \frac{x_{j,k+1} - x_{j,k}}{y_{j,k+1} - y_{j,k}},$$

where c is the sound speed, $c = \sqrt{\gamma p / \rho}$ for a perfect gas. The entries of matrix G can be efficiently expressed in terms of the parameters $\kappa_1, \dots, \kappa_6$ in a *Mathematica* code by using the transformation rules. Let, for example, cp1= κ_1. Then we can introduce the notation cp1 into the entry gg[[1,1]] of the matrix G with the aid of transformation rule
gg[[1,1]] = gg[[1,1]]/.c -> cp1*Ajk/(y[[j,k+1]] - y[[j,k]]),
where Ajk= A_{jk}, y[[j,k]]= $y_{j,k}$, etc. The remaining parameters $\kappa_2, \dots, \kappa_6$ are introduced in the entries of G in a similar way. The first row of G thus obtained is then stored in the file row1.m. After that we compute in a similar way the next rows of G. Such a strategy saves a lot of computer memory, so that only about 2 Mb are needed to compute one row of G. Once we have computed all the rows of matrix G, we can assemble them into a 4×4 matrix. The resulting matrix G takes 1898 lines of text, with 65 symbols in each line on the average.

At the numerical stages of our method, the zeroes of characteristic equation (19) are computed numerically with the aid of the *Mathematica* function

Solve[...]. It is well known [3] that these zeroes are very sensitive to round-off errors when the machine arithmetic of floating-point numbers is used to compute the numerical values of coefficients of equation (19). On the other hand, it is well known that the computer algebra system *Mathematica* performs exact arithmetic operations on rational numbers. In accordance with (23) the coefficients c_j in (19) depend on $\cos \xi_m$ and $\sin \xi_m$, $m = 1, 2$. In order to avoid the introduction of any roundoff errors when computing the numerical values of these functions we have determined these values as the following rational numbers:

$$\cos \xi_m = \begin{cases} -1, & \xi_m = \pi \\ \frac{1-R^2(t_m,\varepsilon)}{1+R^2(t_m,\varepsilon)}, & \xi_m \neq \pi \end{cases} ; \quad \sin \xi_m = \begin{cases} 0, & \xi_m = \pi \\ \frac{2R(t_m,\varepsilon)}{1+R^2(t_m,\varepsilon)}, & \xi_m \neq \pi \end{cases}, \quad (27)$$

where $R(t_m, \varepsilon) =$ Rationalize[N[t_m, $10^{-(e+1)}$], ε], $m = 1, 2$ and $t_m = \tan(\xi_m/2)$; $\varepsilon = 10^{-(e+1)}$, $e \geq 0$, is the user-specified accuracy with which the built-in *Mathematica* function Rationalize[...] converts a floating-point number t_m into a rational number. It is important that the calculation of $\cos \xi_m$ and $\sin \xi_m$ by formulas (27) always ensures the satisfaction of the relation $\cos^2 \xi_m + \sin^2 \xi_m = 1$, $m = 1, 2$.

The values of nondimensional parameters (25) and (26) were also computed in (19) as the rational numbers. As a result, the coefficients c_j of equation (19) are exact for any complex numerical method. Therefore, we can compute the zeroes of (19) exactly, because the *Mathematica* function Solve[...] implements the exact solution formulas at $m = 4$.

For the verification of the above symbolic/numeric method we have used the analytic solution [3] for the necessary stability condition of the linearized Runge-Kutta scheme, which can be obtained from (22) in the particular case where $d_3 = 0$, i.e., $\varepsilon_{2x} = \varepsilon_{4x} = \varepsilon_{2y} = \varepsilon_{4y} = 0$:

$$|\kappa_2| + |\kappa_2\kappa_4| + |\kappa_3\kappa_6| + |\kappa_3\kappa_5|$$
$$+ [(|\kappa_1| + |\kappa_1\kappa_4|)^2 + (|\kappa_1\kappa_6| + |\kappa_1\kappa_5|)^2]^{0.5} \leq f(\alpha_1, \alpha_2), \qquad (28)$$

where

$$f(\alpha_1, \alpha_2) = \frac{1}{\alpha_1} \left[\frac{2\alpha_1 - \alpha_2 + (\alpha_2(\alpha_2 - 4\alpha_1 + 8\alpha_1^2))^{0.5}}{2\alpha_2} \right]^{0.5}. \qquad (29)$$

In the particular case of a uniform rectangular spatial grid in the (x, y) plane we have:

$$x_{j+1,k} = x_{j,k} + h_1, \quad x_{j,k+1} = x_{j,k},$$
$$y_{j+1,k} = y_{j,k}, \quad y_{j,k+1} = y_{j,k} + h_2 \quad \forall j, k, \qquad (30)$$

where h_1 and h_2 are the grid steps along the x- and y-axes, respectively. The substitution of (30) in (26) yields the formulas

$$\kappa_1 = \frac{c\tau}{h_1}, \quad \kappa_2 = \frac{u\tau}{h_1}, \quad \kappa_3 = \frac{v\tau}{h_1}, \quad \kappa_4 = 0, \quad \kappa_5 = \frac{h_1}{h_2}, \quad \kappa_6 = 0.$$

Therefore, the stability condition (28) simplifies at $\alpha_1 = \alpha_2 = 1/2$ to the condition

$$|\kappa_2| + |\kappa_3|\kappa_5 + \kappa_1\sqrt{1 + \kappa_5^2} \leq 2. \tag{31}$$

At the specified cell aspect ratio κ_5 the equality

$$\kappa_1 = (2 - |\kappa_2| - |\kappa_3|\kappa_5)/\sqrt{1 + \kappa_5^2} \tag{32}$$

determines a surface $\kappa_1 = \varphi(\kappa_2, \kappa_3)$ of the stability region of scheme (16) on an uniform rectangular grid in the absence of artificial dissipator. In particular, at the apex of pyramid (32), where $\kappa_2 = \kappa_3 = 0$, we have $\kappa_1 = 2/\sqrt{1 + \kappa_5^2}$. In Table we present the results of numerical computation of κ_1 at the stability region boundary at a user-specified accuracy $\varepsilon = 10^{-2}$ for the computation of κ_1. In this table, κ_{1num} is the value of κ_1 on the stability region boundary obtained by the above presented symbolic-numerical method; $\kappa_{1ex} = 2/\sqrt{1 + \kappa_5^2}$; $\delta\kappa_1 = |\kappa_{1ex} - \kappa_{1num}|$.

Table. Values of κ_1 at point $\kappa_2 = \kappa_3 = 0$ of the stability region boundary of scheme (16) at different values of κ_5

$\kappa_1 \backslash \kappa_5$	$\frac{1}{2}$	1	2	3
κ_{1num}	$\frac{1831}{1024}$ ≈ 1.788086	$\frac{5793}{4096}$ ≈ 1.41414307	$\frac{7325}{8192}$ ≈ 0.894165	$\frac{971}{1536}$ ≈ 0.632162
κ_{1ex}	1.788854	1.414214	0.894427	0.632456
$\delta\kappa_1$	0.000768	0.000093	0.000262	0.000294

It can be seen from the Table that the absolute error $\delta\kappa_1$ is smaller by an order of magnitude than the user-specified accuracy 10^{-2}.

In the general case, where the artificial dissipation coefficients $\varepsilon_{2x}, \varepsilon_{2y}$, ε_{4x}, ε_{4y} are different from zero, we have at first determined the stability region boundary in different sections of a ten-dimensional Euclidean space of $(\varepsilon_{2x}, \varepsilon_{2y}, \varepsilon_{4x}, \varepsilon_{4y}, \kappa_1, \kappa_2, \ldots, \kappa_6)$ points. This has required many runs on a computer. As a result of these runs, we have accumulated the information, which proved to be sufficient for an analytic fitting of all the numerical data obtained. At this fitting we have considered the values $\alpha_1 = \alpha_2 = \frac{1}{2}$ in (29), at which $f(\alpha_1, \alpha_2) = 2$. In this case, we have obtained the von Neumann necessary stability condition of the three-stage Runge-Kutta finite volume method (16) on curvilinear grid in the form

$$\left(\frac{\varepsilon_{2x}}{0.5}\right)^{2.7} + \left(\frac{\varepsilon_{2y}}{0.5}\right)^{2.7} + \left(\frac{\varepsilon_{4x}}{1/8}\right)^{8} + \left(\frac{\varepsilon_{4y}}{1/8}\right)^{8}$$

$$+ \left[\frac{|\kappa_1|\sqrt{(1 + |\kappa_4|)^2 + (|\kappa_5| + |\kappa_6|)^2}}{2 - |\kappa_2|(1 + |\kappa_4|) - |\kappa_3|(|\kappa_5| + |\kappa_6|)}\right]^{4} \leq 1. \tag{33}$$

It is easy to see that in the particular case where $\varepsilon_{2x} = \varepsilon_{2y} = \varepsilon_{4x} = \varepsilon_{4y} = 0$ formula (33) coincides with inequality (28). In accordance with (22) the amplification matrix G is a matrix polynomial of matrix $d_1 A + d_2 B$. It is well known that the matrices $d_1 A$ and $d_2 B$ can be diagonalized simultaneously by the same similarity transformation [5]. By using the sufficient stability criterion [5] for the diagonalizable amplification matrices it easy to prove that the necessary von Neumann stability condition (33) for the linearized Runge-Kutta scheme under consideration is also sufficient for stability.

Substituting expressions (26) for the nondimensional similarity parameters $\kappa_1, \ldots, \kappa_6$ into (33) we can easily obtain the explicit expression for the maximum time step τ allowed by the stability of the Runge-Kutta scheme under study. A simple analysis of this expression shows that in the case of the presence of artificial dissipator, that is in the case where at least one of the four coefficients (25) is different from zero, the maximum time step size allowed by stability reduces in comparison with the case of the absence of artificial dissipation terms.

4   Aerodynamic Computations with Mathematica

The obtained stability condition (33) was used in our aerodynamic code for the computation of the local time step in each cell of a curvilinear computing mesh to implement the principle of local time stepping [2], which accelerates significantly the convergence of the numerical solution to a steady state.

As a test flow problem we have chosen a problem of inviscid gas flow in a channel whose lower wall has a circular arc bump. Since Euler equations are solved, slip conditions are prescribed at walls. This flow problem was proposed as a test case in a GAMM workshop of 1981 and is now often used to assess the accuracy of numerical schemes [6].

The curvilinear grid of quadrilateral cells was generated in the (x, y) plane numerically by a *Mathematica* program, in which we have implemented the multi-surface method [7] for numerical grid generation.

In order to speed up execution in our aerodynamic code we have performed the segmentation of the main computational process into four blocks:
(1) the computation of fluxes in the streamwise direction;
(2) the computation of artificial dissipation terms in the streamwise direction;
(3) the computation of fluxes in the normal direction;
(4) the computation of artificial dissipation terms in the normal direction.
An analysis of these computational blocks has shown that it is possible to execute blocks (1) and (3) with the aid of the same function. The same is true for blocks (2) and (4). As a result, we have written two functions: one of them computes the fluxes on curvilinear grid, and the other function computes the artificial dissipation terms. After that, these two functions were compiled by using the built-in *Mathematica* function Compile[...] in order to speed up the numerical computation.

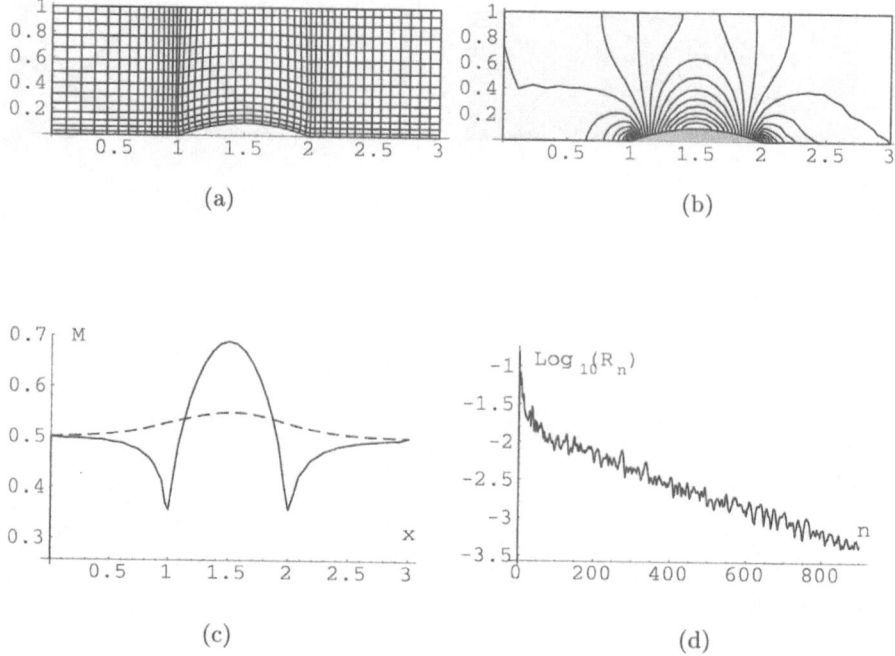

Fig. 2. Inviscid flow through a channel with a circular arc bump in lower wall: subsonic flow at $M_\infty = 0.5$: (a) curvilinear grid of 50×15 nodes; (b) predicted Mach number contours; (c) predicted Mach number profiles along lower wall (solid line) and upper wall (dashed line); (d) convergence history.

We have solved numerically the chosen flow problem for a wide range of the freestream Mach numbers: the subsonic, transonic, and supersonic flow regimes. The thickness-to-chord ratio of the circular arc is 10 % for subsonic and transonic cases and 4 % for the supersonic case. Uniform inlet flow at Mach numbers $M_\infty = 0.5$ (subsonic), 0.675 (transonic) and 1.65 (supersonic) is specified.

As a criterion for the numerical solution convergence to a stationary limit we have checked the inequality $R_n \leq \delta$, where $R_n = \max_{j,k} |\rho_{j,k}^{n+1} - \rho_{j,k}^n|$ is the solution residual, $n = 0, 1, 2, \ldots$, and δ is a user-specified small positive number; we have taken the value $\delta = 10^{-4}$.

Let us denote by τ_{max} the maximum value of the time step τ, which is obtained from (33) if one replaces the $\leq$ symbol with the equality symbol. The actual aerodynamic computations were performed with $\tau = \theta \cdot \tau_{max}$,

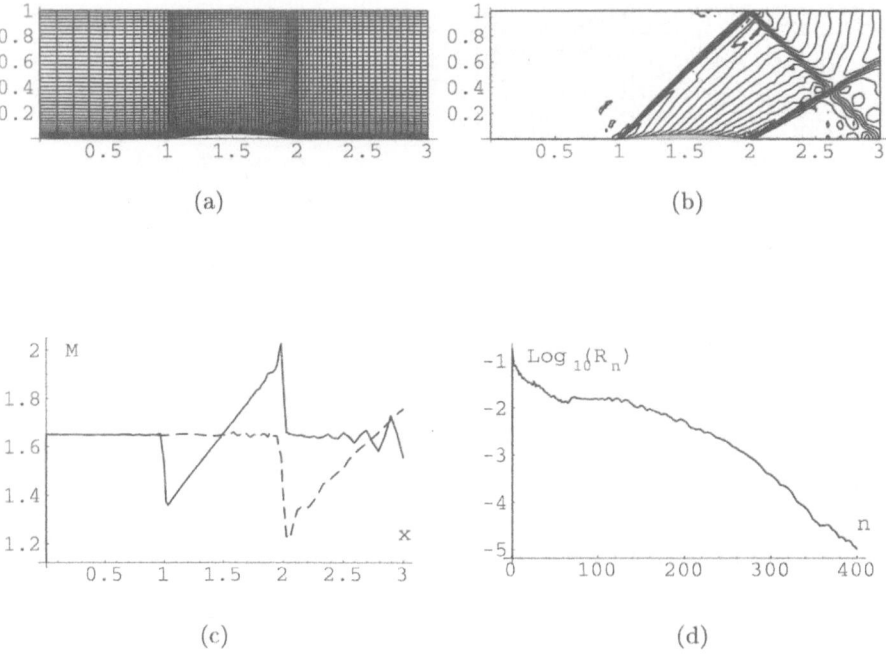

Fig. 3. Inviscid flow through a channel with a circular arc bump in lower wall: supersonic flow at $M_\infty = 1.65$: (a) curvilinear grid of 80×40 nodes; (b) predicted Mach number contours; (c) predicted Mach number profiles along lower wall (solid line) and upper wall (dashed line); (d) convergence history.

where θ is a safety factor, $0 < \theta \leq 1$. In the case of Figs. 2 and 3, the value $\theta = 0.95$ was specified.

In order to check the accuracy of the obtained stability condition (33) we have performed the runs also at the values $\theta > 1$, which correspond theoretically to an unstable regime of computation by scheme (16). At the free stream Mach number M_∞ and $\theta = 1$ the computation still was stable. However, at $\theta = 1.2$ there begins a rapid growth of the solution residual R_n at $n \geq 5$, and already at $n = 11$ the residual R_n exceeds the initial value R_0 by a factor of about 3. Thus, stability condition (33) is sufficiently accurate despite the fact that it was obtained from the linearized finite difference equations.

The results presented in Fig. 2 b,c and Fig. 3 b,c agree well with those of [6]. In particular, the maximum value of the Mach number on the lower wall is 0.693 in our case at $M_\infty = 0.5$; and in [6] it is equal to 0.700 on a mesh of 224×56 nodes.

In the case of supersonic flow at $M_\infty = 1.65$ (see Fig. 3), two oblique shocks are generated at both leading and trailing edges of the airfoil; these shocks are well visible in Fig. 3, b as the subregions, in which different Mach number contours coalesce. An expansion fan caused by the convex airfoil surface is formed between the leading- and trailing-edge shock waves.

5 Conclusion

The purpose of our present aerodynamic computations was twofold:

- validation of the complex stability condition obtained with the aid of *Mathematica*;
- the investigation of the ability of *Mathematica 3.0* to solve numerically sufficiently complex CFD problems.

We can summarize the results of our numerical aerodynamic computations in the *Mathematica* environment as follows.

(i) The presented stability condition, which takes into account both the grid topology and artificial dissipation, is correct. Moreover, the convergence to steady state becomes faster than in the original Jameson's method [2].

(ii) The implementation of the Mathematica function `Compile[...]` in our aerodynamic code speeds up the execution only by a factor of 5/3, instead of the factor of "as large as 20" promised in the *Mathematica* manual.

In connection with the result (ii), the following two ways for the speedup of the numerical computations in the *Mathematica* environment appear to be promising:
(a) the use of functions compiled from FORTRAN or C;
(b) parallelization of the explicit Runge-Kutta time stepping schemes.

References

1. V.G. Ganzha and E.V. Vorozhtsov. *Numerical Solutions for Partial Differential Equations. Problem Solving Using Mathematica*. CRC Press, Boca Raton, New York, London, 1996.
2. A. Jameson, W. Schmidt, and E. Turkel. *Numerical Solution of the Euler Equations by Finite Volume Methods Using Runge Kutta Time Stepping Schemes*. AIAA Paper 81-1259, 1981.
3. V.G. Ganzha and E.V. Vorozhtsov. *Computer-Aided Analysis of Difference Schemes for Partial Differential Equations*. Wiley-Interscience, New York, 1996.
4. A. Jameson and W. Schmidt. Some recent developments in numerical methods for transonic flows. *Computer Methods in Applied Mechanics and Engineering* **51**, 467–493, 1985.
5. R.D. Richtmyer and K.W. Morton. *Difference Methods for Initial-Value Problems*, 2nd Edition. Wiley-Interscience, New York, 1967.

6. J.H. Ferziger and M. Perić. *Computational Methods for Fluid Dynamics.* Springer, Berlin, Heidelberg, New York, 1996.

7. P.R. Eiseman. A multi-surface method of coordinate generation. *Journal of Computational Physics* **33**, 118–150, 1979.

Completion of Linear Differential Systems to Involution*

Vladimir P. Gerdt

Laboratory of Computing Techniques and Automation, Joint Institute for Nuclear Research, 141980 Dubna, Russia

Abstract. In this paper we generalize the involutive methods and algorithms have been devised for polynomial ideals to differential ones generated by a finite set of linear differential polynomials in the differential polynomial ring over a zero characteristic differential field. Given a ranking of derivative terms and an involutive division, we formulate the involutivity conditions which form a basis of involutive algorithms. We present an algorithm for computation of a minimal involutive differential basis. Its correctness and termination hold for any constructive and noetherian involutive division. As two important applications we consider posing of an initial value problem for a linear differential system providing uniqueness of its solution and Lie symmetry analysis of nonlinear differential equations. In particular, this allows to determine the structure of arbitrariness in general solution of linear systems and thereby to find the size of symmetry group.

1 Introduction

Among the properties of systems of analytical partial differential equations (PDEs) which may be investigated without their explicit integration there are compatibility and formulation of an *initial-value problem* providing existence and uniqueness of the solution. The classical Cauchy-Kowalevsky theorem establishes a certain class of quasilinear PDEs which admit posing such an initial-value problem. The main obstacle in investigating other classes of PDE systems of some given order q is existence of *integrability conditions*, that is, such relations for derivatives of order $\leq q$ which are differential but not pure algebraic consequences of equations in the system.

An *involutive* system of PDEs has all the integrability conditions incorporated in it. This means that prolongations of the system do not reveal integrability conditions. Extension of a system by its integrability conditions is called *completion*. The concept of involutivity was invented hundred years ago by E.Cartan [1] in his investigation of the Pfaff type equations in total differentials. For these purposes he used the exterior calculus developed by himself. The Cartan approach was generalized by Kähler[2] to arbitrary systems of exterior differential equations. The underlying completion procedure [3] was implemented in [4,5].

* This work was supported by grant INTAS-96-184 and grants No.96-15-96030, 98-01-00101 from Russian Foundation for Basic Research.

In his study of the formal power series solutions of PDEs, Riquier introduced [6] a class of relevant *rankings* for partial derivatives and considered systems of *orthonomic* equations which are solved with respect to the highest rank derivatives called *principal*. Thereby, these derivatives, by the equations in the system, are defined in terms of the other derivatives called *parametric*. An integrability condition gives a constraint for parametric derivatives, and that of them of the highest ranking becomes the principal derivative. Recently Riquier's class of rankings was generalized in [7].

Janet made the further development of Riquier's approach. He observed [8] that the integrability conditions may occur only from prolongations with respect to certain independent variables called *nonmultiplicative*. Prolongations with respect to the rest of variables called *multiplicative* never lead to integrability conditions. Given a set of principal derivatives, Janet gave the prescription how to separate variables into multiplicative and nonmultiplicative for every equation in the system. He formulated, on this ground, the *involutivity conditions* for orthonomic systems and designed an algorithm for their completion. This approach to completion is known as *Riquier-Janet theory* and was implemented in [9–11].

A system satisfying Janet involutivity conditions is often called *passive*. This involutivity is generally coordinate dependent. On the other hand, the modern *formal theory* of PDEs developed in 60s-70s by Spencer and others (see [12,13]) allows to formulate the involutivity intrinsically, in a coordinate independent way. The formal theory relies on another definition of multiplicative and nonmultiplicative variables which was known to Janet as long ago as in 20s, but called nowadays after Pommaret because of its importance in the technique presented in [12]. The implementation in Axiom of completion based on the formal theory was presented in [14,15].

Thomas in [16] used another separation of independent variables into multiplicative and nonmultiplicative and generalized the Riquier-Janet theory to non-orthonomic algebraic PDEs. Given a system of PDEs, he showed that in a finite number of steps one can: (i) check its compatibility; (ii) if the system is compatible, then split it into a finite number of *simple* systems involving generally both equations and inequalities and such that their equation parts are orthonomic and can be completed to involution. This splitting is similar to that generated by the Rosenfeld-Gröbner algorithm [17].

In paper [18] for Pommaret separation of independent variables it was shown that involutive (passive) basis of a non-differential polynomial ideal is a Gröbner basis. The implementation in Reduce of the proposed completion algorithm for polynomial bases demonstrated a high computational efficiency of the involutive technique. However, Pommaret bases may not exist for positive dimensional ideals unlike Janet and Thomas bases.

The above classical separations of variables into multiplicative and nonmultiplicative are particular cases of *involutive monomial division*, a concept invented and analyzed in [19] (cf. [20]). The polynomial completion algorithms designed for a general involutive division [19,21] were implemented in

Reduce for Pommaret division. Different involutive divisions and completion of monomial sets have also been implemented in Mathematica [22]. In [23] we generalized the algorithm of paper [21] to arbitrary completion ordering.

One more efficient method for the completion of linear PDEs to an involutive form called *standard* which is not based on the separation of variables was developed in [29] and implemented in Maple. The extension of this method to nonlinear PDEs is given in paper [25].

In the present paper we generalize the involutive methods and algorithms devised in [19,21,23] for polynomial ideals to differential ideals generated by a finite set of linear polynomials. We formulate the involutivity conditions for the differential case. If a set satisfies the involutivity conditions it is called an *involutive basis*. Similar to the pure algebraic case, a linear involutive basis is a differential Gröbner basis [26,27] which is not generally reduced. We present an algorithm for computation of a minimal involutive basis. This algorithm is the straightforward generalization of the polynomial involutive algorithm [21,23]. As well as for the latter, the correctness and termination of the former hold for any constructive and noetherian involutive division.

An important application of the involutive method is posing an initial value problem providing the unique solution of a system of PDEs. For linear involutive systems we formulate such an initial value problem and thereby generalize the classical results of Janet [8] to arbitrary involutive divisions. This formulation makes it possible, among other things, to reveal the structure of arbitrariness in general solution. Given a linear involutive basis, we write also the explicit formulae for the Hilbert function and the Hilbert polynomial of the corresponding differential ideal which are the straightforward generalizations of their polynomial analogues [20,22].

Another important application of the new algorithm is *Lie symmetry analysis* of nonlinear differential equations. It is because of the fact that completion to involution is the most general and universal method of integrating the determining system of linear PDEs for infinitesimal Lie symmetry generators [28]. Moreover, an involutive form of determining equations allows to construct the Lie symmetry algebra without their explicit integration [24]. In particular, for an involutive determining system the size of symmetry group can easily be found that for Janet bases was shown in [11]. Though reduced Gröbner bases for the determining equations do not generally reveal information on Lie symmetry groups, and more generally on the solution space, so explicitly as involutive bases, they are also very useful for Lie symmetry analysis as shown in [30]. The facilities of the Maple package devised of the first author and used in the paper go far beyond linear differential systems, and it can also be fruitfully applied to nonlinear systems.

2   Preliminaries

Let $\mathbb{R} = \mathbb{K}\{y_1, \dots, y_m\}$ be a differential polynomial ring [31,32] with the set of differential indeterminates $\{y_1, \dots, y_m\}$, and $\mathbb{K} \subset \mathbb{R}$ is a differential field of zero characteristic with a finite number of mutually commuting derivation operators $\partial/\partial x_1, \ldots, \partial/\partial x_n$. Elements in $\mathbb{R}$ are differential polynomials in $\{y_1, \ldots, y_m\}$. In this paper we use the following notations and conventions:

$f, g, h, p \in \mathbb{R}$ are linear differential polynomials.

$F, G, H \subset \mathbb{R}$ are finite sets of linear differential polynomials.

$\mathcal{F} = \{f = 0 \mid f \in F\}$ is a linear system of PDEs.

$\mathbb{N} = \{0, 1, 2, \ldots\}$ is the set of nonnegative integers.

$\alpha, \beta, \gamma \in \mathbb{N}^n$ are multiindices.

$lcm(\alpha, \beta)$ is the least common multiple of $alpha, beta$.

$X = \{x_1, \ldots, x_n\}$ is the set of independent variables.

$R = K[X]$ is the polynomial ring over the field K of zero characteristic.

$R \supset \mathbb{M} = \{x^\alpha = x_1^{\alpha_1} \cdots x_n^{\alpha_n} \mid \alpha_i \in \mathbb{N}\}$ is the set of monomials in X.

$i = 1, \ldots, n$ indexes derivation operators $\partial_i = \partial/\partial x_i$.

$j = 1, \ldots, m$ indexes indeterminates y_j.

u, v, w are elements in $\mathbb{M}$.

$U, V \subset \mathbb{M}$ are finite monomial sets.

(U) is the monomial ideal in R generated by U.

$deg_i(u)$ is the degree of x_i in $u \in \mathbb{M}$.

$deg(u) = \sum_{i=1}^n deg_i(u)$ is the total degree of u.

$\partial_\alpha y_j = \frac{\partial^{\alpha_1 + \cdots + \alpha_n}}{\partial x_1^{\alpha_1} \ldots \partial x_n^{\alpha_n}} y_j$ is a derivative.

$ord(\partial_\alpha y_j) = \sum_{i=1}^n \alpha_i$ is the order of $\partial_\alpha y_j$.

θ, ϑ are derivatives.

$lcm(\partial_\alpha y_j, \partial_\beta y_j) = \partial_{lcm(\alpha, \beta)} y_j$.

$\prec, \prec_c$ are rankings of derivatives.

$ld(f)$ is the leading derivative in $f \in \mathbb{R}$.

$lc(f) \in K$ is the coefficient of $ld(f)$.

$ld(F)$ is the set of leading derivatives in $F \subset \mathbb{R}$.

$[F]$ is the differential ideal in $\mathbb{R}$ generated by F.

L is an involutive division.

$L(u, U)$ is the set of $(L-)$multiplicative monomials for $u \in U$.

$NM_L(u, U)$ is the set of $L-$nonmultiplicative variables for $u \in U$.

$M_L(u, U)$ is the set of $L-$multiplicative variables for $u \in U$.

$x^\alpha \in \mathbb{M}$ is the monomial associated with the derivative $\partial_\alpha y_j$.

$\cup_{j=1}^m U_j$ is the monomial set associated with the set $ld(F) = \cup_{j=1}^m \{ld_j(F)\}$.

$W = \cup_{j=1}^m \{W_j \mid W_j \subset M\}$ is the complementary set for $\cup_{j=1}^m U_j$.

$\mathcal{G}$ is the set of $L-$generators of W.

$\vartheta = \partial_L \theta$ is a multiplicative prolongation of θ.

$\partial_{x_i} \cdot \theta$ is the nonmultiplicative prolongation of θ w.r.t. x_i.

$\partial_\alpha \cdot \theta$ is a nonmultiplicative prolongation of θ.

$NF_L(p, F)$ is the $L-$normal form of p modulo F.

$NM_L(f, F) \subseteq X$ is the set of $(L-)$nonmultiplicative variables for $f \in F$.

$C_L(F) = \cup_{\theta \in ld(F)} \{\vartheta \mid \vartheta = \partial_L \theta\}$ is the $L-$cone generated by F.

In this paper we distinguish two rankings (c.f. [23]): a *main ranking* and a *completion ranking* denoted by $\succ$ and $\succ_c$, respectively. The main ranking will be used, as usually, for isolation of the leading derivatives in differential polynomials whereas the completion ranking serves for taking the lowest nonmultiplicative prolongations by the normal strategy [19] and thereby controlling the property of partial involutivity introduced in Sect. 4.

3   Basic Concepts and Definitions

Throughout this paper we exploit the well-known algorithmic similarities between pure algebraic polynomial systems and linear differential systems [13,33]. In so doing, the basic algorithmic ideas go back to Janet [8] who invented the constructive approach to study of PDEs in terms of the corresponding monomial sets which is based on the following association between derivatives and monomials:

$$\partial_\alpha y_j = \frac{\partial^{\alpha_1 + \cdots + \alpha_n} y_j}{\partial x_1^{\alpha_1} \cdots \partial x_n^{\alpha_n}} \iff x^\alpha = x_1^{\alpha_1} \cdots x_n^{\alpha_n}. \tag{1}$$

The monomials, associated with the different indeterminates y_j are to be considered as belonging to different monomial sets $U_j \in \mathbb{M}$ indexed by subscript j of the indeterminate.

Definition 1. [32] A total ordering $\prec$ over the set of derivatives $\partial_\alpha y_j$ is called a *ranking* if it satisfies: (i) $\partial_i \partial_\alpha y_j \prec \partial_\alpha y_j$, (ii) $\partial_\alpha y_j \prec \partial_\beta y_k \iff \partial_\gamma \partial_\alpha y_j \prec \partial_\gamma \partial_\beta y_k$ for all $i, j, k, \alpha, \beta, \gamma$. A ranking $\prec$ is said to be *orderly* if $\theta \prec \vartheta$ whenever $ord(\theta) > ord(\vartheta)$.

The association (1) implies the reduction of a ranking $\prec$ to the associated admissible monomial ordering, and throughout the paper we shall assume that

$$\partial_1 \succ \partial_2 \succ \cdots \succ \partial_n \iff x_1 \succ x_2 \succ \cdots \succ x_n. \tag{2}$$

Remark 2. Given a finite set $F \subset \mathbb{R}$ and a ranking $\succ$, set $ld(F)$ of the leading derivatives is partitioned $ld(F) = \cup_j ld_j(F)$ into subsets $ld_j(F)$ corresponding to different indeterminates y_j which occur in $ld(F)$. For an involutive division L defined as follows each subset generates for every its element the separation of independent variables into multiplicative and nonmultiplicative ones.

Definition 3. [19] An *involutive division* L on $\mathbb{M}$ is given, if for any finite monomial set $U \subset \mathbb{M}$ and for any $u \in U$ there is given a submonoid $L(u, U)$ of $\mathbb{M}$ satisfying the conditions:

(a) If $w \in L(u, U)$ and $v|w$, then $v \in L(u, U)$.
(b) If $u, v \in U$ and $uL(u, U) \cap vL(v, U) \neq \emptyset$, then $u \in vL(v, U)$ or $v \in uL(u, U)$.
(c) If $v \in U$ and $v \in uL(u, U)$, then $L(v, U) \subseteq L(u, U)$.
(d) If $V \subseteq U$, then $L(u, U) \subseteq L(u, V)$ for all $u \in V$.

Elements of $L(u, U)$ are called *multiplicative* for u. If $w \in uL(u, U)$, u is called an involutive divisor or $(L-)divisor$ of w. In such an event the monomial $v = w/u$ is called $L-multiplicative$ for u. If u is a conventional divisor of w but not $L-$divisor, then v is called *nonmultiplicative* for u.

Remark 4. Definition 3 for every $u \in U$ provides the partition

$$X = M_L(u, U) \cup NM_L(u, U), \quad M_L \subset L(u, U) \tag{3}$$

of the set of variables $X = \{x_1, \dots, x_n\}$ into subset $M_L(u, U)$ of *multiplicative variables* for u and subset $NM_L(u, U)$ of the remaining *nonmultiplicative variables*. Conversely, if for any finite set $U \subset \mathbb{M}$ and any $u \in U$ the partition (3) of variables into multiplicative and nonmultiplicative is given such that the corresponding submonoid $L(u)$ satisfies the conditions (b)-(d) in Definition 3, then the partition generates an involutive division.

Definition 5. [19] A monomial set U is called $L-autoreduced$ if $uL(u, U) \cap vL(v, U) = \emptyset$ holds for all distinct $u, v \in U$.

Definition 6. [19] A monomial set $\tilde{U}$ is called an $L-completion$ of a set $U \subseteq \tilde{U}$ if

$$(\forall u \in U) \ (\forall w \in \mathbb{M}) \ (\exists v \in \tilde{U}) \ [\ uw \in vL(v, \tilde{U}) \ ].$$

If there exists a finite $L-$completion $\tilde{U}$ of a finite set U, then the latter is called *finitely generated* with respect to L. The involutive division L is *noetherian* if every finite set U is finitely generated with respect to L. If $\tilde{U} = U$, then U is called $L-complete$. An $L-$autoreduced and complete set is called $(L-)involutive$.

Definition 7. [19] Given a monomial set U, the set $\cup_{u \in U} u \mathbb{M}$ is called *the cone* generated by U and denoted by $C(U)$. The set $\cup_{u \in U} u L(u, U)$ is called *the involutive cone* of U with respect to L and denoted by $C_L(U)$.

Thus, the set $\tilde{U}$ is an $L-$completion of U if $C(\tilde{U}) = C_L(\tilde{U}) = C(U)$. Correspondingly, for an involutive set U the equality $C(U) = C_L(U)$ holds.

Whereas noetherity provides existence of a finite involutive basis for any polynomial ideal, another important properties of an involutive division called *continuity* and *constructivity* provide algorithmic construction of involutive bases [19]. Continuity implies involutivity when the local involutivity holds whereas constructivity strengthens continuity and allows to compute involutive bases by sequential examination of single nonmultiplicative prolongations only. We refer to papers [19,21,23] for description of these topics in detail. In those papers some examples of involutive divisions were studied (see also [34]) which include three divisions called after Janet, Thomas and Pommaret, because they have used the corresponding separations of variables for involutivity analysis of PDEs [8,16,12]. Other two divisions called Division I and II were introduced in [21], and a class of involutive divisions called Induced division, since every division in the class is induced by an admissible monomial orderings, was introduced in [23]. All those divisions are constructive and, except Pommaret division, they are noetherian. Below we use three of those divisions defined as follows.

Definition 8. Janet division [8]. Let $U \subset \mathbb{M}$ be a finite set. Divide U into groups labeled by non-negative integers $\alpha_1, \ldots, \alpha_i$ $(1 \leq i \leq n)$:

$$[\alpha_1, \ldots, \alpha_i] = \{ \, u \in U \mid \alpha_j = deg_j(u), \ 1 \leq j \leq i \, \}.$$

Then x_i is multiplicative for $u \in U$ if if $i > 1$ and $deg_1(u) = \max\{deg_1(v) \mid v \in U\}$, or $u \in [\alpha_1, \ldots, \alpha_{i-1}]$ and $deg_i(u) = \max\{deg_i(v) \mid v \in [\alpha_1, \ldots, \alpha_{i-1}]\}$ for $i > 1$.

Definition 9. Pommaret division [12]. For a monomial $u = x_1^{\alpha_1} \cdots x_k^{\alpha_k}$ with $\alpha_k > 0$ the variables $x_j, j \geq k$ are considered as multiplicative and the other variables as nonmultiplicative. For $u = 1$ all the variables are multiplicative.

Definition 10. Lexicographically induced division [23]. A variable x_i is non-multiplicative for $u \in U$ if there is $v \in U$ such that $v \prec_{Lex} u$ and $deg_i(u) < deg_i(v)$, where $\succ_{Lex}$ denotes the lexicographical ordering.

In the sequel Janet, Pommaret and Lexicographically induced divisions will be distinguished by the subscripts J, P and D_{Lex}, respectively.

Example 11. Separation of variables for set $U = \{x_1^2 x_3, x_1 x_2, x_1 x_3^2\}$ and ordering (2) for the above defined three divisions:

Element in U	Separation of variables					
	Janet		Pommaret		Lex. induced	
	M_J	NM_J	M_P	NM_P	$M_{D_{Lex}}$	$NM_{D_{Lex}}$
$x_1^2 x_3$	x_1, x_2, x_3	–	x_3	x_1, x_2	x_1	x_2, x_3
$x_1 x_2$	x_2, x_3	x_1	x_2, x_3	x_1	x_1, x_2	x_3
$x_1 x_3^2$	x_3	x_1, x_2	x_2, x_3	x_1	x_1, x_2, x_3	–

The corresponding L-completions of U are

$$\tilde{U}_J = \{x_1^2 x_3, x_1 x_2, x_1 x_3^2, x_1^2 x_2\},$$
$$\tilde{U}_P = \{x_1^2 x_3, x_1 x_2, x_1 x_3^2, x_1^2 x_2, \ldots, x_1^{i+2} x_2, \ldots, x_1^{j+2} x_3, \ldots\},$$
$$\tilde{U}_{D_{Lex}} = \{x_1^2 x_3, x_1 x_2, x_1 x_3^2, x_1 x_2 x_3\}.$$

where $i, j \in \mathbb{N}$. This example explicitly shows non-noethery of Pommaret division.

Definition 12. Given a finite set $F \subset \mathbb{R}$, a ranking $\succ$ and an involutive division L, the derivative $\vartheta = \partial_\beta y_j$ will be called a *multiplicative prolongation* of $\theta = \partial_\alpha y_j \in ld_j(F)$ and denoted by $\vartheta = \partial_L \theta$, if the associated monomials satisfy $x^\beta \in x^\alpha L(x^\alpha, U_j)$. Otherwise the prolongation will be called *nonmultiplicative*. Respectively, the corresponding prolongation $\partial_\beta f$ of the element $f \in F$ with $ld(f) = \partial_\alpha y_j$ will be called *multiplicative* and denoted by $\partial_L(f)$ or *nonmultiplicative*. The set $C_L(F) = \cup_{\theta \in ld(F)} \{\vartheta \mid \vartheta = \partial_L \theta\}$ will be called the $L-cone$ generated by F. If $\partial_i f$ is a nonmultiplicative prolongation of $f \in F$, we shall write $x_i \in NM_L(f, F)$.

4   Linear Involutive Differential Bases

In this section we generalize the results obtained in papers [19,23] for commutative algebra to differential algebra of linear polynomials. Proofs of the theorems are omitted because of similarity with the proofs of their algebraic analogues.

Definition 13. Given an involutive division L, a finite set $F \subset \mathbb{R}$ of linear differential polynomials, a ranking $\succ$ and a linear polynomial $p \in \mathbb{R}$, we shall say:

1. p is $L-reducible$ *modulo* $f \in F$ if p has a term $a\theta$, $(a \in K \setminus \{0\})$ such that $\theta = \partial_L ld(f)$. It yields the $L-reduction$ $p \to g = p - (a/lc(f)) \partial_\beta f$ where $\partial_\beta ld(f) = \theta$.
2. p is $L-reducible$ *modulo* F if there is $f \in F$ such that p is $L-$reducible modulo f.
3. p is *in* $L-normal$ *form modulo* F, if p is not $L-$reducible modulo F.

We denote the $L-$normal form of p modulo F by $NF_L(p, F)$.

As a $L-$normal form algorithm one can use the following differential analogue of the polynomial normal form algorithm [19]:

Algorithm **InvolutiveNormalForm**:

Input: p, F, L, $\prec$
Output: $h = NF_L(p, F)$
begin
  $h := p$
  while   exist $f \in F$ and a term $a\theta$ $(a \in \mathbb{K} \setminus \{0\})$ of h
    such that $\theta = \partial_L ld(f)$ **do**
    choose   the first such f
    $h := h - (a/lc(f)) \partial_\beta f$ where $\partial_\beta ld(f) = \theta$
  end
end

Correctness and termination of this algorithm is an obvious consequence of Definition 13 and correctness and termination of the polynomial $L-$normal form algorithm [19].

Definition 14. A finite set F is called $L-autoreduced$ if every $f \in F$ is irreducible modulo any other element $g \in F$. An $L-$autoreduced set F is called $(L-)involutive$ if

$$(\forall f \in F) \, (\forall \alpha \in \mathbb{N}^n) \, [\, NF_L(\partial_\alpha f, F) = 0 \,].$$

Given a derivative ϑ and an $L-$autoreduced set F, if there exist $f \in F$ such that $ld(f) \prec_c \theta$ and

$$(\forall f \in F) \, (\forall \alpha \in \mathbb{N}^n) \, (\partial_\alpha ld(f) \prec_c \vartheta) \, [\, NF_L(\partial_\alpha f, F) = 0 \,], \qquad (4)$$

then F is called *partially involutive up to the derivative* ϑ with respect to the ranking $\prec_c$. F is still said to be partially involutive up to ϑ if $\vartheta \prec_c ld(f)$ for all $f \in F$.

Corollary 15. *If $F \subset \mathbb{R}$ is an $L-$involutive set, then every monomial set $U_j \in \mathbb{M}$ $(1 \leq j \leq m)$ associated with $ld_j(F)$ is $L-$involutive.*

Proof. It follows immediately from Definitions 6 and 14. $\qquad\qquad\square$

Theorem 16. *An $L-$autoreduced set $F \subset \mathbb{R}$ is involutive with respect to a continuous involutive division L iff the following (local) involutivity conditions hold*

$$(\forall f \in F) \, (\forall x_i \in NM_L(f, F)) \, [\, NF_L(\partial_{x_i} \cdot f, F) = 0 \,].$$

Correspondingly, partial involutivity (4) holds iff

$$(\forall f \in F) \, (\forall x_i \in NM_L(f, F)) \, (\partial_{x_i} \cdot ld(f) \prec_c \vartheta) \, [\, NF_L(\partial_{x_i} \cdot f, F) = 0 \,].$$

Theorem 17. *If $F \subset \mathbb{R}$ is an $L-$involutive basis of $[F]$, then it is also a differential Gröbner basis.*

The following theorem and corollary give an involutive analogue of Buchberger chain criterion [35] in application to linear differential bases.

Theorem 18. *Let F be a finite $L-$autoreduced set of linear differential polynomials with respect to a continuous involutive division L, and $NF_L(p, F)$ be an algorithm of $L-$normal form. Then the following are equivalent:*

1. *F is an $L-$involutive differential basis of $[F]$.*
2. *For all $g \in F, x \in NM_L(g, F)$ there is $f \in F$ satisfying $\partial_x \cdot ld(g) = \partial_L ld(f)$ and a chain of elements in F of the form*

$$f \equiv f_k, f_{k-1}, \ldots, f_0, g_0, \ldots, g_{m-1}, g_m \equiv g$$

such that

$$NF_L\left(S_L(f_{i-1}, f_i), F\right) = NF_L\left(S(f_0, g_0), F\right) = NF_L\left(S_L(g_{j-1}, g_j), F\right) = 0$$

where $0 \leq i \leq k$ and $0 \leq j \leq m$, $S(f_0, g_0)$ is the conventional differential S-polynomial [27] and $S_L(f_i, f_j) = \partial_x \cdot f_i - \partial_L f_j$ is its special form which occurs in involutive algorithms.

Corollary 19. *Let F be a finite $L-$autoreduced set, and let $\partial_x \cdot g$ be a non-multiplicative prolongation of $g \in F$. If the following holds*

$$(\forall h \in F)\ (\forall \partial_\alpha)\ (\partial_\alpha ld(h) \cdot u \prec_c ld(g \cdot x))\ \ [\ NF_L(h \cdot u, F) = 0\ ],$$

$$(\exists f, f_0, g_0 \in F) \begin{bmatrix} ld(f) = \partial_\beta ld(f_0)\,,\ ld(g) = \partial_\gamma ld(g_0) \\ \partial_x \cdot ld(g) = \partial_L ld(f)\,,\ lcm\,(ld(f_0), ld(g_0)) \prec_c \partial_x \cdot ld(g) \\ NF_L\left(\partial_\beta \cdot f_0, F\right) = NF_L\left(\partial_\gamma \cdot g_0, F\right) = 0 \end{bmatrix},$$

then the prolongation $\partial_x \cdot g$ may be discarded in the course of an involutive algorithm.

5   Completion Algorithm

The below given algorithm **MinimalLinearInvolutiveBasis** is a differential analogue of the polynomial algorithm **MinimalInvolutiveBasis** of paper [23]. In so doing, the conventional (non-involutive) autoreduction which is performed in line 2 of the latter algorithm omitted, as this autoreduction is optional [23].

Validity of the involutive chain criterion used in lines 11 and 22 is provided by Theorem 18 and Corollary 19. The proof of correctness and termination of the differential algorithm is identical to the proof for its polynomial analogue [21,23]. It follows, that if the completion ranking $\succ_c$ is orderly, then, given a generating set of linear differential polynomials and a constructive involutive division, algorithm **MinimalLinearInvolutiveBasis** computes a minimal differential basis whenever the latter exists. If the division is noetherian, the basis is computed for any completion ordering.

Though the output basis for a noetherian division does not depend on the completion ranking, the proper choice of the latter may increase efficiency of computation. For instance, as shown in [23], the lexicographical completion ranking is the most efficient choice for Janet and Lexicographically induced divisions.

Remark 20. If the algorithm **MinimalLinearInvolutiveBasis** takes a conventional differential Gröbner basis of the ideal $[F]$ as an input, then it produces the minimal involutive differential basis just by enlargement of the input set with its irreducible nonmultiplicative prolongations if any. This enlargement is done in the lower **while**-loop.

Algorithm **MinimalLinearInvolutiveBasis**

Input: F, L, $\succ$ (main ranking), $\succ_c$ (completion ranking)
Output: G, a minimal involutive basis of $[F]$

begin	1
choose $g \in F$ with the lowest $ld(g)$ w.r.t. $\prec_c$	2
$T := \{(g, ld(g), \emptyset)\}$; $\quad Q := \emptyset$; $\quad G := \{g\}$	3
for each $f \in F \setminus \{g\}$ **do**	4
$Q := Q \cup \{(f, ld(f), \emptyset)\}$	5
repeat	6
$\quad h := 0$	7
$\quad$ **while** $Q \neq \emptyset$ **and** $h = 0$ **do**	8
$\qquad$ **choose** g in $(g, \theta, P) \in Q$ with the lowest $ld(g)$ w.r.t. $\prec_c$	9
$\qquad Q := Q \setminus \{(g, \theta, P)\}$	10
$\qquad$ **if** $Criterion(g, \theta, T)$ is false $\quad$ **then** $\quad h := NF_L(g, G)$	11
$\quad$ **end**	12
$\quad$ **if** $h \neq 0$ **then** $\quad G := G \cup \{h\}$	13
$\qquad$ **if** $ld(h) = ld(g)$ **then** $\quad T := T \cup \{(h, \theta, P)\}$	14
$\qquad$ **else** $\quad T := T \cup \{(h, ld(h), \emptyset)\}$	15
$\qquad$ **for each** f in $(f, \vartheta, S) \in T$ s.t. $ld(f) \succ_c ld(h)$ **do**	16
$\qquad\quad T := T \setminus \{(f, \vartheta, S)\}$; $\quad Q := Q \cup \{(f, \vartheta, S)\}$; $\quad G := G \setminus \{f\}$	17
$\quad$ **while** exist $(g, \theta, P) \in T$ and $x \in NM_L(g, G) \setminus P$ and, if $Q \neq \emptyset$,	18
$\qquad$ s.t. $ld(\partial_x \cdot g) \prec_c ld(f)$ for all f in $(f, \vartheta, S) \in Q$ **do**	19
$\qquad$ **choose** such (g, θ, P), x with the lowest $ld(\partial_x \cdot g)$ w.r.t. $\prec_c$	20
$\qquad T := T \setminus \{(g, \theta, P)\} \cup \{(g, \theta, P \cup \{x\})\}$	21
$\qquad$ **if** $Criterion(\partial_x \cdot g, \theta, T)$ is false $\quad$ **then** $\quad h := NF_L(\partial_x \cdot g, G)$	22
$\qquad$ **if** $h \neq 0$ **then** $\quad G := G \cup \{h\}$	23
$\qquad\quad$ **if** $ld(h) = ld(\partial_x \cdot g)$ $\quad$ **then** $\quad T := T \cup \{(h, \theta, \emptyset)\}$	24
$\qquad\quad$ **else** $\quad T := T \cup \{(h, ld(h), \emptyset)\}$	25
$\qquad\qquad$ **for each** f in $(f, \vartheta, S) \in T$ with $ld(f) \succ_c ld(h)$ **do**	26
$\qquad\qquad\quad T := T \setminus \{(f, \vartheta, S)\}$; $\quad Q := Q \cup \{(f, \vartheta, S)\}$; $\quad G := G \setminus \{f\}$	27
$\quad$ **end**	28
$\quad$ **until** $Q \neq \emptyset$	29
end	30

$Criterion(g, \theta, T)$ is true if there is $(f, \vartheta, S) \in T$ such that $ld(g) = \partial_L ld(f)$ and $lcm(\theta, \vartheta) \prec_c ld(g)$.

Example 21. [8] The well-known Janet example with three independent and one dependent variables ($n = 3, m = 1$):

$$\begin{cases} \partial_{11} y - x_2 \partial_{33} y = 0\,, \\ \partial_{22} y = 0\,. \end{cases}$$

The above completion algorithm applied for Janet, Pommaret and Lexicographically induced divisions gives the following involutive bases, which coincide for both pure lexicographical and graded lexicographical rankings compatible with (2) and which sorted in the descending lexicographical order:

Gröbner	Involutive Bases	
basis	Janet & Pommaret	Lex. Induced
$\partial_{11}y - x_2\partial_{33}y$	$\partial_{11}y - x_2\partial_{33}y$	$\partial_{112}y - \partial_{33}y$
$\partial_{22}y$	$\partial_{122}y$	$\partial_{11333}y$
$\partial_{233}y$	$\partial_{1233}y$	$\partial_{1133}y$
$\partial_{3333}y$	$\partial_{13333}y$	$\partial_{113}y - x_2\partial_{333}y$
	$\partial_{22}y$	$\partial_{11}y - x_2\partial_{33}y$
	$\partial_{233}y$	$\partial_{22}y$
	$\partial_{3333}y$	$\partial_{223}y$
		$\partial_{2333}y$
		$\partial_{233}y$
		$\partial_{3333}y$

The first column contains the reduced differential Gröbner basis, and Janet and Pommaret bases are identical for this example.

6   Initial Value Problem

The results of this section generalize to arbitrary $L-$involutive linear systems those obtained in Riquier-Janet theory [6,8,16], for Janet and Thomas divisions, as well as in the formal theory [12,13] for Pommaret division, on posing an initial value problem providing uniqueness and existence of solutions.

Definition 22. [6,8] If $\theta \in ld(F)$ is a leading derivative in $F \subset \mathbb{R}$, then $\partial_\alpha \theta$ is called a *principal derivative*. A derivative which is not principal is called *parametric*. The monomial set $W = \{\cup_{j=1}^m W_j \mid W_j \subset \mathbb{M}\}$ associated by (1) with the set of parametric derivatives is called a *complementary set* of F.

Proposition 23. *Given a ranking* $\prec$, *if set F is a linear $L-$involutive basis of differential ideal $[F]$, then the sets of principal and parametric derivatives (complementary set) related to F depend only on $[F]$ and $\prec$ and do not depend on the choice of involutive division L.*

Proof. It follows immediately from the fact that any involutive basis is a Gröbner basis (Theorem 17). $\square$

Lemma 24. (*decomposition lemma*) *Given a noetherian division L and $L-$involutive set $F \subset \mathbb{R}$, every subset W_j in the complementary monomial set of F related to j-th differential indeterminate y_j $(1 \le j \le m)$ can be decomposed as a disjoint union*

$$W_j = \cup_{v \in V_j} vL_v, \quad L_v \subseteq L(v, U_j \cup \{v\}), \qquad (5)$$

where U_j is the $L-$involutive monomial set (not necessarily nonempty) associated with $ld_j(F)$, and $V_j \in \mathbb{M}$ is a finite subset.

Proof. Let U and W be a pair of monomial sets associated with the principal and parametric derivatives of a differential indeterminate in F. The complementary set W can be written as a disjoint union [36]

$$W = W_0 \cup W_1 \cup \cdots \cup W_d \tag{6}$$

where d is the dimension of monomial ideal (U), W_0 is a finite set, and every W_i $(1 \le i \le d)$ is a finite disjoint union[1]

$$W_r = W_{r_1} \cup W_{r_2} \cup \cdots \cup W_{r_k} \tag{7}$$

with

$$W_{r_s} = \{ \, w_{r_s} x_{i_{s_1}}^{\alpha_1} \cdots x_{i_{s_r}}^{\alpha_r} \mid \alpha_t \in \mathbb{N}, \ 1 \le t \le r \, \} \quad (1 \le s \le k). \tag{8}$$

For every $v \in W_0$ we shall take $L_v = \{1\}$ in (5). Thus, for $d = 0$ the decomposition (5) $W = W_0 = \cup_{v \in W_0} \{v\}$ holds trivially. If $d > 0$ we consider the finite set

$$V = W_0 \cup_{r=1}^{d} \cup_{s=1}^{k} \{w_{r_s}\}, \tag{9}$$

where monomials w_{r_s} generate W_{r_s} in accordance with (8).

We claim that elements in set (9), and the decompositions (6), (7) they determine can be written such that the union in $W = \cup_{v \in V} v L_v$ with $L_v \subseteq L(v, U \cup \{v\})$ is disjoint in accordance with (5). To prove the claim we define the degree q of set U as $q = \max\{deg(u) \mid u \in U\}$, and choose all the monomials w_{r_s} generating W_{r_s} in (8) such that $deg(w_{r_s}) = q$. Obviously, this can always be done by appropriate choice of W_0. Let now V_1 be the set $V_1 = \cup_{r=1}^{d} \cup_{s=1}^{k} \{w_{r_s}\}$, and let $\hat{U}$ be a finite L–autoreduced completion of $U \cup V$. The existence of $\hat{U}$ is guaranteed by noetherity of L. Consider now set $\hat{V} = \hat{U} \cap W \supseteq V_1$. Its L–involutivity and property (d) of L in Definition 10 imply

$$(\forall w \in W \setminus W_0) \, (\exists v \in \hat{V}) \, [\, w \in v L(v, T) \subseteq v L(v, U \cup \{v\}) \,].$$

Thus, we obtain the desired decomposition $W = W_0 \cup_{v \in \hat{V}} v L(v, \hat{U})$. Disjointedness of this union follows from that in (7) and Definition 5 of L–autoreduction. This proves the claim and the lemma. $\qquad\square$

Definition 25. Those elements v_{j_k} (parametric derivatives) which, in accordance with (5), generate the whole complementary set W, will be called L–*generators* of the set. The multiplicative variables x_i satisfying $x_i \in L_{j_k}$

---

[1] The union in (7) considered in [36] is not necessarily disjoint. However, unions in (6) and (7) apparently can be rewritten as disjoint by appropriate choice of W_0 and components of W_r.

will be called $(L-)multipliers$ of the generator v_{j_k} and the remaining variables will be called its $(L-)nonmultipliers$. The whole set of $L-$generators of W will be denoted by $\mathcal{G}_L$, and in accordance with (5)

$$\mathcal{G}_L = \cup_{j=1}^m V_j \,. \tag{10}$$

For a non-noetherian division L a complementary set may not have a finite set of $L-$generators as the following example shows.

Example 26. Let division L defined on $\mathbb{M}$ as follows. Variables $x_1, \ldots, x_{n-1}$ are separated into multiplicative and nonmultiplicative by Definition 8. Let variable x_n be also separated by Definition 8 if $deg_n(u) = 0$ and $u \neq 1$, whereas if $deg_n(u) > 0$ or if $u = 1$, x_n be nonmultiplicative for u. Then, monomial set $U = \{x_1^2, x_1 x_2, x_2\}$ is $L-$involutive in $K[x_1, x_2, x_3]$. Its complementary set has the infinite set of $L-$generators: $\mathcal{G}_L = \{1\} \cup \{x_1\} \cup_{i=1}^{\infty} \{x_3^i\}$.

Remark 27. Decomposition (5) and the underlying $L-$generator set (25) are not uniquely defined, and usually a more compact set $\mathcal{G}$ of $L-$generators (with less number of elements) than that constructed in the proof of Lemma 24 can be chosen. For example, for any Janet basis $\mathcal{G}_P$ given by (10) can always be chosen [8] such that

$$(\forall V_j) \, (\forall v \in V_j) \, [\, L_v = J(v, U_j \cup \{v\}) \,] \quad (1 \leq j \leq m), \tag{11}$$

where J stands for Janet set of multiplicative monomials. Since for $\hat{U}_j$, as it constructed in the proof, the inclusion $U_j \cup \{v\} \subseteq \hat{U}_j$ holds, the property (d) in Definition 3 implies $J(v, \hat{U}_j) \subset J(v, U_j \cup \{v\})$. Therefore, the set of Janet generators defined by (11) is a subset of that constructed in the proof of Lemma 24.

For a Pommaret basis in the formal theory [12] decomposition (5) is taken in the form

$$W = W_0 \cup_{\{v \in W \ | \ deg(v)=q\}} v P(v), \tag{12}$$

where $P(v)$ denotes the set of Pommaret multiplicative monomials for v, and q, as in the proof, is the degree of the basis. The number of Pommaret generators in (12) with i multipliers is called i-th *Cartan character*[2] $(1 \leq i \leq n)$ of the basis and will be denoted by σ_q^i.

Example 28. The complementary set of the monomial ideal (U) for $U = \{x_1^2 x_3, x_1 x_2, x_1 x_3^2\}$ in Example 11 is $W = \cup\{x_1^{i+1} \mid i \in \mathbb{N}\} \cup \{x_2^j x_3^k \mid j, k \in \mathbb{N}\}$. Its most compact sets $\mathcal{G}_J$ and $\mathcal{G}_{D_{Lex}}$ together with their multipliers are:

---

[2] Cartan introduced these numbers in his analysis of exterior PDEs [3] and called them *characters*.

Janet division		Lex. induced division	
Generator	Multipliers	Generator	Multipliers
1	x_2, x_3	1	x_2, x_3
x_1	–	x_1	x_1
x_1^2	x_1	–	–

We note that if involutive bases $\tilde{U}_P, \tilde{U}_{D_{Lex}}$, given in Example 11, are sequentially enlarged with every single generator, then the sets of Janet multipliers, in accordance with Remark 27, coincide with the sets of multiplicative variables

$$M_J(1, \tilde{U}_P \cup \{1\}) = \{x_2, x_3\}, \ M_J(x_1, \tilde{U}_P \cup \{1\}) = \emptyset, \ M_J(x_1^2, \tilde{U}_P \cup \{x_1^2\}) = \{x_1\}$$

whereas for lexicographically induced division, every set of multipliers is the proper subset of multiplicative variables

$$M_{D_{Lex}}(1, \tilde{U}_{D_{Lex}} \cup \{1\}) = M_{D_{Lex}}(x_1, \tilde{U}_{D_{Lex}} \cup \{x_1\}) = \{x_1, x_2, x_3\}.$$

Theorem 29. *(uniqueness theorem) Let $\mathcal{F}$ be an $L-$involutive system of linear PDEs for an orderly ranking. Then $\mathcal{F}$ has at most one solution satisfying the following initial conditions: the derivatives associated with $L-$generators of the complementary monomials are arbitrary functions of their multipliers at the fixed values of their nonmultipliers from coordinates of the initial point $x_i = x_i^0$ ($1 \leq i \leq n$)), whereas the generators without multipliers are considered to be arbitrary constants.*

Proof. Involutivity of $\mathcal{F}$ with respect to an orderly ranking implies that the associated complementary monomial set contains all the monomials associated with the parametric derivatives. This statement is an immediate consequence of the well-known fact [36] that for a graded monomial ordering the Hilbert function of a polynomial ideal is defined by the monomial ideal generated by the leading monomials of a Gröbner basis of the polynomial ideal.

Furthermore, by association (1), the decomposition (6) yields that every parametric derivative associated with a monomial in $W \setminus W_0$ is produced by differentiation of the uniquely defined parametric derivative ($L-$generator) with respect to its multipliers. Assigning the fixed values to all these parametric derivatives is obviously equivalent to fixing some function of the multipliers. Therefore, given initial point $x_i = x_i^0$, in addition to the set of arbitrary constants which associated with elements in W_0, all the parametric arbitrariness is determined by functions corresponding to the $L-$generators and which are arbitrary functions of the multipliers at the fixed values of nonmultipliers from coordinates of the initial point. $\qquad \square$

Remark 30. Different involutive divisions give, obviously, equivalent forms of initial value problem providing the uniqueness of solutions. However, given a system of PDEs with an infinite set of parametric derivatives, the writingf of such initial conditions in accordance with Theorem 29 may be more compact for one division than for another. We demonstrate this fact by examples given below.

Theorem 31. *(existence theorem) Let $\mathcal{F}$ be an $L-$involutive linear system for an orderly ranking, and let its coefficients be analytic functions in an initial point $(x_i = x_i^o)$. Then $\mathcal{F}$ has precisely one solution which is analytic in this point if all arbitrary functions in the initial data specified in Theorem 29 are analytic in their arguments taking values from coordinates of the initial point.*

Proof. This is identical to the existence proof in Riquier-Janet theory [6,8] (see also [31]). □

Example 32. The complementary monomial set for Janet system in Example 21 is finite and consists of 12 elements

$$W = \{1, x_1, x_2, x_3, x_1 x_2, x_1 x_3, x_2 x_3, x_3^2, x_1 x_2 x_3, x_1 x_3^2, x_3^3, x_1 x_3^3\}.$$

By Theorem 31, its general solution depends on 12 arbitrary constants.

Example 33. [12] The system of the first order PDEs with four independent and one dependent variables $(n = 4, m = 1)$ and its completion to involution for Janet or Pommaret division for any ranking compatible with (2) are given by

$$\begin{cases} \partial_1 y + x_2 \partial_3 y + y = 0, \\ \partial_2 y + x_1 \partial_4 y = 0, \end{cases} \quad \overset{J,P-\text{completion}}{\Longrightarrow} \quad \begin{cases} \partial_1 y + x_2 \partial_4 y + y = 0, \\ \partial_2 y + x_1 \partial_4 y = 0, \\ \partial_3 y - \partial_4 y = 0. \end{cases}$$

The parametric derivatives $\partial_4^i y$ $(i \in \mathbb{N})$ have the only Janet generator $y \Longleftrightarrow 1$ with the only multiplier x_4. Hence, the initial data providing the unique analytic solution are $y|_{x_1 = x_1^o, x_2 = x_2^o, x_3 = x_3^o} = \phi(x_4)$ with arbitrary function $\phi(x_4)$, analytic at $x_4 = x_4^o$. The system can explicitly be integrated and its general solution is

$$y = e^{-(x_4 - x_4^o)} \phi(x_3 + x_4 - x_1 x_2 + x_1^o x_2^o - x_3^o).$$

The Pommaret generators are y and $\partial_4 y$ without multipliers and with multiplier x_4, respectively. This leads to the initial value problem

$$y|_{x_1 = x_1^o, x_2 = x_2^o, x_3 = x_3^o} = c, \quad \partial_4 y|_{x_1 = x_1^o, x_2 = x_2^o, x_3 = x_3^o} = \psi(x_4)$$

with arbitrary constant c and arbitrary function ψ. This shows that the Janet initial conditions are written more compact than those of Pommaret.

Example 34. [37] The well-known Lewy example with $n = 3, m = 2$ and $\eta_1, \eta_2 \in \mathbb{K}$

$$\begin{cases} \partial_1 y_1 - 2x_3 \, \partial_2 y_1 - \partial_3 y_2 - 2x_1 \, \partial_2 y_2 = \eta_1(x_1, x_2, x_3), \\ \partial_1 y_2 + 2x_1 \, \partial_1 y_1 + \partial_3 y_1 - 2x_3 \, \partial_2 y_2 = \eta_2(x_1, x_2, x_3). \end{cases}$$

This system is involutive for any of Janet, Pommaret or lexicographically induced divisions and the orderly ranking with $\partial_1 y_j \succ \partial_2 y_j \succ \partial_3 y_j$, $y_1 \succ y_2$. Janet generators are y_1, y_2. Each of them has multipliers x_2, x_3. This implies the initial data providing the uniqueness: $y_j|_{x_1 = x_1^\circ} = \phi_j(x_2, x_3)$ $(j = 1, 2)$ with arbitrary functions $\phi_j(x_2, x_3)$. Pommaret and lexicographically induced divisions lead to a less compact writing these conditions.

Remark 35. As shown by Lewy [37] for Example 34, there exist C^∞ functions η_1, η_2 such that the system has no C^∞ (and even C^1) solutions. Therefore, analyticity in the Theorem 31 statement can not be replaced by smoothness.

We conclude this section with explicit formulae for the Hilbert function $HF_{[F]}$ and Hilbert polynomial $HP_{[F]}$ of differential ideal $[F]$ represented by its linear involutive basis F. These formulae are valid for any involutive division and an orderly ranking. For ordinary differential ideals, that is, for the case of single differential indeterminate $(m = 1)$, by association (1), they are the same as in commutative algebra [20,22]. For partial differential case they involve the number m of differential indeterminates

$$HF_{[F]} = m \binom{n+s}{s} - \sum_{j=1}^{m} \sum_{i=0}^{s} \sum_{u \in U_j} \binom{s - deg(u) + \mu(u) - 1}{\mu(u) - 1}, \quad (13)$$

$$HP_{[F]} = m \binom{n+s}{s} - \sum_{j=1}^{m} \sum_{u \in U_j} \binom{s - deg(u) + \mu(u)}{\mu(u)}. \quad (14)$$

Here n is the number of independent variables, U_j is the monomial set associated with the set of leading derivatives $ld_j(F)$, and $\mu(u)$ is the number of multiplicative elements of u.

The first term in the right hand side of (13) is the total number of derivatives of order $\le s$. The triple sum counts the number of principal derivatives among them in accordance with Definition 14 which says that any principal derivative is uniquely obtained by the multiplicative prolongation of one of the leading derivatives in F. Thus, (13) gives the number of parametric derivatives of order $\le s$, and for s large enough it becomes polynomial (14).

In the formal theory [12,13] the Janet formula is used:

$$HP_{[F]} = \sum_{i=1}^{n} \binom{s - q + i - 1}{i - 1} \sigma_q^i.$$

Here the Hilbert polynomial [8] is written in terms of Cartan characters σ_q^i (see Remark 27). Apparently, this is (14), rewritten for Pommaret division in terms of Cartan characters.

7   Lie Symmetry Analysis of PDEs

Lie symmetry methods and their computerization yield a powerful practical
tool for analysis of nonlinear differential equations (see the review article [28]
and references therein for more details). We present here the basic computational formulae and demonstrate, by two simple examples with a single
nonlinear evolution equation, application of the above described involutive
methods to finding the classical infinitesimal symmetries.
Given a finite system of polynomial-nonlinear PDEs

$$ f_k(x_i, y_j, \dots, \partial_\alpha y_j) = 0, \quad (1 \le i \le n, \ 1 \le j \le m, \ 1 \le k \le r) \qquad (15) $$

one looks for one-parameter infinitesimal transformations

$$ \begin{cases} \tilde{x}_i(\lambda) = x_i + \xi_i(x_i, y_j)\lambda + O(\lambda^2), \\ \tilde{y}_j(\lambda) = y_j + \eta_j(x_i, y_j)\lambda + O(\lambda^2), \end{cases} \quad (1 \le i \le n, \ 1 \le j \le m). \qquad (16) $$

The conditions of invariance of (15) under transformations (16) are

$$ \hat{Z}^{(\alpha)} f_k(x_i, y_j, \dots, \partial_\alpha y_j)|_{f_s=0} = 0, \quad (1 \le k, s \le r) \qquad (17) $$

$$ \hat{Z}^{(\alpha)} = \xi_i \partial_{x_i} + \eta_j \partial_{y_j} + \zeta_{j;i} \partial_{y_{j;i}} + \dots + \zeta_{j;\alpha} \partial_{y_{j;\alpha}}, \qquad (18) $$

where $\partial_i y_j$ denoted by $y_{j;i}$, etc.[3] Functions $\zeta_{j;\dots}$ involved in the differential
operator (18) are uniquely computed in terms of functions ξ_i, η_j and their
derivatives by means of the recurrence relations

$$ \zeta_{j;i} = D_i(\eta_j) - y_{j;q} D_i(\xi_q), $$

$$ \zeta_{j;i_1 \dots i_p} = D_{i_p}(\zeta_{j;i_1 \dots i_{p-1}}) - y_{j;i_1 \dots i_{p-1} q} D_{i_p}(\xi_q), $$

where D_i is the total derivative operator with respect to x_i

$$ D_i = \partial_i + y_{j;i} \partial_{y_j} + y_{j;ik} \partial_{y_{j;k}} + \dots $$

The invariance conditions (17) produce the overdetermined system of linear homogeneous PDEs in ξ_i, η_j which is called the *determining system*. Its
particular solution yields an infinitesimal operator of the symmetry group

$$ \hat{Z} = \xi_i \, \partial_{x_i} + \eta_j \, \partial_{y_j}, \qquad (19) $$

and the general solution yields all the infinitesimal operators.

Given initial system (15), integration of the determining system is generally a bottleneck of the whole procedure of constructing these symmetry
operators, and completion the system to involution is the most universal
algorithmic method of its integration [28].

---

[3] In this section the summation over repeated indices is always assumed.

Example 36. [33] Diffusion type equation $y_t + y y_x - t y_{xx} = 0$ $(n = 2, m = 1)$. The symmetry operator (18) of the form

$$\hat{Z} = \xi_1 \, \partial_t + \xi_2 \, \partial_x + \eta \, \partial_y \qquad (20)$$

satisfies the determining system

$$\partial_{yy}\xi_1 = 0, \quad \partial_{yy}\xi_2 = 0, \quad t\,\partial_{yy}\eta - 2t\,\partial_{xy}\xi_2 - 2y\,\partial_y\xi_2 = 0,$$
$$\partial_{xy}\xi_1 + \partial_y\xi_1 = 0, \quad 2t^2\partial_{xy}\eta - t^2\partial_{xx}\xi_2 - yt\,\partial_t\xi_2 + t\,\partial_t\xi_2 + y\,\xi_1 - t\eta = 0,$$
$$t\,\partial_{xx}\eta - y\,\partial_x\eta - \partial_t\eta = 0, \quad t^2\,\partial_{xx}\xi_1 - yt\,\partial_x\xi_1 + 2t\,\partial_x\xi_2 - t\,\partial_t\xi_1 - \xi_1 = 0,$$
$$t\,\partial_{xy}\xi_1 + \partial_y\xi_2 = 0, \quad \partial_x\xi_1 = 0.$$

By choosing the orderly degree-reverse-lexicographical ranking with $\partial_y \succ \partial_x \succ \partial_t$, $\xi_1 \succ \xi_2 \succ \eta$ and applying the completion algorithm of Sect. 5, we obtain the (Pommaret, Janet, lexicographically induced) involutive system

$$\partial_y\xi_1 = 0, \quad \partial_y\xi_2 = 0, \quad \partial_y\eta = 0, \quad \partial_x\xi_1 = 0, \quad \partial_x\xi_2 - \frac{1}{t}\xi_1 = 0,$$

$$\partial_x\eta = 0, \quad \partial_t\xi_1 - \frac{1}{t}\xi_1 = 0, \quad \partial_t\xi_2 - \eta = 0, \quad \partial_t\eta = 0.$$

The generators of parametric derivatives ξ_1, ξ_2, η have no multipliers. Hence, the general solution depends on three arbitrary constants c_1, c_2, c_3, and it can easily be obtained by explicit integration of the involutive system

$$\xi_1 = c_1 t, \quad \xi_2 = c_1 x + c_2 t + c_3, \quad \eta = c_2.$$

Respectively, the Lie symmetry group is three-dimensional. Its symmetry operators $\hat{Z}_1 = t\partial_t + x\partial_x$, $\hat{Z}_2 = t\partial_x + \partial_y$, $\hat{Z}_3 = \partial_x$ form the Lie algebra $[\hat{Z}_1, \hat{Z}_2] = 0$, $[\hat{Z}_2, \hat{Z}_3] = 0$, $[\hat{Z}_1, \hat{Z}_3] = -\hat{Z}_3$.

Example 37. [38] The Harry Dym equation $\partial_t y - y^3 \partial_{xxx} y = 0$ $(n = 2, m = 1)$ which was already used in [28] as an illustrative example. The symmetry operator in the form (20) is now determined by the system

$$\partial_y\xi_1 = 0, \quad \partial_x\xi_1 = 0, \quad \partial_y\xi_2 = 0, \quad \partial_{yy}\eta = 0,$$
$$\partial_{xy}\eta - \partial_{xx}\xi_2 = 0, \quad \partial_t\eta - y^3\partial_{xxx}\eta = 0,$$
$$3y^3\partial_{xxy}\eta + \partial_t\xi_2 - y^3\partial_{xxx}\xi_2 = 0, \quad y\,\partial_t\xi_1 - 3y\,\partial_x\xi_2 + 3\eta = 0.$$

Its Janet and Pommaret involutive form for the same ranking as in the previous example is

$$\partial_{xx}\eta = 0, \quad \partial_y\eta - \frac{1}{y}\eta = 0, \quad \partial_t\eta = 0, \quad \partial_y\xi_2 = 0, \quad \partial_x\xi_2 - \frac{1}{3}\partial_t\xi_1 - \frac{1}{y}\eta = 0,$$
$$\partial_t\xi_2 = 0, \quad \partial_{tt}\xi_1 = 0, \quad \partial_y\xi_t = 0, \quad \partial_x\xi_1 = 0.$$

There are five generators of parametric derivatives $\xi_1, \partial_t \xi_1, \xi_2, \eta, \partial_x \eta$ which have no multipliers that implies the five-dimensional Lie symmetry group. The involutive determining system in this example is also easy to integrate

$$\xi_1 = c_1 + c_2 t, \quad \xi_2 = c_3 + c_4 x + c_5 x^2, \quad \eta = \left(c_4 - \frac{1}{3} c_2 + 2 c_5 x\right) y.$$

This gives the Lie symmetry operators

$$Z_1 = \partial_t, \quad Z_2 = t \partial_t - \frac{1}{3} y \partial_y, \quad Z_3 = \partial_x, \quad Z_4 = x \partial_x + y \partial_y, \quad Z_5 = x^2 \partial_x + 2xy \partial_y$$

with the following nonzero commutators of the symmetry algebra

$$[Z_1, Z_2 = Z_1, \quad [Z_3, Z_4] = Z_4, \quad [Z_3, Z_5] = 2 Z_4, \quad [Z_4, Z_5] = Z_5.$$

8   Conclusion

Most of the above presented definitions, statements and constructive methods can be extended to finite sets of differential polynomials in $\mathbb{R}$ which, given a ranking, are linear with respect to their highest rank (*principal*) derivatives. In Riquier-Janet theory the corresponding systems of PDEs are called *orthonomic*. Their completion to involution, for any constructive and noetherian division, could be done much like linear systems. The essential obstruction here is an non-orthonomic integrability condition. Moreover, even if such an integrability condition is explicitly solvable with respect to its principal derivative, then this leads to non-polynomial orthonomicity, and, thereby, to difficulty in the use of constructive methods of differential and commutative algebra. In the latter case some geometric features of the formal theory may be useful for computational purposes [25].

However, given an orthonomic system of polynomial PDEs and an involutive division L, one can always verify if it is L-involutive. Analytic involutive orthonomic systems admit posing an initial value problem providing the existence and uniqueness of solution. One can, hence, determine arbitrariness in the general solution as it is done in Sect. 6 for linear systems. In particular, the compact general formulae (13) and (14) for the Hilbert function and Hilbert polynomial are also valid for involutive orthonomic equations.

We are going to implement the completion algorithm **MinimalLinearInvolutiveBasis** (Sect. 5) after examination and optimization of its polynomial analogue [21,23]. Though its implementation in Reduce for Pommaret division [19] has already shown its efficiency, the differential case needs more careful analysis of implementation and optimization issues to be applicable to PDEs of practical interest. Thus, in Lie symmetry analysis of relatively small systems it is easy to obtain determining systems of many hundreds equations. Currently, the most efficient completion algorithm for linear systems implemented in some packages for Lie symmetry analysis [28] is that of paper [24]. Its underlying implementations allow to treat hundreds determining equations (cf. [25]). As for significantly larger determining systems, they are hardly tractable by the present day computer algebra tools, whereas there are practical needs in it. In gas dynamics, for instance, the group classification of the system of five second order PDEs describing a viscous heat conducting gas and involving five dependent and four independent variables (three spatial and one temporal) [39], leads to the determining system containing more than 200 000 equations.

In our intention to extract, in the process of implementation, the maximal possible efficiency from the algorithms proposed, we hope, first of all, to detect (heuristically) the most optimal choice of involutive division. As the first step in this direction an implementation of the monomial completion for different divisions has been done in *Mathematica* and for Janet division in C [34].

References

1. Cartan, E.: Sur certaines expressions différentielles a le problème de Pfaff. *Annales Ecole Normale*, 3-e serie, **16**, 1899, 239-332; Sur l'integration des systèmes d'équations aux différentielles totales. Ibid., **18** (1901) 241-311.
2. Kähler, E.: *Einführung in die Theorie der Systeme von Differentialgleichungen*, Teubner, Leipzig, 1934.
3. Cartan, E.: *Les Systèmes Différentielles Extérieurs et leurs Applications Géometriques*, Paris, Hermann, 1945.
4. Arais, E.A., Shapeev, V.P., Yanenko, N.N.: Realization of Cartan's Method of Exterior Differential Forms on an Electronic Computer. *Sov. Math. Dokl.* **15(1)** (1974) 203-205.
5. Hartley, D., Tucker, R.W.: Constructive Implementation of the Cartan-Kähler Theory of Exterior Differential Systems. *J. Symb. Comp.* **12** (1991) 655-667.
6. Riquier, C.: *Les Systèmes d'Equations aux Dérivées Partielles*, Gauthier-Villars, Paris, 1910.
7. Rust, C.J., Reid G.J.: Rankings of Partial Derivatives. In: *Proceedings of IS-SAC'97*, W.Küchlin (ed.), ACM Press, 1997 pp. 9-16.
8. Janet, M.: *Leçons sur les Systèmes d'Equations aux Dérivées Partielles*, Cahiers Scientifiques, IV, Gauthier-Villars, Paris, 1929.
9. Schwarz, F.: The Riquier-Janet Theory and its application to Nonlinear Evolution Equations. *Physica* **11D** (1984) 243-251.
10. Topunov, V.L.: Reducing Systems of Linear Differential Equations to a Passive Form. *Acta Appl. Math.* **16** (1989) 191-206.
11. Schwarz. F.: An Algorithm for Determining the Size of Symmetry Groups. *Computing* **49** (1992) 95-115.
12. Pommaret, J.F.: *Systems of Partial Differential Equations and Lie Pseudogroups*, Gordon & Breach, New York, 1978.
13. Pommaret, J.F.: *Partial Differential Equations and Group Theory. New Perspectives for Applications*, Kluwer, Dordrecht, 1994.

14. Schü, J., Seiler, W.M., Calmet, J.: Algorithmic Methods for Lie Pseudogroups. In: *Modern Group Analysis: Advanced Analytical and Computational Methods in Mathematical Physics*, N.Ibragimov et al (eds.), Kluwer, Dordrecht, 1993, pp. 337-344.
15. Seiler, W.M.: *Applying AXIOM to Partial Differential Equations*. Internal Report 95-17, Universität Karlsruhe, Fakultät Informatik, 1995.
16. Thomas, J.: *Differential Systems*. AMS Publication, New York, 1937.
17. Boulier, F., Lazard, D., Ollivier, F., Petitot M.: Representation for the Radical of a Finitely Generated Differential Ideal. In: *Proceedings of ISSAC'95*, A.H.M. Levelt (ed.), ACM Press, 1995, pp. 158-166.
18. Zharkov, A.Yu., Blinkov, Yu.A.: Involutive Approach to Investigating Polynomial Systems. In: Proceedings of "SC 93", International IMACS Symposium on Symbolic Computation: New Trends and Developments (Lille, June 14-17, 1993). *Math. Comp. Simul.* **42** (1996) 323-332.
19. Gerdt, V.P., Blinkov, Yu.A.: Involutive Bases of Polynomial Ideals. Preprint-Nr. 1/1996, Naturwissenschaftlich-Theoretisches Zentrum, University of Leipzig; *Math. Comp. Simul.* **45** (1998) 519-542.
20. Apel, J.: Theory of Involutive Divisions and an Application to Hilbert Function. *J. Symb. Comp.* **25** (1998) 683-704.
21. Gerdt, V.P., Blinkov, Yu.A.: Minimal Involutive Bases. *Math. Comp. Simul.* **45** (1998) 543-560.
22. Gerdt, V.P., Berth, M., Czichowski, G.: Involutive Divisions in Mathematica: Implementation and Some Applications. In: *Proceedings of the 6th Rhein Workshop on Computer Algebra* (Sankt-Augustin, Germany, March 31 - April 3, 1998), J.Calmet (Ed.), Institute for Algorithms and Scientific Computing, GMD-SCAI, Sankt-Augustin, 1998, pp.74-91.
23. Gerdt, V.P.: Involutive Division Technique: Some Generalizations and Optimizations, Preprint JINR E5-98-151, Dubna, 1998. To be published in the *Proceedings of "CASC'98"* (April 20-24, 1998, St.Petersburg).
24. Reid, G.J.: Algorithms for Reducing a System of PDEs to Standard Form, Determining the Dimension of its Solution Space and Calculating its Taylor Series Solution. *Euro. J. Appl. Maths.* **2** (1991) 293-318.
25. Reid, G.J., Wittkopf, A.D., Boulton A.: Reduction of Systems of Nonlinear Partial Differential Equations to Simplified Involutive Form. *Euro. J. Appl. Maths.* **7** (1996) 635-666.
26. Carra'Ferro, G.: Gröbner Bases and Differential Algebra. *Lec. Not. in Comp. Sci.* **356** (1987) 129-140.
27. Ollivier, F.: Standard Bases of Differential Ideals. *Lec. Not. in Comp. Sci.* **508** (1990) 304-321.
28. Hereman, W.: Symbolic software for the computation of Lie symmetry analysis. In: *CRC Handbook of Lie Group Analysis of Differential Equations, Volume 3: New Trends in Theoretical Developments and Computational methods*, Ibragimov, N.H. et al. (eds.), CRC Press, Boca Raton, 1995, pp. 367-413.
29. Reid, G.J.: Finding Abstract Lie Symmetry Algebras of Differential Equations without Integrating Determaning Equations. *Euro. J. Appl. Maths.* **2** (1991) 319-340.
30. Mansfield, E., Clarkson, P.A.: Application of the Differential Algebra Package diffgrob2 to Classical Symmetries of Differential Equations, *J. Symb. Comp.* **23** (1997) 517-533.

31. Ritt, J.F.: *Differential Algebra*, AMS Publication, New York, 1950.
32. Kolchin, E.R.: *Differential Algebra and Algebraic Groups*, Academic Press, New York, 1973.
33. Gerdt ,V.P.: Gröbner Bases and Involutive Methods for Algebraic and Differential Equations, *Math. Comp. Model.* **25**, No.8/9 (1997) 75-90.
34. Gerdt, V.P., Berth, M., Czichowski, G., Kornyak V.V.: Construction of Involutive Monomial Sets for Different Involutive Divisions. *This volume.*
35. Buchberger, B.: Gröbner Bases: an Algorithmic Method in Polynomial Ideal Theory. In: *Recent Trends in Multidimensional System Theory*, Bose, N.K. (ed.), Reidel, Dordrecht, 1985. pp. 184-232.
36. Cox, D., Little, J., O'Shea D.: *Ideals, Varieties and Algorithms*, 2nd Edition, Springer-Verlag, New York, 1996.
37. Lewy. H.: An Example of a Smooth Linear Partial Differential Equation without Solution, *Ann. Math.* **66** (1957) 155-158.
38. Ablowitz, M.J., Clarkson, P.A.: *Solitons, Nonlinear Evolution Equations and Inverse Scattering*, London Mathematical Society Lecture Notes on Mathematics **149**, Cambridge University Press, Cambridge, UK, 1991.
39. Bublik, V.V.: Group Classification of Equations for Dynamics of Viscous Heat Conducting Gas, In: *Dynamics of Continuous Medium* **113**, Novosibirsk, 1998, pp. 19-21 (in Russian).

Constrained Hamiltonian Systems and Gröbner Bases[*]

Vladimir P. Gerdt[1] and Soso A. Gogilidze[2]

[1] Laboratory of Computing Techniques and Automation, Joint Institute for Nuclear Research, 141980 Dubna, Russia
[2] Institute of High Energy Physics, Tbilisi State University, 38086 Tbilisi, Georgia

Abstract. In this paper we consider finite-dimensional constrained Hamiltonian systems of polynomial type. In order to compute the complete set of constraints and separate them into the first and second classes we apply the modern algorithmic methods of commutative algebra based on the use of Gröbner bases. As it is shown, this makes the classical Dirac method fully algorithmic. The underlying algorithm implemented in Maple is presented and some illustrative examples are given.

1 Introduction

The generalized Hamiltonian formalism invented by Dirac [1] for constrained systems has become a classical tool for investigation of gauge theories in physics [2–4], and a platform for numerical analysis of constrained mechanical systems [5]. Finite-dimensional constrained Hamiltonian systems are part of differential algebraic equations whose numerical analysis is of great research interest over last decade [6] because of importance for many applied areas, for instance, multi-body mechanics and molecular dynamics.

In physics, the constrained systems are mainly of interest for purposes of quantization of gauge theories which play a fundamental role in modern quantum field theory and elementary particle physics. Dirac devised his methods to study constrained Hamiltonian systems just for those quantization purposes. Having this in mind, he classified the constraints in the first and second classes. A first class constrained physical system possesses gauge invariance and its quantization requires gauge fixing whereas a second class constrained system does not need this. The effect of the second class constraints may be reduced to a modification of a naive measure in the path integral. The presence of gauge degrees of freedom (first class constraints) indicates that the general solution of the system depends on arbitrary functions. Hence, the system is underdetermined. To eliminate unphysical gauge degrees of freedom one usually imposes gauge fixing conditions whereas for elimination of other unphysical degrees of freedom occurring because of the second class constraints, one can use the Dirac brackets [2,3,7]. In some special cases one can explicitly eliminate the unphysical degrees of freedom [8].

---

[*] This work was supported in part by Russian Foundation for Basic Research, grant No. 98-01-00101.

Unlike physics, where constrained systems are singular, as they contain internal constraints, mechanical systems are usually regular with externally imposed constraints [9]. Such a system is equivalent to a singular one whose Lagrangian is that of the regular system enlarged with a linear combination of the externally imposed constraints whose coefficients (multipliers) are to be treated as extra dynamical variables. The latter system may reveal extra constraints for the former system providing the consistency of its dynamics.

Therefore, to investigate a constraint Hamiltonian system one has to detect all the constraints involved, and separate them, for physical models, into first and second classes. In his theory [1] Dirac gave the receipt for computation of constraints which is widely known as *Dirac algorithm*, and it has been implemented in computer algebra software [10]. However, the Dirac approach, as a method for computation of constraints, is not yet an algorithm. Even computation of the primary constraints, given a singular Lagrangian, is not generally algorithmic. Moreover, in generation of the secondary, tertiary, etc., constraints by the Dirac method one must verify if a certain function of the phase space variables vanishes on the constraint manifold. Generally, the latter problem is algorithmically unsolvable. Similarly, there are no general algorithmic schemes for separation of constraints into the first and second classes. In physical literature one can find quite a number of particular methods developed for the constraint separation (see, for example, [11,12]). But all of them have non-algorithmic defects. Thereby, being successfully applied to one constrained system, those methods may be failed for another system even of a similar type.

In practice, many constrained physical and mechanical problems are described by polynomial Lagrangians that lead to polynomial Hamiltonians. In this case, as we show in the present paper, one can apply Gröbner bases which nowadays have become the most universal algorithmic tool in commutative algebra [13] and algebraic geometry [14,15]. The combination of the Dirac method with the Gröbner bases technique makes the former fully algorithmic and, thereby, allows to compute the complete set of constraints. Moreover, the constraint separation is also done algorithmically. We show this and present the underlying algorithm which we call *algorithm Dirac-Gröbner*. This algorithm has been implemented in Maple V Release 5, and we illustrate it by examples both from physics and mechanics.

2   Dirac Method

In this section we shortly describe the computational aspects of the Dirac approach to constrained finite-dimensional Hamiltonian systems [1,3].
Let us start with a Lagrangian $L(q, \dot{q}) \equiv L(q_i, \dot{q}_j)$ $(1 \leq i, j \leq n)$ as a function of the generalized coordinates q_i and velocities $\dot{q}_j$[1]. If the Hessian $\partial^2 L / \partial \dot{q}_i \partial \dot{q}_j$

---

[1] We consider only autonomous systems, and there is no loss of generality since time t may be treated as an additional variable.

has the full rank $r = n$, then the system is *regular* and it has no internally hidden constraints. Otherwise, if $r < n$, the Euler-Lagrange equations

$$\dot{p}_i = \frac{\partial L}{\partial q_i} \quad (1 \leq i \leq n) \tag{1}$$

with

$$p_i = \frac{\partial L}{\partial \dot{q}_i} \tag{2}$$

are *singular* or *degenerate*, as not all differential equations (1) are of the second order. There are just $n - r$ such independent lower order equations. By the Legendre transformation [2]

$$H_c(p, q) = p_i q_i - L, \tag{3}$$

we obtain the *canonical Hamiltonian* with momenta p_i defined in (2). In the degenerate case there are *primary constraints* denoted by ϕ_α, which form the *primary constraint manifold* denoted by Σ_0

$$\Sigma_0 : \quad \phi_\alpha(p, q) = 0 \quad (1 \leq \alpha \leq n - r), \tag{4}$$

Thus, the dynamics of the system is determined only on the constraint manifold (4). To take this fact into account, Dirac defined the *total Hamiltonian*

$$H_t = H_c + u_\alpha \phi_\alpha \tag{5}$$

with *multipliers* u_α as arbitrary (non-specified) functions of the coordinates and momenta. The corresponding Hamiltonian equations determine the system dynamics together with the primary constraints

$$\dot{q}_i = \{H_t, q_i\}, \quad \dot{p}_i = \{H_t, p_i\}, \quad \phi_\alpha(p, q) = 0 \quad (1 \leq i \leq n, \ 1 \leq \alpha \leq n - r), \tag{6}$$

where the *Poisson brackets* are defined for any two functions f, g of the dynamical variables p and q as follows

$$\{f, g\} = \frac{\partial f}{\partial p_i} \frac{\partial g}{\partial q_i} - \frac{\partial g}{\partial p_i} \frac{\partial p}{\partial q_i}. \tag{7}$$

In order to be consistent with the system dynamics, the primary constraints must satisfy the conditions

$$\dot{\phi}_\alpha = \{H_t, \phi_\alpha\} \overset{\Sigma_0}{=} 0 \quad (1 \leq \alpha \leq n - r), \tag{8}$$

where $\overset{\Sigma_0}{=}$ stands for the equality, called *a week equality*, on the primary constraint manifold (4). The Poisson bracket in (8) must be a linear combination

---

[2] In this paper summation over repeated indices is we always assumed.

of the constraint functions [3]. Given a constraint function ϕ_α, the consistency condition (8), unless it is satisfied identically, may lead either to a contradiction or to a new constraint. The former case signals that the given Hamiltonian system is inconsistent. In the latter case, if the new constraint does not involve any of multipliers u_α, it must be added to the constraint set, and, hence, the constraint manifold must involve this new constraint. Otherwise, the consistency condition is considered as defining the multipliers, and the constraint set is not enlarged with it.

The iteration of this consistency check ends up with the *complete set of constraints* such that for every constraint in the set condition (8) is satisfied. This is the Dirac method of the constraint computation. As shown in [16], the method is nothing else than completion of the initial Hamiltonian system to involution, and the constraints generated are just *the integrability conditions*. For general systems of PDEs, the completion process is done [17] by sequential prolongations and projections. For Hamiltonian systems, the time derivative of a constraint is its prolongation whereas projection of the prolonged constraint is realized in (8) by computing the Poisson bracket on the constraint manifold.

Let now Σ be the constraint manifold for the complete set of constraints

$$\Sigma : \quad \phi_\alpha(p, q) = 0 \quad (1 \le \alpha \le k). \tag{9}$$

If a constraint function ϕ_α satisfies the condition

$$\{\phi_\alpha(p, q), \phi_\beta(p, q)\} \overset{\Sigma}{=} 0 \quad (1 \le \beta \le k), \tag{10}$$

it is of *the first class*. Otherwise, the constraint function is of *the second class*. The number of the second class constrains is equal to rank of the following $(k \times k)$ *Poisson bracket matrix*, whose elements must be evaluated on the constraint manifold

$$M_{\alpha\beta} \overset{\Sigma}{=} \{\phi_\alpha, \phi_\beta\}. \tag{11}$$

Note that matrix M has even rank because of its skew-symmetry.

If a Lagrangian system $L_0(q, \dot{q})$ is regular with externally imposed *holonomic* constraints $\psi_\alpha(q) = 0$, the system is equivalent [5] to the singular one with Lagrangian $L = L_0 + \lambda_\alpha \phi_\alpha$ and extra generalized coordinates λ_α. Furthermore, the Dirac method can be applied for finding the other constraints inherent in the initial regular system and, hence, not involving the extra dynamical variables.

Therefore, the problem of constraint computation and separation is reduced to manipulation with functions of the coordinates and momenta on the constraint manifold. Generally, there is no algorithmic way for such a manipulation. However, for polynomial functions all the related computations can be done algorithmically by means of Gröbner bases, as we show in the next section.

3   Algorithm Description

Here we describe an algorithm which, given a polynomial Lagrangian whose coefficients are rational numbers, computes the complete set of constraints and separates them into the first and second classes. The algorithm combines the above described Dirac method with the Gröbner bases technique. By this reason we call it algorithm Dirac-Gröbner. All the below used concepts, definitions and constructive methods related to Gröbner bases are explained, for instance, in textbooks [13–15].

At first we present the algorithm under assumption that a polynomial ideal generated by constraints is radical. This is true for most of real practical problems. Next, we indicate how to modify the algorithm to treat the most general (non-radical) case.

Algorithm Dirac-Gröbner

Input: $L(q, \dot{q})$, a polynomial Lagrangian ($L \in Q[q, \dot{q}]$)

Output: Φ_1 and Φ_2, sets of the first and second class constraints, respectively.

1. Computation of the canonical Hamiltonian and primary constraints:
   (a) Construct the polynomial set $F = \cup_{i=1}^n \{p_i - \partial L/\partial \dot{q}_i\}$ in variables $p, q, \dot{q}$.
   (b) Compute the Gröbner basis G of the ideal in ring $Q[p, q, \dot{q}]$ generated by F with respect to an ordering[3] which eliminates $\dot{q}$. Then compute the canonical Hamiltonian as the normal form of (3) modulo G.
   (c) Find the set Φ of primary constraint polynomials as $G \cap Q[p, q]$. If $\Phi = \emptyset$, then stop since the system is regular. Otherwise, go to the next step.

2. Computation of the complete set of constraints:
   (a) Take $G = \Phi$ for the Gröbner basis G of the ideal generated by Φ in $Q[p, q]$ with respect to the ordering induced by that chosen at Step 1(b). Fix this ordering in the sequel.
   (b) Construct the total Hamiltonian in form (5) with multipliers u_α treated as symbolic constants (parameters).
   (c) For every element ϕ_α in Φ compute the normal form h of the Poisson bracket $\{H_t, \phi_\alpha\}$ modulo G. If $h \neq 0$ and no multipliers u_β occur in it, then enlarge set Φ with h, and compute the Gröbner basis G for the enlarged set.
   (d) If $G = \{1\}$, stop because the system is inconsistent. Otherwise, repeat the previous step until the consistency condition (8) is satisfied for every element in Φ irrespective of multipliers u_α. This gives the complete set of constraints $\Phi = \{\phi_1, \ldots, \phi_k\}$.

---

[3] An elimination ordering which induced the degree-reverse-lexicographical one for monomials in p and q is heuristically best for efficiency reasons.

3. Separation of constraints into first and second classes:

   (a) Construct matrix M in (11) by computing the normal forms of its elements modulo G, and determine rank r of M. If $r = k$, stop with $\Phi_1 = \emptyset$, $\Phi_2 = \Phi$. If $r = 0$, stop with $\Phi_1 = \Phi$ and $\Phi_2 = \emptyset$. Otherwise, go to the next step.

   (b) Find a basis $A = \{a_1, \dots, a_{k-r}\}$ of the null space (kernel) of the linear transformation defined by M. For every vector a in A construct a first class constraint as $a_\alpha \phi_\alpha$. Collect them in set Φ_1.

   (c) Construct $(k - r) \times k$ matrix $(a_j)_\alpha$ from components of vectors in A and find a basis $B = \{b_1, \dots, b_r\}$ of the null space of the corresponding linear transformation. For every vector b in B construct a second class constraint as $b_\alpha \phi_\alpha$. Collect them in set Φ_2.

The correctness of Steps 1, 2 and 3(a) of the algorithm is provided by the properties of Gröbner bases [13–15] and by the following facts: (i) the definition (3) of the canonical Hamiltonian implies its independence of $\dot{q}$ on the primary constraint manifold (4); (ii) whenever a multiplier u_α in (5) is differentiated when the Poisson bracket in (8) is evaluated, the corresponding term vanishes on the constraint manifold. The correctness of Steps 3(b) and 3(c) follows from definition (10) of the first class constraints and the correctness of Step 3(a). The termination of algorithm Dirac-Gröbner follows from the finiteness of the Gröbner basis G which is constructed at Step 2(c).

Now consider the most general case when the constraints obtained from (8) lead to a non-radical ideal. It should be noted that the ideal generated by the primary constraint polynomials (Step 1) is always radical. This is provided by linearity of (2) in momenta. However, already the first secondary constraint added may destroy this property of the ideal. Therefore, the algorithm needs one more step, namely, Step 2(e), where the Gröbner basis G of the radical ideal for the polynomial set Φ is computed. Next, every constraint polynomial in Φ is replaced by its normal form modulo G. All the elements with zero normal forms are eliminated from the set. The extra step is also algorithmic. There are algorithms for construction of a basis, and, hence, a Gröbner basis, of the radical of a given ideal, which are built-in in some computer algebra systems (see [13–15] for more details and references). One can also check the radical membership of h at Step 2(c) before its adding to Φ. This check is easily done [13,14], but in any case Step 2, for the correctness of Step 3, must end up with the radical sets Φ and G.

We implemented algorithm Dirac-Gröbner, as it presented above for the radical case, in Maple V Release 5. The implementation is relied on the built-in system facilities for computation and manipulation with Gröbner bases and for linear algebra. Using our Maple code for different examples from physics and mechanics, we experimentally observed that in those infrequent cases when the constraint ideals are non-radical this can easily be detected from the structure of the output set.

4   Examples

In this section we illustrate, by examples from physics and mechanics, the application of algorithm Dirac-Gröbner.

Example 1. $SU(2)$ Yang-Mills mechanics in $0+1$ dimensional space-time [8]. This is a constrained physical model with gauge symmetry. The model Lagrangian is given by $L = \frac{1}{2}(D_t)_i(D_t)_i$, $(D_t x)_i = \dot{x}_i + g\epsilon_{ijk}y_j x_k$ ($1 \leq i, j, k \leq 3$). Here x_i and y_i are the generalized coordinates and tensor ϵ_{ijk} is antisymmetric in its indices with $\epsilon_{123} = 1$. Respectively, the primary constraints and the canonical Hamiltonian are $p_i^y = 0$ and $H_c = \frac{1}{2} - \epsilon_{ijk}x_j p_k y_i$ with the momenta given by $p_i^y = \partial L/\partial \dot{y}_i$ and $p_i = \partial L/\partial \dot{x}_i$. The other constraints in the complete set computed by the algorithm are $\phi_i = \epsilon_{ijk}x_j p_k = 0$, and all the six constraints found are of the first class.

Example 2. Point particle of mass m moving on the surface of a sphere (rigid rotator). The movement is described by the regular Lagrangian $L_0 = \frac{1}{2}m^2(\dot{q_1}^2 + \dot{q_2}^2 + \dot{q_3}^2)/2 \equiv \frac{1}{2}m^2\dot{q}^2$ with the externally imposed holonomic constraint $\phi(q) = q^2 - 1 = 0$. This system is equivalent to the singular Lagrangian system $L = L_0 + \lambda\phi$, where λ is an extra coordinate. There is the only primary constraint $p_\lambda = 0$ ($p_\lambda = \partial L/\partial \lambda$), and the canonical Hamiltonian is $H_c = \frac{1}{2}m^2 p^2 - \lambda\phi(q)$ ($p_i = \partial L/\partial q_i$). The complete set of constraint polynomials for the singular system contains four second class polynomials $\{p_\lambda, \phi(q), p_i q_i, 2m\lambda + p^2\}$. Coming back to the initial regular system, the first and the last polynomials in the set must be omitted since they determine the extra dynamical variables.

Example 3. Singular physical system with both first and second class constraints[4]. The system Lagrangian is $L = q_1(\dot{q}_2 - \dot{q}_3) - \dot{q}_1 q_2$. There are three primary constraint polynomials $\{p_1 + q_2, p_2 - q_1, p_3\}$. The canonical Hamiltonian is $H_c = q_1 q_2$. One more constraint polynomial q_1 is found by the Dirac-Gröbner algorithm. The sets Φ_1 and Φ_2 of the first and second classes are $\{p_2 + q_1, p_3\}$ and $\{p_1 + q_2, q_1\}$, respectively. Note that this system has no physical degrees of freedom (c.f. [16]).

Example 4. Inconsistent singular system [4]: $L = \frac{1}{2}\dot{q}_1^2 + q_2$. There is the single primary constraint $p_2 = 0$. The canonical Hamiltonian is $H_c = p_1^2/2 - q_2$. At Step 2(c) of algorithm Dirac-Gröbner the inconsistency $\dot{p}_2 = 1$ occurs. The algorithm detects this inconsistency and stops.

The above examples are rather small and can be treated by hand. With our Maple code we have already tried successfully much more nontrivial examples. For instance, we computed and separated the constraints for the $SU(2)$ Yang-Mills mechanics in $3 + 1$ dimensional space-time [8]. Surprisingly, this

---

[4] A.Burnel. Private communication.

computation took only a few seconds on an Pentium 100 personal computer though the model Lagrangian and the canonical Hamiltonian are rather cumbersome polynomials of the 4th degree in 21 variables.

References

1. Dirac, P.A.M.: Generalized Hamiltonian Dynamics. *Canad. J. Math.* **2** (1950), 129-148; *Lectures on Quantum Mechanics*, Belfer Graduate School of Science, Monographs Series, Yeshiva University, New York, 1964.
2. Gitman, D.M., Tyutin, I.V.: *Quantization of Fields with Constraints*, Springer-Verlag, Bonn, 1990.
3. Henneaux, M., Teitelboim, C.: *Quantization of Gauge Systems*, Princeton University Press, Princeton, New Jersey, 1992.
4. Prokhorov, L.V., Shabanov, S.V.: *Hamiltonian Mechanics of Gauge Systems*, St. Petersburg University, 1997 (in Russian).
5. Seiler, W.M.: Numerical Integration of Constrained Hamiltonian Systems Using Dirac Brackets. *Math. Comp.* **68** (1999) 661-681.
6. Brenan, K.E., Campbell, S.L., Petzold, L.R.: *Numerical Solution of Intial-Value Problems in Differential-Algebraic Equations*, Classics in Applied Mathematics **14**, SIAM, Philadelphia, 1996.
7. Sundermeyer, K.: *Constrained Dynamics*, Lecture Notes in Physics **169**, Springer-Verlag, New York, Berlin, 1982.
8. Gogilidze, S.A., Khvedelidze, A.M., Mladenov, D.M., Pavel, H.-P.: Hamiltonian Reduction of $SU(2)$ Dirac-Yang-Mills Mechanics, *Phys. Rev.* **D57** (1998) 7488-7500.
9. Arnold, V.I.: *Mathematical Methods of Classical Mechanics*, Graduate Texts in Mathematics **60**, Springer-Verlag, New York, 1978.
10. Tombal, Ph., Moussiaux, A.: MACSYMA Computation of the Dirac-Bergman Algorithms for Hamiltonian Systems with Constraints. *J. Symb. Comp.* **1** (1985) 419-421.
11. Chaichian, M., Martinez, D.L., Lusanna, L.: Dirac's Constrained Systems: The Classification of Second Class Constraints. *Ann. Phys. (N.Y.)* **232** (1994) 40-60.
12. Battle, C., Comis, J., Pons, J.M., Roman-Roy, N.: Equivalence Between the Lagrangian and Hamiltonian Formalism for Constrained Systems. *J. Math. Phys.* **27** (1986) 2953-2962.
13. Becker, T., Weispfenning, V., Kredel, H.: *Gröbner Bases. A Computational Approach to Commutative Algebra*, Graduate Texts in Mathematics **141**, Springer-Verlag, New York, 1993.
14. Cox, D., Little, J., O'Shea, D.: *Ideals, Varieties and Algorithms*, 2nd Edition, Springer-Verlag, New York, 1996.
15. Cox, D., Little, J., O'Shea, D.: *Using Algebraic Geometry*, Graduate Texts in Mathematics **185**, Springer-Verlag, New York, 1998.
16. Seiler, W.M., Tucker, R.W.: Involution and Constrained Dynamics. *J. Phys. A.* **28** (1995) 4431-4451.
17. Pommaret, J.F.: *Partial Differential Equations and Group Theory. New Perspectives for Applications*, Kluwer, Dordrecht, 1994.

Construction of Involutive Monomial Sets for Different Involutive Divisions

Vladimir P. Gerdt[1], Vladimir V.Kornyak[1], Matthias Berth[2], and Günter Czichowski[2]

[1] Laboratory of Computing Techniques and Automation
Joint Institute for Nuclear Research
141980 Dubna, Russia
gerdt@jinr.ru
[2] Department of Mathematics and Informatics
University of Greifswald
D17487 Greifswald, Germany
berth@rz.uni-greifswald.de
czicho@rz.uni-greifswald.de

Abstract. We consider computational and implementation issues for the completion of monomial sets to involution using different involutive divisions. Every of these divisions produces its own completion procedure. For the polynomial case it yields an involutive basis which is a special form of a Gröbner basis, generally redundant. We also compare our *Mathematica* implementation of Janet division to an implementation in C.

1 Introduction and Basic Definitions

In our previous paper [1] we described our first results on implementing in *Mathematica* 3.0 [2] different involutive divisions introduced in [3–5]; the completion of monomial sets to involution for those divisions and application to constructing Hilbert functions and Hilbert polynomials for monomial ideals.

In the present paper we pay more attention to efficient computation and propose some algorithmic improvements. Besides, we shortly describe an implementation of Janet division in C and compare the running times for both implementations. Though in this paper we consider involutivity of monomial ideals, all the underlying operations with involutive divisions and monomials enter in more general completion procedures for polynomial [3,4] and differential systems [9].

Let $\mathbb{N}$ be a set of non-negative integers, and $\mathbb{M} = \{x_1^{d_1} \cdots x_n^{d_n} \mid d_i \in \mathbb{N}\}$ be a set of monomials in the polynomial ring $K[x_1, \ldots, x_n]$ over a field K of characteristic zero. By $deg(u)$ and $deg_i(u)$ we denote the total degree of $u \in \mathbb{M}$ and the degree of variable x_i in u, respectively. For the least common multiple of two monomials $u, v \in \mathbb{M}$ we shall use the conventional notation $lcm(u, v)$. An admissible monomial ordering is denoted by $\succ$, and throughout this paper we shall assume that it is compatible with

$$x_1 \succ x_2 \succ \cdots \succ x_n . \tag{1}$$

Definition 1. [3] An *involutive division* L on $\mathbb{M}$ is given, if for any finite monomial set $U \subset \mathbb{M}$ and for any $u \in U$ there is given a submonoid $L(u, U)$ of $\mathbb{M}$ satisfying the conditions:

(a) If $w \in L(u, U)$ and $v|w$, then $v \in L(u, U)$.
(b) If $u, v \in U$ and $uL(u, U) \cap vL(v, U) \neq \emptyset$,
   then $u \in vL(v, U)$ or $v \in uL(u, U)$.
(c) If $v \in U$ and $v \in uL(u, U)$, then $L(v, U) \subseteq L(u, U)$.
(d) If $V \subseteq U$, then $L(u, U) \subseteq L(u, V)$ for all $u \in V$.

Elements of $L(u, U)$ are called *multiplicative* for u. If $w \in uL(u, U)$ we shall write $u|_L w$ and call u an *(L−)involutive divisor* of w. In such an event the monomial $v = w/u$ is *multiplicative* for u and the equality $w = uv$ will be written as $w = u \times v$. If u is a conventional divisor of w but not an involutive one we shall write, as usual, $w = u \cdot v$. Then v is said to be *nonmultiplicative* for u.

For every monomial $u \in U$, Definition 1 provides the separation

$$\{x_1, \ldots, x_n\} = M_L(u, U) \cup NM_L(u, U), \tag{2}$$

$M_L(u, U) \cap NM_L(u, U) = \emptyset$, of the set of variables into two subsets: *multiplicative* $M_L(u, U) \subset L(u, U)$ and *nonmultiplicative* $NM_L(u, U) \cap L(u, U) = \emptyset$. Conversely, if for any finite set $U \subset \mathbb{M}$ and any $u \in U$ the separation (2) is given such that the corresponding submonoid $L(u, U)$ of monomials in variables in $M_L(u, U)$ satisfies the conditions (b)-(d), then the partition generates an involutive division.

Definition 2. [3] Given an involutive division L, a monomial set U is *involutive* with respect to L or $L−$*involutive* if

$$(\forall u \in U) \ (\forall w \in \mathbb{M}) \ (\exists v \in U) \ [\ uw \in vL(v, U) \ ].$$

In this paper as well as in [1] we shall consider the following eight different involutive divisions studied in [3–5]:

Example 3. Thomas division [6]. Given a finite set $U \subset \mathbb{M}$, the variable x_i is considered as multiplicative for $u \in U$ if

$$deg_i(u) = \max\{deg_i(v) \mid v \in U\},$$

and nonmultiplicative, otherwise.

Example 4. Janet division [7]. Let the set $U \subset \mathbb{M}$ be finite. For each $1 \leq i \leq n$ divide U into groups labeled by non-negative integers $d_1, \ldots, d_i$:

$$[d_1, \ldots, d_i] = \{ \ u \ \in U \mid d_j = deg_j(u), \ 1 \leq j \leq i \ \}.$$

A variable x_i is multiplicative for $u \in U$ if $i = 1$ and $deg_1(u) = \max\{deg_1(v) \mid v \in U\}$, or if $i > 1$, $u \in [d_1, \ldots, d_{i-1}]$ and $deg_i(u) = \max\{deg_i(v) \mid v \in [d_1, \ldots, d_{i-1}]\}$.

Example 5. Pommaret division [8]. For a monomial $u = x_1^{d_1} \cdots x_k^{d_k}$ with $d_k > 0$ the variables $x_j, j \geq k$ are considered as multiplicative and the other variables as nonmultiplicative. For $u = 1$ all the variables are multiplicative.

Example 6. Division I [4]. Let U be a finite monomial set. The variable x_i is nonmultiplicative for $u \in U$ if there is $v \in U$ such that

$$x_{i_1}^{d_1} \cdots x_{i_m}^{d_m} u = lcm(u, v), \quad 1 \leq m \leq [n/2], \quad d_j > 0 \ (1 \leq j \leq m),$$

and $x_i \in \{x_{i_1}, \ldots, x_{i_m}\}$.

Example 7. Division II [4]. For monomial $u = x_1^{d_1} \cdots x_k^{d_n}$ the variable x_i is multiplicative if $d_i = d_{\max}(u)$ where $d_{\max}(u) = \max\{d_1, \ldots, d_n\}$.

Example 8. Induced division [5]. Given an admissible monomial ordering $\succ$ a variable x_i is nonmultiplicative for $u \in U$ if there is $v \in U$ such that $v \prec u$ and $deg_i(u) < deg_i(v)$.

To distinguish these divisions we use the abbreviations T, J, P, I, II, D In the implementation described below, three orderings are used to induce division in Example 8: lexicographical, degree-lexicographical and degree-reverse-lexicographical. For these three induced divisions we shall use the subscripts L, DL, DRL, respectively.

Every of the above divisions generates its own procedure for completion of a monomial set to involution by means of its enlargement with involutively irreducible nonmultiplicative prolongations. Given a monomial basis and an involutive division, the following algorithm **MinimalInvolutiveMonomialBasis** [3] produces the uniquely defined minimal involutive basis of the ideal.

Algorithm **MinimalInvolutiveMonomialBasis:**

Input: U, a finite monomial set
Output: $\bar{U}$, the minimal involutive basis of $Id(U)$

begin	1
$\quad \bar{U} := Autoreduce(U)$	2
$\quad$ **choose** any admissible monomial ordering $\prec$	3
$\quad$ **while** exist $u \in \bar{U}$ and $x \in NM_L(u, \bar{U})$ s.t.	4
$\quad\quad u \cdot x$ has no involutive divisors in $\bar{U}$ **do**	5
$\quad\quad$ **choose** such u, x with the lowest $u \cdot x$ w.r.t. $\prec$	6
$\quad\quad \bar{U} := \bar{U} \cup \{u \cdot x\}$	7
$\quad$ **end**	8
end	9

Here *Autoreduce(U)* stands for the conventional (non-involutive) autoreduction.

2 Implementation Issues

In this section we will describe some observations that allow to speed up the steps of the algorithm **MinimalInvolutiveMonomialBasis** significantly. Some of them are applicable to different divisions, others are concerned with the completion procedure in general. The basic operations on monomial sets are the same for the computation of involutive bases of polynomial [3,4] and differential systems [9], so the improvements described here are relevant for these computations.

Our package provides a framework for studying the effect of using different divisions and optimizations. It is implemented using a "generic programming" approach which allows to start with a straightforward implementation of the algorithm and introduce more efficient procedures for special situations later.

The following statement returns the minimal involutive basis of a monomial set U with respect to Janet division and with lexicographic selection ordering:

```
minimalInvolutiveMonomialBasis[Janet][U,lexorder]
```

To extend the package for a new involutive division (called, say, `newDivision`), one would only have to write the specific version of the function `separation` which computes the multiplicative and nonmultiplicative variables of a monomial $u \in U$ w.r.t. the set U:

```
separation[newDivision][u_,U_]:=...
```

All the other steps in the algorithm would then be executed by functions that are generically defined for any involutive division.

On the other hand, an optimized procedure for a specific situation can be introduced later to override the generic version. The pattern matching mechanism in *Mathematica* dispatches to the specific version wherever it is appropriate.

Monomials are represented as multiindices, i.e. the monomial $x_1^{i_1} \cdot \ldots \cdot x_n^{i_n}$ is represented as the list of its exponents $\{i_1, \ldots, i_n\}$. Thus, the set $U = \{u_1, \ldots, u_m\}$ can be considered as a $m \times n-$ matrix of integers. For every monomial u, we use two additional lists of length n: a list giving the separation of the variables for u, and a similar list containing notes about the prolongations that have already been done.

We will now describe observations that can be used to make the basic operations of the algorithm **MinimalInvolutiveMonomialBasis** faster. Functions like *lcm* will be applied also to multiindices, with the obvious meaning. The set notation is used for lists, assuming that the order of the elements is given somehow. $U = \{u_1, \ldots, u_n\}$ is a list of monomials, and u is always an element of U.

The first step is to compute the separation for each of the input monomials. For globally defined divisions, this is done irrespective of the other monomials in U. For Janet division (Example 4), we made use of the following remark:

Remark 1. When the list U is sorted lexicographically in decreasing order, the groups $[d_1, \ldots, d_i]$ mentioned in the definition are grouped together. These groups are sorted lexicographically with respect to their labels of any fixed length i. The sorted list starts with the group labeled $[d_{1\,max}], d_{1\,max} = \max deg_1 u$, the monomials in $[d_{1\,max}]$ have x_1 as a multiplicative variable. We can split the list into groups given by labels of length 1 and proceed recursively within each of them, next considering degrees in the second variable x_2, and so on.

For a division $D_\succ$ (Example 8) that is induced by some ordering $\succ$, we can use an auxiliary list:

Remark 2. Let the monomials be sorted in descending order: $u_1 \succ \ldots \succ u_n$. We call the elements of the list $\mathrm{cm}(U) := \{m_1, \ldots, m_n | m_i = \mathrm{lcm}(u_i, \ldots, u_n), i = n, \ldots, 1\}$

the cumulated multiples of U. By definition, variable x_j is nonmultiplicative for u_i if and only if it has a higher degree in m_i: $deg_j u_i < deg_j m_i$. Thus, all we have to do is compute the list $\mathrm{cm}(U)$ of cumulated multiples and then compare each $u \in U$ against its corresponding entry in $\mathrm{cm}(U)$.

For Division I, we are not aware of any property that would allow us to accelerate the computation of separations in a manner similar to Janet or Induced divisions.

The following observation can be used to speed up the process of finding a minimal nonmultiplicative prolongation (line 6 of the algorithm). Let us denote the minimal (w.r.t. the chosen ordering $\succ$) nonmultiplicative prolongation by a given variable x with $P_\succ(x)$.

Remark 3. Let U be sorted w.r.t. the completion ordering: $u_1 \succ \ldots \succ u_n$. Let u_i and x be fixed such that $u_i \cdot x$ is a minimal nonmultiplicative prolongation w.r.t. $\succ$. Then $u_i \cdot x$ is an element of the set $\{P_\succ(x_1), \ldots, P_\succ(x_n)\}$.

This follows directly from the minimality of $u_i \cdot x$. Furthermore, u_i is the minimal monomial having x as a nonmultiplicative variable, because $v \cdot x \succ u \cdot x$ implies $v \succ u$.

The remark obviously extends to the more general situation of the algorithm, where some of the nonmultiplicative prolongations have already been considered. We keep a list $P = \{P_\succ(x_1), \ldots, P_\succ(x_n)\}$ of nonmultiplicative prolongations, one for each variable $x_1, \ldots, x_n$, sorted by the completion ordering. Let $v = u_i \cdot x_j$ be the minimal prolongation. It is removed from P and checked for involutive divisors. If v is involutively reducible, we have to add another prolongation w.r.t. *the same variable* x_j to P. Otherwise, we add v to the monomial set and recompute the separations and P.

The next step in the algorithm is to search for an involutive divisor w of a nonmultiplicative prolongation $v = u \cdot x$. In the polynomial case, the efficiency of this search can be even more important, since we may want to involutively reduce every term of a prolonged polynomial. Recall that for an involutively reduced set U, there can be at most one such w. We present now some optimizations that apply to increasingly specialized situations.

The following remark uses a special property of involutive divisions, taking into account that v is a nonmultiplicative prolongation of an element of U.

Remark 4. Let U be an involutively autoreduced set of monomials and $v = u \cdot x$ a nonmultiplicative prolongation of some $u \in U$. If a monomial $w \in U$ is an involutive divisor of v then $deg_x w = deg_x v$.

Since $u \cdot x$ should be involutively reducible by w, we can write $u \cdot x = w \times (u \cdot x/w)$. If $w = v = u \cdot x$, we are done. If $w \neq u \cdot x$ and $w|u$, then $u = w \times (u/w)$, which contradicts our assumption that U is involutively autoreduced.

One can gain even more by considering particular divisions. Consider a Janet-autoreduced set U. Let us denote the *longest common prefix* of two monomials u, v by $lcp(u, v)$, where $lcp(u, v) := (u_1, \ldots, u_k)$ with $(u_1, \ldots, u_k) = (v_1, \ldots, v_k)$, and k the maximal index for which u_k and v_k coincide. If $u_1 \neq v_1$, we define $lcp(u, v) := ()$. More generally, we use $lcp(v, U)$ to denote the longest common prefix that v shares with some monomial from the set U.

Remark 5. Assume that we search for a Janet - involutive divisor w of a monomial v. Then, w is in the class $\mathbb{C}$ defined by the label $lcp(v, U)$. Let $lcp(v, U) = (v_1, \ldots, v_k)$. Every involutive divisor $w = (w_1, \ldots, w_n)$ is also a conventional divisor, thus $w_i \leq v_i, i = 1, \ldots, k$. We show by contradiction that $w_i = v_i =$ for $i = 1, \ldots, k$. Let s be the smallest integer $1 \leq s \leq k$ such that $w_s < v_s$. Then, x_s is nonmultiplicative for w because there exists a monomial in the class $(v_1, \ldots, v_{s-1})$ which has higher degree in x_s, and w is not an involutive divisor of v.

Note that this remark applies to arbitrary monomials v, not only those resulting from a nonmultiplicative prolongation.

Consider a nonmultiplicative prolongation $v = u \cdot x$. For Pommaret division, an involutive divisor w is reverse lexicographically greater than u. For a division that is induced by $\succ$, either $u \cdot x = w$ or $u \succ w$ holds.

These properties together with Remark 3.12 in [1] suggest that one should keep the monomials sorted with respect to some suitable order, and use this order as completion order, too.

Finally, when we find no involutive divisor, we have to add the prolongation to the set and adjust separations for all monomials accordingly. Except for globally defined divisions, this step is potentially very time consuming.

Remark 6. For all divisions discussed so far, the following holds for a monomial $u \in U$: $NM(u, U \cup \{v\}) = NM(u, U) \cup NM(u, \{u, v\})$.

A detailed discussion of this fact can be found in [5]. After adding a monomial v to U, this remark allows us to compute only the "pairwise" separations for every $u \in U$.

Specific divisions give rise to more improvements.

Remark 7. Let v be a monomial, and assume that v has no involutive divisor in the Janet-autoreduced set U. Then, the separation may only change for monomials in the class $lcp(v, U) = (v_1, \ldots, v_k)$. The separation of the variables $x_1, \ldots, x_k$ is left unchanged. Furthermore, the separation of the variables $x_1, \ldots, x_k$ for the new monomial v can be copied from the separation of any of the monomials in the class $lcp(v, U)$.

Remark 8. Consider adding a nonmultiplicative prolongation $v = u \cdot x_j$ to an autoreduced set w.r.t. some induced division $D_{\succ}$.

Only the variable x_j can change from multiplicative to nonmultiplicative, and it can do so only for monomials $s \succ v$ satisfying $deg_j s = deg_j v - 1$.

Not all of the improvements mentioned here were actually implemented in the package. Our experience suggests that sometimes the practical performance in *Mathematica* differs from what one expects from looking at the algorithm. This is due to the interpreted nature of *Mathematica* and its flexible evaluation mechanism. Operations which are performed in the kernel are usually much faster than their equivalent expressed in a user defined function, and it was often a matter of trial and error to decide which variant of an operation one should use for a given division.

In practice, the size of the resulting involutive basis is certainly the dominating factor for the overall running time of the algorithm. It was thus worthwhile to invest more programming work in improvements for those divisions which yield relatively small involutive bases (see below).

The improvements for Janet division resulted in the biggest gain in speed compared to the generic implementation. When the completion ordering is lexicographic, all optimizations described above are applied. For induced divisions $D_{\succ}$, we always use $\succ$ as completion ordering and Remark 2 to recompute the separations. Only for Division I, the time for changing the separations dominates the time for the other basic operations. Division I is also the only division for which the property mentioned in Remark 6 is used. The optimizations for finding an involutive divisor described above have a positive effect for all divisions.

We have applied the package to examples taken from various sources. For each polynomial system, we computed the degree - reverse - lexicographical Gröbner basis and took the resulting set of leading monomials as input to the algorithm **MinimalInvolutiveMonomialBasis**. As we described in [1] the output can then be used to compute the Hilbert function, the Hilbert polynomial and the index of regularity of the corresponding polynomial ideal.

Example 9. [11] Consider a $n \times n$ matrix $A = \left(\alpha_{ij}\right)_{n,n}$ with unspecified entries. The condition $A^2 = 0$ leads to a system of n^2 polynomial equations in the variables $\alpha_{11}, \ldots, \alpha_{1n}, \alpha_{21}, \ldots, \alpha_{nn}$. We treated the leading monomials of the degree reverse lexicographic Gröbner basis, where the variables are ordered according to $\alpha_{11} \succ \ldots \succ \alpha_{1n} \succ \alpha_{21} \succ \ldots \succ \alpha_{nn}$.

Example 10. The system of "n-th cyclic roots" is a well known example. For $n = 4$, it is given by:

$$x_1 + x_2 + x_3 + x_4 = 0,$$
$$x_1 x_2 + x_2 x_3 + x_3 x_4 + x_4 x_1 = 0,$$
$$x_1 x_2 x_3 + x_2 x_3 x_4 + x_3 x_4 x_1 + x_4 x_1 x_=2 = 0,$$
$$x_1 x_2 x_3 x_4 - 1 = 0.$$

Example 11. The Reimer system in 5 variables:

$$1 - 2x_1^2 + 2x_2^2 + 2x_3^2 + 2 * x_4^2 - 2x_5^2 = 0,$$
$$1 - 2x_1^3 + 2x_2^3 + 2x_3^3 + 2 * x_4^3 - 2x_5^3 = 0,$$
$$1 - 2x_1^4 + 2x_2^4 + 2x_3^4 + 2 * x_4^4 - 2x_5^4 = 0,$$
$$1 - 2x_1^5 + 2x_2^5 + 2x_3^5 + 2 * x_4^5 - 2x_5^5 = 0,$$
$$1 - 2x_1^6 + 2x_2^6 + 2x_3^6 + 2 * x_4^6 - 2x_5^6 = 0.$$

Example 12. The Katsura system in 7 variables:

$$x_1^2 - x_1 + 2x_2^2 + 2x_3^2 + 2x_4^2 + 2x_5^2 + 2x_6^2 + 2x_7^2,$$
$$2x_2 x_1 + 2x_2 x_3 + 2x_3 x_4 + 2x_4 x_5 + 2x_5 x_6 + 2x_6 x_7 - x_2,$$
$$2x_3 x_1 + 2x_2 x_4 + 2x_3 x_5 + 2x_4 x_6 + 2x_5 x_7 + x_2^2 - x_3,$$
$$2x_4 x_1 + 2x_2 x_5 + 2x_3 x_6 + 2x_4 x_7 + 2x_2 x_3 - x_4,$$
$$2x_5 x_1 + 2x_2 x_6 + 2x_3 x_7 + 2x_2 x_4 + x_3^2 - x_5,$$
$$2x_6 x_1 + 2x_2 x_7 + 2x_2 x_5 + 2x_3 x_4 - x_6,$$
$$x_1 + 2x_2 + 2x_3 + 2x_4 + 2x_5 + 2x_6 + 2x_7 - 1.$$

The following table shows the results of applying the algorithm **MinimalInvolutiveMonomialBasis** to our examples. In the first three columns, the size of the input is given where m is the number of monomials, n is the number of variables, and d is the maximum total degree of the input monomials. The divisions are indicated by the abbreviations used above. For each division, we give the length of the minimal involutive monomial basis, the number of prolongations considered during completion, the portion of reducible prolongations, and the computation time. Thus, 100% reducible prolongations means that the input is already an involutive basis. An empty entry in the column for Pommaret division means that we did not compute a minimal Pommaret basis because the ideal is not zero dimensional. For the other divisions, it means that the timing is larger than 10000 seconds at our computer[1]. For some examples, bases for two different divisions may coincide. For the fourth cyclic roots (Example 10), the bases for Thomas division and Division I, as well as those for Janet division and the induced division D_{DL} coincide, respectively.

The computations with monomial sets should give at least some hint to the performance of different divisions in the polynomial and differential cases. From our experience, Janet division, generally, and Induced divisions, sometimes, seem to be the most promising in terms of prolongations that have to be considered. Pommaret division – even though it is not noetherian – deserves further investigation, because it is globally defined and rather "compact", too.

3 Conclusion

In addition to the above described implementation of different involutive divisions in *Mathematica* we implemented the completion algorithm for Janet division (Example 4) in C. In this case an input monomial set is represented as an array of lexicographically ordered multiindices and its completion is done with respect to the same order. This choice of completion ordering was motivated by the monotonicity of Janet division with respect to the lexicographical order. The partial involutivity of an intermediate monomial set is preserved in the course of completion and the time for recomputation of the separations is minimized [5].

The set of nonmultiplicative prolongations to be treated is also represented as a lexicographically sorted array of multiindices, that provides the simplest way to choose a minimal prolongation. Every time an irreducible nonmultiplicative prolongation occurs it is inserted in the intermediate monomial set and its nonmultiplicative prolongations are inserted in the prolongation set. The determination of their position in the sorted arrays is performed using the binary search algorithm. In so doing, the check of Janet reducibility of the prolongation under consideration is done in the course of the position determination. This is a rather straightforward procedure that makes use of the partition into prefix-groups as defined in Example 4.

The C implementation was done in GNU C/C++ version 2.81 on a 100 MHz Pentium computer running Windows 95. The running times for examples in the above table are less than 0.01 seconds, except Example 9 for $n = 4$ which took about 5 seconds.

---

[1] a 200 MHz 586 running Linux

Input	Size			Division							
	m	n	d	J	T	P	I	II	D_L	D_{DRL}	D_{DL}
Ex. 11	38	5	8	**55** 190 91% 3.7 s	**4392** 17406 75% 4484 s	**55** 190 91% 3.4 s	—	**151** 503 77% 11 s	**242** 798 74% 48 s	**894** 3994 79% 556 s	**594** 2639 79% 267 s
Ex. 12	41	7	7	**43** 211 99% 3.5 s	—	**43** 211 99% 3.7 s	—	**201** 861 81% 20 s	**201** 892 82% 44 s	**1337** 7600 83% 1500 s	**1346** 7663 83% 1539 s
cyc 4	7	4	6	**7** 14 100% 0.19 s	**98** 242 62% 5.4 s	—	**98** 242 62% 18 s	**25** 55 67% 0.87 s	**41** 92 63% 2.3 s	**9** 20 90% 0.33 s	**7** 14 100% 0.21 s
cyc 5	20	5	8	**23** 76 96% 1.1 s	**1010** 3544 72% 266 s	**23** 76 96% 1.1 s	**1010** 3544 72% 1656s	**93** 297 75% 5.5 s	**154** 488 72% 21 s	**135** 548 79% 21 s	**106** 419 79% 14 s
cyc 6	45	6	9	**46** 194 99% 3.2 s	—	**46** 194 99% 3.1 s	—	**201** 807 81% 19 s	**385** 1527 78% 123 s	**841** 4230 81% 586 s	**972** 4899 81% 754 s
Ex. 9 $n = 3$	25	9	4	**56** 239 87% 4.5 s	—	—	—	**612** 2972 80% 131 s	**531** 2920 83% 313 s	**1711** 9362 82% 2593 s	**1479** 8044 82% 2048 s
Ex. 9 $n = 4$	161	16	6	**1324** 11836 90% 923 s	—	—	—	—	—	—	—

We plan to extend both *Mathematica* and C codes to polynomial and then to linear differential systems. Whereas the highly flexible and easily extensible *Mathematica* code allows one to experiment with different involutive divisions, in the further development of the C code we are going to restrict ourselves to Janet, Pommaret and may be Induced divisions which are more preferable from the computational efficiency point of view.

4   Acknowledgement

The contribution of two of the authors (V.P.G. and V.V.K.) was partially supported by grant INTAS-96-184 and grant from the Russian Foundation for Basic Research No. 98-01-00101.

References

1. Gerdt, V.P., Berth, M., Czichowski, G. (1998). *Involutive Divisions in Mathematica: Implementation and Some Applications*, Proceedings of the 6th Rhein Workshop on Computer Algebra (Sankt-Augustin, Germany, March 31 - April 3, 1998), J.Calmet (Ed.), Institute for Algorithms and Scientific Computing, GMD-SCAI, Sankt-Augustin, 1998.
2. Wolfram, S. (1996) *The Mathematica Book*, Third Edition, Wolfram Media, Inc. and Cambridge University Press.
3. Gerdt, V.P., Blinkov, Yu.A. (1998). Involutive Bases of Polynomial Ideals. *Math. Comp. Simul.* **45**, 519-542.
4. Gerdt, V.P., Blinkov, Yu.A. (1998). Minimal Involutive Bases. *Math. Comp. Simul.* **45**, 543-560.
5. Gerdt, V.P. (1998). Involutive Division Technique: Some Generalizations and Optimizations. Preprint JINR E5-98-151, Dubna. Submitted to CASC'98 (April 20-24, St.Petersburg, Russia).
6. Thomas, J. (1937). *Differential Systems*. American Mathematical Society, New York.
7. Janet, M. (1920). Sur les Systèmes d'Equations aux Dérivées Partielles. *J. Math. Pure et Appl.* **3**, 65-151.
8. Pommaret, J.F. (1978). *Systems of Partial Differential Equations and Lie Pseudogroups*, Gordon & Breach, New York.
9. Gerdt, V.P. (1995). Gröbner Bases and Involutive Methods for Algebraic and Differential Equations. In: *Computer Algebra in Scien= ce and Engineering*, Fleischer, J., Grabmeier, J., Hehl, F.W., Küchlin, W. (eds.), World Scientific, Singapore, pp.117-137; *Math. Comput. Modelling* **25**, No.8/9, 1997, 75-90.
10. Cox, D., Little, J., O'Shea, D. (1996). *Ideals, Varieties and Algorithms. An Introduction to Computational Algebraic Geometry and Commutative Algebra.* 2nd Edition, Springer-Verlag, New-York.
11. Bayer, D., Stillman, M. (1992). Computation of Hilbert Functions. *J. Symb. Comp.* 14, 31-50.

Partial Inverse Heuristic for the Approximate Solution of Non-linear Equations
(Invited Talk)

Gaston H. Gonnet and Allan Bonadio

[1] Informatik E.T.H. Zurich, Switzerland
[2] Waterloo Maple, San Francisco

Abstract. We show how to generate many fix-point iterators of the form $x_{i+1} = F(x_i)$ which could solve a given non-linear equation. In particular, these iterators tend to have good global convergence, and we show examples whereby obscure solutions can be discovered. This methods are only suitable for computer algebra systems, where the equations to be solved can be manipulated in symbolic form. Also, a systematic method for finding most or all solutions to nonlinear equations that have multiple solutions is described. The most successful iterators are constructed to have a small number of occurrences of x_i in F. We use grouping of polynomial terms and expressions in x, e^x and $\ln x$ using known inverse relations to obtain better iterators. Each iterator is tried in a limited way, in the expectation that at least one of them will succeed. This heuristic shows a very good behaviour in most cases, in particular when the answer involves extreme ranges.

1 Introduction

Problem definition. Solving non-linear equations is a classical topic in numerical analysis [7,8,12,14,1,11,10,5]. Many algorithms are well-known and well-studied. Few algorithms give any guarantee that they can find all the roots in a given interval, and the ones which do [13] depend on bounding higher order derivatives. It is fair to say that the behaviour of algorithms under convergence is well understood, and most of them are very efficient. In the absence of convergence, however, the algorithms usually perform a useless walk over the valid domain.

In our experience, the biggest challenge for a zero-finder is this focusing on a convergence area, and not on the performance during convergence. We will use the term *random walk* to describe the sequence of values before the convergence criteria are met, and *refinement* to describe the iterations performed under convergence. In this paper we suggest the use of fixed point iterators to find the first approximations to roots of non-linear equations. These approximate roots may be refined further with other methods.

Convergence, divergence, random walk, invalid domains and slow convergence. Most of the literature is concerned with the refinement phase, which in our experience is the least expensive one. The random walk phase is characterized by one or more of the following scenarios:

(a) *divergence.* The values grow steadily farther from any possible solution. E.g. xe^x when tried on an $x_0 \ll -1$.

(b) *iterating outside valid domains.* This may happen when the user specifies a domain for the solution, e.g. that the solutions be real, or in a given interval, and the computation returns a complex number or a number outside the given interval. Exponent overflow/underflow, division by zero, or other domain errors such as $\arcsin(x)$ where $|x| > 1$ are also symptoms of the same problem.

(c) *convergence to a non-root.* This is the case where the iterator mistakenly converges to a value which is not a root. A good example is the case of $1/x$ for bisection search starting with a positive and a negative value.

(d) *hopelessly slow convergence.* The convergence achieved by an iterator showing linear convergence with a constant very close to 1. Alternatively, showing just linear convergence in a range which is too large. A simple example is using Newton-Raphson on $x^{103} = 0$. For another example, the behaviour shown by $x^{1.001} - x \ln x = 0$ with starting values $x = 10$ and $x = 10^{5000}$ (the solution is $x = 0.7941... \times 10^{3960}$). This problem requires 16609 bisection steps to find the first significant digit of the answer.

(e) *pseudo-stable oscillation.* The iterator gives values belonging to two or more sets in a cyclic sequence. For example, $|x| + 10 - 20e^{-x^2}$ has two zeros at $x = \pm 0.785812...$, but if Newton's method is used, and the iteration is started on an $|x| > 1.911$, the iteration will eventually alternate steadily between $+10$ and -10.

(f) *incomplete multiple solution.* This is a situation where there are many roots, but the rootfinder finds only one of them, or only a few. Most algorithms involve a process where roots are eliminated by algebraic deflation. This leads to an N^2 algorithm as the expression to zero becomes more complicated. For example, $\sin(x) = x/100$ has 63 roots on the real axis.

Witness problems and new algorithms. Usually, advances in most disciplines happen whenever we are confronted with new problems which are not solved by the old theories. In this vein, we present four examples which present serious problems to all systems, in particular to the existing algorithms used in Maple's `fsolve`[2] function.

(1)

$$x^{1.001} - x \ln x = 0$$

for positive x, this equation has two solutions, one small, the other one huge in magnitude.

$$x = 2.721005..., \quad 0.794138... \times 10^{3960}$$

The problem here is to find the large positive root, which was the one wanted by the user who proposed the problem. The large magnitude of the root will make all methods based on classical iterations too slow to converge.

(2)

$$\frac{\sin^{-1} x - \tan x}{x^4} = 0$$

This problem and the next were proposed by Kahan[9]. For positive x, this equation has one solution, $x = 0.9999060124....$ This value is too close to 1, the limit where the function can be evaluated without going into the complex plane. Many algorithms are likely to overshoot (any algorithm based on the derivative or on estimating the derivative is a candidate to overshoot) and will try a value outside the valid range. In this case, the computation is likely to be aborted. To hit the area of convergence without going into values greater than 1 for Newton's method, we would have to start in the range $0.99964 \le x < 1$. This means that an equally spaced grid with at least 2800 values would have to be used.

(3)

$$x^2 + 5 + \ln(|x - \pi|) = 0$$

For positive x, this equation has two roots very close to π, $x = 3.1415923...$ and $x = 3.1415930....$ The difference between each root and π is about 0.348×10^{-6}. The convergence interval for such roots is extremely narrow, and most methods, even when started close to the roots, will diverge away from them. If we would use Newton's iteration, it would converge only if the initial x is within 0.2575×10^{-5} from π. If these initial points were sampled from a uniform grid between 0 and 10, we would need more than 3.8 million points. Graphing software will be often mislead and fail to point these roots.

(4)

$$sin(x) = x/100$$

This equation has 63 real roots in the interval $-96.1 < x < 96.1$, and close-call extrema near $x = \pm 102.4$. The roots come in pairs, each separated by 0.5 to 3.14, closer as you go away from zero. Root pairs occur approximately every 2π. In other words, the roots are systematically spaced; the problem is their multitide. Any good iterator will easily converge to any root given a suitable starting guess. The trick is to find all the roots in a systematic way.

Starting values. When the user does not supply a starting value but supplies a range (or a range is implicit), selecting the starting value is a problem in itself. Ideally we would like to try several starting points in the valid interval, because the iterator may fail for any of the reasons listed above. This suggests the following strategy for all iterators.

```
starting_points := {};
x[0] := most_isolated_valid_point( starting_points );
for i do
    x[i] := F(x[i-1]);
    starting_points := starting_points union {x[i-1]};
    if computation_failed or outside_domain(x[i]) then
        start_again
    else if convergence_achieved then
        successful_finish
    else if i>3 and diverging then
        start_again
    else if acceleration_possible then
        x[i] := acceleration(x[i], x[i-1], ...)
    end if
end do;
```

2   Algorithm of partial inversion

General fixed point iterations. An iterator of the form $x_{i+1} = F(x_i)$ is called a fixed point iterator. The solution of the equation is the fixed point of F. The conditions for convergence are quite straightforward, since a root α of the equation implies $f(\alpha) = 0$, and $\alpha = F(\alpha)$, then

$$x_{i+1} - \alpha = \varepsilon_{i+1} = F(x_i) - F(\alpha) = F'(\xi)\varepsilon_i$$

when ξ is in the interval (x_i, α). So for x where $|F'(x)| < 1$ we have convergence to a root of $f(x)$. Iterators with order of convergence γ satisfy the following asymptotic equation on their errors

$$\varepsilon_{i+1} = O(\varepsilon_i^\gamma)$$

and as a natural consequence, $F'(\alpha) = ... = F^{\gamma-1}(\alpha) = 0$ for integer γ.

Let $\#_x(f)$ be the number of occurrences of the variable x in the algebraic expression for $f(x)$. We will not take into account simplification for the time being, we will just consider the number of occurrences as they appear in the expression as it is written. E.g. $\#_x(x(\sin x - 1)) = 2$, whereas $\#_x(x \sin x - x) = 3$ Of course, any equation for which $\#_x(f) = 1$ is trivial to solve by algebraic isolation, if we know the inverses of all the functions used, even if there are multivalue issues. The cases where $\#_x(f) = 1$ are considered trivial and we will now study the case of $\#_x(f) > 1$ exclusively.

It is easy to see, that if $\#_x(f) = k$, then by algebraic isolation of each of the occurrences of x we can usually compute k iterators of the form $x = F(x)$ derived from $f(x) = 0$. Except for multivalued functions or principal values, all of these iterators will have the same solution set as the original[1]. At this

---

[1] some inverse functions will have to be considered multivalued, and each choice of branch could give a solution. E.g. $\sin x = 1/2$ has infinitely many solutions.

point we will not perform any simplification or any additional manipulation to obtain the iterators. For each occurrence of x we simply isolate it. For example, from $x^{1.001} - x \ln x = 0$ we obtain 3 iterators, namely

$$x^{1.001} - x \ln x = 0 \implies x = (x \ln x)^{1/1.001}$$
$$\implies x = \frac{x^{1.001}}{\ln x}$$
$$\implies x = e^{x^{1.001}/x}$$

and we intentionally did not simplify any of the resulting iterators. As we will see in the next section, it is, in general, possible to obtain more iterators from one equation.

We are now ready to describe the heuristic algorithm. For $f(x) = 0$ we compute all the iterators generated by isolation, $F_1(x)$, $F_2(x)$, ..., $F_k(x)$. For each initial value x_0 we try all the iterators a limited number of times. This is done according to the following procedure

```
for x[0] in set_of_initial_values do
    for m = 1 to k do
        for i = 1 to maximum_iterations do
            x[i] := F[m](x[i-1]);
            if computation_failed or outside_domain(x[i])
                then next m
            else if convergence_achieved
                then return x[i]
            else if i>3 and diverging
                then break
            else if acceleration_possible
                then x[i] := acceleration(x[i],x[i-1],...)
            end if
        end for i
    end for m
end for set_of_initial_values;
```

The idea behind this heuristic is that while it is extremely improbable that all of the iterators will converge, it is also improbable that all of them will fail to converge. By keeping the cost of running each one low, we can try all of them, expecting at least one to succeed. In practice, this heuristic is highly successful even for contrived, ill-behaved examples.

Alternatively, inverses of multivalued functions may give solutions which do not match their principal value. E.g. the iterator for $\sin^{-1} x = \pi$ would be $x = \sin \pi = 0$ which is not a solution. Section 4 describes how to solve these problems.

Evaluation by simulation.

"When you can measure what you are speaking about and express it in numbers you know something about it, but when you cannot measure it, when you cannot express it in numbers, your knowledge is of a meagre and unsatisfactory kind." *Lord Kelvin, 1883.*

In this vein, we have attempted to measure the behaviour of the iterators by simulation. We randomly generate equations to be solved. This is done top down, generating for each node of the expression tree a random operator. The number of occurrences of x is kept between 2 and 10, various functions are given different probabilities, the equation is forced to be a sum of various terms at the top level and polynomials are discarded. The following are 3 examples of such equations

$$x - 3 + \cosh^{-1}(-3 - 7x - 3x^2) = 0$$

$$\left((-8 + 3x - 3x^3 - 3x^4)^4 + \frac{e^{8-4x^4}}{83521} - 15\right)^4 - 7 + x = 0$$

$$x + 1 + 10x^2 + (-11)^{(11+5/2x)} + \frac{8}{7x(5 - \ln(x - 7)/9)} = 0$$

Within the limits of the biases (unknown to us) that this random set of equations may impose, we evaluate the iterators by running and measuring them against these equations.

66644 random equations producing 162314 iterators			
method		failures	
converged to a root	69.50%	converged to a non-root	3.08%
failed	30.50%	diverged	31.85%
average time	2.639	outside domain	43.44%
time per root	3.797	too many iterations	9.59%
		iterator fails	.01%
iterators per equation	2.436	no iterators	12.03%

Table 1. Simple iterators generated by isolating an x to the lhs of the equation

For the simple iterators (not included in the groups in the next section) table 1 shows the results of extensive simulations. It is quite remarkable that about 70% of the equations are solved. This compares extremely favourably to the results for Newton's method shown in table 7.

invert, instead of isolating x. For example, the equation $6x^2 - 9x + 6 - \ln(8+x)$ generates the iterators

$$x = \frac{6x^2 + 6 - \ln(8+x)}{9}$$

$$= \pm \frac{\sqrt{-4 + 6x + 2\ln(8+x)/3}}{2}$$

$$= e^{6x^2 - 9x + 6} - 8$$

For the initial value $x_0 = 1.23$, all these iterators fail. The first one and the third one grow without bound, the positive second iterator converges too slowly and the negative oscillates between one value and its conjugate. For this equation we could instead isolate the polynomial part.

$$6x^2 - 9x + 6 = \ln(8+x)$$

solve it treating the $\ln(8+x)$ as a constant, and obtain two new iterators.

$$x = \frac{9 \pm \sqrt{24\ln(8+x) - 63}}{12}$$

Notice that these new iterators have only one occurrence of x on the rhs, compared to two for the previous ones. The positive choice for this iterator is successful and converges very quickly to $x = 0.7595... + 0.2753...i$. This is not a general rule, we could certainly find examples which show the contrary, but in general it is expected that such groupings will produce better iterators as they capture more information about the inverse.

So we will use the following rule, for each iterator $F(x)$ which is a sum of a polynomial part and a non polynomial part, i.e.

$$x = F(x) = G(x) + p(x)$$

we will produce an iterator which is $x - p(x) = G(x)$ and each iteration consists of evaluating $\beta = G(x)$ and then solving the polynomial $x - p(x) - \beta = 0$. Removing the polynomial part will decrease the number of occurrences of x on the rhs, and hence improve our measure of quality of the iterators. The iterator can be written using Maple's $\mathtt{RootOf}^2$ notation as

$$x_{i+1} = \mathtt{RootOf}(G(x_i) + p(z) - z = 0, z)$$

A polynomial iterator, with degree d on its lhs, will normally have d roots. This has a cardinality advantage over handling a polynomial iterator by its individual terms. If the individual terms of the polynomial are isolated one

---

[2] The notation $\mathtt{RootOf}(F = 0, x)$ stands for the values of x which make $F(x) = 0$. This is Maple's mechanism to represent algebraic numbers, algebraic functions or any root of an equation.

by one, and for each monomial x^k, k roots have to be considered, up to $d(d+1)/2$ iterators could be generated. The drawback is obvious, instead of having a closed form solution for the iterator, we have to solve a polynomial of degree d, and this is typically an iterative process for $d > 2$.

Selecting which root of the polynomial to use is non trivial. When roots are given by a formula, e.g. for $d = 2$, then it is easy to write two iterators, one for each root. But when the roots are found numerically, it is not possible to have a consistent way of using the same root on successive iterations. Actually, the term "same root" does not even make sense for different polynomials, it only makes sense when the roots can be expressed as functions of the coefficients. On the other hand, if the polynomial iterator is converging, we want to select the root which is closest to the iteration value. I.e.

$$x_{i+1} = \text{RootOf}(p(z) - F(x_i), z)$$

and we select the root which is closest to x_i. Since this selection is necessary for convergence, we will use it in every step of the algorithm. Furthermore, many iterative methods for solving polynomials can profit significantly from starting their iterators at an approximation of the root; the correct root could come almost for free. For example, for the solution of the equation

$$x^5 - 6x^4 + 5x^3 - 7x^2 \ln x + 6x - 5 = 0$$

we define the iterator

$$x_{i+1} = \text{RootOf}(z^5 - 6z^4 + 5z^3 + 6z - 5 = 7x_i^2 \ln x_i, z)$$

If we start with $x_0 = 1$, then the rounded roots of the polynomial are

$$-0.526224 \pm 0.844348i, \quad 0.758845, \quad 1.34521, \quad 4.94839$$

The root which is closest to $x_0 = 1$ is $0.758845...$ Hence we set $x_1 = 0.758845....$ For the second iteration the polynomial to solve, is $z^5 - 6z^4 + 5z^3 + 6z - 5 = -1.11236...$ The roots of this polynomial are

$$-0.489123 \pm 0.829261i, \quad 0.586566, \quad 1.44569, \quad 4.94599$$

and the root closest to x_1 is $0.586566...$ which becomes x_2. This process converges quite quickly, $x_3 = 0.561733...$, $x_4 = 0.563302...$, $x_5 = 0.563168...$, etc. This root selection can also be treated as a multiple value function problem, which is discussed in the next section. Table 2 shows the simulation results for polynomial lhs iterators. Almost 64% of the problems for which we can find iterators ($63.81 = 44.64/(1 - 0.5536 \times 0.5426)$) yield a root, in time which is of the same order of magnitude as for the simple iterators.

Substitute all non-polynomials. Another possible way of constructing an iterator is to inspect the equation top-down and force the evaluation of any

66644 random equations producing 59428 iterators	
method	failures
converged to a root 44.64%	converged to a non-root 1.67%
failed 55.36%	diverged 21.22%
average time 1.593	outside domain 18.06%
time per root 3.569	too many iterations 4.79%
	iterator fails 0.00%
iterators per equation .892	no iterators 54.26%

Table 2. Iterators which have a non-linear polynomial in their lhs

subexpression which is a special function, a power to a non-integer exponent, or anything else that is not algebraic. If after this is done, we are left with an expression containing x, this must be a rational polynomial expression. The solution of this is equivalent to the solution of a polynomial and we can proceed as with the previous iterators. For example

$$\frac{x - \sin x}{1 - x^2/2} = \frac{\tan x - x}{1 + x^2/2}$$

for $x_0 = 1.23$ would be handled by evaluating the $\sin x$ and $\tan x$, obtaining

$$\frac{x - 0.94248...}{1 - x^2/2} = \frac{2.8198... - x}{1 + x^2/2}$$

which has the roots $-3.3331...$, $1.2024...$. From these possible values for x_1 we select, as before, the closest to x_0, $x_1 = 1.2024...$. More formally, using Maple's `RootOf` notation, the iterator becomes

$$x_{i+1} = \texttt{RootOf}\left(\frac{z - \sin x_i}{1 - z^2/2} = \frac{\tan x_i - z}{1 + z^2/2}, z\right)$$

Table 3 shows the simulation results for this heuristic. Again, 54% of the problems for which such an iterator could be found were solved.

Transcendental Iterators. The technique of explicitly finding roots of polynomials can be extended to cases involving transcendental functions with multivalued inverse functions.

Consider the equation $\sin x = x/100$. Providing for all solutions of $\sin x$ yields three iterators:

$$x = 100 \sin x$$
$$x = \sin^{-1}(x/100) + 2\pi n$$
$$x = \pi - \sin^{-1}(x/100) + 2\pi n$$

66644 random equations producing 14398 iterators			
method		failures	
converged to a root	11.64%	converged to a non-root	.39%
failed	88.36%	diverged	6.22%
average time	.672	outside domain	3.51%
time per root	5.768	too many iterations	1.15%
		iterator fails	0.00%
iterators per equation	.216	no iterators	88.73%

Table 3. Rational polynomial iterators, obtained by solving all the transcendental subexpressions first

where n iterates over all of the integers and the arcsin returns the principal branch. The first iterator diverges chaotically. The other two, however, either converge to solutions or else fail due to the arcsin evaluating to a complex number ($|x/100| > 1$).

Furthermore, all solutions can be generated by simply using different values of n. For the first equation, values $-15 \le n \le 15$ will yield the even numbered roots, whereas values $-16 \le n \le 15$ will yield the remaining roots when used in the second equation. Other values of n diverge. (The asymmetry comes from the positive sign on the first π; the iterator $x = -\pi - \sin^{-1}(x/100) + 2\pi n$ would supply the same set of roots with $-15 \le n \le 16$). The solution obtained is unrelated to the initial guess used; almost any starting value acceptable to the arcsin converges to the same root for a given choice of iterator and n.

Other special cases. The technique used for polynomials can be extended to other cases, when we know how to solve some transcendental equations. In Maple, the function $W(x)$[2,4,3] is the solution of $W(x)e^{W(x)} = x$. Hence many combinations of powers of x with e^x and with $\ln x$ are invertible. The resulting iterators have a lower number of occurrences of x on the rhs, and are considered better. Some of them are shown in table 4.

equation	iterator
$x^a e^{bx} = F(x)$	$x = \dfrac{aW\left(\frac{bF(x)^{1/a}}{a}\right)}{b}$
$a \ln x + bx = F(x)$	$\dfrac{aW(b\frac{e^{F(x)/a}}{a})}{b}$
$x^x = F(x)$	$e^{W(\ln F(x))}$
$x \ln x = F(x)$	$e^{W(F(x))}$

Table 4. Inverting expressions with the aid of the $W(x)$ function

66644 random equations producing 3174 iterators		
method		failures
converged to a root	1.83%	converged to a non-root .07%
failed	98.17%	diverged .80%
average time	.128	outside domain 1.14%
time per root	6.985	too many iterations .20%
		iterator fails 0.00%
iterators per equation	.048	no iterators 97.79%

Table 5. Iterators generated by solving a lhs involving $\ln x$, e^x and x in terms of $W(x)$

Table 5 shows the simulation results for lhs which can be resolved with the $W(x)$ function. The iterators generated in this way are also very successful in producing roots, just as the non-linear polynomials. In this case however, only 4% of the equations can produce such iterators, and their relative usefulness is decreased. The $W(x)$ function accepts a branch indicator, then as before we can compute an arbitrarily large number of iterators which will normally converge to different roots.

Remove linear term heuristic. At the beginning of this section we saw that an arbitrary iterator $x = \frac{F(x)+ax}{a+1}$ can be constructed for any $a \neq -1$. For a general iterator, if $F'(\alpha) = 0$ the iterator has superlinear convergence. Hence if we have any knowledge about the value of $F'(\alpha)$, we could set $a = -F'(\alpha)$ and improve the convergence order. Even if we only know an approximation of $F'(\alpha)$ then using such an a will mean that the value of the derivative of the new iterator near the root will be small and linear convergence will be accelerated. Knowledge about $F'(\alpha)$ could be inferred from $F'(0)$ or from $F'(\pm\infty)$ when they exist. Iterators modified in this way are shown in table 12 with a †. Table 6 shows the results of simulations of the simple iterators

66644 random equations producing 20656 iterators		
method		failures
converged to a root	12.09%	converged to a non-root .66%
failed	87.91%	diverged 9.24%
average time	.415	outside domain .65%
time per root	3.429	too many iterations 7.74%
		iterator fails 0.00%
iterators per equation	.310	no iterators 81.70%

Table 6. Simple iterators, modified to remove a possible linear term $(-F'(0))$

with $a = F'(0)$. Surprisingly, the results are only marginally better (about 3% better) than the ones for simple iterators, and the roots found are typically the same. This heuristic produced significantly fewer iterators than the simple ones. Hence we do not recommend this heuristic to generate extra iterators.

5   Inverting functions

To generate iterators we often need to invert functions or expressions. For example, if at one point of our isolation process we have the equation

$$x^2 = h(x)$$

we derive $x = \pm\sqrt{h(x)}$. The choice of signs presents a problem. The easiest way to resolve it is to derive two iterators, one for each sign as we have done before. Almost all functions except for lineal polynomials, present this or other problems for isolation.

An alternative to computing inverses which are multiple-valued is the following. We want to compute a value x_{i+1} from a previous value x_i. When there are multiple choices for x_{i+1} we want to select the one with minimal distance to x_i for convergence reasons. I.e. select the x_{i+1} which makes $|x_{i+1} - x_i|$ minimal. This observation is a crucial one for our algorithm. So from $x_{i+1}^2 = h(x_i)$ we will select $x_{i+1} = \pm\sqrt{h(x_i)}$, the sign depending on whether $|x_i - \sqrt{h(x_i)}|$ or $|x_i + \sqrt{h(x_i)}|$ is smaller. This resolves the first problem, the choice between multiple values. For isolating, we use a function Inverse_square. E.g. from $g(x_{i+1})^2 = h(x_i)$ we derive $g(x_{i+1}) =$ Inverse_square$(h(x_i), g(x_i))$, where

```
Inverse_square := proc( rhs, lhs )
    r := sqrt( rhs );
    if abs(r-lhs) <= abs(r+lhs) then r else -r fi
end;
```

In summary, when the result of an isolating step is a multivalued function, we can take two approaches

(a) Enumerate all iterators, either explicitly as in the case for $x^2 = h(x)$ or as a function of an arbitrary integer n as for $\sin x = x/100$.
(b) Leave the choice to be determined during the actual computation, by choosing the one closest to the previous value, and hence improving the chances of convergence.

A second problem that we have with inverting functions is a domain problem, and it can be illustrated with the equation

$$\sqrt{x_{i+1}} = h(x_i)$$

from which we isolate $x_{i+1} = h(x_i)^2$. In this case there is no choice of inverse, but if $h(x_i)$ is negative (or $|\arg h(x_i)| > \pi/2$) then the inverse cannot be computed, as we assume that $\sqrt{x}$ returns its principal value. E.g. for $\sqrt{x} = -1$, isolation gives $x = 1$ which is not a solution of the original equation. Such a situation should be treated as a domain error. In this case we use a new function to define this type of manipulation, $x_{i+1} = \text{Inverse\_sqrt}(h(x_i))$ and

```
Inverse_sqrt := proc( rhs )
    a := argument( rhs );
    if a <= -Pi/2 or a > Pi/2 then
        ERROR( 'cannot invert sqrt' )
    else rhs^2 fi
end;
```

6 Conclusions

We have also run the random tests against several classical methods for finding zeros. Table 7 shows the results for Newton's method and table 8 shows the results for the Secant method. These are shown for comparison, and we can see that both are successful less often and require more time.

66641 random equations			
method		failures	
converged to a root	34.36%	converged to a non-root	2.95%
failed	65.64%	diverged	53.24%
average time	1.595	outside domain	19.94%
time per root	4.644	too many iterations	23.87%
		iterator fails	.00%

Table 7. Newton's method, $x - f(x)/f'(x)$

66641 random equations			
method		failures	
converged to a root	37.40%	converged to a non-root	4.46%
failed	62.60%	diverged	72.81%
average time	2.122	outside domain	7.19%
time per root	5.674	too many iterations	15.53%
		iterator fails	.01%

Table 8. Secant method (2-point method)

It is appropriate to run the witness examples that we proposed in the introduction with this method. We think the results speak for themselves. The results for each equation are shown in tables 9, 10 and 11, where the columns are for each iterator and the rows have the value of each iteration. In all cases, at least one of the iteration gives the values which were considered difficult to find. Table 12 shows other examples, the first two taken from [13] and the rest have been collected by the Maple development group. All these problems had an iterator which was successful.

$(x \ln x)^{1/1.001}$	$\frac{x^{1.001}}{\ln x}$	$e^{x^{0.001}}$	$(\ln x)^{1000}$
1.23	1.23	1.23	1.23
.254976...	5.94285...	2.71884...	$.100017... \times 10^{-683}$
$-.348812... + .00109473...i$	3.34053...	2.72100...	$.186958... \times 10^{3198}$
$.365255... - 1.09527...i$	2.77297...	2.72101...	$.989096... \times 10^{3867}$
$-1.31325... - .616913...i$	2.72159...	converged	$.388442... \times 10^{3950}$
$-2.14588... + 3.31938...i$	2.72101...		$.585638... \times 10^{3959}$
$-10.0449... - .0715578...i$	2.72101...		$.596622... \times 10^{3960}$
$-23.2443... + 31.2573...i$	converged		$.769617... \times 10^{3960}$
diverged			$.791411... \times 10^{3960}$
			$.793839... \times 10^{3960}$
			$.794105... \times 10^{3960}$
			$.794135... \times 10^{3960}$
			converged

Table 9. Partial inverse iterators for solving $x^{1.001} - x \ln x = 0$

Extension to systems of equations. The extension of this idea to systems of equations is quite desirable but non-trivial. If we have k equations with k unknowns, then for each equation we have many freedoms: we can choose the variable on which to construct the iterator, we can choose the iterator, and we can choose the order of the equations. And of course, an iterator for the system consists of k iterator equations, one for each of the individual variables, so we can choose each of these independently. This means that we have a huge number of choices to build an iterator for the entire system for small k, and the number of choices can quickly become astronomical for larger k. It would appear that this number is too high to justify its use. We have some ideas which improve this situation, but these are developed in a separate paper[6], since they are out of the scope of this one.

References

1. Åke Björck and Germund Dahlquist. *Numerical Methods*. Prentice-Hall, 2 edition, 1995.

$\sin\tan x$	$\tan^{-1}\sin^{-1} x$
0.6	0.6
.632004...	.571793...
.668499...	.546785...
.710223...	.524475...
.757788...	.504453...
.811228...	.486381...
.868933...	.469981...
.925654...	.455027...
.970858...	.441327...
.994075...	.428723...
.999439...	.417083...
.999883...	.406296...
.999905...	.396264...
converged	.386907...
	.378155...
	.369947...
	.362231...
	.354961...
	.348096...
	.341601...
	.335445...
	too many iterations

Table 10. Partial inverse iterators for solving $\frac{\sin^{-1}x-\tan x}{x^4}=0$

$\pi + e^{-5-x^2}$	$\pi - e^{-5-x^2}$	$\sqrt{-5-\ln|x-\pi|}$	$-\sqrt{-5-\ln|x-\pi|}$
0.6	0.6	0.6	0.6
3.14629356...	3.13689175...	2.43573211...i	$-2.43573211...i$
3.14159299...	3.14159230...	2.52588218...i	$-2.52588218...i$
3.14159300...	3.14159231...	2.52864327...i	$-2.52864327...i$
converged	converged	2.52872814...i	$-2.52872814...i$
		converged	converged

Table 11. Partial inverse iterators for solving $x^2 + 5 + \ln(|x-\pi|) = 0$

2. Bruce W. Char, Keith O. Geddes, Gaston H. Gonnet, Benton L. Leong, Michael B. Monagan, and Stephen M. Watt. *Maple V Language Reference Manual.* Springer-Verlag, 1991.

3. Rob M. Corless, Gaston H. Gonnet, Dave E. G. Hare, and David J. Jefrey. Lambert's w function in maple. *Maple Technical Newsletter*, (9):12–22, 1993.

4. Rob M. Corless, Gaston H. Gonnet, Dave E. G. Hare, David J. Jefrey, and Donald E. Knuth. On the lambert w function. *Advances in Computational Math*, to appear.

equation		
	iterator	result
$e^x - 6x$		
	$\ln(6x)$	converged to 2.83314...
	$\frac{e^x}{6}$	converged to .20448...
	$-W(-1/6)$	is 0.20448...
	$\frac{e^x-1}{5}$ †	converged to .20448...
$\sin z^2 \ln(1+z) - \cos\sqrt{2}z$		
	$\sqrt{\sin^{-1}\left(\frac{\cos\sqrt{2}z}{\ln(1+z)}\right)}$	diverged
	$-\sqrt{\sin^{-1}\left(\frac{\cos\sqrt{2}z}{\ln(1+z)}\right)}$	too many iterations
	$e^{\frac{\cos\sqrt{2}z}{\sin z^2}} - 1$	too many iterations
	$\frac{\cos^{-1}(\sin z^2 \ln(1+z))}{\sqrt{2}}$	converged to 0.83102...
$\ln(x + \sqrt{\pi+x^2}) - \ln(x-\pi) = 4$		
	$\pi + e^{-4+\ln(x+\sqrt{\pi+x^2})}$	converged to 3.45613...
$-1/2 + 1/2\sqrt{1 - 4\sqrt{\pi} + 4(x-\pi)e^4}$		converged to 50.14201...
$-1/2 - 1/2\sqrt{1 - 4\sqrt{\pi} + 4(x-\pi)e^4}$		diverged
	$\frac{\pi+e^{-4+\ln(x+\sqrt{\pi+x^2})}-e^{-4}x}{1+e^{-4}}$ †	converged to 3.45613...
	$e^{4+\ln(x-\pi)} - \sqrt{\pi} - x^2$	diverged
	$\sqrt{e^{4+\ln(x-\pi)} - \sqrt{\pi}} - x$	converged to 50.14201...
$x^x(1+\ln x) + 32 = 0$		
	$\left(-\frac{32}{1+\ln x}\right)^{1/x}$	falls outside valid domain
	$e^{-32x^{-x}-1}$	converged to $0.46588... \times 10^{-14}$
	$\frac{\ln\left(-\frac{32}{1+\ln(x)}\right)}{\ln x}$	too many iterations
	$e^{W(\ln(-\frac{32}{1+\ln x}))}$	converged to $3.443... + 3.812...i$

Table 12. Examples from various sources, all examples are started from $x_0 = 1.23$

5. J.E. Jr. Dennis and Robert B. Schnabel. *Numerical Methods for Unconstrained Optimization and Nonlinear Equations*. Prentice-Hall, 1983.
6. Gaston H. Gonnet. Solution of non-linear systems of equations using partial inverses. In preparation, 1996.
7. Peter Henrici. *Elements of Numerical Analysis*. John Wiley, New York, 1964.
8. Peter Henrici. *Essentials of Numerical Analysis*. John Wiley, New York, 1982.
9. W. Kahan. Personal communication, 1992. Two equations which Maple's fsolve could not solve.
10. C.T. Kelley. *Iterative Methods for Linear and Nonlinear Equations*. SIAM, 1995.
11. J.M. Ortega and W.C. Rheinboldt. *Iterative Solution of Nonlinear Equations in Several Variables*. Academic Press, 1970.
12. Anthony Ralston. *A First Course in Numerical Analysis*. McGraw-Hill, 1965.
13. Kelly Roach. Symbolic-numeric nonlinear equation solving. In *Proceedings of the 1994 ISSAC*, pages 278–284. ACM Press, Jul 1994.
14. Joe F. Traub. *Iterative Methods for Solution of Equations*. Prentice-Hall, 1964.

Computing Cocycles on Simplicial Complexes[*]

Rocío González–Díaz and Pedro Real

Universidad de Sevilla, Depto. de Matemática Aplicada I,
Avda. Reina Mercedes, 41012 Sevilla, Spain,
e-mails: rogodi@euler.fie.us.es, real@cica.es

Abstract. In this note, working in the context of simplicial sets [17], we give a detailed study of the complexity for computing chain level Steenrod squares [20,21], in terms of the number of face operators required. This analysis is based on the combinatorial formulation given in [5]. As an application, we give here an algorithm for computing cup–i products over integers on a simplicial complex at chain level.

1 Introduction

Cohomology operations are tools for calculating n-cocycles on the cohomology of spaces (see, for example, [16,19]). Unfortunately, up to the present, no symbolic computational system includes *general* methods for finding representative n–cocycles on the cohomology of spaces, algebras, groups, etc. Recently, several methods for finding 2–cocycles representing 2–dimensional cohomology classes of finite groups have been designed (see [4,12,14]). The method established in [14] is based on the general theory presented in [13] and it seems that it can be generalized to higher dimensions without effort.

In this paper, we describe a different procedure based on a combinatorial formulation given in [5] for an important class of chain level cohomology operations called *Steenrod squares*. The formula we obtain in [5] is essentially an explicit simplicial description of the original formula given by Steenrod [20] for the cup–i product on simplicial complexes. We note that a mod–2 explicit formulation of the Steenrod coproduct on the chain of a simplicial set has also been given in (6.2) of Hess [11], using a different method.

We work with simplicial sets [17] which are combinatorial analogs of topological spaces. First, our concern here is to study the "complexity" (in terms of number of face operators involved) of an algorithm for computing (at chain level) the integer cup–i products, using the formulation given in [5]. Finally, as an application, we give an algorithm for computing chain level Steenrod squares on simplicial complexes.

We integrate here tools of Combinatorics and Computer Algebra in a work of Algebraic Topology, opening a door to a computational development in the search for cocycles in any degree (see [1] and [6]). A treatment of some of our methods has already been presented in [7].

---

[*] Partially supported by the PAICYT research project FQM-0143 from Junta de Andalucía and the DGES-SEUID research project PB97-1025-C02-02 from Education and Science Ministry (Spain).

In the literature, there is plenty of information about cup–i products and Steenrod squares (see [23] and [3] for a non–exhaustive account of results). We think that the algorithmic technique explained here could be substantially refined if it is suitably combined with relevant and well–known results on these cohomology operations and with techniques of homological perturbation for manipulating explicit homotopy equivalences (see [2,8–10]).

We are grateful to Prof. Julio Rubio for his helpful suggestions for improving the algorithms showed here.

2   Topological and Algebraic Preliminaries

The aim of this section is to give some simplicial and algebraic preliminaries in order to put into context the problem of computing n–cocycles (via cup–i products and Steenrod squares). Most of the material given in this section can be found in [15], [17] and [19].

A *simplicial set* X is a sequence of sets $X_0, X_1, \ldots$, together with *face operators* $\partial_i : X_n \to X_{n-1}$ and *degeneracy operators* $s_i : X_n \to X_{n+1}$ ($i = 0, 1, \ldots, n$), which satisfy the following simplicial identities:

(s1) $\partial_i \partial_j = \partial_{j-1} \partial_i$ if $i < j$;

(s2) $s_i s_j = s_{j+1} s_i$ if $i \leq j$;

(s3) $\partial_i s_j = s_{j-1} \partial_i$ if $i < j$,

(s4) $\partial_i s_j = s_j \partial_{i-1}$ if $i > j + 1$,

(s5) $\partial_j s_j = 1_x = \partial_{j+1} s_j$.

The elements of X_n are called n–*simplices*. A simplex x is *degenerate* if $x = s_i(y)$ for some simplex y and degeneracy operator s_i; otherwise, x is *non degenerate*.

Let R be a ring which is commutative with unit. Given a simplicial set X, let us denote $C_*(X)$ by the chain complex $\{C_n(X), d_n\}$, in which $C_n(X)$ is the free R–module generated by X_n and $d_n : C_n(X) \to C_{n-1}(X)$ is a R–module map of degree -1 called *differential*, defined by $d_n = \sum_{i=0}^{n} (-1)^i \partial_i$.

Let $s(C_*(X))$ be the graded R–module generated by all the degenerate simplices of X. Since $d_n(s(C_{n-1}(X))) \subset s(C_{n-2}(X))$, then $C_*^N(X) = \{C_n(X)/s(C_{n-1}(X)), d_n\}$ is a chain complex called *the normalized chain complex associated to X*.

Since $d_n\, d_{n+1} = 0$, we can define the *homology* of X, denoted by $H_*(X)$, that is the family of modules $H_n(X) = \mathrm{Ker}\, d_n / \mathrm{Im}\, d_{n+1}$.

Now, the *cochain complex* associated to $C_*^N(X)$, denoted by $C^*(X; R)$, is the free R–module generated by all the R–module maps from $C_*^N(X)$ into R, together with a map called *codifferential* defined by $(\delta^n c)(x) = c(d_{n+1}(x))$ if $x \in C_{n+1}^N(X)$ and $c \in C^n(X; R)$. We will say that $c \in C^n(X; R)$ is a n–*cocycle* if $\delta(c) = 0$, and c is a n–*coboundary* if there exists another cochain $c' \in C^*(X; R)$ such that $c = \delta(c')$.

In this way, we define the *cohomology* of X with coefficients in R by $H^n(X) = \operatorname{Ker} \delta^n / \operatorname{Im} \delta^{n-1}$. Notice that a cocycle c represents a class of cohomology.

3   Complexity for Computing Steenrod Squares

First of all, let us show the explicit formula of the cup–n product $\smile_n$ on $C^*(X; R)$ given in [5]. The chain level Steenrod squares $Sq^i : C^j(X; \mathbb{Z}_2) \to C^{j+i}(X; \mathbb{Z}_2)$ are defined from this operation in a very easy way,

$$Sq^i(c) = c \smile_n c, \text{ where } n = j - i \ .$$

They verify that if c is a j–cocycle, then $Sq^i(c)$ is a $(i+j)$–cocycle.

Theorem 1. [5] *Let R be the ground ring and X a simplicial set. Let $c \in C^p(X; R)$, $c' \in C^q(X; R)$ and $x \in C^N_{p+q-n}(X)$; if n is even, then*

$$c \smile_n c'(x) = \sum_{i_n=n}^{m} \sum_{i_{n-1}=n-1}^{i_n-1} \cdots \sum_{i_0=0}^{i_1-1} (-1)^{A(n)+B(n,m,\bar{i})+C(n,\bar{i})+D(n,m,\bar{i})}$$

$$c(\partial_{i_0+1} \cdots \partial_{i_1-1} \partial_{i_2+1} \cdots \cdot \partial_{i_{n-1}-1} \partial_{i_n+1} \cdots \partial_m \, x)$$
$$\bullet c'(\partial_0 \cdots \partial_{i_0-1} \partial_{i_1+1} \cdots \cdot \partial_{i_{n-2}-1} \partial_{i_{n-1}+1} \cdots \partial_{i_n-1} \, x)$$

and if n is odd, then

$$c \smile_n c'(x) = \sum_{i_n=n}^{m} \sum_{i_{n-1}=n-1}^{i_n-1} \cdots \sum_{i_0=0}^{i_1-1} (-1)^{A(n)+B(n,m,\bar{i})+C(n,\bar{i})+D(n,m,\bar{i})}$$

$$c(\partial_{i_0+1} \cdots \partial_{i_1-1} \partial_{i_2+1} \cdots \cdot \partial_{i_{n-2}-1} \partial_{i_{n-1}+1} \cdots \partial_{i_n-1} \, x)$$
$$\bullet c'(\partial_0 \cdots \partial_{i_0-1} \partial_{i_1+1} \cdots \cdot \partial_{i_{n-1}-1} \partial_{i_n+1} \cdots \partial_m \, x)$$

where $m = p + q - n$, the symbol $\bullet$ is the product in R,

$$A(n) = \begin{cases} 1 & \text{if } n \equiv 3, 4, 5, 6 \bmod 8 \ , \\ 0 & \text{otherwise,} \end{cases}$$

$$B(n, m, \bar{i}) = \begin{cases} \displaystyle\sum_{j=0}^{\lfloor \frac{n}{2} \rfloor} i_{2j} & \text{if } n \equiv 1, 2 \bmod 4 \ , \\[2em] \displaystyle\sum_{j=0}^{\lfloor \frac{n-1}{2} \rfloor} i_{2j+1} + nm & \text{if } n \equiv 0, 3 \bmod 4 \ , \end{cases}$$

$$C(n, \bar{i}) = \sum_{j=1}^{\lfloor \frac{n}{2} \rfloor} (i_{2j} + i_{2j-1})(i_{2j-1} + \cdots + i_0)$$

and

$$D(n, m, \bar{i}) = \begin{cases} (m + i_n)(i_n + \cdots + i_0) & \text{if } n \text{ is odd,} \\ 0 & \text{if } n \text{ is even,} \end{cases}$$

being $\bar{i} = (i_0, i_1, \dots, i_n)$.

As we can see, the general organization of face operators in these formulae is simple in the sense that we distinguish in some way $n + 1$ face operators $\partial_{i_0}, \partial_{i_1}, \dots, \partial_{i_n}$; but the signs involved follow a complicated formula. Working over $\mathbb{Z}_2$, this problem is eliminated.

The aim of this section is to give an idea of the complexity of the algorithm for computing n–cocycles based on the previous formulation.

First of all, let us begin by giving a different description of the cup–n formula. Let us consider an alphabet with only two letters: 0 and 1. So, words in this alphabet are sequences of letters 0 and 1. We count the letters of a word from the left to the right and we will suppose that the first letter on the left is in zero position.

Let m and n be two nonnegative integers such that $n \leq m$. And let $i_0, i_1, \dots, i_n \in \mathbb{Z}$ so that $0 \leq i_0 < i_1 \cdots < i_n \leq m$, then the notation $(i_0, i_1 \dots, i_n)_m$ represents the word with $m + 1$ letters such that there are zeros in the positions $i_0, i_1, \dots, i_n$ and ones in the rest, that is,

$$\overset{i_0}{1\cdots 1\ 0}\ \overset{i_1}{1\cdots 1\ 0}\ \overset{i_2}{1\cdots 1\ 0}\ \overset{i_3}{1\cdots 1\ 0} \cdots \cdots \overset{i_n}{0\ 1\cdots 1}\ .$$

In the word above, by j–*block* $(1 \leq j \leq n)$ we mean the block of ones in $i_{j-1} + 1$ until $i_j - 1$ positions and zero in i_j position. The 0–block has ones in 0 until $i_0 - 1$ positions and zero in i_0 position; and the $(n + 1)$–block has ones in $i_n + 1$ until m positions. That is,

$$\overbrace{1\cdots 1\ 0}^{i_0}\ \overbrace{1\cdots 1\ 0}^{i_1}\ \overbrace{1\cdots 1\ 0}^{i_2} \cdots\cdots \overbrace{1\cdots 1\ 0}^{i_n}\ \overbrace{1\cdots 1}$$

with the labels: 0–block, 1–block, 2–block, ..., n–block, $(n+1)$–block.

Eventually, the $(n + 1)$–block can be the empty word.

Now, given a word $(i_0, i_1, \dots, i_n)_m$ we can make a pair of words denoted by $((i_0, i_1, \dots, i_n)_m^+, (i_0, i_1 \dots, i_n)_m^-)$, in the following way. If n is even, then

– the first word of the pair, denoted by $(i_0, i_1, \dots, i_n)_m^+$, can be obtained from the word $(i_0, i_1, \dots, i_n)_m$ preserving the j–blocks with j odd, that is,

$$\overbrace{1\cdots 1\ 0}^{\text{1–bl.}}\ \overbrace{1\cdots 1\ 0}^{\text{3–bl.}}\ \overbrace{1\cdots 1\ 0}^{\text{5–bl.}} \cdots\cdots \overbrace{1\cdots 1\ 0}^{(n-1)\text{–bl.}}\ \overbrace{1\cdots 1}^{(n+1)\text{–bl.}}\ ;$$

- the second word of the pair, denoted by $(i_0, i_1, \ldots, i_n)_m^-$ can be obtained from the word $(i_0, i_1, \ldots, i_n)_m$ preserving the j–blocks with j even, that is,

$$\overbrace{1 \cdots 1 0}^{\text{0–bl.}} \ \overbrace{1 \cdots 1 0}^{\text{2–bl.}} \ \overbrace{1 \cdots 1 0}^{\text{4–bl.}} \ \cdots \cdots \ \overbrace{1 \cdots 1 0}^{(n-2)\text{–bl.}} \ \overbrace{1 \cdots 1 0}^{n\text{–bl.}} \ .$$

If n is odd, then the procedure is analogous.

Some examples are:

- the word 1101101 represented by $(2, 5)_6$ is associated with the pair of words:

$$((2, 5)_6^+, (2, 5)_6^-) = (110, 1101) \ ;$$

- the word 00110 represented by $(0, 1, 4)_4$ is associated with the pair of words:

$$((0, 1, 4)_4^+, (0, 1, 4)_4^-) = (0, 0110) \ .$$

It is easy to see that we can recover the original word $(i_0, i_1, \ldots, i_n)_m$ from the pair $((i_0, i_1, \ldots, i_n)_m^+, (i_0, i_1, \ldots, i_n)_m^-)$ suitably combining the j–blocks of both words.

For example, if we have the pair

$$(111101011, 011100) \ ,$$

we first count the number of letters (in this case, $m = 14$), we determine the j–blocks in each word of the pair

$$\left(\ \overbrace{11110}^{\text{0–bl.}} \ \overbrace{10}^{\text{1–bl.}} \ \overbrace{11}^{\text{2–bl.}} \ , \ \overbrace{0}^{\text{0–bl.}} \ \overbrace{1110}^{\text{1–bl.}} \ \overbrace{0}^{\text{2–bl.}} \ \right)$$

and finally, we reconstruct the original word alternating the blocks of both words

$$0 \ 11110 \ 1110 \ 10 \ 0 \ 11 = (0, 5, 9, 11, 12)_{14} \ .$$

Identifying the letter 1 in the position k with ∂_k and 0 with the identity, the general formula for the cup–n product admits the following representation:

$$c \smile_n c'(x)$$

$$= \sum_{i_n = n}^{m} \ \sum_{i_{n-1} = n-1}^{i_n - 1} \cdots \sum_{i_0 = 0}^{i_1 - 1} (-1)^{A(n) + B(n, m, \bar{i}) + C(n, \bar{i}) + D(n, m, \bar{i})}$$

$$c((i_0, i_1, \ldots, i_n)_m^+ x) \bullet c'((i_0, i_1, \ldots, i_n)_m^- x) \ .$$

And the problem of counting the number of summands in the formula of the cup–n product is equivalent to that of finding all the possible ways to put $n + 1$ zeros in $m + 1$ possible places, that is,

$$\binom{m+1}{n+1} \ .$$

But, taking into account that c is a p–cochain and c' is a q–cochain, then we only have to consider the summands of the formulae having $q - n$ face operators in the first factor and $p - n$ in the second one. Hence, in an analogous way to [5], a new combinatorial definition of the cup–n product is given in the following theorem.

Theorem 2. *Let R be the ground ring and X a simplicial set. If $c \in C^p(X; R)$, $c' \in C^q(X; R)$ and $x \in C^N_{p+q-n}(X)$, then*

$$c \smile_n c'(x)$$

$$= \sum_{i_n=S(n)}^{m} \sum_{i_{n-1}=S(n-1)}^{i_n-1} \cdots \sum_{i_1=S(1)}^{i_2-1} (-1)^{A(n)+B(n,m,\bar{\imath})+C(n,\bar{\imath})+D(n,m,\bar{\imath})} \tag{1}$$

$$c((i_0, i_1, \ldots, i_n)^+_m x) \bullet c'((i_0, i_1, \ldots, i_n)^-_m x)$$

where $m = p + q - n$, $\bullet$ is the product in R,

$$S(k) = i_{k+1} - i_{k-2} + \cdots + (-1)^{k+n-1} i_n + (-1)^{k+n} \left(\lambda(n) - \left\lfloor \frac{n}{2} \right\rfloor \right) + \left\lfloor \frac{k}{2} \right\rfloor$$

where $\lambda(n) = p$ if n even and $\lambda(n) = q$ if it is not; and $i_0 = S(0)$.

Proof. Let us start with $c \in C^p(X; R)$ and $c' \in C^q(X; R)$. If $n < p$ or $n < q$ then $c \smile_n c'$ is zero because there is no summand in the formula with $q - n$ face operators in the first factor and $p - n$ face operators in the second one. So, let us suppose that $n \leq p$ and $n \leq q$.

If $n = 0$, then $p + q - i_0 = q$ and $i_0 = p$, so $i_0 = p$.

If $n = 1$, then $i_1 - 1 - i_0 = q - 1$ and $p + q - 1 - i_1 + i_0 = p - 1$. So, $i_1 - i_0 - q = 0 = q - i_1 + i_0$ and hence, $i_0 = i_1 - q$ and $i_1 \geq q$.

Let us suppose that n is even (if n is odd, the proof is analogous), then the number of face operators in the first factor of the summands is

$$p + q - n - i_n + \cdots + i_{2k+1} - 1 - i_{2k} + \cdots + i_1 - 1 - i_0 \; , \tag{2}$$

and in the second one

$$i_n - 1 - i_{n-1} + \cdots + i_{2k} - 1 - i_{2k-1} + \cdots + i_2 - 1 - i_1 + i_0 \; . \tag{3}$$

Since, in the formula for $c \smile_n c'$, we only have to consider the summands that the number of face operators in the first factor is $q - n$ and in the second one $p - n$, that is, (2) is $q - n$ and (3) is $p - n$, then

$$p + q - n - i_n + \cdots + i_{2k+1} - 1 - i_{2k} + \cdots + i_1 - 1 - i_0 - p + n$$
$$= i_n - 1 - i_{n-1} + \cdots + i_{2k} - 1 - i_{2k-1} + \cdots + i_2 - 1 - i_1 + i_0 - q + n$$

and hence,

$$i_0 = i_1 - i_2 + i_3 - \cdots - i_n + p - \frac{n}{2} \; . \tag{4}$$

Taking into account in (4) that $i_0 \geq 0$, we get

$$i_1 \geq i_2 - i_3 + \cdots + i_n - p + \frac{n}{2} \ .$$

Using $i_0 \leq i_1 - 1$ in (4), we have

$$i_2 \geq i_3 - i_4 + \cdots + i_{n-1} - i_n + p - \frac{n}{2} + 1 \ .$$

In general, let us suppose that

$$i_k \geq i_{k+1} - i_{k+2} + \cdots + (-1)^{k+n-1} i_n + (-1)^{k+n} \left(p - \frac{n}{2} \right) + \left\lfloor \frac{k}{2} \right\rfloor \ ,$$

for all $1 \leq k \leq \ell$, and let us prove that this expression is true in $\ell + 1$ with ℓ odd (if ℓ is even, the proof is similar). In the case $k = \ell - 1$, since $i_\ell - 1 \geq i_{\ell-1}$, we have

$$i_\ell - 1 \geq i_\ell - i_{\ell+1} + \cdots + (-1)^{\ell+n-2} i_n + (-1)^{\ell+n-1} \left(p - \frac{n}{2} \right) + \frac{\ell-1}{2}$$

and simplifying, we conclude

$$i_{\ell+1} \geq i_{\ell+2} - i_{\ell+3} + \cdots + (-1)^{\ell+n} i_n + (-1)^{\ell+n+1} \left(p - \frac{n}{2} \right) + \frac{\ell+1}{2} \ .$$

$\square$

Now, let us study the number of summands in the formula above. Given a p–cochain c, a q–cochain c' and a nonnegative integer n, the problem of counting all the summands in the formula of $c \smile_n c'$ is equivalent to that of finding all the pairs of words $((i_0, i_1, \ldots, i_n)_m^+, (i_0, i_1, \ldots, i_n)_m^-)$ such that the first word has $q - n$ letters 1 and the second word has $p - n$ letters 1. We obtain the following result.

Theorem 3. *Let R be the ground ring. Let X be a simplicial set and n a nonnegative integer. If $c \in C^p(X; R)$ and $c' \in C^q(X; R)$, then the number of summands taking part in the formula (1) for $c \smile_n c'$ is*

$$\binom{q - \lfloor \frac{n+1}{2} \rfloor}{\lfloor \frac{n}{2} \rfloor} \binom{p - \lfloor \frac{n}{2} \rfloor}{\lfloor \frac{n+1}{2} \rfloor} \ .$$

Proof. First, let us suppose that n is even. Our proof starts with the observation that the first factor of a summand of the formula (1) has $q - n$ face operator if and only if the word $(i_0, i_1, \ldots, i_n)_m^+$ associated to it has $q - n$ letters 1 and $\frac{n}{2}$ letters 0. Then the number of words $(i_0, i_1, \ldots, i_n)_m^+$ having exactly $q - n$ letters 1 is the number of all the possible ways to put $\frac{n}{2}$ zeros in $q - n + \frac{n}{2}$ places,

$$\binom{q - \frac{n}{2}}{\frac{n}{2}} \ .$$

Analogously, the word $(i_0, i_1, \ldots, i_n)_m^-$ associated to the second factor has $p-n$ letters 1 and $\frac{n}{2}+1$ letters 0. Then the number of words $(i_0, i_1, \ldots, i_n)_m^-$ having $p-n$ letters 1 is the number of all the possible ways to put $\frac{n}{2}$ zeros (the last zero can not be changed) in $p - n + \frac{n}{2}$ places, that is,

$$\binom{p - \frac{n}{2}}{\frac{n}{2}} .$$

And the same reasoning applied to the case n odd gives us the result that there are

$$\binom{q - \frac{n+1}{2}}{\frac{n-1}{2}}$$

possible words $(i_0, i_1, \ldots, i_n)_m^+$ with $q - n$ letters 1, and

$$\binom{p - \frac{n-1}{2}}{\frac{n+1}{2}}$$

words $(i_0, i_1, \ldots, i_n)_m^-$ with $p - n$ letters one.   □

Let us see by means of several examples, the improvement of the last formulae of the cup–n product given in Theorem 2 with respect to the first formulae given in Theorem 1. Let us note c_p if $c \in C^p(X; R)$.

Table 1. Number of summands

	in the formula of Theorem 1	in the formula of Theorem 2
$c_3 \smile_2 c_4$	20	6
$c_6 \smile_5 c_6$	28	12
$c_{12} \smile_4 c_{10}$	11,628	1,260
$c_{25} \smile_5 c_{30}$	18,009,460	621,621
$c_{60} \smile_5 c_{70}$	4,925,156,775	68,222,616
$c_6 \smile_5 c_{700}$	162,699,437,009,655	970,224
$c_{60} \smile_{50} c_{60}$	225,368,761,961,739,396	33,701,394,635,724,816
$c_6 \smile_5 c_{7000}$	163,331,343,055,757,216,550	97,902,024

Taking into account that Steenrod squares are defined using cup–n products, the following corollary holds.

Corollary 4. *Let $\mathbb{Z}_2$ be the ground ring. Let i be a nonnegative integer and $c \in C^j(X; \mathbb{Z}_2)$, then the number of summands taking part in the formula of $Sq^i(c)$ is*

$$\binom{\lfloor \frac{m}{2} \rfloor}{\lfloor \frac{n}{2} \rfloor} \binom{\lfloor \frac{m+1}{2} \rfloor}{\lfloor \frac{n+1}{2} \rfloor} ,$$

where $m = i + j$ and $n = j - i$.

4   Simplicial Complexes

Now, let us study a particular simplicial set. A (combinatorial) *simplicial complex* [18,22] is a collection P of nonempty finite subsets of a vertex set V such that if $\tau \subset \sigma \subset V$ and $\sigma \in P$, then $\tau \in P$. If the vertex set is ordered, we call P an *ordered* simplicial complex. To every such ordered simplicial complex we associate a simplicial set $SS(P)$ as follows. The set $SS_n(P)$ consists of all ordered $(n+1)$–tuples $\langle v_0, v_1, \ldots, v_n \rangle$ of vertices (called n–*simplices*), possibly including repetition, such that the underlying set $\{v_0, v_1, \ldots, v_n\}$ is in P (note that $v_0 \leq v_1 \leq \cdots \leq v_n$). This set is endowed with face and degeneracy operators defined by:

$$\partial_i \langle v_0, \ldots, v_n \rangle = \langle v_0, \ldots, v_{i-1}, v_{i+1}, \ldots, v_n \rangle$$

and

$$s_i \langle v_0, \ldots, v_n \rangle = \langle v_0, \ldots, v_i, v_i, \ldots, v_n \rangle \ .$$

Notice that a simplex is degenerate if it has repeated vertices; otherwise, the simplex is non degenerate.

Summing up, a simplicial complex P can be considered as a combinatorial version of a triangulated polyhedron. The strong combinatorial structure in the first one (more precisely, in $SS(P)$) is due to considering the degeneracy operators.

From now on, due to the fact that we will work only with ordered simplicial complexes, we will call them simplicial complexes, and in order to simplify the explanation, we will identify the ordered simplicial complex P with the associated simplicial set $SS(P)$. Then if $v \in P_q$, we will say that the *dimension* of v is q. By abuse of notation, we will say that a simplex belongs to P if it belongs to P_ℓ for some ℓ.

Let x and y be two simplices of P. We will note $x \leq y$ if x is a projection of y. It is clear that a simplicial set can be given by the set of all the simplices with maximal dimensions; and a simplex belongs to P if it is a projection of a maximal simplex of P.

Let x and y be two simplices of a simplicial complex P. Let us define two operations between simplices. Let $\{z \in P : x \leq z \text{ and } y \leq z\}$, then we define $x \cup y$ as the simplex of this set with the smallest dimension (it is easy to see that $x \cup y$ is unique). And let $\{z \in P : z \leq x \text{ and } z \leq y\}$, then $x \cap y$ is the simplex of this set with the highest dimension (observe that $x \cap y$ is unique, too). On the other hand, the formulation of cup–n products given in Theorem 2 on a simplicial complex is the following.

Proposition 5. *Let R be the ground ring and P a simplicial complex with a finite number of vertices. If $c \in C^p(P)$ and $c' \in C^q(P)$, then for a nonnegative integer n, $c \smile_n c' \in C^{p+q-n}(P)$ is defined by the following formulae. Let $m = p + q - n$ and $x = \langle v_0, \ldots, v_m \rangle \in C_m(P)$, then if n is even,*

$$c \smile_n c'(x)$$

$$
= \sum_{i_n=S(n)}^{m} \sum_{i_{n-1}=S(n-1)}^{i_n-1} \cdots \sum_{i_1=S(1)}^{i_2-1} (-1)^{A(n)+B(n,m,\bar{i})+C(n,\bar{i})+D(n,m,\bar{i})}
$$

$$
c(\langle v_0, \ldots, v_{i_0}, v_{i_1}, \ldots v_{i_2}, v_{i_3}, \ldots, v_{i_{n-2}}, v_{i_{n-1}}, \ldots, v_{i_n} \rangle)
$$
$$
\bullet c'(\langle v_{i_0}, \ldots, v_{i_1}, v_{i_2}, \ldots v_{i_3}, v_{i_4}, \ldots, v_{i_{n-1}}, v_{i_n}, \ldots v_m \rangle) \ ;
$$

and if n is odd, the formula is analogous.
  In these formulae, $\bullet$ is the product in R,

$$
S(k) = i_{k+1} - i_{k+2} + \cdots + (-1)^{k+n-1} i_n + (-1)^{k+n} \left\lfloor \frac{m+1}{2} \right\rfloor + \left\lfloor \frac{k}{2} \right\rfloor
$$

for all $0 \leq k \leq n$, and $i_0 = S(0)$.

Proof. Using the formula from Theorem 2, we only have to notice that

$$
\partial_0 \cdots \partial_\ell \langle v_0, \ldots, v_m \rangle = \langle v_{\ell+1}, \ldots, v_m \rangle \ ,
$$
$$
\partial_\ell \cdots \partial_s \langle v_0, \ldots, v_m \rangle = \langle v_0, \ldots, v_{\ell-1}, v_{s+1}, \ldots, v_m \rangle \ ,
$$
$$
\partial_s \cdots \partial_m \langle v_0, \ldots, v_m \rangle = \langle v_0, \ldots, v_{s-1} \rangle \ .
$$

$\square$

For example, the formula

$$c \smile_1 c'(\langle v_0, v_1, \ldots v_m \rangle)$$

$$
= \sum_{j=0}^{p-1} (-1)^{j+(p-1+j)q} c(\langle v_0, \ldots, v_j, v_{j+q}, \ldots, v_m \rangle) \bullet c'(\langle v_j, \ldots, v_{j+q} \rangle)
$$

coincides with that of Steenrod given on p. 293 of [20], up to the sign $(-1)^{p+q}$.

5   Algorithms

We are interested in designing algorithms for computing cocycles using cup–n products. In order to do this, we need the following notation.

  Given a simplicial complex P, two nonnegative integers n and m, and three simplices x, y, z such that $z = x \cup y = \langle v_0, \ldots, v_m \rangle$ is a m–simplex and $x \cap y = \langle v_{i_0}, \ldots, v_{i_n} \rangle$ is a n–simplex, let us define the simplices

$$
z^0 = \langle v_0, \ldots, v_{i_0} \rangle \ ,
$$
$$
z^j = \langle v_{i_{j-1}}, \ldots, v_{i_j} \rangle \quad \text{for } 1 \leq j \leq n \ ,
$$
$$
z^{n+1} = \langle v_{i_n}, \ldots, v_m \rangle \ .
$$

We have the following result.

Proposition 6. *Let R be the ground ring. Let P be a simplicial complex, n a nonnegative integer, $c \in C^p(P)$ and $c' \in C^q(P)$. Let C (resp. C') be the set of non degenerate simplices of P such that $c(x) \neq 0$ if and only if $x \in C$ (resp. $c'(x) \neq 0$ if and only if $x \in C'$). Let $m = p + q - n$ and let $z = \langle v_0, \ldots, v_m \rangle$ be a simplex of P. Define the set*

$$D_z = \{ (x_r, y_s) : x_r \in C, \, y_s \in C', \, x_r \cup y_s = z,$$
$$x_r \cap y_s = \langle v_{i_0}, \ldots, v_{i_n} \rangle \text{ is a } n\text{-simplex with } i_0 = S(0)$$
$$\text{and } x_r = \bigcup_{j \text{ even}} z^j \} \ .$$

Then,

$$c \smile_n c'(z) = \sum_{(x, y) \in D_z} (-1)^{A(n) + B(n, m, \bar{i}) + C(n, \bar{i}) + D(n, m, \bar{i})} c(x) \bullet c'(y)$$

where $\bullet$ is the product in R.

Proof. Using the formula in Proposition 5 for $c \smile_n c'$, it is not difficult to see that a summand of the formula is not zero if the first factor is a simplex of C and the second factor is a simplex of C'. Hence, the simplices $x_r \in C$ and $y_s \in C'$, are both factors of a summand if and only if $x_r \cup y_s = z$, $x_r \cap y_s = \langle v_{i_0}, \ldots, v_{i_n} \rangle$ is a n-simplex with $i_0 = S(0)$ (therefore, the rest of the inequalities $S(k) \leq i_k \leq i_{k+1}$, $1 \leq k \leq n - 1$, and $S(n) \leq i_n \leq m$ are verified) and $x_r = \bigcup_{j \text{ even}} z^j$. $\square$

Translating this result to a more algorithmic language, we obtain the following method in which the output is expressed as a formal sum of simplices.

Procedure 7. *Algorithm for computing cup–n products.*

Input: *the ground ring R,*
   a simplicial complex P,
   a p–cochain c and a q–cochain c'.
Construct the set C of p–simplices so that $x \in C$ if and only if $c(x) \neq 0$.
Construct the set C' so that $y \in C'$ if and only if $c'(y) \neq 0$.
Initially, $D := \{ \ \}$.
for *each $x \in C$ and $y \in C'$,* **do**
   $z := x \cup y = \langle v_0, \ldots, v_m \rangle$,
   if $x \cap y = \langle v_{i_0}, \ldots, v_{i_n} \rangle$ *is a n–simplex with $n = p + q - m$,*
      $i_0 = S(0)$ *and* $x = \bigcup_{j \text{ even}} z^j$ **then**
      $D := D \cup \{(x, y)\}$.
   endif;
endfor;
Let cup := 0.
for *each $(x, y) \in D_z$* **do**
$cup := cup + (-1)^{A(n) + B(n, m, \bar{i}) + C(n, \bar{i}) + D(n, m, \bar{i})} c(x) \bullet c(y) \, z.$
endfor;

Output: *a formal sum, cup $= \sum \lambda_j z_j$, such that*
if λz is a summand of cup ($\lambda \in R$ and z is a m–simplex) then
$c \smile_n c'(z) = \lambda$, where $n = p + q - m$.
Otherwise, $c \smile_n c'(z) = 0$.

Now, in order to compute cocycles, for example, working in $\mathbf{Z}_2$, we need the following formula given in [20]:

$$\delta(c \smile_n c') = u \smile_{n-1} v + v \smile_{n-1} u + \delta u \smile_n v + u \smile_n \delta v \ .$$

It is clear that if both c and c' are cocycles, then the "commutativity" of the cup–$(n-1)$ product will determine the obtention of cocycles via cup–n products. And, in the particular case $c = c'$, the chain level Steenrod squares appear in a natural way. We will develop machinery which takes advantage of this fact in a future work.

The following result is a simple consequence of Proposition 6.

Corollary 8. *Let $\mathbf{Z}_2$ be the ground ring. Let P be a simplicial set and c a j–cocycle. Let C be the set of non degenerate j–simplices of P such that $c(x) = 1$ if and only if $x \in C$. Let i be a positive integer and $z = \langle v_0, \ldots, v_m \rangle$, a $(i+j)$–simplex of P. Define the set*

$$\begin{aligned} D_z = \{ \ (x_r, x_s) : \ & x_r, x_s \in C, \ r < s, \ x_r \cup x_s = z, \\ & x_r \cap x_s = \langle v_{i_0}, \ldots, v_{i_n} \rangle \text{ is a } n\text{--simplex with } n{=}j{-}i, \\ & i_0 = S(0) \text{ and } x_r = \bigcup_{j \ even} z^j \text{ or } x_r = \bigcup_{j \ odd} z^j \ \}. \end{aligned}$$

If the cardinal of D_z is even, then $Sq^i(c)(z) = 0$. Otherwise, $Sq^i(c)(z) = 1$.

In this corollary, we consider only $i > 0$ because it is well–known that $Sq^0(c) = c$.

Using the fact that Steenrod squares $Sq^i(c_j)$ are cup–$(j - i)$ products, we can adapt the Procedure 7 to these operations.

Taking a cochain c as the input datum, the following method gives us the cochains $Sq^i(c)$, with $i > 0$. Since Steenrod squares are cohomology operations, the first step of the algorithm is to determine if c is a cocycle, because in this case, $Sq^i(c)$ are cocycles too. The problem is that the resulting cocycles $Sq^i(c)$ can be coboundaries or not. This difficulty will be studied in the near future in combination with techniques of the homological computation.

Procedure 9. *Algorithm for computing chain level Steenrod squares.*

Input: *a simplicial complex P,*
        a j–cochain c.

Construct the set $C = \{x_1, x_2, \ldots, x_k\}$ of j–simplices so that $x \in C$ if and only if $c(x) = 1$.
Let $O := \{ \ \}$.

for *each* $x_r, x_s \in C$, $r < s$, *and* $x_r \cup x_s$ *is a* $(j+1)$*-simplex* **do**
  $O := O \cup \{(x_r, x_s, x_r \cup x_s)\}$.
endfor;
if O *is empty* **then**
  c *is not a cocycle*
else *let* $co := \{\ \}$.
    for *each* $(x_r, x_s, x_r \cup x_s) \in O$ **do**
      if *there exists a pair* (y, z) *in* co *such that* $x_r \cup x_s = z$ **then**
        if x_r *is not a summand of* y, **then**
          $co := (co \setminus \{(y, z)\}) \cup \{(y + x_r, z)\}$.
        endif;
        if x_s *is not a summand of* y, **then**
          $co := (co \setminus \{(y, z)\}) \cup \{(y + x_s, z)\}$.
        endif;
      else $co := co \cup \{(x_r + x_s, x_r \cup x_s)\}$.
      endif;
    endfor;
endif;
if *there exists some pair in* co *such that*
  the number of summands in the first element is odd **then**
  c *is not a cocycle,*
else *let* $S := 0$.
    for *each* $x_r, x_s \in C$, $r < s$, **do**
    $z = x_r \cup x_s = \langle v_0, \ldots, v_m \rangle$,
      if $x_r \cap x_s = \langle v_{i_0}, \ldots, v_{i_n} \rangle$ *where* $n = 2j - m$,
      $i_0 = S(0)$
      and $x_r = \bigcup_{t \ even} z^t$ *or* $x_r = \bigcup_{t \ odd} z^t$ **then**
        $S := S + z$.
      endif;
    endfor;
endif.

Output: *a formal sum of simplices* S *such that*
      if the m*-simplex* z *is a summand of* S *then*
      $Sq^i(c)(z) = 1$ *where* $i = m - j$,
      and $Sq^i(c)(z) = 0$ *otherwise.*

The previous procedures can be easily implemented using any Computer Algebra package or functional programming language.

References

1. Álvarez, V., Armario, A., González–Díaz, R., Real, P.: Algorithms in Algebraic Topology and Homological Algebra: the problem of the complexity. International workshop CASC'98 (April 1998) Saint Petersburg

2. Brown, R.: The twisted Eilenberg-Zilber Theorem. Celebrazioni Archimedee del secolo XX, Simposio di topologia (Messina, 1964), Ed. Oderisi, Gubbio (1965) 33–37

3. Dieudonné, J.: A history of Algebraic and Differential Topology 1990–1960. Birkhäuser (1989) Boston

4. Ekedahl, T., Grabmeier, J., Lambe, L.: Algorithms for algebraic computations with applications to the cohomology of finite p-groups. Preprint of Department of Math. and Centre for Innovative Computation (1997) University of Wales

5. González–Díaz, R., Real, P.: A combinatorial method for computing Steenrod squares. Methodes Effectives en Geometrie Algebrique MEGA'98 (June 1998) Saint-Malô. J. of Pure and Appl. Algebra (to apear)

6. González–Díaz, R., Real, P.: Una curiosa combinación de Topología, Álgebra y Combinatoria: los cuadrados de Steenrod. La Gaceta de la Real Sociedad Matemática Española **3** (1999) 457–466

7. González–Díaz, R., Real, P.: Computing the action of the Steenrod algebra on the cohomology of polyhedral simplicial sets. International congress IMACS-ACA'98 (August 1998) Prague

8. Gugenheim, V. K. A. M.: On the chain complex of a fibration. Illinois J. Math. **3** (1972) 398–414

9. Gugenheim, V. K. A. M., Lambe, L.: Perturbation theory in Differential Homological Algebra, I. Illinois J. Math. **33** (1989) 56–582

10. Gugenheim, V. K. A. M., Lambe, L., Stasheff, J.: Perturbation theory in Differential Homological Algebra, II. Illinois J. Math. **35 (3)** (1991) 357–373

11. Hess, K.: Perturbation and Transfer of Generic Algebraic Structure. Contemporary Math. **227** (1999) 103–143

12. Horadam, K. J., De Launey, W.: Cocyclic development of designs. J. Algebraic Combin. **2 (3)** (1993) 267–290. Erratum: **1** (1994) 129

13. Lambe, L.: Homological perturbation theory, Hochschild homology and formal group. Deformation theory and quantum groups with applications to mathematical physics (1990) Amherst. Contemp. Math. **134** (1992) 183–218

14. Lambe, L.: An algorithm for calculating cocycles. Preprint of Department of Math. and Centre for Innovative Computation (1997) University of Wales

15. Mac Lane, S.: Homology. Classics in Math. (1995) Springer-Verlag. Reprint of the 1975 edition

16. Massey, W.: Singular Homology Theory. Graduate texts in Math. **56** (1952) Springer-Verlag

17. May, P.: Simplicial objects in Algebraic Topology. Van Nostrand (1967) Princeton

18. Munkres, J. R.: Elements of Algebraic Topology. Addison-Wesley Publishing Company (1984)

19. Spanier, E. H.: Algebraic Topology. McGraw-Hill (1966). Reprinted by Springer-Verlag (1981)

20. Steenrod, N. E.: Products of cocycles and extensions of mappings. Ann. of Math. **48** (1947) 290–320

21. Steenrod, N. E.: Reduced powers of cohomology classes. Ann. of Math. **56** (1952) 47–67

22. Weibel, C. A.: An introduction to Homological Algebra. Cambridge studies in advanced Math. **38** (1994) Cambridge University Press

23. Wood, R. M. W.: Problems in the Steenrod algebra. Bull. London Math. Soc. **30** (1998) 449–517

Bifurcations of Maps in the Software Package CONTENT

W. Govaerts[1,4], Yu. A. Kuznetsov[2,3] and B. Sijnave[4]

[1] Fund for Scientific Research F.W.O., Belgium
[2] Universiteit Utrecht, Mathematisch Instituut, Postbus 80.010, 3508 Utrecht, The Netherlands
[3] Institute of Mathematical Problems of Biology, Russian Academy of Sciences, Pushchino, Moscow Region, 142292 Russia
[4] Department of Applied Mathematics and Computer Science, University of Gent, Krijgslaan 281 (S9), B–9000 Gent, Belgium

Abstract. The qualitative behaviour of iterates of a map can be very complicated. One approach to these phenomena starts with the simplest situation, the case where the map has a fixed point. Under parameter variations, the fixed point typically moves until a bifurcation value is reached and one of three possible more complex phenomena is encountered. These are fold, flip and Neimark - Sacker bifurcations; they are called codimension one phenomena because they generically appear in problems with one free parameter.

The software package CONTENT (CONTinuation ENvironmenT) combines numerical methods (integration, numerical continuation etcetera) with symbolic methods (e.g. symbolic derivatives) and allows (among other things) to numerically continue fixed points and to detect, compute and continue fold points, flip points and Neimark - Sacker points. To the best of our knowledge CONTENT is the only software that allows to detect and compute all codimension two points on such curves, including strong resonances and degenerate Neimark - Sacker bifurcations. The paper provides details on defining systems and test functions implemented in CONTENT for these purposes.

We show the power of the software by studying the behaviour of an electromechanical device that exhibits a complicated bifurcation behaviour, the so - called Sommerfeld's effect. In this example the map is defined by the time integration of a three - dimensional dynamical system over a fixed time interval.

1   Introduction

We briefly review some basic facts about maps, referring to [7] for details. We consider a smooth map

$$u \mapsto F(u, \alpha) \equiv F_\alpha(u), \quad F : \mathbb{R}^n \times \mathbb{R}^m \to \mathbb{R}^n \tag{1}$$

and the numerical continuation of its fixed points, defined as solutions to the equations

$$F(u, \alpha) = u.$$

The eigenvalues of the Jacobian matrix F_u of F are called *multipliers*. The fixed point is asymptotically stable if $|\mu| < 1$ for every multiplier μ. If there exists a multiplier μ with $|\mu| > 1$, then the fixed point is unstable.

While following a curve of fixed points, three codimension–1 bifurcations can occur, namely a fold, a period doubling (flip) or a Neimark - Sacker bifurcation. A fold point is a point where the Jacobian F_u of (1) has one multiplier equal to $+1$. Generically, the curve of fixed points turns at the fold point when a parameter is freed. When the Jacobian has a multiplier equal to -1, the bifurcation is called a period–doubling bifurcation. Generically, two fixed points of F_α^2 bifurcate from the fixed point of F_α. The case where the Jacobian has a conjugate pair of complex multipliers on the unit circle $(e^{\pm i\theta})$, is known as a Neimark - Sacker bifurcation. Typically, at a Neimark - Sacker point a family of closed invariant curves of the map (1) is born. Fig. 1 shows the critical multipliers for the three codimension–1 bifurcations of fixed points.

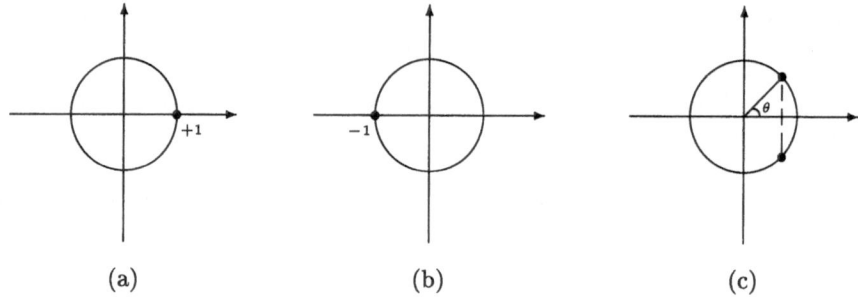

(a)   (b)   (c)

Fig. 1. Critical multipliers at fold(a), flip(b) and Neimark - Sacker (c).

The freely available software package CONTENT [8] allows to numerically continue curves of fixed points of a map if one parameter is freed, to detect and accurately compute fold, flip and Neimark - Sacker bifurcation points if these occur on the fixed point curve. In the present paper we describe how CONTENT continues fold, flip, and Neimark - Sacker bifurcation curves, and locates all codimension - two bifurcation points on these codimension - one curves. In addition, CONTENT computes normal form coefficients at some of the codimension - two points. These are essential data which allow to predict the qualitative behaviour of the iterates of the map near the bifurcation point. Details on the normal form computations will be given elsewhere.

2   Example : the Sommerfeld's effect

The study of the interaction of a source of energy with limited power and an elastic construction was originated in a work of A. Sommerfeld [9]. From

[6] we recall the description of a relatively simple electromechanical system sketched in Figure 2 which exhibits Sommerfeld's effect.

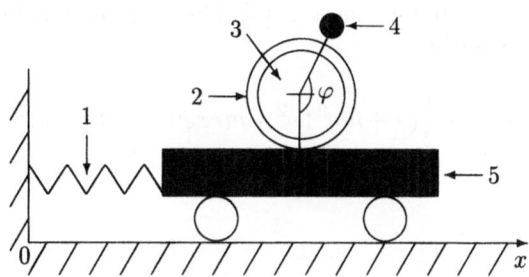

Fig. 2. The electromechanical device

A movable platform (5) is connected to a base point with a visco - elastic connection (1) that is characterized by a stiffness coefficient k and a damping coefficient d. The base point is taken as the origin of the one - dimensional horizontal direction along which one measures the displacement x of the platform. A direct current motor (2) on top of the platform activates a rotor (3). The total mass of the platform and the motor is denoted by M, the mass of the rotor by M_R. The inertial axial moment of the rotor is denoted by J. An unbalanced mass m (4) is fixed to the rotor; e is its eccentricity, i.e. its distance to the central axis of the rotor. The position of this unbalanced mass is described by the angle φ that it forms with the (downward) vertical direction. An important characteristic of the motor is the dependence of the electrical moment Γ of the rotor on the angular speed $\Omega = \frac{d\varphi}{dt}$ of the rotor; we assume that this dependence is linear and represent it as

$$\Gamma(\Omega, u, \Gamma_0, \Omega_0) = \Gamma_0 \left(u - \frac{\Omega}{\Omega_0} \right)$$

where Γ_0, Ω_0 are constants of the motor while u is a control parameter which is proportional to the voltage of the direct current in the energizing circuit. This is obviously an important bifurcation parameter. A further parameter is the axial resistance moment Γ_c of the drum. As usual, g denotes the gravity constant.

The movement of this construction is completely described by x, φ as functions of the time t. For low voltages the system typically converges to a periodic oscillation, the period and amplitude of which are determined by the parameters of the system. If the damping d is high then no bifurcations occur for increasing values of u. However, for small values of d the stability of the periodic orbits breaks down if u is increased sufficiently, irregular movements occur and after some time the system converges to a different periodic orbit. If u is decreased again, a similar jump occurs for a different value of u. For some intermediate values of u two different stable periodic movements are possible. This is called the Sommerfeld effect.

To study the effect numerically, we write down the dynamical equations of the system. We use the Lagrangian formalism which is described in every textbook on classical mechanics, see e.g. [3]. The Lagrangian of the electrome-chanical system is given by

$$L = \frac{1}{2}(M + M_R + m)\dot{x}^2 + \frac{1}{2}(J + me^2)\dot{\varphi}^2 + me\dot{x}\dot{\varphi}\cos(\varphi) - \frac{1}{2}kx^2 + mge\cos(\varphi),$$

with generalized forces

$$Q_x = -d\dot{x}, Q_\varphi = \Gamma - \Gamma_c.$$

The dynamics of the system is now described by the Lagrange equations

$$\frac{d}{dt}\left(\frac{\partial L}{\partial \dot{x}}\right) - \frac{\partial L}{\partial x} = Q_x \, , \, \frac{d}{dt}\left(\frac{\partial L}{\partial \dot{\varphi}}\right) - \frac{\partial L}{\partial \varphi} = Q_\varphi$$

To get explicit compact formulae in nondimensional form we introduce several new parameters

$$M_\Sigma = M + M_R + m, X_* = \sqrt{\frac{J + me^2}{M_\Sigma}}, T_* = \sqrt{\frac{M_\Sigma}{k}}, \gamma_0 = \frac{\Gamma_0}{kX_*^2}, \gamma_c = \frac{\Gamma_c}{kX_*^2},$$

$$\omega_0 = \Omega_0 T_*, \zeta = \frac{d}{2kT_*}, \beta = \frac{gT_*^2}{X_*}, E = \frac{me}{M_\Sigma X_*}.$$

Next we rescale time by introducing $\tau = \frac{t}{T_*}$ and x by introducing $\xi = \frac{x}{X_*}$. We further introduce the new state variables $\omega = \frac{d\varphi}{d\tau}$ and $\eta = \frac{d\xi}{d\tau}$ and use φ as the "new time", assuming implicitly that φ is a monotonous function of time as has to be the case in practical situations. After some tedious computations this leads to the non - autonomous dynamical system

$$\begin{cases} \dot{\xi} = \frac{\eta}{\omega} \\ \dot{\eta} = \frac{1}{\omega D}\left[F_1 - E\cos(\varphi)F_2\right] \\ \dot{\omega} = \frac{1}{\omega D}\left[-E\cos(\varphi)F_1 + F_2\right] \end{cases} \tag{2}$$

where derivatives are taken with respect to φ and $D = 1 - E^2\cos^2(\varphi)$, $F_1 = -\xi - 2\zeta\eta + E\omega^2\sin(\varphi)$, $F_2 = \gamma_0\left(u - \frac{\omega}{\omega_0}\right) - \gamma_c - \beta E\sin(\varphi)$.

Now the map is defined by

$$\begin{pmatrix} \xi(0) \\ \eta(0) \\ \omega(0) \end{pmatrix} \mapsto \begin{pmatrix} \xi(2\pi) \\ \eta(2\pi) \\ \omega(2\pi) \end{pmatrix} \tag{3}$$

where $\xi(\varphi), \eta(\varphi), \omega(\varphi)$ are solutions to (2).

In the numerical study that follows the parameters $E = 0.2$, $\gamma_0 = 4$, $\omega_0 = 1$, $\gamma_c = 0.1$ and $\beta = 2$ are fixed. CONTENT handles not only maps but also ODE's. As a first application of CONTENT we consider the orbit integration of (2) for $\zeta = 0.045$, $u = 0.6$. Starting from the (arbitrarily chosen) point $(1, 1, 1)$ the orbit converges quickly to a stable periodic orbit which we represent in Figure 2 in the (ξ, η) - plane.

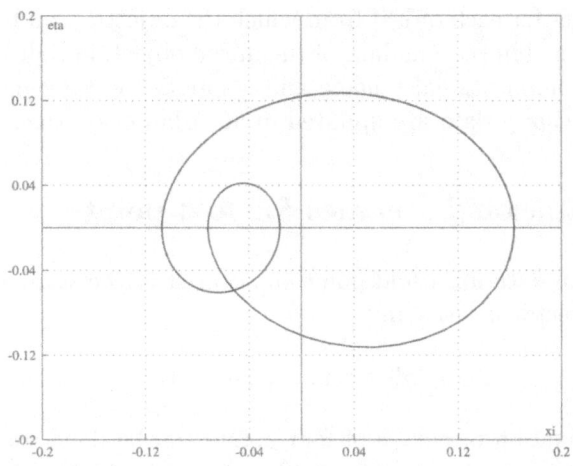

Fig. 3. Projection of a periodic orbit on the (ξ, η) - plane.

As an interesting feature we note that the platform (ξ - component) oscillates twice and with two different amplitudes during one rotation of the rotor.

3   Computational schemes : the general idea

One of the basic ingredients of CONTENT is the continuer which allows to compute curves of solutions to a nonlinear system of equations provided that the number of independent variables is equal to the number of equations plus one and that the resulting system has full rank. The computation of a curve in CONTENT can be done in several ways. This computation always starts from a point of a certain type, which we will further denote as an object O. The method for the computation of a curve starting from O is called a computational scheme and will be denoted as $\mathcal{C}(O)$.

Each object is characterized by its associated bifurcation data, containing the fixed point coordinates and parameter values and certain other data, particular for the object. The auxiliary data are a group of data particular for one computational scheme. They have to be initialized at the starting point of a curve and updated along the computed curve. The union of the auxiliary data and the unknowns of the defining system are called the continuation data.

The development of a computational scheme $\mathcal{C}(O)$ for the computation of a curve of objects of type O starts with writing Starters for $\mathcal{C}(O)$. A curve of objects of type O can start from a point that is archived as object O but sometimes also from other (typically more "specialized") objects. There is a separate Starter for each object from which the object O can be started. The Starters read the bifurcation data of the initial object, initialize the auxiliary data for the computational scheme and compute the tangent vector to the curve. The auxiliary data are updated in an Adapter routine.

4   Computational schemes for fold points

The bifurcation data for a fold point O_{lp} consist of the state and parameter values and a vector v satisfying

$$F_u v = v, \quad \langle v, v \rangle = 1.$$

The continuation of curves of fold points can be done according to two different computational schemes, namely the standard fold curve $\mathcal{C}^s(O_{lp})$ and the bordered fold curve $\mathcal{C}^b(O_{lp})$. The continuation data for the standard fold curve $\mathcal{C}^s(O_{lp})$ coincide with the bifurcation data. In the case of the bordered fold curve $\mathcal{C}^b(O_{lp})$, the continuation data consist of the state variables and the parameters as well as two auxiliary vectors.

4.1   Standard fold curve

The standard fold curve $\mathcal{C}^s(O_{lp})$ is a curve in $\mathbb{R}^{2n+2}$ defined by $2n+1$ equations in the $2n+2$ unknowns $u \in \mathbb{R}^n$, $v \in \mathbb{R}^n$, $\alpha \in \mathbb{R}^2$:

$$\begin{cases} F(u, \alpha) - u & = 0 \\ (F_u(u, \alpha) - I_n) v = 0 \\ \langle v, v \rangle - 1 & = 0 \,. \end{cases}$$

A similar system is used in AUTO97 [1] and its precursors. For detection of bifurcations along the standard fold curve, the following test functions are computed :

$$\begin{cases} \psi_1 = \langle \tilde{w}, v \rangle \\ \psi_2 = \det(A + I_n) \\ \psi_3 = \det(A \odot A - I_m) \\ \psi_4 = \langle w, B(v, v) \rangle \,. \end{cases}$$

Here $A = F_u$, $2m = n(n-1)$ and the vectors v, w and $\tilde{w}$ are such that

$$Av = v, \quad A^T w = w, \quad A^T \tilde{w} = \tilde{w}, \quad \langle v, v \rangle = \langle \tilde{w}, \tilde{w} \rangle = 1, \quad \langle w, v \rangle = 1 .$$

We recall that $\odot$ denotes the bialternate matrix product; if $A_1, A_2 \in \mathbb{R}^{n \times n}$, then $A_1 \odot A_2 \in \mathbb{R}^{m \times m}$ where $2m = n(n-1)$, see [5] or [7]. If $\mu_1, \mu_2, \dots, \mu_n$ are the eigenvalues of A, then $A \odot A$ has the eigenvalues $\mu_i \mu_j$ for $1 \leq i < j \leq n$.
  The multilinear function $B(p, q)$ is defined by

$$B_i(p, q) = \sum_{j,k=1}^{n} \left. \frac{\partial^2 F_i(u, \alpha)}{\partial u_j \partial u_k} \right|_{(u_0, \alpha_0)} p_j \, q_k \tag{4}$$

for $i = 1, 2, \dots, n$.
  The following codimension–two bifurcations can be detected and located as regular zeroes of the above defined testfunctions :

  - Resonance 1:1 (R1) : $\psi_1 = 0, \psi_3 = 0$
  - Fold + Flip (FF) : $\psi_2 = 0$
  - Fold + Neimark–Sacker (FN) : $\psi_1 \neq 0, \psi_3 = 0$
  - Cusp (CP) : $\psi_4 = 0$.

4.2 Bordered fold curve

The bordered fold curve $\mathcal{C}^b(O_{lp})$ is a curve in $\mathbb{R}^{n+2}$ defined by $n+1$ equations in the $n+2$ unknowns $u \in \mathbb{R}^n$, $\alpha \in \mathbb{R}^2$:

$$\begin{cases} F(u, \alpha) - u = 0 \\ g(u, \alpha) \quad\ = 0 . \end{cases}$$

Hereby $g = g(u, \alpha)$ is defined by

$$\begin{pmatrix} F_u - I_n & W_1 \\ V_1^T & 0 \end{pmatrix} \begin{pmatrix} v \\ g \end{pmatrix} = \begin{pmatrix} 0_n \\ 1 \end{pmatrix}$$

where 0_n denotes the n–dimensional nullvector. The auxiliary vectors V_1, $W_1 \in \mathbb{R}^n$ are initially chosen as $V_1 = e_p, W_1 = e_q$ where $e_k \in \mathbb{R}^n$ is the k - th unit vector and p and q are determined by the row and column index of the row and column with minimal pivot elements in the LU–decomposition of $F_u - I_n$. Before continuation is started, V_1 and W_1 are adapted once.
  To detect the same singularities as on the standard fold curve $\mathcal{C}^s(O_{lp})$, the following test functions are computed :

$$\begin{cases} \psi_1 = g'(u, \alpha) \\ \psi_2 = \det(A + I_n) \\ \psi_3 = \det(A \odot A - I_m) \\ \psi_4 = \langle w, B(v, v) \rangle \end{cases}$$

whereby $A = F_u, 2m = n(n-1)$,

$$A\,v = v, \quad A^T w = w, \quad \langle v, v \rangle = \langle v, w \rangle = 1$$

and $B(v, v)$ defined by (4). The scalar $g' = g'(u, \alpha)$ is defined by

$$\begin{pmatrix} F_u - I_n & W_1 \\ V_1^T & 0 \end{pmatrix} \begin{pmatrix} v' \\ g' \end{pmatrix} = \begin{pmatrix} v \\ 0 \end{pmatrix}.$$

The above defined test functions allow CONTENT to detect and localize the same codim 2 singularities as in the standard fold curve.

5   Computational schemes for flip points

The bifurcation data for a flip point O_{pd} consist of the state and parameter values and a vector v satisfying

$$F_u\,v = -v, \quad \langle v, v \rangle = 1$$

with F_u the Jacobian matrix of F from (1).

Two different computational schemes can be used to continue curves of flip points, namely the standard flip curve $C^s(O_{pd})$ and the bordered flip curve $C^b(O_{pd})$. In the case of the standard flip curve, the continuation data coincide with the bifurcation data. The continuation data for the bordered flip curve consist of the state variables and the parameters as well as two auxiliary vectors.

5.1   Standard flip curve

The standard flip curve $C^s(O_{pd})$ is a curve in $\mathbb{R}^{2n+2}$ defined by $2n + 1$ equations in the $2n + 2$ unknowns $u \in \mathbb{R}^n$, $v \in \mathbb{R}^n$, $\alpha \in \mathbb{R}^2$:

$$\begin{cases} F(u, \alpha) - u & = 0 \\ (F_u(u, \alpha) + I_n)\,v = 0 \\ \langle v, v \rangle - 1 & = 0. \end{cases}$$

A similar system is used in AUTO97 [1] and its precursors. For detection of higher bifurcations along the standard flip curve, the following test functions are computed :

$$\begin{cases} \psi_1 = \langle \tilde{w}, v \rangle \\ \psi_2 = \det(A - I_n) \\ \psi_3 = \det(A \odot A - I_m) \\ \psi_4 = \langle w, C(v, v, v) \rangle + 3\,\langle w, B(v, (I_n - A)^{-1} B(v, v)) \rangle. \end{cases}$$

Here $A = F_u$, $2m = n(n-1)$ and the vectors v, w and $\tilde{w}$ are such that

$$A\,v = v, \quad A^T w = w, \quad A^T \tilde{w} = \tilde{w}, \quad \langle v, v \rangle = \langle \tilde{w}, \tilde{w} \rangle = 1, \quad \langle w, v \rangle = 1.$$

The multilinear functions $B(p,q)$ and $C(p,q,r)$ are defined by (4) and

$$C_i(p,q,r) = \sum_{j,k,l=1}^{n} \frac{\partial^3 F_i(u,\alpha)}{\partial u_j \partial u_k \partial u_l}\bigg|_{(u_0,\alpha_0)} p_j\, q_k\, r_l \qquad (5)$$

for $i = 1, 2, \ldots, n$.

The following codim 2 bifurcations can be detected and located as regular zeroes of the above defined testfunctions :

- Resonance 1:2 (R2) : $\psi_1 = 0, \psi_3 = 0$
- Flip + Fold (FF) : $\psi_2 = 0$
- Flip + Neimark–Sacker (FN) : $\psi_1 \neq 0, \psi_3 = 0$
- Degenerate flip (DP) : $\psi_4 = 0$.

5.2   Bordered flip curve

The bordered flip curve $\mathcal{C}^b(O_{pd})$ is a curve in $\mathbb{R}^{n+2}$ defined by $n+1$ equations in the $n+2$ unknowns $u \in \mathbb{R}^n$, $\alpha \in \mathbb{R}^2$:

$$\begin{cases} F(u,\alpha) - u = 0 \\ g(u,\alpha) \quad\;\; = 0 \;. \end{cases}$$

Hereby $g = g(u,\alpha)$ is defined by

$$\begin{pmatrix} F_u + I_n & W_1 \\ V_1^T & 0 \end{pmatrix} \begin{pmatrix} v \\ g \end{pmatrix} = \begin{pmatrix} 0_n \\ 1 \end{pmatrix}$$

where 0_n denotes the $n-$dimensional nullvector. The auxiliary vectors V_1, $W_1 \in \mathbb{R}^n$ are initially chosen as $V_1 = e_p, W_1 = e_q$ where p and q are determined by the row and column index of the row and column with minimal pivot elements in the $LU-$decomposition of $F_u + I_n$. Before continuation is started, V_1 and W_1 are adapted once.

To detect the same codim 2 singularities as on the standard flip curve $\mathcal{C}^s(O_{pd})$, the following test functions are computed :

$$\begin{cases} \psi_1 = g'(u,\alpha) \\ \psi_2 = \det(A - I_n) \\ \psi_3 = \det(A \odot A - I_m) \\ \psi_4 = \langle w, C(v,v,v) \rangle + 3 \langle w, B(v, (I_n - A)^{-1} B(v,v)) \rangle \end{cases}$$

whereby $A = F_u, 2m = n(n-1)$,

$$A v = v, \quad A^T w = w, \quad \langle v, v \rangle = \langle v, w \rangle = 1$$

and $B(v,v), C(v,v,v)$ defined by (4) and (5). The scalar $g' = g'(u,\alpha)$ is defined by

$$\begin{pmatrix} F_u + I_n & W_1 \\ V_1^T & 0 \end{pmatrix} \begin{pmatrix} v' \\ g' \end{pmatrix} = \begin{pmatrix} v \\ 0 \end{pmatrix} \;.$$

The above defined test functions allow CONTENT to detect and localize the same singularities as in the standard flip

6   Computational schemes for Neimark–Sacker points

The bifurcation data for a Neimark–Sacker point O_{ns} consist of the state and parameter values, the scalar κ defined as the real part of the Neimark–Sacker multipliers $e^{\pm i\theta}$ and two vectors V and L. The vector V in the eigenspace of the Neimark–Sacker multipliers whilest L is a vector not orthogonal to the Neimark–Sacker eigenspace and not linearly dependent on V.

Three computational schemes are implemented to continue Neimark–Sacker curves, namely the standard Neimark-Sacker curve $\mathcal{C}^s(O_{ns})$, the bordered biproduct Neimark–Sacker curve $\mathcal{C}^{bp}(O_{ns})$ and the bordered squared Jacobian Neimark–Sacker curve $\mathcal{C}^{bs}(O_{ns})$.

6.1   Standard Neimark–Sacker curve

The standard Neimark–Sacker curve $\mathcal{C}^s(O_{ns})$ is a curve in $\mathbb{R}^{2n+3}$ defined by $2n+2$ equations in the $2n+3$ unknowns $u \in \mathbb{R}^n$, $v \in \mathbb{R}^n$, $\alpha \in \mathbb{R}^2$, $\kappa \in \mathbb{R}$:

$$
\begin{cases}
F(u,\alpha) - u & = 0 \\
(F_u(u,\alpha)^2 - 2\,\kappa\, F_u + I_n)\, v & = 0 \\
\langle v, v \rangle - 1 & = 0 \\
\langle v, L \rangle & = 0\,.
\end{cases}
$$

This method was first used in the software package CANDYS/QA [2]. For detection of codimension - two bifurcations along the standard Neimark–Sacker curve, we compute the following test functions :

$$
\begin{cases}
\psi_1 = \frac{1}{2}\operatorname{Re} e^{-i\theta_0}\left[\langle p, C(q,q,\overline{q})\rangle + 2\langle p, B(q,(I_n - A)^{-1}B(q,\overline{q}))\rangle \right. \\
\qquad \left. + \langle p, B(\overline{q}, (e^{2i\theta_0} I_n - A)^{-1}B(q,q))\rangle\right] \\
\psi_2 = \kappa - 1 \\
\psi_3 = \det(A - I_n) \\
\psi_4 = \det(A + I_n) \\
\psi_5 = \det(A|_{\mathcal{N}^C} \odot A|_{\mathcal{N}^C} - I_m) \\
\psi_6 = \kappa + 1 \\
\psi_7 = \kappa + \frac{1}{2} \\
\psi_8 = \kappa
\end{cases}
$$

where $A = F_u(u,\alpha)$ and the vectors $p, q \in \mathbb{C}^n$ satisfy

$$
A q = e^{i\theta_0} q, \quad A^T p = e^{-i\theta_0} p, \quad \langle \operatorname{Re} q, \operatorname{Im} q \rangle = 0, \quad \langle q, q \rangle = \langle p, q \rangle = 1\,.
$$

The subspace $\mathcal{N}^C$ of $\mathbb{R}^n$ is the orthogonal complement of the critical two–dimensional left eigenspace associated with the pair of multipliers with unit product and $2m = (n-2)(n-3)$. The multilinear functions $B(p,q)$ and $C(p,q,r)$ are as defined in (4) and (5). With these test functions, the following singularities can be detected :

 – Degenerate Neimark–Sacker (DN) : $\psi_1 = 0$

- Fold + Neimark–Sacker (FN) : $\psi_2 \neq 0, \psi_3 = 0$
- Flip + Neimark–Sacker (PN) : $\psi_4 = 0, \psi_6 \neq 0$
- Double Neimark–Sacker (NN) : $\psi_5 = 0$
- Resonance 1:1 (R1) : $\psi_2 = \psi_3 = 0$
- Resonance 1:2 (R2) : $\psi_4 = \psi_6 = 0$
- Resonance 1:3 (R3) : $\psi_7 = 0$
- Resonance 1:4 (R4) : $\psi_8 = 0$

Our defining system of the Standard Neimark - Sacker curve also allows solutions with $\kappa < -1$ or $\kappa > 1$ (in this respect the situation is different from [2]). In this case F_u has two real multipliers μ_1, μ_2 with $\mu_1 \mu_2 = 1$, $\kappa = \frac{\mu_1 + \mu_2}{2}$. Such points are called neutral saddles. The situation is analogous to the case of Hopf bifurcations in equilibria of dynamical systems, cf. [10]. Curves of neutral saddle points often connect seemingly unrelated Neimark - Sacker points, cf. §7. The test function ψ_1 is not defined for neutral saddle points.

6.2   Bordered biproduct Neimark–Sacker curve

The bordered biproduct Neimark–Sacker curve $\mathcal{C}^{bp}(O_{ns})$ is a curve in $\mathbb{R}^{n+2}$ defined by $n + 1$ equations in the $n + 2$ unknowns $u \in \mathbb{R}^n$, $\alpha \in \mathbb{R}^2$:

$$\begin{cases} F(u, \alpha) - u & = 0 \\ g_{11} \, g_{22} - g_{12} \, g_{21} = 0 \end{cases}$$

whereby $g_{ij} = g_{ij}(u, \alpha)$ are components from the 2×2 matrix

$$G = \begin{pmatrix} g_{11} & g_{12} \\ g_{21} & g_{22} \end{pmatrix}$$

defined by

$$\begin{pmatrix} F_u \odot F_u - I_m & W_1 & W_2 \\ V_1^T & d_{11} & d_{12} \\ V_2^T & d_{21} & d_{22} \end{pmatrix} \begin{pmatrix} V \\ G \end{pmatrix} = \begin{pmatrix} O_{m,2} \\ I_2 \end{pmatrix}$$

with $2\,m = n(n - 1)$.

To detect the same singularities as on the standard Neimark–Sacker curve $\mathcal{C}^s(O_{ns})$, the same test functions are computed, except for ψ_5 which is replaced by $\psi_5 = \det(M_1)$ where

$$M_1 = \begin{pmatrix} F_u \odot F_u - I_m & W_1 \\ V_1^T & d_{11} \end{pmatrix} .$$

Neutral saddle points can also be handled with this computational scheme and the same remarks apply as for $\mathcal{C}^s(O_{ns})$.

6.3   Bordered squared Jacobian Neimark–Sacker curve

The bordered squared Jacobian Neimark–Sacker curve $\mathcal{C}^{bs}(O_{ns})$ is a curve in $\mathbb{R}^{n+3}$ defined by $n+2$ equations in the $n+3$ unknowns $u \in \mathbb{R}^n$, $\alpha \in \mathbb{R}^2$, $\kappa \in \mathbb{R}$:

$$\begin{cases} F(u, \alpha) - u = 0 \\ \quad g_{i_1 j_1} \quad\;\; = 0 \\ \quad g_{i_2 j_2} \quad\;\; = 0 \end{cases}$$

whereby $g_{ij} = g_{ij}(u, \alpha)$ are components of the 2×2 matrix G defined by

$$\begin{pmatrix} F_u^2 - 2\kappa F_u + I_n & W_1 & W_2 \\ V_1^T & 0 & 0 \\ V_2^T & 0 & 0 \end{pmatrix} \begin{pmatrix} V \\ G \end{pmatrix} = \begin{pmatrix} O_{n,2} \\ I_2 \end{pmatrix} .$$

A similar method was suggested in [10]. Computational details on starting and adapting the auxiliary data are as in the analogous method for the Hopf bifurcation in ODEs [4]. The same test functions, and as a consequence the same singularities as on the standard Neimark–Sacker curve $\mathcal{C}^s(O_{ns})$ can be calculated; neutral saddle points are handled in the same way.

7   Sommerfeld's effect revisited

We consider again the electromechanical problem from §2. We now compute a fixed point of the map (3) for $u = 0.6$, $\zeta = 0.01$. We then free the parameter u (the most natural bifurcation parameter in the problem) and compute a curve of fixed points of (3) for increasing values of u. In Figure 7 we represent the amplitude of the oscillation

$$A_\xi = \sqrt{\frac{1}{2\pi} \int_0^{2\pi} \|\xi(\varphi)\|^2 d\varphi}$$

as a function of u. This picture contains two fold points labeled LP and two points labeled NS. The lower NS point corresponds to the Neimark-Sacker bifurcation, while the upper one is a neutral saddle. The branch starting from the left is stable but loses stability through a fold bifurcation, the branch starting from the right is also stable but loses stability through a Neimark - Sacker bifurcation. An interesting conclusion is that for some values of u, e.g. $u = 1.2$, the system has two stable fixed points and one unstable fixed point. It is also important that the Neimark-Sacker bifurcation is subcritical ($\psi_1 > 0$), i.e. the stability loss is catastrophic.

To get a more global picture we select in CONTENT the first limit point represented in Figure 7 and continue it numerically, with free parameters u, ζ. We so obtain the wedge - shaped curve in Figure 7. This limit point curve contains three special points, namely two 1:1 resonant points and one cusp

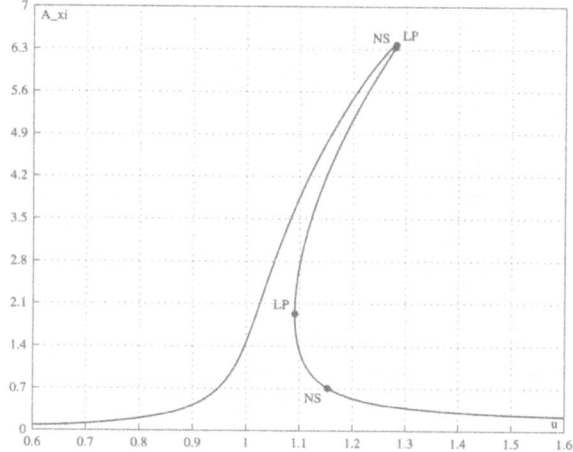

Fig. 4. Amplitude of an oscillation A_ξ as a function of u for $\zeta = 0.01$.

point. The coordinates of the first **R1** point are $\xi = -0.865973$, $\eta = -2.18348$, $\omega = 1.08129$, $\zeta = 0.0214788$, $u = 1.10202$. The coordinates of the second **R1** point are $\xi = -21.0049$, $\eta = -5.68956$, $\omega = 0.718283$, $\zeta = 0.00403959$, $u = 1.62413$.

From each of them a Neimark - Sacker curve can be started. It turns out that the neutral saddle curve connects the two 1:1 resonant points. It is tangential to the limit point curves, as can be expected from the analytical theory of 1:1 resonant points, see [7].

The Neimark - Sacker curve that starts from the left limit point has several strong resonance points, namely two 1:4 (**R4**) and two 1:3 (**R3**) resonant points. The Neimark - Sacker curve that starts from the right limit point contains an **R4** point, an **R3** point and naturally ends in an **R2** point.

The coordinates of the **R4** point in Figure 7 are $\xi = 0.0166885$, $\eta = -0.619325$, $\omega = 1.37933$, $\zeta = 0.00330682$, $u = 1.36438$. The coordinates of the **R3** point are $\xi = 0.0116809$, $\eta = -0.550418$, $\omega = 1.54866$, $\zeta = 0.00209432$, $u = 1.53061$.

The presence of the abovementioned bifurcation points has a profound influence on the qualitative behaviour of the system. Many details about this are given in [6]. We restrict to some remarks concerning the **R4** and **R3** points not discussed in [6]. From the analytical theory [7] we expect unstable period 4 - limit cycles near an **R4** point. CONTENT allows to simulate orbits and look for this phenomenon. We find easily orbits with the predicted behaviour; it is sufficient to replace the value of ξ by 0.2. The resulting orbit is presented

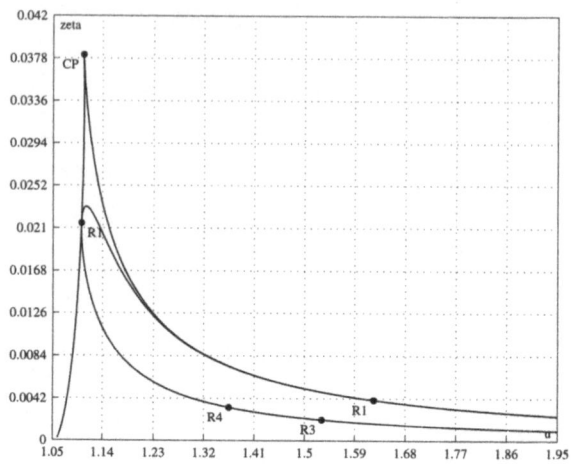

Fig. 5. Fold and Neimark–Sacker curves in (u, ζ)–space.

in Figure 7. Actually, the figure presents a slow transient behavior near the unstable orbit.

In terms of the electromechanical model this means that the platform returns to the same position precisely after 4 revolutions of the rotor.

From the analytical theory [7] we also expect unstable period 3 - limit cycles near an R3 point. It is sufficient to replace the value of ξ by 0.1. The resulting orbit is presented in Figure 7.

References

1. E. J. Doedel, A. R. Champneys, T. F. Fairgrieve, Yu. A. Kuznetsov, B. Sandstede and X. J. Wang, AUTO97 : *Continuation and Bifurcation Software for ordinary differential Equations (with HomCont), User's Guide*, Concordia University, Montreal, Canada (1997).
2. U. Feudel and W. Jansen CANDYS/QA - *A software system for qualitative analysis of nonlinear dynamical systems.* Int. J. Bifurcations and Chaos 4 (1992) 773–794.
3. H. Goldstein, *Classical mechanics*, Addison - Wesley (1950).
4. W. Govaerts, Yu. A. Kuznetsov and B. Sijnave, *Implementation of Hopf and double Hopf continuation using bordering methods*, to appear in ACM Trans. Math. Software.
5. J. Guckenheimer, M. Myers and B. Sturmfels, *Computing Hopf Bifurcations I*, SIAM J. Numer. Anal. 34 (1997) 1–21.
6. A. M. Guskov and Yu. A. Kuznetsov, *Neimark - Sacker bifurcations in the interaction of a source of limited power and an elastic construction*, to appear in Transactions of the Russian Academy of Sciences. (in Russian)

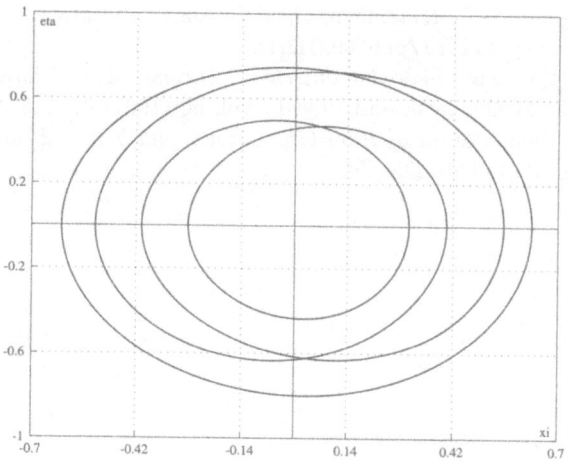

Fig. 6. Orbit near the R4 point in Figure 7.

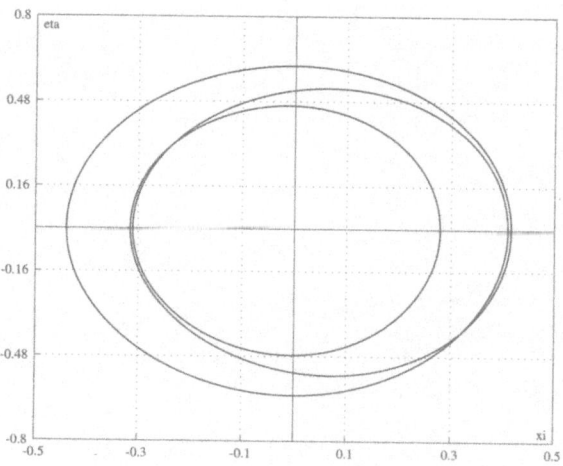

Fig. 7. Orbit near the R3 point in Figure 7.

7. Yu. A. Kuznetsov, *Elements of Applied Bifurcation Theory*, Applied Mathematical Sciences 112, Springer Verlag, (1995, 1998).
8. Yu. A. Kuznetsov and V. V. Levitin, CONTENT :*A multiplatform environment for analyzing dynamical systems*, Dynamical Systems Laboratory, CWI, Amsterdam (1995–1997) (`ftp.cwi.nl/pub/CONTENT`).
9. A. Sommerfeld, *Zur hydrodynamischen Theorie der Schmiermittelreibung*, Zeitschrift für Mathematik und Physik, Vol. 50 (1904) 97–155. (in German)
10. B. Werner, *Computation of Hopf bifurcations with bordered matrices*, SIAM J. Numer. Anal. 33 (1996) 435–455.

Extending a Java Based Framework for Scientific Software-Components

Manfred Göbel[1], Wolfgang Küchlin[2], Stefan Müller[3], and Andreas Weber[2]*

[1] Deutsches Fernerkundungsdatenzentrum, Algorithmen und Prozessoren,
   Deutsches Zentrum für Luft- und Raumfahrt, Oberpfaffenhofen, 82234 Weßling,
   Germany
   manfred.goebel@dlr.de
[2] Arbeitsbereich Symbolisches Rechnen, Wilhelm-Schickard-Institut für
   Informatik, Universität Tübingen, 72076 Tübingen, Germany
   {kuechlin,weber}@informatik.uni-tuebingen.de
   http://www-sr.informatik.uni-tuebingen.de/
[3] Arbeitsbereich Datenbanken und Informationssysteme,
   Wilhelm-Schickard-Institut für Informatik, Universität Tübingen, 72076
   Tübingen, Germany
   muellers@informatik.uni-tuebingen.de
   http://www.informatik.uni-tuebingen.de/db.html

Abstract. A prototypical framework, which was used for building software components for symbolic computation, is extended as follows. First, we demonstrate that the server components can be accessed from other frameworks for collaborative scientific computing, too. Specifically, we incorporate access from the PROGRESS system. Second, we discuss several design issues that arise when encapsulating existing systems as services into the framework. Many of these issues are of a general nature but become relevant in our effort to incorporate the invariant package of MAS and the quantifier elimination package qepcad into our framework.

1 Introduction

In [27,28] we have developed a prototypical framework for building software components for symbolic computation. Using Java, we encapsulated software systems for parallel Gröbner bases computations and for Gröbner basis conversion by the *Fractal Gröbner Walk* [1,2]. Via the Remote Method Invocation (RMI) of Java these specialized software systems are now available from a Java applet and also from general purpose systems such as Maple.

In this paper we discuss several design issues that arose in our continuing work to adapt the prototypical framework to other existing software systems. We discuss them in this context, but they are much more general in nature than this specific work:

– We demonstrate that access to the RMI port from other infrastructures for collaborative scientific computing is possible without any changes on

---

* Supported by *Deutsche Forschungsgemeinschaft* under grant Ku 966/6-1.

the server side. Specifically, we extended the PROGRESS system [3,5,4] in this direction. Since the PROGRESS system is an integral part of the MatSe project for a *"Linkup of Mathematical Servers in the Internet"* [20], our computer algebra servers are now available in this other framework for mathematical servers, too.

- We are currently extending the framework to other server services such as the ones for various computations in invariant theory or for quantifier elimination on real closed fields. Specifically, we are integrating the invariant package of MAS [13], which is a special purpose software system to study polynomial invariants of permutation groups, and the qepcad program [16,7], which allows quantifier elimination on first-order formulas over the field of the reals.
- We now use Java Beans [14] on the client side. Their main use are with respect to the non-algebraic parts of the distributed computation, such as the choice of a compute server.

A major goal of wrapping existing packages as server components of our framework is to make the functionality of these packages available for other systems in a uniform way, especially for general purpose systems such as AXIOM, Maple, Mathematica, MuPad, or Reduce. Thus the situation is the same as the one described in [27] for the Gröbner basis software, to which we refer for the general idea.

The organization of the paper is as follows: In Sec. 2 we describe the PROGRESS system and our extensions to it, which allow it to access our server components via RMI. In Sec. 3 we describe the software packages which we are currently integrating into our framework as new algebraic services. The design issues that arise in this context are discussed in Sec. 4.

2   Accessing Java and RMI Encapsulated Software from Non-Java Systems

2.1   The Progress system

The system PROGRESS [3,5,4] is part of the MatSe project [20]. The goal of MatSe is to build an infrastructure for scientific cooperation via the Internet. The PROGRESS system itself is an object-oriented environment for the definition and manipulation of abstract user-defined data types. Every instance of a defined data type is treated as a PROGRESS object on which appropriate methods can be executed. Pre-defined data types provide methods for accessing various kinds of objects and data on remote hosts. Therefore the system can serve as a platform for the easy integration of algorithms and their transparent usage within a heterogeneous network like the Internet. In conjunction with the generic Web interfaces, PROGRESS opens a market place for computational services, which is also its part in the MatSe project.

A PROGRESS server, called **pgexd** (PROGRESS execution daemon), provides access to various kinds of PROGRESS objects. These objects are stored in files that contain their specification as statements of the PROGRESS language. The PROGRESS language is a simple untyped scripting language. It facilitates the easy definition and easy processing of PROGRESS objects. There are built-in basic object types such as string, boolean, integer, real, list and tuple. Each of those objects provides methods for manipulation and observation, e.g. the method **strlen** can be applied to an object of type string and returns the length of this particular string. The PROGRESS system is extensible in the sense that the definitions of the object types including the provided methods are loaded dynamically. Therefore new object types and methods can be added to the system at any time.

Apart from the basic object types, there are already some additional and more complex object types included the system. One of them is the object type **mdes** (method description), which is used to encapsulate the different services, so that they can all be used in the same way and with the same interface. Figure 1 shows the specification of an **mdes** object which is used to call a service for the generation of random numbers. This object holds several attributes. The attribute **type** defines the input type (here: a PROGRESS tuple containing the sample-size, the mean value and the variance), the attribute **pre** specifies a pre-condition (as a PROGRESS function) that the input parameter must satisfy, and the attribute **rtype** defines the type of the returned object (a PROGRESS list of the computed random numbers). The attribute **method** is the only required attribute and is responsible for the actual service call. In this case, it is a call to a locally available dynamic library function for the computation of the random numbers. The exact syntax of the PROGRESS language is beyond the scope of this paper. For a detailed description see [5].

```
mdes( <|

    type: type(<| samplesize: type("integer"),
                  mu:         type( "real" ),
                  sigsq:      type( "real" )
              |> ),

    pre: '( samplesize > 0 and sigsq > 0.0 ),

    method: method("local:/random.so:normal"),

    rtype: type( [ type( "real" ) ] )

|> )
```

Fig. 1. Method Description Object

210   Manfred Göbel, Wolfgang Küchlin, Stefan Müller, and Andreas Weber

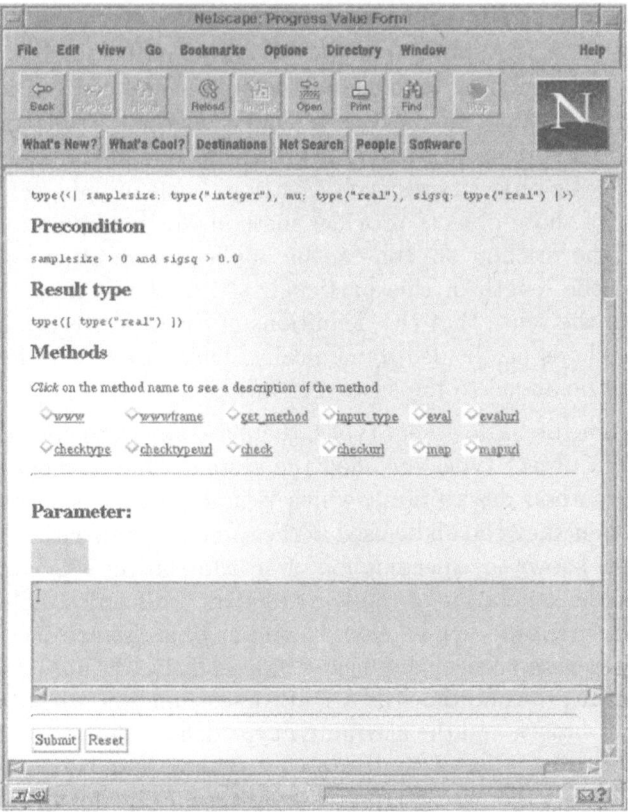

Fig. 2. Generic Web Interface

Every object of type **mdes** provides the method **eval** to evaluate the
encapsulated service with a parameter supplied by the user. As mentioned
above, all these objects are stored as files within the workspace of the
PROGRESS system. They can be accessed via a PROGRESS server by a unique
Uniform Resource Identifier (URI [6]). The core of the PROGRESS server is
the PROGRESS language interpreter which loads the referenced object, inter-
prets it and executes the desired method with the actual parameter. One
special functionality of the PROGRESS server is that it accepts Hyper-Text
Transfer Protocol (HTTP) requests so that it can be contacted with any
Web browser. Upon an HTTP request with a dedicated URI, the server in-
spects the referenced object and generates a generic HTML document, which
is then returned to the client browser and serves as the user interface for
further activities.

Figure 2 shows the HTML document generated by a PROGRESS server when the object of Figure 1 is referenced. This page contains radio buttons for the selection of the desired method, a text area for the specification of an input parameter and a button to submit the request. To generate random numbers simply select the method `eval`, type a correct parameter (according to the type and the precondition) and push the submit button. The PROGRESS server executes the service and sends back an HTML page containing the result.

In a heterogeneous networked environment, especially on the Internet, technologies like Common Object Request Broker Architecture (CORBA) or Java Remote Method Invocation (RMI) [23,25] provide access to already existing algorithms. To enable the use of those algorithms via a PROGRESS system to obtain the generic PROGRESS Web interface, the special communication protocol has to be incorporated into the PROGRESS system. At the moment PROGRESS only supports access to services provided by RMI servers. The next section describes the problems that had to be solved with respect to the communication protocol and the transferred data and gives an example of an already integrated RMI service.

2.2   Progress and RMI

The main problem that we face when we want to call a RMI service out of a PROGRESS server is that general Java objects can not be mapped onto PROGRESS language objects. Every argument that a user has to edit in the PROGRESS user interface when invoking an evaluation of an algorithm or a service call must comply with the PROGRESS language. So if an RMI service requires an argument or delivers a result value for which there is no counterpart in the PROGRESS language, this service can not be integrated into the PROGRESS system.

The only Java objects that can be mapped directly onto PROGRESS objects are the primitive datatypes `int`, `real` and `boolean`, and Java objects of type `String` and `Vector`.

As there exists a Java package used for the communication between Java programs and PROGRESS [15] our approach for the implementation of RMI service calls out of the PROGRESS system is straightforward: We have implemented a small Java wrapper that is invoked whenever a PROGRESS server receives a request for an RMI service. This wrapper transforms the incoming parameter from the PROGRESS language format into Java values, performs the actual RMI service call and converts the resulting Java value back into the corresponding PROGRESS value. This value is given back to the PROGRESS server which sends the result back to the client in the desired form (e.g. as an HTML page if the client is an Internet browser). The communication details are totally hidden within the RMI module of the PROGRESS server.

The simplest way to integrate an RMI service into the PROGRESS system is via an appropriate object of type `mdes` as mentioned above. All neccessary

```
mdes(<|
  description :
        "This method performs a Groebner basis computation",

  type : type( <| var: type("string"),
                  term: type("string") |>),

  method: '(
    argstring <- arg.var; argstring.append("\n");
    argstring.append(arg.term); argstring.append("\n");
    method(
      "rmi://chaq.informatik.uni-tuebingen.de:1099/").eval
      ( <| rmiobject: "ObjectServer",
           rmimethod: ["getGroebnerObject","runParGroebner"],
           arg: [ [ void ],
                  [ [ "parallel", "-m 1", "-L 4 4", "-C 4",
                      "-M 1", "-p 2", "-o 2" ],
                    argstring ] ] |> ) )
|>)
```

Fig. 3. Mdes object for Gröbner basis computation

information required for an RMI service call like the RMI server name, the RMI server port, the name of the remote object and the sequence of methods that must be applied on the remote object can be encapsulated into the mdes object. So the PROGRESS user need only be concerned about the varying input data that servers as the argument to the RMI service call.

Figure 3 shows an example mdes object used to call an RMI service for computing a Gröbner basis. The tuple attribute method holds a PROGRESS function that first builds up the argument string for the RMI call (argstring) out of the users input data (variables and terms). Then this function calls the actual RMI service with the additionally neccessary information (remote object, remote methods and tags for controlling the underlying Gröbner basis solver). As with any mdes object the PROGRESS server provides a generic Web interface, so that this RMI service can now be used via a WWW browser. For ease of use the generated HTML page looks exactly the same as the one described in the previous section. The user does not recognize that the actual service is provided by an RMI server.

In this Section we have dealt with an extension on the client side. The extensions discussed in the following are on the server side.

3   Integrating other Server Packages

Since the integration of the following server packages into our framework is work in progress, we will only give a brief sketch of the packages. The main issue of the second part of this paper are the design considerations in Sec. 4, which came up by the specific integration of these packages but are relevant for further extensions, too.

3.1   The Invariant Package of MAS

The invariant package of the computer algebra package MAS [18] is a workbench for programming and experimenting with polynomial invariants of permutation groups. It is focused on the implementation of reduction and completion procedures with a special emphasis on algorithms for finding representations of polynomials in terms of permutation-invariant basis polynomials. From the programmer's point of view, the invariant package is built of a set of modules and provides a library of algorithms (and data types) for high level programming. The algorithms are based on the classical theorem of E. Noether [21,26] and on algorithms described in [11–13].

The invariant package contains algorithms for

- input and output of permutation groups,
- generation of orbit polynomials,
- checking of invariant properties of polynomials,
- unique separation of polynomials in invariant and remainder polynomials,
- computation of representations and reduction of permutation-invariant polynomials w.r.t. different orbit representations and optimization levels,
- checking of representation and reduction results, and
- embedding of reduction techniques for permutation-invariant polynomials within completion algorithms.

The algorithms are implemented over the integer and rational numbers; they can be used interactively or via command files in the interpreter environment of MAS.

3.2   The quantifier-elimination program qepcad

The qepcad program [16] allows elimination of quantifiers on first-order formulas of the real closed field of the real numbers. Its input is a quantified formula, whose atomic formulas are equations or inequalities involving multivariate integral polynomials. Its output is an equivalent quantifier free formula. Improvements to qepcad are described in [7], which yield much "simpler" output formulas than before. Various other algorithms for the elimination of quantifiers for first-order formulas over the field of the reals have also been implemented over the last years, see e. g. [31,30,19]. Their realizations are available in the Redlog system [9], which is implemented in Reduce. The

Redlog system allows access to qepcad. We use this Redlog interface for our server software, because it allows a simplified access to qepcad: the input is simply one first-order formula; the extraction of the list of free and bounded variables and calculating the number of free variables—which are required as additional input parameters by qepcad—are done in Redlog.

During the last years quantifier elimination on real closed fields has found several applications, see e. g. [17,8] for some examples. So an integration of the functionality of qepcad into one of the general purpose algebra system has been the desire of several researchers for some time. Recently in Mathematica the implementation of an algorithm for quantifier elimination on real closed fields has been the topic of some efforts, which to our knowledge has not been finished yet.

Even if this effort for Mathematica succeeds, access to the qepcad functionality in other general purpose systems without a reimplementation is still of considerable interest.

Using a quantifier elimination package for the stability analysis of differential equations. One of our main motivations to make qepcad available for general purpose systems is the stability analysis of differential equations, cf. [17]. This application is a good example of the interaction of computations done in a general purpose system and of ones done in a very specialized system such as qepcad. No system alone could perform the entire task.

The study of stability problems will in general only be one part of the analysis of the differential equation a user wants to perform among others such as numerical simulations. Since most of the other tasks can be done out of a general purpose algebra system, the differential equation should be represented in the general purpose algebra system as a single source for these various computations.

A stability analysis by quantifier elimination on real closed fields is possible for differential equations that are given by polynomials in the variables and parameters, a class that contains many important examples. The reduction of a stability problem to a quantifier elimination problem involves the use of the Routh-Hurwitz criterion or a similar one for deciding if all roots of a polynomial have a negative real part or not. We refer to [17] for the details of this reduction. All the necessary computations for this reduction such as computing Hurwitz determinants can be done in a general purpose computer algebra system such as Maple or Mathematica. Using suitable symbols for the logical quantifiers and logical connectives, a first-order formula stating a stability property of the differential equation can be built in such a system. Then our system infrastructure can be used to send this formula to a quantifier elimination package such as qepcad. The equivalent quantifier free formula which is computed by qepcad is then send back to the general purpose system and can be used there in the same form as the result of a local function call.

The flow of computations in the local general purpose system and the remote quantifier elimination package for a symbolic stability analysis is sketched in Fig. 4.

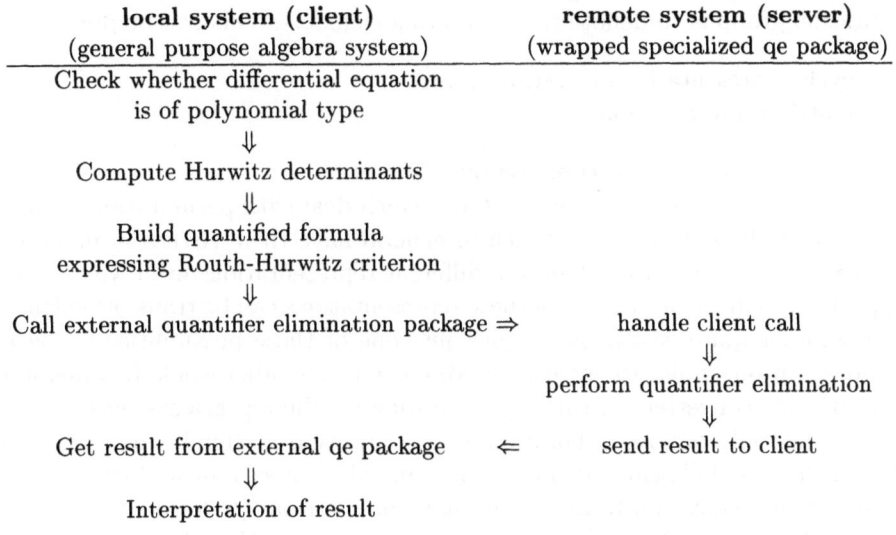

Fig. 4. Flow of computation for symbolic stability analysis

4   Design Issues Arising by these Extensions

4.1   The Common Mathematical Exchange Format

As in [27] we use one of the common mathematical exchange formats to accomplish the data aspect of the communication between a client algebra system and a server algebra component. As in [27] we use the MathBus for this purpose. Another format such as OpenMath would be suited equally well; the choice for the MathBus was primarily because of our existing code base. Converters between MathBus and OpenMath are also one of the goals of our current implementation effort.

The algebraic data types that are handled by the qepcad program are first-order logical formulas involving polynomials. These are already present in the MathBus. Logical quantifiers are not present in all client systems such as Maple, but we can simply choose one representation for them in Maple and extend our Maple to MathBus converter to these data types.

Access to the MAS server involves a new algebraic data type that was not present in the MathBus: permutation groups. Extending the MathBus to a new data type is straight forward: the description of such a new algebraic type just has to be provided in the so called MathBus registry, cf. [33].[1] So we will omit any of these implementation details and will just discuss the following more general problem.

In general, there are several possibilities for representing algebraic data types such as permutation groups. A common possibility to represent a permutation group is to denote the generating elements. This can be done by

- cycle representations in various forms,
- matrix representations

to mention just the most common possibilities.

In general, different algebra systems which deal with permutation groups have made different choices, which in general have their virtues in different contexts. Also very often there are different representations even within one algebra systems. However, all of these representations can be transformed into one another quite easily. So we pick just one of these possibilities (a cycle representation similar to one used in Maple, but any other would be possible) and provide converters to this representation for the algebra systems.

Having only one representation for permutation groups in the exchange format has the following advantage: For any algebra system we have to provide only *one* converter from the internally used format (or formats, if several are used by one system). If we used several representations for permutation groups in the exchange format of the MathBus, then anyone of the algebra system had to provide converters to *all* of the used representations.

The disadvantage of having only one representation is that it might cost more time to transmit data from an algebra system (A) to an algebra system (B): assume that (A) and (B) happen to use a similar representation for the algebraic data to be transmitted. If the exchange format uses another representation, then the time of conversion from (A) to the exchange format and from the exchange format into (B) is higher than in the case that the exchange format provides an additional representation that is similar to the one used by (A) and (B).

In general, the contradictory goals are the speed of transmitting the data structures (including the conversions on client and server side) vs. the implementation effort, which is required if several formats are supported.

Note that a decision for several representations of mathematical data structure in the common exchange format will have consequences for the future: all prospective algebra systems that are included into the framework have to provide support (at least in the form of converters) for all of the formats.

So we propose to provide as few representations as possible, as long as the different representations are "easily convertible" into each other. Intensionally, we have used the rather vague term of "easily convertible" instead of a

---

[1] The situation is similar for OpenMath: a new content dictionary has to be defined for a new algebraic data type.

well defined one like "convertible in linear time", because we think that the choice of the different data types in the exchange format should be governed more by "engineering compromises" than by strictly formal criteria.

Applying this criterion to the case of permutation groups we come to the result of picking just one of the cycle representations and not providing a separate format for a matrix representation in the exchange format. However, if for further applications entirely different representations of groups are needed—e. g. such given by relations—then such a representation should also be included into the common mathematical exchange format, because these might not be easily convertible into the existing ones.

In the case of polynomials we have also chosen to just take one representation for them and the MathBus also provides only one representation for arbitrary precision integers, which is a decimal format. (Strictly speaking the MathBus uses a base 1000000 representation, cf. [33].) With this choice we differ from some of the developments in OpenMath, where recently a content dictionary for polynomials in recursive and distributive representation has been defined [22], or integers can have decimal and binary representations.[2]

We are aware that having binary representations for integers, or recursive and distributive representations for polynomials can have a strong influence on the performance of small grained applications like a component for calculating integral polynomial greatest common divisors, cf. [29]. However, since the framework described in this paper is primarily one for coarse grained components, which are quite common in computer algebra, we think that this issue is not of central importance in our context. Making a decision whether one deals with coarse grained components or small grained components seems to be quite fundamental.

4.2   Drawing the Local-Remote Border

In Fig. 5 we give a schematic view of the communication between a client system and a server system. In general the client and the server will run on different architectures, because otherwise the server software could be downloaded to the client.

There are several options to draw the local-remote border in such a communication. Below we discuss the pros (+) and cons (-) for using the options (a), (b), or (c) in the design of the communication architecture.

Pros and cons of option (a)

+ We have "thin clients".

---

[2] At this point it is debatable whether the different view taken by OpenMath is simply one due to a different interpretation of the term "easily convertible": In this case of integers in binary and decimal representation this might be less a point of discussion than in the case of polynomials in recursive and distributive representation.

	Data types of arguments in interface	Option for local/remote border
Client system		
Java wrapper		
⇕	Strings	(a)
Converter to MathBus format		
MathBus object serialization		
⇕	Objects	(b)
MathBus object de-serialization		
Converter from MathBus format		
⇕	Strings	(c)
Java wrapper		
Server algebra system		

The points (a), (b), or (c) are options for the local-remote border. The second column gives the data types of the objects at these points of the communication.

Fig. 5. Schematic view of client-server communication

+ Access to the server system from other infrastructures which expect string based arguments at the interface (e.g. PROGRESS) is possible.
- Not well suited if algebra system directly supports one of the exchange formats. Some examples are Reduce and OpenMath [10] or the Weyl computer algebra substrate [32] und the MathBus [33]. Because of the many advantages of a common exchange format we assume that this option will be of growing importance.

Pros and cons of option (b)

+ We have "relatively thin clients".
- Access to the server system from other infrastructures, which expect string based arguments at the interface (e. g. PROGRESS) is in general not possible.
  This is a certain disadvantage if Java object serialization is used for the objects of the exchange format (e. g. the dag serialization for the Java OpenMath objects [24]).
  Remark. Any serialized object representation can be converted to a string if a string encoding such as the mime base-64 encoding is used. Such an encoding is used e. g. for the serialized MathBus terms [33] and allows the transport over string biased media such as e-mail. However, the access to these terms from a client system like PROGRESS is as hard as to any binary object serialization, because support for serializing the objects has to be provided by the client system.
+ Well suited, if algebra system supports one of the exchange format.
+ The local-remote interface has to deal with fewer exceptions than is the case with the other options, because the objects are in a consistent syntactic form and no "parse errors" have to be handled.

Pros and cons of option (c)

- We have "relatively fat clients". However, because of the Java specific possibility to distribute the client code dynamically from a server, the drawbacks of this point in a Java context are not as severe as in traditional contexts.
- The client has to know some of the details of the server software, which should be hidden from a client (cf. Fig. 3).
+ Access to the server system from other infrastructures, which expect string based arguments at the interface (e. g. PROGRESS) is possible.
+ Well suited, if client algebra system directly supports one of the exchange formats. The conversion from the exchange format to the format of the server system can be done on client side: simply use the converters from the intermediate format to the server format on the client side.

For the Gröbner basis software we used option (c). In order to gain experience with one of the other possibilities and its elegance, we will use possibility (b) for the MAS server and the qepcad server.

4.3   Use of Java Beans

We have transformed the client-side Java software for the "scripting access" (cf. [27]) to Java Beans [14]. This transformation was applied as well to the existing Java components for the parallel Gröbner basis and Gröbner Walk software as it is used for the new components. Using the techniques of Java Beans and its possibility of having persistent object states that can be changed by the end user has the following advantages.

- The URL of a server can be stored persistently in the bean instance but can nevertheless be changed by a user. Thus the code written in the language of a computer algebra system such as Maple or Mathematica, which is used to access the algebraic service out of this system, does not have to be changed if a new URL is to be used for algebraic service.
- The way of communication between a computer algebra system and the Java Bean can also be stored persistently in the state of the bean instance. Thus only one single Bean is necessary for all the different client algebra systems, independent of their mechanisms of communication (via pipes or via files and the name and location of the files used for communication).
- More elaborate ways of accessing a server (e. g. via a repository that might contain load information of different servers) can be included in the bean instance without change of the algebra software.
- Also information used for access management to the servers can be included in the state of these client-side bean instances.

5   Conclusion

Since there are several conflicting goals when incorporating existing software systems into our prototypical framework, no single "best" solution seems to be possible. Moreover, one has to take into consideration the design decisions of other groups, which gives additional importance to appropriate "Engineering compromises". Although we think that we made reasonable design decisions, it might well be that our answers to the following questions are suboptimal in the context of the design decisions of other groups.

- Which part should be on the server side, which on the client side of the computation?
- Are the parameters to the RMI methods strings or binary objects?

However, a major advantage of our Java based approach is that these parts of the design can be changed without too much effort. So our answers to these questions can be reverted, if an integration with other systems would benefit from a revision.

Moreover, we have shown that our framework can be accessed from other infrastructures for collaborative scientific computing such as the PROGRESS system, too. So the specialized computer algebra software provided by us is made available for further areas of scientific computing.

So we think that the work described in this paper is a step towards the overall goal of achieving an integrated computing environment for scientific computing.

Acknowledgements: We are grateful to T. Hermann and R. Reingruber for implementing parts of the system.

References

1. AMRHEIN, B., AND GLOOR, O.   The Fractal Walk.   In *Gröbner Bases and Applications—Int. Conf. 33 Years of Gröbner Bases* (Feb. 1998), B. Buchberger and F. Winkler, Eds., vol. 251 of *London Mathematical Society Lecture Notes Series*, Cambridge University Press, pp. 305–322.
2. AMRHEIN, B., GLOOR, O., AND KÜCHLIN, W.   On the Walk.   *Theoretical Comput. Sci. 187* (1997), 179–202.
3. BECKER, P. A framework for providing and using algorithms and algorithmic meta knowledge on the Internet. In *Proceedings of the 5th Annual Workshop on Information Technologies & Systems (WITS'95)* (1995), S. Ram and M. Jarke, Eds., no. 95–15 in Aachener Informatik-Berichte, pp. 2–11.
4. BECKER, P. An embeddable and extendable language for large-scale programming on the Internet. In *Proceedings of the 16th International Conference on Distributed Computing Systems (ICDCS'96)* (1996), pp. 594–603.
5. BECKER, P.   *Verteiltes Modell-Management und Objektbanken für diskrete Probleme und diskrete Strukturen.* Dissertation, Wilhelm-Schickard-Institut für Informatik, Universität Tübingen, 1996.

6. BERNERS-LEE, T. Universal Resource Identifiers in WWW. RFC 1630, CERN, June 1994.

7. BROWN, C. W. Simplification of truth-invariant cylindrical algebraic decomposition. In *Proceedings of the 1998 International Symposium on Symbolic and Algebraic Computation (ISSAC '98)* (Rostock, Germany, 1998), O. Gloor, Ed., The Association for Computing Machinery, ACM, pp. 295–301.

8. CHAUVIN, C., MÜLLER, M., AND WEBER, A. An application of quantifier elimination to mathematical biology. In *Computer Algebra in Science and Engineering* (Bielefeld, Germany, Aug. 1994), J. Fleischer, J. Grabmeier, F. W. Hehl, and W. Küchlin, Eds., Zentrum für Interdisziplinäre Forschung, World Scientific, pp. 287–296.

9. DOLZMANN, A., AND STURM, T. *Redlog user manual*. FMI, Universität Passau, 94030 Passau, Germany, 1997. http://www.fmi.uni-passau.de/~redlog/.

10. GAETANO, M., HUCHET, C., AND NEUN, W. The realization of an OpenMath server for REDUCE. In *Computer Algebra in Scientific Computing (CASC-98)—Extended Abstracts* (St. Petersburg, Russia, Apr. 1998), N. N. Vassiliev, Ed., pp. 48–56.

11. GÖBEL, M. Computing bases for permutation-invariant polynomials. *Journal of Symbolic Computation 19* (1995), 285–291.

12. GÖBEL, M. Symideal Gröbner bases. In *Rewriting Techniques and Applications — 7th International Conference (RTA '96)* (New Brunswick, NJ, U. S. A., July 1996), H. Ganzinger, Ed., vol. 1103 of *Lecture Notes in Computer Science*, Springer-Verlag, pp. 48–62.

13. GÖBEL, M. The invariant package of MAS. In *Rewriting Techniques and Applications — 8th International Conference (RTA '97)* (Sitges, Barcelona, Spain, 1997), H. Comon, Ed., vol. 1232 of *Lecture Notes in Computer Science*, Springer-Verlag, pp. 327–330.

14. HAMILTON, G. *JavaBeans*. Sun Microsystems, July 1997. For Version 1.01. http://java.sun.com/beans/.

15. HERMANN, T. Kommunikation zwischen Progress und Java. Studienarbeit, Wilhelm-Schickard-Institut für Informatik, Universität Tübingen, 1997.

16. HONG, H. *Improvements in CAD-Based Quantifier Elimination*. PhD thesis, Ohio State University, Columbus, Ohio, USA, 1990.

17. HONG, H., LISKA, R., AND STEINBERG, S. Testing stability by quantifier elimination. *Journal of Symbolic Computation 24*, 2 (Aug. 1997), 161–187.

18. KREDEL, H. MAS: Modula-2 Algebra System. In *IV International Conference on Computer Algebra in Physical Research* (1990), V. P. Gerdt, V. A. Rostovtsev, and D. V. Shirkov, Eds., World Scientific Publishing, pp. 31–34. http://alice.fmi.uni-passau.de/mas.html

19. LOOS, R., AND WEISPFENNING, V. Applying linear quantifier elimination. *The Computer Journal 5* (1993), 450–462.

20. MATSE PROJECT GROUP. The MatSe project (Linkup of Mathematical Servers in the Internet). URL: http://mmm.wiwi.hu-berlin.de/matse/, 1997.

21. NOETHER, E. Der Endlichkeitssatz der Invarianten endlicher Gruppen. *Math. Ann. 77* (1916), 89–92.

22. OPENMATH CONSORTIUM. OpenMath. URL: www.openmath.org, 1997.

23. ORFALI, R., AND HARKEY, D. *Client/Server Programming with JAVA and CORBA*. Wiley, 1997.

24. POLYMATH DEVELOPMENT GROUP. *Java OpenMath Library.* Centre for Experimental and Constructive Mathematics, Simon Fraser University, Burnaby, BC, Canada, 1997. Version 0.3. `http://pdg.cecm.sfu.ca/openmath/lib/`.
25. SIEGEL, J. *CORBA Fundamentals and Programming.* John Wiley & Sons, New York, 1996.
26. STURMFELS, B. *Algorithms in Invariant Theory.* Texts and Monographs in Symbolic Computation. Springer-Verlag, Wien, 1993.
27. WEBER, A., KÜCHLIN, W., AND EGGERS, B. Parallel computer algebra software as a Web component. *Concurrency: Practice and Experience 10*, 11–13 (1998), 1179–1188.
28. WEBER, A., KÜCHLIN, W., EGGERS, B., AND SIMONIS, V. A parallel Gröbner solver as a Web component. In *Computer Algebra in Scientific Computing (CASC-98)—Extended Abstracts* (St. Petersburg, Russia, Apr. 1998), N. N. Vassiliev, Ed., p. 133.
29. WEBER, A., KÜCHLIN, W., AND HOSS, J. Connecting and reusing computer algebra software via CORBA—a case study. Submitted for the proceedings of the Dagstuhl conference on generic programming.
30. WEISPFENNING, V. Quantifier elimination for real algebra—the cubic case. In *Proceedings of the 1994 International Symposium on Symbolic and Algebraic Computation (ISSAC '94)* (Oxford, July 1994), Association for Computing Machinery, pp. 258–263.
31. WEISPFENNING, V. Quantifier elimination for real algebra—the quadratic case and beyond. *Applicable Algebra in Engineering Communication and Computing 8*, 2 (Feb. 1997), 85–101.
32. ZIPPEL, R. The Weyl computer algebra substrate. In *Design and Implementation of Symbolic Computation Systems — International Symposium DISCO '93* (Gmunden, Austria, Sept. 1993), A. Miola, Ed., vol. 722 of *Lecture Notes in Computer Science*, Springer-Verlag, pp. 303–318.
33. ZIPPEL, R. *The MathBus Term Structure.* Cornell University, Ithaca, NY 14853, U.S.A., 1997. `http://www2.cs.cornell.edu/Simlab/papers/mathbus/mathTerm.htm`.

Symbolic-numeric Investigations for Stability Analysis of Satellite Systems

Sergey A.Gutnik

Institute for Computer Aided Design,
Russian Academy of Sciences,
19/18 2-nd Brestskaya str. Moscow, 123056 Russia

Abstract. An approach for the symbolic-numeric stability analysis of satellite systems correspondingly to structure of gravitational, aerodynamical, gyrostatic and static forces is presented. The satellite system is described by Lagrange differential equations. The equations of motion form a closed system, for which the Jacobi Integral is valid. Stationary solutions of these equations are defined by the multivariate polynomial system.

The algebraic polynomial system has been investigated with the help of both the numerical and symbolic analysis. The symbolic investigation was made by means of Resultant and Grobner Basis methods[7].

The stationary motions of a satellite subject to gravitational, aerodynamical, gyrostatic and static torques is governed by nine algebraic equations with nine parameters - projections of torques vectors onto the frame attached to the body of the satellite. The classes of stationary solutions of these algebraic equations have been found with the help of computer algebra system Maple [8] by applying the Resultant, the Groebner Basis and Factorization methods.

Computation of the surfaces of algebraic equations real solutions is performed numerically by the gradient method. The number of grid points was chosen as a function of curvature. As a result of this work 3D boundary surfaces with equal number of equilibrium positions of a satellite are constructed.

On the base of this methods the problem of defining the equilibrium positions of a satellite in a circular orbit under the influence of external torques was solved [2],[6], [9],[10],[11].

The stability of equilibrium positions are analyzed numerically with Lyapunov's second method. The Jacobi Integral as Lyapunov's function is used.

A symbolic-numeric method is proposed for determining all the equilibrium positions of a satellite with a given gyrostatic torque, with given aerodynamic torque and given principal central moments of inertia. It is shown that 24 isolated equilibrium positions exist when the modulus of the gyrostatic torque vector and the modulus of the aerodynamic torque vector are sufficiently small. The number of isolated equilibrium positions decreases to 8 as the gyrostatic torque increases. The stability of the equilibrium positions are analyzed numerically. We consider the motion of a satellite in a central Newtonian force field. Let statically and dynamically stabilized rotors be mounted in a satellite, where they spin with a constant angular velocity relative to the body of the satellite. A satellite of this type with rotors is called a gyrostat satellite. We shall consider the rotational motion of a gyrostat satellite in a circular orbit under the effect of gravitational and aerodynamic torques. We shall assume that the effect of the atmosphere on the satellite amounts to drag force, applied at the center of pressure and directed opposite the velocity of the center of mass of the the satellite. We shall neglect the entrainment of the atmosphere by the rotating Earth.

The equations of motion of the gyrostat satellite with consideration of the aerodynamic effect can be written in the form [1],[2]:

$$A\dot{p} + (C - B)qr - 3\omega_0^2(C - B)a_{32}a_{33} = \tilde{h}_2 r - \tilde{h}_3 q + \tilde{S}_2 a_1 3 - \tilde{S}_3 a_{12},$$
$$B\dot{q} + (A - C)rp - 3\omega_0^2(A - C)a_{31}a_{33} = \tilde{h}_3 p - \tilde{h}_1 r + \tilde{S}_3 a_1 1 - \tilde{S}_1 a_{13}, \quad (1)$$
$$C\dot{r} + (B - A)pq - 3\omega_0^2(B - A)a_{31}a_{32} = \tilde{h}_1 q - \tilde{h}_2 p + \tilde{S}_1 a_1 3 - \tilde{S}_3 a_{11},$$

Here $\tilde{h}_1 = \sum_{i=1}^{3} J_i \alpha_i \dot{\varphi}_i$, $\tilde{h}_2 = \sum_{i=1}^{3} J_i \beta_i \dot{\varphi}_i$, $\tilde{h}_3 = \sum_{i=1}^{3} J_i \gamma_i \dot{\varphi}_i$, are the projections of the gyrostatic torque vector onto the principal central axes of inertia Ox, Oy, Oz of the satellite; p, q, r are the projections of the absolute angular velocity of the satellite onto the axes Ox, Oy, Oz; A, B, C are the principal central moments of inertia of the satellite; α_i, β_i, γ_i are the constant direction cosines of the symmetry axis of the i-th rotor in the frame $Oxyz$ attached to the satellite; $\dot{\varphi}_i$ is the constant angular velocity of the i-th rotor relative to the body of the satellite; n is the number of rotors; ω_0 is the angular velocity of the center of mass of the satellite in its circular orbit. $\tilde{S}_1 = -a_p Q$, $\tilde{S}_2 = -b_p Q$, $\tilde{S}_3 = -c_p Q$, Q is the atmospheric drug force, a_p, b_p, c_p are the coordinates of the center of pressure of the satellite in the frame $Oxyz$.

If the attitude of the satellite in the orbiting frame $OXYZ$ (the axis OZ is directed along the radius vector of the center of mass of the satellite, the axis OX is directed along the tangent to the orbit, and the axis OY complements the frame to a right-handed coordinate system) is described by means of the Euler angles ψ (precession), ϑ (nutation), and φ (spin) the direction cosines in the transformation matrix between the frames $OXYZ$ and $Oxyz$ and the expressions for p, q and r have the form:

$$
\begin{aligned}
a_{11} &= \cos\psi\cos\varphi - \sin\psi\cos\vartheta\sin\varphi, \\
a_{12} &= -\cos\psi\sin\varphi - \sin\psi\cos\vartheta\sin\varphi, \\
a_{13} &= \sin\psi\sin\vartheta, \\
a_{21} &= \sin\psi\cos\varphi + \cos\psi\cos\vartheta\sin\varphi, \\
a_{22} &= -\sin\psi\sin\varphi + \cos\psi\cos\vartheta\cos\varphi, \\
a_{23} &= -\cos\psi\sin\vartheta, \\
a_{31} &= \sin\vartheta\sin\varphi, \\
a_{32} &= \sin\vartheta\cos\varphi, \\
a_{33} &= \cos\vartheta;
\end{aligned}
\quad (2)
$$

$$p = \dot\psi a_{31} + \dot\vartheta \cos\varphi + \omega_0 a_{21},$$
$$q = \dot\psi a_{32} + \dot\vartheta \sin\varphi + \omega_0 a_{22}, \tag{3}$$
$$r = \dot\psi a_{33} + \dot\vartheta + \omega_0 a_{23}.$$

Equations (1) along with (3) form a closed system of equations of motion of the gyrostat satellite, for which the Jacobi Integral is valid

$$H = \frac{1}{2}(A\bar p^2 + B\bar q^2 + C\bar r^2) + \frac{3}{2}\omega_0^2[(A - C)a_{31}^2 + (B - C)a_{32}^2] +$$
$$+ \frac{1}{2}\omega_0^2[(B - A)a_{21}^2 + (B - C)a_{23}^2] - \omega_0(\tilde h_1 a_{21} + \tilde h_2 a_{22} + \tilde h_3 a_{23}) -$$
$$- (\tilde S_1 a_{11} + \tilde S_2 a_{12} + \tilde S_3 a_{13}), \tag{4}$$

where $\bar p = p - \omega_0 a_{21}$, $\bar q = q - \omega_0 a_{22}$, $\bar r = r - \omega_0 a_{23}$.

Setting $\psi = const$, $\vartheta = const$, $\varphi = const$ in (1) and (3) introducing the notation $\bar h_i = \omega_0 \tilde h_i$, $\tilde S_i = \omega_0^2 \bar S_i$ (i=1,2,3), we obtain the equations

$$(C - B)(a_{22}a_{23} - 3a_{32}a_{33}) = \bar h_2 a_{23} - \bar h_3 a_{22} + \bar S_2 a_{13} - \bar S_3 a_{12},$$
$$(A - C)(a_{21}a_{23} - 3a_{31}a_{33}) = \bar h_3 a_{21} - \bar h_1 a_{23} + \bar S_3 a_{11} - \bar S_1 a_{13}, \tag{5}$$
$$(B - A)(a_{21}a_{22} - 3a_{31}a_{32}) = \bar h_1 a_{22} - \bar h_2 a_{21} + \bar S_1 a_{12} - \bar S_2 a_{11},$$

which determine the equilibrium positions of the gyrostat satellite in the orbiting frame.

Let $A \neq B \neq C$. Substituting the expressions for the direction cosines from (2) in terms of Euler angles into Eqs. (5), we obtain three equations with three unknowns ψ, ϑ, φ. A second procedure for closing Eqs. (5) is to add the following six orthogonality conditions for the direction cosines:

$$a_{i1}a_{j1} + a_{i2}a_{j2} + a_{i3}a_{j3} = \delta_{ij} \tag{6}$$

where δ_{ij} is the Kronecker delta and $(i, j = 1, 2, 3)$. Equations (5) and (6) form a closed system with respect to the direction cosines, which also specifies the equilibrium solutions of the satellite.

We state the following problem for the system of equations (5), (6): determine all nine direction cosines, i.e., to find all the equilibrium positions of the satellite when $A, B, C, \bar h_1, \bar h_2, \bar h_3, \bar S_1, \bar S_2$, and $\bar S_3$ are given.

The problem has been solved only for the special cases in which the total angular momentum of the rotors coincides with one of the axes or lies in one of the coordinate planes of the frame $Oxyz$ [3-5]. In the case $\bar h_1 = \bar h_2 = \bar h_3 = 0$ and $\bar S_1 = \bar S_2 = \bar S_3 = 0$ it has been proved that the system (5), (6) has

24 solutions describing the equilibrium positions of a rigid body. Below, we consider the general case of the problem of the equilibria of a satellite.

Let $\bar{S}_1 = \bar{S}_2 = \bar{S}_3 = 0$. Projecting Eqs. (5) onto the axis of the orbiting frame $OXYZ$, we can obtain algebraic system [6]

$$4(Aa_{21}a_{31} + Ba_{22}a_{32} + Ca_{23}a_{33}) + (\bar{h}_1 a_3 1 + \bar{h}_2 a_3 2 + \bar{h}_3 a_3 3) = 0,$$
$$Aa_{11}a_{31} + Ba_{12}a_{32} + Ca_{13}a_{33} = 0, \quad (7)$$
$$(Aa_{11}a_{21} + Ba_{12}a_{22} + Ca_{13}a_{23}) + (\bar{h}_1 a_1 1 + \bar{h}_2 a_1 2 + \bar{h}_3 a_1 3) = 0,$$

A solution of the system (6), (7) can be obtained using an algorithm for the construction of Groebner bases [7]. The method of Groebner bases is used to solve systems of nonlinear algebraic equations. It comprises an algorithmic procedure for reducing the problem involving polynomials of several variables to the investigation of a polynomial of one variable.

Using a computer algebra system [8], we calculate the Groebner basis of the system of polynomials (6), (7) under the ordering on the total power of the variables [9],[10]. Here we write out the polynomials in the Groebner basis that depend only on variables a_{31}, a_{32}, a_{33}.

$$(B - C)^2 a_{32}^2 a_{33}^2 + (C - A)^2 a_{31}^2 a_{33}^2 + (A - B)^2 a_{31}^2 a_{32}^2 =$$
$$\frac{1}{16}(\bar{h}_1 a_{31} + \bar{h}_2 a_{32} + \bar{h}_3 a_{33})^2 (a_{31}^2 + a_{32}^2 + a_{33}^2),$$
$$4(B - C)(C - A)(A - B)a_{31}a_{32}a_{33} + (\bar{h}_1(B - C)a_{32}a_{33} + \quad (8)$$
$$\bar{h}_2(C - A)a_{31}a_{33} + \bar{h}_3(A - B)a_{31}a_{32})(\bar{h}_1 a_{31} + \bar{h}_2 a_{32} + \bar{h}_3 a_{33}) = 0,$$
$$a_{31}^2 + a_{32}^2 + a_{33}^2 = 1.$$

Introducing the notation $x = a_{31}/a_{32}$, $y = a_{33}/a_{32}$, $h_i = \bar{h}_i/(B - C)$, $\nu = (B-A)/(B-C)$, we deduce the following equations for the determination of x and y.

$$a_0 y^2 + a_1 y + a_2 = 0,$$
$$b_0 y^4 + b_1 y^3 + b_2 y^2 + b_3 y + b_4 = 0, \quad (9)$$

where

$$a_0 = h_3(h_1 - (1 - \nu)h_2 x,),$$
$$a_1 = \nu(4(1 - \nu) - h_3^2)x + (h_1 x + h_2)(h_1 - (1 - \nu)h_2 x),$$
$$a_2 = -\nu)h_3(h_1 x + h_2)x,$$
$$b_0 = -h_3^2,$$
$$b_1 = -2h_3(h_1 x + h_2),$$
$$b_2 = 16(1 +^2 x^2) - (h_1 x + h_2)^2 - h_3^2(1 + x^2),$$
$$b_3 = -2h_3(h_1 x + h_2)(1 + x^2),$$
$$b_4 = 16\nu^2 x^2 - (h_1 x + h_2)^2(1 + x^2).$$

Invoking the resultant concept we eliminate variable y from the equations (9). The equation in x than has the form.

$$p_0 x^{1}2 + p_1 x^{1}1 + \ldots + p_{11}x + p_{12} = 0, \tag{10}$$

whose coefficients depend in a rather complicated way on the parameters ν, h_1, h_2, h_3

$$p_0 = \qquad (1-\nu)^6 p_1 2, p_1 = -(1-\nu)^5 p_1 1, \ldots$$
$$p_{11} = -32h_1^3 h_2^3 (2h_1^2 - 2(1-\nu)h_2^2 + \nu h_3^2 + 4\nu(1-\nu)), p_{12} = -16h_1^4 h_2^2. \tag{11}$$

By the definition of resultant, to every root x of Eq.(10) there corresponds a common root y of the system (9). It can easily be shown that to every real root x of Eq.(10) there correspond 2 solutions for (5),(6). Since the number of real roots of Eq.(10) does not exceed 12, the satellite in a circular orbit can have at most 24 equilibria in the orbiting frame.

Other case when $\bar{h}_1 = \bar{h}_2 = \bar{h}_3 = 0$ and $\bar{S}_1 \neq 0, \bar{S}_2 \neq 0, \bar{S}_3 \neq 0$ is investigated analogously. It can be shown that by reduction of the polynomials (5) and (6) we can then obtain a 12th-degree algebraic equation for x, whose coefficients depends on the parameters ν, S_1, S_2, S_3. This 12th-degree algebraic equation gives 24 equilibrium solutions of the system (5), (6).

Using Eq.(10),(11) we can determined numerically all the relative equilibrium positions of the satellite and analyze their stability. We have analyzed numerically the dependence of the number of real solutions of Eq.(10) on the parameters, using the factorization method [11]. For fixed values of ν and h_3 the number of real roots was determined at the nodes of a uniform grid in the plane (h_1, h_2). Domains with the same number of real solutions were obtained.

An analysis of the results shows that 24 equilibrium satellite attitudes exist for sufficiently small gyrostatic torques; as the magnitude of the gyrostatic torque increases, the domain of existence of the equilibrium solutions diminishes, and for sufficiently large gyrostatic torque the satellite has only 8 equilibrium attitudes.

We shall investigate the stability of the equilibrium solutions $\psi = \psi_0$, $\vartheta = \vartheta_0, \varphi = \varphi_0$ by the second Lyapunov method, using the Jacobi Integral (4) as the Lyapunov function. After the replasement $\psi \to \psi + \psi_0, \vartheta \to \vartheta + \vartheta_0$, $\varphi \to \varphi + \varphi_0$ this integral takes the form

$$H = \frac{1}{2}(A\bar{p}^2 + B\bar{q}^2 + C\bar{r}^2) + (\frac{1}{2}(B-C)(A_{11}\psi^2 + A_{22}\vartheta^2 + A_{33}\varphi^2 +$$
$$2A_{12}\psi\vartheta + 2A_{13}\psi\varphi + 2A_{23}\vartheta\varphi) + O_3(\psi, \vartheta, \varphi), \tag{12}$$

where coefficients A_{ij} depend in a rather complicated way on the parameters $\nu, h_1, h_2, h_3, \psi, \vartheta, \varphi$.

If the right side of the integral (12) is positive-definite for the equilibrium solution under investigation for the system (6), (7), then this solution is stable. Using integral (12), we can numerically analyze the solutions of Eq.(10) stability.

An analysis of the numerical results shows that stable equilibrium positions of the satellite exist for sufficiently large gyrostatic torque. The conditions are obtained for the existence of a stable equilibrium of a gyrostat satellite in a circular orbit in the general case.

References

1. Sarychev V. A., Problems of artificial satellite orientation, in: Spase Research. Results of Science and Technology [in Russian], Vol. 11, VINITI 1978.
2. Sarychev V. A. and Gutnik S. A., Equilibrium positions of a satellite-gyrostat,*Proc. of XXXV-th International Astronautical Congress, IAF*, Lausanne, 1984, p. 356.
3. Anchev A. A., Stabilization of the relative equilibrium of a satellite with flywheel rotors, KOSMICHESKIE ISSLIDOVANIYA, Vol. 4, No. 2, pp. 192, 1966.
4. Roberson R. E., Equilibria of orbiting gyrostats, J. Austronaut. Sci., Vol. 15, No. 5, p. 242, 1968.
5. Longman R. W., Gravity-gradient stabilization of gyrostat satellites, with rotor axes in principal planes, Celestial Mech., Vol. 3, No. 2, p. 169, 1971.
6. Sarychev V. A. and Gutnik S. A., Relative equilibria of a gyrostat satellite. COSMIC RESEARCH (KOSMICHESKIE ISSLIDOVANIYA), Vol. 22, Nos. 3, pp. 257–391, (1984), Plenum Publishing Corporation.
7. Buchberger B., Theoretical Basis for the Reduction of Polynomials to Canonical Forms. SIGSAM Bulletin (1976), pp. 19–29.
8. Char B. W., Geddes K. O., Gonnet G. H., Leong B. L., Monagan M. B., Watt S. M., First Leaves: A Tutorial Introduction to Maple V. Springer- Verlag, 1992.
9. Gutnik S. A., Application of Computer Algebra to Investigation of the Relative Equilibria of a Satellite, *Proceedings of International Symposium on Symbolic and Algebraic Computation* Kiev (1993), ISSAC'93, pp. 63–64. ACM Press.
10. Sarychev V. A. and Gutnik S. A., Equilibria of a Satellite Under the Influence of Gravitational and Static Torques. COSMIC RESEARCH (KOSMICHESKIE ISSLIDOVANIYA), Vol. 32, Nos. 4-5, pp. 386–391, (1995), Plenum Publishing Corporation.
11. Gutnik S. A., Symbolic-numeric methods for solving satellite equilibrium equations, *Proceedings of International Workshop on Symbolic-Numeric Algebra for Polynomials SNAP 96* INRIA Sophia-Antipolis, France (1996), p. 20.

Quantization by Presentation:
The Nambu-Goto String in 1+3 Dimensions

Gerrit Handrich

Fakultät für Physik der Universität Freiburg,
Herrmann-Herder-Str. 3, 79104 Freiburg

Abstract. In a cautious approach to the quantization of the Nambu-Goto string in 1+3 dimensions, correspondence is required for the algebra of observables only. With the help of a presentation of this Poisson algebra the associative quantum algebra may be constructed. A defining relation of the Poisson algebra determines one of the quantum algebra up to a finite number of terms of higher order in $\hbar$. These terms are severely restricted when one requires the correct classical limit for all the relations implied by the defining ones. The ideal generated by the associative defining relations has been computed up to degree five with the help of Mathematica routines specially designed to make use of the $\mathbf{so}(3)$ representation space structure of the algebra. These computations strongly support the consistency of the correspondence postulate for the algebra of observables.

In conventional methods for the quantization of the string like the covariant approach, light-cone gauge fixing or the BRST formalism, at one point or the other there enters the quantization of the unphysical constraint algebra. This algebra picks up a central extension, which in the end leaves us with the well-known problems: Either one loses Lorentz covariance or no acceptable space of physical states can be constructed.

In a more cautious approach correspondence between classical and quantum quantities will only be required for physical degrees of freedom. Not much imagination is required in order to see why the restriction to physical degrees of freedom is usually shunned: The Poisson algebra of observables may be considerably more complicated than the algebra of functions on a space comprising the unphysical degrees.

In the case of the Nambu-Goto theory of closed strings observables have been constructed [1]: cyclically symmetrized iterated integrals. Their value neither depends on the choice of a spacelike surface slicing the string trajectory nor on the parametrization of the one-dimensional object within this hypersurface. The Poisson bracket induced from the canonical one together with the commutative product endows these observables with the structure of a Poisson algebra. This algebra is taken as the starting-point for quantization.

Now, given a Poisson algebra, what are the essentials for the corresponding quantum algebra? We're looking for an associative algebra with the correct classical limit: There should exist a linear bijection between the associative and the Poisson algebra, with the following property: Given an arbitrary relation among elements of the associative algebra, then, after expressing this relation in terms of commutators and anticommutators and after replacing all elements by their classical counterparts with the help of said bijection and substituting the commutator with $i\hbar$ times the Poisson bracket and the anticommutator by twice the commutative product, one finds a Poisson algebra relation in the lowest order of $\hbar$.

A rather direct way to construct this corresponding algebra is by means of a minimal presentation. The Poisson algebra is characterized by a set of generators and defining relations. One can construct an associative algebra on the basis of these data. Every generator of the Poisson algebra corresponds to a generator of the associative algebra. One finds the associative defining relations by replacing the Poisson brackets by $1/i\hbar$ times the commutator and the commutative product by one half of the anticommutator in the Poisson algebra's defining relations. Using the same replacements one constructs a correspondence mapping between the classical and the quantum algebra. By construction, the obtained associative defining relations give the correct classical limit. Still, corrections are allowed that correspond to terms of higher order in $\hbar$.

Can we expect that *all* relations implied by the defining ones have the correct limit? When taking the classical limit one generally finds the correct classical relation in lowest order in $\hbar$ plus further terms which arise due to the non-commutativity of the associative algebra. Problems arise as soon as there are dependencies among the implications of the Poisson algebra's defining relations. In this case the "lowest order" can actually vanish, but the remaining relation for the higher order terms, now of lowest order, does not have any classical analogue. In order to avoid these unwanted relations one has to use the freedom to add higher order terms to the defining relations.

Two tasks are to be accomplished in the course of an explicit construction of the quantum algebra:

- Within the classical algebra one has to compute the multiple Poisson brackets and their products. These expressions have to be brought into a standard form in order to find defining relations.
- The Poisson ideal generated by found relations has to be computed in order to restrict the search for new relations. One needs the corresponding associative ideal in order to gain information about higher order corrections for the defining relations. All elements of this ideal have to be expressed in a suitable standard form (Poincaré-Birkhoff-Witt) in order to find dependencies.

If the algebra is graded it is most appropriate to interweave both tasks when going from one degree to the next one. First, one computes all the implications of relations from lower degrees in the associative algebra. By neglecting the ordering one easily obtains the relations in the Poisson algebra. Additional defining relations for the Poisson algebra can be computed then.

In the case of the Nambu-Goto string in 1+3 dimensions the following situation is found [2]. A relevant part of the algebra is taken into account when one evaluates the observables in the rest frame. In this special frame of reference the algebra is $\mathbb{N}_0$-graded with respect to the Poisson brackets. It is generated by a three-dimensional space of degree zero, a thirteen dimensional space of degree one and an infinite number of mutually Poisson-commuting elements, one of every odd degree $(1, 3, \dots)$. With respect to the Poisson bracket the homogeneous space of degree zero is isomorphic to $\mathbf{so}(3)$ and all homogeneous spaces are $\mathbf{so}(3)$-representation spaces. In addition to degree, all relations must be homogeneous with respect to the highest weight (spin) and weight and, furthermore, with respect to parity $(+$ or $-)$. The generators of degree one fall into three irreducible spaces, characterized by the spin-parities 1^-, 2^- and 2^+. The said mutually Poisson-commuting elements are 0^+, their Poisson-action on the rest of the algebra is conjectured to be semi-direct. One can show that there are no truly polynomial defining relations among the multiple Poisson brackets. The defining relations consist of a part which is linear in multiple Poisson brackets and, generically, a polynomial part in multiple brackets of lower degree. The dimensions of the spaces homogeneous with respect to degree, spin and parity, and therefore the respective numbers of relations, are explicitly known.

In computations it is vital to respect the homogeneities of the relations from the very beginning. We therefore work with the Clebsch-Gordan decomposition of products and Poisson brackets and merely consider one of the weights in an $\mathbf{so}(3)$-irreducible space. One thereby effectively reduces the number of generators and relations, but what is by far more important: The systems of linear relations involved in determining the dimension of an ideal or in the computation of defining relations, have a block form in this basis, which keeps numbers and computation times low. The price one has to pay is that the identities in the Poisson or associative algebra like the Jacobi identity have to be reexpressed in terms of the Clebsch-Gordan decomposed products, now involving 6j-symbols. The Hall and Poincaré-Birkhoff-Witt bases can be modified appropriately [3]. But we do not see how Gröbner basis techniques should be applied. What is a subword when a product is given by the two factors (spaces) plus the spin specifying the decomposition?

As all the defining relations contain a part linear in the Poisson brackets, we can restrict the investigation to the part of the ideal generated by means of the commutator: All dependencies among the ideals generated by the different defining relations can be traced back to this class of relations and all restrictions on new defining relations are found in this way. Hence, one first identifies, for given degree, spin and parity, all Clebsch-Gordan decomposed commutators of a lower degree relation and a generator. Then, the "linear" part has to be expressed in a modified Hall basis, the truly polynomial part in a Poincaré-Birkhoff-Witt basis. Dependencies as well as a set of independent relations are found with the help of the Gauß algorithm.

For the computation of the Poisson brackets a Fortan programme has been developed. The routines dealing with the associative ideal have been implemented with the use of Mathematica. So far the computations up to degree five have been performed [4]. To give an idea of the complexity of the task: the degree five part of the ideal generated by defining relations of lower degree is 105893-dimensional — and there is one further, defining relation.

Out of the initial 95 real parameters, which reflect the freedom in the choice of corrections for the associative defining relations, three remain undetermined after having established the correct classical limit up to degree five. Considering the huge number of dependencies in the ideal — in degree five one finds 569 a priory independent restrictions on 61 parameters — the consistency of our postulates is anything but trivial. We take this as a hint at an underlying structure, the identification of which might enable us to construct the full quantum algebra of observables.

References

1. K. Pohlmeyer: A Group-Theoretical Approach the the Quantization of the Free Relativistic Closed String, Physics Letters **119B** (1982) 100
2. K. Pohlmeyer: The Nambu-Goto Theory of Closed Bosonic Strings Moving in 1+3-Dimensional Minkowski Space: The Quantum Algebra of Observables, Ann. Phys. (Leipzig) **8**,1 (1999) 19
3. G. Handrich: Konstruktion Angepaßter Basen Freier Lie-Algebren, Erzeugt von Vollständigen Multipletten der so(3), Diploma Thesis (unpublished), Freiburg (1996)
4. G. Handrich, C. Nowak: The Nambu-Goto Theory of Closed Bosonic Strings Moving in 1+3-Dimensional Minkowski Space: The Construction of the Quantum Algebra of Observables up to Degree Five, Ann. Phys. (Leipzig) **8**,1 (1999) 51

One Algorithm of Finding Solutions for the Systems with First Integrals

Valentin Irtegov and Tatyana Titorenko

Institute of Systems Dynamics and Control Theory SB RAS,
134, Lermontov str., Irkutsk, 664033, Russia,
E-mail : irteg@icc.ru

Abstract. We discuss the algorithm for finding the relative and absolute stability positions and invariant manifolds of systems of differential equations. The proposed approach is based on the analysis of stationary sets of first integrals of the system. Example applications of this algorithm to mechanical problems are presented. In some stages of solution the tools of computer algebra are used.

The computer algebra allows to considerably change the viewpoint on the efficiency of many classical algorithms. This special viewpoint is bound up with a new estimation of possible amounts of computations performed within a fixed time. This stimulates both the use of above algorithms, what could be time consuming (cumbersome) when performed without any computational support, and their modification to the end of embracing a wider set of problems.

This paper proposes a modification of the well-known Routh's algorithm [1], which finds out stationary solutions for the systems of differential equations which assume first integrals. Our modification of the algorithm is based on a new idea of considering the property of stationarity with respect to only some part of phase variables rather than with respect to all of them.

The Routh's classical algorithm devised for the separation of both solutions and invariant manifolds of systems of differential equations and also for the investigation of their stability, which was extended by A.M.Lyapunov [2], historically derives from Lagrange's theorem on equilibrium stability.

This refined algorithm can be reduced to the analysis of stationary sets for various elements of algebra of the problem's first integrals. It is frequently used in mechanics for the purpose of qualitative investigation of phase space. In some cases, this approach allows to reveal the stationarity for practically all the types of trajectories (invariant manifolds) assumed by the initial problem. This takes place when, for example, the conservative system has "excessive" (in the sense of Liouville integration) number of first integrals [3]. This class includes the equations, which describe the motion of a material point in the central field of gravitation. In this case, the differential equations in the case of two-dimensional problem has the form [4]:

$$\ddot{\varrho} - \varrho\dot{\varphi}^2 = -\frac{\mu}{\varrho^2}; \quad \ddot{\varphi}\varrho^2 + 2\varrho\dot{\varphi}\dot{\varrho} = 0$$

and assume three independent first integrals: (i) the integral of energy

$$H = \frac{1}{2}(\dot{\varrho}^2 + \varrho^2 \dot{\varphi}^2) - \frac{\mu}{\varrho} = h;$$

(ii) the area integral $V_1 = \varrho^2 \dot{\varphi} = m$; and (iii) the Laplace's integral

$$V_2 = -\mu \cos \varphi + m(\dot{\varrho} \sin \varphi + \varrho \dot{\varphi} \cos \varphi) = f_1,$$

where ϱ É φ are the polar coordinates, μ is the gravitation constant, h, m, f_1 are constants of first integrals.

To the end of finding out the stationary solutions on the basis of Routh-Lyapunov's theorem it is necessary to construct a linear combination of these integrals with the constant parameters λ_1 and λ_2:

$$K = \frac{1}{2}(\dot{\varrho}^2 + \varrho^2 \dot{\varphi}^2) - \frac{\mu}{\varrho} - \lambda_1 \varrho^2 \dot{\varphi} - \lambda_2 [-\mu \cos \varphi + m(\dot{\varrho} \sin \varphi + \varrho \dot{\varphi} \cos \varphi)].$$

Stationary conditions for K with respect to all the variables of the problem have the form

$$\frac{\partial K}{\partial \dot{\varrho}} = \dot{\varrho} - \lambda_2 m \sin \varphi = 0;$$

$$\frac{\partial K}{\partial \dot{\varphi}} = \varrho^2(\dot{\varphi} - \lambda_1) - \lambda_2(2\varrho^3 \dot{\varphi} \cos \varphi + \varrho^2 \dot{\varrho} \sin \varphi) = 0;$$

$$\frac{\partial K}{\partial \varrho} = \dot{\varphi}^2 \varrho + \frac{\mu}{\varrho^2} - 2\lambda_1 \varrho \dot{\varphi} - \lambda_2(2\varrho \dot{\varrho} \dot{\varphi} \sin \varphi + 3\varrho^2 \dot{\varphi}^2 \cos \varphi) = 0;$$

$$\frac{\partial K}{\partial \varphi} = \lambda_2 [\mu \sin \varphi + m(\dot{\varrho} \cos \varphi - \varrho \dot{\varphi} \sin \varphi)] = 0.$$

Since the left-hand side of the latter equation coincides (with the precision up to some constant multiplier) with Laplace's second integral, this equation simply imposes a restriction on the constant of this first integral. It must be zero for our stationary solutions ($f_2 = 0$). It can be easily verified that the residual three equations, for the proper choice of λ_1 and λ_2 such that

$$\lambda_1^2 = \frac{\mu^2 - f^2}{m^2}; \qquad \lambda_2 = \frac{f}{m^2}$$

are satisfied after the substitution (in them) of the following relationships between the problem variables:

$$\varrho = \frac{p}{1 + e \cos \varphi}; \qquad \dot{\varrho} = \frac{me}{p} \sin \varphi; \qquad \dot{\varphi} = \frac{m}{\varrho^2}, \qquad (*)$$

where $e = \frac{f}{\mu}$ is the excentricity, $p = \frac{m^2}{\mu}$ is the parameter of the cone section, $f^2 = f_1^2 + f_2^2$ under the condition that constants of the first integrals are related by the equalities:

$$f_2 = 0; \quad h = -m^2; \quad f^2 = \mu^2 + hm^2.$$

Since the first one of above equations (*) defines the cone section, in the capacity of stationary invariant manifolds of our problem we have obtained (with the precision up to the restrictions imposed on the constants of the first integrals) the trajectories of general solutions for the initial differential equations.

In the case where the system has insufficient number of first integrals, the set of steady motions or invariant manifolds may appear to be thin (i.e. can be reduced to simplest equilibrium positions). So, for the purpose of extension of the set of algorithmically found solutions of differential equations of mechanics one can try to employ the approach bound up with separation of the solutions, which are stationary with respect to some part of variables. In this case, there arises a block of problems similar to those which take place in the theory of investigation of stability with respect to some part of variables [5].

Let us plan the sequence of actions in the process of finding solutions stationary with respect to some part of variables.

Let the system of differential equations

$$\dot{x}_i = X_i(x_1, \ldots, x_n, t), \qquad (i = 1, \ldots, n) \tag{1}$$

assume a few smooth first integrals

$$V_0(x_1, \ldots, x_n, t) = c_0, \ldots, V_m(x_1, \ldots, x_n, t) = c_m. \tag{2}$$

Let us compose the following function of these integrals

$$K_0 = V_0(x, t) + \sum_{i=1}^{m} \lambda_i(t) V_i(x, t) \tag{3}$$

and let us require that this function under an appropriate choice of $\lambda_i(t)$, $i = 1 \ldots, m$, and $x_{k+1}(t), \ldots, x_n(t)$, be the first integral for k first equations of the initial system (1) ($\lambda_i(t)$ may probably be considered, if necessary, to be dependent on $x_{k+1}(t), \ldots, x_n(t)$).

$$\dot{x}_j = X_j(x_1, \ldots, x_k, x_{k+1}(t), \ldots, x_n(t), t), \qquad (j = 1, \ldots, k), \tag{4}$$

i.e. we try to find such $\lambda_i(t), i = 1, \ldots, m$, and $x_{k+1}(t), \ldots, x_n(t)$, that

$$\frac{dK_0}{dt} \overset{\text{def}}{\equiv} \sum_{j=1}^{k} \frac{\partial V_0}{\partial x_j} X_j(x, t) + \sum_{j=1}^{k} \sum_{i=1}^{m} \lambda_i(t) \frac{\partial V_i}{\partial x_j} X_j(x, t) + \frac{\partial K_0}{\partial t} \equiv 0. \tag{5}$$

Having the first integral of the partitioned system, find (using the standard procedure) the set wherein this integral has a stationary value. To this end, we write out the stationarity conditions of K_0 with respect to the variables $x_1, \ldots, x_k$:

$$\frac{\partial K_0}{\partial x_l} = f_l(x_1, \ldots, x_k, x_{k+1}(t), \ldots, x_n(t)),$$

$$\lambda_1(t), \dots, \lambda_m(t), t) = 0. \quad (l = 1, \dots, k). \tag{6}$$

Let an isolated solution of the latter system be found:

$$x_l^0 = x_l^0(x_{k+1}(t), \dots, x_n(t), \lambda_1(t), \dots, \lambda_m(t), t). \qquad (l = 1, \dots, k) \tag{7}$$

It can be easily shown that this solution is invariant for system (4). Indeed, calculating derivatives of identity (5) with respect to x_l $(l = 1, \dots, k)$

$$\frac{\partial}{\partial x_l}\left(\frac{dK_0}{dt}\right) = \sum_{j=1}^{k} \frac{\partial}{\partial x_l}\left(\frac{\partial K_0}{\partial x_j}\right) X_j + \frac{\partial}{\partial x_l}\left(\frac{\partial K_0}{\partial t}\right) + \sum_{j=1}^{k} \frac{\partial K_0}{\partial x_j}\frac{\partial X_j}{\partial x_l} \equiv 0$$

and changing the differentiation order we obtain the system

$$\sum_{j=1}^{k} \frac{\partial}{\partial x_j}\left(\frac{\partial K_0}{\partial x_l}\right) X_j + \frac{\partial}{\partial t}\left(\frac{\partial K_0}{\partial x_l}\right) = -\sum_{j=1}^{k} \frac{\partial K_0}{\partial x_j}\frac{\partial X_j}{\partial x_l}. \qquad (l = 1, \dots, k)$$

From the form of the system one can conclude that the solutions, which make zero all of the derivatives $\frac{\partial K_0}{\partial x_l}$ $(l = 1, \dots, k)$, are invariant for system (4).

It remains only to determine the constraints that our procedure imposes on the variables, which have remained "free": $x_{k+1}(t), \dots, x_n(t)$ and parameters $\lambda_1(t), \dots, \lambda_m$. To this end let us replace $x_1, \dots, x_k$ with their stationary values from (7) in the first integrals (2):

$$V_q(x_1^0(x_{k+1}(t), \dots, x_n(t), \lambda_1(t), \dots, \lambda_m(t), t), \dots,$$

$$x_k^0(x_{k+1}(t), \dots, x_n(t), \lambda_1(t), \dots, \lambda_m(t), t),$$

$$x_{k+1}(t), \dots, x_n(t), t) = c_q \qquad (q = 1, \dots, m) \tag{8}$$

and from the relations obtained find $\lambda_1^0(t), \dots, \lambda_m^0(t)$ corresponding to the stationary solution (7)

$$\lambda_j^0 = \lambda_j^0(x_{k+1}(t), \dots, x_n(t), t, c_1, \dots, c_m) \qquad (j = 1, \dots, m). \tag{9}$$

By substituting the values of λ_j^0 into (7) and then the result into some part of differential equations (1), furthermore, into the part corresponding to the variables $x_{k+1}, \dots, x_n$, we obtain equations for $x_{k+1}, \dots, x_n$ for our stationary solution:

$$\dot{x}_{k+1} = X_{k+1}(x_{k+1}, \dots, x_n, t, c_1, \dots, c_m),$$

$$\dots\dots\dots\dots\dots\dots\dots\dots\dots\dots\dots \tag{10}$$

$$\dot{x}_n = X_n(x_{k+1}, \dots, x_n, t, c_1, \dots, c_m).$$

The solutions of the latter system will be parametrized by the constants of first integrals $c_1, \dots, c_m$:

$$x_{k+1} = x_{k+1}^0(t, c_1, \dots, c_m), \dots, x_n = x_n^0(t, c_1, \dots, c_m). \tag{11}$$

When substituting them into (9), and the result into (7), we find the values of all the variables on the given stationary solution

$$x_1^0 = x_1^0(t, c_1, \dots, c_m), \dots, x_k^0 = x_k^0(t, c_1, \dots, c_m), \tag{12}$$

generally speaking, as functions of t and $c_1, \dots, c_m$.

The formulas (11) and (12) define the sought stationary solution of the system (1) in the whole phase space.

The substitution of (9), (11) and (12) into the expression of the first integral K_0 allows us to obtain conditions imposed on the constants of the first integrals which are admissible in our stationary solution.

The algorithm proposed for finding the stationary (with respect to a sub-set of variables) solutions of differential equations with first integrals can be used for investigation of some specific mechanics problems. Furthermore, it is possible to use computer for both constructing the differential equations of motion, finding their first integrals and execution of most procedures of finding solutions, which are stationary with respect to some part of variables: (i) the formulation of stationarity conditions for the first integral, (ii) the analysis of stationarity conditions with the use of Groebner's basis, etc.

In practice, when solving such problems one can use a simpler approach. It is possible to act without verifying all the conditions of above technique. It is sufficient simply to obtain the conditions with respect to some part of the variables of some first integral, and then verify their compatibility with the differential equations of motion.

It is expedient to give a specific example of application of such a heuristic approach. Consider a gyroscope in a gimbal suspension placed in a central field of forces, the axis of the external frame of which has the angle α with respect to the "vertical".

The kinetic energy of this system writes:

$$2T = (A + A^0)\dot{\theta}^2 + ((A + B^0 - C^0)\sin^2\theta + C^0 + C')\dot{\psi}^2 + C(\dot{\varphi} + \dot{\psi}\cos\theta)^2,$$

where A^0, B^0, C^0 are the inertia moments of the internal frame; $A = B, C$ are the inertia moments of the rotor, C' is the inertia moment of external frame; the force function can be represented as follows:

$$U = -z_0(\cos\alpha\cos\theta - \sin\alpha\sin\theta\cos\psi) + \frac{\mu}{2}(D\sin^2\alpha\sin^2\psi$$
$$+ E\sin^2\alpha\sin^2\theta\sin^2\psi + E\cos 2\alpha\sin^2\theta + \frac{1}{2}E\sin 2\alpha\sin 2\theta\cos\psi),$$

where $D = B' - A' + B^0 - A^0$, $E = C^0 - B^0 + C - A$.

The equations of motion assume (the latter can be verified) two first integrals: $H = T - U = h$ and $V = r_0 = \dot{\varphi} + \dot{\psi}\cos\theta = const$.

When removing $\dot{\varphi}$ from H with the help of the second integral, we obtain the integral K with a parameter r_0. Let us use this integral for finding the stationary solutions with respect to a subset of variables (variable $\dot{\psi}$).

The derivative of K with respect to $\dot{\psi}$

$$\frac{\partial K}{\partial \dot{\psi}} = ((A + B^0 - C^0)\sin^2\theta + C^0 + C')\dot{\psi} = 0$$

allows us to find the stationary value $\dot{\psi}^0 = 0$.

Considering that the rest of the variables are the functions of time to be found, let us require that the derivative of K with respect to t due to the equations of motion for $\dot{\psi} = 0$ vanishes.

$$\frac{\partial K}{\partial t} = (A + A^0)\dot{\theta}\ddot{\theta} + \frac{1}{2}(A + B^0 - C^0)\sin 2\theta \dot{\theta}\dot{\psi}^2 - z_0(\cos\alpha\sin\theta\dot{\theta}$$
$$+ \sin\alpha\sin\theta\sin\psi\dot{\psi} - \sin\alpha\cos\theta\cos\psi\dot{\theta}) - \frac{\mu}{2}(D\sin^2\alpha\sin 2\psi\dot{\psi}$$
$$+ E\sin^2\alpha\sin 2\theta\sin^2\psi\dot{\theta} + E\sin^2\alpha\sin^2\theta\sin 2\psi\dot{\psi} + E\cos 2\alpha\sin 2\theta\dot{\theta}$$
$$+ E\sin 2\alpha\cos 2\theta\cos\psi\dot{\theta} - \frac{1}{2}E\sin 2\alpha\sin 2\theta\sin\psi\dot{\psi}) = 0.$$

Having substituted $\dot{\psi} = 0$, we obtain the condition:

$$\dot{\theta}\{(A + A^0)\ddot{\theta} - z_0\cos\alpha\sin\theta + z_0\sin\alpha\cos\theta\cos\psi - \frac{\mu}{2}E(\sin^2\alpha\sin 2\theta\sin^2\psi$$
$$+ \cos 2\alpha\sin 2\theta + \sin 2\alpha\cos 2\theta\cos\psi)\} = 0 \qquad (13)$$

In the case where $\dot{\psi} = 0$, the differential equations of motion of the gyroscope take the form:

1. $C\dot{\varphi} = r_0$;

2. $Cr_0\sin\theta\dot{\theta} - z_0\sin\alpha\sin\theta\sin\psi + \frac{\mu}{2}(D\sin^2\alpha\sin 2\psi$

$$- \frac{1}{2}E\sin 2\alpha\sin 2\theta\sin\psi + E\sin^2\alpha\sin^2\theta\sin 2\psi) = 0; \qquad (14)$$

3. $(A + A^0)\ddot{\theta} - z_0(\cos\alpha\sin\theta - \sin\alpha\cos\theta\cos\psi) - \frac{\mu}{2}E(\sin^2\alpha\sin 2\theta\sin^2\psi$

$$+ \cos 2\alpha\sin 2\theta + \sin 2\alpha\cos 2\theta\cos\psi) = 0.$$

It can be readily seen that the requirement of $\frac{\partial K}{\partial t} = 0$ in the case of $\dot{\psi} = 0$ in the form (13) coincides for $\dot{\theta} \neq 0$ with the latter motion equation (14) when $\dot{\psi} = 0$.

Consequently, all the solutions, which satisfy equations (14) (as well as the conditions $\dot{\psi} = 0$, $\psi = \text{const}$), are the stationary solutions with respect to a subset of variables $(\dot{\psi})$.

Among them we can indicate the following ones:

1. $\dot{\psi} = \psi = 0$; $(A + A^0)\ddot{\theta} - z_0\sin(\alpha - \theta) - \frac{\mu}{2}E\sin 2(\alpha + \theta) = 0.$

These equations describe the pendulum oscillations of the internal frame (for the case of immobile rotor) about a fixed axis normal to the straight line, which connects the force center and the immobile point of the gyroscope's suspension.

$$2.\ \dot{\psi} = 0; \quad \psi = \frac{\pi}{2}; \quad \alpha = \frac{\pi}{2}; \quad \ddot{\theta} = 0; \quad Cr_0\dot{\theta}_0 - z_0 = 0.$$

This is the precession of the gyroscope for the case of "horizontal" axis of the external frame, which is similar to Tabarovsky's precession [6].

References

1. Routh E. *Dynamics of a System of Rigid Bodies*. New York, Dover Publ., 1905 (Moscow, NAUKA Publ., 1983 (in Russian)).
2. Lyapunov A.M. On permanant screw motion of a solid body in a fluid. Collected Works, Moscow, USSR Acad. Sci. Publ., 1 (1954) 276-319 (in Russian).
3. Perelomov A.M. *Integrable Systems of Classical Mechanics and Lie Algebra*. Moscow, Nauka Publ., 1990 (in Russian).
4. Duboshin G.N. *Celestial Mechanics. Principal Problems and Methods*. Moscow, GIF-ML Publ., 1963 (in Russian).
5. Rumyantsev V.V., Oziraner A.M. *On Stability and Stabilization of Motions with Respect to Some Part of Variables*. Moscow, Nauka Publ., 1978 (in Russian).
6. Tabarovsky A.M. On motion and stability of a gyroscope in the gimbal in Newton's central force field. *Appl. Mech. and Math.* 2 (1961) 11 - 19 (in Russian).

Cohomology of Lie Superalgebras of Hamiltonian Vector Fields: Computer Analysis

Vladimir V. Kornyak

Laboratory of Computing Techniques and Automation
Joint Institute for Nuclear Research
141980 Dubna, Russia
kornyak@jinr.ru

Abstract. In this paper we present the results of computation of cohomology for some Lie (super)algebras of Hamiltonian vector fields and related algebras. At present, the full cohomology rings for these algebras are not known even for the low dimensional vector fields. The partial "experimental" results may give some hints for solution of the whole problem. The computations have been carried out with the help of recently written program in C language. Some of the presented results are new.

1 Introduction and basic definitions

There are many applications of the Lie (super)algebra cohomology in mathematics: characteristic classes of foliations; invariant differential operators; MacDonald-type combinatorial identities, etc. (see [1] for details). Besides, the cohomology is used widely in mathematical and theoretical physics [2]: construction of the central extensions and deformations for Lie superalgebras; construction of supergravity equations for N-extended Minkowski superspaces and search for possible models for these superspaces; study of stability for nonholonomic systems like ballbearings, gyroscopes, electro-mechanical devices, waves in plasma, etc.; description of an analogue of the curvature tensor for nonlinear nonholonomic constraints; new methods for the study of integrability of dynamical systems.

General definitions and properties of cohomology of Lie algebras and superalgebras are described in [1]. Let's recall briefly some basic definitions.

A *Lie superalgebra* is a $\mathbf{Z}_2$-graded algebra over a commutative ring K with a unit:

$$L = L_{\bar{0}} \oplus L_{\bar{1}}, \ u \in L_\alpha, \ v \in L_\beta, \ \alpha, \beta \in \mathbf{Z}_2 = \{\bar{0}, \bar{1}\} \implies [u, v] \in L_{\alpha+\beta}$$

The elements of $L_{\bar{0}}$ and $L_{\bar{1}}$ are called *even* and *odd*, respectively. We shall assume K is one of the fields $\mathbf{C}$ or $\mathbf{R}$. By definition, the *Lie product* (shortly, *brackets*) [,] satisfies the following axioms

$$[u, v] = -(-1)^{p(u)p(v)}[v, u], \qquad skew-symmetry,$$
$$[u, [v, w]] = [[u, v], w] + (-1)^{p(u)p(v)}[v, [u, w]], \qquad Jacobi\ identity,$$

where $p(a)$ is the parity of element $a \in L_{p(a)}$.

A *module* over a Lie superalgebra A is a vector space M (over the same field K) with a mapping $A \times M \to M$, such that $[a_1, a_2]m = a_1(a_2m) - (-1)^{p(a_1)p(a_2)}a_2(a_1m)$, where $a_1, a_2 \in A$, $m \in M$. The most important for our purposes are *trivial* (M is arbitrary vector space, e.g., $M = K$; $am = 0$), *adjoint* ($M = A$; $am = [a, m]$) and *coadjoint* ($M = A'$; $am = \{a, m\}$ is coadjoint action) modules.

A *cochain complex* is a sequence of linear spaces C^k with linear mappings d^k

$$0 \to C^0 \xrightarrow{d^0} \cdots \xrightarrow{d^{k-2}} C^{k-1} \xrightarrow{d^{k-1}} C^k \xrightarrow{d^k} C^{k+1} \xrightarrow{d^{k+1}} \cdots,$$

where the linear space $C^k = C^k(A; M)$ is a super skew-symmetric k-linear mapping $A \times \cdots \times A \to M$, $C^0 = M$ by definition. The super skew-symmetry means symmetry w.r.t. transpositions of odd elements of A and antisymmetry for all other transpositions. Elements of C^k are called *cochains*.

The linear mapping d^k (or, briefly, d) is called the *differential* and satisfies the following property: $d^k \circ d^{k-1} = 0$ (or $d^2 = 0$).

The cochains mapped into zero by the differential are called the *cocycles*, i.e., the space of cocycles is

$$Z^k = \text{Ker } d^k = \{C^k \mid dC^k = 0\}.$$

Those cochains which can be represented as differentials of other cochains are called the *coboundaries*, i.e., the space of coboundaries is

$$B^k = \text{Im } d^{k-1} = \{C^k \mid C^k = dC^{k-1}\}.$$

Any coboundary is, obviously, a cocycle.

The non-trivial cocycles, i.e., those of them which are not coboundaries, form the *cohomology*. In other words, the cohomology is the quotient space

$$H^k(A; M) = Z^k / B^k.$$

The explicit form of the differential for a Lie superalgebra is

$$dC(e_0, \ldots, e_q; O_{q+1}, \ldots, O_k) =$$

$$\sum_{i<j}^{q} (-1)^j C(e_0, \ldots, e_{i-1}, [e_i, e_j], \ldots, \widehat{e_j}, \ldots, e_q; O_{q+1}, \ldots, O_k) +$$

$$(-1)^{q+1} \sum_{i=0}^{q} \sum_{j=q+1}^{k} C(e_0, \ldots, e_{i-1}, [e_i, O_j], \ldots, e_q; O_{q+1}, \ldots, \widehat{O_j}, \ldots, O_k) +$$

$$(-1)^{i+1} \sum_{i=q+1}^{k-1} \sum_{j=q+2}^{k} C(e_0, \ldots, e_q; O_{q+1}, \ldots, O_{i-1}, [O_i, O_j], \ldots, \widehat{O_j}, \ldots, O_k) +$$

$$\sum_{i=0}^{q} (-1)^{i+1} e_i C(e_0, \ldots, \widehat{e_i}, \ldots, e_q; O_{q+1}, \ldots, O_k) +$$

$$(-1)^q \sum_{i=q+1}^{k} O_i C(e_0, \ldots, e_q; O_{q+1}, \ldots, \widehat{O_i}, \ldots, O_k).$$

Here e_i and O_i are even and odd elements of the algebra, respectively, and the hat "$\hat{}$" marks the omitted elements.

Here are some properties and statements we use in the sequel.

An algebra and a module are called *graded* if they can be presented as sums of homogeneous components in a way compatible with the algebra brackets and the action of the algebra on the module:

$$A = \oplus_{g \in G} A_g, \quad M = \oplus_{g \in G} M_g, \quad [A_{g_1}, A_{g_2}] \subset A_{g_1+g_2}, \quad A_{g_1} M_{g_2} \subset M_{g_1+g_2},$$

where G is some abelian (semi)group. The grading in the algebra and module induces a grading on cochains and, hence, in the cohomology:

$$C^*(A; M) = \oplus_{g \in G} C_g^*(A; M), \quad H^*(A; M) = \oplus_{g \in G} H_g^*(A; M).$$

This property allows one to compute the cohomology separately for different homogeneous components; this is especially useful when the homogeneous components are finite–dimensional.

If there is an element $a_0 \in A$, such that eigenvectors of the operator $a \mapsto [a_0, a]$ form a (topological) basis of algebra A, then $H^*(A) \simeq H_0^*(A)$. In other words, all the non-trivial cocycles of the cohomology in the trivial module lie in the zero grade component. The element a_0 is called an *internal grading element*. If also eigenvectors of the operator $m \mapsto a_0 m$ form a topological basis of module M, then the same statement holds for the cohomology in the module M: $H^*(A; M) \simeq H_0^*(A; M)$.

In the case of trivial module, the exterior multiplication of cochains provides the cohomology with a structure of graded ring. There are also another multiplicative structures in cohomology, but we shall not use them in this work.

2   Outline of algorithm and its implementation

To compute the cohomology one needs to solve the equation

$$dC^k = 0, \tag{1}$$

and throw away those solutions of (1) which can be expressed in the form

$$C'^k = dC'^{k-1}.$$

In some exceptional cases it is possible to solve equation (1) in closed form. Generally, in the case of Lie superalgebras of vector fields, determining equation (1) is a system of linear homogeneous functional equations with integer arguments. Unfortunately there is no general method for solving such systems in closed form. Hence, we need to carry out the corresponding computation "numerically". There are several packages for computing cohomology of Lie algebras and superalgebras written in *Reduce* [4], [5] and *Mathematica* [2].

244   Vladimir V. Kornyak

Some new results were obtained completely or partially with the help of these packages. However, these packages, being based on general purpose computer algebra systems, appeared to be too inefficient for large real problems. In view of this, we wrote the program in C language [6].

The C code, of total length near 14000 lines, contains about 300 functions realizing top level algorithms, simplification of indexed objects, working with Grassmannian objects, exterior calculus, linear algebra, substitutions, list processing, input and output, etc. As internal structures we use 8 types of lists for different objects. We represent Grassmann monomials by integer numbers using one-to-one correspondence between (binary codes of) non-negative integers and Grassmann monomials. This representation allows one efficiently to implement the operations with Grassmann monomials by means of the basic computer commands.

The program performs sequentially the following steps:

1. *Reading input information.*
2. *Constructing a basis* for the algebra. The basis can be read from the input file; otherwise the program constructs it from the definition of the algebra. Non-trivial computations at this step arise only in the case of divergence-free algebras. The basis elements of such algebras should satisfy some conditions. In fact, we should construct the basis elements of a subspace given by a system of linear equations. The task is thereby reduced to some problem of linear algebra combined with shifts of indices. For example, among the divergence-free conditions for the *special Buttin* algebra $SB(3)$ there are the following two equations

$$ia_{ijk;UV} - (k+1)a_{i-1,j,k+1;VW} = 0,$$

$$ia_{ijk;UW} + (j+1)a_{i-1,j+1,k;VW} = 0.$$

Here $a_{ijk;UV}, \ldots$ are coefficients at the monomials $p^i q^j r^k UV, \ldots$ in the generating function; p, q, r and U, V, W are even and odd variables, respectively. First of all, we have to shift indices j and k in the second equation to reduce the last terms of both equations to the same multi-indices. Then, using some simple tricks of linear algebra, we can easily construct the corresponding basis element

$$E_{ijk} = (k+1)p^i q^j r^k UV - jp^i q^{j-1} r^{k+1} UW + ip^{i+1} q^j r^{k+1} VW.$$

3. *Constructing the commutator table* for the algebra (if this table has not been read from the input file).
4. *Creating the general form* of expressions for coboundaries and determining equations for cocycles.
5. *Transition to a particular grade* in general expressions. At this step expressions for coboundaries take the form $\mathbf{x} = \mathbf{b}t$, equations for cocycles take the form $\mathbf{Z}\mathbf{x} = \mathbf{0}$, where vector $\mathbf{x}$ corresponds to C^k, parameter vector $\mathbf{t}$ corresponds to C^{k-1}, matrices $\mathbf{Z}, \mathbf{b}$ correspond to the differential d. All these vector spaces are finite-dimensional for any particular grade.

6. *Computing the quotient space* $H^k(A; M) = Z^k/B^k$. Here cocycle subspace Z^k is given by relations $\mathbf{Z}\mathbf{x} = \mathbf{0}$, and coboundary subspace B^k is given parametrically by $\mathbf{x} = \mathbf{b}\mathbf{t}$.
Substeps:
(a) Eliminate $\mathbf{t}$ from $\mathbf{x} = \mathbf{b}\mathbf{t}$ to get equations $\mathbf{B}\mathbf{x} = \mathbf{0}$
(b) Reduce both relations $\mathbf{B}\mathbf{x} = \mathbf{0}$ and $\mathbf{Z}\mathbf{x} = \mathbf{0}$ to the canonical form by Gauss elimination. If $\mathrm{rank}\mathbf{B} = \mathrm{rank}\mathbf{Z}$, then there is no non-trivial cocycle; otherwise go to Substep (c).
(c) Set $\mathbf{B}\mathbf{x} = \mathbf{y}$ and substitute these relations into $\mathbf{Z}\mathbf{x} = \mathbf{0}$ to get relations $\mathbf{A}\mathbf{y} = \mathbf{0}$. The *parametric* (non-leading) y's of the last relations are non-trivial cocycles; that is, they form a basis of the cohomology.
In fact, the above procedure is based on the relation for quotient spaces

$$Z/B = \frac{Y/B}{Y/Z},$$

where Y is an artificially introduced space, combining the above x's and y's.
7. *Output the non-trivial cocycles.*

3   Hamiltonian vector fields and related algebras

To define the formal vector fields on the supermanifold of the superdimension $(2n \mid m)$ we consider the sets of even $p_1, \ldots, p_n, q_1, \ldots, q_n$; and odd (called also *Grassmann*) $U_1, \ldots, U_m$ variables, and formal power series $f, g, \ldots$, in these variables. These power series are called *generating functions*, because the vector fields, considered in this work, can be expressed in terms of the derivatives of $f, g, \ldots$ The (super)commutator of vector fields induces the brackets on generating functions. The Lie superalgebra of *Poisson* vector fields $Po(2n \mid m)$ is a set of generating functions with the brackets

$$\{f, g\} = \sum_{i=1}^{n} \left(\frac{\partial f}{\partial p_i} \frac{\partial g}{\partial q_i} - \frac{\partial f}{\partial q_i} \frac{\partial g}{\partial p_i} \right) - (-1)^{p(f)} \sum_{k=1}^{m} \frac{\partial f}{\partial U_k} \frac{\partial g}{\partial U_k}.$$

The *Hamiltonian* superalgebra is a quotient algebra of the Poisson algebra with respect to its center:

$$H(2n \mid m) = Po(2n \mid m)/Z.$$

In the case of purely odd superdimension the *special*, i.e., divergent-free Hamiltonian superalgebra $SH(0 \mid m)$ is possible. This algebra is an ideal of codimension one in the algebra $H(0 \mid m)$. The algebra $SH(0 \mid m)$ contains the subalgebra $O(m)$ and this fact can be used for analysis of the structure of the cohomology ring $H^*(SH(0 \mid m))$. Note that all the algebras depending only on the odd variables are finite-dimensional. It does not mean however that their cohomologies are finite-dimensional too. All the above algebras are graded due to prescribed grading of the variables. The *standard* grading assumes all variables q_i, p_i, U_i have the grade 1.

4   Computations

In the below tables and formulas we use the small $a, b, c, \ldots$ and capital $A, B, C, \ldots$ letters for even and odd cocycles, respectively. The optional superscript and subscript indicate the cochain degree and grade, correspondingly. The letters without indices denote the genuine cocycles, i.e., generating elements of the cohomology ring. Empty position in the tables means the absence of non-trivial cocycles in the given degree and grade. The columns containing only trivial cocycles are omitted. We use the notations p, q for even and U_i for odd variables of the vector field generating functions.

4.1   Special Hamiltonian superalgebra

Table 1. $H_g^n(SH(0|4))$

$n \backslash g$	-6	-4	-2	0	2	4	6
1							
2			a	b	c		
3				d			
4		a^2	ab	b^2	bc	c^2	
5			ad	bd	cd		
6	a^3	a^2b	ab^2	b^3	ac^2	bc^2	c^3

One can see that the cohomology ring $H^*(SH(0\,|\,4))$ is generated by four generators a, b, c, d obeying to the relations $ac - b^2 = 0$ and $d^2 = 0$. The explicit form of the generators given by the computer is

$a = C(U_4, U_4) = C(U_1, U_1) = C(U_2, U_2) = C(U_3, U_3),$

$b = C(U_4, U_1U_2U_3) = C(U_1, U_2U_3U_4) = C(U_2, U_1U_3U_4) = C(U_3, U_1U_2U_4),$

$c = C(U_2U_3U_4, U_2U_3U_4) = C(U_1U_2U_3, U_1U_2U_3) = C(U_1U_2U_4, U_1U_2U_4)$
$\quad = C(U_1U_3U_4, U_1U_3U_4),$

$d = C(U_1U_4, U_2U_4, U_3U_4) + \frac{1}{2}C(U_1U_4, U_1, U_1U_2U_3) + \frac{1}{2}C(U_1U_4, U_4, U_2U_3U_4)$

$\quad + \frac{1}{2}C(U_2U_4, U_2, U_1U_2U_3) - \frac{1}{2}C(U_2U_4, U_4, U_1U_3U_4)$

$\quad + \frac{1}{2}C(U_3U_4, U_3, U_1U_2U_3) + \frac{1}{2}C(U_3U_4, U_4, U_1U_2U_4) = \ldots$

We omitted for brevity the equivalent forms of generator d in the last formula. The cohomology of $SH(0|4)$ has been computed for the first time in [7] by D.Fuks and D.Leites [1] by hand. We present this example here as a rather

---

[1] They missed the cocycle d revealed later by A. Shapovalov with the help of the program written by P.Grozman.

short illustration demonstrating many features of cohomology ring structure. The structure of $H^*(SH(0|m))$ has some peculiarities at $m = 4$. The reason of this is based on the fact that the subalgebra $O(m)$ is not a simple Lie algebra at $m = 4$. Computations for $m = 3, 5, 6$ revealed two generators: even 2-cocycle

$$a = a^2_{-2} = C(U_1, U_1) = \ldots = C(U_m, U_m)$$

and 3-cocycle

$$
\begin{aligned}
d &= d^3_0 = C(U_1 U_2, U_1 U_3, U_2 U_3), & d^2 &= 0,\ m = 3 \\
D &= D^3_5 = C(U_1 U_3 U_4 U_5, U_2 U_3 U_4 U_5, U_3 U_4 U_5) = \ldots, & D^2 &= 0,\ m = 5 \\
d &= d^3_6 = C(U_3 U_4 U_5 U_6, U_4 U_5 U_6, U_1 U_2 U_4 U_5 U_6), & d^2 &= 0,\ m = 6.
\end{aligned}
$$

As we checked, there are no other generators in the case $m = 3$ up to 16-cocycles. Due to some theoretical reason there might be new generator in the degree 7 for $m \geq 5$ but the check of this requires too long computation.

It would be interesting to look how the divergence-free condition and exclusion of a center influence on the structure of cohomology ring. The Tables 2,3 present the cohomology structure for the superalgebras $H(0\,|\,4)$ and $Po(0\,|\,4)$. Our consideration of the multiplicative structure for these cohomologies is very preliminary. In fact, there is a need to write a program for multiplication and comparison of cocycles modulo coboundaries because corresponding computations are rather tedious and error prone. In the Tables 2,3 a^5_{-2} is some linear combination of ad and $a^2 b$, d' is cocycle and α is some 2-cochain. The cocycle $e = C(U_1 \ldots U_m)$ at the even m satisfies the relation $e^2 = 0$ otherwise it is a free generator.

Table 2. $H^n_g(H(0|4))$

$n\backslash g$	-6	-4	-2	0	2	4	6
1					e		
2			a				
3				$d = d' + ae$		$f - e\alpha$	
4		a^2			ed		
5			a^5_{-2}				$g = e\alpha^2$
6	a^3					fd	

4.2 Algebras $H(2|0)$ and $Po(2|0)$

The case of supermanifold with even variables leads to infinite-dimensional algebras and is much more difficult for the analysis. There are a few results concerning the cohomology of Lie algebra $H(2|0)$. In [8] it has been proved

Table 3. $H_g^n(Po(0|4))$

$n\backslash g$	0	2	4	6
1		e		
2	b			
3	d		$f = e\alpha$	
4		$ed, h = b\alpha$		
5	bd			$g = e\alpha^2$
6			$fd, k = b\alpha^2$	

that $\dim H^2(H(2 \mid 0)) \geq 1, \dim H^5(H(2 \mid 0)) \geq 1, \dim H^7(H(2 \mid 0)) \geq 2$ and $\dim H^{10}(H(2 \mid 0)) \geq 1$. In [9] the inequality $\dim H^*(H(2 \mid 0)) \geq 112$ has been obtained. The both works were based on the extraction of some easier to handle subcomplex of the full cohomological complex and application of the computer analysis to this subcomplex. Besides, some facts about $\dim H^q(H(2n \mid 0))$ for low degrees $q \leq n$ are known [10].

Some cocycles from $H^*(Po(2 \mid 0))$ (denoted by p_g^n) and $H^*(H(2 \mid 0))$ (denoted by h_g^n) obtained by the program are presented in the Table 4. We carried out the computations up to degree 10 and grade 4.

Table 4. $H_g^n(Po(2|0))$ and $H_g^n(H(2|0))$

$n\backslash g$	-4	-2	0
2		h_{-2}^2	
3	p_{-4}^3		
4			
5		p_{-2}^5, h_{-2}^5	
6	p_{-4}^6		
7			p_0^7, h_0^7
8		p_{-2}^8	

If we add the grading element G to the algebra than the non-trivial cocycles lie in zero grade only. In this case the space of cochains is finite-dimensional and we can compute the full cohomology. The cohomologies $H^*(Po(2 \mid 0) \oplus G)$ and $H^*(H(2 \mid 0) \oplus G)$ are three dimensional. They are generated by two cocycles $a_0^1 = C(G)$ and a_0^7 and contain also 8-cocycle $a_0^1 a_0^7$. For the case of Hamiltonian algebra the explicit form of a_0^7 is

$$a_0^7 = C(q, p, q^2, pq, p^2, q^3, p^3) - 3C(q, p, q^2, pq, p^2, pq^2, p^2q).$$

In the Poisson case the expression for a_0^7 is much longer.

5   Conclusion

The computation of cohomology is a typical problem with the combinatorial explosion. Nevertheless, some results can be obtained with the help of computer having efficient enough program. On the other hand, the physicists are interested mainly in the second cohomologies describing the central extensions and deformations. Such cohomologies can be computed rather easily even for large algebras. Some essential possibilities remain for increasing the efficiency of the program. Besides, it would be useful also to write a separate program for investigating the multiplicative structure of cohomology ring.

Acknowledgements

I am grateful to V. Gerdt, D. Leites and O. Khudaverdian for fruitful discussions and useful advises. This work was supported in part by INTAS project No. 96-184 and RFBR project No. 98-01-00101.

References

1. Fuks D.B., *Cohomology of Infinite Dimensional Lie Algebras* (Consultants Bureau, New York, 1987).
2. Grozman P., Leites D., *Mathematica*-aided study of Lie algebras and their cohomology. From supergravity to ballbearings and magnetic hydrodynamics **IMS**'97 (to appear)
3. Leites D., Lie superalgebras. In: *Modern Problems of Mathematics. Recent developments*, v. 25, VINITI, Moscow, 1984, 3–49 (in Russian; English translation in: JOSMAR v. 30(6), 1985, 2481–2512)
4. Leites D., Post G., Cohomology to compute. In: Kaltofen E, Watt S.M. (eds.), *Computers and Mathematics*, Springer, NY ea, 1989, 73–81
5. Post G., Hijligenberg N. von, Calculation of Lie algebra cohomology by computer, Memo# 833, Faculty of Appl. Math. Univ. Twente, 1989; id. ibid. #928, 1991
6. Kornyak V.V., A Program for Computing Cohomology of Lie Superalgebras of Vector Fields. Preprint JINR E5-98-380, Dubna. Submitted to *Comput. Phys. Comm.*
7. Fuks D., Leites D., Cohomology of Lie superalgebras, C.r. Acad. Bulg. Sci., **37**, 12, 1984, 1595–1596.
8. Gel'fand I.M., Kalinin D.I., Fuks D.B., On Cohomology of Lie Algebra of Hamiltonian Formal Vector Fields, *Funkts. Anal. Prilozhen.*, **6**, 1972, 25–29 (in Russian)
9. Perchik J. Cohomology of Hamiltonian and related formal vector fields Lie algebras, *Topology*, **15**, 4, 1976, 395–404.
10. Guillemin V.M., Shnider S.D., Some stable results on the cohomology of classical infinite dimensional Lie algebras, *Trans. Amer. Math. Soc.*, **179**, 1973, 275–280.

Computer Algebra Tools in Construction of Renormgroup Symmetries *

Vladimir F. Kovalev

Institute for Mathematical Modelling, Moscow 125047, RUSSIA

Abstract. The method of constructing renormgroup symmetries with perturbative group analysis is reviewed and the use of symbolic packages in finding these symmetries is discussed in application to nonlinear Schrödinger equation. New solutions of boundary value problems for the system of nonlinear optics equations are presented.

1 Introduction

The study of boundary value problems (b.v.p.) of mathematical physics that are described by models based on differential equations (DEs) is substantially affected by the knowledge of the special class of symmetries, namely renormalization group symmetries (RGS). By RGS we mean a symmetry that characterizes a solution of b.v.p. and corresponds to transformations involving both dynamical variables and parameters entering the solution via boundary conditions and equations.

Transformations of this type appeared about forty years ago in quantum field theory (QFT) [1] and were successively used there for improving an approximate solution to restore a correct structure of solution singularity. In the seventies the concept based on renormgroup (RG) transformations (RG-method) was shown to be fruitful in some other fields of microscopic physics [2], more specifically for description of phase transition in large statistical systems like spin lattice, polymers, turbulence, and so on. Later on, symmetry underlying the RG invariance was also found in a number of problems of macroscopic physics like, e.g., mechanics, transfer theory, hydrodynamics. It was established that RG transformations have a close relation to the concept of self-similarity, and the new notion of functional self-similarity [3] was introduced.

The success of the RG-method in QFT and other fields of theoretical physics is due to the fact that it allows to improve the perturbation theory results and to simplify the analysis of a singular behavior of a solution. With the same goal the ideas of the RG-method were later on introduced in mathematical physics. In [4] the RG approach was applied to a system of nonlinear equations that describe the generating of higher harmonics in

---

* This work was partially supported by Russian Foundation for Basic Research, project No. 99-01-00232.

plasma. Here, the admitted exact symmetry group akin to employed in QFT was used to reconstruct the desired nonlinear b.v.p. solution from the perturbative solution. Methods of QFT and Wilson's RG in combination with the concept of intermediate asymptotics [5] were exploited in [6,7] to prove the global existence of solutions and calculate long time asymptotics for classes of nonlinear parabolic equations that describe a variety of physical phenomena, such as groundwater flow under gravity, shock waves dynamics, radiative heat transfer and so on. Later on the "perturbative renormalization group theory" (see [8] and references therein) based on the form of the invariance condition similar to that used in QFT, was developed for a global asymptotic analysis. The geometrical formulation of this perturbative RG theory was presented in [9] on the basis of a classical theory of envelopes.

However, the procedure of finding symmetries underlying the RG invariance in any particular case is usually based upon atypical manipulations [2,6,10], and the construction of a regular approach to revealing RGS is of principal interest. Such an approach has recently been devised [13] for mathematical models of physical systems that are described by DEs. A key idea of a regular method of the RGS construction is based [11,12] on the notion of the functional self-similarity and the well-known fact that such models can be analyzed using algorithms of modern group analysis. The scheme [13] that describes the RGS construction can be given in a concise form as follows.

Firstly, a specific RG-manifold should be constructed. Secondly, some auxiliary symmetry, i.e. the most general symmetry group admitted by this manifold is calculated. Thirdly, this symmetry should be restricted on a particular solution to get RGS. Fourthly, the RGS allows to improve an approximate solution or, in some lucky cases, to get an exact solution. Depending on both a mathematical model and boundary conditions, the first step of this procedure can be realized in different ways. For the purpose of the present study of particular interest is the perturbation method of constructing the RG-manifold which is based on the presence of small parameters. The second step, the calculation of a most general group admitted by the RG-manifold, is a standard procedure in the group analysis and has been described in detail in many texts and monographs – see, for example, [14,15]. This step includes tedious, mechanical computations, and the use of computer algebra tools helps to overcome these difficulties. A detailed review of modern symbolic packages that aid in the investigation of Lie symmetries for systems of DEs can be found, for example, in [15, Vol.3, Part III, p.365]. The symmetry group thus constructed can not as yet be referred to as a renormgroup. In order to obtain this, the next, third step should be made which consists in restricting the group obtained on a solution of b.v.p. This procedure mathematically appears as a "combining" of different coordinates of group generators admitted by the RG-manifold. In some particular cases the procedure of a group restriction can be partially fulfilled while looking for the admitted group. That means that we can use any additional information about the solution of b.v.p. while making the second step of the scheme. The final step, constructing analytical expressions for solutions of b.v.p. on the basis of the RGS obtained, usually presents no specific problems.

In the studies of various physical systems it is common practice that a model which is used to describe the system behavior is based on DEs with small parameters. This is just the situation mentioned above, when the employment of approximate symmetries [16] is a rational way to constructing RGS. Namely, the presence of small parameters allows us to consider a simple subsystem of the original DEs that usually admits an extended symmetry group inherited by the original DEs. Restricting this approximate group on the solution of the b.v.p. yields the desired RGS. With the presence of small parameters it appears natural that coordinates of RGS generators can be expressed as formal power series in these parameters with coefficients that depend upon the form of boundary conditions. For boundary conditions of a special form these series are truncated and a resultant finite sum describes the exact RGS of a b.v.p. for an arbitrary value of the parameter involved. For the boundary conditions of general form and for small values of parameters the restriction to a finite number of terms in power series leads to approximate RGS.

As well as in "traditional" group analysis the problem of finding RGS in the form of power series can also be simplified by the use of computer algebra tools. The symbolic packages that are employed to find symmetries of DEs usually divide the procedure of finding these symmetries into two major steps: deriving the determining equations, and solving them explicitly. It should be emphasized that for our purpose of the RGS construction the second step is of particular significance. Namely, the possibility of doing the second step separately plays the leading role in constructing RGS. Moreover, of great importance is the possibility of operating with linear homogeneous differential equations not necessarily obtained from symmetry analysis. Below we concentrate our attention on constructing the RGS with the help of approximate symmetries and on the use of symbolic package DIMSYM [17] to calculate the RGS in the form of truncated series for a mathematical model based on the extensively used nonlinear Schrödinger equation and quasi-Chaplygin equations.

The paper is organized as follows:

In Section 2, the governing equations for the intensity and the eikonal derivative (related to complex amplitude in nonlinear Schrödinger equation) and the corresponding boundary conditions are presented in the form that is used in nonlinear physics to describe propagation of a powerful plane (two-dimensional) or cylindrical (three-dimensional) light beam. There are two small parameters involved in these equations that describe nonlinear effects and diffraction of a light beam, respectively. The RGS construction is fulfilled in Section 3 both for the plane and cylindrical light beam geometry. It is shown that the coordinates of RG-symmetry operators are expressed as infinite power series in parameters, which characterize the medium nonlinearity and diffraction. For the boundary conditions of special form these series are truncated, and the resultant finite sum describes the exact RGS of a b.v.p. for arbitrary values of the diffraction and the nonlinearity parameters. For the boundary conditions of general form and for small values of parameters involved the restriction to a finite number or terms in the corresponding series leads to the approximate RGS. The use of the symbolic package DIMSYM [17] in order to obtain approximate symmetries and RGS is demonstrated. The result of the use of the DIMSYM package for calculating the exact symmetries as truncated series, i.e. in the form of finite sums is presented and compared to the traditional way of calculating symmetries for basic equations. In Section 4 we demonstrate some applications of the obtained b.v.p. solutions in nonlinear physics. For a number of particular examples that correspond to apriori given beam intensity distribution at the boundary (in the form of a soliton, a "smoothed" step and a gaussian curve) the formulas are presented, which define in a closed analytical form the distribution of both the intensity and the derivative of the eikonal of a light beam in the nonlinear medium. In Section V we make conclusions and discuss other applications.

2   Governing Equations

A starting point is a mathematical model based on the nonlinear Schrödinger equation with cubic nonlinearity for the complex amplitude $\Psi = A \exp(iks)$ that is reduced (by introducing the intensity $I \equiv A^2 = |\Psi|^2$ and eikonal derivative v related to the eikonal s as $\mathbf{v} = \nabla_\perp s$) to the following two partial DEs (see, e.g., [18]) which are considered as a governing system of equations

$$v_t + v v_x - \alpha n_x - \beta \partial_x \left(\left(x^{1-\nu}/\sqrt{n} \right) \partial_x \left(x^{\nu-1} \partial_x \left(\sqrt{n} \right) \right) \right) = 0 \,,$$

$$n_t + n v_x + v n_x + (\nu - 1)\frac{nv}{x} = 0 \,. \tag{1}$$

We assume that a semi-infinite nonlinear medium occupies a half-space $z \geq 0$, the operator $\nabla_\perp$ acts in the plane that is orthogonal to z-axis, the vector $\mathbf{v}$ has a single non-zero component v in this plane, k is a wave number. Dimensionless coordinates t and x in (1) are used to describe the spatial evolution of the eikonal derivative v and the normalized intensity n in the direction inside the nonlinear

medium and in the transverse direction. The parameters α and β define the role of the nonlinear refraction and diffraction, $\nu = 1$ for a plane and $\nu = 2$ for a cylindrical beam geometry.

In what follows we assume that at the entrance of a nonlinear medium (at $t = 0$) the curvature of the beam wave front and the normalized beam intensity distribution n upon the coordinate x are given:

$$v(0,x) = V(x) = -x/T \,, \qquad n(0,x) = N(x) \,. \tag{2}$$

These boundary conditions are typical of the most of applications and describe a focused light beam with a smooth beam intensity distribution.

In the case of vanishing diffraction, $\beta \to 0$, the governing equations (1) are reduced to the system of quasi-Chaplygin equations:

$$v_t + vv_x - \alpha n_x = 0 , \quad n_t + nv_x + vn_x + (\nu - 1)\frac{nv}{x} = 0 . \tag{3}$$

These equations are known in nonlinear optics as nonlinear geometrical optics equations. A peculiarity of the two-dimensional case with $\nu = 1$ is a possibility of linearization of (3) by hodograph transformations. Namely, by using the new variables $\tau = nt$ and $\chi = x - vt$ and introducing the normalized eikonal derivative $w = v/\alpha$ the system (3) may be rewritten in the form of two linear DEs:

$$\tau_w - n\chi_n = 0, \quad \chi_w + \alpha\tau_n = 0 . \tag{4}$$

In three-dimensional case $\nu = 2$ the second equation in (4) reads as

$$\chi_w + \alpha\left[\tau_n + \frac{w}{\chi}\left(\tau_n\chi_w - n\chi_n^2\right)\right] + \frac{\alpha^2 w}{n^2\chi}\left[2n\tau\tau_n - \tau^2\right] = 0 \tag{5}$$

hence the system of governing equations remains nonlinear after hodograph transformations. The procedure of the RGS construction will be discussed below for both systems (1) and (4), (5).

3 Construction of Renormgroup Symmetries

3.1 RGS in Nonlinear Geometrical Optics

Let us consider first the most simple case of a plane geometry ($\nu = 1$) and take into account only nonlinear refraction effects, $\alpha \neq 0$, whilst diffraction is neglected, $\beta = 0$. The first step on the way to obtaining the RGS is the construction of the RG-manifold, which in our case is presented by the system of DEs (4) treated in the extended space of variables which includes not only dependent and independent variables τ, χ, w, n, but also the nonlinearity parameter α and derivatives of arbitrary order of τ and χ with respect to n (and possibly to α). To proceed further we express the coordinates f and g of the group canonical operator, admitted by Eqs. (4),

$$X = f\,\partial_\tau + g\,\partial_\chi \tag{6}$$

as a power series with respect to the nonlinearity parameter

$$f = \sum_{i=0}^{\infty} \alpha^i f^i ; \quad g = \sum_{i=0}^{\infty} \alpha^i g^i . \tag{7}$$

Expansion coefficients f^i and g^i in (7) are found from determining equations that express the invariance condition for the system (4) with respect to group transformations with the operator (6) and are given by an infinite set of equations (provided α is not involved in group transformations)

$$L_0 g^0 = 0 , \qquad\qquad L_0 f^0 - n L_1 g^0 = 0 ,$$
$$L_0 g^i + L_1 f^{i-1} - L_2 g^{i-1} = 0 , \quad L_0 f^i - n L_1 g^i - L_2 f^{i-1} = 0 , \quad i \geq 1 . \tag{8}$$

Here differential operators L_i, $i = 0, 1, 2$, are defined as follows:

$$L_0 = \partial_w + \sum_{s=0}^{\infty} (n\chi_{s+1} + s\chi_s) \partial_{\tau_s} , \quad L_1 = \partial_n + \sum_{s=0}^{\infty} (\tau_{s+1}\partial_{\tau_s} + \chi_{s+1}\partial_{\chi_s}) ,$$
$$L_2 = \sum_{s=0}^{\infty} \tau_{s+1}\partial_{\chi_s} , \qquad \tau_s = \frac{\partial^s \tau}{\partial n^s} , \quad \chi_s = \frac{\partial^s \chi}{\partial n^s} . \tag{9}$$

The solution of determining equations is formally given by a system of recurrence relations:

$$f^i = F^i + \int dw \left\{ (1 - \delta_{i,0}) Z f^{i-1} + n Y g^i \right\} ,$$
$$g^i = G^i + (1 - \delta_{i,0}) \int dw \left\{ Z g^{i-1} - Y f^{i-1} \right\} . \tag{10}$$

Here

$$Y = \partial_n + \sum_{s=0}^{\infty} (\tau_{s+1}\partial_{\tau_s} + \chi_{s+1}\partial_{\chi_s}) , \quad Z = \sum_{s=0}^{\infty} \tau_{s+1}\partial_{\chi_s} , \tag{11}$$
$$\tilde{\tau}_s = \tau_s - w (s\chi_s + n\chi_{s+1}) ,$$

$F^i(n, \chi_s, \tilde{\tau}_s)$ and $G^i(n, \chi_s, \tilde{\tau}_s)$ are arbitrary functions of their arguments, and expressions in brackets before integrating over w should be given in terms of $\tilde{\tau}_s, \chi_s, n, w$.

The procedure of restricting the group obtained (11) on a particular solution of a b.v.p. in order to obtain the RGS consists in checking the invariance conditions for this solution with respect to the RG operator and imposes limitations on the form of functions F^i and G^i. It means that they are not arbitrary functions, but should be chosen in such a way that the relationships

$$f = 0 , \quad g = 0 , \tag{12}$$

which appear as differential constraints (sometimes in particular case simply as algebraic relations), are identically valid on the desired solution of the b.v.p. and satisfy at $\tau = 0$ the boundary conditions (2). Assuming for simplicity the plane phase front at $t = 0$, i.e. $T \to \infty$, these conditions can be written in terms of (τ, χ) as follows:

$$w = 0 , \quad \tau_s = 0 , \quad \chi = H(n) . \tag{13}$$

Provided that the functions F^i, G^i, $i \geq 1$ are also equal to zero in this case, the boundary conditions are fully correlated with the form of functions F^0 and G^0.

For arbitrary boundary conditions, i.e. for the arbitrary function $H(n)$ in (13), these infinite series are of little utility. However, one can take into account only the finite number of terms provided consideration is restricted to small values of the nonlinearity parameter α. It conceptually means that the construction of RGS is based on approximate symmetries [16] (see also [15, Vol.3, Chapt.2]). It enables us to consider a simple subsystem of the original DEs, that results from (4) by dropping the second term in the second equation:

$$\tau_w - n\chi_n = 0, \quad \chi_w = 0. \tag{14}$$

In contrast with the original system of DEs (4), which admits the finite group of Lie-Bäcklund transformations of any given order, the system of DEs (14) admits an infinite-dimensional symmetry group that is characterized by the arbitrary dependence of coordinates f^0 and g^0 of canonical operator (6) upon their arguments. For small values of the parameter α the symmetry of (14) is inherited by (4) up to an arbitrary finite order of this parameter. The type of the inherited symmetry (i.e. the form of functions f and g) is completely defined by relations (10): it may appear as Lie group of point symmetries or Lie-Bäcklund symmetries as well. Restricting this approximate group on the solution of the b.v.p. yields the desired RGS.

The form of this symmetry can hardly be predicted *apriori*, and results only in calculating the complicated integrals in (10). However, instead of direct calculation of integrals one can analyze the system of linear DEs for functions f^i and g^i considering a limited number of determining equations (8), namely $0 \leq i \leq m$. It is important that this procedure can be simplified by the use of modern computer algebra tools. Moreover, one can impose arbitrary restrictions on the form of these functions, e.g. searching for f^i and g^i that are linear in derivatives τ_1 and χ_1: in this case, the RGS operator is obtained that is equivalent to an RGS operator of the point transformation group. It should be noted that in order to obtain the approximate point RGS operator in a standard non-canonical form

$$R = \xi^1 \partial_w + \xi^2 \partial_n + \xi^3 \partial_\alpha + \eta^1 \partial_\tau + \eta^2 \partial_\chi, \tag{15}$$

one can apply the prescribed algorithm directly to the system (4) with the additional assumption that coordinates ξ^j and η^j have the similar representation as (7)

$$\xi^j = \sum_{i=0}^{\infty} \alpha^i \xi^{i,j}; \quad \eta^j = \sum_{i=0}^{\infty} \alpha^i \eta^{i,j}. \tag{16}$$

The possibility of manual intervention in the process of simplifying and solving the determining equations allows one while searching for RGS to add some constraints that "link" the RGS to solutions of the special form. Hence the procedure of group restriction is partially fulfilled while searching for the solutions of group determining equations. The symmetry thus obtained is not a symmetry of the basic system of DEs in the common "classical" meaning, however, it also enables us to obtain information on the structure of the b.v.p. solution.

When analyzing (8) of special interest are such functions f^0 and g^0, for which the infinite series (10) are automatically truncated for some finite value of $i = m$, and finite sums are obtained. In the latter case, two more equations should be added to the list of $2(m + 1)$ Eqs. (8) that guarantee the absence of higher terms with $i > m$,

$$L_1 f^m - L_2 g^m = 0 , \quad L_2 f^m = 0 , \quad m \geq 1 . \tag{17}$$

In order to illustrate the aforesaid a table is presented below which demonstrates the effectiveness of the use of the symbolic package DIMSYM [17] in calculating determining Eqs. (8), (17) and constructing RGS. The first

Table 1.

Form of RGS	Boundary conditions	Additional conditions	Time used (s): new approach	Time used (s): standard approach
canonical	a	yes	24	640
canonical	b	yes	30	640
canonical	c	no	12	-
point	arbitrary	no	8	-
point	arbitrary	yes	20	-

column indicates the form of RGS representation, and the second column contains information on boundary conditions. The third column indicates whether any additional conditions (for example, in the form of (17)) were used in calculating RGS. The next, fourth column shows the "pure" time (in seconds) needed to calculate the RGS (on PC 486 DX2 66) using the prescribed method. The last column shows the time that is needed to find symmetries of governing equations (4) in a standard way (with no ansatz used). This comparison [19,20] makes sense only for truncated series (7), i.e. for exact RGS.

The a), b) and c) cases correspond to the following boundary conditions which differ in the form of the intensity distribution function $N(x)$ at the medium boundary:

a) soliton mode

$$H(n) = \text{Arccosh}\left(\frac{1}{\sqrt{n}}\right) , \tag{18}$$

b) step-like mode (K is a complete elliptic integral)

$$H(n) = \frac{2}{1+\sqrt{n}}\left(K\left(\frac{2n^{1/4}}{1+\sqrt{n}}\right) - \frac{6}{\pi}K\left(\frac{1-\sqrt{n}}{1+\sqrt{n}}\right)\right) , \tag{19}$$

c) gaussian mode

$$H(n) = (\ln(1/n))^{1/2} . \tag{20}$$

The coordinates f and g of the RGS operators

$$R = f\partial_\tau + g\partial_\chi , \tag{21}$$

in all three cases (first three lines of Table 1) have the binomial form $f = f^0 + \alpha f^1$ and $g = g^0 + \alpha g^1$ and are given by formulas:

a) $f^0 = 2n(1-n)\tau_2 - n\tau_1 - 2nw(\chi_1 + n\chi_2) , \quad f^1 = \frac{1}{2}nw^2\tau_2 ,$

$g^0 = 2n(1-n)\chi_2 + (2-3n)\chi_1 ,$ (22)

$g^1 = w(2n\tau_2 + \tau_1) + \frac{w^2}{2}(n\chi_2 + \chi_1) .$

b) $f^0 = n(1-n)\tau_2 - n\tau_1 - nw(\frac{5}{4}\chi_1 + n\chi_2) , \quad f^1 = \frac{1}{4}nw^2\tau_2 ,$

$g^0 = n(1-n)\chi_2 + (1-2n)\chi_1 - \frac{1}{4}\chi ,$ (23)

$g^1 = w\left(n\tau_2 + \frac{3}{4}\tau_1\right) + \frac{w^2}{4}(n\chi_2 + \chi_1) .$

c) $f^0 = 1 + 2n\chi\chi_1 , \quad f^1 = \frac{\tau^2}{n} - 2\tau\tau_1 , \quad g^0 = 0 , \quad g^1 = -2(\tau\chi_1 + \chi\tau_1) .$ (24)

One can easily check that in cases a) and b) the functions f^i, g^i satisfy both (8) and (17), whereas in the case of c) Eqs. (17) are not true. It means that in cases a) and b) we have the exact symmetry group for which the infinite series (7) is truncated, whereas in the last case c) the symmetry obtained is an approximate one. The dependence of coordinates f^i and g^i upon the higher derivatives indicates that in a) and b) cases the operator (21) is the second order Lie-Bäcklund symmetry operator. In the case c) the coordinates

f^i and g^i are linear in derivatives, and the resultant operator is equivalent to the point approximate RGS operator

$$R = -2\chi\partial_w + 2\alpha\tau\partial_n + \left(1 + \frac{\alpha\tau^2}{n}\right)\partial_\tau . \tag{25}$$

The fourth line of Table 1 presents the effectiveness of calculating point symmetry group when using the non-canonical representation (15)-(16) and taking into account only zero order and first order (linear in α) terms. The RGS thus obtained is described by (15) with coordinates ξ^j, η^j that have the binomial form

$$\xi^j = \xi^{0,j} + \alpha\xi^{1,j} , \quad \eta^j = \eta^{0,j} + \alpha\eta^{1,j} . \tag{26}$$

Here

$$\xi^1 = J + (C^1 + C^2)w + \alpha\left(\frac{w^2}{2n}(hJ)_x - \frac{nw^2}{2}J_{nn} - \frac{\tau^2}{2n}J_{xx} - \tau w J_{nx}\right)$$

$$+ \alpha\frac{w^3}{6}I_n , \quad \xi^2 = 2nC^1 - \alpha(wnJ_n + \tau J_x) , \quad \xi^3 = -2\alpha C^2 ,$$

$$\eta^1 = hJ + \tau I + nw(\chi I_n - (HI)_n) + 2nw(nH_n)_n C^1 + (C^1 + C^2)\tau$$

$$- \alpha\left(\frac{nw^2}{2}(hJ)_{nn} + \frac{\tau^2}{2n}((hJ)_{xx} + J_x) + nw\tau\left(\frac{hJ}{n}\right)_n\right)$$

$$- \alpha\left(\frac{nw^2}{2}\tau I_{nn} + \frac{nw^3}{6}(\chi(nI_n)_{nn} - (n(HI)_n)_{nn})\right)$$

$$- \alpha\frac{nw^3}{3}(n(nH_n)_n)_{nn} C^1 ,$$

$$\eta^2 = (\chi - H)I + 2(nH_n)_n C^1 - \alpha\left(w(hJ)_n + \frac{\tau}{n}(hJ)_x\right) - \alpha\tau w I_n$$

$$- \alpha\frac{w^2}{2}(\chi(nI_n^2)_n - (n(HI^2)_n)_n) - \alpha w^2(n(nH_n)_n)_n C^1 ,$$

$J(n, \chi)$ and $I(n)$ are arbitrary functions of their arguments, C^i are arbitrary constants, and $h(n, \chi)$ results from the product $(n\chi_n)$ that should be expressed in terms of n and χ. It is easily checked that the foregoing RGS operator (25) follows from (15), (26) in view of $h(n, \chi) = -(1/2\chi)$, $J = -2\chi$ and $I = C^1 = C^2 = 0$.

The last, fifth line of Table 1 demonstrates the possibility of calculating the point RGS in view of the following additional constraint that is approximately consistent with the form of a solution in the vicinity of beam axis

[21]:

$$\partial_a \chi = \partial_a \tau = 0 \,. \tag{27}$$

As a result, the infinite-dimensional group of point transformations is obtained that gives rise to the operator of RGS for the gaussian beam with the parameter α involved in group transformations

$$R = 2\tau\partial_w + 2n\chi\partial_n + 2\alpha\chi\partial_\alpha - \partial_\chi \,. \tag{28}$$

The construction of RGS for the three-dimensional beam geometry with $\nu = 2$ is fulfilled in a similar way as in the case of $\nu = 1$, and furthermore, the coordinates f^i and g^i are given by formulas akin to (10), though they result from more complicated calculations (see [21] for details), thus attaching particular significance to the use of DIMSYM package. In view of cumbersome formulas for these coordinates the explicit expressions are omitted below, but it should be noted that the main characteristics of the RGS obtained are quite similar to the two-dimensional case. Namely, for small values of the parameter α the infinite-dimensional symmetry group of equations (14) is inherited by the system of Eqs. (4)-(5) up to an arbitrary finite order of this parameter. The type of the inherited symmetry may appear as Lie group of point symmetries or Lie-Bäcklund symmetries as well. Restricting this approximate group on the solution of the b.v.p. yields the desired RGS.

Similarly to the two-dimensional variant one can impose arbitrary additional constraints on f and g that define the type of RGS, for example, the assumption of linear dependence of f and g upon derivatives τ_1, χ_1 which gives rise to the point RGS. And as in case of $\nu = 1$ there also exist specific boundary conditions, for which the infinite series (7) are truncated, and the RGS is the exact symmetry. For example, for the beam with the parabolic initial density profile $H(n) = \sqrt{1 - n}$, the operator of point RGS (15) has the form:

$$R = -2\chi\partial_w + 4\alpha\tau\partial_n + n\left(1 + \frac{2\alpha\tau^2}{n^2}\right)\partial_\tau - \alpha w\partial_\chi \,. \tag{29}$$

Substituting the expressions for the coordinates of this operator directly into group determining equations one can check that the obtained RGS is exact, i.e. it is valid for arbitrary values of α.

3.2   RGS in Nonlinear Wave Optics

The procedure of constructing RGS in nonlinear wave optics is in many respects similar to that in geometrical optics and employs the representation of coordinates φ and ψ of the group canonical operator admitted by (1),

$$Q = \varphi\,\partial_v + \psi\,\partial_n \tag{30}$$

with coordinates φ and ψ in the form of power series in the nonlinearity parameter α and the diffraction parameter β:

$$\varphi = \sum_{i,j=0}^{\infty} \alpha^i \beta^j \varphi^{i,j}, \quad \psi = \sum_{i,j=0}^{\infty} \alpha^i \beta^j \psi^{i,j}. \tag{31}$$

Expansion coefficients $\varphi^{i,j}$, $\psi^{i,j}$ in (31) depend upon t, x, v, n and derivatives of v and n with respect to x of arbitrary order and are found from the solution of an infinite set of equations that are akin to (8). In particular, equations that define zero-order terms $\varphi^0 \equiv \varphi^{0,0}$, $\psi^0 \equiv \psi^{0,0}$ that do not depend upon α and β, and first order terms that are linear in these parameters $\varphi^1 \equiv \alpha \varphi^{1,0} + \beta \varphi^{0,1}$, $\psi^1 \equiv \alpha \psi^{1,0} + \beta \psi^{0,1}$ have the form

$$M_0 \varphi^0 = 0, \ M_1 \psi^0 + M_2 \varphi^0 = 0, \ M_1 \psi^1 + M_2 \varphi^1 + D_t^1 \psi^0 = 0,$$

$$M_0 \varphi^1 + D_t^1 \varphi^0 - \alpha D_x \psi^0 - \beta \left\{ B_n \psi^0 + B_{n_1} \left(D_x \psi^0 \right) + B_{n_2} \left(D_x^2 \psi^0 \right) \right. \tag{32}$$

$$\left. + B_{n_3} \left(D_x^3 \psi^0 \right) \right\} = 0, \ B = D_x \left(\left(D_x \left(x^{\nu-1} D_x \left(\sqrt{n} \right) \right) \right) / x^{\nu-1} \sqrt{n} \right).$$

Here the differential operators are defined as follows:

$$D_t^0 = \partial_t - \sum_{s=0}^{\infty} \left[D_x^s \left(vv_1 \right) \partial_{v_s} + \left(D_x^{s+1} \left(nv \right) + (\nu - 1) D_x^s \left(\frac{nv}{x} \right) \right) \partial_{n_s} \right],$$

$$D_t^1 = \sum_{s=0}^{\infty} \left[D_x^s \left(\alpha n_1 + \beta B \right) \right] \partial_{v_s}, \ D_x = \partial_x + \sum_{s=0}^{\infty} \left[v_{s+1} \partial_{v_s} + n_{s+1} \partial_{n_s} \right], \tag{33}$$

$$M_0 = D_t^0 + v D_x + v_1, \quad M_1 = M_0 + (\nu - 1)(v/x),$$

$$M_2 = n D_x + n_1 + (\nu - 1)(n/x), \quad v_s \equiv \frac{\partial^s v}{\partial x^s}, \ n_s \equiv \frac{\partial^s n}{\partial x^s}.$$

Solutions of linear DEs for φ^i and ψ^i are defined in terms of arbitrary functions (compare to (10)), that depend upon infinite set of invariants of the operator $D_x + D_t^0$. Restricting the group obtained on the solution of the b.v.p. in view of invariance conditions

$$\varphi = 0, \quad \psi = 0, \tag{34}$$

helps to eliminate this arbitrariness. In particular, one can choose the following simple representation for φ^0 and ψ^0:

$$\varphi^0 = \frac{1}{2T^2} D_x \left(x + vT \left(1 - \frac{t}{T} \right) \right)^2,$$

$$\psi^0 = \frac{x^{1-\nu}}{T} \left(1 - \frac{t}{T} \right) D_x \left[nx^{\nu-1} \left(x + vT \left(1 - \frac{t}{T} \right) \right) \right]. \tag{35}$$

Direct substitution of (35) in (34) proves that the functions φ^0 and ψ^0 satisfy the invariance conditions at $t = 0$ for arbitrary boundary data (2). Solving the remaining equations for φ^1 and ψ^1 in view of (35) yields the following result:

a) $\nu = 1$

$$\varphi^1 = D_x \left\{ \beta \left(\frac{1}{\sqrt{N}} \right) \left(\sqrt{N} \right)_{xx} - \beta \left(1 - \frac{t}{T} \right)^2 \left(\frac{1}{\sqrt{n}} \right) D_x \left(D_x \left(\sqrt{n} \right) \right) \right.$$

$$\left. - \alpha n \left(1 - \frac{t}{T} \right)^2 + \alpha \frac{n}{v_1 T} \left(1 - \frac{t}{T} + \frac{1}{v_1 T} \right) \ln n - \alpha \frac{n}{v_1 T} \left(1 - \frac{t}{T} \right) \right\} ,$$

$$\psi^1 = D_x \left\{ \alpha \frac{n n_1}{v_1^2 T} \left(\frac{\ln n}{v_1 T} + \left(1 - \frac{t}{T} + \frac{1}{v_1 T} \right) (\ln n - 1) \right) \right. \tag{36}$$

$$- \alpha \frac{n^2 v_2}{v_1^3 T} \left(\frac{2 \ln n - 1}{v_1 T} + \left(1 - \frac{t}{T} + \frac{1}{v_1 T} \right) \left(\ln n - \frac{3}{2} \right) \right)$$

$$\left. - \alpha T N N_\chi \ln N - \beta t n \left(\left(\sqrt{N} \right)_{xx} / \sqrt{N} \right)_x \right\} .$$

b) $\nu = 2$

$$\varphi^1 = D_x \left\{ S - \left(1 - \frac{t}{T} \right)^2 \left(\alpha n + \frac{\beta}{x \sqrt{n}} D_x \left(x D_x \sqrt{n} \right) \right) \right\} ,$$

$$\psi^1 = -\frac{1}{x} D_x \left(x t n S_\chi \right) , \quad \chi = x - vt , \tag{37}$$

$$S(\chi) = \alpha N(\chi) + \frac{\beta}{\chi \sqrt{N(\chi)}} \partial_\chi \left(\chi \partial_\chi \left(\sqrt{N(\chi)} \right) \right) .$$

Formulas (35), (36), (37) define the third-order Lie-Bäcklund RGS, but in case of $\nu = 2$, the canonical group operator with coordinates (35) and (37) is equivalent to the point RG operator. Just as in the previous section, the RGS obtained appears to be exact for particular boundary conditions, which in the last formula define the dependence of S on χ. It can be verified directly by searching for the exact symmetry of governing Eqs. (1) (DIMSYM package is of use here) that series (31) contain only the zero-order and linear in α and β terms for

$$S = s_0 + s_2 \chi^2 / 2 , \tag{38}$$

whilst bilinear and higher-order terms vanish. It means that in this case the RGS gives rise to the exact b.v.p. solution.

4 Examples of Different B.V.P. Solutions

From the practical standpoint the regular and efficient method of finding the RGS is of great importance since it can be used to obtain the b.v.p.

solutions. The procedure of constructing such solutions make use of invariance conditions of (12), (34) type. Solving the governing equations in view of boundary conditions and invariance conditions yields the desired solution of the b.v.p., which is exact or approximate depending upon the type of RGS used.

For example, the utilization of the second-order Lie-Bäcklund RGS (22) leads to the well-known exact solution [18] of the b.v.p. in nonlinear geometrical optics for the beam with the initial intensity distribution profile in the form of a soliton $N = \cosh^{-2}(x)$ (see also [22,20])

$$v = -2ant \tanh(x - vt) , \quad an^2 t^2 = n \cosh^2(x - vt) - 1 . \qquad (39)$$

Another example of the exact b.v.p. solution in nonlinear geometrical optics based on the utilization of the exact second-order Lie-Bäcklund RGS (23) is related to the initial beam intensity distribution in the form of a "smoothed" step and is described as follows [21,23]:

$$x = vt + \frac{k_1}{n^{1/4}} \left(K\left(k_1\right) - \frac{6}{\pi} K\left(k_2\right) \right) , \qquad (40)$$

$$t = \frac{1}{n\sqrt{\alpha}} \left[\left(\frac{qk_1}{2} K\left(k_1\right) - \frac{2}{k_1} E\left(k_1\right) - \frac{6}{\pi k_1} \left(2E\left(k_2\right) - k_1^2 K\left(k_2\right) \right) \right) \frac{F(\vartheta, k)}{\sqrt{q_2}} \right.$$
$$\left. - k_1 \left(K\left(k_1\right) - \frac{6}{\pi} K\left(k_2\right) \right) \left(\sqrt{q_2} E(\vartheta, k) - \frac{\left((q_2 - \sqrt{n})(\sqrt{n} - q_1) \right)^{1/2}}{n^{1/4}} \right) \right] .$$

Here

$$q = n^{-1/2} \left(1 + n + \frac{v^2}{4a} \right) ; \quad k = \sqrt{\frac{q_2 - q_1}{q_2}} , \quad k_1 = \frac{2}{\sqrt{q + 2}} , \quad k_2 = \sqrt{\frac{q - 2}{q + 2}} ,$$

$$2q_{1,2} = q \mp \sqrt{q^2 - 4}; \quad \vartheta = \arcsin \left[(q_2/\sqrt{n}) \left(\sqrt{n} - q_1 \right)(q_2 - \sqrt{n}) \right]^{1/2} ,$$

and standard notations for the non-complete $F(\vartheta, k)$, $E(\vartheta, k)$ and complete $K(k)$, $E(k)$ elliptic integrals of the first and the second order are used. For the light beam with the initial gaussian profile the approximate analytical solution of the b.v.p. in nonlinear geometrical optics [21,23] arises with the use of the RGS operator (28)

$$x^2 = \left(1 - 2ant^2 \right)^2 \ln \frac{1}{n(1 - \alpha nt^2)} , \quad v = -\frac{2x\,ant}{1 - 2ant^2} . \qquad (41)$$

The behavior of a cylindrical light wave beam in nonlinear medium when diffraction effects are taken into account is obtained by using the RGS (35), (37), where the function $S(x)$ has the form

$$S(x) = \alpha \exp \left(-x^2 \right) + \beta(x^2 - 2) . \qquad (42)$$

The substitution of (42) in (37) in view of (34) leads to the following original analytical formulas for the beam structure [24]:

$$v(t,x) = \frac{x - \chi}{t} , \quad n(t,x) = e^{-\mu^2} \left(1 - \frac{t}{T}\right)^{-1} \frac{\chi}{x} \frac{\beta - \alpha e^{-\chi^2}}{\beta - \alpha e^{-\mu^2}} . \tag{43}$$

Here the functions χ and μ are defined via t and x by the following relations:

$$\beta\mu^2 + \alpha e^{-\mu^2} = \beta\chi^2 + \alpha e^{-\chi^2} + \frac{2t^2\chi^2}{(1 - t/T)^2} \left(\beta - \alpha e^{-\chi^2}\right)^2 ;$$

$$x = \left(1 - \frac{t}{T}\right)\chi\left[1 + \frac{2t^2}{(1 - t/T)^2}\left(\beta - \alpha e^{-\chi^2}\right)\right] . \tag{44}$$

The last example of b.v.p. solution is based on the RGS that arises from (37) in view of (38). For $s_2 = 0$ this RGS gives the well-known exact stationary solution [25], whilst for $s_2 \neq 0$ it describes a converging light beam with a localized initial intensity profile [24].

5   Conclusions

In this paper we have shown that the recently devised method of constructing RGS (in particular, the algorithm based on approximate symmetries) constitutes a powerful tool in analyzing the b.v.p.'s in mathematical physics, especially when used in combination with computer algebra packages. The utilization of symbolic packages with the aim of calculating approximate symmetry groups makes the whole procedure very efficient and enables one to find the RGS in a reasonable time. The promising feature of the described method is a possibility of its application to various mathematical models, based on DEs with small parameters. In this sense the employed mathematical model based on the nonlinear Schrödinger equation appears to be an attractive but not a unique illustration of the capabilities of the method. An argument for the aforesaid is the use of the analogous method to calculate the point approximate RGS for plasma theory equations [4]. It seems also possible to extend this approach for the mathematical models that are not based just on DEs.

References

1. Stueckelberg, E.E.C. and Petermann, A.: La normalisation des constantes dans la théorie des quanta. Helv. Phys. Acta **22** (1953) 499–520; Gell-Mann, M. and Low, F.: Quantum Electrodynamics at Small Distances. Phys. Rev. **95** (1954) 1300–1312; Bogoliubov, N.N. and Shirkov, D.V.: Group in Quantum Electrodynamics. Dokl. Akad. Nauk. SSSR **103** (1955) 203–206; Charge Renormalization Group in Quantum Field Theory. Nuovo Cim. **3** (1956) 845–863

2. Wilson, K.: Renormalization Group and Critical Phenomena. Phys. Rev. **B4** (1971) 3184-3205; de Gennes, P.G.: Scaling Concepts in Polymer Physics. Ithaca (1979); Zinn-Justin, J.: Quantum Field Theory and Critical Phenomena. Clarendon Press Oxford (1978; 1989)

3. Shirkov, D.V.: Renormalization Group, invariance principle and functional self-similarity. Sov. Phys. Dokl. **27** (1982) 197-200; Renormgroup and functional self-similarity in different branches of physics. Theor.& Math. Phys. **60(2)** (1984) 778-782

4. Kovalev, V.F. and Pustovalov, V.V.: Functional self-similarity in a problem of plasma theory with electron nonlinearity. Theor.& Math. Phys. **81** (1990) No.1 1060-1071

5. Barenblatt, G.I.: Scaling, Self-similarity and Intermediate Asymptotics. Cambridge Univ. Press (1996)

6. Goldenfeld, N., Martin, O., and Oono, Y.: Intermediate asymptotics and renormalization group theory. J. Sci. Comput. **4** (1989) 355-372

7. Bricmont, J., Kupiainen, A. and Lin, G.: RG and asymptotics of solutions of nonlinear parabolic equations. Comm. Pure Appl. Math. **47** (1994) 893-922

8. Chen, L.-Y., Goldenfeld, N., and Oono, Y.: The Renormalization group and singular perturbations: multiple-scales, boundary layers and reductive perturbation theory. Phys. Rev. **E 54** (1996) No.1 376-394

9. Kunihiro, T.: A geometrical formulation of the renormalization group method for global analysis. Progr.Theor.Phys. **94** (1995) No.4 503-514

10. Shirkov, D.V.: Renormalization Group in Modern Physics. Intern. J. Mod. Physics **A3** (1988) 1321-1342

11. Shirkov, D.V.: Several topics on Renormgroup Theory; Kovalev, V.F., Krivenko, S.V., and Pustovalov, V.V.: The Renormalization group method based on group analysis. in: "Renormalization group-91", Proc. of Second Intern. Conf., Sept. 1991, Dubna, USSR, Ed. D. V. Shirkov & V. B. Priezzhev, WS Singapore (1992) 1-10; 300-314.

12. Kovalev V.F.: RG-symmetries: constructing and applications. In: Third International Conference "Renormalization group'96", August 26-31, 1996, Dubna. Editors D.V.Shirkov, D.I.Kazakov, V.B.Priezzhev. Dubna (1997) 263-276

13. Kovalev, V.F., Pustovalov, V.V., and Shirkov, D.V.: Group analysis and renormgroup symmetries. J. Math. Phys. **39** (1998) No.2 1170-1188

14. Ovsyannikov, L.V.: Group analysis of differential equations. Academic Press N.-Y. (1982); Ibragimov, N.H.: Transformation groups applied to mathematical physics. Riedel, Dordrecht (1985); Olver, Peter J.: Applications of Lie groups to differential equations. Springer-Verlag N. Y. (1986)

15. CRC Handbook of Lie Group Analysis of Differential Equations, Ed. N.H. Ibragimov. CRC Press, Boca Raton, Florida, USA. Vol.1: Symmetries, Exact Solutions and Conservation Laws, 1994; Vol.2: Applications in Engineering and Physical Sciences, 1995; Vol.3: New Trends in Theoretical Developments and Computational Methods, 1996

16. Baikov, V.A., Gazizov, R.K., and Ibragimov, N.H.: Perturbation methods in group analysis. J. Sov. Math. **55(1)** (1991) 1450-1512

17. Sherring, J.: DIMSYM: symmetry determination and linear differential equations package. LaTrobe University Mathematics Department Research Report (1993) Melbourne, Australia

18. Akhmanov, S.A., Khokhlov, R.V. and Sukhorukov, A.P.: On the self-focusing and self-chanelling of intense laser beams in nonlinear medium. Sov. Phys. JETP **23** (1966) No.6 1025–1033

19. Kovalev, V.F.: Computer algebra tools in a group analysis of quasi-Chaplygin system of equations in: New Computing Techniques in Physics Research IV. Edited by B.Denby and D.Perret-Gallix (World Scientific Publ. Co Pie Ltd., (1995) 229–235

20. Kovalev, V.F. and Pustovalov, V.V.: Group and renormgroup symmetry of a simple model for nonlinear phenomena in optics, gas dynamics and plasma theory. Mathem. Comp. Modelling **25** (1997) No.8/9, 165–179

21. Kovalev, V.F.: Renormgroup symmetries in problems of nonlinear geometrical optics. Theor.& Mathem. Phys. **111** (1997) No.3 686–702

22. Kovalev, V.F.: Group and renormgroup symmetry of quasi-Chaplygin media. J. Nonlin. Mathem. Phys. **3** (1996) No.3-4 351–356

23. Kovalev, V.F., and Shirkov, D.V.: Renormalization group in mathematical physics and some problems of laser optics. J. Nonlin. Opt. Phys.& Materials **6** (1997) No.4 443–454

24. Kovalev V.F.: Renormgroup analysis of singularity in wave beam self-focusing problem. Theor. & Mathem. Phys. (1999) (to appear)

25. Chiao, R., Garmire, E., and Townes, G.: Dynamics and characteristics of the self-trapping of intense light beams. Phys. Rev. Lett. **16** (1966) No. 9 347–349

Where Numerics Can Benefit from Computer Algebra in Finite Difference Modelling of Fluid Flows

Richard Liska[1] and Burton Wendroff[2]

[1] Faculty of Nuclear Sciences and Physical Engineering, Czech Technical
University in Prague, Břehová 7, 115 19 Prague 1, Czech Republic
(liska@siduri.fjfi.cvut.cz, http://www-troja.fjfi.cvut.cz/~liska)
[2] Group T-7, Los Alamos National Laboratory, Los Alamos, NM 87544, USA
(bbw@lanl.gov, http://math.unm.edu/~bbw)

Abstract. We present several examples of the use of computer algebra systems
as a tool in the development and implementation of finite difference schemes modelling fluid flows. Computer algebra is particularly important for transformations
of partial differential equations, posedness and stability analysis. Automatic code
generation provides a reliable way to process large implicit linear or non-linear finite
difference schemes into Fortran code solving them.

1 Introduction

Computer algebra can support the development of numerical finite difference
codes for solving partial differential equations (PDEs) in several stages of
the development process, typically in situations involving processing of large
formulas. The stages include

- deriving of PDEs
- transforming of PDEs
- analysis of PDEs: flux Jacobians for system of conservation laws, posedness analysis
- discretization – transformation of PDEs into finite difference schemes
  (FDSs)
- analysis of FDSs: approximation, modified equation, stability
- code generation – automatic creation of numerical source programs

Some advantages of using a computer algebra system (CAS) in the development of finite difference codes are:

- increased speed of development,
- decreased probability of bugs,
- rapid and accurate modification of exiting programs.

The first two advantages are related to the fact that CAS programs use
higher-level constructs than arrays of number and loops. In fact, it is relatively easy to describe problems in a notation similar to the mathematical

notation used in textbooks and scientific papers. The inputs to a CAS are more compact and have more direct meaning than the code in a typical numerical program. In addition, a CAS allows the user to analytically check properties such as symmetry, truncation error, and stability of the algorithm under development. The last advantage occurs because knowledge of how to develop the algorithm is saved in the CAS, and consequently, minor changes in the algorithm correspond to minor changes in the CAS code.

For most of our symbolic computations we use the general CAS Reduce [1], for quantifier elimination problems we use the general quantifier eliminatin program QEPCAD [2,3] or special quantifier eliminatin approach by Sturm-Habicht sequences [4].

The experience from several fluid flow models for which the application of symbolic computing proved to be essential during different stages will be presented.

Solving of three-dimensional models of fluid flow is very difficult, and in some cases, such as modelling of the global earth's atmosphere or ocean, even impossible with current computer resources. Incompressible, inviscous models described by the Euler equations can, under some assumptions, be simplified by their vertical averaging which eliminates the vertical coordinate, decreases the dimension by one and substantionally speeds up numerical solution of the model. The best known vertically averaged model is the hydrostatic shallow water model, other models differ in the assumption on the vertical component of fluid velocity and are called Green-Naghdi models [5].

Complexity of the Green-Naghdi models is even in 1D rather high, especially for multilayer cases. We have used a CAS for:

- deriving several two-layer Green-Naghdi models [6]
- posedness analysis of several two-layer shallow water and Green-Naghdi models by Fourier analysis [6] (including application of quantifier elimination)
- discretization of two-layer Green-Naghdi models [7]
- code generation for two-layer Green-Naghdi models [7] where up to 550 kB (over 8000 of lines) of numerical Fortran code has been generated for solving complicated fully implicit difference scheme by the Newton method

Developing the model of 2D shallow water fluid flow on the surface of a rotating sphere we have used a CAS for:

- transforming the system of PDEs into a non-orthogonal coordinate system that has been used to construct a suitable uniform discrete grid
- computation of flux Jacobians (the shallow water model is a system of conservation laws) and their eigenvalues needed in adaptive time step control from the stability condition

The shallow water and ideal gas Euler equations are hyperbolic conservation laws for which we have developed centered composite difference schemes based on composing several time steps of an oscillatory Lax-Wendroff type scheme with one time step of a diffusive Lax-Friedrichs type scheme [8]. The direct generalization of the Lax-Wendroff type scheme to 3D was proved to be unstable by the quantifier elimination method developped in [9]. The modified equation of the unstable scheme has helped us to locate the term that cause the instability, and to propose suitable correction of the scheme to stabilize it.

2   Euler equations and vertical averaging

We will deal with inviscous fluid flows described in general by 3D Euler equations (subscripts denote partial derivatives)

$$
\begin{pmatrix} \rho \\ \rho u \\ \rho v \\ \rho w \\ E \end{pmatrix}_t + \begin{pmatrix} \rho u \\ \rho u^2 + p \\ \rho uv \\ \rho uw \\ u(E+p) \end{pmatrix}_x + \begin{pmatrix} \rho v \\ \rho uv \\ \rho v^2 + p \\ \rho vw \\ v(E+p) \end{pmatrix}_y + \begin{pmatrix} \rho w \\ \rho uw \\ \rho vw \\ \rho w^2 + p \\ w(E+p) \end{pmatrix}_z = 0
$$

with density ρ, velocity (u, v, w), total energy E and pressure p which depend on time t and space position (x, y, z). This system is closed by the equation of state which relates the energy E and the pressure p, i.e. for an ideal gas the equation of state is $p = (\gamma - 1)[E - 1/2\rho(u^2 + v^2 + w^2)]$ where γ is a constant of the particular gas.

In many cases one can consider the fluid to be incompressible. When we restrict to 2D space with horizontal coordinate x and vertical coordinate z the incompressible Euler equations in a gravitational field are

$$u_x + w_z = 0, \tag{1}$$

$$\rho(u_t + uu_x + wu_z) = -p_x, \tag{2}$$

$$\rho(w_t + uw_x + ww_z) = -p_z - g\rho, \tag{3}$$

where g is gravitational acceleration.

Solving the full 3D models is very difficult and in some cases, such as modelling global earth's atmosphere or ocean, even impossible with current computer resources, so simplified models are needed. One way to obtain simplified models is to use vertical averaging to eliminate the vertical coordinate z and reduce the dimensionality by one. Before going to 2D vertically averaged models obtained from the full 3D equations we need to understand 1D verticaly averaged models obtained from the 2D equations (1)-(3).

The derivation of vertically averaged models proceeds in the following way. First we assume a form of the dependence of the velocities u, w on the vertical coordinate z. The incompressibility condition (1) and the boundary conditions in the vertical direction result in a mass conservation equation. The vertical momentum equation (3) is integrated over (z, z_1) (z_1 is the top surface of the fluid) to obtain the pressure $p(z)$. The pressure $p(z)$ is substituted into (2) which is then integrated over (z_0, z_1) (z_0 is the bottom profile) to obtain the momentum conservation equation. The mass and momentum conservation equations then form the system of vertically averaged equations.

The procedure outlined in the previous paragraph for a single layer of fluid can be extended to the multiple-layer case with constant density in each layer. Before going to the general multiple-layer case we however need to understand the two-layer models with which we deal in the next section.

3   Vertically averaged models in 1D

In this section we will consider 1D vertically averaged models derived from the 2D incompressible Euler equations (1)-(3). Mostly we will consider two-layer flows.

3.1   Notation for two-layer flows

The notation used in two-layer flows is shown in Fig. 1. The bottom profile is $h_0(x) = z_0(x)$, the thicknesses of the two layers are $h_1(x, t), h_2(x, t)$, the heights of the layers' upper surfaces are $z_1(x, t) = h_0 + h_1, z_2(x, t) = h_0 + h_1 + h_2$, the horizontal velocities are $u_1(x, t), u_2(x, t)$ the vertical velocities are $w_1(x, t), w_2(x, t)$ and the fluid densities in the two layers ρ_1, ρ_2 are constant.

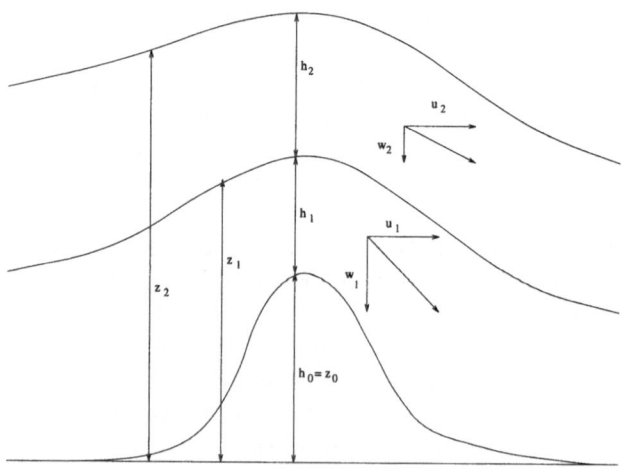

Fig. 1. Notation of thicknesses, heights and velocities for two-layer models.

3.2   Shallow water

The one-layer shallow water model [10] is a well known and widely accepted model of shallow flows. The two-layer shallow water model has been investigated already in [11]. Here we first present the derivation of this model.

We assume that the horizontal velocities u_i do not depend on the vertical coordinate z, i.e. $u_{iz} \equiv 0$, $i = 1, 2$, and that pressure is hydrostatic, $p_{iz} + g\rho_i = 0$. From the incompressibility condition (1) and the vertical boundary conditions we obtain the mass conservation equations

$$h_{it} + (h_i u_i)_x = 0, \quad i = 1, 2. \tag{4}$$

We can integrate the hydrostatic pressure equations, and for free surface flow (i.e. pressure at the upper surface z_2 is zero, $p_2(z_2) = 0$) to obtain pressures $p_2(z) = -\rho_2 g(z - z_2), p_1(z) = \rho_2 g h_2 - \rho_1 g(z - z_1)$. Now we integrate the horizontal momentum equations (2) over each layer $(z_{i-1}, z_i), i = 1, 2$ to obtain momentum equations

$$\int_{z_{i-1}}^{z_i} [\rho_i(u_{it} + u_i u_{ix}) + p_{ix}]d\,z = 0, \quad i = 1, 2,$$

which can be expressed in momentum conservation form as

$$(h_1 u_1)_t + \left(h_1 u_1^2 + \frac{1}{2} g h_1^2\right)_x + \frac{\rho_2}{\rho_1} g h_1 h_{2x} + g h_1 z_{0x} = 0, \tag{5}$$

$$(h_2 u_2)_t + \left(h_2 u_2^2 + \frac{1}{2} g h_2^2\right)_x + g h_2 h_{1x} + g h_2 z_{0x} = 0. \tag{6}$$

The system (4),(5),(6) is the system of four PDEs for four unknowns h_1, h_2, u_1, u_2 depending on x, t.

If we pose the rigid lid boundary condition on the upper surface z_2 we obtain by a similar procedure a system for unknowns are h_1, q, u_1, u_2 depending on x, t where $q = p_1(z_1) = p_2(z_1)$ is the interfacial pressure at the interface z_1 between the layers.

Of course this derivation can be easily done by hand, however we have included it here to show a simple example. The more complicated Green-Naghdi model follows in the next section.

3.3   Green-Naghdi

Here we assume that u_i is independent of z and w_i is linear in z. From one vertical boundary condition and from the incompressibility condition (1) one can derive

$$w_i = d_i z_{i-1} - (z - z_{i-1})u_{ix}, \quad i = 1, 2$$

where d_i is the differential operator

$$d_i = \frac{\partial}{\partial t} + u_i \frac{\partial}{\partial x}$$

The mass conservation equations, which are the same as in the case of the shallow water model (4), follow from the other vertical boundary condition. The pressures are derived by integrating the vertical Euler momentum equation (3)

$$p_2(z) = -\rho_2 \int_{z_2}^{z} (w_{2t} + u_2 w_{2x} + w_2 w_{2z} + g)\mathrm{d}\,z,$$

$$p_1(z) = p_2(z_1) - \rho_1 \int_{z_1}^{z} (w_{1t} + u_1 w_{1x} + w_1 w_{1z} + g)\mathrm{d}\,z,$$

where the integration is trivial as we integrate only low degree polynomials. Having pressures we can derive the momentum equations by integrating again the horizontal Euler momentum euqation (2) over each layer $(z_{i-1}, z_i), i = 1, 2$

$$\int_{z_{i-1}}^{z_i} [\rho_i(u_{it} + u_i u_{ix} + w_i u_{iz}) + p_{ix}]\mathrm{d}\,z = 0, \quad i = 1, 2.$$

The integration again includes only integration of low degree polynomials. The Green-Naghdi momentum equations can be rearranged into the form

$$(z_i - z_{i-1})\mathrm{d}_i u_i + (z_i - z_{i-1})gz_{ix} - A_{ix} - B_i z_{(i-1)x} = \qquad (7)$$
$$-1/\rho_i(z_i - z_{i-1})\mathcal{P}_{ix} \quad, \quad i = 1, 2,$$

where

$$A_i = (z_i - z_{i-1})^2 \mathrm{d}_i \left[\frac{1}{3}(z_i - z_{i-1})u_{ix} - \frac{1}{2}\mathrm{d}_i z_{i-1} \right]$$

$$B_i = (z_i - z_{i-1})\mathrm{d}_i \left[\frac{1}{2}(z_i - z_{i-1})u_{ix} - \mathrm{d}_i z_{i-1} \right]$$

and $\mathcal{P}_i$ is the pressure at the upper surface of the i-th layer. For the free surface case $\mathcal{P}_2 = 0$ and

$$\mathcal{P}_1 = \rho_2 \left[q_2(z_2) - q_2(z_1) + g(z_2 - z_1) \right],$$

where

$$q_i(s) = s\mathrm{d}_i^2 z_{i-1} - \frac{\frac{s^2}{2} - sz_{i-1}}{z_i - z_{i-1}}\mathrm{d}_i \left[(z_i - z_{i-1})u_{ix} \right].$$

So again we have a system of four two-layer Green-Naghdi equations (4) and (7) for four unknowns h_1, h_2, u_1, u_2 depending on x, t. This form of the Green-Naghdi equations looks quite simple, however one has to keep in mind that the momentum equations still include the differential operators d_i which must be expanded before discretization, and this expansion makes the system much more complicated. After the expansion the momentum equation for the first layer (the equation for u_1) reads

$$
\begin{aligned}
&6\rho_2 g h_{2x} h_1 + 3\rho_2 h_1 \left(4h_{2x} h_{1tx} u_2 + 2h_{2x} h_{1tt} + 2h_{2x} h_{1xx} u_2^2 + 2h_{2x} h_{1x} u_{2t} \right.\\
&+ 2h_{2x} h_{1x} u_{2x} u_2 + 2h_{2x} h_{0xx} u_2^2 + 2h_{2x} h_{0x} u_{2t} + 2h_{2x} h_{0x} u_{2x} u_2 - 2h_{2x} u_{2tx} h_2 \\
&- 2h_{2x} u_{2xx} h_2 u_2 + 2h_{2x} u_{2x}^2 h_2 + 4h_{1tx} h_2 u_2 + 4h_{1tx} u_{2x} h_2 + 2h_{1ttx} h_2 \\
&+ 2h_{1xxx} h_2 u_2^2 + 2h_{1xx} u_{2t} h_2 + 6h_{1xx} u_{2x} h_2 u_2 + 2h_{1x} u_{2tx} h_2 + 2h_{1x} u_{2xx} h_2 u_2 \\
&+ 2h_{1x} u_{2x}^2 h_2 + 2h_{0xxx} h_2 u_2^2 + 2h_{0xx} u_{2t} h_2 + 6h_{0xx} u_{2x} h_2 u_2 + 2h_{0x} u_{2tx} h_2 \\
&+ 2h_{0x} u_{2xx} h_2 u_2 + 2h_{0x} u_{2x}^2 h_2 - u_{2txx} h_2^2 - u_{2xxx} h_2^2 u_2 + u_{2xx} u_{2x} h_2^2 \big) \\
&+ 6\rho_1 g h_1 \left(h_{1x} + h_{0x} \right) + \rho_1 h_1 \left(6h_{1x} h_{0xx} u_1^2 + 6h_{1x} h_{0x} u_{1t} + 6h_{1x} h_{0x} u_{1x} u_1 \right.\\
&- 6h_{1x} u_{1tx} h_1 - 6h_{1x} u_{1xx} h_1 u_1 + 6h_{1x} u_{1x}^2 h_1 + 3h_{0xxx} h_1 u_1^2 + 6h_{0xx} h_{0x} u_1^2 \\
&+ 3h_{0xx} u_{1t} h_1 + 9h_{0xx} u_{1x} h_1 u_1 + 6h_{0x}^2 u_{1t} + 6h_{0x}^2 u_{1x} u_1 + 6h_{0x} u_{1x}^2 h_1 \\
&- 2u_{1txx} h_1^2 + 6u_{1t} - 2u_{1xxx} h_1^2 u_1 + 2u_{1xx} u_{1x} h_1^2 + 6u_{1x} u_1 \big) = 0
\end{aligned}
$$

and the second momentum equation for u_2 has similar complexity. We see that the two-layer Green-Naghdi system is a very complicated highly non-linear dispersive system of PDEs (note that the momentum equation includes also second order time derivatives which have to be eliminated before dis-cretization). This system is too complicated to be treated by hand, so for its derivation from the incompressible Euler equations and its analysis and discretization we have used the CAS Reduce.

3.4   Method of well-posedness analysis

Before trying to solve a system of PDEs numerically one need to know if the system is well-posed or ill-posed (briefly, a system is ill-posed if a small change of initial condition can cause a big change, possibly exponentialy growth, in its solution). Here we describe a method of well-posedness analysis.

We start with a nonlinear system of PDEs $\mathbf{E}(\mathbf{u}(x, t)) = 0$. We linearize this system by the substitution $\mathbf{u} = \bar{\mathbf{v}} + \epsilon \tilde{\mathbf{v}}$. The coefficients of ϵ give us a linearized system $\mathbf{L}\,\tilde{\mathbf{v}} = 0$. The standard dispersion analysis of the linear system is done by Fourier transformation in both the x and t variables, which is accomplished by the substitution

$$
\frac{\partial^{n+m} \tilde{\mathbf{v}}}{\partial t^n \, \partial x^m} \to (i\omega)^n (ik)^m \hat{\mathbf{v}}
$$

which results in $\hat{\mathbf{L}}(\omega, k)\,\hat{\mathbf{v}} = 0$. The characteristic polynomial of the matrix $\hat{\mathbf{L}}$ after change of variables $\lambda = \omega/k$ gives

$$
P(\lambda, k) = \det \hat{\mathbf{L}}(\lambda k, k).
$$

Now the roots λ_j of $P(\lambda, k) = 0$ in the limit $|k| \to \infty$ determine well-posedness. We derive the polynomial $P_1(\lambda, k)$ from the polynomial $P(\lambda, k)$ by keeping only the terms of highest degree in k in each coefficient of powers of λ. In most cases $P_1(\lambda, k) = k^m P_2(\lambda)$ and P_2 has real coefficients. In that case the system is ill-posed iff there exists a root λ_j of $P_2(\lambda) = 0$ with non-zero imaginary part. So to avoid ill-posedness we need

$$\forall \lambda \ \ P_2(\lambda, \alpha) = 0 \Rightarrow \lambda \in R$$

(α are parameters of the PDEs system and include also the unperturbed local state variables $\bar{v}$). This is a quantifier elimination problem and can be solved by Sturm-Habicht sequences [4]. All the steps of outlined procedure can be done in a CAS. All posedness analysis has been implemented in the CAS Reduce.

3.5   Results of well-posedness analysis

In this section we present results of posedness analysis for the two-layer shallow water and Green-Naghdi models.

The two-layer shallow water model with free surface produces the polynomial

$$P_1(\lambda) = (\lambda + u_1)^2 (\lambda + u_2)^2 - gh_1(\lambda + u_2)^2$$
$$- gh_2(\lambda + u_1)^2 + g^2 h_1 h_2 (1 - \rho_2/\rho_1)$$

from which by the method of Sturm-Habicht sequences we have derived the following condition of ill-posedness

$$
\begin{aligned}
-256r^3 s^3 &- 128r^2 s^4 - 320r^2 s^3 u^2 + 512r^2 s^3 + 16r^2 s^2 u^4 \\
&- 320r^2 s^2 u^2 - 128r^2 s^2 - 16rs^5 + 48rs^4 u^2 + 192rs^4 - 48rs^3 u^4 \\
&+ 208rs^3 u^2 - 352rs^3 + 16rs^2 u^6 - 416rs^2 u^4 + 208rs^2 u^2 \\
&+ 192rs^2 + 16rsu^6 - 48rsu^4 + 48rsu^2 - 16rs + +16s^5 \\
&- 64s^4 u^2 - 64s^4 + 96s^3 u^4 64s^3 u^2 + 96s^3 - 64s^2 u^6 + 64s^2 u^4 \\
&+ 64s^2 u^2 - 64s^2 + 16su^8 - 64su^6 + 96su^4 - 64su^2 + 16s < 0 \\
\vee 32rs^2 &+ 16rsu^2 + 32rs + 8s^3 - 16s^2 u^2 - 8s^2 + 8su^4 \\
&+ 96su^2 - 8s + 8u^4 - 16u^2 + 8 < 0
\end{aligned}
$$

where we have used the notation $u_1 = 0, gh_i = H_i, i = 1, 2, u_2 = u\sqrt{H_1}$ $r = \rho_2/\rho_1, s = H_2/H_1$.

The two-layer shallow water model with rigid lid is well-posed for

$$(u_1 - u_2)^2 \le g(\rho_1 - \rho_2) \left(\frac{h_1}{\rho_1} + \frac{h_2}{\rho_2} \right)$$

For two-layer Green-Naghdi model with free surface we obtained the polynomial $P_1(\lambda) = (\lambda + u_2)^2 Q(\lambda)$ where $Q(\lambda)$ is quadratic in λ and its discriminant is negative and so the system is unconditionaly ill-posed. The system can however be regularized with a fourth order dissipation.

A similar result holds also for the two-layer Green-Naghdi model with rigid lid which is also unconditionaly ill-posed and can be regularized with a fourth order dissipation.

In [6] we have investigated also other types of verticaly averaged models including piecewise quadratic w, integrations with weight or using point values instead of an integral. The other approximations have parameter regions of well-posedness and regions of ill-posedness.

3.6   Shallow water discretization

The one-layer shallow water model

$$h_t + (hu)_x = 0$$

$$(hu)_t + \left(hu^2 + g\frac{1}{2}h^2\right)_x + ghz_{0x} = 0.$$

is a system of conservation laws $U_t = f_x(U)$.

The Lax-Friedrichs (LF) two-step scheme for a system of conservation laws has a predictor

$$U_{i+1/2}^{n+1/2} = \frac{1}{2}[U_i^n + U_{i+1}^n] + \frac{\Delta t}{2\Delta x}[f(U_{i+1}^n) - f(U_i^n)],$$

and a corrector that is the same shifted by $1/2$ in indices n, i. The Lax-Wendroff (LW) two-step scheme uses the same predictor and the corrector

$$U_i^{n+1} = U_i^n + \frac{\Delta t}{\Delta x}[f(U_{i+1/2}^{n+1/2}) - f(U_{i-1/2}^{n+1/2})].$$

It is well known that the LF scheme is excessively diffusive while the LW scheme produces oscillations behind shocks as can be nicely seen in Fig. 2(a). A composite scheme [7,8], which we donote by LWLFn, is got by replacing every n-th LW step by a LF step (i.e. we do $n - 1$ LW steps and then one LF step) which filters out the LW oscillations. The composite schemes work remarkably well as might be seen in Fig. 2(b). This of course has nothing to do with computer algebra, however we include it here to have some backgroud for the development of composite schemes in 3D in section 5.

The two-layer shallow water system is hyperbolic in some region of state space and ill-posed in the rest so the situation is more complicated, however a variant similar to composite schemes works well.

Numerical example As a simple numerical example to show the basic numerical properties of the LF and LW schemes we presnet here one-layer shallow water fluid flow over a bump, treated already in [10].

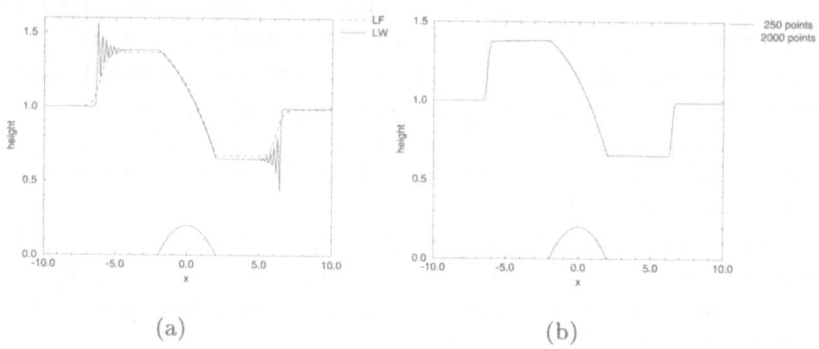

Fig. 2. Heights of a 1D shallow water flow calculated (a) by Lax-Friedrichs and Lax-Wendroff schemes and (b) by the composite LWLF4 scheme with 250 and 2000 points.

3.7 Green-Naghdi discretization

The ill-posedness of the two-layer Green-Naghdi model will certainly cause difficulty with the stability of a numerical method, particularly with an explicit scheme. Although even an implicit scheme also cannot be stable in the usual sense, we decided to try a fully implicit method for the discretization of the Green-Naghdi model.

For the time discretization we employ the simplest method

$$v_t \approx \frac{v^{n+1} - v^n}{\Delta t}$$

and all the remaining terms are discretized at the implicit time level $n + 1$. For space discretization we use standard finite differences on a uniform grid with a five point stencil

$$v_x \approx \frac{-v_{j+2} + 8v_{j+1} - 8v_{j-1} + v_{j-2}}{12\Delta x},$$

$$v_{xx} \approx \frac{-v_{j+2} + 16v_{j+1} - 30v_j + 16v_{j-1} - v_{j-2}}{12\Delta^2 x},$$

$$v_{xxx} \approx \frac{v_{j+2} - 2v_{j+1} + 2v_{j-1} - v_{j-2}}{2\Delta^3 x}.$$

The resulting non-linear scheme is solved by Newton's method, which results in an iterative method. The Newton method uses quite complicated Jacobians of the non-linear scheme which, however, can be easily computed in a CAS. At each iteration step an implicit linear difference scheme has to be solved. As we have a good approximation of the solution of the non-linear equations (the solution from the previous time step), in most cases only one iteration step is needed. We call this method the backward Euler Newton (BEN) scheme.

The discretization of the model, computation of Jacobians and numerical code generation of the kernel part of the numerical program solving the model have been accomplished by the CAS Reduce. For the code generation we are using the Reduce package Gentran [12]. We generate the numerical code in the Fortran programming language. For one-layer Green-Naghdi model we generated about 90 kB or 1600 lines of Fortran source code.

For two-layer Green-Naghdi the BEN scheme resulted in more than 550 kB or 8000 lines of numerical code, as the Jacobians of the non-linear scheme are huge. Being big this code is also slow. We have used an ad-hoc linearization and in products not containing time derivatives the term containing the highest order spatial derivative is taken on the implicit level. For the ad-hoc scheme our code generation tools have generated about 130 kB or 2500 lines of Fortran source code for solving this linear implicit scheme.

4   Shallow water models in 2D

One-layer shallow water models in 2D are well known and might be derived by vertical averaging from the 3D incompressible Euler equations.

4.1   2D Shallow water equations in the plane

The shallow water equations in 2D planar geometry are a system of conservation laws. In [8] we have developped for 2D conservation laws a new LF type two-step scheme using a staggered grid and a corresponding LW type second order scheme that we call the corrected Friedrichs (CF) scheme. The stability analysis of the schemes is done as usual for the scalar advection equation. The LF scheme is a positive and optimally stable scheme (the stability condition is the 1D condition in each coordinate direction). From the amplification factor of the CF scheme one can easily see [8] that it is also optimally stable. For stability analysis we use the Fourier method with the von Neumann stability condition, which can be stated as a quantifier elimination problem. For more details on employing computer algebra in the stability analysis of finite difference schemes see [9] and references there.

4.2   2D Shallow water equations on a sphere

The 2D shallow water equations on a rotating sphere are

$$h_t + \nabla \cdot (h\mathbf{v}) = 0 \tag{8}$$

$$(h\mathbf{v})_t + \nabla \cdot (\mathbf{v}h\mathbf{v}) + gh\nabla H + f\mathbf{r}_0 \times h\mathbf{v} = 0 \tag{9}$$

where h is the thickness of the fluid layer, H is the height of upper surface, $\mathbf{v}$ is horizontal velocity, $\mathbf{r}_0$ is the outward unit radial vector and f is the Coriolis parameter $f = 2\Omega \sin\Theta$, with Ω being the rotation rate of the sphere and Θ the latitude.

In the spherical coordinate system of latitude and longitude the shallow water equations (8)-(9) have singularities at the poles and also there is a big difference of areas of grid cells on the equator and close to the poles. So this coordinate system is not suitable and one needs to use some other one. One possibility is to project the sphere onto a cube and on the six cube faces use either equidistant or equiangular coordinates. We use the equiangular version of gnomonic coordinates as in [13]. Let us briefly review these gnomonic coordinates. For the four regions corresponding to the cube faces around the equator the first coordinate ξ is given by the longitude, i.e. as an angle between two planes going through the rotation axis. The second coordinate η is then the angle of two planes going through the line which passes through the center of the cube and through the centers of the two equatorial faces which neighbor the current face. The grid in the gnomonic coordinates and the regions corresponding to the cube faces are shown in Fig. 3.

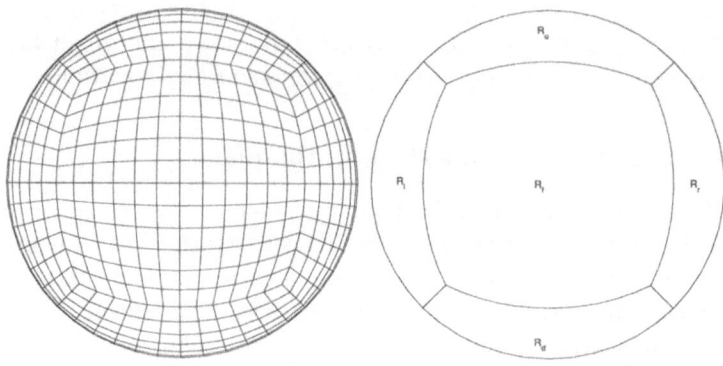

Fig. 3. Equiangular mesh on spherical cube and regions corresponding to six faces of a cube.

The gnomonic coordinate system is a non-orthogonal coordinate system and transforming the shallow water system (8)-(9) to this system is a non-trivial task (note e.g. that we need the divergence of a tensor). For the transformation we have used the CAS Reduce and computed the shallow water equations in the gnomonic sytem in the conservation form

$$h_t + (q^\xi v^\xi h)_\xi + (q^\eta v^\eta h)_\eta$$
$$+ p^\xi v^\xi h + p^\eta v^\eta h = 0,$$
$$(v^\xi h)_t + (q^\xi v^{\xi^2} h + r^{\xi\xi} h^2)_\xi + (q^\eta v^\xi v^\eta h + r^{\xi\eta} h^2)_\eta \qquad (10)$$
$$+ p^\xi v^{\xi^2} h + t^\xi v^\xi v^\eta h + o^\xi h^2 + s^\xi v^\xi h - s^\eta v^\eta h = 0,$$
$$(v^\eta h)_t + (q^\xi v^\xi v^\eta h + r^{\eta\xi} h^2)_\xi + (q^\eta v^{\eta^2} h + r^{\eta\eta} h^2)_\eta$$
$$+ p^\eta v^{\eta^2} h + t^\eta v^\xi v^\eta h + o^\eta h^2 + s^\eta v^\xi h - s^\xi v^\eta h = 0,$$

where

$$(q^\xi, q^\eta) = \left(\frac{\delta}{aC^2D}, \frac{\delta}{aCD^2} \right),$$

$$(p^\xi, p^\eta) = \left(\frac{X(-X^2 + 2Y^2 - 1)}{aC^2D}, \frac{Y(2X^2 - Y^2 - 1)}{aCD^2} \right),$$

$$(r^{\xi\xi}, r^{\xi\eta}, r^{\eta\xi}, r^{\eta\eta}) = \left(\frac{Dg}{2a}, \frac{XYg}{2aD}, \frac{XYg}{2aC}, \frac{Cg}{2a} \right),$$

$$(t^\xi, t^\eta) = \left(\frac{Y(X^2 - 2Y^2 - 2)}{aCD^2}, \frac{X(-2X^2 + Y^2 - 2)}{aC^2D} \right),$$

$$(o^\xi, o^\eta) = \left(-\frac{Xg}{2aD}, -\frac{Yg}{2aC} \right), \quad (s^\xi, s^\eta) = \left(\frac{2\Omega XY^2}{\delta}, \frac{2\Omega CDY}{\delta} \right),$$

$$X = \tan\xi, \quad Y = \tan\eta, \quad \delta = 1 + X^2 + Y^2,$$

$$C = \sqrt{1 + X^2}, \quad D = \sqrt{1 + Y^2}.$$

For adaptive time step computation which we do after each time step we need the eigenvalues of the flux Jacobians. The ξ and η flux Jacobians of the system (10) are

$$\begin{pmatrix} 0 & \frac{\delta}{aC^2D} & 0 \\ \frac{C^2D^2gh - v^\xi\delta}{aC^2D} & \frac{2v^\xi\delta}{aC^2D} & 0 \\ \frac{CDXYgh - v^\xi v^\eta\delta}{aC^2D} & \frac{v^\eta\delta}{aC^2D} & \frac{v^\xi\delta}{aC^2D} \end{pmatrix}, \begin{pmatrix} 0 & 0 & \frac{\delta}{aCD^2} \\ \frac{CDXYgh - v^\xi v^\eta\delta}{aCD^2} & \frac{v^\eta\delta}{aCD^2} & \frac{v^\xi\delta}{aCD^2} \\ \frac{C^2D^2gh - v^\eta\delta}{aCD^2} & 0 & \frac{2v^\eta\delta}{aCD^2} \end{pmatrix}$$

and have the eigenvalues

$$e^\xi_{1,2,3} = \frac{\delta}{aC^2D}v^\xi, \frac{\delta}{aC^2D}v^\xi \pm \frac{1}{aC}\sqrt{\delta gh},$$

$$e^\eta_{1,2,3} = \frac{\delta}{aCD^2}v^\eta, \frac{\delta}{aCD^2}v^\eta \pm \frac{1}{aD}\sqrt{\delta gh}.$$

The flux Jacobians and their eigenvalues have been also computed by the CAS Reduce.

5 Composite difference schemes in 3D

In this section we present an example of a computer algebra application to the development of a new difference scheme for solving a 3D system of conservation laws $u_t = f(u)_x + g(u)_y + h(u)_z$. For more details see [14].

5.1 LF scheme in 3D

The new Lax-Friedrichs scheme for 3D conservation laws is derived in a similar manner as the 2D scheme developed in [8]. The approximation at the center of edges is given by the LF approximate solution of 1D Riemann problems

$$u_{i+1/2,j,k} = \frac{1}{2}(u_{i,j,k} + u_{i+1,j,k}) + C\frac{\Delta t}{\Delta x}(f(u_{i+1,j,k}) - f(u_{i,j,k})),$$

where C is a constant to be discussed later (in this case of LF approximate solution $C = 1/6$). Similar formulas hold for $u_{i,j+1/2,k}, u_{i,j,k+1/2}$. The fluxes at the center of faces are evaluated at the points obtained as the LF approximate solution of corresponding 2D Riemann problems

$$\begin{aligned}
F_{i,j+1/2,k+1/2} = f\Big[&\frac{1}{4}(u_{i,j,k} + u_{i,j+1,k} + u_{i,j,k+1} + u_{i,j+1,k+1}) \\
&+\frac{1}{4}\frac{\Delta t}{\Delta y}(g(u_{i,j+1,k+1/2}) - g(u_{i,j,k+1/2})) \\
&+\frac{1}{4}\frac{\Delta t}{\Delta z}(h(u_{i,j+1/2,k+1}) - h(u_{i,j+1/2,k}))\Big]
\end{aligned}$$

with similar formulas for the other fluxes $G_{i+1/2,j,k+1/2}, H_{i+1/2,j+1/2,k}$. Now the LF predictor is given by

$$\begin{aligned}
u_{i+1/2,j+1/2,k+1/2}^{n+1/2} = \frac{1}{8}&(u_{i,j,k} + u_{i+1,j,k} + u_{i,j+1,k} + u_{i,j,k+1} \\
&+u_{i,j+1,k+1} + u_{i+1,j+1,k} + u_{i+1,j,k+1} + u_{i+1,j+1,k+1}) \\
&+\frac{1}{2}\frac{\Delta t}{\Delta x}(F_{i+1,j+1/2,k+1/2} - F_{i,j+1/2,k+1/2}) \quad\quad (11)\\
&+\frac{1}{2}\frac{\Delta t}{\Delta y}(G_{i+1/2,j+1,k+1/2} - G_{i+1/2,j,k+1/2}) \\
&+\frac{1}{2}\frac{\Delta t}{\Delta z}(H_{i+1/2,j+1/2,k+1} - H_{i+1/2,j+1/2,k})
\end{aligned}$$

with $C = 1/6$ in the center of edges approximation. The LF corrector is the same with the indices n, i, j, k shifted by $1/2$ and primary and dual grids exchanged.

For the scalar advection equation the half step of the LF scheme is the transport projection scheme which is a positive optimally stable scheme.

5.2 CF scheme in 3D

The predictor of the 3D CF scheme is the same as the LF predictor (11). The CF corrector is, as in 1D and 2D, a standard second order scheme with fluxes on the staggered grid and a correction from time level n given by

$$u_{i,j,k}^{n+1} = u_{i,j,k}^n + \frac{1}{4}\frac{\Delta t}{\Delta x}\sum_{J=j}^{j+1}\sum_{K=k}^{k+1}[f(u_{i+1/2,J-1/2,K-1/2}^{n+1/2}) - f(u_{i-1/2,J-1/2,K-1/2}^{n+1/2})]$$

$$+\frac{1}{4}\frac{\Delta t}{\Delta y}\sum_{I=i}^{i+1}\sum_{K=k}^{k+1}[g(u_{I-1/2,j+1/2,K-1/2}^{n+1/2}) - g(u_{I-1/2,j-1/2,K-1/2}^{n+1/2})]$$

$$+\frac{1}{4}\frac{\Delta t}{\Delta z}\sum_{I=i}^{i+1}\sum_{J=j}^{j+1}[h(u_{I-1/2,J-1/2,k+1/2}^{n+1/2}) - h(u_{I-1/2,J-1/2,k-1/2}^{n+1/2})]$$

The problem is that with $C = 1/6$ in the predictor the CF scheme is unconditionaly unstable for scalar advection. Now the question is how to stabilize the scheme.

We have used the modified equation approach to locate the terms responsible for instability. The modified equation is obtained from the finite difference scheme by Taylor expansion of discrete function values and by elimination of all time derivatives except u_t by repeated use of the same equation. The modified equation of the CF scheme (with $C = 1/6$ predictor) calculated by the CAS Reduce for scalar advection $u_t = au_x + bu_y + cu_z$ is for the special case $a = b = c, \Delta x = \Delta y = \Delta z, \lambda = a\Delta t/dx, \mu = b\Delta t/\Delta y, \tau = c\Delta t/\Delta z$

$$U_t = U_x + U_y + U_z + \frac{\Delta x^2}{2}\left[(1 - \lambda^2)\left(\frac{1}{3}(U_{xxx} + U_{yyy} + U_{zzz})\right.\right.$$

$$+\frac{1}{2}(U_{xxy} + U_{xxz} + U_{xyy} + U_{yyz} + U_{xzz} + U_{yzz})\right) + \frac{\lambda^2}{2}U_{xyz}\right] \quad (12)$$

$$-\frac{\Delta x^3}{4}\lambda\left[(1 - \lambda^2)\left(\frac{1}{2}(U_{xxxx} + U_{yyyy} + U_{zzzz}) + U_{xxxy} + U_{xxxz}\right.\right.$$

$$+U_{xyyy} + U_{yyyz} + U_{xzzz} + U_{yzzz} + U_{xxyy} + U_{xxzz} + U_{yyzz})$$

$$+\frac{2 - 3\lambda^2}{2}(U_{xxyz} + U_{xyyz} + U_{xyzz})\right].$$

According to the modified equation approach the coefficient of the fourth order derivatives should be negative for the scheme to be stable. We should be carefull using the modified equation as it is known that this approach has troubles in some cases and we use this stability condition only as a heuristic clue. By inspecting the modified equation (12) we see that instability is probably caused by the terms $u_{xxyz}, u_{xyyz}, u_{xyzz}$ (last line of the formula) that come from the fluxes of type $f(g(h(u)))$ (with arbitrary ordered f, g, h). This leads us to consider variations of the constant C. The predictor with $C = 0$ has coefficients $(1 \pm \lambda)(1 \pm \mu)(1 \pm \tau) \pm \lambda\mu\tau$ which do not include the term $\lambda\mu\tau$, the latter being related to instability.

With $C = 0$ in the predictor the amplification factor of the CF scheme is

$$|g_{CF}|^2 = 1 + 4\frac{(\lambda t_a + \mu t_b + \tau t_c)^2}{(1 + t_a^2)^2(1 + t_b^2)^2(1 + t_c^2)^2} \left[(\lambda t_a \mu t_b + \lambda t_a \tau t_c + \mu t_b \tau t_c)^2 \right.$$
$$\left. + \lambda^2 t_a^2 + \mu^2 t_b^2 + \tau^2 t_c^2 - (1 + t_a^2)(1 + t_b^2)(1 + t_c^2) + 1 \right],$$

where $t_a = \tan(\alpha/2), t_b = \tan(\beta/2), t_c = \tan(\gamma/2)$ $(\alpha, \beta, \gamma$ come from Fourier transformation). For the special case $\lambda = \mu = \tau$ the von Neumann stability condition is

$$\forall t_a, t_b, t_c \ \lambda^4(t_a t_b + t_a t_c + t_b t_c)^2 + \lambda^2(t_a^2 + t_b^2 + t_c^2) + 1$$
$$- (1 + t_a^2)(1 + t_b^2)(1 + t_c^2) \leq 0.$$

The quantifier elimination program QEPCAD has proved that this is equivalent to $27\lambda^8 - 18\lambda^4 + 4\lambda^2 - 1 \leq 0$. Afer checking the stability region by numerical sampling (see [14] for a plot of the stability region) we can conclude that the stability region includes the cube $\max(|\lambda|, |\mu|, |\tau|) < 0.8545$ where $\lambda = 0.8545$ is the only positive real root of the above polynomial.

6   Discussion

We have presented several examples of computer algebra applicaitons during the derivation, analysis and numerical solution of PDEs. In most cases the required symbolic computations are rather simple, such as integration of polynomials during the derivation of verticaly averaged models, Fourier transformation during the posedness or stability analysis, derivation during the transformation of shallow water equations on a sphere into the non-orthogonal coordinate system and Jacobians computation or Taylor expansion during computation of the modified equation. Some of these cases might be computed by hand, however this would reguire several hand re-computations to believe in the correctness of the hand-computed result and we think that the approach employing computer algebra is much more effective. Some other cases, such as posedness analysis of two-layer Green-Naghdi models would be impossible to do by hand.

In cases where we use quantifier elimination during the posedness or stability analysis very advanced and complex computer algebra algorithms are used. The applicability of the general quantifier elimination algorithm implemented in the QEPCAD program is greatly limited by its huge complexity (double exponential in the number of variables). It can solve almost all textbook stability problems and also some research problems, however it fails to solve more complicated problems. The method of Sturm-Habicht sequences has better complexity, but it works only for the special case of quantifier eliminatin problems and tends to produce large results.

A separate issue is numerical code generation the use of which we have demonstrated here on the Green-Naghdi models. For their solution we used a highly non-linear fully implicit scheme, so we needed to generate numerical code for solving a big system of non-linear algebraic equations. For the solution of this system we used Newton's method, which requires construction of the Jacobian and repeated solution of a linear system. For the two-layer Green-Naghdi model we have generated more than a half of megabyte of Fortran source code and we believe that it would be impossible to write such a code by hand. Of course the generated code cannot be maintained by hand and after any change we need to do the code generation again, however, this is not a big problem as typically the code generation is not slow. Another question is that some parts of the numerical sources are still written by hand (e.g. the routines dealing with input and output) and are not machine generated. We however do not see a problem in this as we believe that the developer must understand and control all the numerical sources anyway.

For symbolic computation we have used the CAS Reduce (except QEP-CAD program). This is mostly for historical reasons, for most purposes also other CAS might be used. The exception here is the numerical code generation, as not all major CAS like Maple or Mathematica have such a good code generation package as Gentran (there exist versions for Reduce and Macsyma).

Acknowledgment

Both authors were partially supported by the CHAMMP program of the US DOE. R. Liska was supported in part by the NSF grant CCR-9531828 and by the Ministry of Education of Czech Republic program Kontakt, Project ME 050 (1997) and would like to thank the Institute for Geophysics and Planetary Physics (IGPP) of the Los Alamos National Laboratory for hosting his visits at Los Alamos.

References

1. A. C. Hearn. REDUCE user's manual, version 3.6. Technical Report RAND Publication CP 78 (Rev. 7/95), RAND, Santa Monica, 1995.
2. H. Hong. *Improvements in CAD-based Quantifier Elimination*. PhD thesis, The Ohio State University, 1990.
3. G. E. Collins and H. Hong. Partial cylindrical algebraic decomposition for quantifier elimination. *J. Symb. Comp.*, 12(3):299–328, 1991.
4. L. González-Vega. A combinatorial algorithm solving some quantifier elimination problems. In B.F. Caviness and J.R. Johnson, editors, *Quantifier Elimination and Cylindrical Algebraic Decomposition*, pages 365–375, Wien, 1998. Springer-Verlag.
5. A. E. Green, N. Laws, and P. M. Naghdi. On the theory of water waves. *Proc. R. Soc. Lond. A*, 338:43–55, 1974.

6. R. Liska, L. Margolin, and B. Wendroff. Nonhydrostatic two-layer models of incompressible flow. *Computers and Math. with Applic.*, 29(9):25–37, 1995.

7. R. Liska and B. Wendroff. Analysis and computation with stratified fluid models. *J. Comp. Phys.*, 137:212–244, 1997.

8. R. Liska and B. Wendroff. Composite schemes for conservation laws. *SIAM J. Numer. Anal.*, 35(6):2250–2271, 1998.

9. H. Hong, R. Liska, and S. Steinberg. Testing stability by quantifier elimination. *J. Symbolic Computation*, 24(2):161–187, 1997. Special issue on Applications of Quantifier Elimination.

10. D. D. Houghton and A. Kasahara. Nonlinear shallow fluid flow over an isolated ridge. *Comm. Pure Appl. Math.*, 21:1–23, 1968.

11. D. Houghton and E. Isaacson. Mountain winds. In J. M. Ortega and W. C. Rheinboldt, editors, *Studies in Numerical Analysis*, pages 21–52. SIAM, 1970.

12. B. L. Gates. Gentran user's manual, REDUCE version. Technical report, The RAND Corporation, Santa Monica, 1987.

13. C. Ronchi, R. Iacono, and P.S. Paolucci. The "cubed sphere": A new method fot the solution of partial differential equations in spherical geometry. *J. Comp. Phys.*, 124:93–114, 1996.

14. R. Liska and B. Wendroff. Composite centered schemes for multidimensional conservation laws. In *Proceedings of the Seventh International Conference on Hyperbolic Problems Theory, Numerics, Applications*, Zurich, 1998. To appear.

Effectively Computation of Some Radicals of Submodules of Free Modules

Agustín Marcelo, Félix Marcelo and César Rodríguez

Departamento de Matemáticas, Universidad de Las Palmas de Gran Canaria, Campus de Tafira, 35017 Las Palmas de Gran Canaria, Spain.

Abstract. A new characterization of the radical of a submodule is presented and it is applied to give a computational method for calculating some radicals of submodules of free modules. Two examples of this method are also included.

1 INTRODUCTION

The development of computer systems, such that *CoCoA* and *Macaulay*, specifically designed for computation in Commutative Algebra and Algebraic Geometry, has allowed to tackle new areas of investigation. The extent of the concept of prime ideal from the category of rings to the category of modules has allowed to show that many, but not all, of the results in the theory of rings are also valid for modules. In particular, the important role played by the radical in the study of rings has encouraged several authors to seek whether there are analogue properties for the radical of submodules. (See, for example, Refs. [1], [2], [5]). The main purpose of this work is to provide a computational method which enables us to compute some radicals of submodules of free modules.

In what follows all rings are commutative with identity and all modules are unitary. Let R be a ring and let M be an R-module. A proper submodule N of M is said to be prime if for every $a \in R$, the induced homothety $h_a : M/N \to M/N$, $h_a(\overline{n}) = a \cdot \overline{n}$, is either injective or null . In light of this definition, it turns out that if N is a prime submodule of M then the set of homotheties of R vanishing on M/N, i.e.,$(N : M) = \{a \in R \ / \ aM \subseteq N\} = Ann(M/N)$ is a prime ideal of R (See [3, Proposition 1.1,]). Thus if N is a prime submodule of M with $\mathfrak{p} = (N : M)$ we will say that $N \subset M$ is a $\mathfrak{p}$-prime submodule. Furthermore, it is easily seen that a submodule N of M is called to be $\mathfrak{p}$-prime if $N \neq M$ and, given $r \in R, m \in M$, then $rm \in N$ implies $m \in N$ or $r \in \mathfrak{p} = (N : M)$.

A special class of prime submodules of a module over a domain is given by the ones whose prime ideal in R is the ideal (0). According to [3, Definition 2.1], these prime submodules are called $0-$submodules and it can be proved that a proper submodule N of a module M over a domain R is a $0-$submodule if and only if M/N is a torsion-free module, or equivalently if and only if for every non-zero $a \in R$, $n \in M$, the relation $a \cdot n \in N$ implies that $n \in N$.

The intersection of all prime submodules of M containing a submodule $N \subset M$ is called the radical of N and it is denoted by $\operatorname{rad}_M(N)$ (see [4]). As is well-known, the radical $\sqrt{I}$ of an ideal $I \subset R$ is characterized as the set of elements $a \in R$ such that $a^n \in I$ for some $n \in \mathbb{Z}^+$. A natural question arises as to whether there is a somewhat similar characterization for the radical of a submodule. In [5] it is shown that if R is a principal ideal domain and M a finitely generated R-module then the radical of every submodule $N \subseteq M$ coincides with the submodule generated by its envelope; that is, $\operatorname{rad}_M(N) = \langle E(N) \rangle$, where $E(N)$ is the set of all $x \in M$ for which there exists $a \in R$, $y \in M$ such that $x = a \cdot y$ and $a^n y \in N$ for some $n \in \mathbb{Z}^+$. In this case the module M is said to satisfy the radical formula. In [1] this result has been extended to any Dedekind domain R and any R-module.

In the present work we show that with the aid of the symmetric algebra of a finitely generated module it is possible to get such a characterization for the radical of a submodule. To achieve this aim, to each prime submodule N of a finitely generated R-module M, we first associate a prime ideal of the symmetric algebra of M - called the *expansion* of N - and then we use it in order to obtain a characterization of the radical of a submodule, which is as follows: an element of a finitely generated R-module M belongs to $\operatorname{rad}_M(N)$ if and only if it is contained in the radical of the ideal of the symmetric algebra of M generated by all elements of N. As this result reduces the calculation of $\operatorname{rad}_M(N)$ to that of the radical of an ideal in a symmetric algebra, we apply our characterization to compute some radicals of submodules of free modules by using the algebra computer system *CoCoA3*. To illustrate the whole process we present two examples which reveal the effectiveness of this method.

2   THE EXPANSION OF PRIME SUBMODULES

In this section, to each prime submodule N of an $R-$module M, we associate a prime ideal of the symmetric algebra of M, denoted by $S(M) = \bigoplus_{i \geq 0} S_i(M)$. Throughout this paper we identify $S_0(M)$ (resp. $S_1(M)$) to R (resp. M).

Definition 1. Let M be a finitely generated $R-$module and let N be a $\mathfrak{p}-$prime submodule of M. We define the *expansion* $\mathcal{E}_N$ of N to be the set of all elements $b \in S(M)$ for which there exists an $a \in R$, $a \notin \mathfrak{p}$ such that $a \cdot b \in (\mathfrak{p}, N) \cdot S(M)$.

Proposition 2. *With the above notations and assumptions we have*

1) $\mathcal{E}_N \cap R = \mathfrak{p}$.
2) $\mathcal{E}_N \cap M = N$

Proof. Because $\mathfrak{p}$ is a prime ideal the equality 1) follows directly from the definition of expansion. As for 2) we only need taking into account that N is a prime submodule.

Remark 3. Since the ideal $(\mathfrak{p}, N) \cdot S(M)$ is homogeneous it follows that $\mathcal{E}_N$ is a homogeneous ideal whose homogeneous components are $\mathcal{E}_N = \underset{i \geq 0}{\oplus} \mathcal{E}_{N_i}$, where $\mathcal{E}_{N_i} = \mathcal{E}_N \cap S_i(M)$.

In the remainder of this section we will prove in two stages that $\mathcal{E}_N$ is a prime ideal of $S(M)$, starting with $0-$submodules.

Proposition 4. *Let R be a domain and let N be a $0-$submodule of a finitely generated $R-$module M . Then $\mathcal{E}_N$ is a prime ideal of $S(M)$.*

Proof. First we prove that $\mathcal{E}_{N_i}$ is a $0-$submodule of $S_i(M)$ for every $i \geq 0$. It suffices to show that $S_i(M)/\mathcal{E}_{N_i}$ is torsion free. Indeed, assume $b \in S_i(M)$ is a torsion element in $S_i(M)/\mathcal{E}_{N_i}$. Thus there exists a non-zero element $a \in R$ such that $a \cdot b \in \mathcal{E}_{N_i}$. This implies that there exists $a' \in R$, $a' \neq 0$ such that $a' \cdot (a \cdot b) = (a' \cdot a) \cdot b \in N \cdot S(M)$, so that $b \in \mathcal{E}_{N_i}$. Hence $S(M)/\mathcal{E}_N = \underset{i \geq 0}{\oplus} S_i(M)/\mathcal{E}_{N_i}$ is a torsion-free R-module so that the morphism $S(M)/\mathcal{E}_N \longrightarrow (S(M)/\mathcal{E}_N)_{(0)} = S(M_{(0)})/(\mathcal{E}_N)_{(0)}$ is injective. Moreover since $\mathcal{E}_N/(\mathfrak{p}, N) \cdot S(M)$ is a torsion R-module it follows that $(\mathcal{E}_N)_{(0)} = N_{(0)} \cdot S(M_{(0)})$. Therefore $S(M)/\mathcal{E}_N$ embeds into $S(M_{(0)})/N_{(0)} \cdot S(M_{(0)})$. Finally taking into account that $N_{(0)} \cdot S(M_{(0)})$ is a prime ideal of the ring of polynomials $S(M_{(0)}) = R_{(0)}[x_1, ..., x_r]$, $r = rank M$, with coefficients in a field (for it is generated by polynomials of degree one), we can conclude that $\mathcal{E}_N$ is a prime ideal .

Next we consider the general case.

Proposition 5. *The expansion $\mathcal{E}_N$ of a $\mathfrak{p}$-prime submodule N of a finitely generated R-module M is a prime ideal of $S(M)$.*

Proof. Note that there exists a canonical isomorphism of $R/\mathfrak{p}$-algebras $S(M)/\mathfrak{p}S(M) = S(M/\mathfrak{p}M)$. Then it suffices to prove that $\mathcal{E}_N/\mathfrak{p}S(M)$ is the expansion of the 0-submodule $\overline{N} = N/(N \cap \mathfrak{p}M) \subset M/\mathfrak{p}M$, viewed as an $R/\mathfrak{p}$-module since $S(M)/\mathcal{E}_N = S(M/\mathfrak{p}M)/\mathcal{E}_{\overline{N}}$ and we can apply the above theorem. It is clear that $\mathcal{E}_N/\mathfrak{p}S(M) \subseteq \mathcal{E}_{\overline{N}}$ and the converse inclusion follows taking into account that the kernel of the quotient map $S(M) \longrightarrow S(M/\mathfrak{p}M)$ is just $\mathfrak{p}S(M)$.

3   A CHARACTERIZATION OF RADICALS OF SUBMODULES

We are now ready to deal with the expansion of prime submodules in order to characterize radicals of submodules.

Theorem 6. *Let R be a ring, let M be a finitely generated $R-$module and let Q be a submodule of M. Then an element $m \in M$ belongs to $rad_M(Q)$ if and only if $m \in \sqrt{Q \cdot S(M)}$, or equivalently, $m^\alpha \in Q \cdot S(M)$ for some $\alpha \in Z^+$.*

Proof. First, assume that $m \in rad_M(Q)$. Then we must prove that m belongs to every prime ideal of $S(M)$ containing $Q \cdot S(M)$. Let $\mathfrak{q} \in SpecS(M)$ such that $Q \cdot S(M) \subseteq \mathfrak{q}$. If we set $N = \mathfrak{q} \cap M$, by applying [3, Proposition 1.2], it is routine to show that N is a prime submodule of M. Moreover, since $Q \subseteq N$ we have $m \in N$. Hence $m \in \mathfrak{q}$, so that $m^\alpha \in Q \cdot S(M)$.

Conversely, let $m \in M$ be an element such that $m^\alpha \in Q \cdot S(M)$ for some $\alpha \in Z^+$. Now we only need to show that if N is a prime submodule of M such that $Q \subseteq N$, then $m \in N$. Indeed, let $\mathcal{E}_N$ be the expansion of N. Since $Q \subseteq N$ we have $Q \cdot S(M) \subseteq \mathcal{E}_N$, so that $m^\alpha \in \mathcal{E}_N$ and since $\mathcal{E}_N$ is a prime ideal, it must be $m \in \mathcal{E}_N$. Hence $m \in \mathcal{E}_N \cap M = N$, and the theorem is proved.

4   COMPUTING THE RADICAL OF A SUBMODULE

The task of this section is to apply Theorem 3.1 to calculate some radicals of submodules.

From now on, we denote by $A = R[x_1, ..., x_n] = \bigoplus_{i \geq 0} A(i)$ the positively graded ring of all polynomials over a ring R. If M is an R-module, then there is an exact sequence of R-modules

$$0 \longrightarrow K \longrightarrow F \overset{\pi}{\longrightarrow} M \longrightarrow 0 \tag{1}$$

where F is a free R-module. Given a proper submodule $N \subset M$ we set $L = \pi^{-1}(N)$. If $\{e_1, ..., e_n\}$ is a basis of F, we have an isomorphism $\varphi \colon F \longrightarrow A(1)$, $\varphi(e_i) = x_i$, $1 \leq i \leq n$. We denote by I, J the ideals $\varphi(K) \cdot A$, $\varphi(L) \cdot A$, respectively. Clearly $I \subseteq J$ and from (1) we obtain an exact sequence

$$0 \longrightarrow I \longrightarrow A \longrightarrow S(M) \longrightarrow 0.$$

Moreover, I, J and $\sqrt{J}$ are homogeneous ideals with gradings $I = \oplus_{k \geq 0} I(k)$, $J = \oplus_{k \geq 0} J(k)$, and $\sqrt{J} = \oplus_{k \geq 0} \sqrt{J}(k)$, respectively.

Proposition 7. *With the above notations, the following equality holds true*

$$rad_M(N) = \sqrt{J}(1)/I(1).$$

Proof. From the exact sequence (1) we have $rad_M(N) = rad_F(L)/K$. Moreover, since $\varphi(K) = I(1)$ and $\varphi(L) = J(1)$, we can apply Theorem 3.1 to obtain $rad_M(N) = \sqrt{J}(1)/I(1)$.

Next we apply this result to calculate some radicals of submodules of free modules.

Let $R = k[y_1, ..., y_n]$ be the ring of polynomials over a field k, let $A = R[x_1, ..., x_n]$ and let N be a submodule of a free module F generated by

$\{e_1, ..., e_n\}$. By using the isomorphism $\varphi \colon F \longrightarrow A(1)$ above it turns out that $J = \varphi(N) \cdot A$. So if we know the generators of the submodule N, we only need to replace e_i by x_i to obtain the generators of the ideal J. Once we know this, by using computer algebra systems it is possible to obtain the generators of the ideal $\sqrt{J}$. Finally, taking into account the preceding Proposition it follows that the $\mathrm{rad}_F(N)$ is spanned by the linear generators of $\sqrt{J}$ in the variables $x_1, ..., x_n$. To illustrate the whole process we present the following

Example 8. *Let $R = \mathbb{Q}[x, y, z]$ be the polynomial ring over $\mathbb{Q}$ in three variables and let F be a free R-module with basis $\{e_1, ..., e_4\}$. Let N be the following submodule of F:*

$$N = \langle 3x^2y^2e_1 + 2xz^3e_2,\ 2x^3ye_3 + 3y^2z^2e_4,\ 2y^3ze_1 + 3x^2z^2e_4 \rangle .$$

By replacing $\{e_1, ..., e_4\}$ by $\{a, b, c, d, \}$ respectively, we shall consider the ideal

$$I = \langle 3x^2y^2a + 2xz^3b,\ 2x^3yc + 3y^2z^2d,\ 2y^3za + 3x^2z^2d \rangle .$$

Next by using the package Radical, by M. Caboara, implemented in CoCoA 3.5, we obtain that the $\sqrt{I}$ is given by

$$
\sqrt{I} = \langle\ \frac{4}{9}yz^3ab - x^3zad,\ \frac{4}{9}y^2z^2ab - x^3yad,\ \frac{4}{9}xyz^3b - x^4zd,
$$

$$
xzbc + \frac{27}{8}xzd^2,\ -\frac{8}{27}xybc^2 - xycd^2,\ -\frac{8}{27}xyabc - xyad^2,
$$

$$
yzbcd + \frac{27}{8}yzd^3,\ yzabc + \frac{27}{8}yzad^2,\ x^3yc + \frac{3}{2}y^2z^2d,
$$

$$
-\frac{3}{2}xy^3a - \frac{9}{4}x^3zd,\ -\frac{3}{2}x^2y^2a - xz^3b,\ y^3za + \frac{3}{2}x^2z^2d,
$$

$$
\frac{4}{9}yz^3bd - x^3zd^2,\ x^3zcd + \frac{3}{2}yz^3d^2\ \rangle
$$

Thus the radical of the submodule M of F is

$$
\mathrm{rad}_F(N) = \langle\ \frac{4}{9}xyz^3e_2 - x^4ze_4,\ x^3ye_3 + \frac{3}{2}y^2z^2e_4,\ -\frac{3}{2}xy^3e_1 - \frac{9}{4}x^3ze_4,
$$

$$
-\frac{3}{2}x^2y^2e_1 - xz^3e_2,\ y^3ze_1 + \frac{3}{2}x^2z^2e_4\ \rangle
$$

Example 9. *Let $R = \mathbb{Q}[x, y, z]$ be the polynomial ring over $\mathbb{Q}$ in three variables and let F be a free R-module with basis $\{e_1, ..., e_5\}$. Let N be the following submodule of F:*

$$N = \langle x^2e_1 + y^2e_2,\ x^2ze_2 + y^3e_3,\ y^3ze_3 + x^4e_4,\ xz^3e_4 + y^4e_5 \rangle .$$

By replacing $\{e_1, ..., e_5\}$ by $\{a, b, c, d, e\}$ respectively, we shall consider the ideal

$$I = \langle x^2a + y^2b,\ x^2zb + y^3c,\ y^3zc + x^4d,\ xz^3d + y^4e \rangle .$$

Next we obtain that the $\sqrt{I}$ is given by

$$
\begin{aligned}
\sqrt{I} = \langle\ & x^2a + y^2b,\ ycd^2 + xabe,\ xcd^2 - yb^2e,\ xzd^2 - y^2ae,\ -yzac + x^2bd, \\
& yzb^2 - y^2ac,\ xzb^2 - xyac,\ yz^2b - x^2yd,\ xz^2b - x^3d,\ x^2zb + y^3c, \\
& xz^2a + xy^2d,\ xyd^3 + yza^2e,\ yz^2ae + y^3de,\ x^2d^3 + xza^2e, \\
& yzbd^2 + xya^2e,\ yz^2cd - xy^2be,\ xz^2cd - x^2ybe,\ xz^3d + y^4e, \\
& xza^2c + xyb^2d,\ y^3zc + x^4d,\ xb^2d^3 + ya^3ce,\ xa^3c^2 + xb^4d, \\
& ya^3c^2 + yb^4d,\ yz^4c - x^3y^2e,\ ybd^5 - ya^4e^2,\ xbd^5 - xa^4e^2, \\
& y^2bd^4 - xza^3de,\ yb^3d^3 - xa^4ce,\ -y^2a^2c^3d + xyb^5e\ \rangle
\end{aligned}
$$

Thus the radical of the submodule M of F is

$$
\begin{aligned}
rad_F(N) = \langle\ & x^2e_1 + y^2e_2,\ yz^2e_2 - x^2ye_4,\ xz^2e_2 - x^3e_4,\ x^2ze_2 + y^3e_3, \\
& xz^2e_1 + xy^2e_4,\ xz^3e_4 + y^4e_5,\ y^3ze_3 + x^4e_4,\ yz^4e_3 - x^3y^2e_5\ \rangle
\end{aligned}
$$

Acknowledgement: The authors would like to thank T. Recio for his help to compute radicals of ideals.

References

1. J. Jenkins and P. F. Smith, *On the prime radical of a module over a commutative ring*, Comm. Algebra **20**(12) (1992), 3593–3602.

2. Chin-Pi Lu, *M-radicals of submodules in modules*, Math. Japonica **34**, No. 2 (1989), 21–219.

3. Agustín Marcelo and J. Muñoz Masqué, *Prime Submodules, the Descent Invariant, and Modules of Finite Length*, J. Algebra **189** (1997), 273–293.

4. R. McCasland and M. Moore, *On radicals of submodules of finitely generated modules*, Canad. Math. Bull., **29** (1) (1986), 37–39.

5. —, *On radicals of submodules*, Comm. Algebra **19**(5) (1991), 1327–1341.

Computations on Character Tables of Association Schemes.[*]

Edgar Martínez-Moro

Dept. Matemática Aplicada Fundamental.
Universidad de Valladolid
47002 Valladolid, Castilla, Spain
edgar@vax631.cpd.uva.es // edgar@modulor.arq.uva.es

Abstract. Association schemes are combinatorial objects that allow us solving problems in several branches of mathematics. They have been used in the study of permutation groups and graphs and also in the design of experiments. The author get in touch with this topic through Delsarte's thesis on association schemes and coding theory [6]. All the information of an association scheme can be derived from its table of characters. In this paper we show some techniques for computing the character table and also derive other properties from it, such as the condition for the scheme to be P-polynomial etc. We also work out some characteristics of metrics which are constant over the relations of the scheme such as Lloyd polynomials. The computations are based on the relation between an association scheme and its Bose-Mesner algebra.

Keywords: Association schemes, Bose-Mesner algebra, eigenvalue problems, Gröbner basis, metric and weakly metric schemes, Lloyd polynomial.

1 Introduction and examples.

Throughout this paper we will follow the definition of association scheme given by E. Bannai and T. Ito [2]:

Definition 1. An association scheme with d classes is a pair $\mathcal{S} = (X, \{R_i\}_{i=0}^{d})$, given by a finite set X and a set of relations $\{R_i\}_{i=0}^{d}$ on X, satisfying the following rules:

1. $R_0 = \{(x,x) \mid x \in X\}$ (the diagonal relation)
2. $\{R_i\}_{i=0}^{d}$ is a partition on $X \times X$.
3. $\forall i \in \{0, \ldots d\}$ $\exists j \in \{0, \ldots d\}$ such that $R_i^t = R_j$, where

$$R_i^t = \{(y,x) \mid (x,y) \in R_i\}$$

4. For each election of $i, j, k \in \{0, \ldots d\}$, the number:

$$p_{ij}^k = |\{z \in X \mid (x,z) \in R_i \quad (z,y) \in R_j\}|$$

is constant for all $(x,y) \in R_k$

---

[*] This work was supported by the Spanish Research Council grant DGICYT PB97-0471.

Remark 2. Sometimes association schemes are called cellular rings (usually in Russian literature). We say that the scheme is commutative if $p_{ij}^k = p_{ji}^k$ $\forall i, j, k \in \{0, \ldots d\}$. We say the scheme is symmetric if $R_i^t = R_i$.

We can rewrite the above conditions as matrix relations. Consider the set of square matrices of order $v = |X|$ given by:

$$i = 1, \ldots, d \quad D_i = [D_i(x,y)]_{0 \leq x, y \leq v} \quad D_i(x,y) = \begin{cases} 1 & \text{if } (x,y) \in R_i \\ 0 & \text{elsewhere} \end{cases}$$

Therefore, the conditions $1 - 4$ above are equivalent to:

1'. $D_0 = Id$ (identity matrix)
2'. $\sum_{k=0}^d D_k = J$, where J is the matrix where all entries are 1.
3'. $\forall i \in \{0, \ldots d\}$ $\exists j \in \{0, \ldots d\}$ such that $D_i^t = D_j$
4'. $D_i \cdot D_j = \sum_{k=0}^d p_{ij}^k D_k$

The set of matrices $\{D_i\}_{i=0}^d$ is the generating set of a semisimple algebra $\mathcal{B}$ over $\mathbb{C}$ called **Bose-Mesner algebra** or **adjacency algebra**. All matrices in the set are linearly independent by condition $2'$, hence $\mathcal{B}$ has dimension $d+1$. If the scheme is commutative, it is clear that $D_i D_j = D_j D_i$, and therefore the algebra is commutative. From now on, in sake of brevity, we will write scheme for a commutative symmetric association scheme.

Example 3. Some well known of association schemes:

a) **(Group case)** The association scheme defined by the adjacency matrices given by a regular representation of some group of order $|X|$.
b) **(An all purpose construction)** (See [22]) Let X be endowed with a metric d. Suppose that a subgroup G of the group of isometries of d acts transitively on X. Consider the induced action of G on the set $X \times X$, and let $\{R_i\}_{i=0}^d$ be the orbits of such action where $R_0 = \{(x,x) \mid x \in X\}$. This scheme is an example of a *weakly metric scheme* since all the pairs in the same relation are at the same distance. It is also called 2-orbit scheme and the associated Bose-Mensner algebra is the Hecke algebra or centralizer algebra (see [20]). Classical schemes in coding theory such as Hamming scheme, Lee scheme and modular schemes can be seen as schemes of this type. (See [15,16,22,23]) Recently some new examples of this schemes for two dimensional modulo metrics over complex integers have been found [17,18].
c) **(A non 2-orbit scheme)** Another example which is not a 2-orbit scheme is defined as follows: For q even and $n \geq 3$ let Q be a non degenerate quadric in $PG(n,q)$ (the projective space of dimension n over the finite field with q elements). Let X the set of nonisotropic points distint from the nucleus. Two distint points are related acording as the line through these points is a hyperboloic line, an eliptic line or a tangent. This relations define a 3-association scheme.

2   The adjacency algebra.

2.1   The structure of the Bose-Mensner Algebra.

The products given in (4′) are just the *structure equations* of the algebra $\mathcal{B}$ (for an account on finite generated associative algebras see [8,21]) which extend to the product in $\mathcal{B}$ as usual:

$$\left(\sum_{k=0}^{d} a_k D_k\right)\left(\sum_{k=0}^{d} b_k D_k\right) = \sum_{k=0}^{d}\left(\sum_{i,j=0}^{d} a_i b_j p_{ij}^k\right) D_k \tag{1}$$

Also the product is associative, which gives us some further relations:

$$\sum_{r=0}^{d} p_{ij}^r p_{rk}^s = \sum_{r=0}^{d} p_{jk}^r p_{ir}^s \qquad 0 \le i,j,k,s \le d \tag{2}$$

To give a coordinatized insight of the above conditions we have the following viewpoint (see [21]):
Fixed a basis $B = \{B_1, \ldots, B_n\}$ of $\mathcal{B}$, we associate to each linear combination ϕ of the basis the matrix defined by:

$$\alpha(\phi) = [\phi_j^k]_{j,k=0}^d \qquad \phi(B_j) = \sum_{k=0}^{d} \phi_j^k B_k \tag{3}$$

It is well known that $\phi \mapsto \alpha(\phi)$ is an isomorphism from the algebra of endomorphism of $\mathcal{B}$ to $M_n(\mathbb{C})$. The *structure constants* of the algebra can be arranged in a matrix associated to the endomorphism $\lambda_{D_i} : A \mapsto D_i \cdot A$ as $[p_{i,j}^k]_{k,j=0}^d$ and as the one associated to the endomorphism $\rho_{D_i} : A \mapsto A \cdot D_i$ as $[p_{i,j}^k]_{k,i=0}^d$ (These are called *multiplication matrices*). Therefore, the condition of associativity is similar to say that the right and left $(\rho_{D_i}, \lambda_{D_i})$ regular representations above commute.

2.2   Krein parameters.

Let I be the identity matrix and J the $n \times n$ matrix where all the entries are 1. It is well known (see [1,6]) that $\mathcal{B}$ is a diagonalizable algebra[1] and there is a unique set of primitive idempotents $\{E_0 = \frac{1}{|X|} J, E_1, \ldots, E_d\}$.

Definition 4. The matrix representing the change of base from the base of the adjacency matrices to the idempotent matrices is called **character table**[2] and it is denoted by:

$$P = [p_i(j)]_{i,j=0}^d \tag{4}$$

---

[1] This arises from the fact that $\{D_i\}$ is a set of commuting matrices.(see [13])
[2] The justification for this name is given in [2].

Note that the entries on the ith row are the eigenvalues (counting multiplicities) of the matrix D_i. Also, since we are considering symmetric association schemes, the D_i's are symmetric and the eigenvalues are real. If we consider the algebra $\mathcal{U}$ generated by $\{E_0, E_1, \ldots, E_d\}$ endowed with Hadamard product over the complex numbers, we have that the set of primitive idempotents is the set $\{D_i\}_{i=0}^d$ (see [1]) and:

$$E_j = \sum_{i=0}^d q_i(j) D_i \qquad Q = [q_i(j)]_{i,j=0}^d = |X| P^{-1} \tag{5}$$

The $q_i(j)$'s are called *Krein parameters*. Clearly the association scheme is completely determined by one set of parameters, either the character table or the Krein parameters.

3   Computing the spectrum.

3.1   Computing the eigenvalues.

We define $\mathcal{F} = \{x_i x_j - f_{i,j}\}_{0 \le i \le j \le d} \subset \mathbb{C}[x_0, \ldots, x_d]$ where the $f_{i,j}$ are given by:

$$f_{ij} = \sum_{k=0}^d p_{ij}^k x_k \tag{6}$$

the set of structure equations of the Bose-Mensner algebra[3]. Note that not all the combinations of indices i, j are needed since the algebra is commutative. Also we have fixed x_0 to be the unity (because $I_0 = Id$), therefore we can define:

$$\mathcal{F}' = \{x_i x_j - f'_{i,j}\}_{1 \le i \le j \le d} \cup \{x_0 - 1\} \subset \mathbb{C}[x_0, \ldots, x_d] \tag{7}$$

where $f'_{ij} = p_{ij}^0 + \sum_{k=1}^d p_{ij}^k x_k$. Roughly speaking, we substitute $x_0 = 1$ in $\mathcal{F}$.

The structure constants can be rearranged in such a way that they build the multiplication matrices corresponding to multiplication by D_i:

$$\mathcal{B} \to \mathcal{B} : \quad \beta \mapsto \beta D_i \tag{8}$$

i.e., the element (j, k) of the matrix is the coefficient of D_k in the expansion of $D_i D_j$. From the above matrices we can rebuild any multiplication table for an arbitrary element on $\mathcal{B}$ just by linearity.

The discusion above can be done for the ideal $\mathcal{I}$ generated by $\mathcal{F}$ in a Gröbner basis setting. $\mathcal{F}$ is a reduced Gröbner basis for $\mathcal{I}$ in the total degree order [4] and $V(\mathcal{F})$ (the variety generated by $\mathcal{F}$) is zero-dimensional. As usual

---

[3] i.e. $\mathcal{F}$ is build by the sustitution of D_i by x_i in equations on (4').

[4] This can be shown just computing the S-polynomials

$lt(f)$ will denote the leading term of f and the set of terms will be denoted by:

$$T = \{x_0^{i_0} \ldots x_d^{i_d} \mid i_0, \ldots, i_d \in \mathbb{N}_0\} \tag{9}$$

We define the normal set as:

$$N = \{t \in T \mid \nexists f \in \mathcal{F} \text{ such that } lt(f)|t\} = \{x_i\}_{i=0}^d \tag{10}$$

N is a basis of $\mathbb{C}[x_0, \ldots, x_d] \bmod \mathcal{I}$ and the cardinality of N is just the number of roots of $\mathcal{F}$. We can describe the effect of multipliying an arbitrary element by a fixed $f \in \mathbb{C}[x_0, \ldots, x_d]$ modulo $\mathcal{I}$ just by using the images of multipliying f by each term in N. Hence, if we denote by $\mathrm{nf}(f)$ the normal form with respect $\mathcal{F}$, we conclude that:

$$\mathrm{nf}(f \cdot x_i) = \sum a_{ij}(f)x_i \quad i = 0, \ldots d \tag{11}$$

As usual the complex matrix $A(f) = [a_{ij}(f)]_{i,j=0}^d$ is the multiplication matrix of f. The multiplication tables for the elements in N are particulary important since from them we can rebuild any multiplication table and clearly $A(x_i) = [p_{ij}^k]_{j,k=0}^d$. The following result is a slightly modified version of a theorem in [4].

Theorem 5. *Let $\mathcal{F}$ a Gröbner basis, and let $M_0, \ldots M_d$ the multiplication matrices for $x_0, \ldots, x_d$ defined as above. Let U the unitary matrix such that $U^* M_i U = F_i$ is diagonal for each $i \in \{0, 1, \ldots, d\}$. If we denote the diagonal entries of the matrices F_i as $(u_0^i, \ldots, u_d^i)$ then the points on $V(\mathcal{F})$ counting multiplicity are:*

$$z_j = (x_0^j, \ldots, x_d^j) = (u_j^0, u_j^1, \ldots, u_j^d) \tag{12}$$

i.e. the roots of $\mathcal{F}$ are the eigenvalues of the M_i.

Proof. For a proof of the result see [4] in the case we deal with simple eigenvalues or [19] in the general case. $\square$

Now we are in conditions of state the main theorem in this paper which is a colorary from the result above:

Main theorem. *The character table P of an association scheme $\mathcal{S}$ with structure equations given by $\mathcal{F}$ is given by the non-zero points on $V(\mathcal{F})$.*

We shall need some facts about association schemes given in the section below for proving this result. As a colorary we have:

Corollary 6. *The character table of the association scheme $\mathcal{S}$ in the theorem above is given by the points $(p_0, \ldots, p_d) \in V(\mathcal{F}')$.*

Proof. It follows directly from the main theorem and the definition of $\mathcal{F}$. $\square$

In fact all the discusion above could be reproduced for the ideal $\mathcal{I}'$ generated by $\mathcal{F}'$.

3.2   The intersection algebra.

Definition 7. We define the intersection matrices $M^i, 0 \leq i \leq d$ by:

$$M^i = \left(m^i_{lm}\right)^d_{l,m=0}, \quad \text{where } m^i_{lm} = p^m_{li} \tag{13}$$

i.e. M^i is the multiplication matrix corresponding to D_i in the Bose-Mensner algebra.

Proposition 8. *With the above notation* $M^i M^j = \sum_{k=0}^d p^k_{ij} M^k$

Proof. We give here an alternative proof to the one in [3] pp. 126–127 based on facts of the adjacency algebra. (The one in Cameron's text [3] is purely combinatorial and it is based on counting possible colourings among related elements in X.)

$M^i M^j$ is the multiplication matrix corresponding to the aplication:

$$c : \mathcal{B} \to \mathcal{B} \quad \beta \mapsto c(\beta) = \beta D_i D_j \tag{14}$$

i.e., the k row of the multiplication matrix of c correspond to the expresion of $D_k(D_i D_j)$ in the base of the adjacency matrices.

$$
\begin{aligned}
D_k(D_i D_j) &= \left(\sum_{m=0}^d p^m_{ki} D_m \right) D_j \\
&= \sum_{m=0}^d p^m_{ki} D_m D_j = \sum_{m=0}^d p^m_{ki} \left(\sum_{s=0}^d p^s_{mj} D_s \right)
\end{aligned}
\tag{15}
$$

Therefore, if we denote the (k,s) element in the multiplication matrix of c by $\left(M^i M^j \right)_{ks}$, we have:

$$
\begin{aligned}
\left(M^i M^j \right)_{ks} &= \sum_{m=0}^d p^m_{ki} p^s_{mj} \\
&\overset{(\star)}{=} \sum_{m=0}^d p^m_{ij} p^s_{km} = \left(\sum_{m=0}^d p^m_{ij} M^k \right)_{ks}
\end{aligned}
\tag{16}
$$

Where equality in $(\star)$ holds because the algebra is associative (see equation (2)). So:

$$M^i M^j = \sum_{k=0}^d p^k_{ij} M^k \tag{17}$$

as required.   □

Definition 9. The set of matrices $\{M^i\}_{i=1}^d$ generate an algebra given by $\mathcal{M} = \mathbb{C}[M^1, \ldots, M^d]$ called **intersection algebra** of the scheme.

Proposition 10. *The intersection algebra and the adjacency algebra are isomorphic.*

Proof. Consider the map $\mathcal{B} \to \mathcal{M}$ given by $D_i \mapsto M^i$. Clearly it is an isomorphism since the structure relations in (17) and 4′ are the same.   □

Finally in this section, we give a proof for the main theorem above:

Proof (of the main theorem). Diagonalising the adjacency algebra is just the same as diagonalising the intersection algebra (by the isomorphism above). But diagonalising the intersection algebra is the same as diagonalising the multiplication matrices of the adjacency algebra and the result follows from theorem 5   □

3.3   Examples.

We give here two examples of schemes arising from the theory of error correcting codes.

Example 11. The **Hamming** or **hypercubic** association scheme [14]. In this scheme $X = (\mathbb{Z}/p\mathbb{Z})^n$. and two vectors are i^{th} associates if they are at Hamming distance i [5]. For example, if $p = 2, n = 3$ we have that the Hamming distance is the sorthest path distance on the cube:

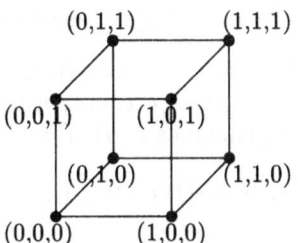

There is a formula for deriving the structure constants in Hamming schemes (see [14]). The variety $\mathcal{F}_H'$ defined by the scheme is given by:

$$\mathcal{F}_H' = \{x_2x_3 - x_1,\ x_1x_3 - x_2,\ x_0 - 1,\ x_1^2 - 2x_2 - 3,$$
$$x_3^2 - 1,\ x_2^2 - 2x_2 - 3,\ x_1x_2 - 2x_1 - 3x_3\} \tag{18}$$

The character table is:

$$Chart(H) = \begin{pmatrix} 1 & 3 & 3 & 1 \\ 1 & 1 & -1 & -1 \\ 1 & -3 & 3 & -1 \\ 1 & -1 & -1 & 1 \end{pmatrix}$$

---

[5] It can be seen as a 2-orbit association scheme (see example 3.b) such that the group acting on X is $(\mathbb{Z}/p\mathbb{Z})^* \wr S_n$.

Example 12. Let $X = \mathbb{Z}_m, m \in \mathbb{N}$ and a radix r $(r < m)$. The subgroup of $\mathbb{Z}_m^*$ generated by r and -1 acts on X by multiplication with orbits $\mathcal{O}_k$. The following relation defines an association scheme on X:

$$x R_k y - x - y \in \mathcal{O}_k \qquad (19)$$

These schemes are called **Clark Liang** schemes. When $m = 9, r = 2$ the orbits are:

$$\mathcal{O}_0 = \{0\}, \; \mathcal{O}_1 = \{-1, 1 - 2, 2, -4, 4\} \; \mathcal{O}_2 = \{-3, 3\}$$

$\mathcal{F}'_{CL}$ is given by:

$$\mathcal{F}'_{CL} = \{x_2{}^2 - 6 - 6x_1 - 3x_2, \; x_0 - 1, \; x_1{}^2 - x_1 - 2, \; x_1 x_2 - 2x_2\} \qquad (20)$$

The character table is:

$$Chart(CL) = \begin{pmatrix} 1 & 2 & 6 \\ 1 & 2 & -3 \\ 1 & -1 & 0 \end{pmatrix}$$

3.4 A remark on ordering of solutions.

From the examples above note that we need to impose some order in the solutions arising from the equations in order to get the appropiate character table. This is usually done by giving a set of common eigenvectors of the matrices. The following result in the book of Bannai and Ito [2] solves this problem without the need of computing the eigenvectors.

Proposition 13 ([2],2.4.). *Let* $\mathbf{v}_i = (p_0(i), p_1(i), \ldots, p_d(i))$, *then* $\mathbf{v}_i$ *is characterized as the unique standarized common right eigenvector of the intersection matrices for the eigenvalues* $p_j(i)$, *i.e.:*

$$M^j \mathbf{v}_i^t = p_j(i) \mathbf{v}_i^t \quad 0 \le i, j \le d$$

3.5 Collecting all the data and applications.

All the data of an association scheme can be derived from the character table. That was our motivation for dealing with those structures. There are lots of results showing this relation (examples can be found in [2,11]). We have already shown some of them such as $PQ = |X|$, which relates P and Q (see equation (5)). Clearly the structure constants can be rebuilt from the matrices P and Q. Most computations for deriving other parameters from P involves the multiplicities m_i; i.e. the rank of E_i. As an example of the facts above we remark here a result of Biggs for computing the multiplicities m_i of the scheme:

$$\sum_{k=0}^{d} \frac{p_k(i)}{p_k(0)} = \frac{|X|}{m_i} \qquad (21)$$

From the above discusion, it follows that any polynomial condition [6] on some parameters derived from an association scheme can be seen as a polynomial condition on the eigenvalues. Moreover, the ideal $\mathcal{I}'$ is radical (see proposition below) and therefore a polynomial condition p on the eigenvalues can be seen as the belonging of p to $\mathcal{I}'$.

Proposition 14. $\mathcal{I}'$ *is a radical ideal on* $\mathbb{C}[x_0, ..., x_d]$, *ie. the variety* $V(\mathcal{I}')$ *is reduced.*

Proof. This follows from the fact that the algebra $\mathcal{B}$ is commutative and semisimple, therefore it contains no nilpotent elements (see [8], colorary 2.2.7).[7]   □

As a corolary is easy to check whether a polynomial condition is fullfilled or not without computing the eigenvalues, just computing the normal form with respect the Gröbner basis above. As an example of application we have the following:

Example 15 (See [23]). The conditions for a code on a weakly metric scheme to be perfect can be expressed as conditions on the eigenvalues of the scheme and the dual inner distribution of the scheme [8]. I.e. they can be seen as polynomials with the eigenvalues as indeterminates and the inner distribution of the code as parameters, therefore, from the above construction, we use the normal form to determine whether it belongs to the ideal or not.

4   P-polynomial schemes.

4.1   Definition and results.

In the theory of association schemes the concept of P-polynomial association scheme play a central role. We say tha a scheme $\mathcal{S} = (X, \{R_i\}_{i=0}^d)$ is P-polynomial if we can reorder the relations R_i so that the corresponding D_i is a polynomial p_i in D_1 with degree i and $p(x_1)$ is a polynomial in x_1 whose roots are the eigenvalues of D_1.

Clearly, if $\mathcal{S}$ is a P-polynomial scheme, and we have reorder the relations as above we have that the set:

$$\{x_0 - 1, p(x_{i_1}), x_{i_2} - p_2(x_{i_1}), \ldots x_{i_d} - p_d(x_{i_1})\}$$

is a reduced Gröbner basis for $\mathcal{I}'$ for a pure lexicographical order where $x_{i_1} < x_{i_j}, j = 2, \ldots, d$. Therefore, by the above discussion, the following proposition holds:

---

[6] For a polynomial condition we mean a set of polynomials that are zero when they are evaluated in the parameters.

[7] It is clear that the elements in the radical of $\mathcal{I}'$ and not in $\mathcal{I}'$ correspond to the nilpotent elements of the algebra.

[8] A code is just a subset of X. For a definition of perfect code and dual inner distribution see [23,22]

Proposition 16. *Let $S = (X, \{R_i\}_{i=0}^d)$ be an association scheme and $\mathcal{I}'$ its associated ideal. S is a P-polynomial scheme if and only if there is an pure lexicographical ordering for the variables x_{i_j} with $x_{i_0} = x_0, x_{i_1} < x_{i_j}, j \neq i_0$ such that*

$$\{x_0 - 1, p(x_{i_1}), x_{i_2} - p_2(x_{i_1}), \ldots x_{i_d} - p_d(x_{i_1})\} \tag{22}$$

is a Gröbner basis for that ordering, and the following conditions on the degree of the polynomials $p, p_1, \ldots, p_d$ are satisfied:

$$degree(p_i) = i \quad \forall i = 2, \ldots, d \quad degree(p) = d$$

4.2   Some worked examples.

Example 17. Schemes in examples 11 ,12 are both P-polynomial schemes (It is a well known fact in combinatorics that Hamming schemes are allways P-polynomial and that schemes with two classes are also P-polynomial). Their respective Gröbner basis for the ordering in the proposition above are[9]:

$$\{x_0 - 1, 6x_3 - x_1^3 + 7x_1, -x_1^2 + 2x_2 + 3, -10x_1^2 + 9 + x_1^4\} \tag{23}$$

for the scheme in example 11 , and:

$$\{-x_2^2 + 6 + 6x_1 + 3x_2, x_0 - 1, -18x_2 - 3x_2^2 + x_2^3\}$$

for the scheme in example 12.

Remark 18. In a P-polynomial scheme we can see the matrices D_i as the *distance matrices* of distance regular graph of diameter d and $|X|$ vertices (See [11]).i.e., two vertices related by R_i are at distance i.

Proposition above allow us checking whether an association scheme is P-polynomial or not, the following example is not P-polynomial ([22]):

Example 19. Consider the Clark Liang scheme given by $m = 31, r = 2$ the orbits are:

$$\mathcal{O}_0 = \{0\}, \ \mathcal{O}_1 = \{\pm 1, \pm 2, \pm 4, \pm 8, \pm 15\}$$
$$\mathcal{O}_2 = \{\pm 3, \pm 6, \pm 7 \pm 12, \pm 14\}, \mathcal{O}_3 = \{\pm 5, \pm 9, \pm 10, \pm 11, \pm 13\}$$

It is well known that this scheme is not P-polynomial. Let us check it by the proposition above. The ideal $\mathcal{I}'$ is given by:

$$\{x_2^2 - 2x_1 - 3x_2 - 4x_3 - 10, \ x_2 x_3 - 4x_1 - 4x_2 - 2x_3, x_0 - 1,$$
$$x_1 x_3 - 2x_1 - 4x_2 - 4x_3, \ x_1 x_2 - 4x_1 - 2x_2 - 4x_3,$$
$$x_1^2 - 3x_1 - 4x_2 - 2x_3 - 10, \ x_3^2 - 4x_1 - 2x_2 - 3x_3 - 10\}$$

---

[9] These are presented and ordered in the same fashion as the output of Maple V r4.

Let $x_1 < x_2, x_3$, the reduced Gröbner basis for a plex. order is:

$$\{x_0 - 1, \; 16\,x_3 - x_1{}^3 + 18\,x_1 + 7\,x_1{}^2 - 40, \; 32\,x_2 + x_1{}^3 + 6\,x_1 - 15$$
$$x_1{}^2 + 120, 80 - 20\,x_1{}^2 + 92\,x_1 - 9\,x_1{}^3 + x_1{}^4\} \tag{24}$$

For $x_2 < x_1, x_3$ is:

$$\{x_0 - 1, \; 16\,x_1 - x_2{}^3 + 18\,x_2 + 7\,x_2{}^2 - 40, \; 32\,x_3 + x_2{}^3 + 6\,x_2 - 15$$
$$x_2{}^2 + 120, 80 + 92\,x_2 - 20\,x_2{}^2 - 9\,x_2{}^3 + x_2{}^4\} \tag{25}$$

For $x_3 < x_1, x_2$ is:

$$\{x_0 - 1, \; 16\,x_3 - x_1{}^3 + 18\,x_1 + 7\,x_1{}^2 - 40, \; 32\,x_2 + x_1{}^3 + 6\,x_1 - 15\,x_1{}^2 + 120,$$
$$80 - 20\,x_1{}^2 + 92\,x_1 - 9\,x_1{}^3 + x_1{}^4\} \tag{26}$$

Therefore, Gröbner basis in (24),(25) and (26) do not fulfill the conditions (on the degree of the polynomials) stated in the proposition and hence the scheme is not P-polynomial.

5   Metric and weakly metric schemes.

Definition 20. We define a quasi-distance on X as a mapping from X^2 to the non-negative real numbers satisfying the triangle inequality. A **weakly metric scheme** (See [22]) is a commutative association scheme with a quasi-distance d constant in the classes of the scheme:

$$\forall (x, y) \in X^2, \quad (x, y) \in R_k \Rightarrow d(a, b) = d(k)$$

Remark 21. By the previous remark, P-polynomial schemes are also weakly metric for the shortest path distance in the graph associated to them. In this case we say that the distance d is graphic.

Remark 22. When d is graphic and $d(k) = k$ we recover the definition of P-polynomial scheme.

Remark 23. Hamming and Clark-Liang schemes are weakly metric for the Hamming distance and modular distance respectively (See [22], for a definition of modular distance see example 25).

Remark 24. A weakly metric scheme could be P-polynomial as scheme, but maybe the graphic metric defined by this fact is not compatible with the metric in the scheme. See the following example:

Example 25. Consider the Clark Liang scheme given by $m = 10, r = 3$ the orbits are:

$$\mathcal{O}_0 = \{0\}, \; \mathcal{O}_1 = \{\pm 1, \pm 3\}, \; \mathcal{O}_2 = \{\pm 2, \pm 4\}, \; \mathcal{O}_3 = \{\pm 5\}$$

And the distance over $\mathbb{Z}_m$ given by the arithmetic modular weight radix r (See [24])[10] This setting defines a weakly metric scheme whose distance mapping is given by:

$$(x, y) \in R_0 \Rightarrow d(x, y) = 0; \qquad (x, y) \in R_1 \Rightarrow d(x, y) = 1;$$
$$(x, y) \in R_2 \Rightarrow d(x, y) = 1; \qquad (x, y) \in R_3 \Rightarrow d(x, y) = 2.$$

Note that elements related by both R_1, R_2 are at the same distance. The ideal $\mathcal{I}'$ for this scheme is given by:

$$\{x_2{}^2 - 3\,x_2 - 4, \; x_1{}^2 - 3\,x_2 - 4, \; x_3{}^2 - 1, \; x_1\,x_2 - 3\,x_1 - 4\,x_3,$$
$$x_1\,x_3 - x_2, \; x_2\,x_3 - x_1, \; x_0 - 1\}$$

A reduced Gröbner basis for the plex. order where $x_3 > x_2 > x_1$ is given by:

$$\{12\,x_3 - x_1{}^3 + 13\,x_1, \; -x_1{}^2 + 3\,x_2 + 4, \; -17\,x_1{}^2 + 16 + x_1{}^4, \; x_0 - 1\}$$

Hence the scheme is P-polynomial, but the distance defined by this fact between elements in R_2 is two, which does not fit with the modular distance.

Definition 26. We define the r Lloyd polynomial of a weakly metric scheme as:

$$\Psi_r(l) = \sum_{d(k) \leq r} p_k(l) \tag{27}$$

When the scheme is metric they become polynomials in one single variable $p_1(l)$. In the general case they are polynomials in g variables $p_{i_1}(l), \ldots p_{i_g}(l)$ where the matrices $D_{i_1}, \ldots D_{i_g}$ span the Bose-Mesner algebra[11]. Proposition above give us a procedure for computing the Lloyd polynomial of a metric association scheme. Also it allows us computing this polynomial for a weakly metric scheme.

---

[10] The arithmetic modular weight of an element $x \in \mathbb{Z}$ is the minimal $t \geq 0$ such there is a representation:

$$x = \sum_{i=1}^{t} a_i r^{n(i)} \quad \mathrm{mod}\; m \quad |a_i| < r, n(i) \geq 0$$

[11] Note that this has a great resemblance with "triangular forms" [12].

Example 27. The Lloyd polynomials for example 11 can be computed from (23) in example 17 and they are:

$$\Psi_0(l) = 1 \qquad \Psi_1(l) = 1 + p_1(l)$$
$$\Psi_2(l) = \Psi_1(l) + \frac{1}{2}\left(p_1(l)^2 - 3\right) \tag{28}$$
$$\Psi_3(l) = \Psi_2(l) + \frac{1}{6}\left(p_1(l)^3 - 7\,p_1(l)\right)$$

Example 28. Note that in some cases Lloyd polynomials of weakly metric schemes can be expressed as polynomials in the single variable $p_1(l)$ even if they are not metric. Following the example in 25 we have:

$$\Psi_0(l) = 1 \qquad \Psi_1(l) = 1 + p_1(l) + \frac{1}{3}\left(p_1(l)^2 - 4\right)$$
$$\Psi_2(l) = \Psi_1(l) + \frac{1}{12}\left(p_1(l)^3 - 13p_1(l)\right) \tag{29}$$

Example 29. Finally, we show another computation of the Lloyd polynomials for another example arising from coding theory. This example shows that it is not always possible the construction on the example before. In this case the Lloyd's polynomials will depend on more than one variable. Consider the Clark Liang scheme given by $m = 8, r = 3$, the orbits are:

$$\mathcal{O}_0 = \{0\}, \ \mathcal{O}_1 = \{\pm 1, \pm 3\}, \ \mathcal{O}_2 = \{\pm 2, \}, \ \mathcal{O}_3 = \{4\}$$

Each of then corresponding to the modular weights $0, 1, 1, 2$ respectively. The associated ideal $\mathcal{I}'$ is generated by:

$$\{x_1{}^2 - 4\,x_2 - 4\,x_3 - 4, \ x_3{}^2 - 1, \ x_0 - 1, \ x_1\,x_2 - 2\,x_1,$$
$$x_1\,x_3 - x_1, \ x_2{}^2 - 2\,x_3 - 2, \ x_2\,x_3 - x_2\}$$

If we compute the reduced Gröbner basis with respect plex. orders we have:

1. $x_1 < x_2, x_3$

    $4x_3 + 4x_2 - x_1{}^2 + 4, 2x_2{}^2 + 4x_2 - x_1{}^2, x_1x_2 - 2x_1, -16x_1 + x_1{}^3, x_0 - 1$

2. $x_2 < x_1, x_3$

    $x_0 - 1, x_1{}^2 - 4x_2 - 2x_2{}^2, x_1x_2 - 2x_1, -x_2{}^2 + 2x_3 + 2, -4x_2 + x_2{}^3$

3. $x_3 < x_1, x_2$

    $x_1{}^2 - 4x_2 - 4x_3 - 4, x_1x_2 - 2x_1, x_1x_3 - x_1, x_2{}^2 - 2x_3 - 2, x_2x_3 - x_2,$
    $x_3{}^2 - 1, x_0 - 1$

In none of the three cases we can achieve the Lloyd polynomials in one variable. If we choose one ordering (for example $x_1 < x_2, x_3$) we have the following expression in two variables of Lloyd's polynomials:

$$\Psi_0(l) = 1 \qquad \Psi_1(l) = 1 + p_1(l) + p_2(l)$$
$$\Psi_2(l) = \Psi_1(l) + \frac{1}{4}\left(p_1(l)^2 - 4p_2(l) + 4\right) \tag{30}$$

6   Conclusions.

We have seen how the properties of symmetric commutative association schemes can be derived from their associated algebras via ideal computations. In particular, Gröbner basis of the ideals $\mathcal{I}'$ associated with then allow us derive some important properties of the schemes such as if they are P-polynomial. We have proved that these ideals are radical, and therefore any polynomial condition on the points $V(\mathcal{I}')$ can be seen as a membership problem which is answered by computing the normal form. All computations proposed are effective since we are dealing with zero-dimensional Gröbner basis[12].

All examples of association schemes in the paper come from the field of coding theory because they are well known and they have been studied before. Anyway, all the properties cited on the paper are general for all association schemes and are checkable by the techniques showed in this paper when the schemes are given in terms of their structure equations.

7   Acknowledgments.

The author would like to thank the help of the groups of *Computer Algebra* and *Error Correcting Codes* (Department of Algebra and Geometry, University of Valladolid) where he is involved. He also would like to thank Santiago Encinas-Carrión for his help in Gröbner basis topics. All examples (orbits, Gröbner basis, etc.) have been computed using Maple V release 4.

References

1. **E. Bannai**: *Subschemes of some association schemes*, Journal of Algebra, 144, 167-188 (1991).
2. **E. Bannai, T. Ito**: *Algebraic combinatorics I: association schemes*, Benjamin-Cumming publishers, (1984).
3. **P.J. Cameron, J.H. Van Lint** *Graphs, codes and designs*. Cambridge University Press (LMS lecture notes 43) (1980).

---

[12] A new Gröbner basis for $\mathcal{I}'$ can be computed just by reordering (FGLM) techniques [9] on the ideal

4. **R.M. Corless**: *Matrix eigenproblems*. SIGSAM Bulletin vol. 30 , n0.4, December 1996 . Issue 118.

5. **D. Cox, J. Little, D. O'Shea**: *Ideals, Varieties and Algorithms*.2nd. edition. Springer-Verlag (1996)

6. **P. Delsarte**: *An algebraic approach to the association schemes of coding theory.*, Technical report, Philips Research Laboratory, 1973

7. **P. Delsarte, V. Levenshtein**: *Association schemes and coding theory.*, IEEE trans. on inf. theory, vol.44, **6** Oct.1998, 2477–2504

8. **Yu.A. Drozd, V.V. Kirichenko**: *Finite dimensional algebras*, Springer Verlag 1994.

9. **J. Faugère, P. Gianni, D. Lazard, T. Mora**: *Efficient Computation of Zero-dimensional Gröbner Bases by Change of Ordering*, J. Symb. Comp, **16**, pp. 329–344 1993.

10. **T. Gateva-Ivanova, V. Latyshev**: *On the recognizable Properties of Associative Algebras*, J. Symb. Comp, **6**, N. 2/3 pp. 371–388 1988.

11. **C.D. Godsil**: *Algebraic combinatorics* Chapman and Hall (1993)

12. **L. González-Vega**: *Symbolic Recipies for Polynomial system solving*. Publicaciones del Dpt. de Matemáticas. Universidad de Cantabria. **6** (1996)

13. **R.A. Horn, C.H. Jonhson**: *Matrix Analysis* Cambridge University Press (1985)

14. **F.J. MacWilliams , N.J.A. Sloane**: *The theory of error correcting codes*. North Holland Mathematical Library **16** (1996)

15. **E. Martínez**: *Combinatorial structure of arithmetic codes.*, PhD Thesis in preparation.

16. **E. Martínez**: *Códigos correctores y álgebra computacional.*, I Jornadas de Matemática Discreta y Algorítmica. Barcelona 1998

17. **E. Martínez, F.J. Galán**: *Combinatorial structure of arithmetic codes.*, Winter School on Coding and Information Theory 1998 (Ebeltoft, Denmark)

18. **E. Martínez,M.A. Borges, M. Borges** : *Combinatorial structure of rings of complex integers with Mannheim metric.*, 1st. Workshop on Combinatorics, Geometry, Coding Theory and related areas. CIMAF'99 La Habana, Cuba, March 1999.

19. **M. Möller, H.J. Stetter**: *Multivariate polynomial equations with multiples zeros solved by matrix eigenproblems*. Numerische Mathematik. **70**,311–329 (1995)

20. **M. Muzychuk**: *On association schemes of the symmetric group S_{2n} acting on partitions of type 2^n.*, 1 Bayreuther Mathematische Schriften **47** (1994) 151–164.

21. **R.S. Pierce**: *Associative algebras*, Graduate Text in Mathematics **88** (1982) Springer-Verlag.

22. **P.Solé**: *On the parameters of codes for the Lee and modular distance.*, Discrete Mathematics 89 (1991), pp. 185–194.

23. **P.Solé**: *A Lloyd theorem in weakly metric association schemes*, Europ. J. Combinatorics **10** 189–196 (1989).

24. **J.H. VanLint**: *Introduction to coding theory* GTM, Springer-Verlag (1982)

Investigation of Subgroup Embeddings
by the Computer Algebra Package GAP*

V.I. Mysovskikh

St.Petersburg State University, Dept. of Math. and Mechanics, St.Petersburg, Petrodvorets, Bibliotechnaya pl. 2, 198904, RUSSIA, e-mail: vimys@pdmi.ras.ru

Abstract. We describe algorithms for testing subgroups of a finite group for subgroup embedding properties. The latter include abnormality, pronormality, paranormality, their weak analogies, the subnormalizer condition and weak normality (in the sense of K.H.Müller). The algorithms are based on the usage of tables of marks (Burnside matrices). This tool allows us to carry out calculations with integers instead of computations with group elements. Our implementation within the computer algebra package GAP is also considered. The respective codes are written in the GAP language. Two long-standing problems in the area were solved with the help of these programs. The respective counterexamples are described.

The goal of the paper is to describe all the algorithms developed by the author for checking subgroup embedding properties like pronormality in finite groups. We also mention here some features of their implementation within the computer algebra package GAP [17]. The subgroup embedding properties under consideration include well-known notions of abnormality [5], pronormality [4] and their weak analogies [1]. Also we deal with polynormality and paranormality (Z.I.Borevich, [1, 2]) as well as with weak normality in the sense of K.H.Müller [8]. Actually, all these properties extend the most important in group theory concept of a normal subgroup and reflect a nice arrangement of the lattice of overgroups [10]. One can prove that all the embedding properties except weak normality are special kinds of polynormal subgroups with certain additional restrictions.

Our methods can be divided into two parts: the first one contains those based on efficient computations in a finite group (represented as a permutation group, or a matrix group, or a finitely presented group, or a polycyclically presented group), while the second one does not fulfil any actual calculations with group elements but uses certain information in the form of a low triangular matrix with integer coefficients. This matrix is known as the table of marks [3], its dimension is equal to the number of conjugacy classes of subgroups of the considered group. In addition to that matrix we need to know the normalizer of any class at least to within conjugacy. Fortunately, these data are available in the GAP library TOM by the record component

---

* The author gratefully acknowledges support of his visit to Lehrstuhl D für Mathematik, RWTH Aachen by the Deutsche Forschungsgemeinschaft in the context of DFG Schwerpunkt "Algorithmische Zahlentheorie und Algebra".

t.normalizer (GAP 3.4.4) or by the attribute NormalizersTom(t) (in the current beta-release GAP 4b5) for t:= TableOfMarks(G), where G is the name of the group under consideration (see [7, 16] for details).

Another important feature of the 2nd type tests for pronormality and weak pronormality is concerned with using the function IntersectionsTom [7] which returns all possible intersections of two conjugacy classes of subgroups as a list of class numbers. It should be noted that codes based on the methods of the second kind are considerably faster than the first ones, since they perform calculations just with integers and exploit only fast standard GAP functions of the same nature. On the other hand, the programs involving computations with group elements do not depend on any library information and therefore are more universal. Algorithms of the first type were considered in [11, 12], the respective codes are accessible with the help of ftp–servers in Aachen and St.Andrews (see, for instance, ftp-gap.dcs.st-and.ac.uk, file "embedsub.g" of 'Deposited Contribution' No. 15). Therefore we limit ourselves here to the second group of methods.

Recall basic definitions and notations. Let G be a finite group. Consider a subgroup $D \leq G$. We apply exponential notation for the conjugation by elements of G. In particular, D^x means the subgroup conjugate to D by an element $x \in G$. Angle brackets denote the subgroup generated by a given set. For an intermediate subgroup $H : D \leq H \leq G$ the normal closure D^H of D in H, i.e. the smallest normal subgroup of H containing D, is well defined. The letter N stands for the normalizer of D in G, i.e. $N = N_G(D)$.

Definition 1. An intermediate subgroup H is said to be D-complete if $D^H = H$, i.e. if there is no proper normal subgroup of H containing D.

Definition 2. A subgroup D is called a paranormal subgroup of G if for any $x \in G$ the subgroup $\langle D, D^x \rangle$ is D-complete.

Definition 3. A subgroup D is said to be pronormal in G if for any $x \in G$ the subgroups D and D^x are conjugate in their join $\langle D, D^x \rangle$.

Definition 4. A subgroup D is said to be abnormal in G if for every $x \in G$ we have the inclusion $x \in \langle D, D^x \rangle$.

Definition 5. D is called a weakly normal subgroup of G if for each $x \in G$ the inclusion $D^x \leq N_G(D)$ implies the equality $D^x = D$.

Definition 6. We say that a subgroup D satisfies the subnormalizer condition in G if for each subgroup H such that $D \leq H \leq N_G(D)$ the inclusion $N_G(H) \leq N_G(D)$ holds.

To define concepts of polynormality, weak pronormality and weak abnormality it is sufficient to replace the subgroup $\langle D, D^x \rangle$ by the larger subgroup $D^{\langle x \rangle}$ in definitions 2, 3, 4 respectively. For a subgroup $D \leq G$ we denote by $L(D,G)$ the lattice of all intermediate subgroups between D and G. It is known [1] that for a polynormal subgroup $D \leq G$ the lattice $L(D,G)$ admits a very simple description: every intermediate subgroup is contained in the unique interval from a D-complete subgroup to its normalizer.

Let G act on a finite set M. For a subgroup $U \leq G$ we define the Burnside mark as the number of its fixed points under the action of G on M:

$$\beta_M(U) = |Fix_M(U)| = |\{m \in M : \forall u \in U : mu = m\}| \ .$$

Take another subgroup $V \leq G$ and consider the transitive action of G on the factorset G/V by the rule $(V_i, g) \mapsto V_i g$ for $g \in G$ and a right coset $V_i \in G/V$. This action defines marks $\beta_{G/V}(U)$ for any $U, V \leq G$. Denote by $\rho_G(V,U) = |\{V^g : g \in G, \ U \leq V^g\}|$ the number of subgroups conjugate to V in G that contain U. Consider also the dual function

$$\nu_G(V,U) = |\{U^g : g \in G, \ U^g \leq V\}| \ .$$

Proposition 7 ([16]). *For any subgroups $U, V \leq G$ we have the equality*

$$\beta_{G/V}(U) = \rho_G(V,U) \cdot |N_G(V) : V| \ .$$

Proposition 8 ([16]). *For arbitrary $U, V \leq G$ the following formula holds*

$$\nu_G(V,U) = \frac{|V|}{|N_G(U)|} \cdot \beta_{G/V}(U) \ .$$

Note also the obvious formulas $\beta_{G/V}(V) = |N_G(V) : V|$ and $\beta_{G/V}(1) = |G : V|$. Therefore, values of ρ and ν can be easily calculated from Burnside marks. Next we choose a representative of each conjugacy class of subgroups of G, number them in monotonic order (with respect to subgroups orders) and denote these subgroups $G_1, G_2, G_3, \ldots, G_n$. Then the table of marks is defined as a $n \times n$ matrix whose (i,j)th element is

$$\mathcal{M}_{i,j} = \beta_{G/G_i}(G_j) \ .$$

The second kind algorithms for checking subgroup embedding properties in finite groups are based on the following author's results (see [14, 15] for details).

Theorem 9. *A subgroup D is polynormal in G if and only if every D-complete intermediate subgroup K satisfies the subnormalizer condition in G.*

Theorem 10. *A polynormal subgroup $D \leq G$ is paranormal in G if and only if for any D-complete intermediate subgroup K and its normalizer $L = N_G(K)$ we have the equality $\nu_G(K,D) = \nu_G(L,D)$.*

Theorem 11. *Let D be a polynormal subgroup of G. Then D is weakly pronormal in G if and only if for any D-complete intermediate subgroup K and its normalizer $L = N_G(K)$ we have the equality $|L : K| = |L \cap N : K \cap N|$.*

Theorem 12. *A weakly pronormal subgroup $D \leq G$ is pronormal in G if and only if for each D-complete subgroup $H \in L(D, G)$ we have the equality $\nu_G(H, D) = |H : N_H(D)|$.*

Theorem 13. *Weak abnormality of D in G is equivalent to any of the following conditions:*
  a) each intermediate subgroup $H : D \leq H \leq G$ is D-complete;
  b) every $H : D \leq H \leq G$ is self-normalizing, i.e. $N_G(H) = H$.

Theorem 14. *A weakly abnormal subgroup D of G is abnormal in G if and only if for any intermediate subgroup H the equality $\rho_G(H, D) = 1$ holds (or, equivalently, $\nu_G(H, D) = |H : D|$).*

Weak normality is the simplest subgroup embedding property for testing with the help of the table of marks. According to definition 5, it can be recognized by usage of only one entry of Burnside matrix or the respective value of the GAP function ContainedTom. Namely, a subgroup D is weakly normal in G if and only if $\nu_G(N, D) = 1$.

We turn next to other embedding properties. Obviously, the most important task for their recognition is to compute all intermediate subroups. At first, we find all *conjugacy classes* of intermediate subgroups with the help of the attribute SubsTom(t). Note that our function IntermClassesSubsTom contains a simple test for orders of intermediate subgroups, i.e. a part of inappropriate subgroups are filtered out at once.

Next, we determine the number of representatives in each conjugacy class by the attribute ContainingTom, which corresponds to the function ρ. This step completes the computation of intermediate subgroups. The code IntermClSubsTom(G, k, 1) for finding all intermediate subgroups between the subgroups number k and 1 is written in a similar way. Since the GAP library TOM contains information about normalizers, we are able to check the subnormalizer condition directly by definition 6. The code IsStand1Tom performs this test.

The next step is concerned with recognition of D-complete subgroups. Unfortunately, it is impossible to find all of them exactly, because the library TOM describes only the partially ordered set of conjugacy classes of subgroups. Our examples show that even in the case of a polynormal subgroup D of G different representatives of one class of intermediate subgroups may have distinct properties. For instance, in the group of order 1944, which will be considered below, there are two intermediate subgroups B, B_1 of order 162. These subgroups are conjugate in G, the subgroup B_1 is D-complete, but B contains the proper normal subgroup F of 54th order such that $D \leq F$. Therefore, B cannot be a D-complete subgroup.

Despite this obstacle, the library TOM allows us to find out all *conjugacy classes* of D-complete subgroups. Obviously, our function IsCompleteSubTom significantly uses information on normalizers with the help of the attribute NormalizersTom.

Using Theorem 9 and combining our functions IsStand1Tom as well as IsCompleteSubTom, we obtain the test IsPolynormalTom(G, d). Straightforward application of Theorem 10 together with a simple test for the equality $\nu_G(K, D) = \nu_G(L, D)$ leads us to the function IsParanormalTom.

In a similar manner, using Theorem 11, our functions IsCompleteSubTom, IsPolynormalTom as well as a simple test for indices, we get the function IsWePronormalTom. The next code IsPronormalTom can be easily obtained with the help of Theorem 12. As it has already been mentioned in introduction, these codes use the attribute IntersectionsTom developed in [7].

Tests for weak abnormality and abnormality can be based on the usage of Theorems 13, 14. However, our implementation makes use of another idea. One can prove that a subgroup D is abnormal in G if and only if it is pronormal in G and $N = D$. The same assertion holds for the respective weak properties. Therefore, it is sufficient to combine our functions IsWePronormalTom, IsPronormalTom with a simple test for the normalizer of D in G.

As an application of the developed algorithms and programs we mention two counterexamples to important conjectures in the area of arrangement of intermediate subgroups. The first one is concerned with the example of polynormal but non-paranormal subgroup in a finite solvable group of 1944th order and briefly described in [13, 14]. It is known [1] that in arbitrary (even infinite) solvable group pronormality and abnormality are equivalent to their weak analogies, i.e. the respective conditions of theorems 12 and 14 are fulfilled automatically. It was supposed for a long time that a similar fact is valid for paranormality as well. Now we show that the condition of theorem 10 is essential even for a finite solvable group.

Consider the group G defined by generators and relations:

$$G = \langle a, b, x, y, z : a^4 = 1,\ b^2 = 1,\ ab = ba,$$
$$x^3 = y^3 = z^3 = 1,\ xy - yx,$$
$$x^a = xy, x^b = x,\ y^a = xy^2,\ y^b = y,\ z^a = xyz,$$
$$z^b = y^2 z^2 [y, z],\ [x, z, x] = 1 \rangle. \quad (1)$$

It can be easily shown that G is a semidirect product of its Sylow subgroups of orders 8 and 243 respectively, the last-mentioned group coincides with the derived subgroup $G' = \langle x, y, z \rangle$ of the exponent 3. It is not difficult to check that $G'' = \langle [x, z], [y, z] \rangle$ is an elementary abelian group of 9th order, hence $G''' = 1$. Consider the subgroup $D = \langle d_1, d_2, d_3 \rangle$, where $d_1 = byx^2a^2y^2$, $d_2 = z[x, z]^2$, $d_3 = [y, z][x, z]$. This non-nilpotent subgroup of 18th order has the normalizer $N = \langle D, z \rangle$ of order 54. Enumeration of all 11 intermediate subgroups and computation of their normalizers shows the polynormality of the subgroup D in G. On the other hand, for the D-complete subgroup $F = \langle D, xy \rangle$, $|F| = 54$ and its normalizer $B = \langle F, z \rangle$, $|B| = 162$ the values $\nu_G(F, D) = 3$ and $\nu_G(B, D) = 6$ do not coincide. Therefore, D is not paranormal in G by Theorem 10.

The second counterexample shows that there exists an unsolvable finite group with a nilpotent polynormal but non-pronormal subgroup. This example was found out in the symplectic group $PSp(4, 4)$ with the help of our codes IsPolynormalTom and IsPronormalTom, which use the library of tables of marks in GAP 4. Namely, two conjugacy classes of cyclic subgroups of 15th order in that group deliver counterexamples. It should be noted that for a nilpotent subgroup of a finite solvable group polynormality is equivalent to pronormality.

Finally, we would like to mention another important problem in the area. Obviously, any paranormal subgroup is necessarily weakly normal. But it is unknown whether the polynormality condition implies weak normality for subgroups of finite groups. The respective fact was proved only for finite supersolvable groups [9]. The author hopes to find out the answer with the help of his codes and the new large library of tables of marks in GAP 4b5.

References

1. Ba, M.S., Borevich, Z.I.: On the arrangement of intermediate subgroups. *Rings and Linear Groups*. Krasnodar (1988), pp. 14–41 (in Russian)
2. Borevich, Z.I., Vavilov, N.A.: Arrangement of intermediate subgroups in the general linear group over a commutative ring. *Trudy Moskovskogo Instituta im. V.A. Steklova AN SSSR*, 1984, v. 165, pp. 24–42 (in Russian).
3. Burnside, W.S.: *Theory of Groups of Finite Order*. Second ed., Cambridge Univ. Press, Cambridge, 1911.
4. Doerk, K., Hawkes, T.: *Finite Soluble Groups*. Walter de Gruyter, Berlin, New York, 1992.
5. Huppert, B.: *Endliche Gruppen. I*. Springer-Verlag, Berlin, 1967.
6. Lux, K., Pahlings, H.: Computational aspects of representation theory of finite groups. II, *Algorithmic Algebra and Number Theory*/ eds. B.H. Matzat, G.-M. Greuel, G. Hiss, Springer-Verlag, Berlin, Heidelberg, New York, 1999, 381–397.
7. Merkwitz, Th.W.: Markentafeln endlicher Gruppen. Diplomarbeit, RWTH Aachen, März 1998.
8. Müller, K.H.: Schwachnormale Untergruppen: eine gemeinsame Verallgemeinerung der normalen und normalisatorgleichen Untergruppen. *Rend. Semin. Mat. Univ. Padova* **36** (1966), 129–157.
9. Mysovskikh, V.I.: On polynormal subgroups of finite supersolvable groups. *Vestnik Leningrad Univ. Math.* **23**, no. 4 (1990), 83–85.
10. Mysovskikh, V.I.: A survey on the lattices of intermediate subgroups and some subgroup embedding properties. Preprint, RWTH Aachen, June 1996.
11. Mysovskikh, V.I.: Testing subgroups of a finite group for some embedding properties like pronormality. *Zap. Nauchn. Sem. Peterb. Otd. Mat. Inst. Steklov* **236** (1997), 119–123 (in Russian).

12. Mysovskikh, V.I.: Speeding up the tests for subgroup embedding properties. *Extended Abstracts of the Workshop CASC'98, St. Petersburg, April 1998*, 98–100.

13. Mysovskikh, V.I.: A counterexample to the long-standing conjecture of Z.I.Borevich by GAP. *Extended Abstracts of the Workshop CASC'98, St. Petersburg, April 1998*, 101–102.

14. Mysovskikh, V.I.: Burnside marks and solution of two problems of Z.I.Borevich on polynormal subgroups. *Doklady Rossijskoj Akademii Nauk*, 1999 (to appear, in Russian).

15. Mysovskikh, V.I.: Subnormalizers and subgroup embedding properties in finite groups. Preprint, St. Petersburg Dept. Steklov Math. Inst., 1999 (in Russian).

16. Pfeiffer, G.: The subgroups of M_{24} or how to compute the table of marks of a finite group. Preprint, RWTH Aachen, 1995.

17. Schönert, M. et al.: *GAP — Groups, Algorithms and Programming*. Lehrstuhl D für Mathematik, RWTH, Aachen, Germany, fifth edition, 1995.

An Investigation into Stability of Conservative Mechanical Systems Using Analytic Calculations

M.A. Novickov

Institute of System Dynamics and Control Theory SB RAS, Irkutsk
134, Lermontov str., 664033, Russia, E-mail : irteg@icc.ru

Abstract. The report is devoted to Beletsky's problem of obtaining slightest sufficient conditions for stability of "cylindrical" precessions of dynamically symmetrical
satellite. Investigation was carried out dependending on values of motion parameter
α and inertia momenta $A, B, C (A = B)$ with respect to principal central axes of
a satellite.

Inasmuch as the stability problem in Lyapunov's sense is neither algebraically nor analytically solvable [1,2] there is an acute problem of obtaining
as soft sufficient stability conditions as possible. One problem in this context
when the second Lyapunov method is used involves obtaining and using good
criteria for the property of having fixed sign of polynomial expressions.

A special class of systems for which the problem under discussion is of
applied interest is represented by conservative mechanical systems. For such
systems, necessary and sufficient stability conditions for stationary motions
often coincide except on the boundary.

Sufficient conditions are obtained from the property of having fixed sign in
some Lyapunov function, which in conservative systems is frequently represented by the first integral or a sheaf of integrals. Their analytic expressions
in the neighborhood of stationary motions [3] as a rule begin with quadratic
terms, and on the stability boundary they represent a quadratic form of fixed
sign.

Higher-order terms, depending on their structure, can lead both to the property of having fixed sign and to alternating signs of analytic expressions of
the above mentioned sheaves of integrals. Hence higher-order terms must be
invoked when investigating the property of having fixed signs of such inhomogeneous forms.

It is significantly more difficult to check such inhomogeneous forms for the
property of having fixed sign when compared with quadratic forms, and this
requires a large number of intermediate calculations and transformations to
the simplest form. A method has been suggested for analyzing the property
of having fixed sign below, which extensively uses substitutions of some algebraic expressions into others; multiplications of series; factorization and
simplification of polynomial expressions; substitutions of numerical values

into algebraic expressions in the process of solving equations; and other operations on processing of results. This manipulation with unwieldy inhomogeneous forms results in the need to apply systems of analytic calculations. The "Mathematica" system and its development. for example, is suited for this purpose.

The property of having fixed sign in inhomogeneous forms, in which the least-order form is of constant signs, can be investigated using the method described below [4].

Let there be a function

$$V(x) = V_{2m}(x_1, \ldots, x_n) + V_*(x_1, \ldots, x_{n+1}) \tag{1}$$

where $n \geq 1$; $m \geq 1$; $x \in R^{n+1}$. We expand (1) into series in which the least-order form $V_{2m}(x_1, \ldots, x_n)$ when $m \geq 1$ is of fixed sign as a function of its variables; $V_*(x)$ is a polynomial whose degree is higher than $2m$. The conditions of the property of having fixed sign of $V(x)$ obviously are equivalent to the absence of real solutions to the equation $V(x) = 0$ in the neighborhood of zero. Such solutions may be sought in the form of parametric branches [5] :

$$x_i = \sum_{j=L}^{\infty} a_{ij}t^j, \quad (i = 1, \ldots, n), \quad a_{ij} \in R, \quad L > M, \quad x_{n+1} = \delta t^M, \tag{2}$$

where $\delta = -1$ is chosen only for even M when $x_{n+1} < 0$, otherwise $\delta = +1$, $(-\epsilon < t < \epsilon)$, and integral positive values of L and M are fitted in the process of constructing the solutions of $V(x) = 0$.

Substitution of the series (2) in $V(x)$ gives:

$$V(x(t)) = W(t) = A_{Q(L)}(a_{ij}, L) t^Q + \ldots, \tag{3}$$

where $A_{Q(L)}(a_{ij}, L)$ is a function of the expansion coefficients of $V(x)$ and of parametrization of (3); Q is the least order in t of the series $V(x(t))$ of parameter t (the initial value of $Q = 2Lm$, we next have $Q \geq 2Lm$); dots denote higher order terms in parameter t.

The initial value of M may be found by constructing Newton polyhedrons [5,6], or it should initially be considered equal to the least common multiple of the numbers $1, 2, \ldots, 2m$. The value of L is determined from the condition:

$$A_{Q(L-1)}(a_{ij}, L-1) \equiv 0, \quad a_{i(M+1)} = 0, \ldots, a_{i(L-1)} = 0, \quad i = 1, 2, \ldots, n;$$

$$A_{Q(L)}(a_{ij}, L) \neq 0, \quad a_{i(M+1)} = 0, \ldots, a_{iL} = 0, \quad i = 1, 2, \ldots, n. \tag{4}$$

Once at the first step the Q, L, M are determined, they can be refined by reducing them by the greatest common divisor D. As a result, we obtain $Q_1 = Q/D$, $L_1 = L/D$, $M_1 = M/D$, and again we designate them as Q, L, M. Let Q/M be represented as an irreducible fraction q/p, and the question of the property of having fixed sign or alternating signs (1) is then solved by

Theorem 1. *In the case when*
1^0 : *a) if* $q = 2l + 1$ *(l is integer), or*
    b) if $q = 2l$, *and* $A_{Q_L}(a_{iL}, L)$ *admits negative values for certain real* a_{ij},
    then $V(x)$ *has alternating signs;*
2^0 : *if* $q = 2l$, *and* $A_{Q_L}(a_{iL}, L) > 0$ *for every real* a_{iL} $(i = 1, \ldots, n)$,
    then $V(x)$ *is of fixed sign;*
3^0 : *if* $A_{Q_L}(a_{iL}, L) \geq 0$ *at even* q, *for every real* $a_{ij} \in R$,
    then $V(x)$ *may be of fixed sign or alternating sign, which is established by invoking higher than order* L *terms of the parameter* t *of the expansion (2) and, accordingly, higher than order* Q *terms in (3).*

Proof. In 1a), we choose the sign of the parameter $t = (\delta x_{n+1})^{1/p}$ at any integer values of p to be opposite to the sign of $A_{Q(L)}(a_{iL}, L)$. Then for odd q, it is always possible to obtain a value of $V(x)$ close to values of $A_{Q(L)}(a_{iL}) \, t^Q < 0$. For values of a different sign of t, we obtain $A_{Q(L)}(a_{iL}) \, t^Q > 0$.
Consequently, when $A_{Q(L)}(a_{iL}) \neq 0$, depending on the sign of t for $A_{Q(L)}(a_{iL}, L) t^Q$, values of different signs are obtained.
In 1b), it is possible to fit values of a_{iL} for $i = 1, 2, \ldots, n$, at which $A_{Q(L)}(a_{iL}) < 0$, and consequently $A_{Q(L)}(a_{iL}) \, t^Q < 0$ irrespective of the sign of t.

Thus, in item 1, the inhomogeneous form (1) is always with alternating signs.

As intimated by the conditions of item 2 of the Theorem, it is impossible to find at least one set of real values of $a_{1L}, \ldots, a_{nL}$, at which $V(x(t))$ would vanish. Since everywhere for any real $a_{1L}, \ldots, a_{nL}$ the value of $V(x(t)) > 0$ at sufficiently small t, at $t \neq 0$ this is equivalent to the property of positive definiteness of $V(x)$.

In item 3, the conditions of the Theorem make it possible to find particular values of the coefficients $a_{1L}^*, \ldots, a_{nL}^*$ of order L in terms of expansions (2) of parametric solutions for $V(x) = 0$. In this case, higher than order L terms of the parameter t should be used to continue the process of seeking branches of solutions of $V(x) = 0$. In doing so, additional terms u_{iL_1} $(L_1 > L)$ are introduced into expansion (2), and again Theorem 1 is applied with the coefficient $A_{Q_1(L_1)}(a_{iL}^*, a_{i(L+1)}, \ldots, a_{iL_1}, L_1)$ at the lower degree t^{Q_1} of parameter t in series (3). The proof is completed.

Thus the property of having fixed sign and the property of having alternative signs are established by the finite order L_1 of expansion (2).

In answering the question of the fixed sign character, it is desirable, in (1), to reduce the degree of M as far as possible, which facilitates the analysis of the expression $A_{Q(L)}(a_{ij}, L)$ as a lower degree polynomial in t.

Theorem 2. *In the analysis of the fixed sign character of the form* $V(x)$ *for the case where* $m = 1$, *one can always assume that* $M = 1$ *in expansion (2).*

Proof. At the value $m = 1$ the least common multiple to the numbers: $1, 2$ will be $M = 2$, and the original value of $Q = 2mL = 2L$. We next consider two possibilities: 1. $L = 2\gamma$ (γ is integer), 2. $L = 2\gamma + 1$.

In the former case the numbers Q, L, and M can be reduced by any greatest common divisor $D = 2$. As a result, we obtain $Q_1 = Q/D = L$, $L_1 = \gamma$, $M_1 = 1$. If Theorem 1 is to be applied, the "refined" series (2) at $M = 1$ may be used in this case.

In the latter case, by Theorem 1, we find $q/p = Q/M = 2L/2 = L = 2\gamma + 1$, the property of alternating signs of the initial form immediately follows, irrespective of the sign of $A_{Q(L)}(a_{iL}, L)$. When $M_1 = 1$ we find $Q_1 = 2\gamma + 1$, $L_1 = \gamma + 1$, and $A_{Q_1(L_1)}(a_{iL_1}, L_1)$ does not vanish identically according to the second condition of (4).

Consequently, when $m = 1$ it is always possible to assume $M = 1$ when analyzing the property of having alternating signs. The proof is completed.

Let us demonstrate the essence of the dynamically symmetric satellite (illustrated by considering the problem of analyzing the stability boundary of precessional motions) whose center of mass uniformly moves in circular Keplerian orbit with angular velocity $\omega_0 = const$ [7].

It is common knowledge that equations of motion of a satellite in canonical variables can be obtained by the Hamiltonian function [7]:

$$H = \frac{1}{2}p_1^2 + \frac{1}{2}\frac{p_2^2}{\sin^2\theta} - p_2\,ctg\theta\cos\psi - \alpha\beta p_2\frac{\cos\theta}{\sin^2\theta} - p_1\sin\psi$$
$$+ \alpha\beta\frac{\cos\psi}{\sin\theta} + \frac{1}{2}\alpha^2\beta^2 ctg^2\theta + \frac{3}{2}(\alpha - 1)\cos^2\theta\,,$$

where ψ, θ and φ are the Euler angles; $\alpha = C/A$ $(0 < \alpha < 2)$; A, $B = A$, C are the principal central moments of inertia of the satellite; $\beta = r_0/\omega_0$; r is the projection of the satellite absolute angular velocity onto the axis of proper rotation $(r = r_0 = const)$; p_1 and p_2 are generalized impulses corresponding to the variables θ and φ.

One kind of stationary motions of the body is exemplified by "cylindrical" precessions:

$$\theta_0 = \frac{\pi}{2}, \quad \psi_0 = \pi, \quad p_{10} = 0,$$

$$p_{20} = 0, \quad (0 < \alpha < 2), \quad (0 < \beta^2 < 1). \tag{5}$$

To investigate the stability of cylindrical precession (5), we introduce deviations from stationary motion:

$$x_1 = \theta - \frac{\pi}{2}, \quad x_2 = \psi - \pi, \quad x_3 = p_1, \quad x_4 = p_2\,.$$

Then the Hamiltonian function of equations of disturbed motion takes the form

$$H_1(x) = \frac{1}{2}\left(\frac{x_4}{\cos x_1} - \sin x_1 \cos x_2 + \alpha\beta\tan x_1\right)^2 + \frac{1}{2}(x_3 + \sin x_2)^2$$

$$-\alpha\beta\cos x_1 \cos x_2 \; - \; \frac{1}{2}\cos^2 x_2 \sin^2 x_1 \; - \; \frac{1}{2}\sin^2 x_2 \; + \; \frac{3}{2}(\alpha \; - \; 1)\sin^2 x_1. \quad (6)$$

The necessary stability conditions (1) were obtained in [7] from the first approximation of differential equations described by function (6) and are expressed by the inequalities:

$$(\alpha\beta \; - \; 1)(\alpha\beta \; + \; 3\alpha \; - \; 4) \geq 0, \qquad\qquad (\alpha\beta \; - \; 1)^2 \; + \; 3\alpha \; - \; 2 \geq 0,$$

$$[(\alpha\beta \; - \; 1)^2 \; + \; 3\alpha \; - \; 2]^2 \; - \; 4(\alpha\beta \; - \; 1)(\alpha\beta \; + \; 3\alpha \; - \; 4) \geq 0.$$

A direct Lyapunov method from the quadratic approximation $H_1(x)$ was used in [7] to obtain sufficient stability conditions represented by a system of inequalities:

$$\alpha\beta \; - \; 1 > 0, \quad \alpha > 1. \qquad\qquad (7)$$

Let us pose the problem of investigating a portion of the boundary of sufficient stability conditions of motions

$$\alpha\beta = 1, \quad \alpha > 1. \qquad\qquad (8)$$

For verifying the property of having fixed sign of $H_1(x)$ with condition (8), we expand it into a Maclaurin series to fourth-order terms using a PC and the *Mathematica* system. As a result, we obtain the following expression needed for further investigations:

$$H_2(x) = \frac{3}{2}(\alpha \; - \; 1)\,x_1^2 \; + \; \frac{1}{2}\,x_2^2 \; + \; x_2 x_3 \; + \; \frac{1}{2}\,x_3^2 \; + \; \frac{1}{2}\,x_4^2 \; + \; [\frac{1}{8} - \frac{1}{2}(\alpha - 1)]\,x_1^4$$

$$+ \; \frac{1}{2}\,x_1^3 x_4 \; + \; \frac{1}{4}\,x_1^2 x_2^2 \; + \; \frac{1}{2}\,x_1^2 x_4^2 \; + \; \frac{1}{2}\,x_1 x_2^2 x_4 \; - \; \frac{1}{24}\,x_2^4 \; - \; \frac{1}{6}\,x_2^3 x_3. \quad (9)$$

The quadratic part $H_2(x)$ equal to $3\,(\alpha \; - \; 1)/2\,x_1^2 \; + \; (x_2 \; + \; x_3)^2/2 \; + \; x_4^2/2$ is of constant sign. It is therefore necessary to use higher than 2nd-order terms in the analysis of the property of having fixed sign of (9). To investigate the property of having fixed sign of $H_1(x)$ we perform a change of variables: $y_1 = x_1$, $y_2 = x_2$, $y_3 = x_2 + x_3$, $y_4 = x_4$. In this case the expression (9) simplifies to

$$H_3(y) = \frac{3}{2}(\alpha \; - \; 1)\,y_1^2 \; + \; \frac{1}{2}\,y_2^2 \; + \; \frac{1}{2}\,y_4^2 \; + \; [\frac{1}{8} - \frac{1}{2}(\alpha - 1)]\,y_1^4 \; + \; \frac{1}{2}\,y_1^3 y_4$$

$$+ \; \frac{1}{4}\,y_1^2 y_2^2 \; + \; \frac{1}{2}\,y_1^2 y_4^2 \; + \; \frac{1}{2}\,y_1 y_2^2 y_4 \; + \; \frac{1}{8}\,y_2^4 \; - \; \frac{1}{6}\,y_2^3 y_3.$$

The resulting inhomogeneous form of $H_3(y)$ of four variables has a quadratic form of constant signs that is definite as a function of three variables. Therefore, we apply the above approach to the analysis of the property of having fixed sign of the inhomogeneous forms when investigating the stability of "cylindrical" precession (5). Since it is possible to represent $H_3(y) = V_2(y_1, y_3, y_4) + V_*(y)$, then at $m = 1$ we use Theorem 2 with the values of $M = 1$, $L = 2$, $Q = 4$, and $\delta = +1$.

A parametric expansion of (2) in this problem has the form:

$$y_2 = t, \quad y_1 = a_2 t^2 + a_3 t^3 + \ldots, \quad y_3 = b_2 t^2 + \ldots, \quad y_4 = c_2 t^2 + \ldots,$$

where all a_i, b_i, c_i $(i \geq 2)$ are real and are subject to definition. On substituting these expressions into $H_3(y)$, we get

$$W(t) = H_3(y(t)) = A_4(a_2, b_2, c_2, 2)t^4 + \ldots,$$

where $A_4(a_2, b_2, c_2, 2) = 3(\alpha - 1)/2 \, a_2^2 + b_2^2/2 + c_2^2/2 + 1/8$, and dots denote higher fourth-order terms. Note that the unwieldy calculations needed in this case were performed in the interactive mode on a PC using the *Mathematica* system.

Since at any real a_2, b_2, c_2, we always have $A_4(a_2, b_2, c_2, 2) \geq 1/8 > 0$, equation $A_4(a_2, b_2, c_2, 2) = 0$ does not allow any real solutions.
Therefore, by the second item of Theorem 1, the function $H_3(y)$ will be positive definite. At the same time the functions $H_2(x)$ and $H_1(x)$ will also be positive definite.

Consequently, when $\alpha\beta = 1$, $\alpha > 1$ the "cylindrical" precession (5) is stable.

We wish to notice in conclusion that computer algebra, as demonstrated in this study, makes it possible to considerably enhance the possibilities of investigating stability and qualitative properties of solutions of differential equations; it can provide expansions into series, substitutions, and control over calculations. As follows from the above and some other examples, the combined use of manual and computer calculations is an effective method.

References

1. Arnold V.I. Additional Chapters of the Theory of Ordinary Differential Equations. Nauka, Moscow (1978) 304 (in Russian).
2. Ilyashenko Yu.S. Analytic insolvability of stability problems and of the problem of a topological classification of singular points of analytic systems of differential equations. Mat. sb. Moscow (1976) V.99, No. 2 162-175 (in Russian).
3. Lyapunov A.M. On Constant Helical Rotations. Collected Works, V.1. Izd. AN SSSR, Moscow (1954) 446 (in Russian).
4. Novickov M.A.. On the property of having fixed sign of analytic functions. In: The Lyapunov Functions Method in the Analysis of System Dynamics. Nauka, Novosibirsk (1987) 256-261 (in Russian).
5. Walker R.J. Algebraic Curves. *IIL*, Moscow (1952) 236 (in Russian).
6. Bryuno A.D. A Local Method for the Non-linear Analysis of Differential Equations. Nauka, Moscow (1979) 255 (in Russian).
7. Beletskii V.V. The Motion of a Satellite with Respect to the Center of Mass in a Gravitational Field. MGU, Moscow (1975) 307 (in Russian).

Superfast Computations with Singular Structured Matrices over Abstract Fields*

V. Y. Pan[1], A. Zheng[2], M. Abu Tabanjeh[2], Z. Chen[2], S. Providence[2]

[1] Dept. Math & Comp. Sci.
Lehman College, CUNY
Bronx, NY 10468
NY, NY 10036
vpan@lcvax.lehman.cuny.edu
[2] Ph.D Programs in Math & Comp. Sci.
Graduate School, CUNY
33 W. 42nd St., NY, NY 10036

Abstract. An effective superfast divide-and-conquer algorithm of Morf, 1980, and Bitmead and Anderson, 1980, computes the solution $x = T^{-1}b$ to a strongly non-singular Toeplitz or Toeplitz-like linear system $Tx = b$. The algorithm is called superfast because it runs in almost linear time, versus cubic time of Gaussian elimination and quadratic time of some known faster solutions. Recently, the algorithm was extended to similar superfast computations with $n \times n$ Cauchy and Cauchy-like matrices. We use randomization to extend this approach to superfast solution of a singular Cauchy-like linear system of equations over any field of constants and, futhermore, to superfast computation of the rank of a Cauchy-like matrix and a basis for its null space. We also ameliorate slightly Kaltofen's superfast solver of singular Toeplitz-like linear systems in an arbitrary field. The algorithms can be easily extended to similar computations with singular Hankel-like and Vandermonde-like matrices. The applications include rational and polynomial interpolation, Padé approximation and decoding Reed-Solomon and algebraic-geometric codes.

1 Introduction

The $n \times n$ dense structured matrices are defined by $O(n)$ parameters, and their structure enables dramatic acceleration of computations with such matrices. For example, an $n \times n$ Toeplitz matrix $T = [t_{i-j}]$ can be multiplied by a vector over any field of constants by using

$$T_{M_v}(n) = O((n \ \log \ n) \log \log n) \qquad (1.1)$$

arithmetic operations [3] versus $2n^2 - n$ for general $n \times n$ matrices (hereafter, we refer to arithmetic operations as *ops*). Furthermore, the well-known divide-and-conquer algorithm of [14], [15], [1] (hereafter, we refer to it as the *MBA algorithm*) rapidly computes the recursive triangular factorization of T, as

* Supported by NSF Grants CCR 9625344 and CCR 9732206 and PSC CUNY Awards 668365 and 669363

well as T^{-1}, det T, and the solution $x = T^{-1}b$ to a linear system $Tx = b$. The algorithm uses

$$T_{RF}(n) = O(T_{M_v}(n) \log n) = O((n \log^2 n) \log \log n)$$

ops over a wider class of Toeplitz-like matrices, having structure of Toeplitz type defined by associated *displacement operators* [12]. The algorithm is called *superfast* because it runs in almost linear time versus both cubic time of Gaussian elimination and quadratic time of some other known fast algorithms such as Levinson's and Trench's [8]. In [2], [22], [21], [16], the MBA algorithm was extended to other structured matrices, in particular, to Toeplitz-like + Hankel-like matrices [2] and to Cauchy-like and Vandermonde-like matrices [22], [21], [16]. The reader is referred to [3], [20], [16], [17] and to the bibliography therein on various applications of structured matrices. In many cases, in particular in application to signal processing, Padé approximation and sparse multivariate polynomial interpolation, one needs to solve singular Toeplitz-like, Vandermonde-like or Cauchy-like linear systems of equations.

Kaltofen in [11] extended the MBA approach to the solution of a singular Toeplitz-like linear system of equations. We will do the same thing in the Cauchy-like case and will also ameliorate slightly the algorithm of [11] in the Toeplitz-like case. Our algorithms use

$$T_{sing}(n) = O(T_{M_v}(n) \log n) \tag{1.2}$$

ops in the Toeplitz-like case (as in [11]) and

$$C_{sing}(n) = O(C_{M_v}(n) \log n) \tag{1.3}$$

ops in the Cauchy-like case. Here,

$$C_{M_v}(n) = O((n \log^2 n) \log \log n) \tag{1.4}$$

is the number of ops sufficient to solve *Trummer's problem* of multiplication of an $n \times n$ Cauchy matrix by a vector over any field of constants $\mathbf{F}$ (cf. [3], p. 130; [7], [21], [22]). If $\mathbf{F}$ supports FFT, then the factor $\log \log n$ in (1.1) and (1.4) can be removed. Our algorithms sample $4n$ random parameters from a fixed finite set S of cardinality $|S|$ in the Cauchy-like case. In Toeplitz-like case, they sample $2n - 2$ parameters (versus order of $n \log n$ in [11]). Our algorithms may fail with a probability at most $2\rho(\rho + 1)/|S|$ where ρ is the rank of the input matrix (versus $4n\rho/|S|$ in [11]), otherwise they produce correct output. Besides being linear solvers, our algorithms (like one of [11]) can be immediately applied to compute (at the same asymptotic computational cost) the rank of a given matrix and a basis for its null-space and to verify the correctness of the output in all cases.

Our study of Toeplitz-like and Cauchy-like computations and, in particular, our asymptotic complexity estimates (1.1), (1.2) and (1.3), (1.4) can be easily extended to the study of Hankel-like and Vandermonde-like computations, respectively. The bound (1.3) is supported directly by our algorithms in the Cauchy-like and Vandermonde-like cases, but in both cases it can be improved to the bound

$$T_{sing}(n) + O(V_{M_v}(n)) = O((n \log^2 n) \log \log n) \qquad (1.5)$$

(assuming that an $n \times n$ Vandermonde matrix can be multiplied by a vector in $V_{M_v}(n)$ ops), by means of some general techniques proposed in [18] for the transformation (at the cost $O(V_{M_v}(n))$) of various computational problems for Cauchy-like and Vandermonde-like matrices to the same problems for Toeplitz/Hankel-like matrices. (In fact, [18] defined such transformations among all the cited classes of structured matrices in all directions.) The difference by logarithmic factor may be not decisive in practice, because of the role of other potential criteria (such as numerical stability and the decrease of the overhead constants hidden in the above "O" notation), so we show all estimates (1.1)-(1.5) and not just (1.1), (1.2), (1.5). Furthermore, we comments on further practical improvement in Remark 3.1.

On various applications of Cauchy-like algorithms, see bibliography in [16], [20] and note that by using the cited transition to Toeplitz/Hankel computations we may save logarithmic factor in the complexity estimates versus ones of [16]. More dramatic improvement of the known record complexity estimates was resulted from the application of our algorithms to the list decoding of Reed-Solomon and algebraic-geometric codes [17], [23], [25]. The bottleneck of the list decoding is the computation of a nonzero vector from the null space of a singular $l \times m$ Vandermonde-like matrix where $l + m = O(n)$, n being the input size of the decoding problem. Application of our algorithms enables immediate decrease of the record complexity of these computations by order of magnitude - from at best quadratic order of n^2 [17], [23], [25] to almost linear order of n (up to a polylogarithmic factor).

We organize our paper as follows. In section 2, we recall some definitions and auxiliary facts. In section 3, we recall the MBA algorithm and the results of [22], [21], [16] on its Cauchy-like extension. In section 4, we apply randomization to extend the latter results to the case of a nonsingular but not strongly nonsingular input matrix. In sections 5 and 6, we cover the extension of Cauchy-like and Toeplitz-like solvers to the singular case. In section 7, we comment on the extension of our algorithms to the Hankel-like and Vandermonde-like cases.

2   Some Definitions and Basic Facts

Definition 2.1. W^T *is the transpose of a matrix or vector* W. $D(v) =$ diag$(v_0, v_1, \cdots, v_{n-1})$ *for* $v = (v_0, v_1, \cdots, v_{n-1})^T$ *is the diagonal matrix with the diagonal entries* $v_0, v_1, \ldots, v_{n-1}$.

Definition 2.2 [3], [4], [9], [10]. *For a field* $\mathbf{F}$ *and for vectors* $q = (q_i)$, $t = (t_j)$, $q_i \neq t_j$, $i, j = 0, \cdots, n-1$, *a matrix* $A \in \mathbf{F}^{n \times n}$ *is a* Cauchy *matrix (denoted by* $C(\mathbf{q}, \mathbf{t})$*) if* $A = (\frac{1}{q_i - t_j})_{i,j=0}^{n-1}$. *A is a* Cauchy-like *matrix if*

$$F_{[D(q),D(t)]}(A) = D(q)A - AD(t) = GH^T, \qquad (2.1)$$

$G, H \in \mathbf{F}^{n \times r}$, *and* $r = O(1)$. *(Clearly,* $r = 1$ *for* $C(\mathbf{q}, \mathbf{t})$.*) The pair of matrices* (G, H^T) *of (2.1) is a* $[D(q), D(t)]$-*generator (or a scaling generator) of length r for A and is denoted by* $s.g._r(A)$. *The minimum r allowing representation (2.1) is equal to* rank $(F_{[D(q)),D(t)]}(A))$ *and is called the* $[D(q), D(t)]$-*rank (or the scaling rank) of A.*

Lemma 2.1 [9]. *Let* A, q, t, $G = [g_1, \cdots, g_r] = (u_i^T)_{i=0}^{n-1} \in \mathbf{F}^{n \times r}$, $H = [h_1, \cdots, h_r] = (v_j^T)_{j=0}^{n-1} \in \mathbf{F}^{n \times r}$ *be as in Definition 2.2, such that (2.1) holds. Then*

$$A = \sum_{m=1}^{r} D(g_m)C(q,t)D(h_m) = \left(\frac{u_i^T v_j}{q_i - t_j}\right)_{i,j=0}^{n-1}, \qquad (2.2)$$

where $C(\mathbf{q}, \mathbf{t})$ *is a Cauchy matrix, and vice versa, (2.2) implies (2.1).*

Lemma 2.2 (cf. [3], [7]). *Given an* $n \times n$ *Cauchy matrix A and an n-dimensional vector v, the product Av can be computed in* $C_{M_v}(n)$ *ops (cf. (1.4)). If A is an $n \times n$ Cauchy-like matrix given with an $s.g._r(A)$, then the product Av can be computed in* $(3n + C_{M_v}(n))r$ *ops.*

Lemma 2.3. *Let* $q_j \in \mathbf{F}^{n \times 1}$, $j = 1, 2, 3$, *where the vectors* q_1 *and* q_3 *share no components. Let* $A_i \in \mathbf{F}^{n \times n}$, $F_{[D(q_i),D(q_{i+1})]}(A_i) = G_i H_i^T$, G_i, $H_i \in \mathbf{F}^{n \times r_i}$, $i = 1, 2$. *Then the matrix* $A = A_1 A_2$ *is a Cauchy-like matrix with* $F_{[D(q_1),D(q_3)]}(A) = GH^T$, $G = [G_1, A_1 G_2]$, $H = [A_2^T H_1, H_2]$, G, $H \in \mathbf{F}^{n \times r}$, $r = r_1 + r_2$. *Furthermore,* $O(r_1 r_2 C_{M_v}(n))$ *ops suffice to compute G and H.*

Lemma 2.4 *Let* $F_{[D(q),D(t)]}(A) = GH^T$, $G = [g_1, \cdots, g_r] \in \mathbf{F}^{n \times r}$, $H = [h_1, \cdots, h_r] \in \mathbf{F}^{n \times r}$. *Then* $F_{[D(t),D(q)]}(A^{-1}) = -UV^T$, *where the matrices* $U = [u_1, \cdots, u_r]$, $V = [v_1, \cdots, v_r]$ *satisfy* $AU = G$, $V^T A = H^T$.

Corollary 2.1. *Under the assumptions of Lemma 2.4, we have* rank $(F_{[D(t),D(q)]}(A^{-1})) \leq r$.

Lemma 2.5. *Let a Cauchy-like matrix A satisfy (2.1) and let $B_{I,J}$ be a* $k \times d$ *submatrix of A,* $1 \leq k, d \leq n$. *Then $B_{I,J}$ is a Cauchy-like matrix with a* $[D(q_I), D(t_J)]$-*generator of a length at most r, where* $I = [i_1, \cdots, i_k]$, $J = [j_1, \cdots, j_d]$, $D(q_I) = \text{diag}(q_{i_1}, \cdots, q_{i_k})$, $D(t_J) = \text{diag}(t_{j_1}, \cdots, t_{j_d})$.

Lemma 2.6. *The matrices $A + B$ and $A - B$ have* $[D(q), D(t)]$-*rank at most $r + r_1$ if A and B have* $[D(q), D(t)]$- *ranks r and r_1, respectively.*

Lemma 2.7 (cf. [4]). *An* $n \times n$ *Cauchy matrix* $C(\mathbf{q}, \mathbf{t})$ *is nonsingular if and only if all the $2n$ components of the vectors q and t are distinct. Every square submatrix of a nonsingular Cauchy matrix is nonsingular.*

Fact 2.1 (cf. Proposition A.6 of [19] or [3], Problem 2.2.11b). *Given an* $s.g._{\tilde{r}}(A) = (G, H)$ *and the scaling rank r of A,* $r < \tilde{r} \leq n$, *one can compute an $s.g._r(A)$ by using* $O(\tilde{r}^2 n)$ *ops.*

3   Recursive factorization of a Cauchy-like matrix

Definition 3.1. *A matrix W is strongly nonsingular if all its leading principal (that is, northwestern) submatrices are nonsingular.*

Hereafter, I and O stand for the identity and null matrices.

$$A = \begin{pmatrix} I & O \\ EB^{-1} & I \end{pmatrix} \begin{pmatrix} B & O \\ O & S \end{pmatrix} \begin{pmatrix} I & B^{-1}C \\ O & I \end{pmatrix}, \tag{3.1}$$

$$A^{-1} = \begin{pmatrix} I & -B^{-1}C \\ O & I \end{pmatrix} \begin{pmatrix} B^{-1} & O \\ O & S^{-1} \end{pmatrix} \begin{pmatrix} I & O \\ -EB^{-1} & I \end{pmatrix}, \tag{3.2}$$

where A is an $n \times n$ strongly nonsingular matrix

$$A = \begin{pmatrix} B & C \\ E & J \end{pmatrix}, \qquad S = J - EB^{-1}C, \tag{3.3}$$

B is a $k \times k$ matrix, and S is an $(n - k) \times (n - k)$ matrix, called the *Schur complement of B in A*. Factorization (3.1) represents block Gauss-Jordan elimination applied to the 2×2 block matrix A of (3.3). If the matrix A is strongly nonsingular, then the Schur complement matrix S can be obtained in $n - k$ steps of Gaussian elimination. By expanding (3.2) we obtain

$$A^{-1} = \begin{pmatrix} B^{-1} + B^{-1}CS^{-1}EB^{-1} & -B^{-1}CS^{-1} \\ -S^{-1}EB^{-1} & S^{-1} \end{pmatrix}. \tag{3.4}$$

Lemma 3.1 [3], [8].   *If A is strongly nonsingular, so are B and S.*

Lemma 3.2 [3], [8].   *Let A be an $n \times n$ strongly nonsingular matrix and let S be defined by (3.3). Let A_1 be a leading principal submatrix of S and let S_1 denote the Schur complement of A_1 in S. Then S^{-1} and S_1^{-1} form the respective southeastern blocks of A^{-1}.*

Lemma 3.3.   *If (3.1) holds, then $\det A = (\det B)\det S$.*

Due to Lemma 3.1, we may extend factorization (3.1) from A to B and S and then recursively continue this factorization process until we arrive at 1×1 matrices (compare [24], [15], [1]). In actual computation, we invert these matrices and then recursively proceed *bottom up*, that is, by using matrix multiplications and subtractions we compute all the matrices defined in the recursive descending process until we arrive at A^{-1}. The entire computation will be called the *CRF (or complete recursive factorization)* of A. We will always assume *balanced* CRFs, where B of (3.3) is a $\lfloor \frac{n}{2} \rfloor \times \lfloor \frac{n}{2} \rfloor$ submatrix of A, and similar balancing is maintained in all subsequent recursive steps. The balanced CRF has depth at most $d = \lceil \log_2 n \rceil$.

Let us summarize our description in the form of a recursive algorithm.

Algorithm 3.1. *Recursive triangular factorization and inversion of a matrix.*

Input: a strongly nonsingular $n \times n$ matrix A of (3.3).

Output: balanced CRF of A, including the matrix A^{-1}.

Computations:

1. Apply Algorithm 3.1 to the matrix B (replacing A as its input) in order to compute the balanced CRF of B (including B^{-1}).

2. Compute the Schur complement $S = J - EB^{-1}C$.

3. Apply Algorithm 3.1 to the matrix S (replacing A as its input) to compute the balanced CRF of S (including S^{-1}).

4. Compute A^{-1} from (3.2).

Clearly, given A^{-1} and a vector b, we may immediately compute the vector $x = A^{-1}b$. If we also seek det A, then it suffices to add the request for computing det B, det S, and det A at stages 1, 3, and 4, respectively.

In application of Algorithm 3.1 to a Cauchy-like matrix or, more generally, to a matrix given by its short scaling generator, all matrix operations are performed with short scaling generators of the auxiliary matrices involved, and this yields the next result (cf. [22], [21], [16]).

Theorem 3.1. *Let A denote an $n \times n$ strongly nonsingular Cauchy-like matrix given with its F-generator of a length r for the operator $F = F_{[D(q),D(t)]}$. Then F-generators of length $O(r)$ of all matrices encountered in the balanced CRF of A (including an $s.g._r(A^{-1})$) as well as the value of det A can be computed by using $O(r^2 C_{M_v}(n) \log n)$ ops and $O(nr \log n)$ words of storage space.*

Remark 3.1 Scaling generator of a Schur complement S of (3.3) has simple explicit expressions via the $s.g._r(A^{-1})$ [16], [21]. Using them simplifies the computation of $s.g._r(S^{-1})$ and similarly at all other stages of the algorithm, though such a simplification decreases the overall asymptotic cost of performing the algorithm only by a constant factor.

4   Ensuring strong nonsingularity

For a nonsingular real or complex matrix A, the matrices $A^T A$ and AA^T are strongly nonsingular. By applying Algorithm 3.1 to these matrices, we may extend Theorem 3.1 to any nonsingular matrix A [22], [21]. For computations in finite fields such a symmetrization does not work, but we will next yield similar results over any field $\mathbf{F}$ by using random parameters always sampled from a fixed finite set $\mathbf{S}$ (in $\mathbf{F}$ or in its extension) independently of each other and under the uniform probability distribution on $\mathbf{S}$. We will keep using definitions of sections 2 and will rely on the following lemma.

Lemma 4.1 *[5]. Let $p(\mathbf{x}) = p(x_1, x_2, \cdots, x_m)$ be a nonzero m-variate polynomial of a total degree d. Let $\mathbf{S}$ be a finite set in the domain of the definition of $p(\mathbf{x})$, let the random values $x_1^*, \cdots, x_m^*$ be sampled from $\mathbf{S}$, and let $\mathbf{x}^* = (x_1^*, x_2^*, \cdots, x_m^*)$. Then probability$(p(\mathbf{x}^*) = 0) \leq d/|\mathbf{S}|$.*

Theorem 4.1. *Let A be an $n \times n$ nonsingular matrix satisfying equation (2.2). Let X be a matrix satisfying $X = YC(q, s)$, where*

$$Y = \sum_{m=1}^{r} D(g_m^*) C(t, q) D(h_m^*) , \qquad (4.1)$$

$C(q, s) = (\frac{1}{q_i - s_j})_{i,j=0}^{n-1}$ is a fixed nonsingular Cauchy matrix, $q \in \mathbf{F}^{n \times 1}$, $t \in \mathbf{F}^{n \times 1}$, $s \in \mathbf{F}^{n \times 1}$, q and t are as in Lemma 2.4, $q_i \neq s_j$, $s_i \neq t_j$ for all i and j, $g_m^* \in \mathbf{F}^{n \times 1}$, $h_m^* \in \mathbf{F}^{n \times 1}$, $m = 1, \cdots, r$, and the $2nr$ components of the $2r$ latter vectors are random values from a fixed finite set $\mathbf{S}$. Then AX has F-rank at most $2r+1$ and, with a probability at least $1 - n(n+1)/|\mathbf{S}|$, is a strongly nonsingular matrix.

Proof. First consider matrix Y of (4.1), where the random vectors g_m^* and h_m^* are replaced by generic vectors whose components are indeterminates. Recall that the $F_{[D(t),D(q)]}$-rank of A^{-1} is at most r, due to Lemma 2.4. Therefore, there exists an assignment of values to the components of the vectors g_m^*, h_m^*, for which we have $AY = I$, and then the matrix $AX = C(q, s)$ is strongly nonsingular (cf. Lemma 2.7). On the other hand, the determinants of the $k \times k$ leading principal submatrices $(AX)_k$ of AX are polynomials of degrees at most $2k$ in the coordinates of g_m^*, h_m^*. Since $AX = C(q, s)$ for a particular assignment, these polynomials are not identically 0 if the components are indeterminates. Therefore, by Lemma 4.1, we obtain

$$probability(\det(AX)_k \neq 0, k = 1, \cdots, n) \geq \prod_{k=1}^{n} \frac{1-2k}{|\mathbf{S}|} \geq \frac{1-n(n+1)}{|\mathbf{S}|}.$$

Corollary 4.1. *Let an $n \times n$ nonsingular Cauchy-like matrix A be given with its F-generator of length r for the operator $F = F_{[D(q),D(t)]}$. Then an $F_{[D(t),D(q)]}$-generator of length at most r for A^{-1} can be computed by means of a randomized algorithm using $2nr$ random parameters (sampled from the set $\mathbf{S}$) and $O(nr^2 \log^3 n)$ ops and failing with a probability at most $\frac{n(n+1)}{|\mathbf{S}|}$.*

Proof. Let us define X as above. By Theorem 4.1, the Cauchy-like matrix AX is strongly nonsingular with a probability at least $1 - n(n+1)/|\mathbf{S}|$, and then, by Theorem 3.1, we may compute the matrices $(AX)^{-1}$ and $A^{-1} = X(AX)^{-1}$ by using a total of $O(C_{M_v}(n)r^2 \log n)$ ops. Due to Lemma 4.1, we also obtain the desired bounds on the number of random parameters used and on the failure probabilities. Finally, we will decrease the length of the computed F-generator of A^{-1} by applying Fact 2.1.

Corollary 4.2. *$\det A$ and ρ=rank A can be computed by using $2nr$ random parameters and $O(C_{M_v}(n)r^2 \log n)$ ops for a matrix A of (2.1), (2.2). If $C(t, q)$ is a nonsingular Cauchy matrix, then (by Lemmas 2.7 and 4.1) the matrix X is strongly nonsingular, with a probability at least $1 - n(n+1)/|\mathbf{S}|$, and (by Theorem 3.1) $\det(AX)$, $\det X$, and $\det A = \frac{\det (AX)}{\det X}$ can be computed at the randomized cost $O(C_{M_v}(n)r^2 \log n)$. Furthermore, with a probability at least $\rho(\rho+1)/|\mathbf{S}|$, $\rho \times \rho$ is the maximum size of a nonsingular leading principal submatrix of AX for the matrix X of Theorem 4.1. Such a size is computed as a by-product of application of Algorithm 3.1 to AX.*

5   Fast Cauchy-like Computations - Singular Case

Studying the solution of a singular Cauchy-like linear system, we will use the next result and definition.

Lemma 5.1 *[11]. Let A be an $n \times n$ matrix of rank ρ with entries from a fixed field $\mathbf{F}$ and suppose that the $\rho \times \rho$ leading principal submatrix A_ρ is nonsingular. Then for a vector y with coordinates from the field $\mathbf{F}$ the vector*

$$x = \begin{pmatrix} A_\rho^{-1} b\,' \\ 0 \end{pmatrix} - y$$

is a solution to $Ax = b$, where the vector $b\,'$ consists of the first ρ coordinates of $b + Ay$, and 0 denotes the null vector of dimension $n - \rho$.

Definition 5.1. *Let A_i be the $i \times i$ leading principal submatrix of A, where $1 \le i \le n$. We say that A has generic rank profile if A_j is nonsingular for all j, $1 \le j \le \mathrm{rank}(A)$.*

The next theorem extends the known results from the Toeplitz-like (cf. [3], p. 206, or [13]) to the Cauchy-like case and can be an alternative to Theorem 4.1 where the input matrix is nonsingular (see Remark 5.1).

Theorem 5.1. *For an $n \times n$ Cauchy-like matrix A of rank ρ represented by an $s.g._r(A)$ and satisfying (2.1) and (2.2), consider the matrix product $\overline{A} = LAM$, where L and M are also Cauchy-like matrices with scaling generators of length 1. Assume the following relations:*

$$F_{[D(s),\ D(q)]}(L) = YZ^T,$$

$$F_{[D(t),\ D(p)]}(M) = XW^T,$$

$$Y^T = [y_1, \cdots, y_n] \in \mathbf{F}^n,\ Z^T = [z_1, \cdots, z_n] \in \mathbf{F}^n,$$

$$X^T = [x_1, \cdots, x_n] \in \mathbf{F}^n,\ W^T = [w_1, \cdots, w_n] \in \mathbf{F}^n,$$

$$L = \left(\frac{y_{i+1} z_{j+1}}{s_i - q_j}\right)_{i,j=0}^{n-1},\ M = \left(\frac{x_{i+1} w_{j+1}}{t_i - p_j}\right)_{i,j=0}^{n-1},$$

where the entries of the matrices Y, Z, X, W are random samples from a fixed finite subset $\mathbf{S}$ of the field $\mathbf{F}$ and where $\mathbf{S}$ does not contain 0. Let s_i, q_j, p_k be all pairwise distinct for $i, j, k = 0, \cdots, n - 1$. Then

   (1) L and M are strongly nonsingular matrices and

   (2) $\overline{A}$ has generic rank profile with a probability at most $1 - \frac{2\rho(\rho+1)}{|\mathbf{S}|}$.

Proof. Part (1) follows from (2.2) and Lemma 2.7 since $\mathbf{S}$ does not contain 0. Let us prove part (2). For an $n \times n$ matrix D, denote by $D_{I,J}$ the determinant of the submatrix of D formed by removing from D all rows not contained in the set I and all columns not contained in the set J. First, let Y, Z, X, and W be generic matrices. For $I = [1, 2, \cdots, i]$, $J = [j_1, j_2, \cdots, j_i]$, $K = [k_1, k_2, \cdots, k_i]$, $i = 1, 2, \cdots, \rho$, we have from the Cauchy-Binet formula that

$$\overline{A}_{I,I} = \sum_J \sum_K L_{I,J} A_{J,K} M_{K,I}.$$

Let us prove that

$$\overline{A}_{I,I} \neq 0 \ for \ i = 1, \ 2, \ \cdots, \ \rho. \tag{5.1}$$

Observe that, for a fixed pair of $J = [j_1, j_2, \cdots, j_i]$ and $K = [k_1, k_2, \cdots, k_i]$, the determinant $L_{I,J}$ has the unique term

$$a y_1 y_2 \cdots y_i z_{j_1} \cdots z_{j_i},$$

where $a \neq 0$ is a constant. Likewise, $M_{K,I}$ has the unique term

$$b x_{k_1} \cdots x_{k_i} w_1 \cdots w_i,$$

where $b \neq 0$ is a constant. Therefore, $\overline{A}_{I,I} \neq 0$ provided that there exists a pair J, K such that $A_{J,K} \neq 0$. This is true for all $i \leq \rho$, since A has rank ρ, and we arrive at (5.1).

Now, we observe that $\overline{A}_{I,I}$ is a polynomial of degree at most $4i$ in the variables $y_m, z_m, x_m, w_m, m = 1, \ldots, n$. Under the random choice of their values, we apply Lemma 4.1 and obtain that $probability(\overline{A}_{I,I} \neq 0, i = 1, \cdots, \rho) \geq \prod_{i=1}^{\rho} (1 - 4i/|\mathbf{S}|) \geq 1 - 2\rho(\rho+1)/|\mathbf{S}|$. This proves part (2) of Theorem 5.1.

Remark 5.1. If the input Cauchy-like matrix is nonsingular, we may apply Theorem 5.1, as an alternative to Theorem 4.1. Application of Theorem 5.1, rather than Theorem 4.1, requires by factor $2/r$ fewer random parameters ($4n$ versus $2nr$) and involves scaling generators of roughly half length ($r+2$ versus $2r+1$), at the small price of doubling the probability of errors ($2n(n+1)/|\mathbf{S}|$ versus $n(n+1)/|\mathbf{S}|$).

To prove Theorem 5.1, we devised a simple algorithm that, for an $n \times n$ Cauchy-like matrix A of rank ρ given with an $s.g._r(A)$, computes a random pair $s.g._1(L)$ and $s.g._1(M)$, where L and M are $n \times n$ matrices such that, with a probability at least $1 - 2\rho(\rho+1)/|\mathbf{S}|$, the matrix $\overline{A} = LAM$ has generic rank profile. Furthermore, based on Lemma 2.3, we computed $s.g._{r+2}(\overline{A})$ by using $O(r^2 C_{M_v}(n))$ ops (cf. (1.4)). Now, we assume that we have been already given $s.g._1(L)$, $s.g._1(M)$, and $s.g._{r+2}(\overline{A})$ for a pair of nonsingular matrices L and M and an $n \times n$ matrix $\overline{A} = LAM$ having generic rank profile and propose the following algorithm, using $O(r^2 C_{M_v}(n) \log n)$ ops (cf. (1.3)).

Algorithm 5.1. *Computation of the largest nonsingular leading principal inverse.*

Input: vectors $\mathbf{q} = (q_i)_{i=0}^{n-1}$, $\mathbf{t} = (t_j)_{j=0}^{n-1}$, $q_i \neq t_j$, $i, j = 0, 1, \cdots, n-1$, and $\mathbf{g}_1, \cdots, \mathbf{g}_{r+2}, \mathbf{h}_1, \cdots, \mathbf{h}_{r+2}$ such that the next matrix has generic rank profile:

$$\overline{A} = \sum_{m=1}^{r+2} D(\mathbf{g}_m) C(\mathbf{q}, \mathbf{t}) D(\mathbf{h}_m).$$

Output: An integer $\rho \leq n$ and vectors $\mathbf{u}_1, \cdots, \mathbf{u}_{\overline{r}}, \mathbf{v}_1, \cdots, \mathbf{v}_{\overline{r}}, \mathbf{u}_m, \mathbf{v}_m \in \mathbf{F}^{n \times 1}$, $m = 1, 2, \cdots, \overline{r}, \overline{r} \leq r + 2$, such that $\rho = \text{rank}(\overline{A})$ and

$$\overline{A}_{\rho}^{-1} = \sum_{m=1}^{\overline{r}} D(\mathbf{u}_m) C(\mathbf{t}, \mathbf{q}) D(\mathbf{v}_m).$$

1. Represent $\overline{A}$ as $\overline{A} = \begin{pmatrix} \overline{B} & \overline{C} \\ \overline{E} & \overline{J} \end{pmatrix}$, cf. (3.3), where $k = \lceil \frac{n}{2} \rceil$, and the $k \times k$ submatrix $\overline{B}$ of $\overline{A}$ is singular if and only if $k > \rho$ (since $\overline{A}$ has generic rank profile). Apply Algorithm 5.1 recursively to the input matrix $\overline{B}$ replacing $\overline{A}$. (Note that we are given an $s.g._r(\overline{B})$.) If $\rho \geq k$, the output of this stage is the desired output of the algorithm. Otherwise, the matrix $\overline{B}$ is nonsingular, and then we obtain $s.g._r(\overline{B}^{-1})$.

2. Apply Algorithm 3.1 to compute an $s.g._r(\overline{S})$ for the matrix $\overline{S} = \overline{J} - \overline{E}\,\overline{B}^{-1}\overline{C}$.

3. Apply the algorithm recursively to the Cauchy-like input matrix $\overline{S}$, replacing $\overline{A}$. Output $\rho = \text{rank}(\overline{A}) = k + \text{rank}(\overline{S})$.

4. By using the definitions and the results of section 2, compute an $s.g._{2r+4}(\overline{A}_\rho^{-1})$ (see further comments below).

5. Apply Fact 2.1, to compute and output $s.g._{r+2}(\overline{A}_\rho^{-1})$.

Let us specify stage 4. Consider the $\rho \times \rho$ leading principal submatrix,
$$\overline{A}_\rho = \begin{pmatrix} \overline{B} & \overline{G} \\ \overline{D} & \overline{R} \end{pmatrix}, \ \overline{G}, \ \overline{D}^T \in \mathbf{F}^{k \times (\rho-k)}, \ \overline{R} \in \mathbf{F}^{(\rho-k) \times (\rho-k)}. \text{ Write } \hat{S} = \overline{R} -$$
$\overline{D}\,\overline{B}^{-1}\overline{G}$. Note that at the preceding stages we have computed $s.g._{r+2}(\overline{G})$, $s.g._{r+2}(\overline{D})$, $s.g._{r+2}(\overline{B}^{-1})$, $s.g._{r+2}(\overline{DB}^{-1})$, $s.g._{r+2}(\overline{B}^{-1}\overline{G})$, and $s.g._{r+2}(\hat{S}^{-1})$ (cf. Theorem 3.1). Represent $\overline{A}_\rho^{-1}$ as follows:

$$\overline{A}_\rho^{-1} = \begin{pmatrix} B_{1,1} & B_{1,2} \\ B_{2,1} & \hat{S}^{-1} \end{pmatrix},$$

where $B_{1,2} = -\overline{B}^{-1}\overline{G}\,\hat{S}^{-1}$, $B_{2,1} = -\hat{S}^{-1}\overline{D}\,\overline{B}^{-1}$, $B_{1,1} = \overline{B}^{-1} - B_{1,2}\overline{D}\,\overline{B}^{-1}$ (cf. (3.4)). Due to Lemma 2.5 and Corollary 2.1, the matrices $B_{1,1}, B_{1,2}, B_{2,1}$, and $\hat{S}^{-1}$ have scaling rank at most $r+2$, and we may apply Algorithm 3.1 and the results of section 2 to compute the respective short scaling generators of these matrices. Let us specify the operators defining these generators. Write $q^{(1)} = (q_i)_{i=0}^{k-1}, \ q^{(2)} = (q_i)_{i=k}^{\rho-1}, \ t^{(1)} = (t_i)_{i=0}^{k-1}, \ t^{(2)} = (t_i)_{i=0}^{\rho-1}$,
$$q^{(0)} = \begin{pmatrix} q^{(1)} \\ q^{(2)} \end{pmatrix} \text{ and } t^{(0)} = \begin{pmatrix} t^{(1)} \\ t^{(2)} \end{pmatrix}.$$
Now obtain that
$$F_{[D(t^{(0)}), \ D(q^{(0)})]}(\overline{A}_\rho^{-1})$$
$$= \begin{pmatrix} D(t^{(1)}) & O \\ O & D(t^{(2)}) \end{pmatrix} \overline{A}_\rho^{-1} - \overline{A}_\rho^{-1} \begin{pmatrix} D(q^{(1)}) & O \\ O & D(q^{(2)}) \end{pmatrix}$$
$$= \begin{pmatrix} F_{[D(t^{(1)}), \ D(q^{(1)})]}(B_{1,1}) & F_{[D(t^{(1)}), \ D(q^{(2)})]}(B_{1,2}) \\ F_{[D(t^{(2)}), \ D(q^{(1)})]}(B_{2,1}) & F_{[D(t^{(2)}), \ D(q^{(2)})]}(\hat{S}^{-1}) \end{pmatrix},$$
which gives us an $s.g._{2r+4}(\overline{A}_\rho^{-1})$.

To solve a singular Cauchy-like linear system $A\overline{x} = \overline{b}$, first compute a vector y that satisfies $LAMy = Lb$ and then recover the vector $x = My$ that satisfies $Ax = b$. Since L and M are nonsingular, rank $(A) = $ rank (LAM).

As a by-product, the algorithm computes rank $(\overline{A})$, which equals rank (A) with a probability at least $1 - 2\rho(\rho + 1)/|\mathbf{S}|$, by Theorem 5.1. By using a standard technique (see e.g. [3], p.110), the algorithm can be immediately extended (at additional cost $O(rC_{M_v}(n))$) to the computation of a basis for the null space of A.

Finally, we observe that, by using $O(rC_{M_v}(n))$ ops, we may verify whether $A\boldsymbol{x} = \boldsymbol{b}$, that is, the overall cost bound for the algorithm covers the cost of the verification of its correctness; furthermore, similar property holds for the rank and null space computation by this approach.

6 Solving Singular Toeplitz-like Linear Systems

We will next follow and slightly improve the known best randomized algorithm of [11] for the solution of a singular Toeplitz-like linear system. (We will use fewer ops and random parameters due to the incorporation of Lemma 6.4 below, which is a result from [19].)

Definition 6.1 *(cf. e.g. [3], Definition 11.1). For an $n \times n$ matrix T, define the two displacements,*

$$F_-(T) = T - Z^T T Z, \quad F_+(T) = T - Z T Z^T, \tag{6.1}$$

where $Z = (z_{i,j})$, is a down shift $n \times n$ matrix, $z_{i,j} = 0$ unless $i = j + 1$, $z_{i,i+1} = 1$. If for a fixed field $\mathbf{F}$ and for $F = F_+$ or $F = F_-$, we have

$$F(T) = G^* H^{*T}; \quad G^*, H^* \in \mathbf{F}^{n \times r}, \tag{6.2}$$

then the pair of matrices (G^*, H^*) is called an F-generator or a displacement generator of T of length r and will be denoted by $d.g._r(T)$. The minimum r allowing the above representation (6.2) is called the F-rank (or displacement rank) of T. T is called a Toeplitz-like matrix if $r = O(1)$.

Lemma 6.1 *[1]. For any $n \times n$ matrix A,*

$$\text{rank } (F_-(A)) - 2 \le \text{rank } (F_+(A)) \le \text{rank } (F_-(A)) + 2.$$

Furthermore, given a $d.g._r(T)$ under $F = F_+$ (resp. $F = F_-$), it suffices to use $O(rT_{Mv}(n))$ ops (for $T_{Mv}(n)$ of (1.1)) in order to compute a $d.g._{r+2}(T)$ under $F = F_-$ (resp. $F = F_+$).

Lemma 6.2 *[12]. Let F_-, F_+, T, G^*, H^*, and r be as in (6.1) and (6.2). Then $F(T) = G^*(H^*)^T = \sum_{i=1}^{r} \mathbf{g}_i^*(\mathbf{h}_i^*)^T$ if*

$$T = \sum_{i=1}^{r} L^T(\mathbf{g}_i^*) L(\mathbf{h}_i^*) \text{ for } F = F_-, \quad T = \sum_{i=1}^{r} L(\mathbf{g}_i^*) L^T(\mathbf{h}_i^*) \text{ for } F = F_+,$$

where $G^* = [\mathbf{g}_1^*, \cdots, \mathbf{g}_r^*]$, $H^* = [\mathbf{h}_1^*, \cdots, \mathbf{h}_r^*]$, and $L(\boldsymbol{v})$ is a lower triangular Toeplitz matrix with the first column $\boldsymbol{v}$.

Lemma 6.3 *(cf. e.g. [3], Corollary 12.1). Let T_1 and T_2 be two Toeplitz-like matrices, given with their F-generators of lengths r_1 and r_2, respectively, for $F = F_+$ or $F = F_-$. Then an F-generator of length at most $r_1 + r_2 + 1$ for the matrix $T_1 T_2$ can be computed at the cost of performing $O((r_1 + r_2)^2 T_{M_v}(n))$ ops (cf. (1.1)). Furthermore, a $d.g._r(UTL)$ for a given $d.g._r(T)$ and a given pair of lower triangular Toeplitz matrices L and U^T can be computed at the cost $2r^2 T_{M_v}(n)$, provided that $F = F_-$.*

Lemma 6.4 (cf. Proposition A.6 of [19] or [3], Problem 2.2.11b). *Given an $d.g._{\tilde{r}}(A) = (G, H)$ and the displacement rank r of A, $r < \tilde{r} \leq n$, one can compute a $d.g._r(A)$ by using $O(\tilde{r}^2 n)$ ops.*

Lemma 6.5 *[12]. Let T be a nonsingular Toplitz-like matrix. Then we have rank $(F_+(T^{-1})) =$ rank $(F_-(T))$.*

Lemma 6.6 *(cf. [15], [1], [3]). Let T be an $n \times n$ strongly nonsingular Toeplitz-like matrix such that*

$$T = \begin{pmatrix} B & C \\ E & J \end{pmatrix}, \qquad S = J - EB^{-1}C,$$

B is a $k \times k$ matrix, and S is the $(n-k) \times (n-k)$ Schur complement of B in T (cf. (3.3)). Let $r = \text{rank}(F_+(T))$. Then

$$\text{rank }(F_-(S^{-1})) = \text{rank }(F_+(S)) \leq r,$$

$$\text{rank }(F_-(B^{-1})) = \text{rank }(F_+(B)) \leq r,$$

$$\text{rank }(F_+(S^{-1})) = \text{rank }(F_-(S)) \leq r + 2,$$

$$\text{rank }(F_+(B^{-1})) = \text{rank }(F_-(B)) \leq r + 2.$$

Proof. The lemma follows from Lemmas 3.2, 6.1, and 6.5.

Theorem 6.1 *[11]. For an $n \times n$ Toeplitz-like matrix T of rank ρ, represented by $d.g._r(T)$ satisfying (6.1) and (6.2), let $\tilde{T} = UTL$, where U^T and L are two unit lower triangular Toeplitz matrices whose $2n-2$ entries are randomly sampled from a subset $\mathbf{S}$ of a fixed field containing the entries of T. Then the matrix $\tilde{T}$ has generic rank profile with a probability at least $1 - \rho(\rho+1)/|\mathbf{S}|$.*

Due to Lemma 6.3, we may compute $d.g._r(\tilde{T})$ at the cost of performing at most $2r^2 T_{M_v}(n)$ ops.

Now, given a $d.g._r(\tilde{T})$ for a matrix $\tilde{T} \in \mathbf{F}^{n \times n}$ having generic rank profile, the following algorithm extends one of [11] and supports (1.2).

Algorithm 6.1. *Computing the largest nonsingular leading principal inverse.*

Input: a field $\mathbf{F}$ and vectors $\tilde{g}_1, \cdots, \tilde{g}_r, \tilde{h}_1, \cdots, \tilde{h}_r$ from $\mathbf{F}^{n \times 1}$ such that the matrix $\tilde{T} = \sum_{i=1}^r L^T(\tilde{g}_i) L(\tilde{h}_i)$ has generic rank profile.

Output: An integer $\rho \leq n$ and vectors $\tilde{u}_1, \cdots, \tilde{u}_r$, $\tilde{v}_1, \cdots, \tilde{v}_r$, $\tilde{u}_m, \tilde{v}_m \in \mathbf{F}^{n \times 1}$, $m = 1, 2, \cdots, r$, such that $\rho = \text{rank}(\tilde{T})$ and $\tilde{T}_\rho^{-1} = \sum_{m=1}^r L(\tilde{u}_m) L^T(\tilde{v}_m)$.

1. Represent $\tilde{T}$ as $\tilde{T} = \begin{pmatrix} \tilde{B} & \tilde{C} \\ \tilde{E} & \tilde{J} \end{pmatrix}$, as in (3.3), for $k = \lceil \frac{n}{2} \rceil$, where the $k \times k$ submatrix $\tilde{B}$ of $\tilde{T}$ is singular if and only if $k > \rho$ (since $\tilde{T}$ has generic rank profile). Apply Algorithm 6.1 recursively to the input matrix $\tilde{B}$ replacing $\tilde{T}$. (Note that the first k components of the given vectors $\tilde{g}_i$ and $\tilde{h}_i$ define a $d.g._r(\tilde{B})$.) If $\rho \geq k$, the output of this stage is the desired output of the algorithm. Otherwise, the matrix $\tilde{B}$ is nonsingular, and then obtain a $d.g._{r+2}(\tilde{B}^{-1})$ for $F = F_-$ and a $d.g._r(\tilde{B}^{-1})$ for $F = F_+$.

2. Apply Lemma 6.3 for $F = F_+$ to compute a $d.g._r(\tilde{S})$ for $\tilde{S} = \tilde{J} - \tilde{E}\,\tilde{B}^{-1}\tilde{C}$.

3. Apply the algorithm recursively to the Toeplitz-like input matrix $\tilde{S}$, replacing $\tilde{T}$. Output $\rho = \text{rank}(\tilde{T}) = k + \text{rank}(\tilde{S})$.

4. By using Definition 6.1 and Lemmas 6.1-6.6, compute $s.g._r(\tilde{T}_\rho^{-1})$ for $F = F_+$.

Let us specify stage 4. Consider the $\rho \times \rho$ leading principal submatrix, $\tilde{T}_\rho = \begin{pmatrix} \tilde{B} & \tilde{G} \\ \tilde{D} & \tilde{R} \end{pmatrix}$, $\tilde{G}$, $\tilde{D}^T \in C^{k \times (\rho-k)}$, $\tilde{R} \in C^{(\rho-k) \times (\rho-k)}$. Write $\check{S} = \tilde{R} - \tilde{D}\,\tilde{B}^{-1}\tilde{G}$. Note that at the preceding stages we have computed $d.g._r(\tilde{G})$ and $d.g._r(\tilde{D})$ for $F = F_-$, $d.g._r(\tilde{B}^{-1})$, $d.g._{2r+1}(-\tilde{B}^{-1}\tilde{G})$, $d.g._{2r+1}(-\tilde{D}\tilde{B}^{-1})$, and $d.g._r(\check{S}^{-1})$ for $F = F_+$. We obtain the following block representation:

$$\tilde{T}_\rho^{-1} = \begin{pmatrix} M_{1,1} & M_{1,2} \\ M_{2,1} & \check{S}^{-1} \end{pmatrix},$$

where $M_{1,2} = -\tilde{B}^{-1}\tilde{G}\,\check{S}^{-1}$, $M_{2,1} = -\check{S}^{-1}\tilde{D}\,\tilde{B}^{-1}$, $M_{1,1} = \tilde{B}^{-1} - M_{1,2}\tilde{D}\,\tilde{B}^{-1}$. By applying Lemmas 6.1-6.6, we compute $d.g._r(\tilde{T}_\rho^{-1})$ for $F = F_+$.

As in the Cauchy-like case of section 5, algorithm 6.1 outputs rank (A) as a by-product and has immediate extension to the computation of a basis for the null space of A.

7   Extensions to Computations with Structured Matrices of Other Classes

Hankel matrices and *Hankel-like matrices* of displacement rank r are obtained from Toeplitz matrices and Toeplitz-like matrices of displacement rank r, respectively, by their pre-multiplication (as well as by their post-multiplication) by the *reflection matrix* J, having ones on its antidiagonal and zero entries elsewhere. (Note that J^2 is the identity matrix.) Toeplitz and Toeplitz-like matrix computations and, in particular, all results of section 6 are immediately extended to Hankel and Hankel-like matrix computations, e.g. $H^{-1} = T^{-1}J$, rank $(H) = \text{rank}(T)$, and the null spaces of H and T are the same where $T = JH$. It is also straightforward to extend Algorithm 6.1 to Hankel and Hankel-like computations directly; moreover (as noted in [21]), Remark 3.1 also applies directly to the Hankel-like Schur complements and

Hankel-like extensions of Algorithms 3.1, 5.1 and 6.1 but not to Toeplitz-like Schur complements and Algorithm 6.1.

$A = (x_i^j)_{i,j=0}^{n-1}$ is an $n \times n$ *Vandermonde matrix* (denoted by $V(\mathbf{x})$). Vandermonde-like structure can be defined in terms of the operator $A \to D^{-1}(\mathbf{t})A - AZ^T$, for a fixed vector $\mathbf{t}$ (or in terms of some similar linear operators [3], [9]): For a field $\mathbf{F}$ and for a vector $\mathbf{t} = (t_i)$, $t_i \neq 0$, $i = 1,\dots,n-1$, we call a matrix $A \in \mathbf{F}^{n\times n}$ a *Vandermonde-like* matrix if

$$D^{-1}(\mathbf{t})A - AZ^T = GH^T; \ G, H \in \mathbf{F}^{n\times r}, \tag{7.1}$$

$r = O(1)$. (Clearly, $r = 1$ for $V(\mathbf{t})$.) Then the pair of matrices (G, H^T) is a $(D^{-1}(\mathbf{t}), Z^T)$-*generator* (or *scaling/displacement generator*) of length r for A, and we have $A = D(\mathbf{t})\sum_{m=1}^r D(\mathbf{g}_m)V(\mathbf{t})L^T(\mathbf{h}_m)$ for $\mathbf{g}_m$, $\mathbf{h}_m$ defined as in Lemma 2.1 and for $L(\mathbf{v})$ defined as in Lemma 6.2. The minimum r in all such representations of A is called the $(D^{-1}(\mathbf{t}), Z^T)$-*rank* of A.

Our study of Cauchy-like matrices in sections 2-5 and, in particular, Theorems 3.1, 4.1, 5.1, Corollaries 4.1, 4.2, Remark 3.1, Algorithm 5.1 and the complexity bound (1.3) can be easily extended to the Vandermonde-like case. On the other hand, the latter bound can be improved to (1.5) for all cited computations with both Cauchy-like and Vandermonde-like input matrices. This is achieved by means of general transformations proposed in [18], which at the cost $V_{M_v}(n)$ reduce such Cauchy-like and Vandermonde-like computations to ones with Toeplitz-like (or, alternatively, Hankel-like) matrices. In particular, for a matrix A of (7.1), the matrix $\overline{A} = V^T(\mathbf{t}^{-1})A$ (where $\mathbf{t}^{-1} = (t_i^{-1})$) has F_--rank r (cf. [3], Proposition 2.12 on p. 193) and shares with the above matrix A its rank and null space (because $V^T(\mathbf{t}^{-1})$ is a nonsingular matrix). The rank and the null space of $\overline{A}$ can be computed based on Algorithm 6.1 at the randomized cost bounded by (1.5). The transition from A to $\overline{A}$ costs $O(V_{M_v(n)})$. On the other hand, $s.g._{\cdot r}(AF^{-1})$ is immediately recovered from (7.1) , where F is the $n \times n$ matrix of discrete Fourier transform [10].

References

1. R.R. Bitmead, B.D.O. Anderson, Asymptotically Fast Solution of Toeplitz and Related Systems of Linear Equations, *Linear Algebra Appl.*, **34**, 103-116, 1980.

2. D. Bini, V. Y. Pan, Improved Parallel Computations with Toeplitz-like and Hankel-like Matrices, *Linear Algebra Appl.*, **188**, **189**, 3-29, 1993.

3. D. Bini, V.Y. Pan, *Polynomial and Matrix Computations, Volume 1: Fundamental Algorithms*, Birkhäuser, Boston, 1994.

4. A. L. Cauchy, Mémorie sur les Fonctions Alternées et sur les Somme Alternées, *Exercises d' Analyse et de Phys. Math.*, **II**, 151-159, 1841.

5. R.A. Demillo, R.J. Lipton, A Probabilistic Remark on Algebraic Program Testing, *Information Process. Letters*, **7**, **4**, 193-195, 1978.

6. N. Gastinel, Inversion d'une Matrice Generalisant la Matrice de Hilbert, *Chiffres* , **3**, 149-152, 1960.
7. A. Gerasoulis, A Fast Algorithm for the Multiplication of Generalized Hilbert Matrices with Vectors, *Math. Comp.*, **50, 181**, 179-188, 1987.
8. G.H. Golub, C.F. Van Loan, *Matrix Computations*, Johns Hopkins Univ. Press, Baltimore, Maryland, 1996 (third edition).
9. I. Gohberg, V. Olshevsky, Complexity of Multiplication with Vectors for Structured Matrices, *Linear Algebra Appl.*, **202**, 163-192, 1994.
10. G. Heinig, Inversion of Generalized Cauchy Matrices and the Other Classes of Structured Matrices, *Linear Algebra for Signal Processing, IMA Volume in Math. and Its Applications*, **69**, 95-114, Springer, 1995.
11. E. Kaltofen, Analysis of Coppersmith's Block Wiedemann Algorithm for the Parallel Solution of Sparse Linear Systems, *Mathematics of Computation*, **64, 210**, 777-806, 1995.
12. T. Kailath, S.Y. Kung, M. Morf, Displacement Ranks of Matrices and Linear Equations, *J.Math. Anal. Appl.*, **68, 2**, 395-407, 1979.
13. E. Kaltofen, B. D. Saunders, On Wiedemann's Method for Solving Sparse Linear Systems, *Proc. AAECC-5, Lecture Notes in Computer Science*, **536**, 29-38, Springer, Berlin, 1991.
14. M. Morf, Fast Algorithms for Multivariable Systems, Ph.D. Thesis, *Stanford University*, Stanford, California, 1974.
15. M. Morf, Doubling Algorithms for Toeplitz and Related Equations, *Proc. IEEE Intern. Conf. on ASSP*, 954-959, IEEE Comp. Soc. Press, 1980.
16. V. Olshevsky, V. Y. Pan, A Unified Superfast Algorithm for Boundary Rational Tangential Interpolation Problem and for Inversion and Factorization of Dense Structured Matrices, *Proc. 39th Ann. Symp. Foundations of Computer Science*, IEEE Computer Society Press, 192-201, 1998.
17. V. Olshevsky, M. A. Shokrollahi, A Displacement Approach to Efficient Decoding of Algebraic-Geometric Codes, *Proc. 31st Ann. Symp. on Theory of Computing*, ACM Press, New York, 1999.
18. V.Y. Pan, On Computations with Dense Structured Matrices, *Math. of Computation*, **55, 191**, 179-190, 1990.
19. V.Y. Pan, Parametrization of Newton's Iteration for Computations with Structured Matrices and Applications, *Computers and Mathematices (with Applications)*, **24, 3**, 61-75, 1992.
20. V. Y. Pan, M. AbuTabanjeh, Z. Chen, E. Landowne, A. Sadikou, New Transformations of Cauchy Matrices and Trummer's Problem, *Computer and Math. (with Applics.)*, **35, 12**, 1-5, 1998.
21. V. Y. Pan, M. Abu Tabanjeh, Z. Chen, S. Providence, A. Sadikou, Transformations of Cauchy Matrices for Trummer's Problem and a Cauchy-like Linear Solver, *Proc. of 5th Annual International Symposium on Solving Irregularly Structured Problems in Parallel (Irregular98)*, (A. Ferreira, J. Rolim, H. Simon, S.-H. Teng Editors), *Lecture Notes in Computer Science*, **1457**, 274-284, Springer, 1998.
22. V. Y. Pan, A. Zheng, Fast Cauchy-like and Singular Toeplitz-like Matrix Computations, MSRI Preprint No. 1999-013, *Math. Science Research Institute, Berkeley, California*, 1999.
23. M. A. Shokrollahi, H. Wasserman. Decoding Algebraic-Geometric Codes Beyond the Error-Correction Bound, *Proc. 30th Annual Symp. on Theory of Computing*, 241-248, ACM Press, New York, 1998.

24. V. Strassen, Gaussian Elimination Is Not Optimal, *Numer. Math.*, **13**, 354-356, 1969.
25. M. Sudan, Decoding of Reed-Solomon Codes Beyond the Error-Correction Bound, *J. of Complexity*, **13**, 180-193, 1997.

From Modeling to Simulation with Symbolic Computation:
An Application to Design and Performance Analysis of Complex Optical Devices

Yves A. Papegay*

SAGA Team – INRIA, BP 93, F-06902 SOPHIA ANTIPOLIS CEDEX

Abstract. The design and performance analysis of a complex optical instrument, such as an interferometer, leads to the study of a very large model: a set of equations that relate the parameters of the instrument. Problems are then to compute performances with respect to some fixed parameters or to find optimal values of parameters with respect to some required performances. Due to complexity of the models involved, there is no cpmletely automatic method to solve these problems. However, Computer Algebra, through the CIRCE package presented in this paper, can be an invaluable tool to define and store models, to express some parameters or performances as functions of other parameters, and then to generate dedicated numerical simulation.

1 Introduction

Computer algebra systems basically allow formula manipulation, equations solving, and numerical code generation. Hence, they should be naturally helpful tools for any modeling–simulation process. But they are not widely used for that purpose. To correct this situation, we identified, designed and implemented in the CIRCE library some necessary functionnalities and communication skills.

MAPLE[1], enhanced with the CIRCE library provides a computational environnement for defining, storing, retrieving, refining and specializing mathematical models and to generate efficent and dedicated numerical simulators of these models. It has been successfully used during the design and performance analysis stages of complex optical devices in the French aerospace industry, in the framework of the Infrared Atmospheric Sounding Interferometer[2] project.

In this paper, we define precisely what we mean by modeling–simulation process, what are the functionnalities of the CIRCE environment and how it works.

---

* http://www.inria.fr/saga/papegay – Yves.Papegay@inria.fr

2   The Modeling-Simulation Process

Mathematical modeling followed by numerical simulation is a process of crucial importance to study the performances of optical devices in the aerospace industry. During the design stage of such optical instruments, this process is used a lot of time to ensure consistency between functional requirements and definition of the instrument.

A model is a mathematical description of the instrument and of the physical laws which govern its behaviour. It consists of a set of variables and a set of equations relating those variables.

Once a model is given, it is possible to identify some of its variables as known input parameters. A simulation consists in solving the equations of the model to compute the other variables in term of the input parameters. From a set of numerical input data, it produces numerical results.

2.1   About Modeling

There is two kind of basic modeling operations: to choose a parameter for decribing some feature of the instrument or to instantiate a relation describing a physical (or a mathematical) law by the corresponding parameters.

Writing a physical model of an optical device is a lot of work, growing with the complexity of the device. But it amounts to a sequence of basic modeling operations by dividing the instrument in several sub-systems (lenses, sensors, etc ...), separating the different behaviours (geometrical, electrical, thermical, etc ...), and gradually refining the model.

Computations involved in writing a physical model are manipulations on analytical expressions like storage and retrieval of the basic formulas in a database, substitutions and simplifications. Properties like validity domains or physical meaning are naturally attached to the parameters. That results in constraints or assumptions attached to the equations.

2.2   About Simulation

Simulation is a two-stories process. Solving the equations of the model for a given set of unknown variables – representing the output parameters – function of the input parameters produces a computational algorithm. Applying this algorithm to a set of numerical data leads to a numerical (eventually graphical) result.

Different computational algorithm can be produced by simulation, from the same model, depending on the choice of the input parameters: in a performance analysis problem, inputs are the characteristics of the instrument, and in a sizing problem inputs are fixed limits for performances.

Automatic resolution of models is not an easy problem: equations should be selected, ordered and solved, either anatycally, or through a delayed call to a numerical solving method.

Implementation of the computational algorithm into a programming language well suited for efficient numerical computation (Fortran or C for example) is a lot of work if not done automatically.

3 Using circe

3.1 At the Modeling Stage

A CIRCE model is a collection of three MAPLE objects for relations, constants, and variable parameters. Physical units are attached to parameters, as well as comments if needed.

Several tools for creating a model from scratch, by retrieving a model in a library, by merging several models or by replacing part of a model by a sub-model are provided. When creating a model, CIRCE concerns mainly with management of relations and parameters: checking that relations are expressed in terms of declared parameters, checking the consistency of the physical units of the parameters on both side of the relations, avoiding ambiguous uses of names when merging or refining models, ...

A module for attaching numerical domains to parameters, validity domains to the relations and checking the consistency of the relations is currently being implemented.

3.2 At the Simulation Stage

CIRCE computes an hypergraph describing the dependencies of the parameters of the model through its relations: vertices are subset of variables and there is an oriented edge between two vertices if it is possible to express all the variables of the second vertex in term of the variables of the first vertex by using (solving) equations of the model. Such an expression can be analytical or involve a numerical method.

Algorithms and heuristics have been implemented to solve the following crucial problems:

1. given a set of input variables and a set of output variables, is it possible to express the output variables in terms of the input variables ?
2. given a set of input variables and a set of output variables such as it is possible to express the output variables in terms of the input variables, what is their expressions ?
3. given a set of input variables and a set of output variables such as it is not possible to express the output variables in terms of the input variables, find an extended set of input variables such as it is possible to express the output variables in terms of the variables of the new set.

Once the expression is computed of the output parameters in terms of the input parameters, CIRCE may produce the corresponding C or Fortran code, possibly linked with routines of numerical libraries like NAG or IMSL.

4 Practical Experiments

A significant example of the use of CIRCE is a study of the signal-to-noise ratio in an infrared-operating optical instrument: A model has been built by merging three models specifying respectively fundamental relations on radiometric performances, intensity of the collected signal and noises depending on the detection device.

For a given set of data defining the geometry of the instrument (size of the pupil, sattelite altitude, ground pixel size, etc ...) a numerical simulator has been generated in PV-WAVE[1] as well as another simulator computing the size of the pupil of the interferometer against an established performance in term of signal-to-noise ratio.

5 Conclusion

With the help of CIRCE, MAPLE offers to the engineers and researchers a toolbox to develop, manipulate and analyse physical models and to generate automatically efficient numerical simulators.

This toolbox is quite different from other packages already developped for modelling and simulation: its purpose is not to provide specific models for a specific area of physics but to help building models in a general way, to use the power of computer algebra to automatically express output parameters in term of input parameters, and to take benefit of the code generation features for better performances and to save huge amount of human work.

References

1. Char, B.W. Geddes, K.O. Gonnet, G.H. Monagan, M.B. and Watt, S.M.: MAPLE Reference Manual. WATCOM Publications Limited, Waterloo, Ontario, 5th edition, 1988.
2. Javelle, P. and Cayla, F.: IASI Instrument Overview. Proc. 5th International Workshop on Atmospheric Science from Space Using Fourier Transform Spectrometry, Tokyo, 1994.

---

[1] a Visual Data Analysis Software based on the IMSL library

A Symbolic Numeric Environment for Analyzing Measurement Data in Multi-Model Settings (Extended Abstract)

Christoph Richard[1] and Andreas Weber[2]*

[1] Institut für Theoretische Physik, Universität Tübingen, 72076 Tübingen, Germany
christoph.richard@uni-tuebingen.de

[2] Arbeitsbereich Symbolisches Rechnen, Universität Tübingen, 72076 Tübingen, Germany
weber@informatik.uni-tuebingen.de
http://www-sr.informatik.uni-tuebingen.de/

Abstract. We have built a complete system which allows the analysis of measurement data arising from scientific experiments. Within the system, it is possible to fit parameter-dependent curves to given data points numerically in order to obtain estimates of experimental quantities. The system provides moreover a convenient tool to test different theoretical models against a given experiment: We use the computer algebra system Maple not only as a graphical interface to visualize the data but mainly as a symbolic calculator to investigate and to implement solutions of the underlying theory. The system has been used successfully in a project with researchers from the department of chemistry.

1 Introduction

An important issue in the daily work of a scientist is the analysis of measurement data of an experiment. Very often mathematical models in form of parametric functions are available that describe the outcome of an "ideal" experiment. The task is then to determine the "correct" model and to estimate parameter values from the given data.

The least square method invented by Gauß [4] is a major tool for (linear) curve fitting and is available in many software systems. Many experiments, however, cannot be described using linear functions, and there are indeed generalizations of the method — non-linear least-square fit algorithms — which work for a much more general setting. Although much less common than algorithms for the Gaussian least square method, several implementations of non-linear least-square fit algorithms are available. E. g., the so called "non-linear tool-box" of the Matlab system [3] contains an implementation of the Levenberg-Marquardt algorithm for non-linear least-square fit. The functions whose parameters have to be estimated by the non-linear least-square algorithm have to be given as Matlab programs. Using the Matlab system

---
* Supported by *Deutsche Forschungsgemeinschaft* under grant Ku 966/6-1.

alone will leave some tedious work to the user, since the functions which are supposed to describe the experiment have to be coded as Matlab functions – for each of the competing models.

Using a combination of symbolic and numeric systems we have built an environment that allows a comparatively easy numerical analysis of measurement data arising from scientific experiments with respect to various mathematical models. The system will have its main use in situations where different theoretic descriptions are available which should be tested against the available empiric data, such that the best model for a given experiment can be picked without much effort. The symbolic part of our system is currently implemented on top of the computer algebra system Maple [1], the numeric part on top of a library based on algorithms described in [4].

2   Building Blocks of the System

All steps of the data analysis are done within the Maple graphical user interface environment. A Maple worksheet has been designed for the visualization and manipulation of data. Typing one-line commands, the user can perform all steps of data analysis such as reading data from experiment, visualizing data curves, selecting data points for numerical data fitting, perform fits, comparing numerical and experimental results. The numerical data analysis is done by fitting parameter-dependent functions, which are suggested from theory, against the given data curves. These functions are commonly characterized by (sets of) ordinary differential equations for the quantity of measurement. The Maple environment is well suited to clarify the theoretical description since Maple has a number of specialized tools which allow an extensive analysis of such functions.

The example discussed in Sec. 3 shows prototypically such a multi-step formulation:

- A chemical reaction can be described by a differential equation.
- A solution for the differential equation has to be found and verified.
- Simpler models for specialized cases can be developed.
- The chemical reaction cannot be observed directly, but only some resulting effect.
  The resulting effect can be described by some other mathematical means (e. g. as the integral of some simpler effect).
- The computer algebra system can be used to obtain solutions to tasks like symbolic integration, finding symbolic solutions for differential equations and simplifying results for the final parameter dependent function.

Having obtained a parameter dependent function which is supposed to describe the process under consideration correctly, this function can be tested against the experimental data using the Levenberg-Marquardt algorithm for non-linear least-square fit [4]. In order to perform the numerical analysis with appropriate speed, this algorithm is implemented as an external C-routine which is called from the data-worksheet. The routine requires a C-function as one of its arguments, which returns values for the function to be fitted and its Jacobian. Thus we have to provide the C-Code of the function and its Jacobian and compile it together with a driver routine. The code-generation is done by a special Maple-worksheet which guides the user through the necessary tasks step by step. The code generated by Maple is highly optimized with respect to common subexpression elimination — the methods implemented in Maple can compete with the ones used by the best optimizing compilers.

3   Example: An Antigen-Antibody-Reaction

Our system was used to analyze a special type of antigen-antibody reaction. This example arose from a collaboration with researchers from the department of chemistry, when we tried to analyze the setting giving in [2]. The reaction between antigen and antibody is an equilibrium reaction. The change of concentration during the reaction is described by the following differential equation (cf. [2, p. 23 eqn.(18)]):

$$\frac{\partial c_{AgAk}(t)}{\partial t} = k_{ass}(c_{0,Ak} - c_{AgAk}(t))(c_{0,Ag} - c_{AgAk}(t)) - k_{diss}c_{AgAk}(t) \quad (1)$$

with positive constants
$\quad\quad k_{ass}$:   association rate,
$\quad\quad k_{diss}$:   dissociation rate,
$\quad\quad c_{AgAk}$: concentration of connected antibody binding points,
$\quad\quad c_{0,Ag}$: starting concentration of antigen,
$\quad\quad c_{0,Ak}$: starting concentration of antibody.
We are mainly interested in estimates of the reaction constants k_{ass} and k_{diss}. For a complete determination, it is necessary to analyze the reaction away from its stationary state. It is therefore useful to implement nonlinear techniques for parameter estimation.

Solution of the differential equation. We use the computer algebra system Maple to analyze and to solve the given differential equation. Maple contains specialized tools for the analysis of ordinary differential equations (ODE's). Given an ODE, the `odeadvisor` command classifies it according to standard text books and displays a help page including related information for solving it. Using these symbolic tools of Maple, it was possible to find an explicit solution of the ODE without consulting textbooks on differential equations.

Form of the signal curve. As explained in [2], the concentration c_{AgAk} of connected antibody binding points cannot be observed directly, but only the one of a derivate, $c_{Ak,bind}$. Moreover, only the cumulative concentration is measured by the experiment. However, we know that

$$c_{Ak,bind}(t) = \frac{1}{2}\left(c_{0,Ak} - \frac{c_{AgAk}(t)^2}{c_{0,Ak}}\right), \qquad (2)$$

$$\text{signal} = \text{off} + F \int c_{Ak,bind}(t)\, dt \quad, \qquad (3)$$

off and F being (unknown) scaling constants of the experimental setup, cf. [2]. The symbolic expression for $c_{AgAk}(t)^2$, which was found by explicitly solving the corresponding ODE, can be integrated symbolically by Maple. Thus we can derive a closed expression for the signal curve. Since this expressions depends on the parameters we are interested in, a least square fit of signal to the empiric measurement data will provide estimates for the parameters of interest.

A limiting case: the integrated first order time law. Although it is possible to analyze the antigen-antibody reaction using the full solution, we also considered a limiting case in order to have a comparison between the most general description and a simpler one, which had been considered previously, cf. [2]. This limiting case refers to experiments where the antibody concentration is much lower than the concentration of antigen. In this case, the reaction can be described by the differential equation

$$\frac{\partial c_{AgAk}(t)}{\partial t} = k_{ass}c_{0,Ag}(c_{0,Ak} - c_{AgAk}(t)) - k_{diss}c_{AgAk}(t). \qquad (4)$$

This ODE can be solved quite easily in symbolic form by Maple and also the integration which is required for the signal curve (cf. equation 3) could be done symbolically.

Results. In the figure below the measurement data of one of the experiments described in [2] are given, together with the theoretic signal curves of the general law and the law for the limiting case, whose parameters have been fitted by the Levenberg-Marquardt algorithm. Both functions can be fitted quite well, and their graphs almost coincide. The parameter estimates we got are $k_{ass} = 5.02 \cdot 10^6$ and $k_{diss} = 0.00034$.

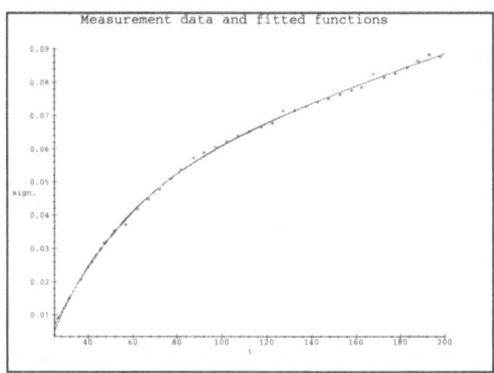

Acknowledgement. We are grateful for the possibility to collaborate with Alexander Jung from the department of chemistry.

References

1. CHAR, B. W., GEDDES, K. O., GONNET, G. H., BENTON, L. L., MONAGAN, M. B., AND WATT, S. M. *Maple V Language Reference Manual.* Springer-Verlag, New York, 1991.
2. JUNG, A. Markierungsfreie Untersuchung der Kinetik von Antigen-Antikörper-Wechselwirkungen in homogener Phase. Diplomarbeit, Universität Tübingen, 1998.
3. MATHWORKS INC. Matlab 5, 1997. `http://www.mathworks.com/products/matlab/`.
4. PRESS, W. H., TEUKOLSKY, S. A., VETTERLING, W. T., AND FLANNERY, B. P. *Numerical Recipes in C: The Art of Scientific Computing*, second ed. Cambridge University Press, 1992.

Geometric Interpretation of Strong Inconsistency in Knowledge Based Systems*

E. Roanes-Lozano[1], E. Roanes-Macías[1], L. M. Laita[2]

[1] Universidad Complutense de Madrid, Dept. Algebra, Edificio "Almudena", c/ Rector Royo Villanova s/n, 28040-Madrid, Spain
[2] Universidad Politécnica de Madrid, Dept. Artificial Intelligence, Campus de Montegancedo, Boadilla del Monte, 28660-Madrid, Spain

Abstract. This paper distinguishes between two different kinds of inconsistency of rule-based Knowledge Based Systems (KBSs) constructed on multi-valued logics, which we have denoted "weak inconsistency" and "strong inconsistency", respectively. While "weak inconsistency" is the inconsistency studied in the verification related references listed at the end of the article, "strong inconsistency" is introduced in this paper. "Strong inconsistency" is a particular case of "weak inconsistency". An interesting interpretation in terms of polynomial ideals and (discrete) algebraic varieties is provided. Finally, an implementation in the Computer Algebra System (CAS) Maple is included. This implementation provides both a visualization of "strong inconsistency" and symbolic results (directly handling truth tables).

Keywords. *Verification. KBSs. Multivalued Logics. Algebraic Varieties. Visualization.*

1 Introduction

The straightforward way to deal with propositional logic is based on directly handling truth tables [16]. But the most exciting approach (from our point of view) relates Logic and Algebra and usually makes use of Gröbner Bases (GB) to deal with effective calculi. The latter was introduced in [8] and [7] for bivalued logics (a similar approach, not using GB, is presented in [10]). It was extended to multivalued logics in [2] and [5], revisited in [14] and reorganized using residue class rings and interpretations borrowed from Algebraic Geometry (using algebraic varieties) in [17]. Considering a residue class ring has the advantage of providing not only effective methods but also an algebraic model.

Once this model has been provided, an obvious extension is to address KBS consistency [15,11] (a state of the art in KBS verification can be found in [9]). We have also applied this approach to study possibly conflicting signaling and switch positions in railway interlocking systems [18] and to study

---

* Partially supported by projects DGES PB96-0098-C04-03 and DGES PB96-0098-C04-01 (Spain).

the consistency of the knowledge contained in a particular set of Medical Appropriateness Criteria (for coronary artery surgery), including uncertainty and provided in table format [12,13].

This model is also used in this article to distinguish between two different kinds of KBS inconsistency (that we have denoted "weak" and "strong" inconsistency, respectively).

2   Basic Notions

In this section, we briefly summarize the KBS theory of knowledge extraction and verification used in this paper [17,14]. An introductory book to the logics used is [19].

2.1   Introductory Note About Multi-Valued Propositional Logics

Let us consider a p-valued propositional logic $(\mathcal{C}, F_1, ..., F_n)$, where $\mathcal{C}$ is the set of propositions and $F_1, ..., F_n$ are the logical connectives (binary or unary). If the propositional variables are $X_1, X_2, ..., X_m$, then $\mathcal{C}$ is the set of well-constructed formulas using $F_1, ..., F_n$ and $X_1, X_2, ..., X_m$.

The connectives F_i are usually defined by a truth table or functionally (for instance: maximum), using valuations, i.e., a mapping is given as follows

$$\tilde{F}_i : \{0, 1, ..., p-1\}^{\mathrm{arity}(F_i)} \to \{0, 1, ..., p-1\}$$

together with the definitions below.

Definition 1. A valuation of the propositional variables is a mapping

$$v : \{X_1, X_2, ..., X_m\} \to \mathbb{Z}_p \ .$$

Definition 2. For each valuation of the propositional variables, v, a valuation, v^*, of the formulas is obtained. This mapping $v^* : \mathcal{C} \to \mathbb{Z}_p$ is the natural extension of v and can be defined recursively as follows: *let $Q \in \mathcal{C}$*

$$v^*(Q) = \begin{cases} v(Q) & , & \text{if } Q \in \{X_1, X_2, ..., X_m\} \\ \tilde{F}_i(v^*(Q')) & , & \text{if } F_i \text{ is unary and } Q = F_i(Q') \\ \tilde{F}_i(v^*(Q'), v^*(Q'')) & , \text{if } F_i \text{ is binary and } Q = F_i(Q', Q'') \end{cases}$$

As the values of all valuations determine a propositional formula, having constructed $\mathcal{C}$, a logical connective F_i can be identified with a function $F_i : \mathcal{C}^{\mathrm{arity}(F_i)} \to \mathcal{C}$. In this paper, such F_i are called *"logical functions"*.

2.2   Introductory Note About KBSs

Definition 3. A rule-based *Knowledge Based System* or *Expert System* (denoted *KBS*) is a set of "rules", "facts" and "integrity constraints".

Definition 4. A KBS *rule* is an implication between a conjunction of propositional variables $X[i]$ and a disjunction of propositional variables, such

$$\circ X[1] \wedge \circ X[2] \wedge ... \circ X[n] \rightarrow \bullet(\circ X[n+1] \vee .... \vee \circ X[s]) \ .$$

Under a Boolean logic, the symbols "$\circ$" can be replaced by the symbol $\neg$ or no symbol at all ($\neg X$ means "not-X").

Under a three-valued logic, the symbols "$\circ$" can be replaced by symbols $\Box$, $\Diamond$, $\neg$, a combination of these symbols (for instance $\Diamond \neg X$) or no symbol at all. $\Box X$ means "it is necessary that X holds", X means "X holds", $\Diamond X$ means "it is possible that X holds". Observe that under a p-valued logic where $p > 3$, there are more of these unary connectives.

The symbol "$\bullet$" refers to the degree of certainty of the whole rule or the certainty of the conclusions and is to be replaced similarly (only in the multi-valued case).

Definition 5. A *literal* is a variable preceded or not by the symbol $\neg$ (if we are in bivalued logic) or by $\neg$, $\Diamond$, L... or by a combination of these symbols (in the multi-valued case).

Definition 6. A *potential fact* in a set of rules is any literal, which stands in the antecedent of some rule(s) in the set but not in the consequent of any rule in the set.

Definition 7. Any potential facts that are stated (in each case) will be called *facts*.

Definition 8. The experts sometimes add that, X and Y, for example, cannot occur simultaneously. This is termed an *integrity constraint* (IC). Then:

– if the logic is Boolean: the negation of the formula concerned: $\neg(X \wedge Y)$
– if the logic is multi-valued: a strong negation of the formula, like: $\Box \neg(X \wedge Y)$

(denoted NIC) is added to the KBS as new information.

Definition 9. A rule is *fired* if all the literals in the antecedent are facts (firing corresponds to the extraction of tautological consequences).

Definition 10. If a literal is in the consequent of one rule and is a part of the antecedent of another rule and the first rule can be fired, then we will say that this literal is a *derived fact*.

Definition 11. A rule is also *fired* if all the literals in the antecedent are facts or derived facts (firing corresponds to the extraction of tautological consequences).

Example 12. Let us take a very simple example of KBS (based on Boolean logic). For the sake of simplicity, the consequents consist of only one element, despite the fact that they are generally disjunctions of elements.

Rule 1. $A \wedge \neg B \to C$
Rule 2. $C \to D$
Rule 3. $D \to \neg E$
Rule 4. $F \to E$

Letters like A, or letters preceded by $\neg$, such as $\neg B$, are examples of literals. The potential facts are A, $\neg B$ and F. As mentioned above, "fact" is any potential fact, which it is of interest to single out.

If A and $\neg B$ are the facts, then by firing Rule 1, C is obtained. C appears in the antecedent of Rule 2, so the literal C is a derived fact and Rule 2 can be fired. Then D is also a derived fact, and Rule 3 can also be fired.

An integrity constraint (denoted IC) is, for example, $A \wedge \neg E$. Thus we have new information to be added to the KBS, the NIC: $\neg(A \wedge \neg E)$.

2.3   Tautological Consequence. Contradictory Domains

From now onwards, let $0, \mu$ be the values assigned to "false" and "true", respectively (in the multi-valued case).

Definition 13. A propositional formula A_0 is a *tautological consequence* of the propositional formulae $A_1, A_2, ..., A_m$, denoted $\{A_1, A_2, ..., A_m\} \models A_0$, iff for any truth-valuation v, such that $v(A_1) = v(A_2) = ... = v(A_m) = \mu$, then $v(A_0) = \mu$.

Definition 14. In this context, $\{A_1, A_2, ..., A_m\}$ is called a *contradictory domain* iff $\{A_1, A_2, ..., A_m\} \models A$, where A is any formula of the language in which $A_1, A_2, ..., A_m$ are expressed.

The name *contradictory domain* comes from the fact that, if all formulae follow from $\{A_1, A_2, ..., A_m\}$, contradictory formulae, in particular, follow. This will be the case for:

- A formula that can only take the truth value "false", such as $P \wedge \neg P$ in Boolean logic.
- A formula that can only take the truth value "false", such as $\Box P \wedge \Box \neg P$ in multi-valued logic.
- A formula that can never take the truth value "true", such as $P \wedge \neg P$ in multi-valued logic (observe that not only $\Box P \wedge \Box \neg P \models P \wedge \neg P$ but also $P \wedge \neg P \models \Box P \wedge \Box \neg P$).

Example 15. Taking the same example as before. Let us consider the KBS formed by rules 1, 2, 3 and 4 and the facts A, $\neg B$ and F. The firing of the rules would lead to the logical contradiction $E \wedge \neg E$. Therefore, this is a contradictory domain.

Example 16. Suppose now that the formula NIC is added in a KBS formed only by the rules 1, 2 and 3. A and $\neg B$ are considered as facts. In this case, the firing of the rules gives the IC, which contradicts the NIC. This too would be a contradictory domain.

3 Strong and Weak Inconsistency (Multi-Valued Case)

In the multivalued case, it could happened that not only all formulae follow from the set of formulae $\{A_1, A_2, ..., A_m\}$, but even that formula $A_1 \wedge A_2 \wedge ... \wedge A_m$ is itself always false. Therefore, from here onwards, we shall make the following distinction in the multivalued case:

Definition 17. If $A_1 \wedge A_2 \wedge ... \wedge A_m$ can take only the truth value "false", we shall say that there is *strong inconsistency*. If $\{A_1, A_2,...,A_m\}$ is a contradictory domain, we shall say that there is *weak inconsistency*.

Proposition 18. *Independently of the number of truth values (p) of the logic:*

$$\text{strong inconsistency} \Rightarrow \text{weak inconsistency.}$$

Proof. $\{A_1, A_2,...,A_m\} \models A_1 \wedge A_2 \wedge ... \wedge A_m$, that is a contradictory formula (by hypotheses). □

Proposition 19. *If the logic is Boolean:*

$$\text{weak inconsistency} \Rightarrow \text{strong inconsistency.}$$

(this result is not true if the logic is multi-valued, as we shall see from the examples given in section 5).

Proof. If there is weak inconsistency in $\{A_1, A_2,...,A_m\}$, for any formula A: $\{A_1, A_2,...,A_m\} \models A$. In particular $\{A_1, A_2,...,A_m\} \models contradiction$, and therefore $A_1 \wedge A_2 \wedge ... \wedge A_m \to contradiction$, so $A_1 \wedge A_2 \wedge ... \wedge A_m$ must take only the truth value "false". □

Example 20. Let us take a simple example of a KBS, similar to the KBS considered in Example 15, but based on Lukasiewicz's three-valued logic:

Rule 1. $A \wedge \neg B \to C$
Rule 2. $C \to D$
Rule 3. $D \to \neg E$
Rule 4. $F \to E$

Let us consider the KBS formed by rules 1, 2, 3 and 4 and facts A, $\neg B$ and F. The firing of the rules would lead to $E \wedge \neg E$, which can never be true. Therefore there is weak inconsistency.

There is no strong inconsistency (the conjunction of rules and facts can take other truth values rather than "false"). If, e.g., A, B, C, D, E and F take the truth value "indeterminate", the conjunction of rules and facts takes the truth value "true" (in Kleene's logic: if A, B, C, D, E and F take the truth value "undecided", this conjunction takes the truth value "undecided").

Example 21. Consider now the KBS based on Lukasiewicz's three-valued logic:

Rule 1. $A \rightarrow \Box B$
Rule 2. $B \rightarrow \Box C$
Rule 3. $C \rightarrow \neg A$

Let us consider the KBS formed by rules 1, 2 and 3 and fact $\Box A$. The firing of the rules would lead to $\Box A \wedge \neg A$, which can never be true. Therefore there is weak inconsistency.

In this case there is also strong inconsistency, as

$$\Box A \wedge (A \rightarrow \Box B) \wedge (B \rightarrow \Box C) \wedge (C \rightarrow \neg A)$$

can only take the truth value "false".

4   The Polynomial Model. Interpretation of Inconsistency

From now onwards, we shall assume that p is prime. The case of multi-valued logics with a non-prime number of truth values r can also be addressed by embedding into a p-valued logic, where p is the least prime greater than r. The reason for doing this is that the base field of the corresponding polynomial ring (to be described below) would be $\mathbb{Z}_r$, and for r not prime it is not even an integral domain. The following result, which we do not prove [3,2,5] is the key to this embedding.

A p-valued propositional logic that has the same language as the given r-valued propositional logic is constructed (let $r-1$ and $p-1$ be the truth values corresponding to "true" in the r-valued and p-valued logics, respectively). The truth table of each connective c_j in the p-valued propositional logic is given by the function

$$H_j : \mathbb{Z}_p^{s_j} \longrightarrow \mathbb{Z}_p$$

$$H_j(u_1, ..., u_{s_j}) = \delta(H_j'(\min(u_1, r-1), ..., \min(u_{s_j}, r-1)))$$

where $(u_1, ..., u_{s_j}) \in \mathbb{Z}_p^{s_j}$, H_j' is the truth table of the connective c_j in the r-valued propositional logic and δ is the bijective function

$$\delta : \{0, 1, ..., r-2, r-1\} \rightarrow \{0, 1, ..., r-2, p-1\}$$

defined as follows[1]

$$\delta(u_i) = \begin{cases} u_i & \text{, if } u_i \neq r-1 \\ p-1 & \text{, if } u_i = r-1 \end{cases}$$

Then, $\{A_1, A_2, ..., A_m\} \models A_0$ in the r-valued logic iff $\{A_1, A_2, ..., A_m\} \models A_0$ in the p-valued one, and, consequently, a propositional formula in the r-valued logic is a tautology if and only if it is a tautology in the p-valued one[2].

4.1   Translation of Logical Formulae into Polynomials

As p is assumed to be prime, $\mathbb{Z}_p$ is a field. Let $x_1, x_2, ..., x_m$ be polynomial variables, and let us consider the residue class ring

$$\mathcal{A} = \mathbb{Z}_p[x_1, x_2, ..., x_m]/I \quad ; \quad I = <x_1^p - x_1, x_2^p - x_2, ..., x_m^p - x_m > .$$

This ring provides a model for $\mathcal{C}$, with the homomorphism

$$\varphi : (\mathcal{C}, \vee, \wedge, \neg) \longrightarrow (\mathcal{A}, f_\vee, f_\wedge, f_\neg)$$

defined as follows

$$\varphi(X_i) = x_i \ ; \ i = 1, 2, ..., m$$
$$\varphi(contradiction) = 0$$

and for any logical function F_i

$$\varphi(F_i(Q, R)) = f_i(q, r) \ , \ \text{if } F_i \text{ is binary}$$
$$\varphi(F_i(Q)) = f_i(q) \ , \ \text{if } F_i \text{ is unary} \ .$$

The $f's$ are adjusted so that the image of f and the respective F are equal.

Let F be a binary connective, $\varphi(F(Q, R)) = f(q, r)$. For any valuation of formulas v^*, if $v^*(Q) = h$ and $v^*(R) = j$, then $v^*(F(Q, R)) = f(h, j)$. The ordered pair (h, j) can be identified with a point Ω of the affine space $\mathbb{Z}_p^2$.

Let F be a unary connective, $\varphi(F(Q)) = f(q)$. For any valuation of formulas v^*, if $v^*(Q) = j$, then $v^*(F(Q)) = f(j)$. Number j can be identified with a point Ω of the affine space $\mathbb{Z}_p$.

The information contained in the KBS is translated into polynomials. In the Boolean case, a polynomial translation of the connectives is

$$f_\neg(q) = 1 - q + I$$
$$f_\vee(q, r) = q + r + qr + I$$
$$f_\wedge(q, r) = qr + I$$
$$f_\rightarrow(q, r) = 1 + q(1 + r) + I$$

---

[1] In [3], as 0 and 1 are the truth values corresponding to "false" and "true", respectively, being 2, 3,..., $r-1$ the other truth values, the function δ is not needed.

[2] This result holds in general for $p \geq r$ even when p would not be a prime number, but this case is not considered in this article.

In the three-valued case (p=3) of Lukasiewicz's Logic with modal connectives, a polynomial translation of the connectives is (see [14])

$$f_\neg(q) = 2 - q + I$$
$$f_\Diamond(q) = 2q^2 + I$$
$$f_\Box(q) = q^2 + 2q + I$$
$$f_\vee(q, r) = q^2 r^2 + q^2 r + qr^2 + 2qr + q + r + I$$
$$f_\wedge(q, r) = 2q^2 r^2 + 2q^2 r + 2qr^2 + qr + I$$
$$f_\rightarrow(q, r) = 2q^2 r^2 + 2q^2 r + 2qr^2 + qr + 2q + 2 + I$$

Under minimal requirements of good behaviour of the logic, the following theorem can be proved (see [17] for details).

Theorem 22. *A formula A_0 is a tautological consequence of $\{A_1, A_2,$ ..., $A_m\}$ ($\{A_1, A_2, ..., A_m\} \models A_0$) iff the polynomial translation of the negation of A_0 belongs to the (polynomial) ideal generated by the polynomial translation of the negations of $A_1, A_2, ..., A_m$, i.e.*

$$\{A_1, A_2, ..., A_m\} \models A_0 \quad - \quad f_\neg(\varphi(A_0)) \in < f_\neg(\varphi(A_1)), ..., f_\neg(\varphi(A_m)) > + I$$

where $A_1, ..., A_m$ can be rules, facts and integrity constraints.

4.2   Weak Inconsistency and Polynomial Ideals

The fact that 1 belongs to a polynomial ideal is equivalent to this ideal being the whole ring. Therefore, $1 \in < f_\neg(\varphi(Rules)), f_\neg(\varphi(Facts)), f_\neg(\varphi(NICs)) > + I$ is equivalent to saying that any formula in the KBS can be obtained by forward firing [15,11]. So:

Corollary 23. *There is weak inconsistency iff*

$$1 \in < f_\neg(\varphi(Rules)), f_\neg(\varphi(Facts)), f_\neg(\varphi(NICs)) > + I \ .$$

This can be checked very easily using Gröbner Bases [6,4,1]. So, we have an effective method of checking weak inconsistency (see [15] and applications [12,18] for details).

4.3   Strong Inconsistency and Algebraic Varieties

But what about strong inconsistency? What is the meaning of strong inconsistency in the polynomial model? As seen in Example 20, weak inconsistency does not imply strong inconsistency.

Let us denote by $V(I)$ the algebraic variety corresponding to the polynomial ideal I (that is, the set of points of the respective affine space which satisfy all polynomials in the ideal I).

Lemma 24. *i) In $\mathbb{Z}_p[x_1, x_2, ..., x_m]$ there are non-zero ideals which variety is the whole affine space.*
ii) In $\mathcal{A} = \mathbb{Z}_p[x_1, x_2, ..., x_m]/I$; $I =< x_1^p - x_1, x_2^p - x_2, ..., x_m^p - x_m >$, the only ideal which variety is the whole affine space is the zero ideal.

Proof. i) For example the value of $x^2 + x \in \mathbb{Z}_2[x]$ is 0 in $0, 1$. Consider therefore $<x^2 + x>$.
The same occurs with $x^3 * (x - 1) * (x - 2)^2 \in \mathbb{Z}_3[x]$. Its value in $0, 1, 2$ is 0.
ii) Case I: Univariate polynomials. If $0, 1, ..., p-1$ are roots of a polynomial in $\mathcal{A} = \mathbb{Z}_p[x]/<x^p - x>$, then the polynomial is either 0 or it can be factorized as

$$x \cdot (x - 1) \cdot x \cdot ... \cdot (x - (p - 1)) \cdot ...$$

Therefore, if it is $\neq 0$, it is of degree $\geq p$. But in $\mathcal{A}$ all polynomials are simplified to polynomials of degree $< p$, so this polynomial simplifies to 0.
Case II: Multivariate polynomials. It can be proved by applying the previous case to the intersections of the hypersurface by hyperplanes parallel to the "vertical" axis. $\qquad\square$

Theorem 25. *There is strong inconsistency iff*

$$V(<\varphi(Rules \wedge Facts \wedge NICs)>+I)$$

is the whole (respective) affine space.

Proof. $Rules \wedge Facts \wedge NICs$ can take only the truth value "false" — polynomial $\varphi(Rules \wedge Facts \wedge NICs)$ can take only the value 0 — $V(<\varphi(Rules \wedge Facts \wedge NICs)>+I)$ is the whole (respective) affine space. $\qquad\square$

Corollary 26. *There is strong inconsistency iff $< \varphi(Rules \wedge Facts \wedge NICs)>+I$ is the zero ideal of $\mathcal{A} = \mathbb{Z}_p[x_1, x_2, ..., x_m]/I$.*

Proof. It follows from Lemma 24 ii) and Theorem 25. $\qquad\square$

Corollary 27. *The implication: strong inconsistency $\Rightarrow$ weak inconsistency (already seen in Proposition 18) can also be interpreted from the point of view of Algebraic Geometry.*

Proof. If there is strong inconsistency, according to the previous lemma

$$<\varphi(Rules \wedge Facts \wedge NICs)>+I =<0>+I .$$

Therefore $\varphi(Rules \wedge Facts \wedge NICs) = 0$ (in $\mathcal{A}$). As the De Morgan's laws hold,

$$\varphi(\neg(Rules) \vee \neg(Facts) \vee \neg(NICs)) =$$
$$\varphi(\neg(Rules \wedge Facts \wedge NICs)) =$$
$$(\mu - 1) - \varphi(Rules \wedge Facts \wedge NICs) = (\mu - 1) - 0 = \mu - 1$$

(an invertible) in $(\mathcal{A})$. But

$$\varphi(\neg(Rules) \vee \neg(Facts) \vee \neg(NICs)) \in$$
$$< f_\neg(\varphi(Rules)), f_\neg(\varphi(Facts)), f_\neg(\varphi(NICs)) > +I$$

and therefore $< f_\neg(\varphi(Rules)), f_\neg(\varphi(Facts)), f_\neg(\varphi(NICs)) > +I = <1>$. □

5 Appendix: Maple V.5 Implementation

5.1 Implementation of Procedures

Procedure whenFalse has the following inputs:

- pol is the function to be plotted,
- p is the number of truth values of the logic,
- lvar is the list of propositional variables that appear in pol.

It is considered that 0 and $p-1$ are the truth values corresponding, respectively, to "false" and "true".

According to the number of propositional variables in pol (i.e., the length of list lvar), dibuja_1, _2 or _3 is executed. If j is such number, the polynomial translation of the formula is considered to be in

$$\mathcal{A} = \mathbb{Z}_p[x_1, x_2, ..., x_j]/ < x_1^p - x_1, x_2^p - x_2, ..., x_j^p - x_j >$$

whose corresponding affine space is $\mathbb{Z}_p^j$. Therefore, if $j > 3$ nothing can be plotted. If $j = 1, 2, 3$, then $\mathbb{Z}_p^j$ will be a line or a plane or the usual three dimensional space, respectively.

Auxiliary procedures dibuja_x check when the formula is false. If it is never false, they answer: the variety is empty. Otherwise, they create and plot a list of points. If it is always false, they underline: the variety is the whole affine space. As discussed above, the variety is the whole affine space iff there is strong inconsistency.

For the sake of brevity, only whenFalse and dibuja_1 are detailed below.

```
> whenFalse:=proc(pol,p,lvar)
>    if nops(lvar)>3
>       then print('Too many variables: maximum 3')
>          elif nops(lvar)=3 then dibuja_3(pol,p,lvar)
>             elif nops(lvar)=2 then dibuja_2(pol,p,lvar)
>                elif nops(lvar)=1 then dibuja_1(pol,p,lvar)
>       fi;
> end:

> dibuja_1:=proc(pol,p,lvar)
>    local i,lispunt;
>    lispunt:=[];
```

```
>   for i from 0 to p-1 do
>     if subs(lvar[1]=i,pol) mod p = 0
>       then lispunt:=[op(lispunt),[i,0]]
>     fi;
>    od;
>   if lispunt<>[]
>     then if nops(lispunt)=p
>             then print('The variety is the whole affine space!
>          fi;
>          plot(lispunt,x=0..p-1,y=-0.03..0.03,
>                 color=red,labels=[lvar[1],''],
>                 style=POINT,symbol=CIRCLE,
>                 tickmarks=[p,1],scaling=constrained)
>       else print('The variety is empty')
>    fi;
>  end:
```

Polynomial expression of the connectives for Boolean logic:

```
> '&and':=(M,N)->M*N mod 2:
> '&or':=(M,N)->M+N+M*N mod 2:
> neg:=M->1+M mod 2:
> '&imp':=(M,N)->1+M*(1+N) mod 2:
> '&iff':=M,N->(M &imp N) &and (N &imp M) mod 2:
```

Polynomial expression of the connectives for Lukasiewicz's three-valued logic:

```
> '&and3':=(M,N)->2*M^2*N^2+2*M^2*N+2*M*N^2+M*N mod 3:
> '&or3':=(M,N)->M^2*N^2+M^2*N+M*N^2+2*M*N+M+N mod 3:
> neg3:=M->2-M mod 3:
> pos3:=M->2*M^2 mod 3:
> nec3:=M->M^2+2*M mod 3:
> '&imp3':=(M,N)->2*M^2*N^2+2*M^2*N+2*M*N^2+M*N+2*Q+2 mod 3:
> '&iff3':=(M,N)->(M &imp3 N) &and (N &imp3 M) mod 3:
```

In Maple, functions '&...' are infix, meanwhile usual functions are pre-fix. The final 3 is included in the names of the functions corresponding to Lukasiewicz's three-valued logic in order to distinguish these from the Boolean functions. Other similar assignations should be made to deal with p-valued logics, where $p > 3$.

5.2   Examples

Example 28. If $(x \wedge y) \vee (z \wedge t)$ is introduced, there are too many variables, and nothing can be plotted (three-valued logic):

```
> whenFalse( (x &and3 y) &or3 (z &and3 t), 3, [x,y,z,t] );
        Too many variables: maximum 3
```

Example 29. When is $\neg\Diamond q$ false in three-valued logic (Fig. 1)? (2 represents "true"):

```
> whenFalse( neg3(pos3(q)), 3, [q] );
```

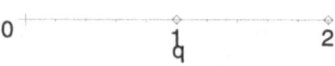

Fig. 1.

Example 30. When is $q \wedge r$ false in Boolean logic (Fig. 2)? (1 represents "true"):

```
> whenFalse( q &and r, 2, [q,r] );
```

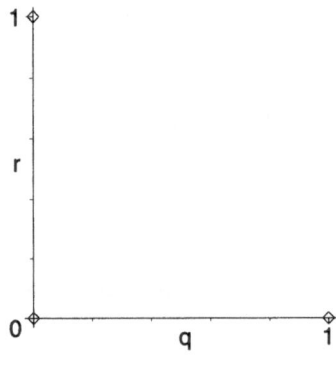

Fig. 2.

Example 31. When is $\neg(\neg q \vee (r \wedge s))$ false in three-valued logic (Fig. 3)?

```
> whenFalse( neg3(neg3(q) &or3 (r &and3 s)), 3, [q,r,s] );
```

Example 32. When is $q \wedge \neg q$ false in Boolean logic?

```
> whenFalse( q &and neg(q), 2, [q] );
        The variety is the whole affine space!!!
```

(The figure is omitted). So, there would be strong inconsistency (and also weak inconsistency) if this formula followed from the rules, facts and integrity constraints.

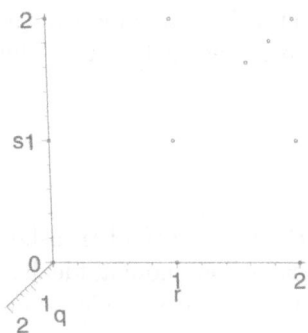

Fig. 3.

Example 33. When is $q \wedge \neg q$ false in Lukasiewicz's logic?

```
> whenFalse( q &and3 neg3(q), 3, [q] );
```

(The figure is omitted, but not all point are marked). So, there would be weak inconsistency (but not strong inconsistency) if this formula followed from the rules, facts and integrity constraints.

Example 34. Let us revisit the KBS of Example 21 (Fig. 4):

```
> whenFalse( nec3(a) &and3 (a &imp3 nec3(b))
>              &and3 (b &imp3 nec3(c))
>              &and3 (c &imp3 nec3(a)), 3, [a,b,c] );
     The variety is the whole affine space!!!
```

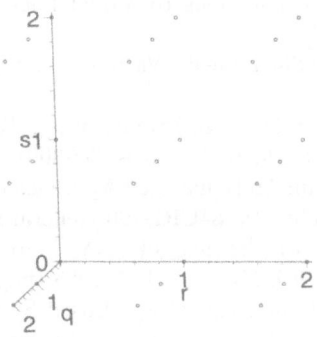

Fig. 4.

So, there is strong (and weak) inconsistency in this case.

Note that this implementation can handle far more complicated formulae. These trivial examples have been included to illustrate the theory, not the possibilities of the method.

6   Conclusion

We have suggested here the possibility of translating inconsistency in terms of algebraic varieties instead of polynomial ideals. This allows different cases of inconsistency to be detected and provides another interesting connection between Logic and Algebra.

7   Acknowledgments

We would like to thank Professor Reiner Haehnle for a suggestion during the reviewing process of [14], that was the starting point for this article.

References

1. V. Adams, P. Loustanau: An Introduction to Gröbner Bases. Graduate Studies in Mathematics 3, American Mathematical Society, 1994.
2. J.A. Alonso, E. Briales: Lógicas Polivalentes y Bases de Gröbner In: C. Martin (editor): Actas del V Congreso de Lenguajes Naturales y Lenguajes Formales, 1989 (pages 307-315).
3. J.A. Alonso: Métodos Algebraicos de Razonamiento Automático (Ph.D. Thesis). Pub. Univ. de Sevilla, 1988.
4. B. Buchberger: Applications of Gröbner Bases in non-linear Computational Geometry. In: J.R. Rice (editor): Mathematical Aspects of Scientific Software. IMA Volumes in Math. and its Applications, vol. 14. Springer-Verlag, 1988.
5. J. Chazarain, A. Riscos and J.A. Alonso, E. Briales: Multi-valued Logic and Gröbner Bases with Applications to Modal Logic. J. Symbolic Computation 11, 1991 (pages 181-194).
6. D. Cox, J. Little, D. O'Shea: Ideals, Varieties, and Algorithms. Springer-Verlag, 1991.
7. J. Hsiang: Refutational Theorem Proving using Term-Rewriting Systems. Artificial Intelligence, vol. 25, 1985 (pages 255-300).
8. D. Kapur, P. Narendran: An Equational Approach to Theorem Proving in First-Order Predicate Calculus. In: 84CRD296 General Electric Corporate Research and Development Report, Schenectady, NY, March 1984, rev. Dec. 1984. Also in: Proceedings of the 9th IJCAI, vol. 2, 1985 (pages 1146-1153).
9. L.M. Laita, L. de Ledesma: Knowledge-Based Systems Verification. In: Kent, J.G. Williams (editors): Encyclopedia of Computer Science and Technology. Marcel Dekker, 1997 (pages 253-280).
10. L. M. Laita, L. de Ledesma, E. Roanes L., E . Roanes M.: An Interpretation of the Propositional Boolean Algebra as a k-algebra. Effective Calculus. In: J. Campbell, J. Calmet (editors): Proceedings of AISMC-2. LNCS (num. 958). Springer-Verlag, 1995 (pages 255-263).

11. L.M. Laita, E. Roanes L.: A Computer Algebraic Method for Verification and Deduction in KBSs: Theory and Implementation. In: Proceedings of the 12th ECAI. Budapest Univ., 1996 (pages 5-10).
12. L.M. Laita, E. Roanes L., V. Maojo: Inference and Verification in Medical Appropriateness Criteria Using Gröbner Bases. In: J. Calmet, J. Plaza (editors): Artificial Intelligence and Symbolic Computation. Int. Conf. AISC'98. LNAI (num. 1476). Springer-Verlag, 1998 (pages 183-194).
13. L.M. Laita, E. Roanes L., V. Maojo, A. Díaz: A Logic and Computer Algebra Approach to a Decision-making Problem in Medicine. Revista de la Real Academia de Ciencias. To appear.
14. L.M. Laita, E. Roanes L., L. de Ledesma, J.A. Alonso: A Computer Algebra Approach to Verification and Deduction in Many-Valued Knowledge Systems. Soft-Computing. To appear.
15. E. Roanes L., L. M. Laita, E. Roanes M.: Maple V in A.I.: The Boolean Algebra Associated to a KBS. CAN Nieuwsbrief **14**, April 1995 (pages 65-70).
16. E. Roanes L.: Introducing Propositional Multi-Valued Logics with the Help of a CAS. Proceedings of the Int. Soc. for Analysis, Appl. and Computing (ISAAC) Conf. 1997. Kluwer. To appear.
17. E Roanes L., L.M. Laita, E. Roanes M.: A Polynomial Model for Multivalued Logics with a Touch of Algebraic Geometry and Computer Algebra. Special Issue "Non-Standard Applications of CA", in Mathematics and Computers in Simulation, **45/1-2** (1998), 83-99.
18. E. Roanes L., L.M. Laita, E. Roanes M.: An Application of an AI Methodology to Railway Interlocking Systems Using Computer Algebra. In: A. P. del Pobil, J. Mira, M. Ali (editors): Tasks an Methods in Applied Artificial Intelligence. IEA-98-AIE. LNAI (num. 1416). Springer-Verlag, 1998 (pages 687-696).
19. R. Turner: Logics for Artificial Intelligence. Ellis Horwood, 1984.

Indices and Solvability for General Systems of Differential Equations
(Invited Talk)

Werner M. Seiler

Lehrstuhl für Mathematik I, Universität Mannheim, 68131 Mannheim, Germany
Email: `seiler@euler.math.uni-mannheim.de`
WWW: `http://iaks-www.ira.uka.de/iaks-calmet/werner/werner.html`

Abstract. We consider general systems of ordinary and partial differential equations from a geometric point of view. This leads to simple interpretations of various index concepts introduced for differential algebraic equations. Especially, we obtain natural generalisations of these concepts to partial differential equations.

1   Introduction

Most of the literature on differential equations is concerned with so-called *normal* systems. In the case of ordinary differential equations this means that the system can be written in explicit form $\dot{u} = \phi(t, u)$ for some vector-valued function $u(t)$. For partial differential equations the condition of normality is more restrictive: it requires the existence of a distinguished independent variable t such that the system can be written in the form $u_t = \phi(t, x, u, u_x)$ where x represents the remaining independent variables (i. e. they satisfy the conditions of the Cauchy-Kowalevsky theorem).

From a theoretical point of view the restriction to normal systems is not very severe in the case of ordinary differential equations. Neglecting singularities any system can at least locally be transformed into an explicit form. In concrete applications one often either cannot explicitly construct or for some reasons does not want to perform this transformation. As a consequence, *differential algebraic equations* [1,8] or more generally *implicit equations* of the form $\Phi(t, u, \dot{u}) = 0$ have found much attention lately.

Simplifying a bit, a system of ordinary differential equations is not normal, if it contains equations of different order. In the usually considered case of first order systems this means that some of the equations are algebraic. The transformation to a normal system is performed by solving these *constraints* and thus eliminating some of the dependent variables. In contrast, a non-normal system of partial differential equations contains usually equations of different class (see Sect. 2.2) and not of different order. In general, no transformation to a normal system exists.

Non-normal systems of partial differential equations are either under- or overdetermined and occur in many applications. For example the field equations of a gauge theory cannot be normal, as the presence of the gauge symmetry implies underdeterminacy. Inverse problems like the construction of a potential for a given force often lead to overdetermined systems. A characteristic property of such systems is the possible existence of integrability conditions. The process of constructing all non-trivial integrability conditions for a given system is often called *completion*.

Already in the late 19th century mathematicians started to study general systems of differential equations and to design completion algorithms. Most notable among these classical approaches is the Janet-Riquier theory [9]; the first geometric approach was the Cartan-Kähler theory [2]. We will use the *formal theory* [18,19] combining elements of both approaches.

All these theories have remained comparatively "exotic". Restricted to ordinary differential equations they become straightforward. Thus it is not surprising that for this special case they have been rediscovered many times in various fields. For differential algebraic equations there exist at least three more or less independently developed approaches [21,22,33] which may be considered as specialisations of the general completion theory. For constrained Hamiltonian systems the same holds for the Dirac theory [6].

A unifying treatment of these two fields was given in [30]. The purpose of this article is to extend the results presented there to infinite dimensional systems. We will give geometric versions of several index definitions proposed in the literature which can be directly applied to partial differential equations.

In order to make this article as self-contained as possible, the next section provides an introduction into formal theory. Section 3 contains various index definitions for general systems of differential equations plus a discussion of their meaning. Relations between the different indices are studied in Sect. 4. Finally, some conclusions are given.

2   Formal Theory of Differential Equations

It is beyond the scope of this article to provide an in-depth introduction to formal theory. For this we must refer to the literature [18,19]. We will give here a brief overview following the presentation in [25]. Section 2.4 contains some simple examples; Sect. 2.5 specialises the theory to ordinary differential equations where it becomes much simpler.

2.1   Jet Bundle Formalism

Although the whole theory can be presented in a coordinate-free manner, we will use throughout local coordinates. Our notations are as follows. The independent variables of the differential equation are denoted by $x^1, \ldots, x^n$; they are local coordinates for the base space X. The dependent variables or unknown functions are denoted by $u^1, \ldots, u^m$. Together with the x^i they form bundle coordinates for a fibre bundle $\pi : \mathcal{E} \to X$. For derivatives we use a multi-index notation. A multi-index μ is an ordered tuple $[\mu_1, \ldots, \mu_n]$ of integers; its length is defined as $|\mu| = \sum \mu_i$. Then we denote the derivative $\partial^{|\mu|} u^{\alpha} / \partial (x^1)^{\mu_1} \cdots \partial (x^n)^{\mu_n}$ by p_{μ}^{α}.

The q-th order *jet bundle* $\mathcal{J}_q \mathcal{E}$ is again a fibre bundle with bundle coordinates $(x^i, u^{\alpha}, p_{\mu}^{\alpha})$ with $|\mu| \leq q$. A point in such a space may be considered as an equivalence class of functions where two functions are equivalent, if they possess identical Taylor series up to order q. A *differential equation* $\mathcal{R}_q$ of order q is defined as a (fibred) submanifold of $\mathcal{J}_q \mathcal{E}$. Locally, we may describe it by some equations $\Phi^{\tau}(x^i, u^{\alpha}, p_{\mu}^{\alpha}) = 0$ where $\tau = 1, \ldots, p$ and recover thus the usual point of view. Note that we do not require that $p = m$! Furthermore this definition makes no distinction between a single equation and a system.

Jet bundles of different order are naturally related by projections: If $r > q$, we define the map $\pi_q^r : \mathcal{J}_r \mathcal{E} \to \mathcal{J}_q \mathcal{E}$ which simply "forgets" all derivatives of higher order than q. For a given differential equation $\mathcal{R}_q \subset \mathcal{J}_q \mathcal{E}$ there exist two natural operations: *prolongation* yields an equation $\mathcal{R}_{q+1} \subset \mathcal{J}_{q+1} \mathcal{E}$ of order $q + 1$; *projection* leads to an equation $\mathcal{R}_{q-1}^{(1)} = \pi_{q-1}^q (\mathcal{R}_q) \subset \mathcal{J}_{q-1} \mathcal{E}$ of order $q - 1$. More generally, we will denote by $\mathcal{R}_q^{(s)}$ the equation obtained by s prolongations with subsequent projection: $\mathcal{R}_q^{(s)} = \pi_q^{q+s} (\mathcal{R}_{q+s})$.

In the classical language, prolongation corresponds to differentiating each equation $\Phi^{\tau} = 0$ with respect to all independent variables. To obtain a local representation of a projected system is in general rather difficult, especially for nonlinear equations, as it requires algebraic elimination.

2.2   Involutive Differential Equations

A key concept in formal theory is *involution*. We approach it in a computational manner considering the order by order construction of the general power series solution for a given differential equation $\mathcal{R}_q$. We make the ansatz $u^{\alpha}(x) = \sum_{|\mu| \geq 0} \frac{a_{\mu}^{\alpha}}{\mu !} (x - x_0)^{\mu}$, enter it into a local description $\Phi^{\tau} = 0$ and evaluate the arising equations at $x = x_0$. This yields an algebraic system for the Taylor coefficients a_{μ}^{α} up to order q. Then we do the same with the prolonged equation $\mathcal{R}_{q+1}$ and get a linear system (usually underdetermined) for the Taylor coefficients of order $q + 1$. This procedure can be repeated with higher prolongations $\mathcal{R}_{q+r}$ as often as one wishes.

This approach produces a valid series solution only, if at no order integrability conditions appear. Otherwise we cannot be sure whether we have correctly identified all conditions the Taylor coefficients must satisfy. Assume for example that we stop at some order $q_0 > q$ but that at a higher order $q_1 > q_0$ an integrability condition of, say, order $q + 1$ was hidden. This additional condition on the coefficients of order $q + 1$ was ignored in our construction and hence we obtained a series with too many free coefficients.

The differential equation $\mathcal{R}_q$ is called *formally integrable*, if $\mathcal{R}_q^{(r)} = \mathcal{R}_q$ holds for all $r \geq 0$. In other words, no matter how often we prolong such an equation, we never find an integrability condition and thus the above described order by order construction of power series solutions can be pursued without problems. Unfortunately, no finite criterion is known to decide whether or not a given differential equation $\mathcal{R}_q$ is formally integrable. This leads to the idea of involution: an involutive equation is formally integrable but possesses in addition further properties which allow for a finite test.

The easiest way to understand involution is to pose the following question: if we use the above outlined construction of the general power series solution, how many Taylor coefficients at some order $q + r$ will be determined by the differential equation and how many can be chosen freely. The former ones are called *principal coefficients*; the latter ones *parametric coefficients*.

The answer is encoded in the *symbol* $\mathcal{M}_q$ of the differential equation $\mathcal{R}_q$. The symbol is a matrix, namely the principal part of the linearisation of $\mathcal{R}_q$. Its formal definition goes as follows. Let a local description of $\mathcal{R}_q$ be given by $\Phi^\tau(x, u, p) = 0$. For each derivative p_μ^α of order q we introduce an unknown a_μ^α (note that we consider only the derivatives of maximal order). The symbol is the matrix of the following linear system in these unknowns a_μ^α

$$\mathcal{M}_q : \left\{ \sum_{\alpha=1}^{m} \sum_{|\mu|=q} \frac{\partial \Phi^\tau}{\partial p_\mu^\alpha} a_\mu^\alpha = 0, \qquad \tau = 1, \ldots, p. \right. \tag{1}$$

The symbol $\mathcal{M}_{q+r}$ of the prolonged system $\mathcal{R}_{q+r}$ appears in our construction of power series solutions as the matrix of the linear system for the Taylor coefficients a_μ^α of order $q + r$. Thus the number of principal coefficients of order $q + r$ is given by rank $\mathcal{M}_{q+r}$. In order to predict this number based solely on the symbol $\mathcal{M}_q$, we introduce the *class* of a multi-index $\mu = [\mu_1, \ldots, \mu_n]$ as the smallest index k such that $\mu_k \neq 0$.

We order the columns of $\mathcal{M}_q$ – corresponding to the unknowns a_μ^α – so that columns for unknowns with a multi-index of higher class are always to the left of columns for unknowns with a multi-index of lower class. Otherwise the ordering does not matter. Then we compute a row echelon form of $\mathcal{M}_q$ and denote by $\beta_q^{(k)}$ the number of rows where the pivot sits in a column for an unknown with a multi-index of class k.

The symbol $\mathcal{M}_q$ is called *involutive*, if rank $\mathcal{M}_{q+1} = \sum_{k=1}^{n} k\beta_q^{(k)}$. This definition sounds rather mysterious, but one can rather easily see that this sum is a lower bound for rank $\mathcal{M}_{q+1}$ (this follows from an analysis of the pivots of $\mathcal{M}_{q+1}$). It is also easy to show that the prolongation of an involutive symbol is again involutive. Thus for involutive symbols $\mathcal{M}_q$ one can derive by induction a closed form expression for rank $\mathcal{M}_{q+r}$ depending only on the $\beta_q^{(k)}$.

The differential equation $\mathcal{R}_q$ is *involutive*, if it is formally integrable and if its symbol is involutive. One can show that if $\mathcal{M}_q$ is involutive and $\mathcal{R}_q^{(1)} = \mathcal{R}_q$, i.e. no integrability conditions appear in the next prolongation, then $\mathcal{R}_q$ is formally integrable and thus involutive. This yields an effectively checkable criterion for involution: involution of the symbol is a matter of some linear algebra and we need only one prolongation. The numbers $\beta_q^{(k)}$ encode the size of the solution space [26].

2.3 Solvability and Completion

The most important property of an involutive system $\mathcal{R}_q$ is that it possesses formal power series solutions. In the case of analytic systems we can even prove the convergence of the series and obtain an existence and uniqueness theorem for analytic solutions: the *Cartan-Kähler theorem*. Its proof sheds some further light on the above analysis of symbols based on the class.

We assume for simplicity that we have a first order equation. Then equations of lower order are algebraic constraints and can again (at least in principle) be treated by solving them and eliminating some dependent variables. The remaining equations are collected into subsystems according to their class. If we consider in the equations of class k the independent variables $x^{k+1}, \ldots, x^n$ as parameters (which is possible as by definition of the class no derivatives with respect to these variables appear), they form a normal system and the Cauchy-Kowalevsky theorem yields the existence and uniqueness of analytic solutions. These solutions are now taken as initial data for the normal system formed by the equations of class $k + 1$ and so on.

This construction could actually be performed for any formally integrable system. However, there remains one final point. After eventually treating the subsystem of class n we obtain solutions depending on all variables x^i. But in the previous steps we always considered some of them as constant parameters and it is not clear whether the final solutions still solve all equations of lower class. But if the system is involutive, one can prove by one more application of the Cauchy-Kowalevsky theorem that this is indeed the case.

The question naturally arises what happens, if one encounters a system which is not involutive. The (perhaps surprising) answer is given by the *Cartan-Kuranishi theorem*. It states that (under some regularity assumptions) any differential equation can either be made involutive by a finite number of prolongations and projections or it is inconsistent and has thus no solutions. This process is called *completion*.

The proof of the Cartan-Kuranishi theorem provides a simple completion algorithm consisting of two nested loops. The inner one prolongs the system until its symbol becomes involutive. The outer one then checks whether integrability conditions have occurred. If yes, they are added and the whole procedure starts again. Otherwise we have reached an involutive system. It is relatively straightforward to implement this algorithm in a computer algebra system.[1] An AXIOM implementation is described in [24,27].

The Cartan-Kuranishi theorem represents a rather deep result in formal theory. The main point is to show that the above outlined algorithm indeed terminates. Especially for the inner loop this is highly nontrivial. The fact

---

[1] There are a number of technical subtleties which pose some real problems.

that any symbol becomes involutive after a finite number of prolongations is sometimes called the *prolongation theorem*. Its proof is usually based on cohomological techniques. The termination of the outer loop stems from a simple Noetherian argument.

In any case we can conclude that the question of (local) solvability for analytic equations is completely answered by our completion algorithm. If no inconsistencies, i.e. integrability conditions of the form $0 = 1$, appear, the equation possesses analytic solutions. Note that analyticity is a necessary condition here! Already for smooth equations further obstacles to local solvability may appear (of so-called Lewy type [11, Chapt. 8]).

Completion (by our algorithm or any other like the ones coming from Janet-Riquier theory) represents essentially the only *systematic* way to prove the consistency of a general system of differential equations. For many systems consistency can be simply shown by exhibiting trivial solutions like $u^\alpha \equiv 0$, but obviously this cannot be done systematically.

2.4   Examples

As a first simple example, we consider the first order differential equation $\mathcal{R}_1$ defined by the two equations $u_z - yu_x = 0$ and $u_y = 0$. If we take the natural ordering $x^1 = x$, $x^2 = y$ and $x^3 = z$, the symbol $\mathcal{M}_1$ is the matrix $\begin{pmatrix} 1 & 0 & y \\ 0 & 1 & 0 \end{pmatrix}$ which is already in row echelon form. Its first row is of class 3 and the second one of class 2; hence $\beta_1^{(3)} = \beta_1^{(2)} = 1$ and $\beta_1^{(1)} = 0$. Prolongation leads to the second order system $\mathcal{R}_2$ defined by the six additional equations $u_{zz} - yu_{xz} = u_{yz} - yu_{xy} - u_x = u_{xz} - yu_{xx} = 0$ and $u_{xy} = u_{yy} = u_{yz} = 0$. It is easy to see that all these equations are independent and that one can eliminate all second order derivatives in one of the equations. Thus rank $\mathcal{M}_2 = 5 = 3\beta_1^{(3)} + 2\beta_1^{(2)} + \beta_1^{(1)}$ and consequently $\mathcal{M}_1$ is involutive and we have already finished the inner loop of the completion algorithm.

However, the elimination yields the integrability condition $u_x = 0$. Thus $\mathcal{R}_1$ is not involutive and we must start again with the projected system $\mathcal{R}_1^{(1)}$ defined by the three equations $u_x = u_y = u_z = 0$. It is left as an exercise to the reader to show that $\mathcal{R}_1^{(1)}$ is involutive. Here we have an example of a so-called finite type system with a finite-dimensional solution space, as its general solution is obviously $u(x, y, z) \equiv \text{Const.}$

A classical example due to Janet where several iterations through both loops of the completion algorithm are needed is given by the second order system $\mathcal{R}_2$ defined by $u_{zz} - yu_{xx} = 0$ and $u_{yy} = 0$. Full details to this example can be found in [20]; here we can only sketch the main steps. The symbol becomes involutive after two prolongations. However, there arises the integrability condition $u_{xxy} = 0$. The symbol of the corresponding system $\mathcal{R}_3^{(1)}$ becomes involutive again only after two prolongations which also lead to an integrability condition: $u_{xxxx} = 0$. The corresponding system $\mathcal{R}_4^{(2)}$ is formally integrable but not yet involutive, as its symbol needs one more prolongation in order to become involutive. Thus our completion algorithm ends with the system $\mathcal{R}_5^{(2)}$ from which it is easy to deduce that it is also of finite type with a 12-dimensional solution space.

A well-known example of a non-normal system are *Maxwell's equations* of electrodynamics. In field strength formulation they represent a system of eight differential equations for six field components:

$$\epsilon \partial_t \boldsymbol{E} - \operatorname{curl} \boldsymbol{H} = 0, \quad \mu \partial_t \boldsymbol{H} + \operatorname{curl} \boldsymbol{E} = 0, \tag{2}$$

$$\operatorname{div} \boldsymbol{E} = 0, \quad \operatorname{div} \boldsymbol{H} = 0. \tag{3}$$

If we take the time t as independent variable x^4, we have six equations of class 4, namely the six evolution equations (2). The two divergence laws (3) are of class 3. There is no need for a completion of Maxwell's equations, as one can easily check that they form already an involutive system.

In the numerical solution of the initial value problem for Maxwell's equations one often follows precisely the strategy of the proof of the Cauchy-Kowalevsky theorem outlined above. One first determines a time-independent solution of (3) and uses it as initial data for the hyperbolic system (2). Involution of Maxwell's equations guarantees that the such obtained solutions satisfy the divergence laws at all times t. Of course, this holds only for the exact solutions! Numerical solutions often violate (3) and the sometimes observed problem of spurious solutions also seems to be related to neglecting the divergence laws [10].

As a final example for some of the effects appearing in general systems of partial differential equations we consider the system

$$\partial_{xx} u - \partial_{xt} v = 0, \quad \partial_{tt} v - \partial_{xt} u = 0. \tag{4}$$

With two equations for two unknown functions, (4) would traditionally be considered as a welldetermined system. In fact, it is underdetermined: if u, v are any solution of (4), $u + \partial_t \Lambda$, $v + \partial_x \Lambda$ are also solutions for *any* function $\Lambda(t, x)$ and we can choose either u or v completely arbitrary.

The simple explanation is that while (4) is involutive, it is not normal! No matter how we order the independent variables, we have always one equation of class 1. In fact, (4) is nothing else than Maxwell's equations in $1 + 1$ dimensions in potential instead of field strength formulation. And it is well-known that in this form we have a gauge symmetry. But the field equations of a gauge theory can never be normal and are always underdetermined.

2.5   Ordinary Differential Equations

Formal theory becomes rather simple when applied to ordinary differential equations. The most important simplification comes from the fact that the symbol of an ordinary differential equations is always involutive. This is rather trivial, as there is only one independent variable and all equations are of the same class. Hence in our completion algorithm we can skip the inner loop.

The completion takes the following simple form. All equations are prolonged. Then one checks for integrability conditions. If some arise, they are added. Now we must check whether the prolongation of these new equations leads to further integrability conditions. If not the completion has finished. In the case of a semi-explicit system the completion can be further simplified. Here it suffices to prolong only the constraint equations, as the prolongations of the true differential equations drop out during the subsequent projection.

This can be seen as follows. A semi-explicit system has the form

$$\mathcal{R}_1 \ : \ \begin{cases} \dot{u} = \phi(t, u, v), \\ 0 = \psi(t, u, v) \end{cases} \tag{5}$$

where u, v may be vectors. The prolonged system is given by

$$\mathcal{R}_2 \ : \ \begin{cases} \dot{u} = \phi(t, u, v), & 0 = \psi(t, u, v), \\ \ddot{u} = \phi_t + \phi_u \dot{u} + \phi_v \dot{v}, & 0 = \psi_t + \psi_u \dot{u} + \psi_v \dot{v}, \end{cases} \tag{6}$$

Projecting back to the $\mathcal{J}_1 \mathcal{E}$ eliminates the equation for $\ddot{u}$. Thus

$$\mathcal{R}_1^{(1)} \ : \ \begin{cases} \dot{u} = \phi(t, u, v), \\ 0 = \psi_t + \psi_u \phi + \psi_v \dot{v}, \\ 0 = \psi(t, u, v). \end{cases} \tag{7}$$

One obtains the same system by only prolonging the constraints $\psi = 0$. The equations in (7) are not necessarily algebraically independent, but it requires only linear algebra to transform $\mathcal{R}_1^{(1)}$ into semi-explicit form. Thus in the next step of the completion it suffices again to prolong only the constraints. Geometrically, the constraints define the submanifold $\mathcal{R}_0^{(1)} = \pi_0^1(\mathcal{R}_1) \subset \mathcal{E}$.

In this simple form the completion algorithm has been rediscovered many times. A prominent example is given by the Dirac algorithm for constrained Hamiltonian systems [6]. Although the prolongations are "disguised" behind Poisson brackets, the Dirac algorithm corresponds for finite-dimensional systems exactly to completing the Hamiltonian equations of motion to an involutive system [31]. But for field theories the Dirac algorithm does in general not suffice to prove consistency of the field equations, as it does not check all possible integrability conditions.

For general differential algebraic equations similar algorithms have already been presented several times [21,22,33]. Their results are more or less identical with ours for systems where all approaches can be applied. Some of them go beyond the results presented here in admitting singularities or less regular solutions. We have excluded many kinds of singularities by defining a differential equation as a submanifold.

Most of these articles propose a slight variant of the completion algorithm. We prolong first and then project, whereas they reverse the operations and first project and then prolong. But this yields equivalent results. We showed already above that in the case of a semi-explicit system, it suffices to prolong only the constraints. Their projection can be interpreted as a kind of transformation into a semi-explicit form, as it produces just these constraints, i.e. the system $\mathcal{R}_0^{(1)}$. Hence if they subsequently prolong these, they obtain exactly the same result as if they first prolonged and then projected.

3   Index Definitions

In the literature on differential algebraic equations there is an abundance of index definitions. We do not attempt to give an overview; a general discussion of indices was recently given by Campbell and Gear [3]. We rather concentrate on the two mainly used types: differentiation and perturbation indices.

Given an implicit first order ordinary differential equation $\mathcal{R}_1$ locally described by $\Phi^\tau(t, u^\alpha, \dot{u}^\alpha) = 0$, we can roughly explain the ideas behind these two classes of indices as follows. *Differentiation indices* count the number of prolongations needed to obtain an equation with some specific property. For "the" differentiation index this property is that all first order derivatives $\dot{u}^\alpha$ can be computed explicitly as a function of the basic variables t, u^α.

Perturbation indices stem from estimates for the difference between solutions of $\mathcal{R}_1$ and solutions of a perturbed equation $\tilde{\mathcal{R}}_1$. The index says up to which order derivatives of the perturbations enter the estimate. Typically, differentiation indices are easier to compute than perturbation indices, but the latter ones are more important for the numerical analysis. Thus there is much interest in relating the two classes of indices.

3.1   Differentiation and Determinacy Index

The most widely used index in the theory of differential algebraic equations is "the" differentiation index. It is often defined via the so-called derivative array of $\mathcal{R}_1$. The kth array consists of the equations up to the k-th prolongation, i.e. it forms a local representation of $\mathcal{R}_{1+k}$.

Classically, one defines the differentiation index of a first order system as the smallest number ν such that all first order derivatives can be uniquely determined as functions of the independent and the dependent variables from the equations in the νth derivative array. In the language of formal theory this idea can be expressed intrinsically using the symbol.

Definition 1. The *differentiation index* of the differential equation $\mathcal{R}_q$ is the smallest integer $\nu = r + s$ such that $\dim \mathcal{M}_{q+r}^{(s)} = 0$.

In this form the definition can be applied to partial differential equations, too. Applied to first order differential algebraic equations it coincides with the usual one. Then $q = 1$ and, as discussed in the Sect. 2.5, we can always choose $r = 0$. The vanishing of the symbol $\mathcal{M}_1^{(\nu)}$ means nothing else than that all first order derivatives are principal and thus determined by equations.

However, for partial differential equations this definition is not very useful, since for most of them one never obtains a vanishing symbol. A vanishing symbol signals a finite dimensional solution space and this occurs only for very overdetermined equations. Consequently, we rephrase the definition in such a way that it remains unchanged for ordinary differential equations but makes more sense for partial differential equations.

Definition 2. The *determinacy index* of the differential equation $\mathcal{R}_q$ in n independent and m dependent variables is the smallest integer $\nu_d = r + s$ such that for $\mathcal{R}_{q+r}^{(s)}$ we find $\beta_{q+r}^{(n)} = m$.

For ordinary differential equations Def. 2 is equivalent to Def. 1, since for them $n = 1$ and the dimension of the symbol is $m - \beta_1^{(1)}$. For partial differential equations the condition in Def. 2 is much weaker than the one in Def. 1. Only underdetermined equations like (4) do not have a finite determinacy index. This fact explains the new name: the determinacy index ν_d counts the number of prolongations needed to decide whether $\mathcal{R}_q$ is underdetermined.[2] In general, it contains no further information.

Especially, ν_d contains generally *no* information about the solvability of the equation. This can easily be seen by considering the following differential algebraic equation in m dependent variables u^α

$$
\mathcal{R}_1 : \begin{cases} \dot{u}^\alpha = \phi^\alpha(t, u^\beta), & \alpha = 1, \ldots, m, \\ \psi^\tau(t, u^\beta) = 0, & \tau = 1, \ldots, m' < m. \end{cases} \tag{8}
$$

Obviously for such an equation $\nu = \nu_d = 0$. But prolonging the algebraic constraints may lead to further constraints or even to an inconsistency.

The determinacy index ν_d is determined during the completion algorithm described in Sect. 2.3. In general, one does not have to go through the full algorithm, if one is only interested in ν_d, since the condition $\beta_{q+r}^{(n)} = m$ is typically satisfied already at an earlier stage.

For ordinary differential equations there exists a simple geometric interpretation of the determinacy index ν_d. As soon as one has prolonged the equation ν_d times, one can compute a vector field such that any solution of the differential algebraic equation corresponds to an integral curve of it (but not necessarily vice versa!). Reich [22] called this uniquely determined field the *corresponding vector field*.

For its geometric construction we consider the equation $\mathcal{R}_1^{(\nu_d)}$ obtained after ν_d prolongations (and subsequent projections). Its algebraic part is described intrinsically by $\mathcal{R}_0^{(\nu_d+1)} = \pi_0^1(\mathcal{R}_1^{(\nu_d)}) \subset \mathcal{E}$. We restrict the inverse of

---

[2] An involutive differential equation $\mathcal{R}_q$ is underdetermined, iff $\beta_q^{(n)} < m$ [25,28].

the projection $(\pi_0^1)^{-1}$ to $\mathcal{R}_0^{(\nu_d+1)}$. Its image at each point is m-dimensional, as the fibre dimension of $\mathcal{J}_1 \mathcal{E}$ over $\mathcal{E}$ is m for ordinary differential equations. The dimension of the intersection of this image with $\mathcal{R}_1^{(\nu_d)}$ is dim $\mathcal{M}_1^{(\nu_d)}$. Since ν_d was defined such that this symbol vanishes, the intersection consists of a single point (under some mild regularity assumptions) and can naturally be identified with a (non-autonomous) vector field.

For partial differential equations there does not exist an analogue to the corresponding vector field. Here we have only the concept of *local solvability*. Recall that a point in the qth order jet bundle $\mathcal{J}_q \mathcal{E}$ may be interpreted as a power series truncated at order q. For an involutive equation $\mathcal{R}_q$ to every point $P \in \mathcal{R}_q$ there exists at least one formal power series solution whose truncation at order q corresponds to P. The striking difference to ordinary differential equations is that there this series is unique whereas for partial differential equations there exist in general infinitely many such series.

The corresponding vector field should not be confused with a so-called *underlying equation* which may also be considered as a vector field in the case of ordinary differential equations. While we have seen that the corresponding vector field is unique but only defined on the constraint manifold $\mathcal{R}_0^{(\nu_d+1)}$, an underlying equation is never unique but defined everywhere.

For an arbitrary differential equation $\mathcal{R}_q$ in n independent and m dependent variables, we call another equation $\tilde{\mathcal{R}}_q$ underlying, if it satisfies: (i) $\mathcal{R}_q \subset \tilde{\mathcal{R}}_q$, (ii) $\tilde{\mathcal{R}}_{q-1}^{(1)} = \mathcal{J}_{q-1}\mathcal{E}$, (iii) $\beta_q^{(n)} = m$ and all other $\beta_q^{(k)}$ vanish. The first condition implies that every solution of $\mathcal{R}_q$ is also a solution of $\tilde{\mathcal{R}}_q$ (but not necessarily vice versa); the second condition says in a geometric way that there are no lower order equations in $\tilde{\mathcal{R}}_q$ and the third condition requires that $\tilde{\mathcal{R}}_q$ is normal. (iii) can be omitted in the case of ordinary differential equations, as there it is implied by (ii). This is not the case for partial differential equations. In the case of Maxwell's equations the evolution part (2) may be considered as an underlying equation.

3.2   Integrability and Involution Index

The next index concept we consider is directly related to the solvability of the considered differential equation. As already mentioned several times a formally integrable equation possesses at least formal power series solutions. In the analytic case the Cartan-Kähler theorem even yields the convergence of these series. In view of these facts it appears more naturally to consider the following indices instead of ν_d.

Definition 3. The *formal integrability index* of the differential equation $\mathcal{R}_q$ is the smallest integer $\nu_f = r + s$ such that $\mathcal{R}_{q+r}^{(s)}$ is formally integrable. The *involution index* of the differential equation $\mathcal{R}_q$ is the smallest integer $\nu_i = r + s$ such that $\mathcal{R}_{q+r}^{(s)}$ is involutive.

In principle, ν_f prolongations suffice to prove the consistency of a given differential equation. However, in practice we need $\nu_i \geq \nu_f$ prolongations, since we know no finite criterion to decide formal integrability except completion to an involutive equation. In the case of ordinary differential equations $\nu_f = \nu_i$, as their symbols are always involutive (cf. Sect. 2.5).

We outlined above for differential algebraic equations the construction of the corresponding vector field. It can be performed as soon as the symbol vanishes. If $\nu_f > \nu_d$ and we apply this construction to the different equations $\mathcal{R}_1^{(\nu_d)} \supset \mathcal{R}_1^{(\nu_d+1)} \supset \cdots \supset \mathcal{R}_1^{(\nu_f)}$, this field does not really change; only its domain of definition shrinks at each step as more and more constraints are added. Once $\mathcal{R}_1^{(\nu_f)}$ is reached (and it is not empty), every integral curve of the corresponding vector field represents a solution of the differential algebraic equation. At the previous steps only the converse holds. Thus the field defined by $\mathcal{R}_1^{(\nu_f)}$ represents a geometric version of what is often called *state space form* of the differential algebraic equation.

For linear differential algebraic equations the integrability index ν_f coincides with the *strangeness index* introduced by Kunkel and Mehrmann [12,13] (they called the co-dimension of the constraint manifold $\mathcal{R}_1^{(0)}$ the strangeness of $\mathcal{R}_1$). To some extent ν_f may also be considered as a geometric version of the *uniform differentiation index* ν_{ud} introduced by Campbell et al. [3,4]. When ν_{ud} is defined, it ensures like ν_f the consistency of the equations and thus the existence and uniqueness of solutions.

There are two main differences between ν_f and ν_{ud}. The fact that the definition of ν_{ud} is based on $\mathcal{R}_{1+s}$ instead of $\mathcal{R}_1^{(s)}$ (i.e. that no projections are performed) is not important, as it does not influence the obtained index values. The first difference is that Condition (A4) of [3,4] excludes the possibility of trivial integrability conditions, as they always appear in overdetermined systems. Thus ν_{ud} is not defined for systems of the form (8).

The second and more important difference is that in formal theory ranks are always evaluated *on* the submanifolds $\mathcal{R}_1^{(s)}$, whereas the definition of ν_{ud} requires constant ranks in open neighbourhoods of solutions. Effectively this forbids algebraic manipulations of the equations and can lead to very different values of the two indices.

We demonstrate this effect on a simple three-dimensional system taken from [3]: $\sin(\dot{y})y + x = 0$, $\sin(\dot{z})z + y = 0$, and $z = 0$. The submanifold $\mathcal{R}_1$ defined by these equations can equivalently be described by the equations $x = y = z = 0$. Thus it is trivial to see that $\mathcal{R}_1$ becomes formally integrable after one prolongation and $\nu_f = 1$. As the two sets of equations are of course not equivalent in an open neighbourhood of $\mathcal{R}_1$, one obtains a different value for the uniform differentiation index, namely $\nu_{ud} = 3$.

3.3 Perturbation Index

The perturbation index was introduced by Hairer et al. [7]; it is an analytic concept and thus cannot be geometrically expressed like the above differentiation indices. But we will show in Sect. 4.2, how formal theory can be useful for estimating the perturbation index.

Hairer et al. introduced this index only for differential algebraic equations. In principle it can straightforwardly be extended to partial differential equations, as already shown in [5]. But there are a number of problems making it rather difficult to formulate a rigorous general theory. This begins already with the question of what function spaces and norms should be used. We will not discuss these points but for simplicity restrict ourselves to smooth functions with the supremum norm. We do not expect serious changes, if more general spaces and norms, especially other L^p norms, are used.

Let $\mathcal{C}^\infty(D)$ denote the space of smooth $\mathbb{R}^m$-valued functions defined on some domain $D \subset \mathbb{R}^n$ and $\|\cdot\|$ the usual Euclidean norm in $\mathbb{R}^m$. For $f \in \mathcal{C}^\infty(D)$ we denote the supremum norm by $\| f \|_\infty = \sup_{x \in D} \| f(x) \|$. Furthermore we introduce on $\mathcal{C}^\infty(D)$ for $\ell \in \mathbb{N}$ the Sobolev type norms

$$\| f \|_\ell = \sum_{0 \leq |\mu| \leq \ell} \| \frac{\partial^{|\mu|} f}{\partial x^\mu} \|_\infty . \tag{9}$$

Partial differential equations are usually accompanied by initial or boundary conditions. In order to accommodate for this we take the following simple approach. Let $D' \subset D$ be a subdomain, typically of lower dimension, and introduce on $\mathcal{C}^\infty(D')$ similar norms denoted by $\| \cdot \|'_\infty$ etc. The conditions are then written in the form $\Psi^\sigma(x, u, p)\big|_{D'} = 0$. This comprises most kinds of initial or boundary conditions. The highest derivative in Ψ^σ determines the order of the conditions.

Definition 4. Let $\Phi^\tau(x, u, p) = 0$ be a system of differential equations and let $U(x)$ be a smooth solution of it defined on some domain D and satisfying some initial/boundary conditions of order k on a domain $D' \subset D$. The system has the *perturbation index* ν_p along this solution, if ν_p is the smallest integer such that for solutions $\hat{U}(x)$ of the perturbed system $\Phi^\tau(x, u, p) = \delta^\tau(x)$ there exists an estimate

$$\| \hat{U}(x) - U(x) \| \leq C \left(\| \hat{U} - U \|'_k + \| \delta \|_{\nu_p - 1} \right) , \tag{10}$$

whenever the right hand side is sufficiently small. The constant C may depend only on the domains D, D' and on the functions Φ^τ.

In the case of first order differential algebraic equations this reduces to the definition of Hairer et al. [7]. D' contains then only the initial point x_0 and the initial conditions do not depend on derivatives; the norm $\| \cdot \|'_0$ is simply the Euclidean norm on $\mathbb{R}^m$. This definition is almost identical to the one proposed by Campbell and Marszalek [5]. The main difference is that we do not include the order k of the initial/boundary conditions into the index.

There exist several ways to interpret the functions δ^τ appearing in (10). Hairer et al. considered them mainly as *defect*, i.e. they assumed that the functions $\hat{U}$ are given and that entering them into the differential equations yields δ. As indicated by the phrasing of Def. 4 we take another point of view and consider δ^τ as a perturbation of the original differential equation.

This approach allows us immediately to generalise the definition of the perturbation index ν_{p}. Let $\tilde{\Phi}^\tau (x, u, p, \delta_1, \ldots, \delta_t)$ be some functions depending smoothly on the $\delta_j(x)$ and their derivatives up to some order $\bar{q}$ such that $\tilde{\Phi}^\tau (x, u, p, 0, \ldots, 0) = \Phi^\tau (x, u, p)$. Note that there are no restrictions on the number of perturbations δ_j, on $\bar{q}$ or on the way $\tilde{\Phi}^\tau$ depends on them. Now we can replace in Def. 4 the condition that $\hat{U}$ be a solution of $\Phi^\tau (x, u, p) = \delta^\tau$ by the condition that $\hat{U}$ be a solution of $\tilde{\Phi}^\tau (x, u, p, \delta) = 0$.

For arbitrary systems $\Phi^\tau = 0$ the perturbations δ_j cannot be chosen freely, as in general they must satisfy *compatibility conditions* in order to ensure that the system $\tilde{\Phi}^\tau (x, u, p, \delta) = 0$ has solutions: in the case of the trivial system $\dot{u} = 0$ and $u = 0$, the perturbed system $\dot{u} = \delta_1$, $u = \delta_2$ is solvable only when $\dot{\delta}_2 = \delta_1$.

Basically this is also the point of view taken by Campbell and Marszalek [5] who speak of *forcing functions* or *input* instead of perturbations. These terms are motivated by control theory and indicate that in principle it is at any time possible to change the meaning of u and δ, i.e. to consider δ as the dependent variables of the differential equation and u as perturbation. Obviously such changes in the interpretation of the equation will in general lead to different values of the perturbation index.

Thus formally it makes no problem to generalise the notion of a perturbation index to partial differential equations. However, it is a more delicate matter to decide whether this generalisation makes sense. For differential algebraic equations satisfying a Lipschitz condition it is straightforward to show (based on Gronwall's lemma) that for normal systems, i.e. explicit systems of the form $\dot{u} = \phi(t, u)$, we have $\nu_{\mathrm{p}} = 0$. In the case of partial differential equations this is less obvious.

For *linear* normal systems one may take a semigroup approach and consider the partial differential equation as an abstract ordinary differential equation on some function (Banach) space $\mathcal{B}$. Let the equation be $\dot{u} = Au$ where the operator A is the infinitesimal generator of a semigroup $T(t)$. It is a classical result (see e.g. [23]) that the solution $U(t)$ of the initial value problem $\dot{u} = Au + \delta(t)$, $u(0) = u_0$ with some $\mathcal{B}$ valued function δ satisfies

$$u(t) = T(t)u_0 + \int_0^t T(t-s)\delta(s) \, ds \,. \tag{11}$$

If the operators $T(t)$ are bounded, this leads directly to an estimate of a form similar to Def. 4 for $\nu_{\mathrm{p}} = 0$.

Note that these simple considerations apply only for perturbed equations of the form $\Phi^\tau (x, u, p) = \delta^\tau$. If one uses more general perturbations $\tilde{\Phi}^\tau (x, u, p, \delta) = 0$, one must be careful even in the case of a differential algebraic equation, as the equation may not be structurally stable and thus completely change its properties under a perturbation.

4   Relations between the Indices

After having defined all these indices we exhibit now some relations between them. In the case of differentiation indices we restrict ourselves to some elementary consequences of formal theory. In Sect. 4.2 we discuss how an estimate for the perturbation index ν_p can be obtained as the involution index of the perturbed system.

4.1   Differentiation Indices

By definition any involutive system is formally integrable. But a formally integrable system requires in general some prolongations to become involutive. Of course no projections are needed, as all non-trivial integrability conditions are already included in the system. Thus we get $\nu_f \leq \nu_i$. An example where $\nu_f < \nu_i$ was given in Sect. 2.4. A similarly trivial result is the inequality already discussed above: $\nu_d \leq \nu_f$. Recall that even for differential algebraic equations it is possible to have here a strict inequality!

To find for partial differential equations an upper bound for the difference $\nu_i - \nu_f$ requires a fairly deep result from formal theory. We mentioned already in Sect. 2.3 the prolongation theorem stating that every symbol becomes involutive after a finite number of prolongations. A proof of it yielding an upper bound for the number of prolongations was given by Sweeny [32]. This bound depends only on the order q of the differential equation, the number n of independent and the number m of dependent variables and can be expressed in form of a recursion relation [18].

If we denote by $\hat{q}(n, m, q)$ the upper bound for the order at which the symbol $\mathcal{M}_q$ becomes involutive, then

$$\hat{q}(n, m, q) = \hat{q}\left(n, m\binom{q+n-1}{n}, 1\right),$$

$$\hat{q}(n, m, 1) = m\left(\frac{\hat{q}(n-1, m, 1) + n}{n-1}\right) + \hat{q}(n-1, m, 1) + 1, \tag{12}$$

$$\hat{q}(0, m, 1) = 0.$$

Obviously, $\hat{q}$ grows rapidly; e. g. $\hat{q}(4, 4, 1) = 13.151.182.504$. Fortunately, it usually drastically overestimates the number of prolongations actually needed. It is not known whether this bound is sharp, i. e. whether there really exist symbols where one needs such a huge number of prolongations.

Consider the following simple system where both equations are of order q

$$\mathcal{R}_q : \begin{cases} u_{x\cdots x} = 0, \\ u_{y\cdots y} = 0. \end{cases} \tag{13}$$

$\mathcal{R}_q$ is formally integrable but not involutive. One can show that its symbol becomes involutive after $q-1$ prolongations [29]. But evaluation of (12) yields $q^4/4 + q^3/2 + 9q^2/4 + 2q + 2$ for this system.

Note that this result yields only a bound for the difference $\nu_i - \nu_t$ and not on ν_i. This can be seen from the discussion of the completion algorithm in Sect. 2.3. The considerations above apply only to its inner loop. The termination of the outer loop was shown with a Noetherian argument giving no indications about the number of iterations needed.

For ordinary differential equations the situation is much simpler. As discussed in Sect. 2.5 they always possess an involutive symbol and we can skip the inner loop in our completion algorithm. This entails that the final involutive system is of the same order as the original system and it is straightforward to give an upper bound: $\nu_t = \nu_i \leq \dim \mathcal{R}_q$. Namely, in the worst case we add one integrability condition in each iteration of the outer loop. But as soon as we have added $\dim \mathcal{R}_q$ equations, we obtain a system with a zerodimensional solution space. Such a system must be either formally integrable or inconsistent, as no more independent equations can be added.

4.2   Perturbation Indices

In general it is rather difficult to obtain estimates like the one required by Def. 4 of the perturbation index ν_p. Thus there is much interest in relating ν_p with differentiation indices which we can (at least in principle) determine algorithmically. We follow here a slightly different route: we try to bound ν_p by the involution index not of $\mathcal{R}_q$ but of the perturbed equation $\tilde{\mathcal{R}}_q$.

We begin by considering linear differential equations. Let $\Phi^\tau(x, u, p) = 0$ be a local representation of the equation $\mathcal{R}_q$. As in Sect. 3.3 we associate to this local representation the perturbed equation $\tilde{\mathcal{R}}_q$ defined locally by $\Phi^\tau(x, u, p) = \delta^\tau(x)$. Now we can apply the completion algorithm of Sect. 2.3. Since we are dealing with a linear system, this algorithm will require only linear operations. Hence the finally obtained involutive equation $\tilde{\mathcal{R}}_{q+\tilde{r}}^{(\tilde{s})}$ possesses a local representation of the form $\psi^\sigma(x, u, p) = F^\sigma(x, \delta, \partial_x \delta, \dots)$. If some of the ψ^σ vanish, we have found compatibility conditions $F^\sigma(x, \delta, \partial_x \delta, \dots) = 0$ which the perturbations must satisfy. So these are automatically determined during the completion of $\tilde{\mathcal{R}}_q$.

Let $\tilde{\nu}_i = \tilde{r} + \tilde{s}$ be the involution index of $\tilde{\mathcal{R}}_q$. As we performed $\tilde{\nu}_i$ prolongations during the completion, in the right hand sides F^σ no derivatives of δ of order higher than $\tilde{\nu}_i$ appear. Now we can apply the ideas used in the proof of the Cartan-Kähler theorem outlined in Sect. 2.3. According to these we can construct the solutions of $\tilde{\mathcal{R}}_{q+\tilde{r}}^{(\tilde{s})}$ by solving a sequence of normal subsystems using the results of one step as initial data for the next step.

At each step the solution can be expressed in the form (11), i. e. an integral over the right hand side appears. Collecting all these expressions we can deduce an estimate of the form (10) with $\nu_p \leq \tilde{\nu}_i$. ν_p will be less than $\tilde{\nu}_i$, if the highest order derivatives of δ appear only in the compatibility conditions and not as right hand sides of equations involving the unknown functions u. In any case we can conclude that the involution index $\tilde{\nu}_i$ of the perturbed equation $\tilde{\mathcal{R}}_q$ represents an upper bound for the perturbation index ν_p of the original equation $\mathcal{R}_q$.

For nonlinear equations or more general forms of perturbations the situation is not so clear. But this is not surprising, as in these cases we could not even show that the perturbation index of normal systems generally vanishes. Nevertheless $\tilde{\nu}_i$ should at least give some indications about the size of ν_p. As in the linear case the involutive equation $\tilde{\mathcal{R}}_{q+\tilde{r}}^{(\tilde{s})}$ will depend on derivatives of δ up to order $\tilde{\nu}_i$ and it is therefore only reasonable to assume that in an estimate of the form (10), these derivatives should appear.

So far we have neglected the fact that in Def. 4 ν_p was defined along a specific solution $\hat{U}$ and of course ν_p may take different values along different solutions. For this reason Campbell and Gear [3] introduced the *maximum perturbation index* ν_{mp} as the maximal value of ν_p on the solution space of the differential equation. Obviously $\tilde{\nu}_i$ represents an upper bound of ν_{mp}, as the arguments above are independent of the choice of a specific solution $\hat{U}$.

5 Conclusions

We have shown in this article how many of the index concepts appearing in the literature on differential algebraic equations find a simple geometric interpretation within the framework of the formal theory. The first to point out this connection and to apply it to concrete numerical problems were Le Vey and Tuomela (see [14] and references therein).

This new interpretation is interesting for several reasons. The perhaps most important one is that it allows us to extend the theory to general systems of partial differential equations. We also think that it provides useful insights. For example, it emphasises that in such systems the main problems typically come from equations of lower class and not of lower order. This is a completely new phenomenon not present in differential algebraic equations. For this reason we do not think that the sometimes found terminology "partial differential algebraic equation" (PDAE) is a very good one.

We believe that it will be the main challenge in the numerical analysis of such general systems to develop robust methods to handle this situation which appears naturally in a number of important applications (we mentioned already electrodynamics, but the same holds e. g. for the dynamics of incompressible fluids). Two simple approaches are either to use an underlying equation or to follow the ideas of the method of lines.

In the first case one follows directly the strategy of the Cartan-Kähler theorem and considers equations of lower class as constraints on the initial data for the equations of maximal class which are taken as underlying equation. However, in general one will have to take measures against a numerical "drift off the constraints." Further problems like spurious solutions arise, if one imposes not only initial but also boundary conditions, as it is usually the case. A thorough discussion for the special case of Maxwell's equations can be found in [10].

In a method of lines approach one would keep the derivatives with respect to x^n and discretise all other derivatives. If equations of lower class are present, they will become purely algebraic equations; thus we arrive naturally at a differential algebraic equation. For semi-linear systems of the form $Au_t + Bu_{xx} + F(u) = f(t, x)$ where at least one of the matrices A, B is singular, this approach has been studied in detail in [15–17].

Actually, most attempts to define (differentiation) indices for partial differential equations that can be found in the literature are based on such semi-discretisations (or closely related integral transforms). This is in marked contrast to differential algebraic equations where indices are defined without reference to a numerical method. The same holds for our generalisation to partial differential equations which are furthermore defined for completely arbitrary systems and not only special classes.

Discretisation based indices cannot capture general structural properties of a given differential equation. But it should be very useful to compare them with discretisation independent indices like the ones introduced in this article (some steps in this direction can already be found in [5]). Intuitively one would want that both indices coincide. If the discretisation based index was higher, this could indicate that unnecessary complications have been introduced. Conversely, if it was lower, one might have lost some important features of the differential equation during the discretisation. Of course, this requires that one develops comparable indices.

Another useful insight provided by formal theory concerns an important difference between differentiation and perturbation indices. All of our differentiation indices are defined *intrinsically*, i.e. they depend only on the manifold $\mathcal{R}_q$ and not on any specific local representation $\Phi^\tau(x, u, p) = 0$. Hence they remain invariant under algebraic manipulation of the equations or under changes of coordinates; they really capture structural properties of the differential equation.

In contrast, the perturbation index ν_p will in general have a different value after algebraic manipulations or changes of coordinates. The same holds for our estimate $\tilde{\nu}_f$. Of course, $\tilde{\nu}_f$ is defined intrinsically for $\tilde{\mathcal{R}}_q$, however the definition of this submanifold is not intrinsic but depends on the chosen representation $\Phi^\tau(x, u, p) = 0$ of $\mathcal{R}_q$.

Finally, it should be remarked that we made implicitly a number of assumptions in this article. Most notably we had to assume that our equations are sufficiently smooth, so that our completion algorithm can be performed; equations with discontinuous terms should be treated with much care. We omitted any discussion of branchings in the completion algorithm. In general, involution is a local property and index values may vary on the manifold $\mathcal{R}_q$.

We also ignored the problem of δ-regularity which makes the formal analysis much more complicated, if characteristic coordinates are used.

All our solvability results apply only to analytic systems and solutions. This is of course much to restrictive for applications and due to the fact that the only general existence and uniqueness theorem for normal systems of partial differential equations is the Cauchy-Kowalevsky theorem requiring analyticity. However, the step by step technique of the proof of the Cartan-Kähler theorem can also be applied in other situations, if more general results are available. For example, in [25,28] the uniqueness theorem of Holmgren was generalised from normal linear systems to arbitrary involutive ones. Analogously one could prove much stronger existence and uniqueness theorems for Maxwell's equations (or other equations with similar structure) based on classical theorems for special classes of normal systems.

Acknowledgements

I thank the organisers, especially V.P. Gerdt, for the invitation to speak at CASC '99 and to write this article. I thank G. Le Vey and J. Tuomela for drawing my attention to this topic and S.L. Campbell for some useful discussions of the uniform differentiation index. This work has been supported by Deutsche Forschungsgemeinschaft.

References

1. K.E. Brenan, S.L. Campbell, and L.R. Petzold. *Numerical Solution of Initial-Value Problems in Differential-Algebraic Equations*. Classics in Applied Mathematics 14. SIAM, Philadelphia, 1996.
2. R.L. Bryant, S.S. Chern, R.B. Gardner, H.L. Goldschmidt, and P.A. Griffiths. *Exterior Differential Systems*. Mathematical Sciences Research Institute Publications 18. Springer-Verlag, New York, 1991.
3. S.L. Campbell and C.W. Gear. The index of general nonlinear DAEs. *Numer. Math.*, 72:173–196, 1995.
4. S.L. Campbell and E. Griepentrog. Solvability of general differential algebraic equations. *SIAM J. Sci. Comp.*, 16:257–270, 1995.
5. S.L. Campbell and W. Marszalek. The index of an infinite dimensional implicit system. *Math. Model. Syst.*, 1:1–25, 1996.
6. P.A.M. Dirac. Generalized Hamiltonian dynamics. *Can. J. Math.*, 2:129–148, 1950.
7. E. Hairer, C. Lubich, and M. Roche. *The Numerical Solution of Differential-Algebraic Equations by Runge-Kutta Methods*. Lecture Notes in Mathematics 1409. Springer-Verlag, Berlin, 1989.
8. E. Hairer and G. Wanner. *Solving Ordinary Differential Equations II*. Springer Series in Computational Mathematics 14. Springer-Verlag, Berlin, 1996.
9. M. Janet. Sur les Systèmes d'Équations aux Dérivées Partielles. *J. Math. Pure Appl.*, 3:65–151, 1920.

10. B.N. Jiang, J. Wu, and L.A. Povelli. The origin of spurious solutions in computational electrodynamics. *J. Comp. Phys.*, 125:104–123, 1996.

11. F. John. *Partial Differential Equations*. Applied Mathematical Sciences 1. Springer-Verlag, New York, 1982.

12. P. Kunkel and V. Mehrmann. Canonical forms for linear differential-algebraic equations with variable coefficients. *J. Comp. Appl. Math.*, 56:225–251, 1994.

13. P. Kunkel and V. Mehrmann. A new look at pencils of matrix valued functions. *Lin. Alg. Appl.*, 212/213:215–248, 1994.

14. G. Le Vey. Some remarks on solvability and various indices for implicit differential equations. *Num. Algo.*, 19:127–145, 1998.

15. W. Lucht and K. Strehmel. Discretization based indices for semilinear partial differential algebraic equations. Technical Report 97-40, Fachbereich Mathematik und Informatik, Universität Halle-Wittenberg, 1997.

16. W. Lucht, K. Strehmel, and C. Eichler-Liebenow. Linear partial differential algebraic equations I: Indexes, consistent boundary/initial conditions. Technical Report 97-17, Fachbereich Mathematik und Informatik, Universität Halle-Wittenberg, 1997.

17. W. Lucht, K. Strehmel, and C. Eichler-Liebenow. Linear partial differential algebraic equations II: Numerical solution. Technical Report 97-18, Fachbereich Mathematik und Informatik, Universität Halle-Wittenberg, 1997.

18. J.F. Pommaret. *Systems of Partial Differential Equations and Lie Pseudogroups*. Gordon & Breach, London, 1978.

19. J.F. Pommaret. *Partial Differential Equations and Group Theory*. Kluwer, Dordrecht, 1994.

20. J.F. Pommaret and A. Haddak. Effective methods for systems of algebraic partial differential equations. In T. Mora and C. Traverso, editors, *Proc. MEGA '90*, pages 411–426. Birkhäuser, Boston, 1991.

21. P.J. Rabier and W.C. Rheinboldt. A geometric treatment of implicit differential algebraic equations. *J. Diff. Eq.*, 109:110–146, 1994.

22. S. Reich. On an existence and uniqueness theory for nonlinear differential-algebraic equations. *Circ. Sys. Sig. Proc.*, 10:343–359, 1991.

23. M. Renardy and R.C. Rogers. *An Introduction to Partial Differential Equations*. Texts in Applied Mathematics 13. Springer, New York, 1993.

24. J. Schü, W.M. Seiler, and J. Calmet. Algorithmic methods for Lie pseudogroups. In N. Ibragimov, M. Torrisi, and A. Valenti, editors, *Proc. Modern Group Analysis: Advanced Analytical and Computational Methods in Mathematical Physics*, pages 337–344. Kluwer, Dordrecht, 1993.

25. W.M. Seiler. *Analysis and Application of the Formal Theory of Partial Differential Equations*. PhD thesis, School of Physics and Materials, Lancaster University, 1994.

26. W.M. Seiler. On the arbitrariness of the general solution of an involutive partial differential equation. *J. Math. Phys.*, 35:486–498, 1994.

27. W.M. Seiler. Applying AXIOM to partial differential equations. Internal Report 95-17, Universität Karlsruhe, Fakultät für Informatik, 1995.

28. W.M. Seiler. Generalized tableaux and formally well-posed initial value problems. Preprint Lancaster University, 1995.

29. W.M. Seiler. Involution and symmetry reductions. *Math. Comp. Model.*, 25:63–73, 1997.

30. W.M. Seiler. Numerical analysis of constrained Hamiltonian systems and the formal theory of differential equations. *Math. Comp. Simul.*, 45:561–576, 1998.

31. W.M. Seiler and R.W. Tucker. Involution and constrained dynamics I: The Dirac approach. *J. Phys. A*, 28:4431–4451, 1995.
32. J.W. Sweeny. The D-Neumann problem. *Acta Math.*, 120:223–251, 1968.
33. A. Szatkowski. Geometric characterization of singular differential algebraic equations. *Int. J. Sys. Sci.*, 23:167–186, 1992.

Decomposing Systems of Polynomial Equations

Rainer Steinwandt[*]

Institut für Algorithmen und Kognitive Systeme,
Professor Dr. Th. Beth, Arbeitsgruppe Computeralgebra,
Fakultät für Informatik,
Universität Karlsruhe, Germany

Abstract. The notion of sequential decomposition of k-correspondences is introduced. This is motivated by the use of functional decompositions of polynomials, rational functions, and rational mappings for the simplification of the solution of certain systems of polynomial equations. Sequential decompositions of k-correspondences can be used to express the "generic solution" of certain kinds of polynomial equations in a simpler way, in some sense. It is shown how Gröbner basis techniques can be applied to compute this kind of decompositions effectively.

1 Introduction

In this paper we treat the simplification of polynomial systems of equations whose solution(s) depend on the choice of free parameters. More precisely, let

$$\{\vec{f}\} := \{f_1, \ldots, f_l\} \subseteq k[\vec{a}, \vec{x}] := k[a_1, \ldots, a_m, x_1, \ldots, x_n] \qquad (1)$$

denote a finite set of polynomials where k is a field. We embed k in a universal domain Ω in the sense of [36], i.e. Ω is algebraically closed and of infinite transcendence degree over k. We are interested in determining the common zeros of $\vec{f}$ in Ω^n after having specialized $\vec{a}$ to some fixed value $\vec{\alpha} \in \Omega^m$. The interest in this kind of equations can be motivated by a problem in the design of diffractive optical systems, for instance, where one looks for a decomposition of a given regular matrix $A \in \mathrm{GL}_n(\mathbb{C})$ into an alternating product of circular and diagonal matrices (see [1,26]). Here $\vec{a}$ specify the entries of the linear mapping to be decomposed and the indeterminates $\vec{x}$ represent the coefficients of the circulant and diagonal "composition factors".

Another example for a system of equations of the form (1) arises in the context of the *threedimensional resection problem* in geodesy (see [13] and Sect. 5.2). Finally, it is worth mentioning that we obtain an ordinary system of polynomial equations in $k[\vec{x}]$ for the special case $m = 0$.

There are at least two important general kinds of simplification for the kind of problem mentioned:

---

[*] grant DFG - GRK 209/3-98 "Beherrschbarkeit komplexer Systeme"

- Decomposition into irreducible components.
- Introduction of intermediate steps/functional decomposition.

Decomposition into irreducible components can be motivated geometrically: Any common zero $(\vec{\alpha}, \vec{\xi}) \in \Omega^m \times \Omega^n$ of $\vec{f}$ may be taken for a point lying in the Zariski closed set

$$\mathcal{Z}(\vec{f}) := \{(\vec{\alpha}, \vec{\xi}) \in \mathbb{A}^m \times \mathbb{A}^n \mid f_i(\vec{\alpha}, \vec{\xi}) = 0, i = 1, \ldots, l\}.$$

Conversely, any point in this set gives rise to a common zero of $\vec{f}$ for some specific value of $\vec{a}$.

Decomposing into irreducibles now simply means to look at each irreducible component of $\mathcal{Z}(\vec{f})$ individually. In terms of polynomials this (geometric) simplification corresponds to the computation of associated primes of the radical of the ideal determined by $\vec{f}$ in $\Omega[\vec{a}, \vec{x}]$, i.e., we have

$$\sqrt{\langle \vec{f} \rangle} = \mathfrak{P}_1 \cap \ldots \cap \mathfrak{P}_r$$

for some prime ideals $\mathfrak{P}_1, \ldots, \mathfrak{P}_r$. In particular, after specializing $\vec{a}$ to some $\vec{\alpha} \in \Omega^m$ we can determine $\mathcal{Z}(\mathfrak{P}_1), \ldots, \mathcal{Z}(\mathfrak{P}_r)$ separately and in parallel in order to obtain the required solutions for $\vec{x}$. For computational purposes it may be useful to restrict oneself to the computation of the associated primes of $\sqrt{\langle \vec{f} \rangle} \trianglelefteq k[\vec{a}, \vec{x}]$, thus avoiding to change into Ω. This kind of decomposition into k-irreducible components can be illustrated nicely by univariate polynomials: Instead of computing the roots of $x^6 + x^5 + x^4 - 5x^2 - 5x - 5 = (x^4 - 5)(x^2 + x + 1) \in \mathbb{Q}[x]$ directly we can determine the roots of the two (over $\mathbb{Q}$) irreducible factors separately.

The computation of associated prime ideals is closely related to the problem of computing primary decompositions and has been subject of extensive research already. For details on this topic we refer to [9] and the references given there.

Introduction of intermediate steps/functional decomposition offers a different kind of decomposition. To illustrate this we can reuse the above univariate example: To obtain a root of the irreducible factor $x^4 - 5 \in \mathbb{Q}[x]$ we have to extract a fourth root. This task can be divided into consecutively taking square roots via the functional decomposition $x^4 - 5 = g(h(x))$ where $g(y) = y^2 - 5$ and $h(x) = x^2$. More generally, a (nontrivial) functional decomposition of a univariate polynomial allows the simplification—we postpone a discussion of the precise meaning—of equations of the form $p(x) = a$ where a can be specialized to some fixed value in Ω.

By passing from the functional decomposition of univariate polynomials (see, e.g., [5,34,35]) to the functional decomposition of univariate rational functions ([37,3,4]) it is possible to simplify the solution of equations of the form $n(x)/d(x) = a$ resp. $n(x) - a \cdot d(x) = 0$, where $n(x), d(x) \in k[x]$ (to take care of vanishing denominators we may like to add the condition $x_0 \cdot$

$d(x) = 1$ where x_0 is a new indeterminate). The functional decomposition of multivariate polynomials is discussed in [10] and [11], for instance. By passing to systems of multivariate rational functions and imposing restrictions on the values for $\vec{a}$ and $\vec{x}$ we reach at the decomposition of rational mappings between affine varieties and their "inverses" which is considered in [29]. Here the equations whose solution is to be simplified are of the form

$$n_1(x_1, \ldots, x_n) - a_1 \cdot d_1(x_1, \ldots, x_n) = 0$$

$$\vdots$$

$$n_l(x_1, \ldots, x_n) - a_l \cdot d_l(x_1, \ldots, x_n) = 0$$
$$x_0 \cdot d_1(x_1, \ldots, x_n) \cdot \ldots \cdot d_l(x_1, \ldots, x_n) - 1 = 0$$

with additional restrictions on the possible values for $\vec{a}$ and $\vec{x}$. Finally, we want to mention the functional decomposition of single algebraic functions which is discussed in [21]. Here the equation to be simplified is given by a bivariate polynomial $f(a, x) \in k[a, x]$.

All these functional decompositions provide some kind of "sequential decomposition" by dividing the process of solving a particular form of equations into (potentially simpler) steps. In the present paper we want to seize this idea of sequential decomposition in order to be able to simplify the solution of the system of equations determined by the prime ideals $\mathfrak{P}_i$ which naturally occur after having computed a decomposition of the Zariski closed set $\mathcal{Z}(\vec{f})$ into (k-)irreducible components as mentioned above. In more detail, the paper is organized as follows: In the next section the notion of sequential decomposition is motivated and—after recalling some terminology from elementary algebraic geometry—defined formally. Thereafter some basic properties of sequential decompositions are given, and the problem of finding this kind of decompositions automatically is discussed. Finally, we give three examples: In the first one we derive a decomposition of a system of equations which is of the form as considered in [1] and [26] in the context of a problem in diffractive optics. The second one is based on a problem in geodesy (see [13]). As an example in positive characteristic we look at a special instance of the Zariski closed sets considered in [12, p. 127, Ex. 12].

2   Motivation and preliminaries

Before defining formally what we mean by a sequential decomposition we have to clarify the notion of "simplifying an equation". For this we resume the introductory example of the univariate polynomial decomposition $x^4 - 5 = g \circ h$ where $g(y) = y^2 - 5$, $h(x) = x^2$. The key here is that instead of solving one equation of degree 4 we have to solve several equations of lower degree, namely 2. The idea behind this is that solving nonlinear equations may require an extension of a given ground field. In the example we pass from the ground field $\mathbb{Q}$ to the extension $\mathbb{Q}(\sqrt[4]{5})$ where a solution of the equation $x^4 - 5$ can be expressed. The decomposition $f = g \circ h$ allows to split this field extension into the (algebraically) simpler steps $\mathbb{Q} \lesssim \mathbb{Q}(\sqrt{5}) \lesssim \mathbb{Q}(\sqrt[4]{5})$. This point of view where field operations $+, -, \cdot, ^{-1}$ are taken for "cheap" and extending a ground field ("extracting roots") is regarded as "expensive" is consistent with [37] and [29]. The use of intermediate fields for the decomposition of multivariate polynomials has also been suggested in [17].

We want to carry over the idea of characterizing simplicity—and therewith decompositions—via intermediate fields to systems of equations given by a prime ideal. For this it is convenient to adopt a more geometric point of view: Instead of speaking of decompositions of the system of equations given by a prime ideal $\mathfrak{P} \trianglelefteq k[\vec{a}, \vec{x}]$ we also speak of decompositions of the k-variety $\mathcal{Z}(\mathfrak{P})$.[1] More precisely, $\mathcal{Z}(\mathfrak{P})$ can be described as a correspondence between affine m- and affine n-space:

Definition 1. (cf. [22, Ch. IV, Sect. 5]) Let $A \subseteq \mathbb{A}^m$, $X \subseteq \mathbb{A}^n$ be k-varieties, $R \subseteq A \times X$ a k-subvariety. Then R is called a *k-correspondence between A and X* and also denoted by $R : A \to X$. For $(\vec{\alpha}, \vec{\xi}) \in R$ we say that $\vec{\alpha} \in A$ *corresponds to $\vec{\xi} \in X$ under R*.

One may object that one should not use the notation $R : A \to X$ as R is not necessarily (the graph of) a function. One motivation for using this notation is the fact that an important class of k-correspondences consists of the (graphs of) rational maps (see [22, Ch. IV, Sect. 3]).

Determining the solution of a system of equations $\vec{f}(\vec{a}, \vec{x}) = \vec{0}$ for a "generic" fixed value $(\vec{\alpha}) \in \Omega^m$ of $(\vec{a})$ where $\mathfrak{P} := \langle \vec{f} \rangle \trianglelefteq k[\vec{a}, \vec{x}]$ is prime now translates into finding the points to which $(\vec{\alpha})$ corresponds to under the correspondence $\mathcal{Z}(\mathfrak{P})$. Hence, for $(\vec{\alpha}, \vec{\xi}) \in \mathcal{Z}(\mathfrak{P})$ a (functional/sequential) decomposition of $\mathcal{Z}(\mathfrak{P})$ should be related to an intermediate field of $k(\vec{\alpha}, \vec{\xi})/k(\vec{\alpha})$: Knowing $\vec{\alpha}$ the usual field operations in $k(\vec{\alpha})$ are "cheap", whereas for expressing $\vec{\xi}$ we have to pass into the extension field $k(\vec{\alpha}, \vec{\xi})$.

Intuitively, a decomposition should consider all "sufficiently generic" elements $(\vec{\alpha}, \vec{\xi}) \in \mathcal{Z}(\mathfrak{P})$ simultaneously. To make this more precise the notion of *generic point* is useful:

Definition 2. (cf. [22, Ch. II, Sect. 3]) Let $\mathfrak{Q} \trianglelefteq k[\vec{x}]$ be prime, and denote by x_i the image of x_i under the canonical ring homomorphism

$$k[\vec{x}] \twoheadrightarrow k[\vec{x}]/\mathfrak{Q} \hookrightarrow k(\vec{x}) := \mathrm{Quot}(k[\vec{x}]/\mathfrak{Q}).$$

Then $\mathcal{Z}(\mathfrak{Q})$ is refered to as a *model of $k(\vec{x})$*, and we call $(\vec{x}) := (x_1, \dots, x_n)$ a *generic point of $\mathcal{Z}(\mathfrak{Q})$ over k*.

All $(\vec{\alpha}, \vec{\xi}) \in \mathcal{Z}(\mathfrak{P})$ can be obtained from a generic point $(\vec{a}, \vec{x})$ of $\mathcal{Z}(\mathfrak{P})$ through specialization, and conversely every specialization of $(\vec{a}, \vec{x})$ yields a

---

[1] We follow the convention that a k-variety is a Zariski closed set $\mathcal{Z}(\mathfrak{P})$ given by some prime ideal $\mathfrak{P} \trianglelefteq k[\vec{Z}]$ (cf. [22]).

zero of $\mathfrak{P}$ (see [22, Ch. II, Sect. 3]). So it seems appropriate to relate decompositions of $\mathcal{Z}(\mathfrak{P})$ to intermediate fields of $k(\vec{a}, \vec{x})/k(\vec{a})$ with $(\vec{a}, \vec{x})$ a generic point of $\mathcal{Z}(\mathfrak{P})$. One problem with this point of view is the fact that we do not necessarily have all constants, i.e. elements of k, at our disposal: For instance, solving $x^4 - a \in \mathbb{C}[a, x]$ for any fixed value $a := \alpha \in \mathbb{C}$ corresponds to the trivial extension $\mathbb{C}(\alpha) = \mathbb{C} \leq \mathbb{C}(\alpha, \sqrt[4]{\alpha}) = \mathbb{C}$, although $\sqrt[4]{\alpha}$ possibly can not be written as a rational expression in the original coefficients and α. The problem here is that all the coefficients of $x^4 - a$ are contained in the proper subfield $\mathbb{Q}$ of $\mathbb{C}$ already. One may therefore argue that instead of relating functional decompositions of $\mathcal{Z}(\mathfrak{P})$ to intermediate fields of $k(\vec{a}, \vec{x})/k(\vec{a})$ one should relate them to intermediate fields of $k'(\vec{a}, \vec{x})/k'(\vec{a})$ where k' denotes the subfield of k generated by the coefficients in a given generating set of $\mathfrak{P}$ over the prime field of k (in the example $x^4 - a$ we had $k' = \mathbb{Q}$). The drawback here is that the field k' depends on the chosen generating set, of course; as a simple example think of the sets $\{x - a, x + a\}$ and $\{x - \sqrt{-1} \cdot a, x + \sqrt{-1} \cdot a\}$ which in $\mathbb{Q}(\sqrt{-1})[a, x]$ generate the same ideal. We do not aim at decomposing a particular representation of $\mathcal{Z}(\mathfrak{P})$ but rather the k-correspondence $\mathcal{Z}(\mathfrak{P})$ itself. Therefore we need a notion of functional/sequential decomposition which is independent of the chosen representation/generating system of $\mathfrak{P}$. To this end we define k' via an "optimal" representation of $\mathfrak{P}$—as the minimal field of definition of $\mathfrak{P}$:

Definition 3. (cf. [22, Ch. III, Sect. 2]) Let $\mathfrak{I} \trianglelefteq k[\vec{x}]$ be an ideal. Then among the subfields k' of k such that $\mathfrak{I}$ has a basis with coefficients in k there is a smallest field k_0 which is contained in all the others. We call k_0 the *minimal field of definition of* $\mathfrak{I}$ and denote it by $k_{\mathfrak{I}}$.

In particular by Hilbert's basis theorem $k_{\mathfrak{I}}$ is finitely generated over the prime field of k. Note, it makes sense to speak of the minimal field of definition of an ideal, but it does not make sense to define the smallest field over which a variety can be defined: E.g., for x transcendental over $\mathbb{F}_2$, $i \in \mathbb{N}$ arbitrary we have $\{x\} = \mathcal{Z}(Z^{2^i} - x^{2^i})$, i.e. $\{x\}$ is the zero set of a polynomial in $\mathbb{F}_2(x^{2^i})$, and we have the infinitely decreasing chain of fields $\mathbb{F}_2(x^2) \supsetneq \mathbb{F}_2(x^4) \supsetneq \mathbb{F}_2(x^8) \supsetneq \mathbb{F}_2(x^{16}) \supsetneq \cdots$

It is worth mentioning, however, that the proof of the existence of the minimal field of definition given in [22, Ch. III, Sect. 2] can easily be generalized from ideals in polynomial rings $k[\vec{x}]$ to one-sided ideals in semigroup rings $k[S]$ (see Appendix A).

Finally, before stating a formal definition of what we mean by a sequential decomposition we adopt the following notation from [36]:

Definition 4. Let $k(\gamma_1, \ldots, \gamma_n)/k$ be a finitely generated extension of fields,

$$\mathfrak{P}_{(\vec{\gamma})/k} := \{ f \in k[\vec{x}] \mid f(\vec{\gamma}) = 0 \} .$$

Then $\mathfrak{P}_{(\vec{\gamma})/k}$ is called the *ideal determined by* $(\vec{\gamma})$ *over* k.

In other words, $\mathfrak{P}_{(\vec{\gamma})/k}$ is the set of relations (syzygies) which are satisfied by $\vec{\gamma}$ over k, and $\mathcal{Z}(\mathfrak{P}_{(\vec{\gamma})/k})$ is a model of $k(\vec{\gamma})$. We remark that in [27] instead of $\mathfrak{P}_{(\vec{\gamma})/k}$ the denotation $J_{k(\vec{\gamma})/k}$ is used. In order to emphasize the dependence on $\vec{\gamma}$ we prefer to use the former notation here.

3   Sequential decompositions and intermediate fields

We have now all the ingredients needed for stating

Definition 5. Let $R : A \to X$ be a k-correspondence with defining prime ideal $\mathfrak{R} := \mathcal{I}(R) = \left\{ f \in k[\vec{a}, \vec{x}] \mid \forall (\vec{\alpha}, \vec{\xi}) \in R : f(\vec{\alpha}, \vec{\xi}) = 0 \right\}$, $(\vec{a}, \vec{x})$ a generic point of R over $k_{\mathfrak{R}}$.

Then a *sequential decomposition of R resp.* $\mathfrak{R} = \mathfrak{P}_{(\vec{a}, \vec{x})/k_{\mathfrak{R}}} \cdot k[\vec{a}, \vec{x}]$ *of arity* r is a pair

$$\left(\mathfrak{P}_{(\vec{x})/k_{\mathfrak{R}}(\vec{a}, \vec{w})}, \mathfrak{P}_{(\vec{w})/k_{\mathfrak{R}}(\vec{a})} \right) \in k_{\mathfrak{R}}(\vec{a}, \vec{w})[\vec{x}] \times k_{\mathfrak{R}}(\vec{a})[w_1, \ldots, w_r]$$

where $k_{\mathfrak{R}}(\vec{a}) \le k_{\mathfrak{R}}(\vec{a}, w_1, \ldots, w_r) \le k_{\mathfrak{R}}(\vec{a}, \vec{x})$.

If $k_{\mathfrak{R}}(\vec{a}) \lneq k_{\mathfrak{R}}(\vec{a}, \vec{w}) \lneq k_{\mathfrak{R}}(\vec{a}, \vec{x})$, i.e., $k_{\mathfrak{R}}(\vec{a}, \vec{w})$ is a proper intermediate field, the decomposition is called *proper*. Otherwise it is called *improper*.

From the preceding discussion the motivation behind this definition is clear:

1. We start by knowing $k_{\mathfrak{R}}$ and $\vec{a}$, and have to define the intermediate results $\vec{w}$ by means of equations involving "known" coefficients: $\mathfrak{P}_{(\vec{w})/k_{\mathfrak{R}}(\vec{a})}$
2. Having solved these equations we can now additionally use fractions involving these solutions. So to define equations for the solutions $\vec{x}$ we can use coefficients in $\mathrm{Quot}(k_{\mathfrak{R}}(\vec{a})[\vec{w}]/\mathfrak{P}_{(\vec{w})/k_{\mathfrak{R}}(\vec{a})}) \simeq k_{\mathfrak{R}}(\vec{a}, \vec{w})$: $\mathfrak{P}_{(\vec{x})/k_{\mathfrak{R}}(\vec{a}, \vec{w})}$

Before going on we illustrate Definition 5 by two simple examples:

Example 6. For the prime ideal $\langle x^4 - a \rangle \trianglelefteq \mathbb{Q}(\sqrt{-1})[a, x]$ we have the chain of fields

$$\mathbb{Q}(a) \le \mathbb{Q}(a, x^2) \le \mathbb{Q}(a, x) = \mathrm{Quot}(\mathbb{Q}[a, x]/\langle x^4 - a \rangle)$$

(the minimal field of definition is $\mathbb{Q}$ here). Setting $w := x^2$ this corresponds to the sequential decomposition

$$\left(\mathfrak{P}_{(x)/\mathbb{Q}(a, w)}, \mathfrak{P}_{(w)/\mathbb{Q}(a)} \right) = \left(\langle x^2 - w \rangle, \langle w^2 - a \rangle \right) \in \mathbb{Q}(a, w)[x] \times \mathbb{Q}(a)[w].$$

In other words, instead of extracting one fourth root we extract two square roots.

Example 7. For $\langle x^6 - 6x^4 - 6x^3 + 12x^2 - 36x + 1 \rangle \trianglelefteq \mathbb{Q}[x]$ (whose generator is the minimal polynomial of $\sqrt{2} + \sqrt[3]{3}$ over $\mathbb{Q}$) we have the chain of fields

$$\mathbb{Q} \le \mathbb{Q}(\sqrt{2}) \le \mathbb{Q}(\sqrt{2} + \sqrt[3]{3})$$

(note that $\sqrt{2} = (48\alpha^5 + 27\alpha^4 - 320\alpha^3 - 468\alpha^2 + 879\alpha - 1092)/755$ where $\alpha = \sqrt{2} + \sqrt[3]{3}$). This corresponds to the sequential decomposition

$$(\mathfrak{P}_{(\sqrt{2}+\sqrt[3]{3})/\mathbb{Q}(\sqrt{2})}, \mathfrak{P}_{(\sqrt{2})/\mathbb{Q}}) = (\langle x^3 - 3\sqrt{2} \cdot x^2 + 6x - 2\sqrt{2} - 3 \rangle, \langle w^2 - 2 \rangle)$$
$$\in \mathbb{Q}(\sqrt{2})[x] \times \mathbb{Q}[w]$$

which, e.g., can be used for representing the number field $\mathbb{Q}(\sqrt{2} + \sqrt[3]{3})$ in a computer algebra system as a tower of fields instead of representing it as a primitive extension.

While in these two examples the extension $k(\vec{a}, \vec{x})/k(\vec{a})$ is algebraic, in general this extension may also be transcendental. To describe the phenomena which can occur in the transcendental case it is helpful to introduce some additional terminology. Again, it is helpful to commence with a small example:

Example 8. Consider the equation

$$x_1{}^2 - x_2{}^2 - a^2 = 0 \tag{2}$$

with coefficients in $\mathbb{Q}$. To solve this equation for x_1 and x_2 we can fix x_2 to obtain a quadratic equation for x_1. As a chain of fields this "strategy" reads

$$\mathbb{Q}(a) \le \mathbb{Q}(a, x_2) \le \mathbb{Q}(a, x_1, x_2) = \text{Quot}(\mathbb{Q}[a, x_1, x_2]/\langle x_1{}^2 - x_2{}^2 - a^2 \rangle)$$

where the first extension is purely transcendental, and the second one algebraic. This chain corresponds to the—somewhat degenerate—decomposition

$$(\langle x_1{}^2 - x_2{}^2 - a^2, x_2 - x_2 \rangle, \langle 0 \rangle) \in \mathbb{Q}(a, x_2)[x_1, x_2] \times \mathbb{Q}(a)[w]$$

of $\langle x_1{}^2 - x_2{}^2 - a^2 \rangle \trianglelefteq \mathbb{Q}[a, x_1, x_2]$ resp. the $\mathbb{Q}$-correspondence defined hereby.

The zero ideal in the decomposition of Example 8 reflects the fact that a purely transcendental field extension does not provide an algebraic simplification; rather it can be understood as a fixing of "free parameters" (x_2 in this example). In this interpretation fixing a transcendence basis of an extension $k_\mathfrak{R}(\vec{a}, \vec{x})/k_\mathfrak{R}(\vec{a})$ means to fix all free parameters (cf. [29] for an analogous interpretation when dealing with rational mappings). To distinguish degenerate decompositions as in the previous example from others we make

Definition 9. A sequential decomposition $(\mathfrak{P}_{(\vec{a})/k_\mathfrak{R}(\vec{a}, \vec{w})}, \mathfrak{P}_{(\vec{w})/k_\mathfrak{R}(\vec{a})})$ is refered to as *degenerate* if the field extension $k_\mathfrak{R}(\vec{a}, \vec{w})/k_\mathfrak{R}(\vec{a})$ is purely transcendental. Otherwise the decomposition is called *non-degenerate*.

Besides being degenerate the above decomposition of $\langle x_1{}^2 - x_2{}^2 - a^2 \rangle$ has another undesirable property (cf. the notion of "strong decomposition" in [29]): Taking this decomposition for a strategy to solve (2) we are left to solve a quadratic equation for x_1 after having fixed x_2. However, by fixing $x_1 + x_2$ instead of x_2 we could solve for $x_1 + x_2$ and $x_1 - x_2$—and therefore also for x_1 and x_2—without extracting any roots, as

$$x_1 - x_2 = \frac{a^2}{x_1 + x_2} \in \mathbb{Q}(a, x_1 + x_2).$$

In terms of fields this phenomenon is a consequence of the fact that $\mathbb{Q}(a, x_2)$ is contained in the purely transcendental extension $\mathbb{Q}(a, x_1 + x_2)$ of $\mathbb{Q}(a)$. To distinguish this kind of decompositions from those which cannot be "strengthened via a fixing of parameters" we parallel [29, Definition 4]:

Definition 10. Let R be a k-correspondence with defining prime ideal $\mathfrak{R}$, $(\mathfrak{P}_{(\vec{x})/k_{\mathfrak{R}}(\vec{a},\vec{w})}, \mathfrak{P}_{(\vec{w})/k_{\mathfrak{R}}(\vec{a})}) \in k_{\mathfrak{R}}(\vec{a}, \vec{w})[\vec{x}] \times k_{\mathfrak{R}}(\vec{a})[w_1, \ldots, w_r]$ a proper nondegenerate sequential decomposition of R resp. $\mathfrak{R}$.

Then this decomposition is called *strong* if there is no field k' such that both $k_{\mathfrak{R}}(\vec{a}, \vec{w}) < k' \leq k_{\mathfrak{R}}(\vec{a}, \vec{x})$ and $k'/k_{\mathfrak{R}}(\vec{a})$ is purely transcendental. Otherwise the decomposition is called *weak*.

The problem of deciding effectively whether a sequential decomposition is proper can be solved by means of a field membership test (cf. [33,19,29]), for instance, but we are not aware of an algorithm to decide in general whether a sequential decomposition is degenerate or strong. A reason for the difficulties in developing such algorithms is indicated in the following connection to invariant theory: Let $x_1, \ldots, x_n$ be algebraically independent over $k_{\mathfrak{R}}(\vec{a})$, G a subgroup of $\mathrm{GL}_n(k_{\mathfrak{R}}(\vec{a}))$ operating on $k_{\mathfrak{R}}(\vec{a})(\vec{x})$, $k_{\mathfrak{R}}(\vec{a})(\vec{w}) := k_{\mathfrak{R}}(\vec{a})(\vec{x})^G$ the field of invariants under the operation of G. In this situation an algorithm to decide whether the sequential decomposition determined by $\vec{w}$ is nondegenerate could in particular decide whether $k_{\mathfrak{R}}(\vec{a})(\vec{x})^G/k_{\mathfrak{R}}(\vec{a})$ is purely transcendental, a problem which is known to be hard (cf., e.g., [20]).

Of course, there are some trivial cases: E.g., for $k_{\mathfrak{R}}(\vec{a}, \vec{w})/k_{\mathfrak{R}}(\vec{a})$ algebraic the corresponding decomposition is necessarily strong (provided that $k_{\mathfrak{R}}(\vec{a}, \vec{w})$ is a proper intermediate field). On the other hand, if the extension $k_{\mathfrak{R}}(\vec{a}, \vec{x})/k_{\mathfrak{R}}(\vec{a})$ is purely transcendental there are no strong decompositions of the corresponding R resp. $\mathfrak{R}$.

It is convenient to introduce an equivalence relation between sequential decompositions which reflects our point of view of taking field operations as "cheap" and passing into extensions as "expensive" (cf. [29, Def. 2]):

Definition 11. Let R be a k-correspondence with defining prime ideal $\mathfrak{R} \trianglelefteq k[\vec{a}, \vec{x}]$, $(\mathfrak{P}_{(\vec{x})/k_{\mathfrak{R}}(\vec{a},\vec{w})}, \mathfrak{P}_{(\vec{w})/k_{\mathfrak{R}}(\vec{a})})$ and $(\mathfrak{P}_{(\vec{x})/k_{\mathfrak{R}}(\vec{a},\vec{w}')}, \mathfrak{P}_{(\vec{w}')/k_{\mathfrak{R}}(\vec{a})})$ decompositions of arity r and r' of R resp. $\mathfrak{R}$. Then we call these decompositions *equivalent* if $r=r'$ and $k_{\mathfrak{R}}(\vec{a}, \vec{w}) = k_{\mathfrak{R}}(\vec{a}, \vec{w}')$, and we write

$$(\mathfrak{P}_{(\vec{x})/k_{\mathfrak{R}}(\vec{a},\vec{w})}, \mathfrak{P}_{(\vec{w})/k_{\mathfrak{R}}(\vec{a})}) \simeq (\mathfrak{P}_{(\vec{x})/k_{\mathfrak{R}}(\vec{a},\vec{w}')}, \mathfrak{P}_{(\vec{w}')/k_{\mathfrak{R}}(\vec{a})}).$$

We can formulate the following analogue of [37, Prop. 4] resp. [29, Lemma 1]:

Lemma 12. *Let $R : A \to X$ be a k-correspondence R with defining prime ideal $\mathfrak{R}$ and generic point $(\vec{a}, \vec{x})$ over $k_{\mathfrak{R}}$. For $r \in \mathbb{N}$ let*

- $\mathcal{D}_r := \{(\mathfrak{P}_{(\vec{x})/k_{\mathfrak{R}}(\vec{a},\vec{w})}, \mathfrak{P}_{(\vec{w})/k_{\mathfrak{R}}(\vec{a})}) : (\mathfrak{P}_{(\vec{x})/k_{\mathfrak{R}}(\vec{a},\vec{w})}, \mathfrak{P}_{(\vec{w})/k_{\mathfrak{R}}(\vec{a})})$ *is a sequential decomposition of R of arity r}* be the set of all sequential decompositions of R of arity r and

- $\mathcal{K}_r := \{k(\vec{a}, w_1, \ldots, w_r) : k_{\mathfrak{R}}(\vec{a}) \leq k(\vec{a}, \vec{w}) \leq k_{\mathfrak{R}}(\vec{a}, \vec{x})\}$ *the collection of intermediate fields of* $k_{\mathfrak{R}}(\vec{a}, \vec{x})/k_{\mathfrak{R}}(\vec{a})$ *which over* $k_{\mathfrak{R}}(\vec{a})$ *can be generated by* r *elements.*

Then for each $r \in \mathbb{N}$ *there is a one-to-one correspondence between* $\mathcal{D}_r / \simeq$ *and* $\mathcal{K}_r$.

Proof. Let $r \in \mathbb{N}$ be arbitrary but fixed, and define the mapping

$$\varphi_r : \mathcal{D}_r / \simeq \longrightarrow \mathcal{K}_r, [(\mathfrak{P}_{(\vec{x})/k_{\mathfrak{R}}(\vec{a}, \vec{w})}, \mathfrak{P}_{(\vec{w})/k_{\mathfrak{R}}(\vec{a})})] \mapsto k(\vec{a}, \vec{w})$$

where $[\cdot]$ denotes the residue class w. r. t. $\simeq$. Since there is always an improper decomposition contained in $\mathcal{D}_r$ and $k_{\mathfrak{R}}(\vec{a}) \in \mathcal{K}_r$ the domain and codomain are non-empty and both well-definedness and injectivity of φ_r are immediate from Definition 11.

For an arbitrary intermediate field $k' \in \mathcal{K}_r$ we can choose a finite generating set $w_1, \ldots, w_r$ of k' over $k(\vec{a})$. Then k' is the image of the element $[(\mathfrak{P}_{(\vec{x})/k_{\mathfrak{R}}(\vec{a}, \vec{w})}, \mathfrak{P}_{(\vec{w})/k_{\mathfrak{R}}(\vec{a})})]$ under φ_r, and hence φ_r is surjective. $\quad\square$

Corollary 13. *For* $k_{\mathfrak{R}}(\vec{a}, \vec{x})/k_{\mathfrak{R}}(\vec{a})$ *finite and simple, e. g. for* char $k = 0$ *and* $k_{\mathfrak{R}}(\vec{a}, \vec{x})/k_{\mathfrak{R}}(\vec{a})$ *finite, the number of non-equivalent sequential decompositions of* R *of fixed arity* $r \in \mathbb{N}$ *is finite.*

Proof. Immediate from Lemma 12 as by the primitive element theorem (see [23, Ch. V, Theorem 4.6]) in this situation each $\mathcal{K}_r$ is finite. $\quad\square$

In positive characteristic we can encounter the phenomenon that a correspondence which corresponds to a finite field extension permits infinitely many non-equivalent decompositions of a fixed arity: E. g., for $\mathfrak{R} = \langle x_1^2 - a_1, x_2^2 - a_2 \rangle \trianglelefteq \mathbb{F}_2[\vec{a}, \vec{x}]$ we have to consider the purely inseparable extension

$$\mathbb{F}_2(a_1, a_2) \leq \mathbb{F}_2(a_1, a_2, x_1, x_2) = \text{Quot}(\mathbb{F}_2[\vec{a}, \vec{x}]/\langle x_1^2 - a_1, x_2^2 - a_2 \rangle)$$

which has infinitely many intermediate fields (cf. [23, Ch. V, Ex. 24]).

In the next section where we deal with the problem of computing sequential decompositions we will indicate a possibility to circumvent this difficulty without abandoning the above characteristic-independent characterization of sequential decompositions.

4   Computing sequential decompositions

According to the above discussion finding a (proper) sequential decomposition of a k-correspondence R with defining prime ideal $\mathfrak{R} \trianglelefteq k[\vec{a}, \vec{x}]$ splits into three parts:

1. Determining the minimal field of definition $k_{\mathfrak{R}}$ of $\mathfrak{R}$.
2. Identifying a (proper) intermediate field $k_{\mathfrak{R}}(\vec{a}, \vec{w})$ of $k_{\mathfrak{R}}(\vec{a}, \vec{x})/k_{\mathfrak{R}}(\vec{a})$.

3. Computing $\mathfrak{P}_{(\vec{w})/k_{\mathfrak{R}}(\vec{a})}$ and $\mathfrak{P}_{(\vec{x})/k_{\mathfrak{R}}(\vec{a},\vec{w})}$.

The first part can be accomplished by computing any reduced Gröbner basis G of $\mathfrak{R}$: The minimal field of definition $k_{\mathfrak{R}}$ is the field generated by the coefficients in G over the prime field of k (see [30], cf. also [27]). The reason why this method works is quite simple: By means of Buchberger's algorithm G can be derived from each finite generating set of $\mathfrak{R}$ without making use of field extensions.

Before discussing Step 2—determining an intermediate field—we first deal with the last step, because ideals of the form $\mathfrak{P}_{(\vec{u})/k_{\mathfrak{R}}(\vec{v})}$ (where $\vec{u}, \vec{v} \in k_{\mathfrak{R}}(\vec{a}, \vec{x})$) will also prove useful for determining certain intermediate fields.

4.1 Computing $\mathfrak{P}_{(\vec{u})/k_{\mathfrak{R}}(\vec{v})}$

One possibility to determine a generating set of $\mathfrak{P}_{(\vec{u})/k_{\mathfrak{R}}(\vec{v})}$ is based on Gröbner basis techniques involving tag variables (see [33], [19], [27]). Another approach for computing $\mathfrak{P}_{(\vec{u})/k_{\mathfrak{R}}(\vec{v})}$ which makes use of the so-called Chow form is suggested in [32].

We want to give an alternate method for computing $\mathfrak{P}_{(\vec{u})/k_{\mathfrak{R}}(\vec{v})}$ which does not involve tag variables. For this let $u_1, \ldots, u_l, \vec{v} \in k_{\mathfrak{R}}(\vec{a}, \vec{x})$. E. g., by means of the following procedure which chooses a maximal over $k_{\mathfrak{R}}(\vec{v})$ algebraically independent subset of $\{\vec{u}\}$ we can determine a transcendence basis $\mathcal{T} \subseteq \{\vec{u}\}$ of $k_{\mathfrak{R}}(\vec{u}, \vec{v})/k_{\mathfrak{R}}(\vec{v})$ without involving tag variables (for a possibility to determine the transcendence degrees without tag variables cf. [32, Procedure 1]).

Procedure 1

In: $u_1, \ldots, u_l, \vec{v} \in k_{\mathfrak{R}}(\vec{a}, \vec{x})$
Out: a transcendence basis $\mathcal{T}$ of $k_{\mathfrak{R}}(\vec{u}, \vec{v})/k_{\mathfrak{R}}(\vec{v})$

$(t, \Lambda, \mathcal{T}) \leftarrow (\mathrm{transdeg}(k_{\mathfrak{R}}(\vec{u}, \vec{v})/k_{\mathfrak{R}}(\vec{v})), \{1, \ldots, l\}, \emptyset)$
while $\mathrm{card}(\mathcal{T}) < t$ **do**
  choose $\lambda \in \Lambda$
  $\Lambda \leftarrow \Lambda \setminus \{\lambda\}$
  if $\mathrm{card}(\mathcal{T}) < \mathrm{transdeg}(k_{\mathfrak{R}}(\vec{v})(\mathcal{T} \cup \{u_\lambda\})/k_{\mathfrak{R}}(\vec{v}))$
    then $\mathcal{T} \leftarrow \mathcal{T} \cup \{u_\lambda\}$
od
return $\mathcal{T}$

After a suitable renaming we may assume that $\mathcal{T} = \{u_1, \ldots, u_t\}$. For $i = t+1, \ldots, l$ we denote by $m_i(y_i)$ the minimal polynomial of u_i over the field $k_{\mathfrak{R}}(\vec{v}, u_1, \ldots, u_{i-1})$. In particular we can express each $m_i(y_i)$ in the form

$$m_i(y_i) = y_i^{\deg(m_i)} + \sum_{j=0}^{\deg(m_i)-1} c_{ij}(u_1, \ldots, u_{i-1}) \cdot y_i^{\,j}$$

for some $c_{ij} \in k_{\mathfrak{R}}(\vec{v})(y_1, \dots, y_{i-1})$ which are—as a result of possibly existing algebraic relations among $\vec{u}$—in general not uniquely determined. We may assume that the c_{ij} are reduced to lowest terms. Moreover, if for the numerator $n_{ij}(\vec{y})$ of $c_{ij}(\vec{y}) = n_{ij}(\vec{y})/d_{ij}(\vec{y})$ the relation $n_{ij}(\boldsymbol{u}_1, \dots, \boldsymbol{u}_{i-1}) = 0$ holds, then we set $c_{ij} := 0$; for $c_{ij} = 0$ we set $d_{ij} := 1$. With these conventions define

$$m_i' := y_i{}^{\deg(m_i)} + \sum_{j=0}^{\deg(m_i)-1} c_{ij}(y_1, \dots, y_{i-1}) \cdot y_i{}^j.$$

After clearing denominators we obtain irreducible polynomials

$$\widetilde{m}_i := \mathrm{lcm}(d_{i0}, \dots, d_{i\,\deg(m_i)-1}) \cdot m_i' \in k_{\mathfrak{R}}(\vec{v})[y_1, \dots, y_i].$$

By construction no coefficient of $\widetilde{m}_i \in k[y_1, \dots, y_{i-1}][y_i]$ is contained in $\mathfrak{P}_{(\vec{u})/k_{\mathfrak{R}}(\vec{v})}$ whereas $\widetilde{m}_{t+1}, \dots, \widetilde{m}_l \in \mathfrak{P}_{(\vec{u})/k_{\mathfrak{R}}(\vec{v})}$. In fact, we can derive a generating set of $\mathfrak{P}_{(\vec{u})/k_{\mathfrak{R}}(\vec{v})}$ from these polynomials (cf. [31, 26.] and the representation of prime ideals in the *Primbasissätze* in [15, Ch. II, §§2,3] and [25]).

Lemma 14. *With the above notation let $D := \mathrm{lcm}\{d_{\mu\nu} : t < \mu \le l, 0 \le \nu < \deg(m_\mu)\}$. Then we have the equality $\langle \widetilde{m}_{t+1}, \dots, \widetilde{m}_l \rangle : D^\infty = \mathfrak{P}_{(\vec{u})/k_{\mathfrak{R}}(\vec{v})}$.*

Proof. "$\subseteq$": Let $p \in \langle \widetilde{m}_{t+1}, \dots, \widetilde{m}_l \rangle : D^\infty$, i.e., $D^s \cdot p \in \langle \widetilde{m}_{t+1}, \dots, \widetilde{m}_l \rangle$ for some $s \in \mathbb{N}$. By construction $D^s \notin \mathfrak{P}_{(\vec{u})/k_{\mathfrak{R}}(\vec{v})}$, and hence from $\mathfrak{P}_{(\vec{u})/k_{\mathfrak{R}}(\vec{v})}$ being prime we know that $p \in \mathfrak{P}_{(\vec{u})/k_{\mathfrak{R}}(\vec{v})}$.
"$\supseteq$": We show that for $0 \le i \le l$ the inclusion

$$\mathfrak{P}_{(\vec{u})/k_{\mathfrak{R}}(\vec{v})} \cap k_{\mathfrak{R}}(\vec{v})[y_1, \dots, y_i] \subseteq \langle \widetilde{m}_{t+1}, \dots, \widetilde{m}_i \rangle : D_i{}^\infty \trianglelefteq k_{\mathfrak{R}}(\vec{v})[y_1, \dots, y_i]$$

holds where $D_i := \mathrm{lcm}\{d_{\mu\nu} : t < \mu \le i, 0 \le \nu < \deg(m_\mu)\}$. For $0 \le i \le t$ this is trivial as in this case $\mathfrak{P}_{(\vec{u})/k_{\mathfrak{R}}(\vec{v})} \cap k_{\mathfrak{R}}(\vec{v})[y_1, \dots, y_i] = \langle 0 \rangle$ by construction. Regarding the inclusion as proven for i we verify it for $i + 1$: Let $p \in \mathfrak{P}_{(\vec{u})/k_{\mathfrak{R}}(\vec{v})} \cap k_{\mathfrak{R}}(\vec{v})[y_1, \dots, y_{i+1}]$, say $p = \sum_{j=0}^s g_j \cdot y_{i+1}{}^j$ where $g_j \in k_{\mathfrak{R}}(\vec{v})[y_1, \dots, y_i]$, $s \in \mathbb{N}$. If $g_s(\boldsymbol{u}_1, \dots, \boldsymbol{u}_i) = 0$ then by induction hypothesis we have

$$g_s \in \langle \widetilde{m}_{t+1}, \dots, \widetilde{m}_i \rangle : D_i{}^\infty \subseteq \langle \widetilde{m}_{t+1}, \dots, \widetilde{m}_{i+1} \rangle : D_{i+1}{}^\infty,$$

and it is sufficient to verify $p - g_s \cdot y_{i+1}{}^s \in \langle \widetilde{m}_{t+1}, \dots, \widetilde{m}_{i+1} \rangle : D_{i+1}{}^\infty$. We may therefore w.l.o.g. assume that $g_s(\boldsymbol{u}_1, \dots, \boldsymbol{u}_i) \ne 0$.

Assume that s is smaller than the degree of m_{i+1} resp. $\widetilde{m}_{i+1}$ as a polynomial in y_{i+1}. From $p \in \mathfrak{P}_{(\vec{u})/k_{\mathfrak{R}}(\vec{v})}$ we obtain $\sum_{j=0}^s g_j(\boldsymbol{u}_1, \dots, \boldsymbol{u}_i) \cdot \boldsymbol{u}_{i+1}{}^j = 0$ where $g_s(\boldsymbol{u}_1, \dots, \boldsymbol{u}_i) \ne 0$—in contradiction to m_{i+1} being the minimal polynomial of $\boldsymbol{u}_{i+1}$ over $k_{\mathfrak{R}}(\vec{v})(\boldsymbol{u}_1, \dots, \boldsymbol{u}_i)$. Hence our assumption was wrong. We can therefore find a polynomial $q \in k_{\mathfrak{R}}(\vec{v})[y_1, \dots, y_{i+1}]$ and a nonnegative integer $\mu < \deg(m_{i+1})$ such that $D_{i+1}{}^\nu \cdot p - q \cdot \widetilde{m}_{i+1} = \sum_{j=0}^\mu a_j \cdot y_{i+1}{}^j$ for some $\nu \in \mathbb{N}$, $a_j \in k_{\mathfrak{R}}(\vec{v})[y_1, \dots, y_i]$.

Since $D_{i+1}{}^\nu \cdot p - q \cdot \widetilde{m}_{i+1} \in \mathfrak{P}_{(\vec{u})/k_{\mathfrak{R}}(\vec{v})}$ and μ is smaller than the degree of $\widetilde{m}_{i+1}$ as a polynomial in y_{i+1} we can argue as above to conclude that $a_j(\boldsymbol{u}_1, \ldots, \boldsymbol{u}_i) = 0$ for all $j = 0, \ldots, \mu$. In other words we have $a_j(y_1, \ldots, y_i) \in \mathfrak{P}_{(\vec{u})/k_{\mathfrak{R}}(\vec{v})} \cap k_{\mathfrak{R}}(\vec{v})[y_1, \ldots, y_i]$ which according to the induction hypothesis is contained in $\langle \widetilde{m}_{t+1}, \ldots, \widetilde{m}_i \rangle : D_i^\infty$. So we have

$$D_{i+1}{}^\nu \cdot p \in (\langle \widetilde{m}_{t+1}, \ldots, \widetilde{m}_i \rangle : D_i^\infty) \cdot k_{\mathfrak{R}}(\vec{v})[y_1, \ldots, y_{i+1}] +$$
$$\langle \widetilde{m}_{i+1} \rangle \cdot k_{\mathfrak{R}}(\vec{v})[y_1, \ldots, y_{i+1}]$$

and hence $p \in \langle \widetilde{m}_{t+1}, \ldots, \widetilde{m}_{i+1} \rangle : D_{i+1}^\infty$. $\qquad\square$

In our concrete situation $\boldsymbol{u}$ and $\boldsymbol{v}$ are given as elements of $k_{\mathfrak{R}}(\vec{a}, \vec{x})$. So to compute the minimal polynomials $m_{t+1}, \ldots, m_l$—from which we can easily derive $\widetilde{m}_{t+1}, \ldots, \widetilde{m}_l$—without tag variables we can compute generators of $\mathfrak{P}_{(\vec{a}, \vec{x})/k_{\mathfrak{R}}(u_1, \ldots, u_{i-1}, \vec{v})}$, $i = t+1, \ldots, l$ as described in [29] and then apply [28, Algorithm 3.2]. Although the latter algorithm has actually been designed for intermediate fields of purely transcendental extensions it can be applied here, as this restriction is not needed in the proof of its correctness. This fact has already been exploited in the computation of the Chow form in [32]. Note that by using tag parameters as described in [28], [29] we obtain the required explicit expressions of the coefficients in terms of $\boldsymbol{u}_1, \ldots, \boldsymbol{u}_{i-1}$.

Finally, to compute the stable quotient $\langle \widetilde{m}_{t+1}, \ldots, \widetilde{m}_l \rangle : D^\infty$ we can, for instance, use a Gröbner basis computation w. r. t. an elimination orderering involving $l+1$ variables (see [6, Prop. 6.37]). Alternatively we can use iterated ideal quotients as suggested in [2]—thereby requiring only l variables.

4.2   Identifying an intermediate extension

Algebraic extensions As indicated in Corollary 13 for $k_{\mathfrak{R}}(\vec{a}, \vec{x})/k_{\mathfrak{R}}(\vec{a})$ being separable and finite the situation is rather simple, because by the primitive element theorem the number of intermediate fields of this kind of extension is finite. Moreover, all of these intermediate fields can be identified, e. g., by means of a minimal primary decomposition of $\mathfrak{P}_{(\vec{a}, \vec{x})/k_{\mathfrak{R}}(\vec{a})} \cdot k_{\mathfrak{R}}(\vec{a}, \vec{x})[\vec{a}, \vec{x}]$ (see [29, Lemma 4]; for other techniques to compute intermediate fields cf. [24] and the references given there).

For $k_{\mathfrak{R}}(\vec{a}, \vec{x})/k_{\mathfrak{R}}(\vec{a})$ an arbitrary algebraic extension [29, Lemma 4] can be applied to identify intermediate extensions $k_{\mathfrak{R}}(\vec{a}, \vec{w})$ where $k_{\mathfrak{R}}(\vec{a}, \vec{w})/k_{\mathfrak{R}}(\vec{a})$ or $k_{\mathfrak{R}}(\vec{a}, \vec{x})/k_{\mathfrak{R}}(\vec{a}, \vec{w})$ is separable algebraic. So the most critical case when dealing with an algebraic extension is the situation where $k_{\mathfrak{R}}(\vec{a}, \vec{x})/k_{\mathfrak{R}}(\vec{a})$ is purely inseparable. As already illustrated above by the example $\mathfrak{R} = \langle x_1{}^2 - a_1, x_2{}^2 - a_2 \rangle \trianglelefteq \mathbb{F}_2[\vec{a}, \vec{x}]$ here we can encounter the unpleasant phenomenon that the number of intermediate fields is infinite, although we are dealing with a finite algebraic extension. To circumvent this phenomenon we first recall

Lemma 15. *([23, Ch. VIII, Ex. 5]): Let $k_\Re(\vec{a}, \vec{x}) = k_\Re(\vec{a}, x_1, \ldots, x_n)$ be a finite separable extension of $k_\Re(\vec{a})$ and choose over $k_\Re(\vec{a})$ transcendental elements $t_1, \ldots, t_n \in \Omega$. Then we have $k_\Re(\vec{t})(\vec{a}, \vec{x}) = k_\Re(\vec{t})(\vec{a}, \sum_{i=1}^n t_i x_i)$.*

If we accept the "padding" of $k_\Re$ by the purely transcendental elements $\vec{t}$ as an innocuous operation, this lemma suggests that in the case of a finite separable extension instead of looking at intermediate fields of $k_\Re(\vec{a}, \vec{x})/k_\Re(\vec{a})$ we could alternatively look at intermediate fields of $k_\Re(\vec{t})(\vec{a}, \sum_{i=1}^n t_i x_i)/k_\Re(\vec{t})(\vec{a})$. As the latter extension also makes sense in positive characteristic and as a simple extension has only finitely many intermediate fields we could use it as an—admittedly not completely satisfactory—substitute for a finite extension $k_\Re(\vec{a}, \vec{x})/k_\Re(\vec{a})$ with infinitely many intermediate fields. Following this interpretation one could think of defining a sequential (t-)decomposition as a pair $(\mathfrak{P}_{(\vec{x})/k_\Re(\vec{t})(\vec{a},\vec{w})}, \mathfrak{P}_{(\vec{w})/k_\Re(\vec{t})(\vec{a})}) \in k_\Re(\vec{t})(\vec{a}, \vec{w})[\vec{x}] \times k_\Re(\vec{t})(\vec{a})[w_1, \ldots, w_r]$ where $k_\Re(\vec{t})(\vec{a}) \leq k_\Re(\vec{t})(\vec{a}, \vec{w}) \leq k_\Re(\vec{t})(\vec{a}, \sum_i t_i x_i)$ (cf. Definition 5). We do not want to pursue this topic any further here, however, and direct our attention to transcendental extensions.

Transcendental extensions Having in mind the interpretation that adjoining transcendental elements to $k_\Re(\vec{a})$ corresponds to a fixing of free parameters we are especially interested in those intermediate fields $k_\Re(\vec{a}, \vec{w})$ of $k_\Re(\vec{a}, \vec{x})/k_\Re(\vec{a})$ which contain a transcendence basis hereof: It seems natural to fix the free parameters first and to solve for the remaining indeterminates thereafter.

Owing to the convenient properties of separable algebraic extensions it is desirable to choose generators $\vec{w}$ which contain a *separating* transcendence basis of the extension $k_\Re(\vec{a}, \vec{x})/k_\Re(\vec{a})$, if the latter is separably generated. To verify constructively whether there is a separating transcendence basis we can use the following theorem whose proof can be turned into a procedure for computing a separating transcendence basis in the affirmative case:

Theorem 16. *([36, Ch. I, Theorem 2]) Let $k(\gamma_1, \ldots, \gamma_n)/k$ be a finitely generated extension of fields, $\operatorname{transdeg}(k(\gamma_1, \ldots, \gamma_n)/k) = t$, $P \subseteq k[x_1, \ldots, x_n]$ a finite basis of the ideal determined by $\vec{\gamma}$ over k. Then the following statements are equivalent:*

(i) $k(\vec{\gamma})$ is separably generated over k.

(ii) The rank of the matrix $\left(\frac{\partial p}{\partial x_i}(\vec{\gamma}) \right)_{p \in P, i=1,\ldots,n}$ is equal to $n - t$.

To determine a separating transcendence basis if the matrix in Theorem 16 is of rank $n - t$ we can use the following observation in Weil's proof of the above statement:

Corollary 17. *With the notation of Theorem 16 let the rank of the matrix $\left(\frac{\partial p}{\partial x_i}(\vec{\gamma}) \right)_{p \in P, i=1,\ldots,n}$ be $n - t$, and choose subsets $P' \subseteq P$, $I' \subseteq \{1, \ldots, n\}$ of* *cardinality* $n - t$ *such that* $\det\left(\left(\frac{\partial p}{\partial x_i}(\vec{\gamma})\right)_{p \in P', i \in I'}\right) \neq 0.$ *Then* $\{\gamma_i : i \in I'\}$ *is a separating transcendence basis of* $k(\gamma_1, \dots, \gamma_n)/k$.

Proof. See the proof of [36, Ch. I, Theorem 2].   □

It is worth remarking that in characteristic zero Theorem 16 also enables us to compute the transcendence degree (and via Corollary 17 also a transcendence basis) of a finitely generated extension $k(\gamma_1, \dots, \gamma_n)/k$ without making use of Gröbner basis techniques if a finite generating set of the ideal determined by $\vec{\gamma}$ over k is known:

Corollary 18. *With the notation of Theorem 16 let* $char(k) = 0$. *Then*

$$\text{transdeg}(k(\gamma_1, \dots, \gamma_n)/k) = n - \text{rank}\left(\left(\frac{\partial p}{\partial x_i}(\vec{\gamma})\right)_{p \in P, i=1, \dots, n}\right).$$

Proof. For $char(k) = 0$ any transcendence basis is separating. Thus the claim follows immediately from Theorem 16.   □

5   Examples

5.1   An example from diffractive optics

As explained in [1] and [26] the design of certain setups in diffractive optics can be reduced to the solution of polynomial equations of the form $A = D_1 \cdot C \cdot D_2$ where A is a matrix with complex entries (depending on a mapping which is to be realized optically), D_1 and D_2 are diagonal matrices whose entries are to be found, and C is a circulant matrix whose entries are also to be constructed. In the case of 4×4 matrices we obtain the system of equations

$$\begin{pmatrix} a_{11} & a_{12} & a_{13} & a_{14} \\ a_{21} & a_{22} & a_{23} & a_{24} \\ a_{31} & a_{32} & a_{33} & a_{34} \\ a_{41} & a_{42} & a_{43} & a_{44} \end{pmatrix} = \begin{pmatrix} d_1 & 0 & 0 & 0 \\ 0 & d_2 & 0 & 0 \\ 0 & 0 & d_3 & 0 \\ 0 & 0 & 0 & d_4 \end{pmatrix} \cdot \begin{pmatrix} c_1 & c_2 & c_3 & c_4 \\ c_4 & c_1 & c_2 & c_3 \\ c_3 & c_4 & c_1 & c_2 \\ c_2 & c_3 & c_4 & c_1 \end{pmatrix} \cdot \begin{pmatrix} d_5 & 0 & 0 & 0 \\ 0 & d_6 & 0 & 0 \\ 0 & 0 & d_7 & 0 \\ 0 & 0 & 0 & d_8 \end{pmatrix}$$

where we look for the possible complex values of the c_i, d_j for given complex values of the a_{mn}. Expanding the above matrix product we obtain the (binomial) ideal

$\Re = \langle a_{11} - d_1 c_1 d_5, a_{12} - d_1 c_2 d_6, a_{13} - d_1 c_3 d_7, a_{14} - d_1 c_4 d_8,$
$\quad a_{21} - d_2 c_4 d_5, a_{22} - d_2 c_1 d_6, a_{23} - d_2 c_2 d_7, a_{24} - d_2 c_3 d_8,$
$\quad a_{31} - d_3 c_3 d_5, a_{32} - d_3 c_4 d_6, a_{33} - d_3 c_1 d_7, a_{34} - d_3 c_2 d_8,$
$\quad a_{41} - d_4 c_2 d_5, a_{42} - d_4 c_3 d_6, a_{43} - d_4 c_4 d_7, a_{44} - d_4 c_1 d_8\rangle$
$\quad \trianglelefteq \mathbb{Q}[a_{11}, a_{12}, a_{13}, a_{14}, a_{21}, a_{22}, a_{23}, a_{24}, a_{31}, a_{32}, a_{33}, a_{34}, a_{41}, a_{42}, a_{43}, a_{44},$
$\qquad d_1, d_2, d_3, d_4, c_1, c_2, c_3, c_4, d_5, d_6, d_7, d_8].$

E. g., by means of the computer algebra system Singular 1.2.2 this ideal is easily verified to be prime and of dimension 12, and hence defines a twelve-dimensional $\mathbb{Q}$-correspondence $R : \mathbb{A}^{16} \to \mathbb{A}^{16}$ in the sense of Definition 1 (we set $\Omega := \mathbb{C}$). Using the lexicographical term order with $a_{32} > a_{33} > a_{34} > a_{42} > a_{43} > a_{44} > d_2 > d_3 > d_4 > c_1 > c_2 > c_3 > c_4 > d_6 > d_7 > d_8$ we obtain the following reduced Gröbner basis for the extension $\mathfrak{R}^e := \mathfrak{R} \cdot \mathbb{Q}(a_{11}, a_{12}, a_{13}, a_{14}, a_{21}, a_{22}, a_{23}, a_{24}, a_{31}, a_{41}, d_1, d_5)[a_{32},$ $a_{33}, a_{34}, a_{42}, a_{43}, a_{44}, d_2, d_3, d_4, c_1, c_2, c_3, c_4, d_6, d_7, d_8]$ of $\mathfrak{R}$ (to perform this computation one can use a computer algebra system like MAGMA V2.4-BETA, for instance):

$$\left\{ a_{32} - \frac{a_{14}a_{22}a_{31}}{a_{11}a_{24}}, a_{33} - \frac{a_{14}a_{22}a_{23}a_{31}}{a_{12}a_{21}a_{24}}, a_{34} - \frac{a_{14}a_{23}a_{31}}{a_{13}a_{21}}, a_{42} - \frac{a_{13}a_{22}a_{41}}{a_{11}a_{23}}, \right.$$

$$a_{43} - \frac{a_{13}a_{14}a_{22}a_{41}}{a_{11}a_{12}a_{24}}, a_{44} - \frac{a_{14}a_{22}a_{41}}{a_{12}a_{21}}, d_2 - \frac{a_{21}d_1}{a_{14}d_5} \cdot d_8, d_3 - \frac{a_{21}a_{31}d_1}{a_{14}a_{24}d_5{}^2} \cdot d_8{}^2,$$

$$d_4 - \frac{a_{13}a_{21}{}^2 a_{41} d_1}{a_{14}{}^2 a_{23}a_{24}d_5{}^3} \cdot d_8{}^3, c_1 - \frac{a_{11}}{d_1 d_5}, c_2 - \frac{a_{11}a_{12}a_{21}}{a_{14}a_{22}d_1 d_5{}^2} \cdot d_8,$$

$$c_3 - \frac{a_{11}a_{12}a_{13}a_{21}{}^2}{a_{14}{}^2 a_{22}a_{23}d_1 d_5{}^3} \cdot d_8{}^2, c_4 - \frac{a_{11}a_{12}a_{13}a_{21}{}^3}{a_{14}{}^2 a_{22}a_{23}a_{24}d_1 d_5{}^4} \cdot d_8{}^3,$$

$$\left. d_6 - \frac{a_{12}a_{13}a_{21}{}^2}{a_{14}{}^2 a_{23}a_{24}d_5{}^2} \cdot d_8{}^3, d_7 - \frac{a_{13}a_{21}}{a_{14}a_{24}d_5} \cdot d_8{}^2, d_8{}^4 - \frac{a_{14}{}^3 a_{22}a_{23}a_{24}d_5{}^4}{a_{11}a_{12}a_{13}a_{21}{}^3} \right\}$$

From this we can derive that $\mathfrak{R}^e$ is zero-dimensional and that $\mathbb{Q}(\vec{a}) := \mathbb{Q}(\{a_{ij} : 1 \leq i, j \leq 4\})$ is equal to the purely transcendental extension $\mathbb{Q}(\{a_{ij} : 1 \leq i, j \leq 4 \text{ and } (i, j) \notin \{(3,2), (3,3), (3,4), (4,2), (4,3), (4,4)\}\})$ of $\mathbb{Q}$ (the meaning of the boldface letters is consistent with the above—cf. Definition 2). Moreover, we can conclude that $\{d_1, d_5\}$ forms a (necessarily separating) transcendence basis of the extension $\mathbb{Q}(\vec{a}, \vec{x})/\mathbb{Q}(\vec{a})$ where $(\vec{x}) := (d_1, \ldots, d_8, c_1, \ldots, c_4)$. The Gröbner basis also shows that in fact $\mathbb{Q}(\vec{a}, \vec{x}) = \mathbb{Q}(\vec{a}, d_1, d_5, d_8)$.

Since $x^4 - (a_{14}{}^3 a_{22}a_{23}a_{24}d_5{}^4)/(a_{11}a_{12}a_{13}a_{21}{}^3) \in \mathbb{Q}(\vec{a}, d_1, d_5)[x]$ ("the 'last' element of the Gröbner basis with d_8 replaced by x") is irreducible we know that the extension $\mathbb{Q}(\vec{a}, \vec{x})/\mathbb{Q}(\vec{a}, d_1, d_5)$ is (separable) algebraic of degree four with primitive element d_8. Looking at the minimal polynomial of d_8 over $\mathbb{Q}(\vec{a}, d_1, d_5)$ it is natural to choose $w := d_8{}^2$ (with minimal polynomial $w^2 - (a_{14}{}^3 a_{22}a_{23}a_{24}d_5{}^4)/(a_{11}a_{12}a_{13}a_{21}{}^3) \in \mathbb{Q}(\vec{a}, d_1, d_5)[x]$) as a generator of an intermediate field of $\mathbb{Q}(\vec{a}, \vec{x})/\mathbb{Q}(\vec{a}, d_1, d_5)$. In summary, we have the following chain of fields to define a sequential decomposition of R:

$$\mathbb{Q}(\vec{a}) \leq \mathbb{Q}(\vec{a}, d_1, d_5, d_8{}^2) \leq \mathbb{Q}(\vec{a}, \vec{x})$$

In terms of ideals this chain is reflected in the following decomposition of R (resp. $\mathfrak{R}$): $(\mathfrak{P}_{(\vec{x})/\mathbb{Q}(\vec{a}, d_1, d_5, d_8{}^2)}, \mathfrak{P}_{(d_1, d_5, d_8{}^2)/\mathbb{Q}(\vec{a})})$ with $\mathfrak{P}_{(\vec{x})/\mathbb{Q}(\vec{a}, d_1, d_5, d_8{}^2)} =$

$$\left\langle d_1 - d_1, d_2 - \frac{a_{21}d_1}{a_{14}d_5} \cdot d_8, d_3 - \frac{a_{21}a_{31}d_1}{a_{14}a_{24}d_5{}^2} \cdot d_8{}^2, d_4 - \frac{a_{13}a_{21}{}^2 a_{41}d_1}{a_{14}{}^2 a_{23}a_{24}d_5{}^3} \cdot d_8{}^3, \right.$$

$$c_1 - \frac{a_{11}}{d_1 d_5}, c_2 - \frac{a_{11}a_{12}a_{21}}{a_{14}a_{22}d_1 d_5{}^2} \cdot d_8, c_3 - \frac{a_{11}a_{12}a_{13}a_{21}{}^2}{a_{14}{}^2 a_{22}a_{23}d_1 d_5{}^3} \cdot d_8{}^2,$$

$$c_4 - \frac{a_{11}a_{12}a_{13}a_{21}{}^3}{a_{14}{}^2 a_{22}a_{23}a_{24}d_1 d_5{}^4} \cdot d_8{}^3, d_5 - d_5, d_6 - \frac{a_{12}a_{13}a_{21}{}^2}{a_{14}{}^2 a_{23}a_{24}d_5{}^2} \cdot d_8{}^3,$$

$$\left. d_7 - \frac{a_{13}a_{21}}{a_{14}a_{24}d_5} \cdot d_8{}^2, d_8{}^2 - w \right\rangle \text{ and}$$

$$\mathfrak{P}_{(d_1, d_5, w)/\mathbb{Q}(\bar{a})} = \left\langle w^2 - \frac{a_{14}{}^3 a_{22}a_{23}a_{24}d_5{}^4}{a_{11}a_{12}a_{13}a_{21}{}^3} \right\rangle.$$

So for a "generic" choice of the a_{ij}, computing the corresponding c_l and d_l splits into the solution of two quadratic (and several linear) equations.

5.2   An example from geodesy

In the context of the *threedimensional resection problem* in [13] the following system of equations with rational coefficients is considered:

$$x_1{}^2 + 2a_{12}x_1 x_2 + x_2{}^2 + a_{00} = 0$$
$$x_2{}^2 + 2b_{23}x_2 x_3 + x_3{}^2 + b_{00} = 0$$
$$x_3{}^2 + 2c_{31}x_3 x_1 + x_1{}^2 + c_{00} = 0$$

Here the solutions for the indeterminates x_1, x_2, x_3 depend on the values of the parameters $a_{00}, a_{12}, b_{00}, b_{23}, c_{00}, c_{31}$ (for the interpretation of the variables and parameters see [13]). This system has been solved in [18, Sect. 2.7.2] where the parameters are taken for algebraically independent. As already mentioned in [13] and [18] a more classical approach to this problem which dates about 150 years earlier can be found in [16]. To see that this system resp. the Zariski closed set defined hereby allows a sequential decomposition in the sense of Definition 5 we first note that the corresponding ideal

$$\langle x_1{}^2 + 2a_{12}x_1 x_2 + x_2{}^2 + a_{00}, x_2{}^2 + 2b_{23}x_2 x_3 + x_3{}^2 + b_{00}, x_3{}^2 + 2c_{31}x_3 x_1 + x_1{}^2 + c_{00} \rangle$$

in $\mathbb{Q}[a_{00}, a_{12}, b_{00}, b_{23}, c_{00}, c_{31}, x_1, x_2, x_3]$ is prime (this can, e.g., be checked via a computer algebra system).

Decompositions of the $\mathbb{Q}$-correspondence defined through this ideal are characterized by intermediate fields of the algebraic extension

$$\mathbb{Q}(a_{00}, a_{12}, b_{00}, b_{23}, c_{00}, c_{31}, x_1, x_2, x_3)/\mathbb{Q}(a_{00}, a_{12}, b_{00}, b_{23}, c_{00}, c_{31}) \tag{3}$$

where $a_{00}, a_{12}, b_{00}, b_{23}, c_{00}, c_{31}$ are algebraically independent over $\mathbb{Q}$.

The minimal polynomial of x_3 over $\mathbb{Q}(a_{00}, a_{12}, b_{00}, b_{23}, c_{00}, c_{31})$ is of degree 8, and one can verify that $x_1, x_2 \in \mathbb{Q}(a_{00}, a_{12}, b_{00}, b_{23}, c_{00}, c_{31}, x_3)$ already, i.e., x_3 is a primitive element for the extension (3). Moreover, the minimal polynomial of x_3 is of the form $Z^8 + \alpha_6 \cdot Z^6 + \alpha_4 \cdot Z^4 + \alpha_2 \cdot Z^2 + \alpha_0$ where $\alpha_i \in \mathbb{Q}(a_{00}, a_{12}, b_{00}, b_{23}, c_{00}, c_{31})$, and one easily verifies that $x_3{}^2$ generates a proper intermediate field of (3), and hence gives rise to a proper sequential decomposition of arity 1. So for a "generic" choice of the parameters a_{00}, a_{12}, $b_{00}, b_{23}, c_{00}, c_{31}$ we can determine x_1, x_2, and x_3 through the solution of an equation of degree two, an equation of degree four, and linear equations.

5.3   An example in positive characteristic

Our last example is based on a concrete instance of the type of varieties considered in [12, p. 127, Ex. 12]: Set $(f_1, f_2, f_3) := (a^2 + a + 1, a^3 + a^2 + 1, a^5 + a^3 + 1) \in \mathbb{F}_2[a]^3$. Then the Zariski closed set $R := \mathcal{Z}(f_1 - x_1{}^3, f_2 - x_2{}^3, f_3 - x_3{}^3) \subseteq \mathbb{A}^1 \times \mathbb{A}^3$ turns out to be an $\mathbb{F}_2$-correspondence with $[\mathbb{F}_2(a, \vec{x}) : \mathbb{F}_2(a)] = 3^3$.

As the extension $\mathbb{F}_2(a, x_2, x_3)/\mathbb{F}_2(a)$ is of degree 3^2 only, the elements x_2, x_3 generate a proper intermediate field of $\mathbb{F}_2(a, \vec{x})/\mathbb{F}_2(a)$. Hence for any tuple of generators $(\vec{w})$ of $\mathbb{F}_2(a, x_2, x_3)$ over $\mathbb{F}_2(a)$ we have a decomposition $(\mathfrak{P}_{(\vec{x})/\mathbb{F}_2(a,\vec{w})}, \mathfrak{P}_{(\vec{w})/\mathbb{F}_2(a)})$ of R.

Acknowledgement

The author is indebted to Jörn Müller-Quade for many helpful discussions.

A   On the minimal field of definition of an ideal

By means of some marginal technical modifications of the proof of [22, Ch. III, Theorem 7] we obtain

Theorem 19. *Let S be a semigroup, k a field with prime field k_0, $\mathfrak{I} \subseteq k[S]$ a one-sided ideal in the semigroup ring $k[S]$. Then there is a subfield $k_\mathfrak{I} \leq k$ such that*

(i) $\mathfrak{I}$ has a basis $G \subseteq k_\mathfrak{I}[S]$, and
(ii) if $F \subseteq k[S]$ is any basis for $\mathfrak{I}$ then $k_\mathfrak{I} \leq k_0(\{a_s : \exists p \in F \text{ with } p = \sum_{s \in S} a_s \cdot s\})$.

Proof. We restrict ourselves to stating the proof for left ideals, as the modifications for right ideals are straightforward.

Let $B \subseteq S$ be such that $\{b + \mathfrak{I} : b \in B\}$ is a basis of the k-vector space $k[S]/\mathfrak{I}$, $C := S \setminus B$ the complement of B in S. By construction there are for each $c \in C$ uniquely determined $\alpha_{cb} \in k$ such that

$$c - \sum_{b \in B} \alpha_{cb} \cdot b \in \mathfrak{I}$$

and $\alpha_{cb} = 0$ for all but finitely many $b \in B$. We claim that $k_\mathfrak{I} := k_0(\{\alpha_{cb} : b \in B, c \in C\})$ has the desired properties:

(i): Let $f \in \mathfrak{I}$, say $f = \sum_{c \in C} \beta_c \cdot c + \sum_{b \in B} \beta_b \cdot b$ where only finitely many of the $\beta_c, \beta_b \in k$ are non-zero. After adjusting the coefficients in the second sum we can write

$$f = \sum_{c \in C} \beta_c(c - \sum_{b \in B} \alpha_{cb} \cdot b) + \sum_{b \in B} \gamma_b \cdot b$$

where all the sums are finite. By construction f and the $c - \sum_{b \in B} \alpha_{cb} \cdot b$ are contained in $\mathfrak{I}$, and hence also $\sum_{b \in B} \gamma_b \cdot b \in \mathfrak{I}$. Due to the vector space basis property of $\{b + \mathfrak{I} : b \in B\}$ we therefore have $\gamma_b = 0$ for all $b \in B$. In other words $G := \{c - \sum_{b \in B} \alpha_{cb} \cdot b : c \in C\}$ is a basis of $\mathfrak{I}$ with $G \subseteq k_{\mathfrak{I}}[S]$.

(ii): Let $F \subset k[S]$ be an arbitrary basis for $\mathfrak{I}$, $k_F := k_0(\{a_s : \exists p \in F \text{ with } p = \sum_{s \in S} a_s \cdot s\})$, $c \in C$ arbitrary but fixed. Then for suitable $g_f \in k[S]$ (where only finitely many of the g_f are non-zero) we can write

$$c - \sum_{b \in B} \alpha_{cb} \cdot b = \sum_{f \in F} g_f f. \tag{4}$$

It is sufficient to prove that the g_f can be chosen from k_F. Equation (4) then implies that $\alpha_{cb} \in k_F$ for each b, and as $c \in C$ was arbitrary we get $k_{\mathfrak{I}} \leq k_F$ as required.

For this aim we introduce for each g_f a polynomial G_f which is obtained by replacing each of the finitely many nonzero "coefficients" γ_{fs} in g_f by an indeterminate x_{fs}: $g_f = \sum_{s \in S} \gamma_{fs} \cdot s \mapsto G_f = \sum_{s \in S} x_{fs} \cdot s$ with $x_{fs} = 0$ if $\gamma_{fs} = 0$. By rearranging the summands we obtain

$$\sum_{f \in F} G_f f = \sum_{c \in C} l_c(\overrightarrow{x_{fs}}) \cdot c + \sum_{b \in B} l_b(\overrightarrow{x_{fs}}) \cdot b$$

where $l_c(\overrightarrow{x_{fs}}), l_b(\overrightarrow{x_{fs}}) \in k_F[\overrightarrow{x_{fs}}]$ are linear polynomials with coefficients in k_F. From (4) we know that the linear system of equations

$$l_c(\overrightarrow{x_{fs}}) = 1$$
$$l_{c'}(\overrightarrow{x_{fs}}) = 0, \quad c' \in C \setminus \{c\}$$

has a solution in k. All the coefficients of this linear system of equations are contained in k_F. Therefore, we may deduce that there is also a solution $(\overrightarrow{\delta_{fs}})$ for $(\overrightarrow{x_{fs}})$ with all of the δ_{fs} being contained in k_F. Denoting by g'_f the element of $k[S]$ obtained from G_f by specializing $(\overrightarrow{x_{fs}}) \mapsto (\overrightarrow{\delta_{fs}})$ we obtain

$$\sum_{f \in F} g'_f f = c - \sum_{b \in B} \epsilon_{cb} \cdot b$$

for some $\epsilon_{cb} \in k_F$. Since $\{b + \mathfrak{I} : b \in B\}$ is a vector space basis of $k[S]/\mathfrak{I}$ and $\sum_{f \in F} g'_f f \in \mathfrak{I}$ the ϵ_{cb} must coincide with the α_{cb} for all $b \in B$, and we are done. □

References

1. Harald Aagedal, Thomas Beth, Jörn Müller-Quade, and Michael Schmid. Algorithmic design of diffractive optical systems for information processing. In Tommaso Toffoli, Michael Biafore, and João Leão, editors, *Proceedings of the Fourth Workshop on Physics and Computation PhysComp96*, pages 1–6. New England Complex Systems Institute, November 1996.

2. Cesar Alonso, Jaime Gutierrez, and Thomas Recio. An implicitization algorithm with fewer variables. *Computer Aided Geometric Design*, 12:251–258, 1995.

3. Cesar Alonso, Jaime Gutierrez, and Tomas Recio. A rational function decomposition algorithm by near-separated polynomials. *J. Symb. Comput.*, 19(6):527–544, 1995.

4. Cesar Alonso, Jaime Gutierrez, and Tomas Recio. A decomposition algorithm for rational functions by quasi-separated polynomials. *Extr. Math.*, 11(3):475–479, 1996.

5. David R. Barton and Richard Zippel. Polynomial Decomposition Algorithms. *Journal of Symbolic Computation*, 1(2):159–168, June 1985.

6. Thomas Becker and Volker Weispfenning. *Gröbner Bases: A Computational Approach to Commutative Algebra*. Graduate Texts in Mathematics. Springer, New York, 1993. In cooperation with Heinz Kredel.

7. Wieb Bosmar, John Cannon, and Catherine Playoust. The Magma Algebra System I: The User Language. *Journal of Symbolic Computation*, 24:235–265, 1997.

8. Bruce W. Char, Keith O. Geddes, Gaston H. Gonnet, Benton L. Leong, Michael B. Monagan, and Stephen M. Watt. *Maple V Language Reference Manual*. Springer, New York; Berlin; Heidelberg, 1991.

9. Wolfram Decker, Gert-Martin Greuel, and Gerhard Pfister. Primary Decomposition: Algorithms and Comparisons. Preprint, Universität Kaiserslautern, 1998. At the time of writing this reference was available electronically at the URL http://kbibmp3.ub.uni-kl.de/Preprint/PS/no_series_20.ps.gz.

10. Matthew T. Dickerson. The Functional Decomposition of Polynomials. Technical Report CORNELLCS//TR89-1023, Cornell University, Computer Science Department, July 1989.

11. Matthew T. Dickerson. General polynomial decomposition and the $s-1$-decomposition are NP-hard. *Int. J. Found. Comput. Sci.*, 4(2):147–156, 1993.

12. Michael D. Fried and Moshe Jarden. *Field Arithmetic*. Ergebnisse der Mathematik und ihrer Grenzgebiete; 3. Folge, Band 11. A Series of Modern Surveys in Mathematics. Springer, Berlin, Heidelberg, 1986.

13. Erik W. Grafarend, Peter Lohse, and Burkhard Schaffrin. Dreidimensionaler Rückwärtsschnitt; Teil II: Dreistufige Lösung der algebraischen Gleichungen — Strecken —. *Zeitschrift für Vermessungswesen*, 114(3):127–137, 1989.

14. G.-M. Greuel, G. Pfister, and H. Schönemann. Singular version 1.2 User Manual. In *Reports On Computer Algebra*, number 21. Centre for Computer Algebra, University of Kaiserslautern, June 1998. At the time of writing available at the URL http://www.mathematik.uni-kl.de/~zca/Singular.

15. Wolfgang Gröbner. *Algebraische Geometrie—Band 2: Arithmetische Theorie der Polynomringe*. BI-Hochschultaschenbücher, 1970.

16. Johann August Grunert. Das Pothenot'sche Problem, in erweiterter Gestalt; nebst Bemerkungen über seine Anwendung in der Geodäsie. *Archiv der Mathematik und Physik*, 1:238–248, 1841.

17. Jaime Gutierrez and Rosario Rubio San Miguel. Polynomial Multivariate Decomposition. Abstract of a talk at the 1998 IMACS Conference on Applications of Computer Algebra in Prague, Czech Republic, August 1998. At the time of writing this reference was available electronically at the URL http://www-troja.fjfi.cvut.cz/aca98/sessions/geom/rubio/index.html.

18. Michael Kalkbrener. *Three Contributions to Elimination Theory*. PhD thesis, Johannes Kepler University, Linz, Austria, 1991.

19. Gregor Kemper. An Algorithm to Determine Properties of Field Extensions Lying over a Ground Field. IWR Preprint 93-58, Heidelberg, October 1993.

20. Gregor Kemper and Gunter Malle. Invariant rings and fields of finite groups. IWR Preprint 98-01, Heidelberg, 1998.

21. Dexter Kozen, Susan Landau, and Richard Zippel. Decomposition of Algebraic Functions. *Journal of Symbolic Computation,*.22(3):235–246, September 1996.

22. Serge Lang. *Introduction to Algebraic Geometry*. Number 5 in Interscience Tracts in Pure and Applied Mathematics. Interscience Publishers, New York, London, 1958.

23. Serge Lang. *Algebra*. Addison-Wesley Publishing Company, Inc., 3rd edition, 1993.

24. D. Lazard and A. Valibouze. *Computing subfields: Reverse of the primitive element problem*, volume 109 of *Progress in Mathematics*, pages 163–176. Birkhäuser, Boston, 1993.

25. Sandra Licciardi and Teo Mora. Implicitization of hypersurfaces and curves by the Primbasissatz and basis conversion. In *Proceedings of the 1994 International Symposium on Symbolic and Algebraic Computation*, pages 191–196. The Association for Computing Machinery, Inc. (ACM), July 1994. At the time of writing this reference was available electronically at the URL `ftp://ftp.disi.unige.it/pub/person/MoraF/oxford.ps.gz`.

26. Jörn Müller-Quade, Harald Aagedal, Thomas Beth, and Michael Schmid. Algorithmic design of diffractive optical systems for information processing. *Physica D*, 120:196–205, 1998.

27. Jörn Müller-Quade and Martin Rötteler. Deciding Linear Disjointness of Finitely Generated Fields. In Oliver Gloor, editor, *Proceedings of the 1998 International Symposium on Symbolic and Algebraic Computation*, pages 153–160. The Association for Computing Machinery, Inc. (ACM), August 1998.

28. Jörn Müller-Quade and Rainer Steinwandt. Basic Algorithms for Rational Function Fields. *Journal of Symbolic Computation*, 27(2):143–170, 1999.

29. Jörn Müller-Quade, Rainer Steinwandt, and Thomas Beth. An application of Gröbner bases to the decomposition of rational mappings. In Bruno Buchberger and Franz Winkler, editors, *Gröbner Bases and Applications*, volume 251 of *London Mathematical Society Lecture Note Series*, pages 448–462. Cambridge University Press, 1998.

30. Lorenzo Robbiano and Moss Sweedler. Ideal and Subalgebra Coefficients. *Proc. Am. Math. Soc.*, 126(8):2213–2219, 1998.

31. Abraham Seidenberg. Constructions in Algebra. *Trans. Am. Math. Soc.*, 197:273–313, 1974.

32. Rainer Steinwandt and Jörn Müller-Quade. Freeness, Linear Disjointness, and Implicitization—a Classical Approach. To appear in *Beiträge zur Algebra und Geometrie/Contributions to Algebra and Geometry*.

33. Moss Sweedler. Using Groebner Bases to Determine the Algebraic and Transcendental Nature of Field Extensions: return of the killer tag variables. In Gérard Cohen, Teo Mora, and Oscar Moreno, editors, *Applied Algebra, Algebraic Algorithms and Error-Correcting Codes 10th International Symposium, AAECC-10*, volume 673 of *LNCS*, pages 66–75, Berlin; Heidelberg, 1993. Springer.

34. Joachim von zur Gathen. Functional Decomposition of Polynomials:The Tame Case. *Journal of Symbolic Computation*, 9(3):281–300, March 1990.

35. Joachim von zur Gathen. Functional Decomposition of Polynomials:The Wild Case. *Journal of Symbolic Computation*, 10(5):437–452, November 1990.

36. André Weil. *Foundations of algebraic geometry*, volume 29 of *Colloquium publications*. American Mathematical Society, Providence, Rhode Island, rev. and enl. edition, 1946.

37. Richard Zippel. Rational Function Decomposition. In Stephen M. Watt, editor, *Proceedings of the 1991 International Symposium on Symbolic and Algebraic Computation, ISSAC'91*, pages 1–6, Baltimore, 1991. ACM Press.

Polynomials with Coefficients of Limited Accuracy

Hans J. Stetter

Tech.Univ. Vienna

Abstract. In Scientific Computing, data often have a limited accuracy. With polynomial modelling functions, this affects the meaningful accuracy of their zeros. We derive constructive criteria for judging the validity of approximate zeros relative to inaccuracies in the polynomials.

1 Introduction

We consider polynomials in their function as a *modelling tool* of Scientific Computing; throughout, coefficients and variables take values in $\mathbb{R}$ or $\mathbb{C}$. Moreover, we assume that some coefficients are only known to a *limited accuracy*. This may reflect the limited accuracy of measured or observed data or the effect of previous numerical computation. This assumption that polynomials may have a "tolerance" has far-reaching consequences for their mathematical and computational treatment. But *linear algebra* has accepted this assumption a long time ago; it has led to the enormous growth of *numerical linear algebra* into one of the supporting pillars of Scientific Computing. In an analogous fashion, the presently evolving *numerical polynomial algebra* studies the modifications and extensions of classical polynomial algebra necessary to accomodate the presence of inaccurate data and inexact computation. An outstanding token of this new development is the Strategic Alliance between the scientific software houses Maple and NAg announced at the ISSAC98.

In this paper, we consider the *zero sets* of polynomials with tolerances, i.e. of a dense set of neighboring polynomials; thus, an isolated zero spreads into a *set of pseudozeros*. For univariate polynomials, *pseudozero domains* have been considered by various authors (cf., e.g., [9],[14],[2]); we extend this concept to multivariate systems in a sufficiently general form to cover the needs of interesting situations. It is well-known that – even for linear systems (see e.g. [1]) – the computational determination of the curious shapes of pseudozero domains is enormously expensive. Therefore, we concentrate on the practical question: Given an approximate zero (from whatever source), how can we ascertain that it is a pseudozero, i.e. that it is an *exact* zero of a polynomial (system) which we cannot distinguish from the specified one because of the indetermination in its data. We derive the general criterion which a pseudozero of a 0-dimensional system has to pass. Moreover, we show how to ascertain that specified approximations to *several different zeros* can be considered as exact zeros of the *same* polynomial (system) within the tolerance neighborhood of the specified polynomial (system). This problem has no analog in numerical linear algebra and appears not to have been considered so far. Our algorithmic test for such *simultaneous pseudozeros* also permits the solution of various related problems. At the end, a few illustrative examples will demonstrate the usefulness of our results.

When applied to *overdetermined* systems of polynomials with a tolerance, our approach removes the discontinuities of potential zeros of such systems; the greatest common divisor problem for univariate polynomials is a special case. This will be treated in a separate publication.

2   Polynomials with Tolerances

Situations with geometric aspects are a typical source of polynomial systems; e.g., many problems in *robotics* permit such a formulation where some coefficients represent lengths and angles of robotic agents and relative positions of objects to be manipulated. It is obvious that these data have only a limited meaningful accuracy. In other areas of Scientific Computing (e.g. biology or economy), the indetermination of some coefficients may amount to several percent! In most real-life situations, the coefficient 4.865 in a polynomial $p(x, y) := x^3 - 2.913\, x^2y + 4.865\, xy^2 - 0.649\, y^3$ does not signify that precise rational number but rather *any real number* from a sufficiently small neighborhood of 4.865, say from the interval [4.864, 4.866]. The boundaries of that neighborhood are themselves *not sharply defined*: The appropriate interpretation is that there is an indetermination *of order* 10^{-3}.

The continued use of traditional mathematics under these circumstances is made possible through the consideration of the *backward error*: If the result of an approximate evaluation of a specified approximate mathematical model can be interpreted as the *exact* result of a mathematical model which lies *within the tolerance range* of the specification, we accept it as a *meaningful result*. This concept has become standard in the omnipresent manipulations of linear algebra (linear equations, eigenproblems, least squares problems etc.); but it has barely entered the world of algebraic computations in the narrower sense: *Computer algebra systems*, from Mupad via Maple and Mathematica to the more refined and specialized packages, assume data to be *exact as specified* and they perform *exact mathematical operations* only, using integer arithmetic with unlimited wordlength. None of them has procedures for a backward error analysis. A treatment of this aspect is also absent from the textbook literature in constructive algebra, even from recent volumes. I believe that this is a significant reason for the surprisingly small impact of computer algebra systems on real-life scientific computing.

For polynomials over $\mathbb{R}$ or $\mathbb{C}$, the formalization of a *tolerance* is straightforward; all related notions in the literature are special cases of Definition 2.1 below. We describe the general case of polynomials in $\mathbb{C}[x_1, \ldots, x_s]$; the specialization to real coefficients and/or one variable is immediate. With the usual notation

$$x^j := x_1^{j_1} x_2^{j_2} \ldots x_s^{j_s}, \quad j \in \mathbb{N}_0^s, \tag{1}$$

a polynomial in s variables with *support* $J \subset \mathbb{N}_0^s$ may be written as

$$p(x) = \sum_{j \in J} a_j x^j. \tag{2}$$

The *tolerance* associated with p is specified by a nonnegative vector $e \in \mathbb{R}^{|J|}$ whose components $e_j \geq 0$ refer to the coefficients $a_j, j \in J$. Let

$$J' := \{j \in J : e_j > 0\} \neq \emptyset, \quad M := |J'| \leq |J|. \tag{3}$$

Definition 2.1 : The *e-neighborhood* $N(p,e)$ of the polynomial p with tolerance e consists of those polynomials $\tilde{p} \in \mathbb{C}[x_1, \ldots, x_s]$, $\tilde{p}(x) = \sum \tilde{a}_j x^j$, which satisfy

$$\tilde{a}_j = 0, \quad j \notin J, \qquad \tilde{a}_j = a_j, \quad j \in J \setminus J', \tag{4}$$

$$\left\| \left(\ldots, \frac{|\tilde{a}_j - a_j|}{e_j}, \ldots, j \in J' \right) \right\|^* \leq 1. \quad \square \tag{5}$$

Intuitively, this says: A polynomial $\tilde{p}$ is an e-neighbor of p if it has the same support as p, if it has the coefficient a_j of p for each vanishing e_j, and if its remaining coefficients $\tilde{a}_j$ differ from those of p only by an order e_j.

The norm $\|..\|^*$ in (5) is a vector norm in $(\mathbb{R}^M)^*$; for $\|b^T\|^* = \max_{j \in J'} |b_j|$, e.g., (5) requires

$$|\tilde{a}_j - a_j| \leq e_j, \quad j \in J'. \tag{6}$$

More generally, we consider an *absolute norm* on $\mathbb{R}^M := \{u = \begin{pmatrix} u_1 \\ \vdots \\ u_M \end{pmatrix} \}$, i.e. a norm for which $\||u|\| = \|u\|$. Then $\|..\|^*$ denotes the associated *dual norm* (operator norm), i.e.

$$\|v^T\|^* := \sup_{u \neq 0} \frac{|v^T u|}{\|u\|}. \tag{7}$$

The following norms are most common:

$$\|u\|_1 := \sum_j |u_j|, \qquad \|v^T\|_1^* := \max_j |v_j|;$$
$$\|u\|_\infty := \max_j |u_j|, \qquad \|v^T\|_\infty^* := \sum_j |v_j|;$$
$$\|u\|_2 := (\sum_j |u_j|^2)^{\frac{1}{2}}, \qquad \|v^T\|_2^* := (\sum_j |v_j|^2)^{\frac{1}{2}}.$$

With (5), the $\|..\|_1^*$ norm appears most appropriate as shown by (6): here, the requirements on the individual coefficients of $\tilde{p}$ remain *separated*.

But we must keep in mind the conceptual background of our formalization: The e_j are *orders of magnitude* rather than precise scaling factors; accordingly, the $\cdots \leq 1$ in (5) must be interpreted in a soft fashion. In some concrete situation, e.g., a $\tilde{p}$ with a "distance" 5 (in place of 1) from p may still be acceptable while 500 is inacceptable in any case; conversely, we may sometimes have reservations in accepting an approximate result where $\tilde{p}$ has a distance .3 from p. Actually, the intuitive interpretation of (5) below Definition 2.1 is the best guideline; it implies:

a_j is *exact*, e.g. integer	$e_j = 0$;
a_j has m meaningful decimal digits after its point	$e_j \approx 10^{-m}$;
a_j has m meaningful decimal digits	$e_j \approx \|a_j\| \, 10^{-m}$.

An a_j *vanishing* in p will normally be considered as *exact*; then j is not an element of the support J of p and of all $\tilde{p} \in N(p, e)$. If, on the other hand, the monomial x^j is permitted to have a tiny non-zero coefficient in a neighboring $\tilde{p}$, then $j \in J' \subset J$ and $e_j > 0$.

The extension of the tolerance concept to a *system* of polynomials

$$P = \{p_\nu \in \mathbb{C}[x_1, \ldots, x_s], \ \nu = 1(1)n\} \tag{8}$$

is straightforward:

Definition 2.2: For a specified system (8), let

$$E := \{e_\nu \text{ (tolerances of the } p_\nu), \ \nu = 1(1)n\};$$

then the E-neighborhood $N(P, E)$ of the system P is

$$N(P, E) := \{\tilde{P} = \{\tilde{p}_\nu\}, \ \tilde{p}_\nu \in N(p_\nu, e_\nu), \ \nu = 1(1)n\} . \quad \square \tag{9}$$

A more general concept (e.g. with a matrix norm over all polynomials of the system) does not appear meaningful.

If (some of) the polynomials p_ν in the system P have *real* coefficients, their indetermination should generally be restricted to the real domain. Definitions 2.1 and 2.2 remain literally valid; but it must be clear whether the tolerance relates to a variation in $\mathbb{R}$ or in $\mathbb{C}$.

Variations in $\mathbb{C}$ of real or complex coefficients may often be specified in terms of real and imaginary parts. In orders of magnitude, the specifications

$$\left.\begin{array}{c} |\text{Re } (\tilde{a}_j - a_j)| \\ |\text{Im } (\tilde{a}_j - a_j)| \end{array}\right\} \leq e_j \quad \text{and} \quad |\tilde{a}_j - a_j| \leq e_j$$

may be considered as equivalent. If necessary, problems with complex coefficients may be replaced by equivalent real problems.

While the e-neighborhoods of Definition 2.1 are a natural formalization for the limited accuracy inherent in most polynomials in "real life", they carry a severe handicap: They depend crucially on the particular *representation* chosen for the polynomials under consideration! A shift of the origin, e.g., will generally lead to a serious change in the support J and in the values of the e_j. On the other hand, an extension of the tolerance concept to representations in terms of other basis functions (e.g. Chebyshev polynomials in place of monomials) is straightforward. In any case, one should choose the appropriate representation *before* one considers values for the tolerance.

Finally, note that we consider *each* polynomial (system) in $N(p, e)$ or $N(P, E)$ resp. as an *equally valid* representation of the problem to be solved. Also, we are not interested in polynomial neighborhoods with arbitrary (i.e. large) tolerance vectors $e \in \mathbb{R}_+^M$; it is implicitly assumed that the e_j are *small* quantities, relative to the level of the $|a_j|$.

3   Pseudozero Domains

Our treatment of data with limited accuracy is based on the *backward error principle*: An approximate result is *meaningful* if it is the exact result for a problem within the tolerance neighborhood of the specified problem. In Scientific Computing, a meaningful result is generally all one can hope to obtain. From this point of view, the concept of a zero of a polynomial (system) over $\mathbb{C}$ must be replaced by that of a pseudozero:

Definition 3.1: A value $z \in \mathbb{C}^s$ is a *pseudozero* of a polynomial p or of a system P of such polynomials, with tolerance e or E resp., if it is a zero of some polynomial $\tilde{p}$ or system $\tilde{P}$ in $N(p, e)$ or $N(P, E)$ resp.   □

Definition 3.2: The *pseudozero domain* of a polynomial p or a system P with tolerance e or E resp. is the set of all pseudozeros :

$$
\begin{aligned}
Z(p, e) \\
Z(P, E)
\end{aligned}
:= \left\{ z \in \mathbb{C}^s : \begin{array}{l} \exists\, \tilde{p} \in N(p, e) : \quad \tilde{p}(z) = 0 \\ \exists\, \tilde{P} \in N(P, E) : \tilde{P}(z) = 0 \end{array} \right\} \quad □ \quad (10)
$$

The term "pseudozero" appears to have evolved only during the past decade (cf. e.g. [14]); but the associated concept has informally been used for a long time. Its formalization paralleled that of the backward error principle; various terms have been used by various authors (e.g. "root neighborhoods" in [9]). For linear equations, the papers by Oettli and Prager ([10],[11]) have been seminal.

Univariate polynomials and 0-dimensional systems of multivariate polynomials generally have more than one zero. Consequently, their pseudozero domains generally decompose into disjoint components:

Definition 3.3: Each maximal connected subset of a pseudozero domain is called a *pseudozero component*.   □

Theorem 3.1 (Mosier [9]): Consider a pseudozero component $Z_\mu(p, e)$ of a polynomial $p \in \mathbb{C}[x]$ with tolerance e. If Z_μ is bounded, each polynomial $\tilde{p} \in N(p, e)$ has the same number of zeros in $Z_\mu(p, e)$ counting multiplicities.

Proof: By definition, there exists a $\tilde{p}^* \in N(p, e)$ with a zero $z \in Z_\mu$; let $m_\mu \geq 1$ be the total number of zeros of $\tilde{p}^*$ in Z_μ (counting multiplicities). Now consider some other $\tilde{p} \in N(p, e)$: Due to the convexity of $N(p, e)$ induced by (5), each polynomial

$$p_t(x) := (1 - t)\,\tilde{p}^*(x) + t\,\tilde{p}(x)\,, \quad t \in [0, 1]\,, \tag{11}$$

is in $N(p, e)$. The zeros of the p_t are continuous functions of their coefficients and hence of t; for any fixed $t \in [0, 1]$, all zeros are in $Z(p, e)$. Since the pseudozero components are disjoint and bounded, no zero can move from one component to another or disappear to ∞ or appear from there; thus all p_t have the same number of zeros in Z_μ.

Multiple zeros must be counted with their multiplicity r since they may arise from the confluence of r zeros (as t changes) or split into r zeros.   □

Pseudozero components of a univariate polynomial of degree d can only be unbounded if $e_d \geq |a_d| > 0$, i.e. if the leading coefficient a_d may vanish within its tolerance so that $N(p, e)$ contains polynomials of a lower degree than d. Thus, for Theorem 3.1, one could also require the polynomials to be monic; but this would be a stronger and less convenient assumption.

Definition 3.4: The *multiplicity* of a bounded pseudozero component $Z_\mu(p, e)$ is the common number of zeros in Z_μ of all polynomials in $N(p, e)$. □

As stated at the end of section 2, we assume that all polynomials in $N(p, e)$ are equally meaningful representatives of a hypothetical "true" polynomial $p^* \in N(p, e)$. Thus, when we consider one particular zero z_0 of p^*, with $z_0 \in Z_0(p, e)$, any value $\tilde{z}_0 \in Z_0(p, e)$ must be considered as a meaningful representative of z_0. The pseudozero component Z_0 represents the *indetermination* associated with that zero; its size and shape display the sensitivity of that zero w.r.t. the small changes in p admisssible in $N(p, e)$. They are thus immediately related with the *condition* of that zero w.r.t. corresponding changes in the coefficients of p.

Proposition 3.2: The condition of a specified simple zero z_0 of a polynomial $p \in \mathbb{C}[x]$ w.r.t. a coefficient a_j is determined by

$$\Delta z_0 = -\frac{z_0^j}{p'(z_0)}\,\Delta a_j + O(|\Delta a_j|^2)\,. \tag{12}$$

Proof: By first order perturbation analysis.   □

In principle, the boundaries in $\mathbb{C}$ of a pseudozero component can be computed and plotted with the help of Theorem 4.2; but the associated effort prohibits this except for experimental purposes (cf. the plots in [9], [14]).

If the component $Z_0(p, e)$ has multiplicity 1 and e is sufficiently small, the correct *order of magnitude* of the diameter of Z_0 may be found from (12) by linear superposition of the potential effects of the nonvanishing e_j. This order of magnitude limits the accuracy to which the computational determination of z_0 is meaningful with the tolerance e: If Z_0 has a diameter of $O(10^{-4})$, e.g., it is not meaningful to compute and to *report* more than 5 decimal digits (behind the point) of an approximation $\tilde{z}_0$, and the 5th digit must be considered uncertain.

If the multiplicity m of Z_0 is greater than 1, p' has zeros inside Z_0 and (12) cannot be used while the pseudozero component is still well-defined. It is obvious from counterexamples that these m zeros cannot have arbitrary relative positions within Z_0 for a $\tilde{p} \in N(p, e)$; on the other hand, the indetermination of p generally prohibits a specification of their relative position, e.g. whether there are two real zeros or a conjugate complex pair in the case of a real polynomial. We will say that a pseudozero component $Z_0(p, e)$ of a multiplicity $m > 1$ represents an *m-cluster* of zeros of p under the tolerance e; cf. section 6.

Before we turn to systems of polynomials, let us shortly consider the case of univariate polynomials with *real* coefficients, i.e. we assume that $p \in \mathbb{R}[x]$ *and* $\tilde{p} \in \mathbb{R}[x]$ for all $\tilde{p} \in N(p, e)$; cf. the remark before the end of section 2.

Theorem 3.3: For $p \in \mathbb{R}[x]$ with $N(p, e) \subset \mathbb{R}[x]$, a pseudozero component Z_μ of multiplicity 1 satisfies either $Z_\mu \subset \mathbb{R}$ or $Z_\mu \cap \mathbb{R} = \emptyset$.

Proof: Under the assumptions, the pseudozero domain $Z(p, e)$ must be symmetric to the real axis. Thus, a connected pseudozero component Z_μ containing real *and* non-real points would also have to be symmetric to the real axis. Take some $\tilde{z} \in Z_\mu, \tilde{z} \notin \mathbb{R}$: There exists $\tilde{p} \in N(p, e)$ with $\tilde{p}(\tilde{z}) = 0$ which implies $\tilde{p}(\tilde{z})^* = \tilde{p}(\tilde{z}^*) = 0$ which contradicts the multiplicity 1.   □

Corollary 3.4: Under the assumptions of Theorem 3.3, a pseudozero component Z_μ with $\emptyset \neq Z_\mu \cap \mathbb{R} \neq Z_\mu$ has at least multiplicity 2.

In our discussion of pseudozero domains of multivariate polynomial systems $P \subset \mathbb{C}[x_1, \ldots, x_s]$ with a tolerance E according to Definition 2.2, we will restrict our attention to situations where P as well as *all systems* in $N(P, E)$ are *consistent* and *0-dimensional* so that the zero sets $Z(\tilde{P})$ of the systems $\tilde{P} \in N(P, E)$ are non-empty and do not contain manifolds. Therefore, we assume (without significant loss of generality) that the number n of polynomials p_ν in P is equal to the number s of variables. (Naturally, this is not sufficient; we must exclude the appearance of *singular polynomial systems* in $N(P, E)$ which are the generalization of consistent singular linear systems; cf. [13]).

As in the univariate case, we further assume that the complete pseudozero domain $Z(P, E)$ is *bounded* in $\mathbb{C}^s$; this excludes the vanishing or appearing of zeros to/from infinity as $\tilde{P}$ varies in $N(P, E)$ and implies that all systems in $N(P, E)$ have the same number of isolated zeros. For systems, this boundedness hypothesis cannot be expressed in terms of the leading coefficients as easily as for one univariate polynomial. It requires that all systems in $N(P, E)$ must be *generic* w.r.t. their BKK-number given by the mixed volume of the support polytopes of the p_ν, cf. e.g. [8]; this implies the invariance of the number of zeros for $\widetilde{P} \in N(P, E)$ and the boundedness of the pseudozero domain. The BKK-number takes the sparsity of the joint support $J = \{J_\nu, \ \nu = 1(1)s\}$ of the systems in $N(P, E)$ fully into account.

Under the above assumptions, the pseudozero domain $Z(P, E)$ of a system P with tolerance E generally decomposes into a number of maximal connected bounded subsets, the *pseudozero components*, for which Definition 3.3 remains valid literally. As in the univariate case, we have

Theorem 3.5: Under the above assumptions, each system $\widetilde{P} \in N(P, E)$ has the same number of zeros (counting multiplicities) in a fixed pseudozero component Z_μ of $Z(P, E)$.

Proof: We can copy the proof of Theorem 3.1 if we have convinced ourselves of the continuity of the zeros as functions of the coefficients in the $\widetilde{P} \in N(P, E)$. Because of the assumed uniform 0-dimensionality in $N(P, E)$, the Jacobian $\widetilde{P}'$ can only be singular at a finite number of isolated points for each $\widetilde{P} \in N(P, E)$. At all other points $x \in \mathbb{C}^s$, $\widetilde{P}'(x)$ is regular and, by the inverse function theorem, a full neighborhood of $\widetilde{P}(x)$ is mapped differentiably onto a full neighborhood of x. Thus, generally, a zero of (cf. (11))

$$P_t(x) := (1 - t)\,\widetilde{P}^*(x) + t\,\widetilde{P}(x)\,, \quad t \in [0, 1]\,, \tag{13}$$

moves smoothly as a function of t because, at some $\bar{t} \in [0, 1]$, a small increment of t in P_t may be interpreted as a small perturbation of $P_{\bar{t}}$ which is a $\widetilde{P} \in N(P, E)$.

If a zero $z(t)$ of P_t coincides with a singularity of P_t' on its way from $z(0)$ to $z(1)$, we can either locally replace the linear homotopy (13) by a different one which guides $z(t)$ around the isolated singularity, or we can refer to the analysis of perturbations of poynomial systems at a multiple zero presented in [12]: No zeros can be gained or lost if the path of several $z(t)$ passes through a common multiple zero $z(\bar{t})$.   □

As a consequence of Theorem 3.5, we can transfer Definition 3.4 of the multiplicity of a pseudozero component to polynomial systems with a tolerance. Also, Theorem 3.3 and Corollary 3.4 can be extended to pseudozero components of *real* multivariate systems which contain only one zero.

The remarks about the interpretation of pseudozero components given after Definition 3.4 hold analogously for multivariate systems, except for the fact that even a rough computation of the boundaries of the domain $Z(P, E)$ is practically impossible for $s > 2$. The more will it be important to have practical criteria for $\tilde{z} \in Z(P, E)$ which are the main object of this paper.

4   Pseudozero Checking

For polynomial systems P with a tolerance E, it is sufficient to obtain approximations which lie in the associated pseudozero domain $Z(P, E)$. Thus, *any* computational zero finding procedure should verify the membership in $Z(P, E)$ of a computed approximate zero $\tilde{z}$ independently of its genesis:

$$\tilde{z} \in Z(P, E) \ ? \tag{14}$$

In view of Definition 3.1, we expect that a specified point $\tilde{z} \in \mathbb{C}^s$ can be a pseudozero of $P = \{p_\nu, \nu = 1(1)n\}$ with tolerance E only if its *residuals* $p_\nu(\tilde{z})$, $\nu = 1(1)n$, are sufficiently small. The precise specification of "sufficiently small" turns out to be surprisingly simple.

For the proof of the general *pseudozero criterion*, we recall an elementary fact about dual norms from linear algebra (cf. (7)):

Lemma 4.1: Consider an arbitrary norm $||..||$ on $\mathbb{R}^M$ and its dual norm $||..||^*$. For any $u \in \mathbb{R}^M$, $||u|| = 1$, there exists $v^T \in (\mathbb{R}^M)^*$, $||v^T||^* = 1$, such that $v^T u = 1$.

Proof: The dual counterpart of (7) is $\sup_{||v^T||^*=1} |v^T u| = ||u||$. Since the sup is over a compact set, it is attained by some v_0^T. If $v_0^T u = -1$, take $v^T = -v_0^T$. $\square$

We consider the situation of Definition 2.1: A polynomial $p \in \mathbb{C}[x_1, \ldots, x_s]$ with tolerance vector $e \in \mathbb{R}^{|J'|}$, J' and M from (3), and the neighborhood $N(p, e)$, with arbitrary but fixed absolute norm $||..||$ and dual norm $||..||^*$.

Theorem 4.2 (Pseudozero Criterion): $z \in \mathbb{C}^s$ is in $Z(p, e)$ *if and only if*

$$|p(z)| \leq \left\| \begin{pmatrix} \vdots \\ e_j |z|^j \\ \vdots \\ {}_{j \in J'} \end{pmatrix} \right\| . \tag{15}$$

Proof:
a) Assume $z \in Z(p, e)$: By Definition 3.1, there exists $\tilde{p} \in N(p, e)$ with $\tilde{p}(z) = 0$. Hence

$$|p(z)| = |\tilde{p}(z) - p(z)| = \left| \sum_{j \in J'} (\tilde{a}_j - a_j) z^j \right| \leq \sum_j \frac{|\tilde{a}_j - a_j|}{e_j} \cdot e_j \, |z|^j$$

$$\leq \left\| (\ldots \frac{|\tilde{a}_j - a_j|}{e_j} \ldots) \right\|^* \cdot \left\| \begin{pmatrix} \vdots \\ e_j |z|^j \\ \vdots \end{pmatrix} \right\|$$

which implies (15) by (5).

b) Assume (15): Let

$$\gamma := \frac{p(z)}{\|(e_j|z|^j)\|} \in \mathbb{C}, \quad \bar{\gamma} := |\gamma| \le 1. \tag{16}$$

Let

$$u := \begin{pmatrix} \vdots \\ e_j|z|^j \\ \vdots \end{pmatrix} \Big/ \|(e_j|z|^j)\| \in \mathbb{R}^M, \quad \|u\| = 1,$$

and $v^T \in (\mathbb{R}^M)^*$ such that $\|v^T\|^* = 1$, $v^T u = 1$ (cf. Lemma 4.1). Assume (at first) $z^j \ne 0$ for all $j \in J'$; then, with (16),

$$1 = v^T u = \frac{\gamma}{p(z)} \cdot \sum_{j \in J'} v_j e_j |z|^j = \frac{\gamma}{p(z)} \cdot \sum_{j \in J'} \left(\frac{v_j e_j |z|^j}{z^j} \right) \cdot z^j$$

or

$$p(z) = \gamma \cdot \sum_{j \in J'} \bar{e}_j \, z^j =: \gamma \cdot \bar{e}(z), \quad \text{with } \bar{e}_j := \frac{v_j e_j |z|^j}{z^j}. \tag{17}$$

If $z^j = 0$ for some j, we set $\bar{e}_j = v_j e_j$ which leaves (17) unaffected.

Let $\tilde{p}(x) := p(x) - \gamma \cdot \bar{e}(x)$; then $\tilde{p}(z) = 0$ by (17) and $\tilde{p}$ is in $N(p, e)$:

$$\|\tilde{p} - p\|_e^* := \bar{\gamma} \cdot \|(\dots \frac{|\bar{e}_j|}{e_j} \dots)\|^* = \bar{\gamma} \cdot \|v^T\|^* = \bar{\gamma} \le 1. \quad \square$$

Corollary 4.3 (Pseudozero Criterion for Systems): $z \in \mathbb{C}^s$ is in $Z(P, E)$ if and only if

$$|p_\nu(z)| \le \left\| \begin{pmatrix} \vdots \\ e_{\nu j} |z|^j \\ \vdots \\ j \in J_\nu' \end{pmatrix} \right\|, \quad \nu = 1(1)n. \tag{18}$$

Proof: By Definitions 3.1 and 3.2, Theorem 4.2 extends immediately to systems. $\square$

Historical Remarks: For *linear* systems, the pseudozero criterion (with the 1-norm) was published by Oettli and Prager in 1964; cf. [10], [11]. For *one univariate polynomial* and the 1-norm, Mosier ([9]) proved it in 1986 (without reference to Oettli/Prager or Lemma 3.1); Toh/Trefethen used the 2-norm version in [14]. In their book ([2]), Chatelin/Fraissé have put these results in the more general framework of a posteriori backward error analysis. Systems of multivariate polynomials appear not to have been considered so far. $\square$

For the purpose of pseudozero checking, a multivariate polynomial is nothing but a *sum of terms*. Thus, the simplicity of (15) is not so surprising but rather a confirmation of the adequacy of the neighborhood concept of section 2 and the pseudozero concept of section 3. For the 1-norm, which is the most natural norm to be used in the neighborhood definition (cf. (5)), (15) and (18) take the even more intuitive form

$$|p_\nu(z)| \leq e_\nu(|z|), \quad \text{with } e_\nu(x) := \sum_{j \in J'_\nu} e_{\nu j} x^j, \quad \nu = 1(1)n. \tag{19}$$

This is also the original formulation of Oettli/Prager for linear equations (with a notation adapted to linear algebra).

For a specified z, (18) and (19) display which indetermination in the polynomial (system) is primarily responsible for the admissible margin in the residual(s). This margin depends not only on the sizes of the $e_{\nu j}$ but also on the *position* of the approximate zero z under investigation. The *tolerance polynomial(s)* $e_{(\nu)}$ in (19) may be extremely sparse, even for dense polynomials $p_{(\nu)}$, because a good number of coefficients may be integer and have vanishing tolerance components.

In applying the pseudozero criterion (15), we must remember the assumptions underlying our analysis: There are no "better" or "worse" polynomials $\tilde{p}$ in $N(p, e)$, and the components e_j of e are orders of magnitude rather than precise numbers. From this point of view, we may consider an approximate zero $\tilde{z}$ as a meaningful result even if $|p(\tilde{z})|$ violates the inequality by a small margin. On the other hand, we should not attempt a further "improvement" of $\tilde{z}$ if $\overline{\gamma} < 1$ say by one order of magnitude. For a polynomial with tolerance e, a further improvement of a zero, e.g. by a Newton step, is meaningful only if $\overline{\gamma} \geq O(1)$.

In the pseudozero criterion for systems, the

$$\gamma_\nu := p_\nu(z) / \|(e_{\nu j}|z|^j)\|, \quad \nu = 1(1)n, \tag{20}$$

(cf. (16)) will generally have different values and $z \in N(p_\nu, e_\nu)$ may hold for some ν but not for others; one should primarily reduce the residuals of those p_ν for which $|\gamma_\nu| \geq O(1)$. A step of Newton's method is the perfect tool for doing so since it determines a correction Δz of the approximate zero z from

$$p'_\nu(z) \cdot \Delta z = -p_\nu(z), \quad \nu = 1(1)n; \tag{21}$$

here $p'_\nu(z)$ is the gradient vector of p_ν at z. If $|p_{\nu'}(z)| \gg |p_\nu(z)|$, $\nu \neq \nu'$, Δz is essentially chosen to achieve a reduction of $|p_{\nu'}(z)|$.

The pseudozero criterion is *sharp* in the following sense:

Corollary 4.4: In the situation of Theorem 4.2, with $\overline{\gamma}$ from (16), we have

$$z \in Z(p, \delta e) \quad \text{for } \delta \geq \overline{\gamma}, \tag{22}$$
$$z \notin Z(p, \delta e) \quad \text{for } 0 \leq \delta < \overline{\gamma}. \tag{23}$$

The polynomial $\tilde{p}(x) := p(x) - \gamma \cdot \bar{e}(x)$ of the proof of Theorem 4.2 is the *unique* polynomial in $N(p, \bar{\gamma} e)$ with $\tilde{p}(z) = 0$.

Proof: Cf. the proof of Theorem 4.2.   □

Corollary 4.4 exhibits $\bar{\gamma}$ as the lower limit for the δ-values which permit a polynomial $\tilde{p} \in N(p, \delta e)$ with $\tilde{p}(z) = 0$. Here, $\bar{\gamma}$ may be smaller or greater than 1 ; in principle, $\bar{\gamma}$ is defined for arbitrary values of $z \in \mathbb{C}$. $\bar{\gamma} e$ is a *backward error* of the approximate zero z for the specified polynomial p because it describes the minimal data perturbation necessary for z to become an exact zero. The backward error concept can also be applied for approximate zeros of polynomials with *exact* coefficients; then it requires the meaningful choice of a *fictitious* tolerance vector e. Cf. section 7.2 for an example.

For systems, the analog to Corollary 4.4 is

Corollary 4.5: In the situation of Theorem 4.3, with (20) and $\bar{\gamma} := \max_\nu |\gamma_\nu|$,

$$z \in Z(P, \delta E) \quad \text{for } \delta \geq \bar{\gamma}, \tag{24}$$

$$z \notin Z(P, \delta E) \quad \text{for } 0 \leq \delta < \bar{\gamma}. \tag{25}$$

This establishes $\bar{\gamma} E$ as a backward error of an approximate zero z of the specified polynomial system P.

5   Simultaneous Pseudozeros

It is intuitively clear that an *arbitrary* set of points $\{z_\mu\}$, with each z_μ from a different pseudozero component, will generally *not* consist of zeros of the *same* neighboring polynomial (system). Thus, the concept of pseudozero domains (Definition 3.1) is not sufficiently powerful to answer the following natural question: Given two (or more) points z_μ in $\mathbb{C}^s$ which are approximations for two (or more) different isolated zeros of a (system of) polynomial(s) with tolerance; is there a polynomial (system) in $N(p, e)$ or $N(P, E)$ resp. such that the z_μ are exact zeros of that *one* polynomial (system) *simultaneously* ?

Consider $p \in \mathbb{C}[x_1, \ldots, x_s]$ with tolerance e, and $M = |J'| > 1$; cf. (3).

Definition 5.1: A set of $z_\mu \in \mathbb{C}^s$, $\mu = 1(1)m \leq M$, is a *set of simultaneous pseudozeros* of p with tolerance e if

$$\exists \tilde{p} \in N(p, e) : \quad \tilde{p}(z_\mu) = 0, \, \mu = 1(1)m. \quad \square \tag{26}$$

While $z_\mu \in Z(p, e)$, $\mu = 1(1)m$, is a trivial necessary condition, a necessary and sufficient condition is given by

Theorem 5.1: In the situation just described, consider the linear manifold $\mathcal{E}$ in the $\mathbb{C}^M$ of the $\bar{e}_j, j \in J'$, defined by

$$\sum_{j \in J'} \bar{e}_j z_\mu^j + p(z_\mu) = 0, \quad \mu = 1(1)m. \tag{27}$$

$\{z_\mu\}$ is a set of simultaneous pseudozeros of p with tolerance e *if and only if*

$$\bar{\gamma} := \min_{\bar{e} \in \mathcal{E}} \|(\dots \frac{|\bar{e}_j|}{e_j} \dots)\|^* \leq 1. \tag{28}$$

Proof: a) Assume (28) and let $\bar{e}_0 \in \mathcal{E} \subset \mathbb{C}^M$ satisfy

$$\|(\dots \frac{|\bar{e}_{0j}|}{e_j} \dots)\|^* \leq 1. \tag{29}$$

Then $\tilde{p}(x) := p(x) + \sum_{j \in J'} \bar{e}_{0j} x^j$ is in $N(p,e)$ and, for $\mu = 1(1)m$,

$$\tilde{p}(z_\mu) = p(z_\mu) + \sum_{j \in J'} \bar{e}_{0j} z_\mu^j = 0 \quad \text{by (27)}.$$

b) Assume (26) and let $\bar{e}(x) := \tilde{p}(x) - p(x) = \sum \bar{e}_{0j} x^j$. Because of $\tilde{p} \in N(p,e)$, $\bar{e}_0 = (\bar{e}_{0j})$ satisfies (29); also because of $\tilde{p}(z_\mu) = 0, \mu = 1(1)m$, we have (27) so that $\bar{e}_0 \in \mathcal{E}$ and (29) implies (28). □

Remark: Obviously, the criterion (28) may also be formulated as

$$\exists \bar{e} \in \mathcal{E} : \|(\dots \frac{|\bar{e}_j|}{e_j} \dots)\|^* \leq 1. \tag{30}$$

In the situation of Theorem 5.1, $\bar{\gamma} e$ is a *simultaneous backward error* of the set $z_\mu, \mu = 1(1)m$, of approximate zeros of the specified polynomial p. Relative to the individual backward errors $\bar{\gamma}_\mu e$ of the zeros z_μ, we have

$$\bar{\gamma} e \geq \max_{\mu=1(1)m} \bar{\gamma}_\mu e . \tag{31}$$

However, equality is generally *not* attained in (31) since the norm distance of the linear manifold $\mathcal{E}$ from the origin is, generally, strictly larger than each of the norm distances of the hyperplanes (27) which intersect in $\mathcal{E}$. Cf. sections 7.2 and 7.3 for examples.

If we have a 0-dimensional system $P = \{p_\nu\}$ with tolerance E and a set $\{z_\mu\} \subset \mathbb{C}^s$ as previously, we must request that the z_μ are *simultaneous* pseudozeros of *each* of the p_ν. Then there exists *one* system $\tilde{P} \in N(P, E)$ which has all the z_μ as zeros. Thus we have to check (28) for the n manifolds $\mathcal{E}_\nu$ defined by (27) for the different p_ν and e_ν. The linear parts of the $\mathcal{E}_\nu$ will generally not be identical because the tolerance supports J'_ν of the tolerances e_ν may differ. A simultaneous backward error of the set of the z_μ is defined in an analogous fashion.

5.1   Simultaneous pseudozero checking

Unfortunately, condition (28) cannot be turned into an *explicit* criterion as it has been possible for $m = 1$ with arbitrary norms but it must rather be tested algorithmically. The fact that (27)/(28) is equivalent to (15) for $m = 1$ is easily confirmed with the help of Lemma 4.1.

For $m = M$, on the other hand, the manifold $\mathcal{E}$ defined by (27) consists of one point $\bar{e} = (\bar{e}_j, \ j = 1(1)M)$ only (if the associated matrix is regular) which may be computed and used in checking (28). M is generally not large as it counts only the nonvanishing coefficients with a limited acuracy.

For $1 < m < M$, we must find the minimal norm distance from the origin in real or complex M-space of a linear manifold of dimension $(M - m)$. We consider only the two practically relevant cases.

1-norm :   Here, (28) takes the form

$$\min_{\bar{e} \in \mathcal{E}} \ \max_{j \in J'} \ \frac{|\bar{e}_j|}{e_j} \leq 1 \tag{32}$$

For a *real* polynomial with a *real* tolerance neighborhood $N(p, e)$ and for *real* zeros z_μ, (28) becomes a *linear program* in the real variables $\bar{e}_j$ and $\bar{\gamma}$:

$$\min \ \bar{\gamma} \quad \text{with (27)} \quad \text{and} \quad \begin{aligned} \bar{\gamma} &\geq 0, \\ \bar{e}_j - e_j \bar{\gamma} &\leq 0, \quad j \in J', \\ -\bar{e}_j - e_j \bar{\gamma} &\leq 0, \quad j \in J'. \end{aligned} \tag{33}$$

Such linear programs can be solved by widely available packaged software.

It may be advantageous to solve the linear equality conditions (27) for m of the $\bar{e}_j$ (say $\bar{e}_{j_1}, \ldots, \bar{e}_{j_m}$) so that (33) becomes an optimization problem

$$\bar{\gamma} = \min_{\bar{e}_{j_{m+1}}, \ldots, \bar{e}_{j_M}} f(\bar{e}_{j_{m+1}}, \ldots, \bar{e}_{j_M}), \tag{34}$$

in the $M - m + 1$ variables $\bar{\gamma}$ and $\bar{e}_{j_{m+1}}, \ldots, \bar{e}_{j_M}$ only, where the piecewise linear convex function f originates form the solving of (27) for the $\bar{e}_{j_\mu}$, $\mu = 1(1)m$. For (34), one can use a descent along edges of the graph of f. Since this function f remains a piecewise smooth, *convex* function when the original problem (27)/(28) is posed in *complex* s-space, this approach is feasible for the algorithmic determination of $\bar{\gamma}$ in general.

2-norm :   From linear algebra we know that the closest point to the origin on a linear manifold is the intersection with the orthogonal subspace. In our case, we have also to take account of the weights $1/e_j$ in (28). For a formal treatment, we write the manifold $\mathcal{E}$ as

$$A^H \bar{e} \ = \ b,$$

with $A^H := (z_\mu^j) \in \mathbb{C}^{m \times M}$, $b := (-p(z_\mu)) \in \mathbb{C}^m$. By a generalized QR decomposition, we find a weighted Hermitian basis for the row space of A^H:

$$A^H \ = \ R^H Q_1^H, \tag{35}$$

where R^H is lower triangular, and the rows q_μ^H of $Q_1^H \in \mathbb{C}^{m \times M}$ satisfy $Q_1^H E Q_1 = I$, with $E := \mathrm{diag}\,(e_1^2, \ldots, e_M^2)$. Q_1^H and Q_1 may be extended into full bases Q^H and Q of the $\mathbb{C}^M$ which satisfy

$$Q^H E Q = I \quad \text{or} \quad Q^{-1} E^{-1} Q^{-H} = I. \qquad (36)$$

Consider $\bar{e}_0 \in \mathbb{C}^M$ which satisfies (cf. (35))

$$Q^H \bar{e}_0 = \begin{pmatrix} Q_1^H \bar{e}_0 \\ Q_2^H \bar{e}_0 \end{pmatrix} = \begin{pmatrix} R^{-H} b \\ 0 \end{pmatrix}. \qquad (37)$$

$\bar{e}_0$ is the point on $\mathcal{E}$ which minimizes $\|(\ldots |\bar{e}_j|/e_j \ldots)\|_2^*$, and

$$\|(..|\bar{e}_j|/e_j..)\|_2^* = \bar{e}_0^H E^{-1} \bar{e}_0 = \bar{e}_0^H Q \, Q^H \bar{e}_0 = b^H R^{-1} R^{-H} b. \qquad (38)$$

These algorithmic procedures could easily be implemented in packages dealing with polynomials. Like condition (15) in section 4, condition (28) is not to be interpreted as a strict disjunction but rather as $\cdots \leq O(1)$; cf. the discussion after Corollary 4.3. Other observations from section 4 also remain valid in the more general context.

Obviously, the size of $\bar{\gamma}$ in (28) depends strongly on the moduli of the residuals $p(z_\mu)$. However, as simple examples show, the reduction of one individual $|p(z_\mu)|$ may increase the value of the minimum. On the other hand, if all $|p(z_\mu)|$ are decreased proportionally then $\bar{\gamma}$ is decreased accordingly. Therefore, one Newton step for *each* z_μ will generally decrease the minimum significantly. Also, if one (or a few) of the $|p(z_\mu)|$ is (are) *much* larger than the others, its (their) reduction will generally decrease the minimum.

5.2   Restricted pseudozero domains

Simultaneous pseudozeros may also be considered from a different point of view: Assume that we have *fixed* a pseudozero z_1 of a univariate polynomial p with tolerance e; this *restricts* the potential localities for the remaining pseudozeros because they must be exact zeros of a polynomial $\tilde{p} \in N(p, e)$ with $\tilde{p}(z_1) = 0$.

Definition 5.2: For $z_1 \in Z(p, e)$,

$$Z(p, e \,|\, z_1) := \{z \in \mathbb{C} : \exists \tilde{p} \in N(p, e) \text{ with } \tilde{p}(z_1) = 0 : \tilde{p}(z) = 0\} \qquad (39)$$

defines a *restricted pseudozero domain.* $\square$

Theorem 5.2: $z \in Z(p, e \,|\, z_1)$ if and only if z and z_1 are simultaneous pseudozeros of p with tolerance e.

Proof: Follows immediately from Definitions 5.2 and 5.1. $\square$

It is obvious that we may restrict remaining pseudozeros further by fixing more than one pseudozero, as long as the fixed pseudozeros are *simultaneous* pseudozeros. When $M < d$ pseudozeros have been fixed for a univariate polynomial p of degree d with a tolerance with $|J'| = M$, the remaining $d - M$ pseudozeros are uniquely determined (except in some singular cases) so that $Z(p, e \,|\, z_1, \ldots, z_M)$ consists only of $d - M$ isolated points.

All considerations above apply immediately to 0-dimensional multivariate systems P with a tolerance E. Situations where restricted pseudozero domains play are role are abundant in Scientific Computing. Theorem 5.2 reduces the associated test to the simultaneous pseudozero criterion of Theorem 5.1.

6   Situations with Simultaneous Pseudozeros

6.1   A complex pseudozero in a real polynomial

For a real polynomial p with a tolerance e, the pseudozero criterion (15) is not sufficient to decide whether a *non-real* approximate zero z may be a zero of a *real* polynomial $\tilde{p} \in N(p, e)$: The polynomial constructed in the proof of Theorem 4.2 is not real in this case. Obviously, the reality of $\tilde{p}$ requires that z and z^* are simultaneous pseudozeros of p.

If we consider the real and imaginary parts of $\tilde{p}(z) = \tilde{p}(z^*) = 0$, we obtain the condition (28) for the *real* linear manifold $\mathcal{E}$ defined by

$$\sum_{j \in J'} \bar{e}_j \operatorname{Re} z^j + \operatorname{Re} p(z) = 0, \qquad \sum_{j \in J'} \bar{e}_j \operatorname{Im} z^j + \operatorname{Im} p(z) = 0. \qquad (40)$$

Naturally, if M permits, we may also consider several complex pseudozeros or a mixture of real and complex pseudozeros for a real polynomial p with a real neighborhood $N(p, e)$. The considerations may be extended to real 0-dimensional systems in an obvious way.

6.2   Multiple pseudozeros

Definition 6.1: An approximate zero z of the polynomial (system) p or P with tolerance e or E resp. is an *m-fold pseudozero* of p or P resp. if there exists a $\tilde{p} \in N(p, e)$ or $\tilde{P} \in N(P, E)$ resp. such that z is an exact m-fold zero of $\tilde{p}$ or $\tilde{P}$ resp. The set of all m-fold pseudozeros of p or P will be denoted by $Z^{(m)}(p, e)$ of $Z^{(m)}(P, E)$ resp.   □

We consider the case of one *univariate* polynomial p with tolerance e first; here, an m-fold zero z of $\tilde{p}$ is characterized by

$$\tilde{p}^{(\mu)}(z) = 0, \quad \mu = 0(1)(m - 1). \qquad (41)$$

With $\tilde{p}(x) = p(x) + \sum_{j \in J'} \bar{e}_j x^j$ as previously, (41) takes the form

$$\sum_{j \in J'} \binom{j}{\mu} \bar{e}_j z^{j - \mu} + \frac{1}{\mu!} p^{(\mu)}(z) = 0, \quad \mu = 0(1)(m - 1). \qquad (42)$$

(42) defines a linear manifold $\mathcal{E}^{(m)}(z)$ in $\mathbb{C}^M$, generally of dimension M-m, which takes the place of (27) in Theorem 5.1.

Corollary 6.1: $z \in \mathbb{C}$ is an m-fold pseudozero of $p \in \mathbb{C}[x]$ with tolerance e if and only if $\mathcal{E}^{(m)}(z)$ satisfies (28) or (30). A necessary condition is $z \in Z(p^{(\mu)}, e^{(\mu)})$, $\mu = 0(1)(m-1)$ where $e^{(\mu)}$ is the tolerance for $p^{(\mu)}$ derived from th tolerance $e^{(0)} = e$ of p.

The residuals $\frac{1}{\mu!} p^{(\mu)}(z)$ in (42) which must be small for an m-fold pseudozero, are the coefficients of the first m terms of an expansion of p in powers of $\xi := x - z$; cf. (43) below. An analogous expansion in powers of $\xi = (\xi_1, \ldots, \xi_s)$, with $\xi_\sigma := x_\sigma - z_\sigma$, in the case of a system P of multivariate polynomials reveals the number and the structure of linearly independent *directional derivatives* of P which nearly vanish at z; the associated algorithmic procedure has been derived in [12], for exact coefficients. A generalization to systems with a tolerance will be presented in a separate publication.

6.3 Pseudozero components of a multiplicity > 1, univariate case

The establishment of some zero as an m-fold pseudozero implies that the associated pseudozero component has multiplicity (at least) m. However, an arbitrary z in a pseudozero component of multiplicity m will generally not be an m-fold pseudozero. Therefore, if the smallness of the first $m > 1$ coefficients in an expansion of p in powers of $\xi := x - z$ raises the expectation that z is an m-fold pseudozero but z does not sytisfy the criterion of Corollary 6.1, we would like to find a correction Δz for z such that $z + \Delta z$ is likely to satisfy the test (42)/(28) for an m-fold pseudozero.

For this purpose, we denote the m zeros of p near z whose presence is indicated by the smallness of the expansion coefficients, by $z_\mu =: z + \zeta_\mu$, and rewrite our polynomial p of degree $d \geq m$ in the form

$$\bar{p}(\xi) := p(z + \xi) =: r_0(\xi) + \xi^m r_1(\xi) + \xi^{2m} r_2(\xi) + \ldots ; \qquad (43)$$

this polynomial must have a divisor $\prod_{\mu=1}^{m} (\xi - \zeta_\mu) =: \xi^m - q(\xi)$ of degree m :

$$\bar{p}(\xi) = (\xi^m - q(\xi)) \, s_1(\xi) + (\xi^m - q(\xi))^2 \, s_2(\xi) + \ldots \qquad (44)$$

In (43)/(44), the polynomials r_ν, s_ν, and q are all of maximal degree $(m-1)$ and the expansions terminate when they reach degree d. Note that – under our assumptions – r_0 must have very small coefficients throughout while the constant term r_{10} of r_1 must be of $O(1)$.

The leading coefficient q_{m-1} of $q(\xi) = \sum_{\mu=0}^{m-1} q_\mu \xi^\mu$ satisfies

$$\Delta z := \frac{1}{m} q_{m-1} = \frac{1}{m} \sum_{\mu=1}^{m} \zeta_\mu ; \qquad (45)$$

in this sense, $z + \Delta z$ is the *center* of the assumed cluster $\{z_\mu\}$. If we regard the m-cluster as a perturbed m-fold zero of a neighboring polynomial p or $\bar{p}$

resp., then a first order perturbation analysis establishes $z + \Delta z$ or Δz resp. as the location of this m-fold zero; cf. [12].

Good approximations for the coefficients q_μ of $q(\xi)$ can be found by a Newton step for the nonlinear system in q and the s_ν obtained by equating (43) and (44), with $q = 0$ and $s_\nu = r_\nu$, $\nu \geq 1$, as starting approximations. In [12], it has been shown that – for q – this Newton step becomes simply

$$
\begin{pmatrix}
r_{10} & & & \\
r_{11} & r_{10} & & 0 \\
\vdots & & \ddots & \\
r_{1,m-1} & \cdots & r_{11} & r_{10}
\end{pmatrix}
\begin{pmatrix}
q_0 \\
q_1 \\
\vdots \\
q_{m-1}
\end{pmatrix}
= -
\begin{pmatrix}
r_{00} \\
r_{01} \\
\vdots \\
r_{0,m-1}
\end{pmatrix}
; \qquad (46)
$$

the $r_{\nu\mu}$ are the coefficients of the $r_\nu(\xi)$ in (43), and $r_{10} = O(1)$ remarked above. Thus, the desired correction (45) can easily be obtained.

For $m > 2$, the existence of an m-fold pseudozero is not a necessary condition for a pseudozero component of multiplicity m as shown by counterexamples. In [9], it has been proved that a 2-fold pseudozero does exist in a pseudozero component of multiplicity $m \geq 2$. In [7], it has been shown that an m-fold pseudozero exists in a certain starshaped region containing the m-cluster.

The establishment of a multiplicity $m > 1$ for a pseudozero component can – in principle – only be interpreted as the presence of an m-cluster of zeros in that component. If we have succeeded in establishing a point in that component as an m-fold pseudozero, then we can claim that – within the tolerance specified – our polynomial p *possesses an m-fold zero*. This is a more meaningful assertion in the following sense:

For a sufficiently small tolerance vector e, assume that $Z^{(m)}(p, e)$ is nonempty and consists of one component associated with the only m-cluster of zeros of p lying in the enclosing pseudozero component $Z_0(p, e)$. Let $\gamma \in (0, 1)$ be such that $Z^{(m)}(p, \delta e) \neq \emptyset$ for $\delta \geq \gamma$ and $\overline{\gamma} > \gamma$ such that $Z_0(p, \delta e)$ has exact multiplicity m for $\gamma \leq \delta < \overline{\gamma}$. Then, as δ varies in $(\gamma, \overline{\gamma})$

- the diameter of $Z^{(m)}(p, \delta e)$ is $O(\|\delta e\|)$,
- the diameter of $Z_0(p, \delta e)$ is $O(\|\delta e\|^{\frac{1}{m}})$.

In this sense, the determination of an m-fold pseudozero is a *well-conditioned* problem while – as is well-known – the determination of individual cluster zeros is increasingly ill-conditioned as m gets larger. The fact that the position of an m-fold polynomial zero is well-conditioned w.r.t. perturbations of the polynomial which leave the multiplicity of the zero invariant has been observed and analyzed by W. Kahan in his seminal paper [7].

7 Examples

7.1 Pseudozeros and meaningful accuracy

In their paper [4], Emiris and Mourrain consider a perturbed model for the conformations of cyclohexane consisting of the polynomial system

$$P(x) := \begin{pmatrix} 1.313x_2^2x_3^2 + .959x_2^2 + 1.389x_2x_3 + .774x_3^2 - .310 \\ 1.269x_3^2x_1^2 + .755x_3^2 + 1.451x_3x_1 + .917x_1^2 - .365 \\ 1.352x_1^2x_2^2 + .837x_1^2 + 1.655x_1x_2 + .838x_2^2 - .413 \end{pmatrix} = 0 ;$$

the tolerance of all entries is $.5 \cdot 10^{-3}$. They display numerically computed approximations for the 4 real zeros to 10 digits. However, the approximate zeros obtained by *rounding their numerical results to 3 digits* are valid pseudozeros under the above tolerance:

With $\tilde{z} = (.368, .320, .297)$, we have to 5 digits (cf. (18))

$$|P(\tilde{z})| = \begin{pmatrix} .00035 \\ .00047 \\ .00020 \end{pmatrix} < E(|\tilde{z}|) = \begin{pmatrix} .00065 \\ .00067 \\ .00068 \end{pmatrix} .$$

By Corollary 4.3, this proves that $\tilde{z}$ is the exact zero of a system which rounds to P so that it is not meaningful to display more than 3 or 4 digits of the zeros of P – no matter how they have been computed.

7.2 Conjugate complex pairs of zeros

Consider

$$p(x) = x^4 + x^3 + x^2 + x + 1 ,$$

with approximate zeros (exact zeros rounded to 3 digits)

$$\tilde{z}_{1,2} = .309 \pm .951\,\mathrm{i} , \quad \tilde{z}_{3,4} = -.809 \pm .588\,\mathrm{i} .$$

With a fictitious tolerance $e = (1, 1, 1, 1, 1) \times 10^{-4}$, we obtain $\overline{\gamma} = .50$ for $\tilde{z}_1$ or $\tilde{z}_2$ as individual complex zeros. For the *conjugate complex pair* $\tilde{z}_{1,2}$ and a *real* neighboring $\tilde{p}$, the relevant quantity $\overline{\gamma}$ of (28) is .92. For both conjugate complex pairs $\tilde{z}_{1,2}, \tilde{z}_{3,4}$ together, the *simultaneous backward error* is approx. $2.5\,e$.

7.3 Clusters and multiple pseudozeros

Consider the univariate polynomial (cf. [6])

$$p(x) := x^4 - 2.83088\,x^3 + 0.00347\,x^2 + 5.66176\,x - 4.00694 .$$

3 of the exact zeros of p are close to $\sqrt{2}$: 1.41421, 1.41481, 1.41607 (to 5 digits). This suggests that there exist neighboring polynomials $\tilde{p}$ with a triple zero. Candidates for such a triple zero z are

- the arithmetic mean of the clustered zeros of p ;
- the zero of p'' at the cluster ;
- the zero of the linear pseudo g.c.d. $(-4.0023\,x + 5.6634)$ of p, p', p''.

All three approaches yield $z = 1.41503$ (to 5 digits).

Let us assume that all coefficients of p (except the leading one) are of limited accuracy. Then the dimension of the manifold $\mathcal{E}^{(3)}(z)$ of (42) is 1; its closest point to the origin in terms of $\max_j |\bar{e}_j|$ is obtained for

$$\bar{e}_3 = -4.15 \cdot 10^{-6}, \; \bar{e}_2 = 6.63 \cdot 10^{-6}, \; \bar{e}_1 = 3.61 \cdot 10^{-6}, \; \bar{e}_0 = -6.63 \cdot 10^{-6}.$$

Thus, for a tolerance vector e with $e_j = 10^{-5}$, $j = 0(1)3$, we have $\bar{\gamma} = .663 < 1$ and the existence of a polynomial $\tilde{p} \in N(p, e)$ with a triple zero at z.

Therefore, the clustered part of the zero set of p is much more adequately described by a triple pseudozero at 1.41503 (or – equivalently – by a 3-cluster about that value) than by the above 3 exact zeros of p: All polynomials in $N(p, e)$ possess 3 zeros in the respective pseudozero domain with an arithmetic mean ≈ 1.41503, while the positions of the *individual* cluster zeros vary very strongly with a variation of $\tilde{p}$. E.g., the 3 relevant zeros of

$$\tilde{p}(x) := x^4 - 2.83087x^3 + 0.00348x^2 + 5.66177x - 4.00693 \in N(p, e)$$

are 1.38583 and $1.42963 \pm 0.02578\,i$ which indicates the large size of the associated pseudozero domain Z_0. The set $Z^{(3)}(p, e)$, on the other hand, has a diameter of only $\approx 3 \cdot 10^{-6}$.

7.4   Reduction of a rational function

Let the transfer function of a stable dynamical system (cf., e.g., [3]) be modelled originally by the rational function

$$r(x) := \frac{3.8764x^5 + 2.0388x^4 + 20.1975x^3 + 7.3914x^2 + 10.8241x + 0.2211}{x^6 + 2.0807x^5 + 11.3926x^4 + 15.5498x^3 + 9.2691x^2 + 7.0977x + 0.1430} =: \frac{p(x)}{q(x)},$$

where all floating-point numbers have an accuracy limited by $1 \cdot 10^{-4}$. In [3], it has been shown how a lower degree approximation of such a model may be determined through the solution of a diagonal quadratic system of polynomial equations. However, since p and q have almost a common zero near $-.0207$ it is much simpler to use this fact for the reduction of the rational function.

The test for the pseudozero property of $z_0 = -.0207$ yields

$$\left.\begin{array}{l} |p(z_0)| = .0000295 \\ |q(z_0)| = .0000865 \end{array}\right\} \leq e(|z_0|) = .000102$$

so that z_0 is indeed a pseudozero of numerator and denominator. Division of p and q by $(x - z_0)$ and omission of the remainder yields (to 4 digits)

$$r_0(x) = \frac{3.8764x^4 + 1.9586x^3 + 20.1570x^2 + 6.9742x + 10.6797}{x^5 + 2.0600x^4 + 11.3500x^3 + 15.3149x^2 + 8.9521x + 6.9124}.$$

This simpler model of the system is correct within the accuracy of the given data and provides meaningful frequency responses for the system.

8   Conclusions

We have shown how the *validity* of an approximate zero of a univariate polynomial or of a 0-dimensional polynomial system may be established relative to *potential inaccuracies* present in some coefficients: We verify whether there exists a neighboring polynomial (system) within a specified tolerance for which the given value is an exact zero. For a set of several approximate zeros, we verify the existence of a neighboring polynomial (system) which has them as exact zeros simultaneously; this makes it also possible to verify the multiplicity of pseudozeros. When the system is assumed to have exact coefficients, our approach establishes the backward error of numerically computed zeros.

This pseudozero approach can also be applied to overdetermined polynomial systems where genuine zeros generally do not exist; this will be explained in a separate publication. Furthermore, the approach can also be applied to positive-dimensional polynomial systems with a tolerance; here a number of new aspects appear. These are currently investigated in a joint project with Prof. Wu Wenda of the Mathematics Mechanization Research Center of the Chinese Academy of Sciences.

References

1. W. Barth, E. Nuding: Optimale Lösung von Intervallgleichungssystemen, Computing **12** (1974) 117 - 125
2. F. Chaitin-Chatelin, V. Frayssé: Lectures on Finite Precision Computations, Software - Environments - Tools, SIAM, Philadelphia, 1996
3. B. Hanzon, J.M. Maciejowski, C.T. Chou: Model Reduction in H_2 Using Matrix Solutions of Polynomial Equations, Univ.Cambridge TR F-INFENG/TR.314, 1998
4. I.Z.Emiris, B. Mourrain: Computer Algebra Methods for Studying and Computing Molecular Conformations, Algorithmica, to appear
5. V. Hribernig: Sensitivity of Algebraic Algorithms, PhD Thesis, TU Vienna, 1995
6. V. Hribernig, H.J. Stetter: Detection and Validation of Clusters of Polynomial Zeros, J.Symb.Comp. **24** (1997) 667 - 681
7. W. Kahan: Conserving Confluence Curbs Ill-condition; Comp. Science UC Berkeley Tech.Rep. 6, 1972
8. T.Y. Li: Numerical Solution of Multivariate Polynomial Systems by Homotopy Continuation Methods, Acta Numerica **6** (1997) 399 - 436
9. R.G. Mosier: Root Neighborhoods of a Polynomial, Math.Comp. **47** (1986) 265 - 273
10. W. Oettli, W. Prager: Compatibility of Approximate Solutions of Linear Equations with Given Error Bounds for Coefficients and Right Hand Sides, Numer.Math. **6** (1964) 405 - 409
11. W. Oettli: On the Solution Set of a Linear System with Inaccurate Coefficients, SIAM J.Num.Anal. **2** (1965) 115 - 118

12. H.J. Stetter: Analysis of Zero Clusters in Multivariate Polynomial Systems, in: Proceed. ISSAC 96 (Ed. Y.N. Lakshman), 127 - 136
13. H.J. Stetter, G.H. Thallinger: Singular Polynomial Systems, in: Proceed. ISSAC 98 (Ed. O. Gloor), 9 - 16
14. K.-C. Toh, L.N. Trefethen: Pseudozeros of Polynomials and Pseudospectra of Companion Matrices, Numer.Math. **68** (1994) 403 - 425
15. L.N. Trefethen: Pseudospectra of Matrices, in: Numerical Analysis (Eds: D.F. Griffiths, G.A. Watson), Longman, 1991

Localization of Roots of a Polynomial not Represented in Canonical Form

Alexei Yu. Uteshev

Faculty of Applied Mathematics, St. Petersburg State University, Bibliotechnaya pl. 2, Petrodvorets, 198904, St. Petersburg, RUSSIA, e-mail: irina@utesh.spb.su

Abstract. The root isolation problem for the polynomial equation not represented in the canonical form can sometimes be solved without evaluation of the coefficients of powers of the variable. We investigate the approach based on representing first the equation in the equivalent determinantal (Hankel or block Hankel) form, and employing then Hermite's root separation method. We illustrate this for the problems of eigenvalues localization, estimation of sensitivity of the roots of the parameter dependent polynomial and nonlinear optimization.

1 Introduction

PROBLEM 1. Find the number of the eigenvalues of a matrix $A_{n \times n}$ lying in the given interval $]a, b[$.

To solve this problem, it would appear at first glance that a canonical representation for the characteristic polynomial $\det(A - x\,I)$ would be needed. The number in question could then be found via, for example, Sturm series construction. However, much simpler algorithm is provided by the following

Theorem 1 (Cauchy). *For a symmetric matrix A one has:*

$$\#\{x \in \mathbb{R} \mid \det(A - x\,I) = 0, \ a < x < b\}$$
$$= P(1, \Delta_1(a), \ldots, \Delta_n(a)) - P(1, \Delta_1(b), \ldots, \Delta_n(b)) \ . \tag{1}$$

Here $\Delta_j(x)$ is the jth leading principal minor of the matrix $A - x\,I$ while P stands for the number of permanences of sign [1].

Thus the stated problem is reduced to that of evaluation of the pair of **numerical** determinants $\det(A - a\,I)$ and $\det(A - b\,I)$ (if both are computed via Gaussian algorithm, then their leading minors will be found at the intermediate steps). Hence, for this problem, the canonical representation for the characteristic polynomial is not obligatory. Similar reasonings hold for several other problems where one does not need the detailed information about every root of polynomial equation, but that one about either a particular root or about a property valid for the whole set of roots (like, for instance, establishing the stability for the linear differential system of equations).

---

[1] Hereinafter we assume for simplicity that none of the sequences of minors contain two consecutive zeros.

We will discuss here three such problems: localization of eigenvalues of matrix (S2), estimation of sensitivity of the roots of a univariate polynomial to the variations of its coefficients (S3) and finding the maximum of a multivariate polynomial (S4).

2   Separation of polynomial roots via Hermite's method

We first sketch some results of the method [5], [6]. For the polynomials

$$f(x) = a_0 x^n + \cdots + a_n \quad \text{and} \quad g(x) = b_0 x^m + \cdots + b_m \quad (a_0 \neq 0, b_0 \neq 0)$$

from $\mathbb{R}[x]$ we want to estimate the relative distribution of their roots. For this aim, find the coefficients of the principal parts of the following Laurent expansions

$$\frac{f'(x)}{f(x)} = \sum_{k=0}^{\infty} \frac{s_k}{x^{k+1}} \quad \text{and} \quad \frac{g(x)f'(x)}{f(x)} = L(x) + \sum_{k=0}^{\infty} \frac{h_k}{x^{k+1}} \ . \tag{2}$$

These coefficients can be calculated recursively via the coefficients of $f(x)$ and $g(x)$: $s_0 = n, s_1 = -a_1/a_0, \ldots,$

$$s_k = \begin{cases} -(a_1 s_{k-1} + a_2 s_{k-2} + \cdots + a_{k-1} s_1 + a_k k)/a_0 & \text{if } k < n, \\ -(a_1 s_{k-1} + a_2 s_{k-2} + \cdots + a_n s_{k-n})/a_0 & \text{if } k \geq n; \end{cases} \tag{3}$$

$$h_k = b_0 s_{k+m} + b_1 s_{k+m-1} + \cdots + b_m s_k \ , \tag{4}$$

while, on the other hand, they give the values for the symmetric polynomials of the roots $\lambda_1, \ldots, \lambda_n$ of $f(x)$:

$$s_k = \sum_{j=1}^{n} \lambda_j^k \quad \text{and} \quad h_k = \sum_{j=1}^{n} g(\lambda_j)\lambda_j^k \ .$$

On evaluating these numbers for $k = 0, \ldots, 2n - 2$, compose the Hankel matrices

$$S = [s_{j+k}]_{j,k=0}^{n-1} \quad \text{and} \quad H = [h_{j+k}]_{j,k=0}^{n-1} \tag{5}$$

and compute their leading principal minors S_j and H_j for $j = 1, \ldots, n$.

Theorem 2 (Jacobi, Hermite, Sylvester). *All the roots of $f(x)$ are distinct iff $S_n \neq 0$. Under this condition, one has:*

$$\#\{x \in \mathbb{R} \mid f(x) = 0\} = P(1, S_1, \ldots, S_n) - V(1, S_1, \ldots, S_n) \ . \tag{6}$$

If $H_n \neq 0$ then

$$\#\{x \in \mathbb{R} \mid f(x) = 0, \ g(x) > 0\} = P(1, H_1, \ldots, H_n) - V(1, S_1, \ldots, S_n) \ .$$

Here V stands for the number of variations of sign.

The following result gives a relationship between the determinants of the matrices (5) with the **discriminant** $\mathcal{D}(f)$ and the **resultant** $\mathcal{R}(f,g)$:

Corollary 3. *One has:*

$$S_n = \mathcal{D}(f)/a_0^{2n-2} \quad \text{and} \quad H_n = S_n \prod_{1 \le j \le n} g(\lambda_j) = S_n \mathcal{R}(f,g)/a_0^m . \tag{7}$$

Theorem 4 (Joachimstahl). *If $\Delta_j(x)$ stands for the jth leading principal minor of the matrix*

$$[s_{j+k}x - s_{j+k+1}]_{j,k=0}^{n-1} \tag{8}$$

then, provided that $S_n \ne 0$, one has

$$\#\{x \in \mathbb{R} \mid f(x) = 0, \ a < x < b\}$$

$$= V(1, \Delta_1(a), \ldots, \Delta_n(a)) - V(1, \Delta_1(b), \ldots, \Delta_n(b)) , \tag{9}$$

Corollary 5. *One has $\Delta_n(t) \equiv S_n f(t)/a_0$.*

Theorem 4 claims that the sequence of the leading principal minors of matrix (8) plays the role of the Sturm series for the root separation problem. The distinction with the canonical Sturm sequence constructed via Euclidean algorithm is that the degrees of polynomials increase with the polynomial $f(x)$ standing at the end.

The last fact is of primary importance for justification of the idea of the present paper. The point is that in several real-life problems we are not granted apriori the canonical representation for the polynomial equation. (Recall, for instance, Problem 1.) Thus, to construct the Sturm sequence for $f(x)$, one first need to find the coefficients a_j. Theorem 1 provides an alternative approach for root separation in which the canonical representation for $f(x)$ becomes unnesesary. To extend that theorem to the non-symmetric matrices, let us utilize the fundamental property of the matrix analysis [4]:

$$s_k = \text{\textbf{trace }} A^k \text{ for } k = 0, \ldots, 2n - 1 .$$

Thus the entries of matrix (8) can be evaluated indirectly, i.e. without finding the coefficients of $\det(A - x I)$. One will be able to separate the eigenvalues with the aid of (9).

Example 6. Isolate the Le Verrier matrix [2] eigenvalues:

$$A = \begin{pmatrix} -5.509882 & 1.870086 & 0.422908 & 0.008814 \\ 0.287865 & -11.811654 & 5.711900 & 0.058717 \\ 0.049099 & 4.308033 & -12.970687 & 0.229326 \\ 0.006235 & 0.269851 & 1.397369 & -17.596207 \end{pmatrix} \tag{10}$$

Solution. First, compute the powers of A within the 10 digits accuracy:

$$A \longrightarrow A^2 = A \cdot A \begin{array}{l} \nearrow A^4 = A^2 \cdot A^2 \longrightarrow A^5 = A \cdot A^4 \\ \searrow A^7 = A^4 \cdot A^3 \\ \searrow A^3 = A^2 \cdot A \nearrow A^6 = A^3 \cdot A^3 \end{array}$$

(the scheme illuminates a possible parallelization of the computations). Find then their traces:

$$s_1 = -47.888430, \quad s_2 = 698.7441983, \quad s_3 = -11329.70086, \quad s_4 = 192458.4988,$$

$$s_5 = -3332643.947, \quad s_6 = 58167599.57, \quad s_7 = -1018740709 .$$

For matrix S given by (5), all the minors S_j are positive. Thus, by (6), all the eigenvalues are real and distinct. Computing the (numerical!) determinant of matrix (8) for $x = 0$, one obtains

$$V(1, \; 47.888430, \; 54318.1319, \; 0.13755989 \times 10^9, \; 0.681478 \times 10^{13}) = 0 ,$$

therefore all the eigenvalues are negative. Further substitutions give the bounds for eigenvalues: one in $]-6, -5[$, one in $]-8, -7[$, two in $]-18, -17[$. One can even find an eigenvalue approximation on this way — only watching the variations in signs of the minors on bisecting the interval. For example, $x_{min} \approx -17.863$ with the error appearing in the next digit. This is a good result in comparison with, e.g. the matrix power method [2]. The latter gives the same accuracy only after computing 220 powers of matrix A.   □

3   Sensitivity

PROBLEM 2. Let the polynomial $f(x)$ be squarefree. For a perturbed polynomial

$$F(x) := f(x) + \varepsilon x^j , \quad (0 \le j < n)$$

evaluate the nearest to zero **critical values** for a parameter ε, i.e. those ones on passing through which, the number of real roots alters.

The critical values we are looking for are the real roots of the discriminant

$$\mathcal{F}(\varepsilon) = \mathcal{D}_x(F(x)) .$$

To find the canonical representation of $\mathcal{F}(\varepsilon)$, one can utilize any method of the resultant computation. Then one will be faced with the problem of localization of the roots of $\mathcal{F}(\varepsilon)$. Consider, for example, the Wilkinson polynomial [8]

$$F(x) = \prod_{1 \le k \le 20} (x + k) + \varepsilon x^{19} . \tag{11}$$

The coefficients of $\mathcal{F}(\varepsilon)$ computed for (11) happen to be of the order $\geq 10^{275}$, whereas those of the initial polynomial $F(x)$ do not exceed 10^{20}. Therefore, to estimate the sensitivity of the roots of one polynomial one should find the roots of another polynomial with more complicated coefficients. To break up this vicious circle, let us represent $\mathcal{F}(\varepsilon)$ as the determinant of a suitable symmetric matrix.

Theorem 7. *The following equality*

$$\mathcal{F}(\varepsilon) \equiv \mathcal{R}_x(\Phi(x), G(x) + \varepsilon) \tag{12}$$

is valid up to a numerical factor independent of ε. Here

$$\Phi(x) := f(x) - \frac{1}{j} f'(x)x, \quad G(x) := \frac{1}{j} \tilde{q}_{j-1}(x) f'(x) \ ,$$

while $\tilde{q}_{j-1}$ stands for the remainder on dividing $\left[\frac{a_n - \Phi(x)}{a_n x} \right]^{j-1}$ by $\Phi(x)$.

Proof. Using the properties of the resultant and the discriminant [3] one obtains [2]:

$$\mathcal{D}(F) = \mathcal{R}(F, F') = \mathcal{R}(F(x) - \frac{1}{j} F'(x)x, F'(x)) = \mathcal{R}(\Phi(x), F'(x)) \ .$$

Furthermore, for the roots of $\Phi(x)$ the following conditions are equivalent:

$$F'(x) = 0 \quad \Longleftrightarrow \quad \frac{f'(x)}{jx^{j-1}} + \varepsilon = 0 \quad \Longleftrightarrow \quad \frac{1}{j} f'(x) [q_1(x)]^{j-1} + \varepsilon = 0,$$

where the polynomial $q_1(x) := (a_n - \Phi(x))/(a_n x)$ evidently satisfies the identity $x q_1(x) + \Phi(x)/a_n \equiv 1$. By representing now the resultant $\mathcal{R}(\Phi(x), F'(x))$ via the roots of $\Phi(x)$, we derive (12). $\qquad\square$

To compute the resultant in the right-hand side of (12) one may utilize (7). Indeed, let us state the root separation problem as the one of finding

$$\#\{x \in \mathbb{R} \mid \Phi(x) = 0, G(x) + \varepsilon > 0\}$$

with the aid of Theorem 2. The corresponding matrix H given by (5) will be ε-dependent and, according to (7) and (12), $\det H = \mathcal{F}(\varepsilon)$ up to a numerical factor. The minors $H_j(\varepsilon)$ of this matrix allow one to separate the roots of $\mathcal{F}(\varepsilon)$:

$$\#\{x \in \mathbb{R} \mid \mathcal{F}(\varepsilon) = 0, \ a < \varepsilon < b\}$$
$$= \#\{x \in \mathbb{R} \mid \Phi(x) = 0, \ G(x) + b > 0\} - \#\{x \in \mathbb{R} \mid \Phi(x) = 0, \ G(x) + a > 0\}$$
$$= P(1, H_1(b), \dots, H_n(b)) - P(1, H_1(a), \dots, H_n(a)) \ .$$

---

[2] The computations were performed up to numerical factors.

Example 8. Find the ε-tolerance for polynomial (11).

Solution. To simplify computations, we will apply the above algorithm not to the polynomial (11) but to $x^{20} F(1/x)$ (exploiting the fact that $\mathcal{D}(a_0 x^n + a_1 x^{n-1} + \cdots + a_n) = \mathcal{D}(a_0 + a_1 x + \cdots + a_n x^n)$ if $a_0 \neq 0$, $a_n \neq 0$). Although the entries of the corresponding matrix H are large:

$$h_0 = 20\,\varepsilon + \frac{1526934632973194983028884449810912753}{13673334576273000766260480000000},$$

$$h_1 = -\frac{7381}{2835}\varepsilon - \frac{8130697380917576953985024810214437 22061}{77527807047467914344696921600000000}, \ldots$$

but they are not that huge as the coefficients of powers of ε in its determinant. We do not aim to compute the latter, i.e. the **symbolic** determinant. Instead of this, we evaluate **numerical** determinants obtained on specializing ε. Every such a computation provides one with the information about the exact number of roots of $\mathcal{F}(\varepsilon)$ lying on the left and on the right from the substituted value. For instance, on computing three numerical determinants for $\varepsilon \in \{0, 1, -1\}$, it can be concluded that 8 roots reside in $]-1, 0[$ and 7 roots reside in $]0, 1[$. On dividing these intervals further, one can even obtain approximations for critical values: polynomial (11) keeps all its roots real for

$$-1.3508 \times 10^{-10} < \varepsilon < +1.4213 \times 10^{-10}.$$

This approves the striking fact of high sensitivity of the roots of (11) established empirically by Wilkinson. □

4   Optimization

PROBLEM 3. Find the maximum of the parameter dependent polynomial

$$-x_1^4 - x_2^4 - x_3^4 + \varepsilon\, x_1^2 x_2 x_3 + \varepsilon\, x_1 x_2^2 x_3 + 2\, x_1 x_2 x_3 - x_1 \ . \tag{13}$$

Formally, the critical values of a polynomial $F(X)$, $X := (x_1, x_2, x_3)$ are contained among the real roots of the discriminant

$$\mathcal{F}(z) := \mathcal{D}_X(F(X) - z) = \mathcal{R}_X\left(\partial F/\partial x_1, \partial F/\partial x_2, \partial F/\partial x_3, F(X) - z\right). \tag{14}$$

Practical evaluation of $\mathcal{F}(z)$ is possible via the Gröbner basis construction for the ideal generated by $\partial F/\partial x_1, \partial F/\partial x_2, \partial F/\partial x_3$ and $F - z$ w.r.t. the lexicographical ordering $x_1 \succ x_2 \succ x_3 \succ z$. However, this is usually a very time-consuming task. Let us recall, however, that our goal **is not** the construction of canonical form for $\mathcal{F}(z)$ but merely evaluation of its maximal root. The latter will be possible if we manage to represent $\mathcal{F}(z)$ in determinantal form. Let us state again the zero-localization problem: find

$$\# \left\{ X \in \mathbb{R}^3 \mid \partial F/\partial x_1 = 0, \partial F/\partial x_2 = 0, \partial F/\partial x_3 = 0, F - z > 0 \right\} \ . \tag{15}$$

For evaluating this number, we will utilize the multivariate counterparts of the results of §2, and we begin with a brief outlook at the algorithms of Hermite's method in $\mathbb{R}^3$ [7]. For the system of equations

$$f_1(X) = 0, \quad f_2(X) = 0, \quad f_3(X) = 0 \text{ with } f_j(X) \in \mathbb{R}[X], \quad \deg f_j = n_j \quad (16)$$

we want to find the number of its real solutions $\Lambda_p = (\alpha_p, \beta_p, \gamma_p)$ satisfying the given inequality $g(X) > 0$, with $g(X) \in \mathbb{R}[X]$, $\deg g = m$. Using the recursive (in the number of variables) construction of the multivariate resultant [7], one can compute the **eliminants**

$$\mathcal{X}_j(x_j) := \mathcal{R}_{X \setminus \{x_j\}}(f_1(X), f_2(X), f_3(X)), (j = 1, 2, 3)$$

together with their linear representations, i.e. to find $M_{jk}(X) \in \mathbb{R}[X]$ satisfying the identities:

$$M_{j1}(X)f_1(X) + M_{j2}(X)f_2(X) + M_{j3}(X)f_3(X) \equiv \mathcal{X}_j(x_j) \ . \quad (17)$$

ASSUMPTION 1. Let $\deg \mathcal{X}_j = N := n_1 n_2 n_3$.
This condition is fulfilled provided that

$$\mathcal{A}_0 := \mathcal{R}_{y_1, y_2}\left(f_{1n_1}(y_1, y_2, 1), f_{2n_2}(y_1, y_2, 1), f_{3n_3}(y_1, y_2, 1)\right) \neq 0 \ , \quad (18)$$

where $f_{jn_j}(X)$ stands for the **leading form** of f_j in expansion of the latter in decreasing powers of the variables. The generic system (16) usually obeys this restriction which is just a constructive version of the Bézout theorem [1] claiming that the number of solutions of (16) usually equals N.

Let us intoduce the following polynomials:

$$\mathcal{V}(X) = \det\left[M_{jk}(X)\right]_{j,k=1}^3 \quad \text{and} \quad \mathcal{J}(X) = \textbf{Jacobian}\,(f_1, f_2, f_3) \ .$$

Consider the expansions of the following fractions in the negative powers of x_1, x_2 and x_3:

$$\frac{\mathcal{V}(X)}{\mathcal{X}_1(x_1)\,\mathcal{X}_2(x_2)\,\mathcal{X}_3(x_3)} = \mathcal{L}_0(X) + \sum_{j_1, j_2, j_3 = 0}^{\infty} \frac{d_{j_1 j_2 j_3}}{x_1^{j_1+1} x_2^{j_2+1} x_3^{j_3+1}} \ ,$$

$$\frac{\mathcal{V}(X)\mathcal{J}(X)}{\mathcal{X}_1(x_1)\,\mathcal{X}_2(x_2)\,\mathcal{X}_3(x_3)} = \mathcal{L}_1(X) + \sum_{j_1, j_2, j_3 = 0}^{\infty} \frac{s_{j_1 j_2 j_3}}{x_1^{j_1+1} x_2^{j_2+1} x_3^{j_3+1}} \ ,$$

$$\frac{\mathcal{V}(X)\mathcal{J}(X)g(X)}{\mathcal{X}_1(x_1)\,\mathcal{X}_2(x_2)\,\mathcal{X}_3(x_3)} = \mathcal{L}_2(X) + \sum_{j_1, j_2, j_3 = 0}^{\infty} \frac{h_{j_1 j_2 j_3}}{x_1^{j_1+1} x_2^{j_2+1} x_3^{j_3+1}} \ .$$

Here $\mathcal{L}_j$ is of the form

$$\frac{A_1(X)\mathcal{X}_1(x_1) + A_2(X)\mathcal{X}_2(x_2) + A_3(X)\mathcal{X}_3(x_3)}{\mathcal{X}_1(x_1)\,\mathcal{X}_2(x_2)\,\mathcal{X}_3(x_3)} \ , \text{ with } A_j(X) \in \mathbb{R}[X] \ .$$

We will be interested, however, only in the coefficients of the terms with negative powers of all the variables. By construction, they can be expressed rationally in terms of the coefficients of f_1, f_2, f_3 and g. On the other hand, these coefficients give the values for certain symmetric functions of the solutions Λ_p:

Theorem 9 (Jacobi). *Under Assumption 1, one has:*

$$s_{j_1 j_2 j_3} = \sum_{p=1}^{N} \alpha_p^{j_1} \beta_p^{j_2} \gamma_p^{j_3} \quad \text{and} \quad h_{j_1 j_2 j_3} = \sum_{p=1}^{N} \alpha_p^{j_1} \beta_p^{j_2} \gamma_p^{j_3} g(\Lambda_p) . \tag{19}$$

From the coefficients $d_{j_1 j_2 j_3}, s_{j_1 j_2 j_3}$ and $h_{j_1 j_2 j_3}$ construct the $N \times N$ block Hankel matrices D, S and H of similar structure. For instance,

$$S := \left[\tilde{S}_{K+L} \right]_{K,L=0}^{n_3-1}, \quad \tilde{S}_K := [S_{k+\ell,K}]_{k,\ell=0}^{n_2-1}, \quad S_{k,K} := [s_{i+j,k,K}]_{i,j=0}^{n_1-1} .$$

ASSUMPTION 2. Let $\det D \neq 0$.

This gives the restriction not on the whole set of the coefficients of system (16) but only on those of the leading forms $f_{jn_j}(X)$. Indeed, it turns out that

$$\det D = \Omega / A_0^{n_1+n_2+n_3-2}$$

where Ω is a product of $n_1 + n_2 + n_3 - 3$ polynomials in the coefficients of the leading forms $f_{jn_j}(X)$ (subresultants of resultant (18)).

Let us now compute the leading principal minors S_j and H_j $(j = 1, \ldots, N)$ for matrices S and H.

Theorem 10. *If $S_N \neq 0$ then all the solutions of (16) are distinct and*

$$\#\{X \in \mathbb{R}^3 \mid (16)\} = P(1, S_1, \ldots, S_N) - V(1, S_1, \ldots, S_N) .$$

If $H_N \neq 0$ then

$$\#\{X \in \mathbb{R}^3 \mid (16) , g(X) > 0\} = P(1, H_1, \ldots, H_N) - V(1, S_1, \ldots, S_N) . \tag{20}$$

Corollary 11. *One has:*

$$S_N = \det D \prod_{1 \leq p \leq N} \mathcal{J}(\Lambda_p) ,$$

$$H_N = S_N \prod_{1 \leq p \leq N} g(\Lambda_p) = S_N \mathcal{R}_X(f_1, f_2, f_3, g) / A_0^m . \tag{21}$$

Let us employ the above results for finding the number (15). We set $f_j(X) := \partial F / \partial x_j$ and $g(X) := F(X) - z$. It turns out that the conditions of Assumptions 1 and 2 are fulfilled provided that the leading form of the expansion of $F(X)$ in decreasing powers of variables is negatively definite, i.e. max F is finite. (For (13) they are satisfied if $|\varepsilon| < 4/\sqrt[4]{54}$.) The corresponding block-Hankel matrix H depends now on z. To obtain the symbolic representation for its determinant — which, due to (21), coincides with (14)— is rather complicated. It is much simpler to localize its roots using formula (20):

$$\# \left\{ X \in \mathbb{R}^3 \mid \partial F/\partial x_1 = 0, \partial F/\partial x_2 = 0, \partial F/\partial x_3 = 0, \ a < F < b \right\}$$
$$= P(1, H_1(a), \ldots, H_N(a)) - P(1, H_1(b), \ldots, H_N(b)) \ .$$

One can find the number of critical values of $F(X)$ remained below and above the "water-level" $z = a$ via consideration of the signs of the **numerical** minors of det $H(a)$. After localizing the value of max $F(X)$ within the desired accuracy it is possible to restore the components of the corresponding critical point Λ_p as the appropriate rational functions of this value with the aid of the minors of matrix $H(z)$ (cf. §4 of [7]).

The determinantal representation helps also in the case of an additional parameter dependency, like the one in (13). It is possible to estimate the behaviour of max $F(X)$ according to variation of ε. The proposed approach can also be extended to the constrained optimization problem (cf. §6 of [7]).

5   Conclusions

The outlined approach to the above three problems can be summarized as follows: for several practical problems concerning the root isolation it is not obligatory to aim at the canonical representation of a considered polynomial. For such problems, it is cheaper, sometimes, to restrict the desires to the search of the determinantal representation of the polynomial. Instead of computing this determinant **symbolically**, i.e. for all the values of the variable, we evaluate **numerical** determinants obtained on specialization of this variable.

References

1. Bikker, P., Uteshev, A.Yu.: On the Bézout construction of the resultant. Tech.Report **99-01** (1999) RISC-Linz.
2. Fadeev D.K., Fadeeva, V.N.: *Computational Methods of Linear Algebra.* (1963) San Francisco. Freeman
3. Bôcher, M.: *Introduction to Higher Algebra.* (1964) New York. Dover
4. Horn, A.G., Johnson, C.R.: *Matrix Analysis.* **1** (1986) Cambridge. Cambridge university press
5. Krein M.G., Naimark M.A.: The method of symmetric and Hermitian forms in the theory of the separation of the roots of algebraic equations. *Linear Multilin. Algebra.* **10(4)** (1981) 265–308

6. Uteshev, A.Yu., Shulyak, S.G.: Hermite's method of separation of solutions of systems of algebraic equations and its applications. *Linear Algebra Appl.* **177** (1992) 49–88
7. Uteshev, A.Yu., Cherkasov, T.M.: The search for the maximum of a polynomial. *J.Symbolic Computation.* **25(5)** (1998) 587–618
8. Wilkinson, J.H.: The evaluation of zeros of ill-conditioned polynomials. *Numer. Math.* **1** (1959) 150–180

On Normalization of a Class of Polynomial Hamiltonians: From Ordinary and Inverse Points of View

Yoshio Uwano[1], Nikolai Chekanov[2], Vitaly Rostovtsev[3], and Sergue Vinitsky[4]

[1] Department of Applied Mathematics and Physics,
Kyoto University, Kyoto 606-8501, Japan
[2] Department of Mathematics, Belgorod State University, Belgorod, Russia
[3] Laboratory of Computer Techniques and Automations, Joint Institute for Nuclear Research, Dubna, Moscow Region 141980, Russia
[4] Bogoliubov Laboratory of Theoretical Physics, Joint Institute for Nuclear Research, Dubna, Moscow Region 141980, Russia

Abstract. In this paper, the normalization of a class of polynomial Hamiltonians based on the symbolic computing is disscussed from both the ordinary and the inverse direction-points of view. The truncated three-particle Toda linear chain(3-TLC) and the regularized system of a planar hydrogen atom with the linear Stark effect (HLSE) are taken as examples to demonstrate the symbolic-computational approach to the ordinary and the inverse normalization problems.

1 Introduction

It is widely known that the Birkhoff-Gustavson normal form (BGNF) expansion works effectively to study a behavior of nonlinear dynamical systems; the Hénon-Heiles system and Toda linear chain (TLC) are often taken as typical examples [1] to describe such an efficiency.

Since a core part of the BGNF expansion is made on the polynomial algebra [2], it fits very well the symbolic computing on computers: For example, the symbolic computing program named GITA realizes the algebraic procedure of converting power-series Hamiltonians into their BGNF [3] with REDUCE 3.3 or later versions of REDUCE.[1].

One of the aims of this paper is to demonstrate how the normalization into BGNF works around integrable systems. Although one might not think it necessary to normalize the integrable Hamiltonian systems, the normalization of integrable systems is worth discussing especially in the case where they admit the trajectories tending to singularities; the truncated three-particle Toda linear chain (3-TLC) is taken as an example to demonstrate how the normalization works in the integrable-system case.

The other aim of this paper is to present a symbolic computaional approach to an 'inverse' problem of normalization recently posed by one of the

---

[1] The authors are trying to implement the same procedure with Maple V

authors (YU) with the aim of an application of quantum studies to certain BGNF systems [4–6]. The inverse problem reads as follows: '*Identify a class of dynamical systems which are reduced to the same BGNF up to a certain order*'. To solve it, the symbolic computing program named GITA^{-1} has been proposed by the authors [7], which will be reviewed in this paper together with an application to the regularized system of planar hydrogen atom with the linear Stark effect (HLSE) [8]. It is shown that a class of Liouville-type systems share the same BGNF with the regularized system of HLSE.

The aim of this talk is also to review another symbolic computing program named ANFER (*Algorithm of Normal Form Expansion and Restoration*) for the inverse problem proposed by the authors (YU and SV) [9]. ANFER is expected to work more effectively than GITA^{-1} does from various points of view; less steps of procedures, less memory expenses, and so on. The system of Hénon-Heiles type will be taken as a very simple but intuitive example to show how ANFER restores the Hénon-Heiles Hamiltonian from its BGNF expansion.

The contents of this paper are organized as follows. In Section 2, a brief reveiw of the ordinary normalization problem is given. In Section 3, the structures of GITA and GITA^{-1} for the general n-degree-of-freedom case is presented briefly. In Section 4, the direct problem of 3-TLC is discussed to show the normalization is effective not only for non-integrable systems but also for integrable ones. In Section 5, the run of the inverse problem of HLSE is demonstrated to show the way to identify a class of Hamiltonian systems which share certain BGNF Hamiltonian in common. In Section 6, the formulation of the inverse normalization problem and algorithm of ANFER are presented. In Section 7 a simple test example of the ANFER run is considered.

2   The Ordinary and Inverse Normalization Problems

In this Section, we review the ordinary problem of the BGNF expansion very briefly following [2]. Let $(\mathbf{R}^n \times \mathbf{R}^n, d\vartheta_n)$ be the phase space endowed with the canonical symplectic 2-form, $d\vartheta_n = \sum_{j=1}^n dp_j \wedge dq_j$, where (q, p) are the Cartesian coordinates of $\mathbf{R}^n \times \mathbf{R}^n$. Let us consider the Hamiltonian system on $(\mathbf{R}^n \times \mathbf{R}^n, d\vartheta_n)$ which admits a stable equilibrium point in a resonance of equal frequencies. Without loss of generality, such an equilibrium point can be put at the origin of $\mathbf{R}^n \times \mathbf{R}^n$, so that around it the Hamiltonian $H(q, p)$ of such a system is assumed to be expanded into a power series,

$$H(q,p) = \frac{1}{2} \sum_{j=1}^n \left(p_j^2 + q_j^2 \right) + \sum_{k=3}^{\infty} H_k(q,p), \tag{1}$$

where $H_k(q, p)$ $(k = 3, 4, \cdots)$ are homogeneous polynomials of degree k in (q, p).

The conversion of H into a BGNF power series is made as follows. Let us consider a local canonical transformation, $(q, p) \rightarrow (\xi, \eta)$ around the origin of

$\mathbf{R}^n \times \mathbf{R}^n$ which is associated with a *type-2* generating function [1],

$$W(q,\eta) = \sum_{j=1}^{n} q_j \eta_j + \sum_{k=3}^{\infty} W_k(q,\eta), \qquad (2a)$$

where $W_k(q,\eta)$ $(k = 3, 4, \cdots)$ are homogeneous polynomials of degree k in (q,η). On choosing $W(q,\eta)$ suitably, the $H(q,p)$ is converted to the power series, say $G(\xi,\eta)$, through

$$H(q, \frac{\partial W}{\partial q}) = G(\frac{\partial W}{\partial \eta}, \eta), \qquad (3a)$$

which is written in the form

$$G(\xi,\eta) = \frac{1}{2} \sum_{j=1}^{n} (\eta_j^2 + \xi_j^2) + \sum_{k=3}^{\infty} G_k(\xi,\eta), \qquad (4a)$$

where $G_k(\xi,\eta)$ $(k = 3, 4, \cdots)$ are homogeneous polynomials of degree k in (ξ,η) subject to the Poisson-commuting relation,

$$\left\{ \frac{1}{2} \sum_{j=1}^{n} (\eta_j^2 + \xi_j^2) , \ G_k(\xi,\eta) \right\} = 0. \qquad (4b)$$

Definition 2.1   *Let $D_{q,\eta}$ be the differential operator*

$$D_{q,\eta} = \sum_{j=1}^{n} \left(q_j \frac{\partial}{\partial \eta_j} - \eta_j \frac{\partial}{\partial q_j} \right) \qquad (5)$$

associated with the variables (q,η) and let $f(q,\eta)$ be a power series or a polynomial in (q,η). Then f is said to be normal (resp. non-normal) to $D_{q,\eta}$ if $f \in Ker(D_{q,\eta})$ (resp. $f \in Im(D_{q,\eta})$).

We have the following fact [2] known well:

Theorem 2.2   *For any Hamiltonian $H(q,p)$ in the form of (1), there exists uniquely the pair of the BGNF, $G(\xi,\eta)$, in the form of (4) and the non-normal type-2 generating function $W(q,\eta)$ in the form of (2a), which satisfies (3a).*

Theorem 2.2 provides the ordinary problem of the BGNF expansion in the following form:

Definition 2.3   (The ordinary problem)   *Convert a power-series (or a polynomial Hamiltonian $H(q,p)$ of the form (1) into a BGNF power series $G(\xi,\eta)$ of the form (4) through a canonical transformation associated with a non-normal type-2 generating function $W(q,\eta)$ of the form (2a).*

In view of Definition 2.3 defining the ordinary problem, the inverse problem is defined as follows:

Definition 2.4 (The inverse problem) *For a given BGNF in the form (4), identify all possible power series $H(q,p)$ in the form (1), which are normalized to the given BGNF through the canonical transformations associated with the type-2 generating functions.*

It should be remarked here that we will present an alternative expression for the inverse problem posed below in Section 6, which will be a key to organize the algorithm ANFER .

3   A Review of GITA and GITA^{-1}

Let $H_{IN}(q,p)$ and $H_{OUT}(q,p)$ be the *input* and the *output* Hamiltonians, which are expressed as

$$H_\lambda(q,p) = \sum_{h=2}^\infty H_\lambda^{(h)}(q,p) \quad \text{with} \quad H_\lambda^{(2)}(q,p) = \frac{1}{2}\sum_{k=1}^n (p_k^2 + q_k^2), \qquad (6)$$

where $H_\lambda^{(h)}$ $(\lambda = IN, OUT, \; h = 3,4,\cdots)$ is a degree-h homogeneous polynomial in (q,p) expressed as

$$H_\lambda^{(h)}(q,p) = \sum_{|\alpha|+|\beta|=h} c_\lambda^{(h)}(\alpha,\beta) q^\alpha p^\beta \quad \text{with} \quad \begin{cases} q^\alpha p^\beta = q_1^{\alpha_1}\cdots q_n^{\alpha_n} p_1^{\beta_1}\cdots p_n^{\beta_n}, \\ |\alpha| = \sum_{k=1}^n \alpha_k, \; |\beta| = \sum_{k=1}^n \beta_k, \end{cases}$$

$$(7)$$

Let $G_{IN}(\xi,\eta)$ and $G_{OUT}(\xi,\eta)$ be the *input* and the *output* BGNF Hamiltonian,

$$G_\lambda(\xi,\eta) = \sum_{j=1}^\infty G_\lambda^{(2j)}(\xi,\eta) \quad \text{with} \quad G_\lambda^{(2)}(\xi,\eta) = \frac{1}{2}\sum_{k=1}^n (\eta_k^2 + \xi_k^2), \qquad (8)$$

where $G_\lambda^{(2j)}$ $(\lambda = IN, OUT, \; j = 2,3,\cdots)$ is a degree-$2j$ homogeneous polynomial in (ξ,η) expressed as

$$G_\lambda^{(2j)}(\xi,\eta) = \sum_{|\alpha|+|\beta|=2j} \gamma_\lambda^{(2j)}(\alpha,\beta) \xi^\alpha \eta^\beta \quad \text{with} \quad \{G_\lambda^{(2)}, G_\lambda^{(2j)}\} = 0. \quad (9)$$

In equation (9), α and β are multi-indices used in the same way as in equation (7), and $\{\cdot,\cdot\}$ is the canonical Poisson bracket associated with the position variables ξ and the momentum ones η. The coefficients $\gamma_\lambda^{(2j)}(\alpha,\beta)$, $(j = 2,3,\cdots)$ are found by solving the key BGNF equation

$$H_\lambda(q, \frac{\partial W}{\partial q}) = G_\lambda(\frac{\partial W}{\partial \eta}, \eta). \qquad (10)$$

Here $W_\lambda(q,\eta)$ is the generating function of the form (2), which should be identified together with $G_\lambda(\xi,\eta)$ as the solutions of (10). We will not get the identification of $W_\lambda(q,\eta)$ in detail here (see [2,3]).

Let us denote by P_ℓ the space of degree-ℓ homogeneous polynomials in $2n$ variables with real coefficients, which can be identified with the vector space $\mathbf{R}^{N(n,\ell)}$, where $N(n,\ell)$ indicates the number of degree-ℓ monomials in $2n$ variables allowed to exist. Then, denoting such a correspondence by $\iota_\ell : P_\ell \to \mathbf{R}^{N(n,\ell)}$, we associate the vectors, $c_\lambda^{(h)}$ and $\gamma_\lambda^{(2j)}$, with H_λ and G_λ by

$$c_\lambda^{(h)} = \iota_h(H_\lambda^{(h)}) \in \mathbf{R}^{N(n,h)} \quad \text{and} \quad \gamma_\lambda^{(2j)} = \iota_{2j}(G_\lambda^{(2j)}) \in \mathbf{R}^{N(n,2j)}, \quad (11)$$

respectively. Further, using ι_ℓ, we express the differential operator D (5), restricted on P_ℓ by the matrix $M^{(\ell)}$ acting on $\mathbf{R}^{N(n,\ell)}$; $\iota_\ell \circ D = M^{(\ell)} \circ \iota_\ell$.

After the preparatory work done above, the hth order part of equation (10) is put into the series of algebraic equations,

$$\gamma_\lambda^{(h)} = M^{(h)}\{c_\lambda^{(h)} + \Phi^{(h)}(c_\lambda^{(h-1)}, \cdot, \cdot, c_\lambda^{(2)})\} \quad (j = 3, 4, \cdots), \quad (12)$$

for $\gamma_\lambda^{(h)}$ ($\lambda = IN, OUT$) [2,8], which are just the equations solved by GITA. Note that $\gamma_\lambda^{(2j+1)}$ ($\lambda = IN, OUT$) turn out to vanish [8].

We are now in position to present what GITA^{-1} computes: Let us recall the inverse problem posed in Section 1, which is put in the following: '*For a given H_{IN}, identify all the possible (or a part of) H_{OUT} subject to $G_{IN} = G_{OUT}$ up to a certain order*'. Since $G_{IN} = G_{OUT}$ can read $\gamma_{IN}^{(h)} = \gamma_{OUT}^{(h)}$ ($h = 2, 3, \cdots$), GITA^{-1} solves the series of equations,

$$M^{(h)}c_{OUT}^{(h)} = \gamma_{IN}^{(h)} - M^{(h)}\Phi^{(h)}(c_{OUT}^{(h-1)}, \cdot, \cdot, c_{OUT}^{(2)})\} \quad (j = 3, 4, \cdots), \quad (13)$$

for $c_{OUT}^{(h)}$, where $\gamma_{IN}^{(h)}$ are determined beforehand from H_{IN} through GITA (*i.e.* (6)-(12)). In the subsequent Sections, we demonstrate how GITA and GITA^{-1} (*i.e.* (6)-(13)) work in REDUCE 3.3 or later versions of REDUCE in the direct problem of 3-TLC and in the inverse problem of HLSE.

4   The Truncated Three-Particle Toda Linear Chain

Let us consider the example of an integrable system: three identical particles on the line governed by the Toda Hamiltonian [10]. The original Toda Hamiltonian can be reduced to the two-dimensional one:

$$H = \frac{1}{2}(p_1^2 + p_2^2) + \frac{1}{4}\{\exp\ (\xi) + \exp\ (\eta) + \exp\ (\zeta)\}, \quad (14a)$$

$$\xi = \sqrt{2}q_1 + \sqrt{\frac{2}{3}}q_2, \quad \eta = -\sqrt{2}q_1 + \sqrt{\frac{2}{3}}q_2, \quad \zeta = -2\sqrt{\frac{2}{3}}q_2, \quad \xi + \eta + \zeta = 0. \quad (14b)$$

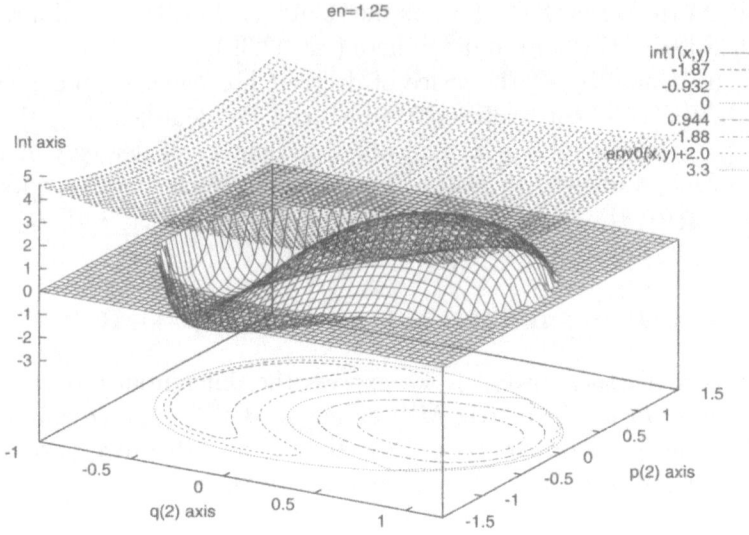

Fig. 1. Exact integral of motion 3-TLC (15)

It is easy to verify that the Hamiltonian system (14) possesses additional integral of motion (see Fig.1) in the form

$$I = \frac{4}{3}p_1(p_1^2 - 3p_2^2) + (p_1 - \sqrt{3}p_2)\exp\ (\xi) + (p_1 + \sqrt{3}p_2)\exp\ (\eta) - 2p_1\exp\ (\zeta).$$
$$(15)$$

Note that the ansatz $q_1 = \sqrt{6}x$, $q_2 = \sqrt{6}y$, $p_1 = \sqrt{6}p_x$, $p_2 = \sqrt{6}p_y$ and $H \to 6H$ brings the expressions (14) and (15) to the same ones as in the book [11]. As the Toda Hamiltonian has the C_{3v} symmetry its power expansion is determined fully through the two invariant functions $f = q_1^2 + q_2^2$ and $g = q_1^2 q_2 - \frac{1}{3}q_2^3$. Below the first power terms of the Taylor series for Hamiltonian (14) are written:

$$H - \frac{3}{4} = \frac{1}{2}(p_1^2 + p_2^2) + \frac{1}{2}(q_1^2 + q_2^2) + \frac{1}{\sqrt{6}}(q_1^2 q_2 - \frac{1}{3}q_2^3) + \frac{1}{12}(q_1^2 + q_2^2)^2$$

$$+ \frac{\sqrt{6}}{36}(q_1^2 + q_2^2)(q_1^2 q_2 - \frac{1}{3}q_2^3) + \frac{1}{180}[(q_1^2 + q_2^2)^3 + 2(q_1^2 q_2 - \frac{1}{3}q_2^3)^2] + \dots \quad (16a)$$

or

$$H - \frac{3}{4} = \frac{1}{2}(p_1^2 + p_2^2) + \frac{1}{2}f + \frac{1}{\sqrt{6}}g + \frac{1}{12}f^2 + \frac{\sqrt{6}}{36}fg + \frac{1}{180}(f^3 + 2g^2)$$

$$+ \frac{1}{90\sqrt{6}}f^2 g + \frac{1}{15120}f(3f^3 + 16g^2) + \dots \quad (16b)$$

Thus, it is seen that any truncated Toda's polynomial series generates a generalized Henon-Heiles Hamiltonian. Here a surprising situation arises: while the full Toda Hamiltonian (14) is integrated, its power expansion truncated in any finite degree presents a nonintegrable system 3-TCL.

In some manner this phenomenon may be explained by the behavior of the negative Gaussian curvature(NGC) domain on the respective potential energy surface PES of the Hamiltonian (16). The NGC domain on the PES indeed emerges if the highest degree (n_{max}) in the truncated series (16) is an odd number and, on the contrary, if the highest degree is an even number then such NGC domain does not appear at all. The emergence of the NGC domain is linked with the saddle points on the PES. Moreover, if we take into account more and more terms in the expansion (16) then the NGC domain moves upwards on the PES and in the case of the infinite series the NGC region vanishes.

Below we have constructed the Birkhoff-Gustavson normal form and the approximate integrals of motion for some truncated Toda's Hamiltonians in order to understand a dependence of the structure of phase space on the inclusion of highest degree polynomial Hamiltonian (16). As an example, we present now the normal forms in the sixth $s_{max} = 6$ approach all but which are obtained for the different highest degree of Toda's series from the value $n_{max} = 3$ (Henon-Heiles's Hamiltonian) to $n_{max} = 5$. These Birkhoff-Gustavson normal forms are expressed below in the action-angle variables and are obtained with the aid of the GITA procedure:

$$\xi_\nu = \sqrt{2I_\nu}\cos(\varphi_\nu), \quad \eta_\nu = \sqrt{2I_\nu}\sin(\varphi_\nu), \quad (\nu = 1, 2).$$

$n_{max} = 3, \quad s_{max} = 6.$

$$G_3^{(6)} = (\frac{7}{1296}I_1^3 - \frac{7}{108}I_1^2 I_2 - \frac{7}{36}I_1^2 - \frac{7}{5184}I_1 I_2^2 + \frac{7}{432}I_2^3 - \frac{7}{144}I_2^2)cos(2\varphi_2)$$

$$-\frac{155}{3888}I_1^3 - \frac{7}{108}I_1^2 I_2 + \frac{7}{5184}I_1 I_2^2 + \frac{35}{1296}I_2^3 - \frac{7}{144}I_2^2 - \frac{1}{12}I_1^2 + 2I_1 \quad (17a)$$

$n_{max} = 4, \quad s_{max} = 6.$

$$G_4^{(6)} = (\frac{22}{81}I_1^3 + \frac{1}{18}I_1^2 I_2 - \frac{1}{9}I_1^2 - \frac{11}{162}I_1 I_2^2 - \frac{1}{72}I_2^3 + \frac{1}{36}I_2^2)cos(2\varphi_2)$$

$$-\frac{2}{243}I_1^3 + \frac{1}{18}I_1^2 I_2 + \frac{11}{162}I_1 I_2^2 - \frac{5}{216}I_2^3 - \frac{1}{36}I_2^2 + \frac{1}{3}I_1^2 + 2I_1 \quad (18a)$$

$n_{max} = 5, \quad s_{max} = 6.$

$$G_5^{(6)} = (\frac{4}{81}I_1^3 - \frac{1}{108}I_1^2 I_2 - \frac{1}{9}I_1^2 - \frac{1}{81}I_1 I_2^2 + \frac{1}{432}I_2^3 + \frac{1}{36}I_2^2)cos(2\varphi_2)$$

$$-\frac{32}{243}I_1^3 - \frac{1}{108}I_1^2 I_2 + \frac{1}{81}I_1 I_2^2 + \frac{5}{1296}I_2^3 - \frac{1}{36}I_2^2 + \frac{1}{3}I_1^2 + 2I_1 \quad (19a)$$

The second integrals in the corresponding approximation are also obtained by GITA procedure up to terms of degree s_{max} as quadratic form [3]

$$I^{(2)}(\xi[s_{max}], \eta[s_{max}]) = G(\xi[s_{max}], \eta[s_{max}]) - \sum_{\nu=1,2} \frac{1}{2}(\xi_\nu^2[s_{max}] + \eta_\nu^2[s_{max}]).$$

To obtain the integral in the original coordinates, GITA expresses the final variables $(\xi_\nu, \eta_\nu) = (\xi_\nu[s_{max}], \eta_\nu[s_{max}])$ in terms of variables $(q_\nu = \xi_\nu[2], p_\nu = \eta_\nu[2])$ making $(s_{max} - 2)$ coordinate transformations $\nu = 1,2;\ s = 3,4,5,\ldots,$ s_{max} in accordance with eqs.(10)and definition of the generation function via coefficiens $W^{(s)}(\xi[s-1], \eta[s])$

$$\xi_\nu[s] = \frac{\partial W^{(s)}}{\partial \eta_\nu[s]}(\xi[s-1], \eta[s]), \quad \eta_\nu[s-1] = \frac{\partial W^{(s)}}{\partial \xi[s-1]}(\xi[s-1], \eta[s]).$$

As an example we present the integrals (see Fig.2-4) in the explicit form : $n_{max} = 3, \quad s_{max} = 6.$

$$I^{(2)} = -\frac{385}{124416}p_2^6 + \frac{3311}{41472}p_2^4 p_1^2 - \frac{385}{41472}p_2^4 q_2^2 - \frac{1589}{41472}p_2^4 q_1^2 - \frac{5}{288}p_2^4$$

$$+\frac{1225}{5184}p_2^3 p_1 q_2 q_1 + \frac{7}{18\sqrt{6}}p_2^3 p_1 q_1 - \frac{2849}{41472}p_2^2 p_1^4 + \frac{287}{6912}p_2^2 p_1^2 q_2^2 - \frac{7}{18\sqrt{6}}p_2^2 p_1^2 q_2$$

$$-\frac{35}{256}p_2^2 p_1^2 q_1^2 - \frac{5}{144}p_2^2 p_1^2 - \frac{385}{41472}p_2^2 q_2^4 + \frac{5}{216\sqrt{6}}p_2^2 q_2^3$$

$$+\frac{245}{2304}p_2^2 q_2^2 q_1^2 - \frac{5}{144}p_2^2 q_2^2 + \frac{23}{72\sqrt{6}}p_2^2 q_2 q_1^2 + \frac{763}{41472}p_2^2 q_1^4$$

$$+\frac{1}{16}p_2^2 q_1^2 - \frac{7}{5184}p_2 p_1^3 q_2 q_1 - \frac{7}{54\sqrt{6}}p_2 p_1^3 q_1 + \frac{217}{5184}p_2 p_1 q_2^3 q_1$$

$$-\frac{7}{36\sqrt{6}}p_2 p_1 q_2^2 q_1 - \frac{791}{5184}p_2 p_1 q_2 q_1^3 - \frac{7}{36}p_2 p_1 q_2 q_1$$

$$-\frac{7}{36\sqrt{6}}p_2 p_1 q_1^3 + \frac{847}{124416}p_1^6 - \frac{2821}{41472}p_1^4 q_2^2 + \frac{7}{54\sqrt{6}}p_1^4 q_2$$

$$+\frac{847}{41472}p_1^4 q_1^2 - \frac{5}{288}p_1^4 + \frac{1771}{41472}p_1^2 q_2^4 - \frac{37}{216\sqrt{6}}p_1^2 q_2^3 - \frac{91}{2304}p_1^2 q_2^2 q_1^2$$

$$+\frac{1}{16}p_1^2 q_2^2 + \frac{1}{8\sqrt{6}}p_1^2 q_2 q_1^2 + \frac{623}{41472}p_1^2 q_1^4 - \frac{5}{144}p_1^2 q_1^2 - \frac{545}{124416}q_2^6$$

$$+\frac{5}{216\sqrt{6}}q_2^5 + \frac{943}{41472}q_2^4 q_1^2 - \frac{5}{288}q_2^4 - \frac{5}{108\sqrt{6}}q_2^3 q_1^2 - \frac{1537}{41472}q_2^2 q_1^4 - \frac{5}{288}q_1^4$$

$$-\frac{5}{144}q_2^2 q_1^2 - \frac{5}{72\sqrt{6}}q_2 q_1^4 - \frac{49}{124416}q_1^6 \qquad (17b)$$

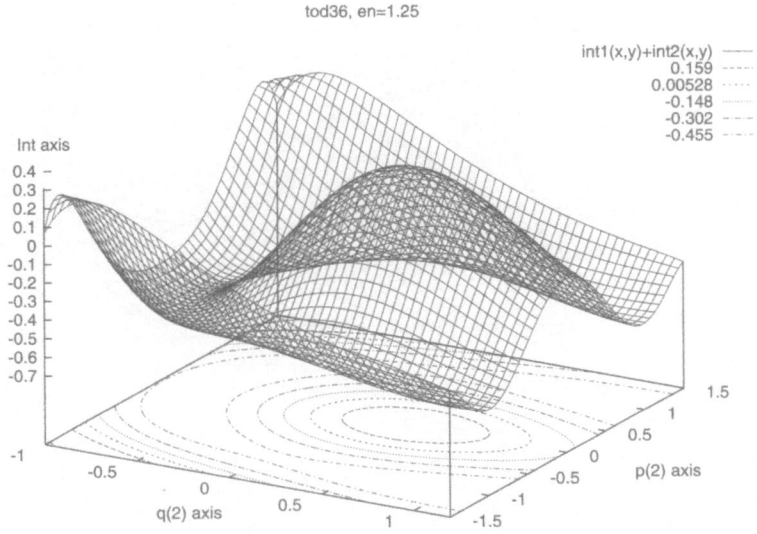

Fig. 2. Approximate integral of motion 3-TLC(17b) $n_{max} = 3, s_{max} = 6$

$n_{max} = 4, \quad s_{max} = 6.$

$$I^{(2)} = \frac{35}{7776}p_2^6 + \frac{77}{2592}p_2^4 p_1^2 + \frac{35}{2592}p_2^4 q_2^2 - \frac{143}{2592}p_2^4 q_1^2 + \frac{1}{72}p_2^4$$

$$+\frac{55}{324}p_2^3 p_1 q_2 q_1 + \frac{2}{9\sqrt{6}}p_2^3 p_1 q_1 + \frac{7}{2592}p_2^2 p_1^4 - \frac{11}{432}p_2^2 p_1^2 q_2^2 - \frac{2}{9\sqrt{6}}p_2^2 p_1^2 q_2$$

$$-\frac{25}{432}p_2^2 p_1^2 q_1^2 + \frac{1}{36}p_2^2 p_1^2 + \frac{47}{2592}p_2^2 q_2^4 - \frac{1}{54\sqrt{6}}p_2^2 q_2^3$$

$$+\frac{1}{48}p_2^2 q_2^2 q_1^2 + \frac{1}{36}p_2^2 q_2^2 + \frac{5}{18\sqrt{6}}p_2^2 q_2 q_1^2 - \frac{17}{2592}p_2^2 q_1^4$$

$$+\frac{1}{12}p_2^2 q_1^2 + \frac{41}{324}p_2 p_1^3 q_2 q_1 - \frac{2}{27\sqrt{6}}p_2 p_1^3 q_1 + \frac{19}{324}p_2 p_1 q_2^3 q_1$$

$$-\frac{1}{9\sqrt{6}}p_2 p_1 q_2^2 q_1 + \frac{13}{324}p_2 p_1 q_2 q_1^3 - \frac{1}{9}p_2 p_1 q_2 q_1$$

$$-\frac{1}{9\sqrt{6}}p_2 p_1 q_1^3 + \frac{49}{7776}p_1^6 - \frac{157}{2592}p_1^4 q_2^2 + \frac{2}{27\sqrt{6}}p_1^4 q_2$$

$$+\frac{49}{2592}p_1^4 q_1^2 + \frac{1}{72}p_1^4 - \frac{11}{2592}p_1^2 q_2^4 - \frac{7}{54\sqrt{6}}p_1^2 q_2^3 + \frac{1}{144}p_1^2 q_2^2 q_1^2$$

$$+\frac{1}{12}p_1^2 q_2^2 + \frac{1}{6\sqrt{6}}p_1^2 q_2 q_1^2 + \frac{53}{2592}p_1^2 q_1^4 + \frac{1}{36}p_1^2 q_1^2 + \frac{79}{7776}q_2^6$$

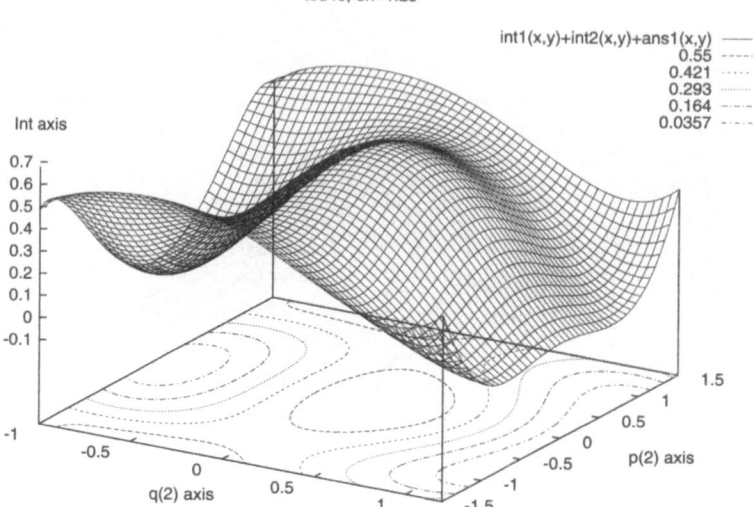

Fig. 3. Approximate integral of motion 3-TLC(18b) $n_{max} = 4, s_{max} = 6$

$$-\frac{1}{54\sqrt{6}}q_2^5 + \frac{1}{2592}q_2^4 q_1^2 + \frac{1}{72}q_2^4 + \frac{1}{27\sqrt{6}}q_2^3 q_1^2 + \frac{131}{2592}q_2^2 q_1^4 + \frac{1}{72}q_1^4$$

$$+\frac{1}{36}q_2^2 q_1^2 + \frac{1}{18\sqrt{6}}q_2 q_1^4 + \frac{53}{7776}q_1^6 \tag{18b}$$

$n_{max} = 5, \quad s_{max} = 6.$

$$I^{(2)} = -\frac{35}{15552}p_2^6 + \frac{175}{5184}p_2^4 p_1^2 - \frac{35}{5184}p_2^4 q_2^2 - \frac{205}{5184}p_2^4 q_1^2 + \frac{1}{72}p_2^4$$

$$+\frac{95}{648}p_2^3 p_1 q_2 q_1 + \frac{2}{9\sqrt{6}}p_2^3 p_1 q_1 - \frac{175}{5184}p_2^2 p_1^4 - \frac{5}{846}p_2^2 p_1^2 q_2^2 - \frac{2}{9\sqrt{6}}p_2^2 p_1^2 q_2$$

$$-\frac{25}{288}p_2^2 p_1^2 q_1^2 + \frac{1}{36}p_2^2 p_1^2 - \frac{11}{5184}p_2^2 q_2^4 - \frac{1}{54\sqrt{6}}p_2^2 q_2^3$$

$$+\frac{35}{864}p_2^2 q_2^2 q_1^2 + \frac{1}{36}p_2^2 q_2^2 + \frac{5}{18\sqrt{6}}p_2^2 q_2 q_1^2 + \frac{5}{5184}p_2^2 q_1^4$$

$$+\frac{1}{12}p_2^2 q_1^2 + \frac{25}{648}p_2 p_1^3 q_2 q_1 - \frac{2}{27\sqrt{6}}p_2 p_1^3 q_1 + \frac{23}{648}p_2 p_1 q_2^3 q_1$$

$$-\frac{1}{9\sqrt{6}}p_2 p_1 q_2^2 q_1 - \frac{31}{648}p_2 p_1 q_2 q_1^3 - \frac{1}{9}p_2 p_1 q_2 q_1$$

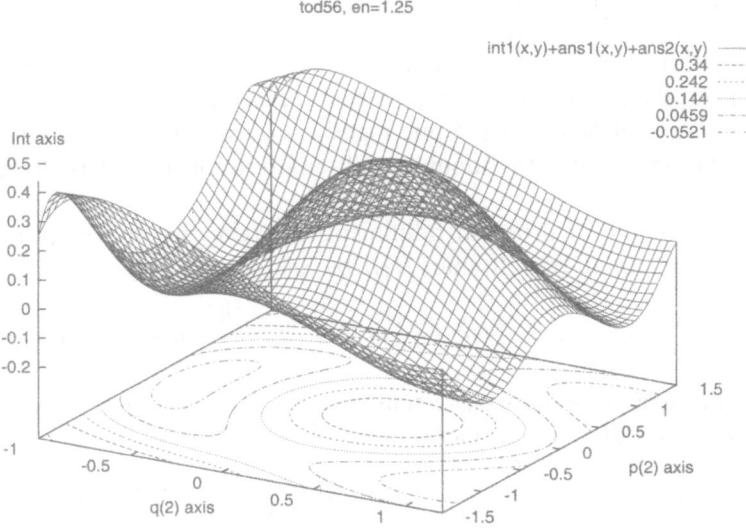

tod56, en=1.25

int1(x,y)+ans1(x,y)+ans2(x,y) ——
0.34 ·······
0.242 ·······
0.144 ·······
0.0459 - - - -
-0.0521 - · - ·

Fig. 4. Approximate integral of motion 3-TLC(19b) $n_{max} = 5, s_{max} = 6$

$$-\frac{1}{9\sqrt{6}}p_2 p_1 q_1^3 + \frac{35}{15552}p_1^6 - \frac{275}{5184}p_1^4 q_2^2 + \frac{2}{27\sqrt{6}}p_1^4 q_2$$

$$+\frac{35}{5184}p_1^4 q_1^2 + \frac{1}{72}p_1^4 + \frac{59}{5184}p_1^2 q_2^4 - \frac{7}{54\sqrt{6}}p_1^2 q_2^3 - \frac{19}{864}p_1^2 q_2^2 q_1^2$$

$$+\frac{1}{12}p_1^2 q_2^2 + \frac{1}{6\sqrt{6}}p_1^2 q_2 q_1^2 + \frac{43}{5184}p_1^2 q_1^4 + \frac{1}{36}p_1^2 q_1^2 + \frac{53}{15552}q_2^6$$

$$-\frac{1}{54\sqrt{6}}q_2^5 + \frac{23}{5184}q_2^4 q_1^2 + \frac{1}{72}q_2^4 + \frac{1}{27\sqrt{6}}q_2^3 q_1^2 + \frac{73}{5184}q_2^2 q_1^4 + \frac{1}{72}q_1^4$$

$$+\frac{1}{36}q_2^2 q_1^2 + \frac{1}{18\sqrt{6}}q_2 q_1^4 + \frac{43}{15552}q_1^6 \qquad (19b)$$

The above integrals (17b)–(19b) and corresponding Poincare sections are presented in Figs. 2-4. One can observe how the sequence of these sections step by step tends to the limited section of the exact Toda integral (15) which is shown in Fig.1. Note that the approximate integrals of motion will describe well theoretically the regular phase trajectories similar to other generalization of the Henon-Heiles dynamical system [12]. In this way one may expect to find additional criteria of a true choice of BGNF structure related to exact integrals.

5 GITA^{-1} and the Inverse Problem of HLSE

GITA^{-1} consists of a core part and a subsidiary part. The core part is derived from GITA [3] and the subsidiary part contains the procedures characteristic of GITA^{-1} , both of which are put together in a single file. The procedure list and the input data (the input Hamiltonian) are loaded at the beginning of running GITA^{-1} .

As an example of program fulfillment, we take the inverse problem of HLSE. Let the input Hamiltonian H_{IN} be

$$H_{IN}(q,p) = \frac{1}{2}(p_1^2 + p_2^2 + q_1^2 + q_2^2) + \frac{8}{3}\varepsilon(q_1^4 - q_2^4), \qquad (20)$$

the Hamiltonian of regularized system of HLSE [8]. The input BGNF Hamiltonian, G_{IN}, for H_{IN} is calculated up to the fourth order to be

$$G_{IN}^{(4)}(\xi,\eta) = \varepsilon(\xi_1^2 + \xi_2^2 + \eta_1^2 + \eta_2^2)(\xi_1^2 + \eta_1^2 - \xi_2^2 - \eta_2^2), \qquad (21)$$

where ε is a parameter. The vector $\gamma_{IN}^{(4)}$ in equation (13) is hence fixed by the coefficients, $\gamma_{IN}^{(4)}(\alpha_1, \alpha_2, \beta_1, \beta_2)$, of $G_{IN}^{(4)}$ through (10). It is worth noting that all these preliminary calculations can be made by GITA.

The GITA^{-1} starts with generating the field P_ℓ to describe the output Hamiltonian $H_{OUT}^{(4)}$ all of whose coefficients $c_{OUT}^{(4)}(\alpha, \beta)$ are unidentified. Next, eqs. (6)-(12) with $\lambda = OUT$ are proceeded in GITA^{-1} to calculate $G_{OUT}^{(4)}$, all of whose coefficients, $\gamma_{OUT}^{(4)}(\alpha, \beta)$, expressed in terms of $c_{OUT}^{(4)}(\alpha, \beta)$, are unidentified. On equating G_{IN} with G_{OUT} in GITA^{-1} , equation (13) takes the following form:

$$\begin{aligned} 3c_{OUT}^{(4)}(0,4,0,0) + c_{OUT}^{(4)}(0,2,0,2) + 3c_{OUT}^{(4)}(0,0,0,4) &= -8\varepsilon, \\ 3c_{OUT}^{(4)}(4,0,0,0) + c_{OUT}^{(4)}(2,0,2,0) + 3c_{OUT}^{(4)}(0,0,4,0) &= 8\varepsilon, \end{aligned} \qquad (22)$$

where the coefficients, $c_{OUT}^{(4)}(k_1, k_2, \ell_1, \ell_2)$, not listed in (22) are set to zero.

Applying the subroutine SOLVE in REDUCE to equation (22), we have

$$\begin{aligned} c_{OUT}^{(4)}(0,0,4,0) &= u(4), & c_{OUT}^{(4)}(0,0,0,4) &= u(2), \\ c_{OUT}^{(4)}(0,4,0,0) &= (-3u(2) - u(1) - 8\varepsilon)/3, & c_{OUT}^{(4)}(0,2,0,2) &= u(1), \\ c_{OUT}^{(4)}(4,0,0,0) &= (-3u(4) - u(3) + 8\varepsilon)/3, & c_{OUT}^{(4)}(2,0,2,0) &= u(3), \end{aligned}$$

as the solution of equation (22), where $u(i)$ ($i = 1, 2, 3, 4$) denote the unidentified constants 'arbcomplex(i)' introduced automatically in SOLVE.

Finally, we identify the output Hamiltonian to be

$$\begin{aligned} H_{OUT}^{(4)}(q,p) = \ & u(4)p_1^4 + u(2)p_2^4 + u(3)q_1^2 p_1^2 + u(1)q_2^2 p_2^2 \\ & + \frac{1}{3}\{-3u(4) - u(3) + 8\varepsilon\}q_1^4 + \frac{1}{3}\{-3u(2) - u(1) - 8\varepsilon\}q_2^4, \end{aligned} \qquad (23)$$

which admits G_{IN} given by equation (21) as the BGNF. Note that if all the $u(i)$ vanish in equation (23), H_{OUT} becomes identical with H_{IN} given by (20).

On setting $u(2) = u(4) = 0$ in equation (23), H_{OUT} becomes

$$H_{OUT}(q, p) = \frac{1 + 2u(3)q_1^2}{2}p_1^2 + \frac{1 + 2u(1)q_2^2}{2}p_2^2$$

$$+ q_1^2 + \frac{1}{3}\left\{-u(3) + 8\varepsilon\right\}q_1^4 + q_2^2 - \frac{1}{3}\left\{u(1) + 8\varepsilon\right\}q_2^4.$$

Surprisingly, H_{OUT} turns out to be a Hamiltonian admitting the separation of variables, which provides an integrable system accordingly. Although it seems to be incidental that we encounter such integrable systems after GITA^{-1}, one may expect to find a class of integrable systems whose Hamiltonians reduce to a given BGNF Hamiltonian.

6   The Inverse Problem and Algorithm of ANFER

To pose the inverse problem appropriately to the ordinary problem given by Def. 2.3, we look at equation (3a), the key equation of the ordinary problem, in more detail: Let us regard $-W(q, \eta)$ (see (2)) as the non-normal type-3 generating function [13] associated with the canonical transformation, $(\xi, \eta) \to (q, p)$ through the relation

$$\xi = -\frac{\partial(-W)}{\partial \eta}, \qquad p = -\frac{\partial(-W)}{\partial q}.$$

Then equation (4) can read that $H(q, p)$ is restored from its BGNF series $G(\xi, \eta)$ through the canonical transformation associated with the non-normal type-3 generating function $-W(q, \eta)$. Hence we pose the inverse problem as follows:

Definition 6.1 (The inverse problem) *For a given BGNF in the form (4) identify all possible pairs of the power series $H(q, p)$ in the form (1) and the non-normal type-3 generating function,*

$$S(q, \eta) = -\sum_{j=1}^{n} q_j \eta_j - \sum_{k=3}^{\infty} S_k(q, \eta), \tag{2b}$$

which satisfy

$$H(q, -\frac{\partial S}{\partial q}) = G(-\frac{\partial S}{\partial \eta}, \eta). \tag{3b}$$

Since we usually dealt with the BGNF polynomials of even order, it would be better to restrict the inverse problem to the following form:

Definition 6.2 (The restricted inverse problem) *For a given BGNF, $G(\xi, \eta)$, in 2ρth order polynomial, identify all the possible pairs* *of the 2ρth order Hamiltonian $H(q,p)$ in the form (1) and the 2ρth order non-normal type-3 generating function $S(q,\eta)$ in the form of (2b), which satisfy equation (3b) up to the 2ρth order.*

Remark: For any 2ρth order BGNF $G(\xi,\eta)$, 2ρ is the highest order up to which both $H(q,p)$ and $S(\eta,q)$ can be identified completely.

We present an algorithm of solving equation (3b), part of ANFER , up to 2ρth order, where $G(\xi,\eta)$ is a 2ρ-th order polynomial in BGNF to be inverted.

Like in the case of solving the ordinary problem [2], we have to deal with a highly combinatorial problem of picking up the homogeneous part of degree k ($3 \leq k \leq 2\rho$) from equation (3b). To settle this problem, it is of great use to consider the composition of canonical transformations as follows.

Let us define a series of canonical transformations,

$$\varphi_r : (\xi^{(r-1)},\eta^{(r-1)}) \to (\xi^{(r)},\eta^{(r)}) \quad \text{with} \quad (\xi^{(2)},\eta^{(2)}) = (\xi,\eta) \quad (r = 3,4,\cdots),$$

associated with the type-3 generating functions,

$$S^{(r)}(\xi^{(r)},\eta^{(r-1)}) = -\sum_{j=1}^{n}\xi_j^{(r)}\eta_j^{(r-1)} - S_r(\xi^{(r)},\eta^{(r-1)}) \quad (r = 3,4,\cdots),$$

where S_r is the homogeneous part of degree r of the generating function $S(q,\eta)$ in the form (2b). Using the $\{\varphi_r\}$'s we have the following Lemmas:

Lemma 6.1   *The composition, $\varphi_r \circ \varphi_{r-1} \circ \cdots \circ \varphi_3$, ($3 \leq r$) of the canonical transformations, $\varphi_3,\cdots,\varphi_r$, is generated by the type-3 generating function of the form*

$$\tilde{S}^{(r)}(\xi^{(r)},\eta^{(2)}) = \sum_{k=3}^{r-1}\left(\sum_{j=1}^{n}\xi_j^{(k+1)}\eta_j^{(k)}\right) + \sum_{s=3}^{r}S^{(s)}(\xi^{(s)},\eta^{(s-1)}), \qquad (24)$$

where $(\xi^{(s)},\eta^{(s-1)})$ ($s = 3,\cdots,r$) on the r. h. s. of (24) are regarded as the functions of $(\eta^{(2)},\xi^{(r)})$ through $\varphi_3,\cdots,\varphi_r$.

Lemma 6.2   *Let $H^{(r)}(\xi^{(r)},\eta^{(r)})$, be the power series determined by*

$$H^{(r)}(\xi^{(r)},-\frac{\partial\tilde{S}^{(r)}}{\partial\xi^{(r)}}) = G(-\frac{\partial\tilde{S}^{(r)}}{\partial\,eta^{(2)}},\eta^{(2)}) \qquad (r = 3,4,\cdots). \qquad (25)$$

Then up to rth order, $H^{(r)}(q,p)$ is identical with $H(q,p)$ determined by (2b).

With account of Lemma 6.2, solving equation (3b) up to 2ρth order amounts to solving equation (25). Since equation (25) is put together with Lemma 6.1 to imply

$$H^{(r)} \circ \varphi_r \circ \cdots \circ \varphi_3 = G \qquad (r = 3,4,\cdots),$$

we see that the $H^{(r)}$'s satisfy the equations

$$H^{(r)}(\xi^{(r)}, -\frac{\partial S^{(r)}}{\partial \xi^{(r)}}) = H^{(r-1)}(-\frac{\partial S^{(r)}}{\partial \eta^{(r-1)}}, \eta^{(r-1)}) \quad (r = 3, 4, \cdots) \qquad (26a)$$

with

$$H^{(2)}(\xi^{(2)}, \eta^{(2)}) = G(\xi^{(2)}, \eta^{(2)}), \qquad (26b)$$

which are the basic equations of constructing ANFER .

We proceed to solve equations (26a) up to $r = 2\rho$ now. Equating the kth order homogeneous part $(k = 2, 3, \cdots, 2\rho)$ in (26a), we have

$$H_k^{(r)}(\xi^{(r)}, \eta^{(r-1)}) = H_k^{(r-1)}(\xi^{(r)}, \eta^{(r-1)}) \qquad (27a)$$

for $k = 2, \cdots, r - 1$,

$$H_r^{(r)}(\xi^{(r)}, \eta^{(r-1)}) = (D_{q,\eta} S_r)(\xi^{(r)}, \eta^{(r-1)}) + H_r^{(r-1)}(\xi^{(r)}, \eta^{(r-1)}) \qquad (27b)$$

for $k = r$, and

$$H_k^{(r)}(\xi^{(r)}, \eta^{(r-1)}) = H_k^{(r-1)}(\xi^{(r)}, \eta^{(r-1)}) + \Theta_k^{(r)}(\xi^{(r)}, \eta^{(r-1)}) \qquad (27c)$$

for $k = r + 1, \cdots, 2\rho$. The $\Theta_k^{(r)}(\xi^{(r)}, \eta^{(r-1)})$ in (27c) is the homogeneous polynomial of degree k $(k = r + 1, \cdots, 2\rho)$ given by [3]

$$\Theta_k^{(r)}(\xi^{(r)}, \eta^{(r-1)})$$

$$= \sum_{|\alpha|=1}^{[\frac{k-2}{r-2}]} \frac{1}{\alpha!} \left[\left(\frac{\partial S_r}{\partial \eta} \Big|_{(\xi^{(r)}, \eta^{(r-1)})} \right)^\alpha \left(\left(\frac{\partial}{\partial \xi^{(r-1)}} \right)^\alpha H_{k-(r-2)|\alpha|}^{(r-1)} \right) \Big|_{(\xi^{(r)}, \eta^{(r-1)})} \right.$$

$$\left. - \left(\frac{\partial S_r}{\partial q} \Big|_{(\xi^{(r)}, \eta^{(r-1)})} \right)^\alpha \left(\left(\frac{\partial}{\partial \eta^{(r)}} \right)^\alpha H_{k-(r-2)|\alpha|}^{(r)} \right) \Big|_{(\xi^{(r)}, \eta^{(r-1)})} \right]$$

$$(28a)$$

where $[\cdot]$ denotes the Gauss symbol, and $\alpha = (\alpha_1, \cdots, \alpha_N)$ is the multi-index with nonnegative-integer valued components associating the notations,

$$|\alpha| = \sum_{j=1}^n \alpha_j, \qquad \left(\frac{\partial S_r}{\partial q} \right)^\alpha = \left(\frac{\partial S_r}{\partial q_1} \right)^{\alpha_1} \cdots \left(\frac{\partial S_r}{\partial q_n} \right)^{\alpha_n},$$

$$\left(\frac{\partial S_r}{\partial \eta} \right)^\alpha = \left(\frac{\partial S_r}{\partial \eta_1} \right)^{\alpha_1} \cdots \left(\frac{\partial S_r}{\partial \eta_n} \right)^{\alpha_n}, \qquad (28b)$$

$$\left(\frac{\partial}{\partial \xi} \right)^\alpha = \frac{\partial^{\alpha_1}}{\partial \xi_1^{\alpha_1}} \cdots \frac{\partial^{\alpha_n}}{\partial \xi_n^{\alpha_n}}, \quad \left(\frac{\partial}{\partial \eta} \right)^\alpha = \frac{\partial^{\alpha_1}}{\partial \eta_1^{\alpha_1}} \cdots \frac{\partial^{\alpha_n}}{\partial \eta_n^{\alpha_n}}.$$

In ANFER , equations (27) are solved recursively from $r = 3$ to $r = 2\rho$ as follows: Let us assume that $H^{(2)}, \cdots H^{(r-1)}$ and $S^{(3)}, \cdots, S^{(r-1)}$ (i.e.,

$S_3, \cdots, S_{r-1})$ have been identified already. Then it turns out that equations (27) are closed for $H_k^{(r)}$ ($k = 2, \cdots, 2\rho$) and S_r. Since equation (27a) means merely an incrementation, we start with solving equation (27b). A key of solving equation (27b) is the direct-sum decomposition induced by the operator $D_{\xi^{(r)}, \eta^{(r-1)}}$ (see (5)) of the vector spaces of kth order homogeneous polynomials of $(\xi^{(r)}, \eta^{(r-1)})$ denoted by $V_k(\xi^{(r)}, \eta^{(r-1)})$;

$$V_k(\xi^{(r)}, \eta^{(r-1)}) = \mathrm{Ker}\left(D_{\xi^{(r)}, \eta^{(r-1)}}^{(k)}\right) \oplus \mathrm{Im}\left(D_{\xi^{(r)}, \eta^{(r-1)}}^{(k)}\right), \qquad (29a)$$

where

$$D_{\xi^{(r)}, \eta^{(r-1)}}^{(k)} = D_{\xi^{(r)}, \eta^{(r-1)}}\big|_{V_k(\xi^{(r)}, \eta^{(r-1)})}. \qquad (29b)$$

Accordingly, decomposing $H_r^{(r)}$ and $H_r^{(r-1)}$ as

$$H_r^{(r-1)} = H_r^{(r-1),N} + H_r^{(r-1),I}, \qquad \left(\begin{array}{c} (H_r^{(r-1),N} \in \mathrm{Ker}\left(D_{\xi^{(r-1)}, \eta^{(r-1)}}^{(r)}\right), \\ H_r^{(r-1),I} \in \mathrm{Im}\left(D_{\xi^{(r-1)}, \eta^{(r-1)}}^{(r)}\right) \end{array}\right),$$

$$H_r^{(r)} = H_r^{(r),N} + H_r^{(r),I}, \qquad \left(\begin{array}{c} (H_r^{(r),N} \in \mathrm{Ker}\left(D_{\xi^{(r)}, \eta^{(r)}}^{(r)}\right), \\ H_r^{(r),I} \in \mathrm{Im}\left(D_{\xi^{(r)}, \eta^{(r)}}^{(r)}\right) \end{array}\right),$$

we can rewrite (27b) as a pair of equations:

$$H_r^{(r),N}(\xi^{(r)}, \eta^{(r-1)}) = H_r^{(r-1),N}(\xi^{(r)}, \eta^{(r-1)}), \qquad (30a)$$

and

$$H_r^{(r),I}(\xi^{(r)}, \eta^{(r-1)}) = (D_{q,\eta}^{(r)} S_r)\big|_{(\xi^{(r)}, \eta^{(r-1)})} + H_r^{(r-1),I}(\xi^{(r)}, \eta^{(r-1)}). \qquad (30b)$$

Equation (30a) obviously identifies $H_r^{(r),N}$ to be equal to $H_{r-1}^{(r),N}$. In contrast with (30a), a pair of unidentified functions, $H_r^{(r),I}$ and S_r, exists in equation (30b), so that we cannot get rid of an ambiguity in the identification; we identify

$$H_r^{(r),I} : \text{chosen arbitrarily as long as it is in } \mathrm{Im}\left(D_{\xi^{(r)}, \eta^{(r-1)}}^{(r)}\right), \qquad (31a)$$

and

$$S_r(\xi^{(r)}, \eta^{(r-1)}) = \left(\left(D_{\xi^{(r)}, \eta^{(r-1)}}^{(r)}\big|_{\mathrm{Im}\left(D_{\xi^{(r)}, \eta^{(r-1)}}^{(r)}\right)}\right)^{-1} H_r^{(r),I}\right). \qquad (31b)$$

Once one has solved (27b), $H_k^{(r)}$ ($k = r + 1, \cdots, 2\rho$) are identified by (27c) with simple substitutions.

After repeating the process described above from $r = 3$ to $r = 2\rho$, $H^{(2\rho)}(q, p)$ thus obtained identifies the inverted Hamiltonian $H(q, p)$ (see (2b)) up to the 2ρth order. In ANFER, the above described process (24)–(31) has been implemented with Reduce 3.3 or its later version.

7   Example

7.1   Introduction

In this short note we solve the ordinary problem for simple test Hamiltonian,

$$K(q,p) = \frac{1}{2}(p^2 + q^2) + q^3. \tag{32}$$

The homogeneous 4th order term of its BGNF is obtained by the direct way. The inverse problem is solved also following the algorithm ANFER. Through out this note, numbers of the variables are reduced as far as such a reduction causes no confusions.

7.2   The Ordinary Problem

Since we would like to convert K into the BGNF up to the 4th order, it is convenient to denote by K_k $(k = 3, 4)$, the kth order part of K;

$$K_3(q,p) = q^3, \qquad K_4(q,p) = 0. \tag{33}$$

Let us further assume the type-2 generating function $W(q, \eta)$ and the BGNF $G(\xi, \eta)$ to be in the power series form,

$$W(q, \eta) = q\eta + \sum_{k=3}^{\infty} W_k(q, \eta),$$

and

$$G(\xi, \eta) = \frac{1}{2}(\eta^2 + \xi^2) + \sum_{\ell=2}^{\infty} G_{2\ell}(\xi, \eta),$$

where W_k (resp. $G_{2\ell}$) stand for the homogeneous k (resp. 2ℓ)th order parts of W (resp. G).

According to the algorithm of BG(Birkhoff-Gustavson)- normalization, what we have to solve is a system of equations[2],

$$G_3(q, \eta) + D_{q,\eta} W_3 = K_3(q, \eta), \tag{34a}$$

and

$$G_4(q, \eta) + D_{q,\eta} W_4 = K_4(q, \eta) + \frac{\partial W_3}{\partial q} \cdot \frac{\partial K_3}{\partial \eta} - \frac{\partial W_3}{\partial \eta} \cdot \frac{\partial G_3}{\partial q}$$

$$+ \frac{1}{2}\left(\frac{\partial W_3}{\partial q}\right)^2 - \frac{1}{2}\left(\frac{\partial W_3}{\partial \eta}\right)^2 \equiv \tilde{K}_4(q, p) \tag{34b}$$

for both G and W, where

$$D_{q,\eta} = q\frac{\partial}{\partial \eta} - \eta\frac{\partial}{\partial q}.$$

---

[2] G_3 vanishes from the definition of BGNF

On introducing the complex variable z by

$$z = q + i\eta, \quad \bar{z} = q - i\eta$$

equation (34a) may be rewritten as[2]

$$i(z\partial - \bar{z}\bar{\partial})W_3 = \frac{1}{8}(z^3 + 3z^2\bar{z} + 3z\bar{z}^2 + \bar{z}^3),$$

with

$$\partial = \frac{\partial}{\partial z}, \quad \bar{\partial} = \frac{\partial}{\partial \bar{z}},$$

so that we have

$$G_3(\xi, \eta) = 0, \quad W_3(q, \eta) = -\frac{i}{24}\left(z^3 + 9z^2\bar{z} - 9z\bar{z}^2 - \bar{z}^3\right). \quad (35)$$

We now proceed to the solution of (34b). Using the relations

$$\frac{\partial}{\partial q} = \partial + \bar{\partial}, \quad \frac{\partial}{\partial \eta} = i(\partial - \bar{\partial}),$$

we have

$$\frac{\partial K_3}{\partial \eta} = 0, \quad \frac{\partial W_3}{\partial q} = -\frac{i}{2}(z^2 - \bar{z}^2), \quad \frac{\partial W_3}{\partial \eta} = -\frac{1}{4}(z^2 - 6z\bar{z} + \bar{z}^2), \quad (36)$$

Hence equations (35) and (36) are combined with equation (33) to put equation (34b) into the form

$$G_4(q, \eta) + D_{q,\eta}W_4 = \tilde{K}_4,$$

where

$$\tilde{K}_4 = \frac{1}{32}(-5z^4 + 12z^3\bar{z} - 30z^2\bar{z}^2 + 12z\bar{z}^3 - 5\bar{z}^4).$$

Since $D_{q,\eta}W_4$ cannot be normal we have

$$G_4(\xi, \eta) = -\frac{15}{16}z^2\bar{z}^2.$$

7.3   The Inverse Problem

In this Section, we solve the inverse problem for the harmonic oscillator Hamiltonian, the BGNF for the Hamiltonian K given by (32). Let $H(q, p)$ and $S(q, \eta)$ be the 4th order polynomial Hamiltonian and the 4th order type-3 generating function of the form

$$H(q, p) = \frac{1}{2}(p^2 + q^2) + H_3(q, p) + H_4(q, p)$$

and
$$S(q, \eta) = -q\eta - S_3(q, \eta) - S_4(q, \eta),$$

where H_k (resp. S_k) ($k = 3, 4$) stand for the homogeneous kth order parts of H (resp. S). The inverse problem is the problem of identifying all the H whose BGNF is identical with the harmonic oscillator up to the 4th order.

We apply the algorithm of *ANFER* (24)-(31) to the present case: Following the notation of Section 6, we define the starting Hamiltonian $H^{(2)}$ to be

$$H_2^{(2)}(q, \eta) = \frac{1}{2}(\eta^2 + q^2), \qquad H_3^{(2)}(q, \eta) = 0, \qquad H_4^{(2)}(q, \eta) = -\frac{15}{16}z^2\bar{z}^2.$$

Then at the stage of $r = 3$, equation (27b) is solved as

$$H_3^{(3)}(q, \eta) = c_1 z^3 + c_2 z^2 \bar{z} + \bar{c}_2 z \bar{z}^2 + \bar{c}_1 \bar{z}^3 \tag{37a}$$

with

$$S_3(q, \eta) = -i\left(\frac{c_1}{3}z^3 + c_2 z^2 \bar{z} - \bar{c}_2 z \bar{z}^2 - \frac{\bar{c}_1}{3}\bar{z}^3\right), \tag{37b}$$

where c_j ($j = 1, 2$) are complex numbers arbitrarily chosen, and $\bar{c}_j$ their complex conjugate. Accordingly, we have

$$\frac{\partial S_3}{\partial q} = -i(c_1 + c_2)z^2 - 2i(c_2 - \bar{c}_2)z\bar{z} + i(\bar{c}_1 + \bar{c}_2)\bar{z}^2,$$

$$\frac{\partial S_3}{\partial \eta} = (c_1 - c_2)z^2 + 2(c_2 + \bar{c}_2)z\bar{z} + (\bar{c}_1 - \bar{c}_2)\bar{z}^2, \tag{38}$$

$$\frac{\partial H_3^{(3)}}{\partial \eta} = i(3c_1 - c_2)z^2 + 2i(c_2 - \bar{c}_2)z\bar{z} - i(3\bar{c}_1 - \bar{c}_2)\bar{z}^2,$$

where $H_3^{(2)}(q, \eta) = 0$, and $H_4^{(3)}(q, \eta)$ turns out to be

$$\begin{aligned}
H_4^{(3)}(q, \eta) = {}&2(-c_1^2 - c_1 c_2 + c_2^2)z^4 \\
&+ 4(-c_1 c_2 + 2c_1 \bar{c}_2 - c_2 \bar{c}_2)z^3 \bar{z} \\
&+ 4(2\bar{c}_1 c_2 - \bar{c}_1 \bar{c}_2 - c_2 \bar{c}_2)z\bar{z}^3 \\
&+ 2(-\bar{c}_1^2 - \bar{c}_1 \bar{c}_2 + \bar{c}_2^2)\bar{z}^4 \\
&+ (6c_1 \bar{c}_1 + 6c_2 \bar{c}_2 - \frac{15}{16})z^2 \bar{z}^2.
\end{aligned} \tag{39}$$

Substituting equations (37)–(39) in equation (27b) with $r = 4$, we have the following: The non-normal part of $H_4^{(4)}$ denoted by $H^{(4),I}$ can be chosen to be arbitrarily non-normal, *i.e.*,

$$H_4^{(4),I}(q, \eta) = f_1 z^4 + f_2 z^3 \bar{z} + \bar{f}_2 z \bar{z}^3 + \bar{f}_1 \bar{z}^4,$$

where f_1 and f_2 are arbitrary complex numbers. In contrast with this, the normal part, denoted by $H_4^{(4),N}$, is determined uniquely to be

$$H^{(4),N}(q,\eta) = (6c_1\bar{c}_1 + 6c_2\bar{c}_2 - \frac{15}{16})z^2\bar{z}^2.$$

To summarize, we see that all the 4th order polynomial Hamiltonians of the form

$$H(q,\eta) = \frac{1}{2}z\bar{z} + \left(c_1 z^3 + c_2 z^2\bar{z} + \bar{c}_2 z\bar{z}^2 + \bar{c}_1\bar{z}^3\right)$$

$$+[f_1 z^4 + f_2 z^3\bar{z} + \bar{f}_2 z\bar{z}^3 + \bar{f}_1\bar{z}^4$$

$$+(6c_1\bar{c}_1 + 6c_2\bar{c}_2 - \frac{15}{16})z^2\bar{z}^2] + \mathcal{O}_4, \tag{40}$$

share $G = (1/2)(\eta^2 + \xi^2)$ as the BGNF up to the 4th order, where $c_1, c_2, f_1, f_2 \in \mathbf{C}$ can be chosen arbitrarily.

The type-3 generating function $S(q,\eta)$ is identified up to 3rd order[3],

$$S(q,\eta) = -q\eta - i\left(\frac{c_1}{3}z^3 + c_2 z^2\bar{z} - \bar{c}_2 z\bar{z}^2 - \frac{\bar{c}_1}{3}\bar{z}^3\right) + \mathcal{O}_3.$$

7.4   Restoring Test Example

We wish to show that the Hamiltonian K defined by equation (32) is in the form of equation (40). Indeed, setting

$$c_1 = 1/8, \quad c_2 = 3/8, \quad f_1 = f_2 = 0, \tag{41}$$

in equation (40), we immediately obtain K. Further, equation (41) is put together with equation (35) to show that $W(q,\eta)$ is equal, up to 3rd order[4], to $S(q,\eta)$ with (41). Thus the normalization of K into G, the BGNF, and the restoration of G to K are completed.

8   Concluding Remarks

We would like to make a few remarks on the peculiarities of the realization of GITA^{-1}. (i) In generating the field P_ℓ and equation (13), we have used REDUCE to implement the combinatorial algorithms and the list processing. (ii) As is seen from the algorithm (6)–(13) presented in Section 3, GITA^{-1} is proceeded by tracing back the procedures of GITA in principle. Since AN-FER might have the performance features different from GITA^{-1}, we may expect that GITA and GITA^{-1} can be put together with ANFER to provide a unified symbolic computing program for various calculation around the BGNF expansion and integrable models in future.

---

[3] To identify H up to 4th order, it is sufficient to identify S up to 3rd order.

Acknowledgements

The authors are grateful to Dr. Dimitry Pavlov and Dr. Denis Proskurin for their help and useful discussions at the preparation of this paper. The authors (NC, VR and SV) thank the Russian Foundation for Basic Research for its support of the present research by Grant No. 98-02-16160.

References

1. M.C. Gutzwiller, M.C.: Chaos in Classical and Quantum Mechanics. Springer, New York, 1990
2. Moser, J.K.: Lectures on Hamiltonian Systems. Memoires of AMS, No.81, 1-60 AMS, Providence (1968)
3. Basios, V., Chekanov, N.A., Markovski, B.L., Rostovtsev, V.A., Vinitsky, S.I.: GITA: A REDUCE program for the normalization of polynomial Hamiltonians. Comp. Phys. Commun. **90** (1995) 355-368
4. Uwano, Y.: Degeneracy of energy levels in a Maslov-quantized perturbed 1:1 resonant oscillator. A quantum counterpart of a Hamiltonian pitchfork bifurcation. J.Phys. **A28** (1995), 2041-2055; 6481.
5. Uwano, Y.: A geometric approach to a quantum counterpart of a saddle-node bifurcation in a 1:1 resonant perturbed oscillator. Int. J. Bifurcation and Chaos **8**(1998), 641-650.
6. Uwano, Y.: A Note on Quantum Pitchfork/Saddle-Node Bifurcations in a Perturbed Oscillator with Four-Parameters. to appear in Proc. of III International Workshop on Cllasical and Quantum Integrable Systems (1998, Yerevan, Armenia)
7. Chekanov, N.A., Rostovtsev, V.A., Uwano, Y.,Vinitsky, S.I.: "Inverse-GITA: Symbolic Algorithm for an Inverse Problem of the Birkhoff-Gustavson Normal Form Method". Submitted to Comp. Phys. Commun.
8. Chekanov, N.A., Hongo, M., Rostovtsev, V.A., Uwano, Y.,Vinitsky, S.I.: "Inverse-GITA" for an Inverse Problem of the Birkhoff-Gustavson Normal Form Method. Phys. Atom. Nucl. **61** N11 (1998) 1918-1922
9. Uwano, Y. and Vinitsky, S.I.: An Inverse Problem of the Bikhoff-Gustavson Normal Form Expansion and ANFER, an Algorithm of Normal Form Expansion and Restoration (was presented for the talk in the workshop, "Dynamical Systems and Differential Geometry", (Kobe, Jan. 25-27, 1999)), in preparation for Inverse Problem.
10. Toda, M.: The theory of nonlinear lattice. Springer-Verlag, N.Y. (1981)
11. Lichtenberg, A., Liberman, M.: Regular and stochastic motion. Springer Verlag Berlin-Heidelberg NY (1983)
12. Bolotin, Yu.L., Chekanov, N.A., Inopin, E.V, Gonchar, V.Yu., Tarasov, V.N.: Stochastic Nuclear Dynamics. Sov. J. At. Nucl. Phys. **50** (1989) 878-929
13. Goldstein, H.: *Classical Mechanics* 2nd. Ed., Addison-Wesley Reading, Mass. 1980

On Multivariate Polynomial Decomposition

Joachim von zur Gathen[1], Jaime Gutierrez[2] and Rosario Rubio[2]

[1] FB Mathematik-Informatik
Universität-GH Paderborn
D-33095 Paderborn, Germany
gathen@math.uni-paderborn.de
[2] Departamento de Matemáticas, Estadística y Computación
Universidad de Cantabria, Spain
{jaime, sarito}@matesco.unican.es

Abstract. In this paper, we discuss the decomposition problem for multivariate polynomials and the possible definitions of decomposable/indecomposable polynomial. We also present a polynomial time algorithm for decomposing multivariate polynomials over an arbitrary field.

1 Introduction

1.1 The Univariate Rational Function Decomposition Problem

If $\mathbb{K}$ is a field, and $g(X), h(X) \in \mathbb{K}[X]$ of degree greater than one, then $f(X) = g(X) \circ h(X) = g(h(X)) \in \mathbb{K}[X]$ is their (functional) composition, and we say that $f(x)$ is a *decomposable* polynomial. The functional univariate decomposition problem over $\mathbb{K}[X]$ can be stated as follows: given $f(X) \in \mathbb{K}[X]$, determine whether there exist $g(X), h(X) \in \mathbb{K}[X]$, of degree greater than one, such that $f(X) = g(h(X))$ and in the affirmative case, compute them.

Univariate polynomial decomposition is an important and interesting problem with a large number of applications in computer science and computational algebra. In fact, most major computational algebra systems (AXIOM, MAPLE, MATHEMATICA, REDUCE) support polynomial decomposition for univariate polynomials. Over the last ten years, there have been new results in the area of univariate polynomial decomposition. For some time this problem was considered computationally hard: the security of a cryptographic protocol was based on its hardness, see Cade ([1985]). In 1985, Barton and Zippel, and later Alagar and Thanh, gave algorithms for the solution, obtaining when a nontrivial polynomial decomposition exists and computing it. In both cases, the algorithms were of exponential time, required polynomial factorization and worked only over fields of characteristic 0. In 1986, Kozen and Landau gave the first polynomial time algorithms for the solution to this problem. Their first algorithm requires $O(r^3 s^2)$ or $O(n^3)$ time while their second algorithm, which uses the Fourier Transform, requires only $O(s^2 r \log r)$ or $O(n^2)$ time. Their algorithms work over any commutative ring in the "tame case" (i.e., the ring contains a multiplicative inverse of r, the degree of $g(X)$), and assuming that the polynomial involved is monic. Independently, Gutierrez, Recio and Ruiz de Velasco in [1989] presented a similar algorithm, this algorithm runs in sequential time $O(n^2)$ and $O(n \log^2 n)$ in parallel. Von zur Gathen ([1990]) has given faster algorithms in the tame case. His algorithm requires only $O(n \log^2 \log \log n)$ time, or $O(n \log^2 n)$ when $\mathbb{K}$ supports a Fourier transform. Later, several new papers have been published on different extensions and variations of this problem (see von zur Gathen ([1990]), Alonso ([1994]), Binder ([1995]), von zur Gathen and Weiss ([1995]), Casperson, Ford, MacKay ([1996])).

The generalization of the decomposition problem to rational functions, (which has several specific applications, see Alonso, Gutierrez and Recio ([1995])) is more involved. Zippel ([1991]) presented the first polynomial time algorithm to decompose any rational function with an algorithm which is valid for univariate rational functions over any field in which one can factor polynomials. However, the exact running time is not calculated. Alonso, Gutierrez and Recio ([1995]) presented two exponential time algorithms to decompose rational functions, but in the practice (not in theory), more efficient than Zippel's method. FRAC is a MAPLE package, which is designed for performing computation in the rational function field, where the main tool is the functional decomposition, see Alonso, Gutierrez and Recio ([1994]).

From the mathematical point of view, it is well known that a univariate rational function $f \in \mathbb{K}(X)$ is *indecomposable* if and only if $\mathbb{K}(f) \subseteq \mathbb{K}(X)$ is a simple algebraic extension, because by Lüroth's theorem, every field $\mathbb{F}$ containing $\mathbb{K}$ and contained in $\mathbb{K}(X)$ is generated by one rational function $h(X) \in \mathbb{K}(X)$, i.e., $\mathbb{F} = \mathbb{K}(h)$. So, the univariate rational function decomposition problem is equivalent to determine intermediate fields $\mathbb{F}$, $\mathbb{K}(f) \subset \mathbb{F} \subset \mathbb{K}(X)$. There exists only a finite number of them and, if $\mathbb{F}$ contains a non-constant polynomial, then $\mathbb{F}$ is generated by a polynomial $h(X)$.

The next question that arises is: What about the decomposition problem for multivariate polynomials? In the following, we would like to define different multivariate polynomial decompositions in such a way they include the most interesting and difficult problems.

1.2   The Multivariate Rational Function Decomposition Problem

Let $\mathbb{K}$ be an arbitrary field. As usual, we denote by $\mathbb{K}(X_1, \ldots, X_n) = \mathbb{K}(\underline{X})$ the field of rational functions in the variables $X_1, \ldots, X_n$ over the field $\mathbb{K}$. The previous subsection and comments suggest the following question.

Problem 1. Given a list of r rational functions $(f_1, \ldots, f_r)$ in $\mathbb{K}(\underline{X})$, we wish to know if there exist $h_1, \ldots, h_m \in \mathbb{K}(\underline{X})$ such that $\mathbb{K}(f_1, \ldots, f_r) \subset \mathbb{K}(h_1, \ldots, h_m) \subset \mathbb{K}(\underline{X})$, and, in the affirmative case to compute $h_1, \ldots, h_m$

and $g_1(Y_1, \ldots, Y_m), \ldots, g_r(Y_1, \ldots, Y_m) \in \mathbb{K}(Y_1, \ldots, Y_m)$ such that, for every $i \in \{1, \ldots, r\}$:

$$f_i = g_i(h_1, \ldots, h_m).$$

We know that any field $\mathbb{F}$ containing $\mathbb{K}$ and contained in $\mathbb{K}(\underline{X})$ is finitely generated over $\mathbb{K}$. So, this problem is equivalent to computing intermediate fields $\mathbb{F}$, with $\mathbb{K}(f_1, \ldots, f_r) \subset \mathbb{F} \subset \mathbb{K}(\underline{X})$.

According to this problem, we consider the following concept.

Definition 2. A polynomial $f \in \mathbb{K}[X_1, \ldots, X_n] = \mathbb{K}[\underline{X}]$ is *decomposable* if and only if there exists a field $\mathbb{F}$ such that $\mathbb{K}(f) \subset \mathbb{F} \subset \mathbb{K}(\underline{X})$.

Let us point out some facts about Problem 1 and Definition 2.

The general techniques developed for decomposition problems all lead to divide the problem into two parts. Given $(f_1, \ldots, f_r)$ and assuming there is a decomposition $f_i = g_i(h_1, \ldots, h_m)$, then:

1. compute the candidates $(h_1, \ldots, h_m)$'s;
2. compute $(g_1, \ldots, g_r)$ given $(h_1, \ldots, h_m)$.

Determining $(g_1, \ldots, g_r)$ from $(f_1, \ldots, f_r)$ and $(h_1, \ldots, h_m)$ is just a subfield membership problem, for instance see Sweedler ([1993]) for a solution to this part. As usual, the hardest step is to find $(h_1, \ldots, h_m)$.

If the characteristic of $\mathbb{K}$ is zero we know that there exists a finite of number fields $\mathbb{F}$ if and only if the transcendence degree of $\mathbb{K}(f_1, \ldots, f_r)$ over $\mathbb{K}$ is the number of variables n. In this case, any field $\mathbb{F}$ containing $\mathbb{K}(f_1, \ldots, f_r)$ is at most generated by $n + 1$ rational functions, see Schinzel ([1982]). Of course, there exist methods to determine the algebraic or transcendental nature of $\mathbb{K}(\underline{X})$ over $\mathbb{K}(f_1, \ldots, f_r)$ which include the computation of the index, in case of a algebraicity, or of the transcendental degree, in case the extension is transcendental. But, if the list is a polynomial f with a number of variables greater than 1, then we immediately determine infinite intermediate fields $\mathbb{F}$ such that $\mathbb{K}(f) \subset \mathbb{F} \subset \mathbb{K}(\underline{X})$. This last comment suggests that we should add some "limitations" to the subfields $\mathbb{F}$.

Finally, it is important to point out that if the given list of rational functions is a list of polynomials, in general $\mathbb{F} = \mathbb{K}(h_1, \ldots, h_m)$ is generated by non-polynomial rational functions h_i.

As we have seen, the multivariate rational function decomposition problem differs from the univariate one.

Anyway, a complete solution to this problem seems to be more difficult than the decomposition for univariate rational functions. But even "non-trivial" partial solutions would be an aid for algebraic simplification and evaluation questions; for instance, bivariate functional decomposition modulo the ideal of the circle (see Hommel and Kovács ([1992]) and Gutierrez and Recio ([1998])) is used for the symbolic simplification of the inverse kinematic equations. See Gutierrez and Rubio ([1999]) for partial results of the general Problem 1.

1.3   One Type of Decomposable Multivariate Polynomial

In von zur Gathen ([1990]), one finds the following definition.

Definition 3. A polynomial $f(X_1, \ldots, X_n) \in \mathbb{K}[\underline{X}]$ of (total) degree rs is *decomposable* if there exist $g(Y) \in \mathbb{K}[Y]$ and $h(X_1, \ldots, X_n) \in \mathbb{K}[\underline{X}]$ of degrees r, s respectively, such that:

$$f(X_1, \ldots, X_n) = g(h(X_1, \ldots, X_n)).$$

The decomposition problem is to decide if a multivariate polynomial f is *decomposable* and in the affirmative case, to compute the polynomials $g(Y)$ and $h(X_1, \ldots, X_n)$. If the field has more than $m + 1$ elements and r not divisible by the characteristic of the field $\mathbb{K}$, von zur Gathen's algorithm can be performed with $O(mn(m+1)^n \log m)$ operations. This bound is favourably better than the estimate of Dickerson's algorithm (1989), which uses less than N^3 operations if the dense representation of $f(X_1, \ldots, X_n)$ has N terms.

This interesting decomposition problem is a special case of the multivariate rational function decomposition Problem 1. In fact, the above question is equivalent to the following:

"Given a multivariate polynomial f, compute intermediate 1-transcendental degree fields $\mathbb{F}$ such that $\mathbb{K}(f) \subset \mathbb{F} \subset \mathbb{K}(X_1, \ldots, X_n)$ ".

Actually, there exists a finite number of them and they are generated by one multivariate polynomial.

1.4   Reduced Gröbner Bases and Decomposable Multivariate Polynomial

The following kind of multivariate polynomial decomposition problem is motivated by the study of the bearing of reduced Gröbner basis computation under polynomial composition, see Hong ([1996], [1998]). This problem can be stated as follows: Let G be a reduced Gröbner basis —under some term ordering— of the ideal generated by H, where H is a finite set of polynomials in the variables $X_1, \ldots, X_n$; let Θ be a polynomial map, that is, $\Theta = (\vartheta_1, \ldots, \vartheta_n)$ is a list of n polynomials in the variables $X_1, \ldots, X_n$. Now, we consider two new polynomial sets: H^* and G^*, obtained from H and G, respectively, by replacing X_i with ϑ_i. A natural question that arises is: *Under which circumstances is G^* the reduced Gröbner basis of the ideal generated by H^* under the same term ordering?* Gutierrez and Rubio ([1998]) gave a complete answer: this happens if and only if the composition by Θ is "compatible" with the term ordering and Θ is a list of permuted univariate and monic polynomials. This problem has two natural applications. One of them is in the computation of reduced Gröbner bases of the ideal generated by composed polynomials: so, in order to compute a reduced Gröbner basis of

H^*, we first compute a reduced Gröbner basis G of H and carry out the composition on G, obtaining a reduced Gröbner basis of H^*. This seems more efficient than computing a reduced Gröbner basis of H^* directly. On the other hand, the opposite application is decomposing the input polynomials $f \in H$ as $f = g(\vartheta_1(X_1), \ldots, \vartheta_n(X_n))$, where $\vartheta_i(X_i)$ is an univariate polynomial in the variable X_i, and then check if the composition by $\Theta = (\vartheta_1, \ldots, \vartheta_n)$ is "compatible" with the term ordering. This problem suggest the study the following concept.

Definition 4. A polynomial $f(X_1, \ldots, X_n) \in \mathbb{K}[\underline{X}]$ is *decomposable* if there exist univariate non-constant polynomials $h_i(X_i) \in \mathbb{K}[X_i]$, for $i = 1, \ldots, n$ and $g(Y_1, \ldots, Y_n) \in \mathbb{K}[\underline{Y}]$ such that:

$$f(X_1, \ldots, X_n) = g(h_1(X_1), \ldots, h_n(X_n)).$$

Similarly, the decomposition problem is to decide if a multivariate polynomial f is *decomposable* and in the affirmative case, to compute the polynomials $g(\underline{Y})$ and $h_1(X_1), \ldots, h_n(X_n)$.

Again, this decomposition problem is a special case of Problem 1. In fact, the above question is equivalent to the following field extension algebraic problem:

"Given a multivariate polynomial f, compute intermediate fields $\mathbb{F}$ such that $\mathbb{K}(f) \subset \mathbb{F} \subset \mathbb{K}(X_1, \ldots, X_n)$ and $\mathbb{F}$ is generated by non-constant polynomials of $\mathbb{K}(X_i)$, for all $i = 1, \ldots, n$."

Moreover, there exists a finite number of them and they are generated by n univariate polynomials $h_i(X_i)$, for all i.

1.5   Decomposable Multivariate Polynomial

The generalization of decomposable multivariate polynomial that we suggest is the following.

Definition 5. We say that a multivariate polynomial f is *decomposable* if and only if there exist $i \in \{1, \ldots, n\}$ and an intermediate field $\mathbb{F}$ such that :

$$\mathbb{K}(X_1, \ldots, X_{i-1}, f, X_{i+1}, \ldots, X_n) \subset \mathbb{F} \subset \mathbb{K}(\underline{X}).$$

This definition involves all the definitions of decomposition of multivariate polynomials that we have shown.

In this paper, we will show that every decomposition of a multivariate polynomial of the Definition 3 and Definition 4 is also a decomposition in the new sense of the above definition, but no conversely. We will see that there exists a finite number of fields $\mathbb{F}$ and that every such field $\mathbb{F}$ is determined by one multivariate polynomial $h \in \mathbb{K}[\underline{X}]$. Moreover, we will see this decomposition implies a strong simplification in the degree of the given polynomial f. We also present an algorithm in polynomial time to compute all intermediate fields $\mathbb{F}$.

The remaining of the paper is divided in three sections. In Section 2 we give the solution of the decomposition problem over factorial domains. Besides we study and solve the general problem of finding (and defining) a complete decomposition into indecomposable elements, clarifying the polynomial decomposition over general rings (question proposed in von zur Gathen ([1990])). We state some uniqueness results concerned with this decomposition and we present an algorithm in polynomial time to find the complete decomposition over any arbitrary factorial domain in which one can factor elements. As a consequence, in Section 3, we recover the decomposition of a

decomposable multivariate polynomial. In Section 4, we give three algorithms for decomposing multivariate polynomials based on Hensel's lifting method.

2   Decomposition over Factorial Domains

In this section, we provide an algorithm to decompose univariate polynomials with coefficients in a factorial domain. A part of these results are in Gutierrez ([1991]).

2.1   Definitions and Basic Results

We denote by R a commutative ring with identity. It is very useful, in order to work with functional decomposition of polynomials, to consider the near-rings of polynomials $(R[X], +, \circ)$, see Pilz and So ([1980]).

If R is a domain, the *units* in the near-ring $R[X]$ are the linear polynomials $aX + b$, where a is an unit in the ring R.

As usual $R_0[X]$ will denote the set of all polynomials over R whose constant term is zero, that is:
$$R_0[X] := \{f(X) \in R[X] / f(X) \circ 0 = f(0) = 0\}.$$
$R_0[X]$ is a subnear-ring and agrees with the zero-symmetric part of the near-ring of polynomials $R[X]$.

Given a polynomial $f(X)$, we denote the degree of $f(X)$ by $deg(f(X))$.

Definition 6. As in ring theory, we say that an element $f(X) \in R[X]$ is *indecomposable* provided that:

1. $f(X)$ is non-constant and non-unit.
2. If $f(X) = g(X) \circ h(X), (g(X), h(X) \in R[X])$ implies $g(X)$ or $h(X)$ is a unit.

Otherwise we say $f(X)$ is *decomposable* .

Of course, if $R = \mathbb{K}$ is a field, then $f(X) \in \mathbb{K}[X]$ a non-zero and non-unit polynomial is indecomposable if $f(X) = g(X) \circ h(X), (g(X), h(X) \in \mathbb{K}[X])$ implies $deg(g(X)) = deg(f(X))$ or $deg(h(X)) = deg(f(X))$.

A *decomposition* of $f(X)$ is a set of polynomials $f_1(X), \ldots, f_m(X) \in R[X]$ such that:

$$f(X) = f_1(X) \circ f_2(X) \circ \cdots \circ f_m(X).$$

The $f_i(X)$ are called the *components* of the decomposition. A *complete decomposition* is one where all the components are indecomposable.

We say that a polynomial $f(X) \in R$ is *primitive* if the greatest common divisor of its coefficients is 1.

Proposition 7. *The subnear-ring $RX := \{aX | a \in R\}$ is isomorphic to ring R.*

Remark 8. If $R = \mathbb{K}$ is a field, every polynomial $f(X)$ has a complete decomposition in $\mathbb{K}[X]$ with a strong uniqueness property when the characteristic of the field does not divide the $deg(f(X))$, see Gutierrez and Recio ([1998]) or von zur Gathen ([1990]).

Remark 9. We note that if R is a domain the degree is multiplicative with respect to composition, but if we take as $R = \mathbb{Z}_4$, the ring of integers modulo 4, then:

$$2X^4 + X^3 = X^3 \circ (2X^2 + X)$$

is a decomposition (tame case), but notice it is not a complete decomposition as Definition 6, because $2X^2 + X$ is a unit in the near-ring $\mathbb{Z}_4[X]$:

$$X = (2X^2 + X) \circ (2X^2 + X).$$

Remark 10. In order to determine a complete decomposition of a polynomial $f(X)$ over a domain R, we observe that the assumption "R factorial domain" can not be omitted as Proposition 7 shows.

Notation 11. In this section, we will denote by D a unique factorization domain and by $\mathbb{K}$ its field of fractions.

In order to get a complete decomposition of $f(X)$, we can assume –without loss of generality– that $f(X)$ is in $D_0[X]$; in fact, $f(X) = a_n X^n + \cdots + a_1 X + a_0 = (X + a_0) \circ (a_n X^n + \cdots + a_1 X)$ is indecomposable if and only if $a_n X^n + \cdots + a_1 X$ is indecomposable.

2.2   The Composition Gauss' Lemma

The key lemma to prove the complete decomposition of $f(X)$ is the composition Gauss' lemma.

Lemma 12. *Let* $g(X), h(X) \in D_0[X]$ *be primitive polynomials. Then their composition is also a primitive polynomial.*

Proof. Suppose $g(X), h(X) \in D_0[X]$ are primitive but $f(X) = g(X) \circ h(X)$ is not. Then there exists an irreducible element $p \in D$ such that p does not divide all the coefficients of $g(X)$ and $h(X)$ but p divide $f(X)$.
We consider the domain $B = D/(p)$. We now apply the composition ring homomorphism of $D[X]$ onto $B[X]$ (i.e. ring and near-ring homomorphism), see Pilz and So ([1980]). We arrive to a contradiction since B is a domain and $g(X)$ and $h(X)$ are polynomials in $B[X]$ with positive degree then $g(X) \circ h(X)$ has to be a polynomial with positive degree in $B[X]$.

The following result gives the relation between the decomposition of a polynomial over the factorial domain and over its field of fractions.

Theorem 13. *If* $f(X) \in D_0[X]$ *is primitive then* $f(X)$ *is indecomposable in* $D[X]$ *if and only if is indecomposable in* $\mathbb{K}[X]$.

An immediate consequence of Proposition 7 and Theorem 13 is the existence of a complete decomposition:

Corollary 14. *Given* $f(X) \in D[X]$ *a non-constant and non-unit polynomial, there exist* $f_1(X), f_2(X), \ldots, f_m(X) \in D[X]$ *indecomposable polynomials such that:*
$$f(X) = f_1(X) \circ f_2(X) \circ \cdots \circ f_m(X).$$

2.3   The Algorithm

The following algorithm solves the decomposition problem over factorial domains, interesting running time appears in the tame case.

Algorithm 15.
Input: $f(X) = a_n X^n + a_{n-1} X^{n-1} + \cdots + a_1 X + a_0 \in D[X]$ of degree $n = rs$.
Output: $g(X), h(X) \in D[X]$ with $f(X) = g(X) \circ h(X)$ and $deg(g(X)) = r$, if such a decomposition exists; and "no decomposition" otherwise.
A.1 Find $\alpha, \beta \in D$ such that $f(X) = (\alpha X + \beta) \circ f'(X)$ where $f'(X) \in D_0[X]$ is primitive.
Take $\alpha = G.C.D(a_n, a_{n-1}, \ldots, a_1), \beta = a_0$.
A.2 Apply a decomposition polynomial algorithm over $\mathbb{K}[X]$ with input $f'(X)$. If no decomposition of $f'(X) \in \mathbb{K}[X]$ exists, return "no decomposition".

If $f'(X) = g'(X) \circ h'(X)$ is returned with $h'(X) \in \mathbb{K}_0[X]$ and monic,

$$h'(X) = X^s + \frac{b_{s-1}}{c_{s-1}}X^{s-1} + \cdots + \frac{b_1}{c_1}X.$$

Return:

$$g(X) = (\alpha X + \beta) \circ g'(X) \circ \frac{X}{\delta} \quad \text{and} \quad h(X) = \delta X \circ h'(X),$$

where $\delta = L.C.M(c_{s-1}, c_{s-2}, \ldots, c_1)$.

We have the degree is multiplicative with respect to composition of polynomials, using Lemma 12 and Theorem 13 we see that the algorithm determines correctly whether $f(X) \in D[X]$ has a decomposition with the required degrees, and if so, computes a decomposition. If we suppose that one can factor elements in the domain $\mathbb{K}$ and since the number of divisors of $deg(f(X)) = n$ is finite, we obtain an algorithm to compute a complete decomposition into indecomposable polynomials over $D[X]$.

2.4   Analysis

This algorithm works over any factorial domain, but if we are working in the tame case, that is, where the degree of $f(X)$ does not divide the characteristic of the domain D (therefore without any restriction, if the characteristic is zero), we will get the following running time:

In step **A.1**, we calculate the $G.C.D(a_n, a_{n-1}, \ldots, a_1)$ in the factorial domain D. It requires $n - 1$ GCD's calculations. In step **A.2**, we can use von zur Gathen's decomposition algorithm that requires a total of $O(M_D(n) \log n)$ arithmetic operations, where $M_D : \mathbb{N} \longmapsto \mathbb{R}$ is such that the product of two polynomials in $D[X]$ of degree at most n can be computed with $O(M(n))$ operations. This last computation is mostly dominated by step **A.1**. For example, if D is a ring of polynomials with coefficients in a field $\mathbb{F}$, $D :=$ $\mathbb{F}[X_1, \ldots, X_n]$, the number of arithmetic operations in the field $\mathbb{F}$ is clearly dominated by the computing of the $G.C.D.$ of the polynomial coefficients of $f(X) \in \mathbb{F}[X_1, \ldots, X_n][X]$.

2.5   Uniqueness

Finally, we obtain some interesting results about the "uniqueness" of a decomposition of $f(X)$, which will let us study the multivariate decomposition problem in next section.

Corollary 16. *Let $f(X) \in D[X]$ be of degree $n = rs$ such that r does not divide the characteristic of D. Then the following holds: If $f(X) = g(X) \circ*

$h(X) = g'(X) \circ h'(X)$ with $deg(g(X)) = deg(g'(X)) = r$ and $h(X), h'(X) \in D_0[X]$, then $h(X)$ and $h'(X)$ are associated in $\mathbb{K}$.

In particular, if they are indecomposable polynomials over $D[X]$, then they are associated in $D[X]$.

Proof. The polynomial returned $h'(X)$ in the algorithm is unique (see Gutierrez, Recio and Ruiz de Velasco ([1989])). The remainder of the proof is a trivial consequence of the algorithm.

Corollary 17. *Let $f(X) \in D[X]$ be a decomposable polynomial. If $char(D)$ does not divide $deg(f(X))$, then the following statements hold:*

i) *There exists, except associated polynomials, a unique complete decomposition of $f(X)$: $[w_1(X), \ldots, w_r(X), f_1(X), \ldots, f_s(X)]$ with the following conditions:*

1. $f(X) = w_1(X) \circ \cdots \circ w_r(X) \circ f_1(X) \cdots \circ f_s(X)$.
2. $deg(w_i(X)) = 1, \forall i = 1, \ldots, r$.
3. $deg(f_i(X)) > 1, \forall i = 1, \ldots, s$.
4. $w_i(X) \in D_0[X], \forall i = 2, \ldots, r$.
5. $f_i(X) \in D_0[X], \forall i = 1, \ldots, s$.
6. *Having calculated polynomials $f_1(X), \ldots, f_{i-1}(X)$, $f_i(X)$ satisfies that $deg(f_i(X)) = minimum\{deg(h(X)) \mid h(X))$ is a good candidate for the polynomial: $w_1(X) \circ \cdots \circ w_r(X) \circ f_1(X) \cdots \circ f_i(X)\}$.*

ii) *Let*

$$f(X) = m_1(X) \circ m_2(X) \circ \cdots \circ m_r(X) \circ g_1(X) \circ g_2(X) \circ \cdots \circ g_u(X)$$

$$= n_1(X) \circ n_2(X) \circ \cdots \circ n_s(X) \circ h_1(X) \circ h_2(X) \circ \cdots \circ h_v(X)$$

be two complete decompositions of $f(X)$ in $D[X]$ with $deg(m_i(X)) = 1$, for all i, $deg(n_j(X)) = 1$, for all j, $deg(g_k(X)) > 1$, for all k and $deg(h_l(X)) > 1$, for all l. Then,
$$m_1(X) \circ m_2(X) \circ \cdots \circ m_r(X) = n_1(X) \circ n_2(X) \circ \cdots \circ n_s(X)$$
and
$$g_1(X) \circ g_2(X) \circ \cdots \circ g_u(X) = h_1(X) \circ h_2(X) \circ \cdots \circ h_v(X)$$
with $r = s$, $u = v$ and the sequences $< deg(g_j(X)) >$, $< deg(h_j(X)) >$ are permutations of each other.

3   Multivariate Polynomial Decomposition

In this section, we will apply the decomposition of polynomial over factorial domains, (when the factorial domain is a polynomial ring with coefficients over a field) to the multivariate decomposition problems. First, we prove that a multivariate polynomial f is decomposable in the sense of Definition 5 if and only if it is a decomposable univariate polynomial, considered as univariate polynomial in the variable X_i, for some i :

Proposition 18. *Let* $f(X_1, \ldots, X_n) \in \mathbb{K}[\underline{X}]$ *be a multivariate polynomial and* $D = \mathbb{K}[X_1, \ldots, X_{i-1}, X_{i+1}, \ldots, X_n]$. *Then the following statements are equivalent:*

1. *There exist* $i \in \{1, \ldots, n\}$ *and an intermediate field* $\mathbb{F}$, *such that:*

$$\mathbb{K}(X_1, \ldots, X_{i-1}, f, X_{i+1}, \ldots, X_n) \subset \mathbb{F} \subset \mathbb{K}(\underline{X}).$$

2. *There exists* $i \in \{1, \ldots, n\}$ *such that* f *is a decomposable univariate polynomial over the factorial domain* $D[X_i]$.

In this case, there is a finite number of fields $\mathbb{F}$. *Moreover, there exists* $h \in \mathbb{K}[\underline{X}]$ *such that* $\mathbb{F} = \mathbb{K}(X_1, \ldots, X_{i-1}, h, X_{i+1}, \ldots, X_n)$ *and for some multivariate polynomial* g, $f = g(X_1, \ldots, X_{i-1}, h, X_{i+1}, \ldots, X_n)$.

As a consequence of the above result and Subsection 1.5, we have an algorithm to compute a decomposition of the multivariate polynomial f in the sense of Definition 4. So, in order to know if a polynomial $f(X_1, \ldots, X_n) \in \mathbb{K}[X_1, \ldots, X_n]$ has a multivariate decomposition, we have to decompose the polynomial $f(X_1, \ldots, X_n)$ over $D := \mathbb{K}[X_1, \ldots, X_{i-1}, X_{i+1}, \ldots, X_n]$ considered as polynomial in the variable X_i with coefficients in D for all variable X_i. If the polynomial has a decomposition, say $g(X_i), h(X_i) \in D[X_i]$, we have that:

$$f = g(X_1, \ldots, X_{i-1}, h(X_1, \ldots, X_n), X_{i+1}, \ldots, X_n).$$

Now, we will see that decompositions of a multivariate polynomial in the sense of Definition 3 and Definition 4 are included in this more general decomposition.

Remark 19. Given a multivariate polynomial $f \in \mathbb{K}[\underline{X}]$. We have:

1. If $f = g(h)$ where $g \in \mathbb{K}[Y]$ and $h \in \mathbb{K}[\underline{X}]$, then f is decomposable in the sense of Definition 5. Moreover, we can
   get at the same decomposition, except constants in $\mathbb{K}$.
2. If $f = g(h_1(X_1), \ldots, h_n(X_n))$, where $h_i(X_i) \in \mathbb{K}[X_i]$, for $i = 1, \ldots, n$, then f is decomposable in the sense of Definition 5. Moreover, we can get at the same decomposition, except constants in $\mathbb{K}$.

Proof. It is immediate to check that Definition 5 is more general than Definition 3 and Definition 4. For the first statement just take $g(X_1, \ldots, X_n) = g(X_1)$, and for the second one, $g(X_1, \ldots, X_n) = g(X_1, h_2, \ldots, h_n)$. The remainder is a trivial consequence of the uniqueness, see Corollary 16 and Corollary 17.

Therefore, we have a new definition of multivariate polynomials which includes the two previous multivariate decompositions Definitions 3 and 4. But these two decompositions are not related between them.

Example 20.
i) Let $f(X_1, X_2) = g(X_1^2 + X_1 X_2^2 - X_2^3 + X_2^2)$, where $g(Y) = Y^3 + Y^2 + Y + 1$. f is decomposable in the sense of Definition 3 but it is not in the sense of Definition 4.
ii) Let $f(X_1, X_2) = g(X_1^2, X_2^3 + X_2^2)$, where $g(Y_1, Y_2) = Y_1 * Y_2 + Y_2^2 + Y_1 + 1$. f is decomposable in the sense of Definition 4 but it is not in the sense of Definition 3.

Now, we show an example illustrating that there exist indecomposable polynomials, in the sense of Definition 3 and Definition 4, but decomposable in the sense of Definition 5.

Example 21. The polynomial $f = X_1^2 - 3 + X_2^2 X_1^4 - X_1 X_2^2 + X_2 X_1^4 + X_1 - 2X_2^2 X_1^3 - X_2^2 X_1^6 - 2X_2^3 X_1^6 + 2X_2^2 + 2X_2^4 X_1^3 - X_2^4 X_1^6 + 2X_2^3 X_1^3 - X_2^4 - 2X_2^2 X_1^3$, has a decomposition as Definition 5: $f = g(X_1, h)$, where $g = Y_1^2 - 2 - Y_1 Y_2 - Y_2^2$ and $h = (X_1^3 - 1) X_2^2 + X_2 X_1^3 - X_1 + 1$. But the polynomial $f(X_1, X_2)$ is "indecomposable" according to Definition 3 and 4.

In some sense, the multivariate decomposition based on the factorial domains is just a special case of the general Definition 2.

Example 22. The polynomial $f(X_1, X_2) = X_1^2 X_2^3 + 2X_1^2 X_2^2 + X_1^3 X_2 + X_1^3 + 3X_1^2 X_2 + X_1 X_2^3 - 5X_1 X_2^2 - 5X_1 X_2 + X_1^2 - 6X_2^2$ can be decomposed as $g(h_1, h_2)$, where $h_1 = X_1 X_2^2 + X_1^2 - 7X_2, h_2 = X_1 X_2 + X_1 + X_2$ and $g(Y_1, Y_2) = Y_1 Y_2 + Y_2^2$. But it is indecomposable as Definition 5.

Another interesting fact, which we have not talked about yet, is the behaviour of the degrees. We know (see Proposition 18) that multivariate decomposition based on Definition 5 puts conditions on the degrees of the new polynomials, contrary to Definition 2.

Example 23. The polynomial $f(X_1, X_2) = -X_1 X_2 - 1 - X_1^2 - X_2^2$ can be decomposed as $g(X_1 X_2 - 1, X_1 + X_2)$ where $g(Y_1, Y_2) = Y_1 - Y_2^2$. We have f is decomposable as Definition 2 and in some sense this decomposition is simpler but we still have polynomials of the same degree as f.

One of the main reason for decomposing polynomials is to obtain new "simpler" polynomials. So it is important to highlight what kind of simplification can we get with this decomposition. By the algorithm, if f is decomposable in the sense of Definition 5, $deg_{X_i}(h_i) \le deg_{X_i}(f)$. So one interesting decomposition would be:

Definition 24. We say that f has a *non-trivial decomposition* if we can write $f(X_1, \ldots, X_n) = g(X_1, \ldots, X_{i-1}, h, X_{i+1}, \ldots, X_n)$ where $i = 1, \ldots, n$ and $g, h \in \mathbb{K}[X_1, \ldots, X_n]$ with $deg_{X_i}(h_i) \leq deg_{X_i}(f)$.

This is a possible definition for non-trivial decomposition, but there exist more definitions that can be suitable for other purposes.

4   Algorithms Based on Hensel's Lifting Method

In this section, we will say that f is a decomposable polynomial if and only if it is decomposable in the sense of Definition 4, that is:
"*A polynomial $f(X_1, \ldots, X_n) \in \mathbb{K}[\underline{X}]$, is decomposable if there exist uni-variate non-constant polynomials $h_i(X_i) \in \mathbb{K}[X_i]$, for $i = 1, \ldots, n$ and $g(Y_1, \ldots, Y_n) \in \mathbb{K}[\underline{Y}]$ such that:*

$$f(X_1, \ldots, X_n) = g(h_1(X_1), \ldots, h_n(X_n)).$$"

We will show algorithms for computing the decomposition of multivariate polynomials in the sense of the above definition. These algorithms are based on Hensel's lifting method. First we calculate the univariate polynomials $h_1(X_1), \ldots, h_n(X_n)$ and afterwards, we will see how to find out the multivariate polynomial $g(X_1, \ldots, X_n)$.

First of all, we need to fix some notations and facts.

Remark 25.
1. We will work in a computable field $\mathbb{K}$ in the tame case, that is, such that the degree of the polynomials are relatively prime with the characteristic of the field. We will denote by $O(M(m))$ the number of the arithmetic operations in order to compute the product of two univariate polynomials in $\mathbb{K}[X]$ of degree at most m.
2. Given the multivariate polynomial $f(X_1, \ldots, X_n)$ with total degree m, we will write $f(X_i) := f(0, \ldots, 0, X_i, 0, \ldots, 0)$.
3. Given a list of natural numbers $(d_1, \ldots, d_n)$ and assuming there is a decomposition $f(X_1, \ldots, X_n) = g(h_1(X_1), \ldots, h_n(X_n))$ with $deg(h_i) = d_i$. Then d_i divides m, in particular $d_i \leq m$. On the other hand, according to Corollaries 16 and 17, they are unique univariate and monic polynomials $h_i(X_i) \in \mathbb{K}[X_i]$ verifying simultaneously:
   3.1 $f(X_1, \ldots, X_n) = g(h_1(X_1), \ldots, h_n(X_n))$.
   3.2 $deg(h_i) = d_i$.
   3.3 $h_i(0) = 0$.

Theorem 26. *Let f be a polynomial in $\mathbb{K}[X_1, \ldots, X_n]$ with degree m. For any list $(d_1, \ldots, d_n)$, where $d_i \leq deg_{X_i}(f)$, we can compute, if there exist, the unique polynomials $h_1(X_1), \ldots, h_n(X_n)$ satisfying the above items (Remark 25(3)) , in $O(nM(m) \log m)$ arithmetic operations.*

Once we have the right-handed polynomials for the decomposition, it only remains the computation of g. In the following, we present three algorithms.

Input :
$f(X_1, \ldots, X_n)$ a multivariate polynomial of degree m and $d = (d_1, \ldots, d_n)$ a list of integers such that $d_i \leq deg_{X_i}(f)$.

Output:
$g(X_1, \ldots, X_n), h_1(X_1), \ldots, h_n(X_n)$ polynomials with coefficients in $\mathbb{K}$ such that $f = g(h_1(X_1), \ldots, h_n(X_n))$ and $deg(h_i) = d_i, \forall i = 1, \ldots, n$, if such decomposition exists; and "no decomposition", otherwise.

Algorithm 27. The following algorithm is performed in $O\left(\binom{m+n}{n}^3\right)$ arithmetic operations.

A.1 For each $i \in \{1, \ldots, n\}$ calculate the unique monic and zero-symmetric polynomial $h_i(X_i)$ of degree d_i such that $f(X_i) = g_i(h_i(X_i))$ for some polynomial $g_i(X_i)$. If such decomposition does not exist, return "no decomposition".
A.2 Solve the system equation: $f(X_1, \ldots, X_n) = g(h_1(X_1), \ldots, h_n(X_n))$. If such system has no solution, return "no decomposition". Otherwise, return $g(X_1, \ldots, X_n)$ and $h_1(X_1), \ldots, h_n(X_n)$.

Algorithm 28. The following algorithm is performed in:
$$O\left(\binom{m+n}{n} n M((m+1)^{n-1})\right).$$
A.1 For each $i \in \{1, \ldots, n\}$ calculate the unique monic and zero-symmetric polynomial $h_i(X_i)$ of degree d_i such that $f(X_i) = g_i(h_i(X_i))$ for some polynomial $g_i(X_i)$. If such decomposition does not exist, return "no decomposition".
A.2 Let h_i^0 be the lowest monomial in h_i. Let $j = 1, g = 0$ and $\hat{f} = f$.

a) If $\hat{f}$ does not depend on X_j, take $j = j + 1$ and go to next step. Otherwise, choose p a monomial of $\hat{f}$ with minimal degree in X_j. Take P the monomial such that $p = P(h_1^0, \ldots, h_n^0)$. If P doesn't exist, return "no decomposition". If P exists, take $g = P + g$ and $\hat{f} = \hat{f} - P(h_1, \ldots, h_n)$.
b) If $j > n$ return g and $h_1, \ldots, h_n$, otherwise repeat step **a)**.

Algorithm 29. The following algorithm is performed in:
$$O\left(\binom{m+n}{n} n M((m+1)^{n-1})\right).$$
A.1 For each $i \in \{1, \ldots, n\}$ calculate the unique monic and zero-symmetric polynomial $h_i(X_i)$ of degree d_i such that $f(X_i) = g_i(h_i(X_i))$ for some polynomial $g_i(X_i)$. If such decomposition does not exist, return "no decomposition".
A.2 Compute $g := Normalform(f, G, <)$, where $<$ is the lexicographic order for $X_1 > \cdots > X_n > t_1 > \cdots > t_n$ and $G = \{h_1(X_1) - t_1, \ldots, h_n(X_n) - t_n\}$ is a Gröbner basis with respect to $<$. If $g \in \mathbb{K}[t_1, \ldots, t_n]$, return g and $h_1, \ldots, h_n$. Otherwise, return "no decomposition".

Acknowledgments

This research is partially supported by the National Spanish project PB97-0346 and "Acción Integrada Alemana-Española" HA1997-0124.

References

[1985] Alagar, V. S., Thanh, M.: Fast polynomial decomposition algorithms. Proceedings of EUROCAL'85. Vol. II. Lecture Notes in Comput. Sci., 204, Springer (1985), 150–153

[1994] Alonso, C.: Desarrollo, análisis e implementación de algoritmos para la manipulación de variedades paramétricas. Departamento de Matemáticas, Estadística y Computación. Universidad de Cantabria. Thesis (1994), Spain

[1994] Alonso, C., Gutierrez, J., Recio, T.: FRAC: A Maple package for computing in the rational function field $K(x)$. In the book Maple V: Mathematics and Its Application. Birkhauser, (1994) 107-115

[1995] Alonso, C., Gutierrez, J., Recio, T.: A rational function decomposition algorithm by near-separated polynomials. J. Symbolic Comput. 19 (1995), no. 6, 527–544

[1985] Barton, R., Zippel, R.: Polynomial decomposition algorithms. J. Symbolic Comput. 1 (1985), no. 2, 159-168

[1995] Binder, F.: Polynomial decomposition. Diplomarbeit, University of Linz, June (1995)

[1985] Cade, J.: A new public-key cipher which allows signatures. Proc. 2nd SIAM Conf. on Appl. Linear Algebra (1985), Raleigh NC

[1996] Casperson, D., Ford, D., MacKay, J.: Ideal decomposition and subfields. J. Symbolic Comput. 21 (1996), no. 2, 133-137

[1989] Dickerson, M.: Functional decomposition of polynomials. Tech. Rep. 89-1023, Dep. of Computer Science, Cornell University, (1989) Ithaca NY

[1990a] Gathen, J. von zur: Functional decomposition of polynomials: the tame case. J. Symbolic Comput. 9 (1990), no. 3, 281-299

[1990b] Gathen, J. von zur: Functional decomposition of polynomials: the wild case. J. Symbolic Comput. 10 (1990), no. 5, 437-452

[1995] Gathen, J. von zur, Weiss, J.: Homogeneous bivariate decompositions. J. Symbolic Comput. 19 (1995), no. 5, 409–434

[1991] Gutierrez, J.: A polynomial decomposition algorithm over factorial domains. Rep. Acad. Sci. Canada 13 (1991), no. 2-3, 81–86.

[1989] Gutierrez, J., Recio, T., Ruiz de Velasco, C.: Polynomial decomposition algorithm of almost quadratic complexity. Proc. AAECC-6/88. Lecture Notes in Comput. Sci., 357, Springer (1989), 471–475

[1998] Gutierrez, J., Recio, T.: Advances on the simplification of sine-cosine equations. J. Symbolic Comput. 26 (1998), no. 1, 31–70

[1998] Gutierrez, J., Rubio, R.: Reduced Gröbner basis under composition. J. Symbolic Comput. 26 (1998), no. 7, 433–444

[1999] Gutierrez, J., Rubio, R.: The multivariate rational function decomposition problem. Tech. Report Dept. Matemáticas y Computación. Universidad de Cantabria, (1999) Spain

[1992] Hommel, G., Kovács, P.: Simplification of symbolic inverse kinematic transformations through functional decomposition. Proc. of the Conference Adv. in Robotics, Ferrara, (1992) 88-95

[1998] Hong, H.: Gröbner basis under composition I. J. Symbolic Comput. **25** (1998), no. 5, 643-663

[1996] Hong, H.: Gröbner basis under composition II. Proc. ISSAC-96, ACM press, (1996)

[1989] Kozen, D., Landau, S.: Polynomial decomposition algorithms. J. Symbolic Comput. **7** (1989), no. 5, 445-456

[1980] Pilz, G., So, Y.: Near-rings of polynomials and polynomial functions. J. Austral. Math. Soc. Ser. A, **29** (1980), no. 1, 61-70

[1993] Sweedler, M.: Using Groebner bases to determine the algebraic and transcendental nature of field extensions: return of the killer tag variables. Proc. AAECC-10/93, Lecture Notes in Comput. Sci., 673, (1993) 66-75

[1982] Schinzel, A.: Selected topics on polynomials. Ann Arbor, University of Michigan Press. (1982)

[1991] Zippel, R.: Rational Function Decomposition. Proc. of ISSAC-91. ACM press, (1991), 1-6

Complexity of Monomial Evaluations and Duality

Nikolai N. Vassiliev

Steklov Mathematical Institute of Russian Academy of Sciences,
St. Petersburg Branch; e-mail: vasiliev@pdmi.ras.ru

Abstract. We give a matrix representation for the problem of joint evaluation of monomial sets. This approach leads to a relation between the problem of evaluation of m monomials in p variables and p monomials in m variables. A relation between multiplicative complexities of these dual problems is given.

Key words: monomials, complexity, duality, computer algebra

1 Introduction

The problem of fast evaluation of sets of powers or more generally sets of monomials has rather a long history, and the most essential result about asymptotical complexity was obtained by N. Pippenger [1]. In this paper we present a new approach to constructing the algorithms for monomial evaluations and for estimating their multiplicative complexity. Our approach is based on matrix reformulation of this problem and the resulting duality between the problems of evaluating m monomials in p variables and p monomials in m variables.
Let

$$y_i = \prod_{j=1}^{p} x_j{}^{n_{ij}}, \quad i = 1, .., m$$

be a set of p monomials in m variables. We represent these monomials via an integer matrix

$$N = (n_{ij}), \quad i = 1, \ldots, m; \quad j = 1, \ldots, p.$$

This general problem of computation of values of monomials is important for many polynomial computer algebra algorithms. For example, monomial evaluations are one of the most important parts of algorithms for manipulating the sparse polynomials. Even simple particular cases of the problem like the problem of fast evaluation of sets of powers are far from triviality and lead to very beautiful mathematical constructions like the additive chains [2]. Many hypotheses about additive chains are still unsolved. But in asymptotic sense the question about multiplicative complexity of the problem of joint evaluation of the set of monomials was solved. The following estimate was proved in [1].

Theorem 1. *Multiplicative complexity $L(N)$ of evaluation of a set of m monomials of n variables satisfies inequality*

$$L(N) < \min(m,p)\log_2(d) + o(\log_2(d)),$$

where $d = \max(n_{ij})$, $i = 1,\dots,p$; $j = 1,\dots,m$.

It is evident that this estimate can be well applicable if the maximal degree of a variable appearing in the set of monomials is much larger than the number of monomials and the number of variables. In many practical problems we face another case, where the number of monomials or number of variables are rather large whereas the maximal degree is bounded. Such a case appears, for example, in the problem of evaluating dense polynomials without adaptation of coefficients. One of the most essential steps of an algorithm described in [3] is the evaluation of special constructed monomial sets.

2   Decomposition of Monomial Evaluations

We consider computational schemes for such monomial sets, which consist of a sequence of simple multiplication steps. The computational scheme computes a monomial set S, if the set of results contains the set S. The multiplicative complexity $L(S)$ of a monomial set S is a minimal number of multiplication steps in the scheme which computes S.

We start with rather a simple observation. Each factorization of matrix N into a product $N = R*S$ decomposes the problem corresponding to monomial set S into a sequence of two monomial evaluations corresponding to matrices R and S.

Let

$$n_{ij} = \sum_{k=1}^{l} r_{ik}s_{kj}.$$

Thus,

$$y_i = \prod_{k=1}^{l} v_k^{s_{ki}},$$

where

$$v_k = \prod_{i=1}^{m} x_i^{r_{ik}}.$$

This fact implies that if we denote by $L(N)$ the multiplicative complexity of the monomial problem corresponding to matrix $N = N_1 N_2 \dots N_k$ then

$$L(N) \leq \sum_{i=1}^{k} L(N_i).$$

Again, each evaluation scheme for monomial set S can be represented as a decomposition of "elementary" monomial substitutions. Each of them has complexity equal to 1. Such elementary substitutions may be represented by matrices of the following type:

$$\begin{pmatrix} 1 & 0 & 0 \ldots 0 \\ 0 & 1 & 0 \ldots 0 \\ 0 & 0 & 1 \ldots 0 \\ \vdots & \vdots & \vdots \ddots \vdots \\ 0 & 0 & 0 \ldots 1 \\ \ldots 1 \ldots 1 \ldots \end{pmatrix}$$

Each row of such elementary matrix except for only one contains one and only one element equal to 1 but in general case not only on the diagonal. The multiplication step corresponds in this matrix to one row only, which contains exactly two units. In addition, all these rows of the elementary matrix are different from each other. Thus, the construction of computational scheme for monomial evaluation corresponding to matrix N reduces to factorizing N into a product of a set of elementary matrices.

It follows from the foregoing that there exists a very interesting and non-trivial duality relating the problem of evaluation of m monomials in p variables and the problem of evaluation of p monomials in m variables. Indeed, if $N = N_1 \times N_2 \times \ldots \times N_{L(N)}$, where N_i are elementary matrices corresponding to steps of a minimal computational scheme, then $^t N =^t N_1 \times^t N_2 \times \ldots \times^t N_{L(N)}$. Matrices $^t N_i$ may not be elementary ones, but it is easy to see that each matrix $^t N_i$ can be represented as a product of no more than two elementary ones. Indeed, monomial substitution corresponding to this matrix can be computed using no more than two multiplications.

Then we have

Proposition 2. *Let N be an integer matrix corresponding to an evaluation of monomial set S. If all the rows of the matrix $^t N$ are different from each other, then the following inequality holds:*

$$L(N) \leq 2L(^t N). \tag{1}$$

The limiting condition for the rows of matrix $^t N$ is essential, what can be illustrated by the following example.

Example. Each computation of the monomial $y = x_1 x_2 \ldots x_k$ needs $k - 1$ multiplications while the dual task corresponding to column represents only one trivial monomial x_1^1.

Inequality (1) cannot be improved.

Let us indeed consider the computation of monomial

$$y = x_1 x_2^2 x_3^4 \ldots x_k^{2^k}.$$

The dual task is the problem of computation of a set of powers $\{x,\ x^2,\ x^4,\ \ldots x^{2^k}\}$, which evidently need $(k-1)$ multiplications.

To show that

$$L(x_1 x_2^2 x_3^4 \ldots x_k^{2^k}) = 2(k-1)$$

we consider any computational scheme for the monomial y. Obviously it contains at least one step, which is a multiplication by the variable x_1. Eliminating this step from computation we get the scheme for computation of the monomial $x_2^2 x_3^4 \ldots x_k^{2^k}$. Consequently eliminating $k-1$ steps – multiplications by variables $x_1, x_2, \ldots, x_{k-1}$ we get a scheme for computation of one power $x_k^{2^k}$. It needs no less than $(k-1)$ multiplications. We have proved that

$$L(x_1 x_2^2 x_3^4 \ldots x_k^{2^k}) \geq 2(k-1).$$

The equality follows from formula $y = ((\ldots ((x_k^2) x_{k-1}^2 \ldots) x_2^2) x_1$.

Finally, the Pippenger's exact asymptotic estimate of multiplicative complexity of evaluation of m monomials in p variables can be proved using this approch too.

Let

$$y_i = \prod_{j=1}^{p} x_j^{n_{ij}}, \quad i = 1, .., m$$

and

$$d = \max(n_{ij})_{i=1,\ldots,m}^{j=1,\ldots,p}.$$

Let us choose the radix 2^s and integer l such as $2^{ls} \geq d$. We have the representation

$$n_{ij} = \sum_{k=0}^{l} a_{ij}^k 2^{ks}.$$

To get the computational scheme with lowest asymptotic complexity we can use a representation of matrix N as a product

$$\begin{pmatrix} a_{11}^0 & a_{11}^1 & \cdots & a_{11}^l & a_{12}^0 & a_{12}^1 & \cdots & a_{12}^l & \cdots & a_{1p}^0 & a_{1p}^1 & \cdots & a_{1p}^l \\ a_{21}^0 & a_{21}^1 & \cdots & a_{21}^l & a_{22}^0 & a_{22}^1 & \cdots & a_{22}^l & \cdots & a_{2p}^0 & a_{2p}^1 & \cdots & a_{2p}^l \\ \vdots & \vdots & \ddots & \vdots & \vdots & \vdots & \ddots & \vdots & \ddots & \vdots & \vdots & \ddots & \vdots \\ a_{m1}^0 & a_{m1}^1 & \cdots & a_{m1}^l & a_{m2}^0 & a_{m2}^1 & \cdots & a_{m2}^l & \cdots & a_{mp}^0 & a_{mp}^1 & \cdots & a_{mp}^l \end{pmatrix} \times$$

$$\begin{pmatrix} 1 & 0 & \ldots & 0 \\ 2 & 0 & \ldots & 0 \\ \vdots & \vdots & & \vdots \\ 2^l & 0 & \ldots & 0 \\ 0 & 1 & \ldots & 0 \\ \vdots & \vdots & & \vdots \\ 0 & 2^l & \ldots & 0 \\ \vdots & \vdots & & \vdots \\ 0 & 0 & \ldots & 1 \\ 0 & 0 & \ldots & 2 \\ \vdots & \vdots & \vdots & \vdots \\ 0 & 0 & \ldots & 2^l \end{pmatrix}$$

if $p \leq m$ and

$$\begin{pmatrix} 1\,2\,\ldots\,2^l\,0\,0\,\ldots\,0\,\ldots\,0\,0\,\ldots\,0 \\ 0\,0\,\ldots\,0\,1\,2\,\ldots\,2^l\,\ldots\,0\,0\,\ldots\,0 \\ \vdots\,\vdots\,\ddots\,\vdots\,\vdots\,\vdots\,\ddots\,\vdots\,\ddots\,\vdots\,\vdots\,\ddots\,\vdots \\ 0\,0\,\ldots\,0\,0\,0\,\ldots\,0\,\ldots\,1\,2\,\ldots\,2^l \end{pmatrix} \times$$

$$\begin{pmatrix} a^0_{11} & a^0_{21} & \ldots & a^0_{m1} \\ a^1_{11} & a^1_{21} & \ldots & a^1_{m1} \\ \vdots & \vdots & \ldots & \vdots \\ a^l_{12} & a^l_{22} & \ldots & a^l_{m2} \\ a^0_{12} & a^0_{22} & \ldots & a^0_{m2} \\ a^1_{12} & a^1_{22} & \ldots & a^1_{m2} \\ \vdots & \vdots & \ldots & \vdots \\ a^l_{12} & a^l_{22} & \ldots & a^l_{m2} \\ \vdots & \vdots & \ldots & \vdots \\ a^0_{1p} & a^0_{2p} & \ldots & a^0_{mp} \\ a^1_{1p} & a^1_{2p} & \ldots & a^1_{mp} \\ \vdots & \vdots & \ldots & \vdots \\ a^l_{1p} & a^l_{2p} & \ldots & a^l_{mp} \end{pmatrix}$$

if $p \geq m$.

3   Conclusions

We have described an approach to monomial evaluations based on a matrix re-formulation of the problem. Any factorization of the matrix $N = N_1 N_2 \ldots N_k$ gives us a decomposition of the problem into a sequence of problems, which correspond to matrices N_i. We have considered also the relation between complexity of the problem of evaluation of a set of p monomials in m variables represented by matrix $N = N_{i,j}$, $i = 1, \ldots, m$, $j = 1, \ldots, p$ and complexity of dual problem for evaluation of a set of m monomials in p variables represented by matrix ${}^t N$.

It would also be very interesting to generalise this approach from standard monomial evaluations to noncommutative case. In particular, the most important case for many computer algebra algorithms operating with Lie polynomials is the problem of evaluation of monomial sets in free Lie algebra what leads to non-associative and anticommutative case.

The algorithms based on matrix decomposition described in the paper are implemented by author in package COMPMON for computer algebra system Maple V. The package generates straight line programs with lowest complexity for effective computing of monomial sets.

References

1. Pippenger N. On the evaluation of powers and monomials, *SIAM. J. Comput.*, v. 9, No. 2, p. 230-250, 1980.
2. Knuth D. *The Art of Programming*, vol. 2, Addison-Wesley Pub. Co., 1969.
3. Vassiliev N.N. Evaluations of sparse polynomials and the synthesis of evaluating programs. *Internat. Conf. on Comp. Algebra and Appl. Theor. Phys.*, Dubna, p. 154-159, 1984.

On the Simplification of Nonlinear DAE Systems in Analog Circuit Design

Tim Wichmann[1], Ralf Popp[2], Walter Hartong[2], and Lars Hedrich[2]

[1] Institut für Techno- und Wirtschaftsmathematik e. V.
Erwin-Schrödinger-Str, D-67663 Kaiserslautern, Germany
email: wichmann@itwm.uni-kl.de
[2] Institute of Microelectronic Systems
University of Hanover, Callinstr.34, D-30167 Hannover, Germany
email: {popp, hartong, hedrich}@ims.uni-hannover.de

Abstract. The behavior of nonlinear analog circuits is described by a set of differential algebraic equations (DAE). In this paper we present a symbolic simplification algorithm for such DAE systems which generates an approximative system. Besides the mathematical background we explain several local and global simplification techniques that are applied to the system. Each modification step is controlled by an error calculation. To achieve a maximum number of simplifications and to avoid unnecessary modifications an optimized order, the so called *ranking*, is needed. We will present two different ranking methods and will show the results on an example.

1   Introduction

In the last few years symbolic methods for analyzing the behavior of analog circuits have become more and more popular. In comparison with numerical simulations, for example with SPICE [12], which are the usual analyzing methods, symbolic techniques provide a deeper insight into the circuit's behavior. Nevertheless, symbolic results can be too large to be human-interpretable and understandable, so simplification techniques for symbolic formulas have to be applied.

Up to now, most work has been done on linear circuits and the results are quite satisfactory for this class of systems. There is a variety of different techniques (like simplification before, during, and after generation, see [4,5] for more information on this), which, for example, perform the symbolic extraction of the dominant expressions for transfer functions or poles and zeros, based on error controlled approximations. This allows the designer to gain deeper insights into the behavior of complex circuits, a numerical simulator would not be able to.

These techniques were extended and applied to nonlinear systems, e.g. mentioned in [2]. Even for quite small nonlinear circuits the describing system of equations can be very huge. The example circuit considered in Chap. 5, for example, is described by 46 equations in 46 variables. Containing only two transistors this is a very simple circuit – examples like the μA741 operational amplifier consist of 23 transistors. There are two major reasons for applying simplifications:

1. The original set of equations is too big to be human-interpretable or understandable, respectively, so one has to simplify the equations to gain insights into the behavior.
2. The numerical simulation of the original system is very time consuming; the simplification techniques allow the generation of a smaller system which can be simulated faster and behaves like the original system within the given error bound.

The simplification techniques now generate a smaller set of equations which describe the behavior of the circuit accurate within a user given error bound. To achieve 1. or 2., different strategies have to be applied – the user has to decide what he is interested in before starting the algorithm.

In this paper we present an overview of the simplification techniques for nonlinear differential algebraic systems of equations (*DAE systems*) arising in analog circuit design, as well as a new ranking algorithm for term deletion. Chapter 2 gives a short introduction of the mathematical background and introduces some notions arising in circuit design. Chapter 3 presents the simplification techniques. Two ranking algorithms are shown in Chap. 4, and Chap. 5 finally gives a small example.

2   Background

The behavior of a nonlinear analog circuit can be described mathematically by a set of ordinary differential equations f and a set of algebraic constraints g:

$$f(x(t), x'(t), y(t), u(t)\,;p) = 0 \quad \text{for all } t \tag{1}$$

$$g(x(t), y(t), u(t)\,;p) = 0 \quad \text{for all } t \ . \tag{2}$$

They originate from Kirchhoff's current and voltage laws and the circuit element characteristics. The latter can be linear equations (like $U = R \cdot I$ for linear resistances), ordinary differential equations (like $I = C \cdot U'$ for linear capacitances), nonlinear equations (like $I = I_s(e^{U/nU_T} - 1)$ for diodes), or even a set of nonlinear equations and ordinary differential equations (e.g. the Gummel-Poon model for BJT transistors). This system of equations can be set up using for example the sparse-tableau analysis (STA) or the modified nodal analysis (MNA). Symbolic analysis tools like Analog Insydes generate the equations automatically starting from a netlist based input [6].

In (1) and (2), x denotes the vector of variables $x = (U, I)$ of the internal voltages and currents, u and y denote the input and output, respectively; they all depend on the time $t \in \mathbb{R}$. We are working on single-input/single-output systems (SISO), so we have:

$$u : \mathbb{R} \to \mathbb{R} \ , \tag{3}$$

$$x : \mathbb{R} \to \mathbb{R}^k \ , \tag{4}$$

$$y : \mathbb{R} \to \mathbb{R} \ . \tag{5}$$

The dimension k of x depends on the analysis method: the modified nodal analysis, for example, yields smaller dimensions than the sparse-tableau analysis.

Besides these variables, the system contains symbolic parameters $p = (p_1, \dots, p_N)$. They represent the circuit element values, like, for example, a value R_1 of a resistor or a value V_{in} of an independent voltage source. Numerical values for these parameters have to be inserted, if the system is solved numerically. We call such a set of numerical values $(\pi_1, \dots, \pi_N) \in \mathbb{R}^N$ for the parameters p a *design point*.

Equations (1) and (2) can be combined to a symbolic nonlinear differential algebraic system of equations:

$$F(x(t), x'(t), y(t), u(t) ; p) = 0 \quad \text{for all } t \ . \tag{6}$$

See Chap. 5 for an example.

To analyze the behavior of the DAE system (6) there are several standard techniques, which are all pure numeric algorithms, thus they require a design point $\pi \in \mathbb{R}^N$ to be inserted for the symbolic parameters p. We distinguish the following techniques which are common in circuit analysis:

DC Analysis. During a DC analysis the dynamical behavior of the system is omitted, i.e., all time derivatives are set to zero, and a constant input signal $u(t) = u \in \mathbb{R}$ is applied. Then all time dependencies can be neglected, so we are interested in the output $y \in \mathbb{R}$, such that

$$F(x, 0, y, u ; \pi) = 0 \quad \text{for a } x \in \mathbb{R}^k \ . \tag{7}$$

A point $(x, u) \in \mathbb{R}^k \times \mathbb{R}$ which fulfills (7) is called *operating point*.

DC-Transfer Analysis. This method, also called *DT analysis*, performs several DC analyses for different input signals: for inputs $u_1, \dots, u_\mu \in \mathbb{R}$ one is interested in the corresponding outputs $y_1, \dots, y_\mu \in \mathbb{R}$, such that

$$F(x_i, 0, y_i, u_i ; \pi) = 0 \quad \text{for all } i \ , \tag{8}$$

for some $x_1, \dots, x_\mu \in \mathbb{R}^k$.

AC Analysis. The AC analysis is a small signal analysis. It examines the behavior in the neighborhood of an operating point; thus the system is linearized at the operating point yielding a set of linear equations. Once the system is linear, the superposition principle holds, so it can be shifted to the origin, omitting the offset given by the operating point. After Laplace-transforming the linear system and rewriting it in the frequency variable s, the transfer function H with $y(s) = H(s)u(s)$ can be computed. For different frequencies $\omega_1, \ldots, \omega_\nu \in \mathbb{R}$ the AC analysis evaluates the transfer function at the points $j\omega_i$ (where j denotes the imaginary unit as usual in electrical engineering), i.e., it calculates

$$y_i := H(j\omega_i) \quad \text{for all } i \ . \tag{9}$$

The complex values of y_i are then splitted into phase and magnitude.

If this is done for several operating points $(x_1, y_1), \ldots, (x_\mu, y_\mu)$ we speak of a *multiple AC analysis*.

Transient Analysis. This analysis method calculates the time-dependent (*transient*) behavior of the system. For a given time-dependent input signal $u : T \to \mathbb{R}$ (where T is an interval) one is interested in the output $y : T \to \mathbb{R}$, such that

$$F(x(t), x'(t), y(t), u(t)\,;\pi) = 0 \quad \text{for all } t \in T \ , \tag{10}$$

for some differentiable $x : T \to \mathbb{R}^k$.

This analysis method requires a numerical algorithm which can solve nonlinear DAE systems. An operating point (see DC analysis) can be used as starting point for a numerical DAE solver.

According to the DC and the DC-transfer analysis we introduce the following notation: if F denotes the DAE system (6), then let F_{DC} denote the projection of F which cancels the second argument:

$$F_{\mathrm{DC}}(x, y, u\,;p) := F(x, 0, y, u\,;p) \quad \text{for all } x \in \mathbb{R}^k \text{ and } y, u \in \mathbb{R} \ . \tag{11}$$

Thus F_{DC} neglects the dynamical behavior of F.

3   Simplification Techniques

To obtain a simplified system of equations, the algorithm performs several simplification techniques on (6). A *simplification* can either be an algebraic manipulation (like substitution of a variable) or a modification of the equations (like deletion of a term) which results in a new, approximative system. The latter requires a numeric simulation to determine the error caused by the modification. Algebraic manipulations are exact operations, so no error tracking is needed there.

The order in which each modification technique is applied influences the rate of simplification. At the end of this chapter we will suggest an order which turned out to be useful in our examples.

The simplification techniques can be divided into two groups: the so called *global* and *local* simplifications.

Global Simplifications. The global simplifications affect the whole DAE system in one step. They include:

1. Elimination of variables
2. Deletion of variables' time derivatives
3. Substitution of variables by constant values

In the notions of above, 1. is an algebraic manipulation which does not need an error calculation. Nevertheless it has to be taken into account that the elimination of variables might cause convergence problems of numerical solvers. Substitution of variables which occur in exponential functions, for example, can cause such problems.

The observation that some variables' dynamical behavior does not affect the output signal (e.g., they do not lie on the signal path) and others can be treated as constant (e.g., they adjust the operating point) motivates 2. and 3.

Local Simplifications. The local simplification techniques operate on single terms of one equation in (6) expanded to sum-of-products form. We apply the following local simplifications:

1. Deletion of terms
2. Substitution of terms by constant values
3. Linearization of terms

They originate from the observation that some terms of a summation participate a very small part to the whole sum and thus can be simplified or even neglected. Which techniques to apply depends on the design goal (see Chap. 1). Linearization, for example, might speed up the simulation time but might on the other hand decrease the readability.

As mentioned above, the application order of the different simplification techniques influences the rate of simplification. Just as much within one technique the application order on the different parts of the system affects the number of modifications until the error bound is reached. So an optimized order within one simplification technique is necessary for two reasons: those parts of the system should be modified first, which cause only a small error, in order to apply as many modifications as possible until the error bound is reached. Moreover the modification of parts which cause an overflow of the error should be avoided, in order to perform as less unnecessary calculations as possible.

An algorithm that predicts the influence on the error a modification step will cause is called *ranking algorithm*. The suggested order within one simplification technique is called *ranking*. After each step, performed in the ranking order, within one modification technique the influence on the output will be computed numerically, enabling us to detect wrong rankings. For that reason the design of a good ranking algorithm is a trade off between accurate ranking prediction and computational efficiency. The different modification techniques require different ranking methods; in Chap. 4 we present two of them.

After each modification of the system we perform a numerical simulation in order to calculate the influence on the output variable due to the modification. It depends on the given problem which simulation method has to be used. In most cases several different simulations will be done with all errors combined in a suitable way to the overall error. One common way is to perform a DC-transfer analysis together with a multiple AC analysis (see Chap. 2) yielding the DC and the AC error:

$$\varepsilon_{\mathrm{DC}} := \|(\widetilde{y}_1 - y_1, \ldots, \widetilde{y}_\mu - y_\mu)\| \, , \tag{12}$$

$$\varepsilon_{\mathrm{AC}} := \frac{1}{\mu} \sum_{i=1}^{\mu} \|(\widetilde{y}_{i1} - y_{i1}, \ldots, \widetilde{y}_{i\nu} - y_{i\nu})\| \, , \tag{13}$$

where y_i resp. y_{ij} denote the results of the original system and $\widetilde{y}_i$ resp. $\widetilde{y}_{ij}$ denote the results of the modified system. Note, that we do not specify which norm has to be used since this depends on the given problem, too. Both errors are afterwards combined to the overall error:

$$\varepsilon := \lambda \cdot \varepsilon_{\mathrm{DC}} + \rho \cdot \varepsilon_{\mathrm{AC}} \, . \tag{14}$$

Again the weights λ and ρ depend on the given problem.

To summarize this chapter Fig. 1 shows the general flow of the simplification algorithm. The simplification techniques are applied in the following order:

1. Elimination of variables
2. Deletion of variables' time derivatives
3. Substitution of variables by constant values
4. Deletion of terms
5. Substitution of terms by constant values
6. Linearization of terms
7. Elimination of variables

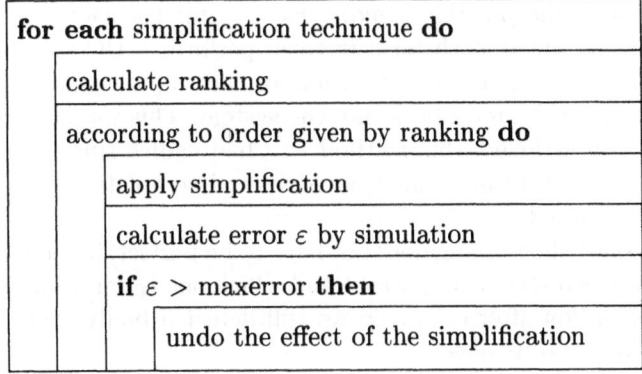

Fig. 1. The simplification algorithm

4   Ranking Methods for Local Simplifications

4.1   Substitution by Constant Values

The ranking algorithm for the substitution of terms by constant values uses the standard deviation as measurement for the influence. It is optimized for applications where the error is calculated via a DC-transfer analysis. If the standard deviation is small the term is assumed to be constant and thus can be substituted by a numerical value. The mean value is used as substitution value.

Let δ be the current term to be substituted and let (x_i, u_i) be the operating points according to the inputs $u_1, \ldots, u_\mu \in \mathbb{R}$. Substituting the values of the operating points for the variables occuring in δ as well as a design point π we calculate the mean value and the standard deviation:

$$m := \frac{1}{\mu} \sum \delta(x_i, u_i) \ , \tag{15}$$

$$\sigma := \left(\sum \left(\delta(x_i, u_i) - m \right)^2 \right)^{1/2} \tag{16}$$

Then terms are sorted with increasing standard deviation as ranking and are substituted be their mean value until the error bound is reached.

4.2   Term Deletion

The ranking algorithm for term deletion we will now present is designed for applications where the error calculation is based on a DC-transfer and a multiple AC analysis. Thus the algorithm consists of two parts which try to predict the influence on the DC-transfer as well as on the AC behavior.

DC Ranking. One possible ranking method for the DC influence would
be the following: delete each term in turn, perform a DC-transfer analysis,
i.e., perform a complete newton iteration for each input value, determine the
error and re-insert the term back into the system. This would yield a perfect
ranking, but nevertheless this method is a bad choice since it is very time
consuming: for each term in the system several complete newton iterations
have to be computed.

As mentioned the ranking does not have to be perfect, it should just give a
good idea of which term is important and which one is not. Since we perform
an error calculation after each step we will detect a badly ranked term and
will be able to undo its effect.

The idea of our new ranking method is to calculate just the first step of
a newton iteration and to use the step size as the influence prediction. For
this let F be the DAE system (6) and let $\widetilde{F}$ be the system which originates
from F by deletion of one term in one equation. Let $u \in \mathbb{R}$ and let (x^*, y^*)
be the corresponding operating point, i.e., $F_{DC}(x^*, y^*, u; \pi) = 0$. Note, that
we again inserted the design point here. In general (x^*, y^*) is no operating
point of $\widetilde{F}$ to the input u any more.

Now we perform the first step of a newton iteration on $\widetilde{F}_{DC}$ starting
in (x^*, y^*) with the input u applied:

$$(x^{(1)}, y^{(1)}) := (x^*, y^*) - J_{\widetilde{F}_{DC}}^{-1}(x^*, y^*, u; \pi) \cdot \widetilde{F}_{DC}(x^*, y^*, u; \pi) , \qquad (17)$$

where $J_{\widetilde{F}_{DC}}$ denotes the Jacobian of $\widetilde{F}_{DC}$ with respect to x and y. Then we
calculate the step size:

$$\begin{aligned} \Delta x :&= \left\| (x^*, y^*) - (x^{(1)}, y^{(1)}) \right\| \\ &= \left\| J_{\widetilde{F}_{DC}}^{-1}(x^*, y^*, u; \pi) \cdot \widetilde{F}_{DC}(x^*, y^*, u; \pi) \right\| . \end{aligned} \qquad (18)$$

The ranking is based upon the following assumption:

*If the deletion of a term causes only a small deviation
of the solution (x^*, y^*), then also Δx is small.*

It is easy to construct examples where this assumption fails and errors of first
and second kind occur. But keep in mind that the ranking method is just a
predictor of influences; since we perform error checking we will detect such
errors. Our experiments showed that this assumption holds in most cases for
real world problems – errors of first and second kind do not occur very often.

This procedure is now applied to the DC transfer analysis. Let $u_1, \ldots ,$
$u_\mu \in \mathbb{R}$ be the input signals. For each u_i let (x_i^*, y_i^*) be the corresponding
operating point of F. Then let Δx_i denote the step sizes calculated as above.
They are combined to the overall DC error prediction for term deletion:

$$\varepsilon_{DC} := \| (\Delta x_1, \ldots, \Delta x_\mu) \| . \qquad (19)$$

The calculation of the ranking is quite fast compared to the complete newton iteration. Using the Sherman-Morisson formula [7] it can even be made faster. As above let $F = (F_1, \ldots, F_n)^T$ be the DAE system (6) and let $\widetilde{F} = (\widetilde{F}_1, \ldots, \widetilde{F}_n)^T$ be the DAE system which originates from F by deletion of the term δ in equation l, i.e.,

$$\widetilde{F}_i = F_i \qquad \text{for } i \neq l \ , \tag{20}$$
$$\widetilde{F}_l = F_l - \delta \ . \tag{21}$$

Now let us compare the Jacobians of F and $\widetilde{F}$. There holds:

$$J_{\widetilde{F}}^{(i)} = J_F^{(i)} \qquad \text{for } i \neq l \ , \tag{22}$$
$$J_{\widetilde{F}}^{(l)} = J_F^{(l)} - \text{grad}_{(x,y)}\delta \ , \tag{23}$$

Where the index $^{(i)}$ denotes the i-th row of a matrix. With $u := e_l$ and $v := -\text{grad}_{(x,y)}\delta$ the difference of both Jacobians can be written as:

$$J_{\widetilde{F}} = J_F + uv^T \ . \tag{24}$$

Under this circumstances the Sherman-Morisson theorem can be applied:

Theorem 1 (Sherman-Morisson). *Let $A \in \mathbb{C}^{n \times n}$ regular and let u, $v \in \mathbb{C}^n$. Finally let $\widetilde{A} := A + uv^T$. Then there holds:*

i) $\widetilde{A}$ is regular if and only if $\quad 1 + v^T A^{-1} u \neq 0$.
ii) If $\widetilde{A}$ is regular, then

$$\widetilde{A}^{-1} = A^{-1} + \Delta^{-1} \ , \tag{25}$$

where

$$\Delta^{-1} := -\frac{1}{1 + v^T A^{-1} u} A^{-1} u v^T A^{-1} \ . \tag{26}$$

Proof. See [14].

This yields the following formula (cf. (18)):

$$\Delta x = \|(J_F^{-1} - (1 + v^T J_F^{-1} e_l)^{-1} J_F^{-1} e_l v^T J_F^{-1}) \cdot \delta e_l\| \ . \tag{27}$$

Note that $\widetilde{F} = F - \delta e_l$ and so

$$\widetilde{F}_{\text{DC}}(x^*, y^*, u\,; \pi) = F_{\text{DC}}(x^*, y^*, u\,; \pi) - \delta e_l = -\delta e_l \ , \tag{28}$$

since (x^*, y^*) is an operating point of F.

Using the Sherman-Morisson formula there is no need to calculate the inverse Jacobian of $\widetilde{F}$ for each term. Instead it suffices to calculate the inverse Jacobian of F once and to use the above formula for each term.

AC Ranking. For the AC ranking the system F is linearized and Laplace-transformed yielding the linear system F_{lin} in the frequency variable s. After deleting one term in F, we linearize and Laplace-transform as above and obtain the approximate linear system $\widetilde{F}_{\text{lin}}$. For a specific frequency s let (x^*, y^*) and $(\widetilde{x}, \widetilde{y})$ denote the solution of F_{lin} and $\widetilde{F}_{\text{lin}}$, respectively. Note, that the solutions can exactly be computed in one step, no numerical iteration is necessary here, since we work on linear systems. Then the error is given by

$$\Delta x = \|(x^*, y^*) - (\widetilde{x}, \widetilde{y})\| \ . \tag{29}$$

Again we apply this procedure to a multiple AC analysis, that is, the system is linearized in several operating points $(x_1, y_1), \ldots, (x_\mu, y_\mu)$ and for each linearization the error Δx_{ik} is computed at different frequency points $j\omega_1$, $\ldots, j\omega_\nu$. All errors are afterwards combined to the overall AC error a term deletion causes:

$$\varepsilon_{\text{AC}} := \left\| \left(\|(\Delta x_{11}, \ldots, \Delta x_{1\nu})\|, \ldots, \|(\Delta x_{\mu 1}, \ldots, \Delta x_{\mu\nu})\| \right) \right\| \ . \tag{30}$$

Finally both errors are combined yielding the total predicted error caused by a term deletion:

$$\varepsilon = \lambda \cdot \varepsilon_{\text{DC}} + \rho \cdot \varepsilon_{\text{AC}} \ . \tag{31}$$

Terms are sorted with increasing values of ε as ranking.

5   Example

Figure 2 shows the schematic of a simple RTL (resistor transistor logic) circuit. It consists of two bipolar junction transistors and four resistors. The independent voltage source V_{CC} provides the power supply. The input signal is given by V_{in}, the output voltage is measured at node *out*. The transistors are modeled using the Gummel-Poon equations (see [9]). The designpoint is given by the following numerical values:

$$V_{\text{CC}} = 5\,\text{V}, \ R_{\text{B1}} = 10^4\,\Omega, \ R_{\text{B2}} = 10^4\,\Omega, \ R_{\text{C1}} = 10^3\,\Omega, \ R_{\text{C2}} = 10^3\,\Omega \ . \tag{32}$$

Furthermore we will focus on the DC behavior of the circuit. Thus we choose a DC-transfer analysis method with the following input values:

$$V_{\text{in}} \in \{ -2\,, -1.5, -1, -0.5, 0, 0.5, 0.75, 1, 1.1, 1.2, 1.3,$$
$$1.4\,, 1.6, 1.8, 2, 2.2\} \ . \tag{33}$$

The result of a DC-transfer analysis of the original system with this input values is shown in Fig. 3.

Using the modified nodal analysis the describing DAE system consists of 46 equations in 46 variables with a total number of 144 terms. Figure 4 gives

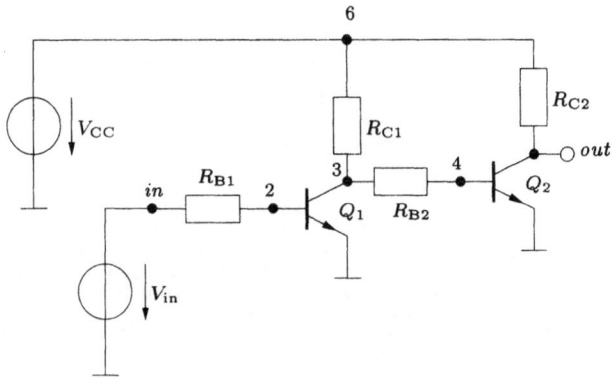

Fig. 2. Schematics of the RTL circuit

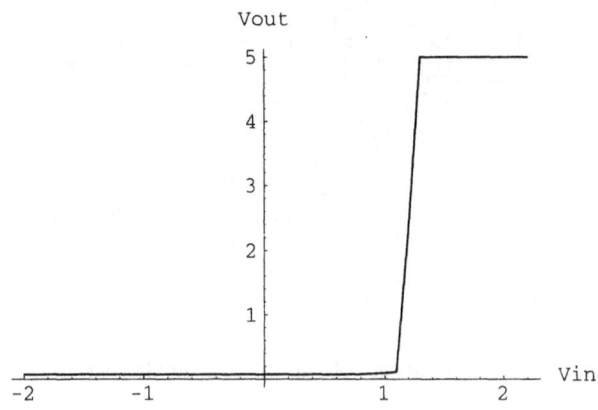

Fig. 3. DC-transfer plot of the original system

an impression of the complexity of this system. It is printed in Mathematica output format [13].

This system of equations is far too complex to be interpretable. The simplification algorithm is now applied to obtain a simplified system having design goal 1. in mind (see Chap. 1).

The measurement of the maximal deviation is used as the error function:

$$\varepsilon_{DC} = \max_{i=1,\dots,16} (|y_i - \widetilde{y}_i|) \ . \tag{34}$$

The simplifications are performed until the maximal error $\varepsilon_{max} = 0.02$ is reached. The resulting DAE system consists of four equations in four variables with a total number of 17 terms (Fig. 5). It can be seen from Figure 6 that the simplified system describes the DC behavior very well. The solid line shows the DC-transfer behavior of the original system, the dots show the

$$\{\text{I\$BC\$Q1[t]} + \text{I\$BE\$Q1[t]} + \frac{\text{V\$2[t]} - \text{V\$input[t]}}{\text{RB1}} == 0,$$

$$-\text{I\$BC\$Q1[t]} + \text{I\$CS\$Q1[t]} + \frac{\text{V\$3[t]} - \text{V\$4[t]}}{\text{RB2}} + \frac{\text{V\$3[t]} - \text{V\$6[t]}}{\text{RC1}} == 0,$$

$$\text{I\$BC\$Q2[t]} + \text{I\$BE\$Q2[t]} + \frac{-\text{V\$3[t]} + \text{V\$4[t]}}{\text{RB2}} == 0,$$

$$\text{I\$VCC[t]} + \frac{-\text{V\$3[t]} + \text{V\$6[t]}}{\text{RC1}} + \frac{\text{V\$6[t]} - \text{V\$output[t]}}{\text{RC2}} == 0,$$

$$\text{I\$VIN[t]} + \frac{-\text{V\$2[t]} + \text{V\$input[t]}}{\text{RB1}} == 0,$$

$$-\text{I\$BC\$Q2[t]} + \text{I\$CS\$Q2[t]} + \frac{-\text{V\$6[t]} + \text{V\$output[t]}}{\text{RC2}} == 0,\ \text{V\$6[t]} == \text{VCC},\ \text{V\$input[t]} == \text{VIN},$$

I\$CS\$Q1[t] == CCS\$Q1[t] VCS\$Q1′[t], VCS\$Q1[t] == V\$3[t], V\$2[t] - V\$3[t] ==
VBC\$Q1[t] + RBB\$Q1[t] (IB\$Q1[t] + CBC\$Q1[t] VBC\$Q1′[t] + CBE\$Q1[t] VBE\$Q1′[t]),
V\$2[t] == VBE\$Q1[t] + RBB\$Q1[t] (IB\$Q1[t] + CBC\$Q1[t] VBC\$Q1′[t] + CBE\$Q1[t] VBE\$Q1′[t]),
V\$2[t] - V\$3[t] == VBX\$Q1[t], IB\$Q1[t] == I\$BC\$Q1[t] +
    I\$BE\$Q1[t] - CBC\$Q1[t] VBC\$Q1′[t] - CBE\$Q1[t] VBE\$Q1′[t] - CJX\$Q1[t] VBX\$Q1′[t],
IC\$Q1[t] == -I\$BC\$Q1[t] + CJX\$Q1[t] VBX\$Q1′[t] - CCS\$Q1[t] VCS\$Q1′[t],
ICC\$Q1[t] == $1. \times 10^{-16}$ ($-1 + \text{E}^{38.6473\ \text{VBE\$Q1[t]}}$),
3. IFX\$Q1[t] == 3. ICC\$Q1[t], IFXS\$Q1[t] == IFX\$Q1′[t],
0 == -qb\$Q1[t] RBB\$Q1[t], z\$Q1[t] == 0, qb\$Q1[t] == 1., IC\$Q1[t] qb\$Q1[t] ==
    $1. \times 10^{-16}$ ($-\text{E}^{38.6473\ \text{VBC\$Q1[t]}} + \text{E}^{38.6473\ \text{VBE\$Q1[t]}} - 1.\ (-1. + \text{E}^{38.6473\ \text{VBC\$Q1[t]}})\ \text{qb\$Q1[t]}$) +
    $1. \times 10^{-12}$ ($-(1. + 1.\ \text{qb\$Q1[t]})\ \text{VBC\$Q1[t]} + \text{VBE\$Q1[t]}$),
IB\$Q1[t] == $1. \times 10^{-16}$ (1. ($-1. + \text{E}^{38.6473\ \text{VBC\$Q1[t]}}$) + 0.01 ($-1. + \text{E}^{38.6473\ \text{VBE\$Q1[t]}}$)) +
    $1. \times 10^{-12}$ (1. VBC\$Q1[t] + 0.01 VBE\$Q1[t]),
CBE\$Q1[t] == 0, CBC\$Q1[t] == 0, CCS\$Q1[t] == 0, CJX\$Q1[t] == 0,
I\$CS\$Q2[t] == CCS\$Q2[t] VCS\$Q2′[t], VCS\$Q2[t] == V\$output[t], V\$4[t] - V\$output[t] ==
VBC\$Q2[t] + RBB\$Q2[t] (IB\$Q2[t] + CBC\$Q2[t] VBC\$Q2′[t] + CBE\$Q2[t] VBE\$Q2′[t]),
V\$4[t] == VBE\$Q2[t] + RBB\$Q2[t] (IB\$Q2[t] + CBC\$Q2[t] VBC\$Q2′[t] + CBE\$Q2[t] VBE\$Q2′[t]),
V\$4[t] - V\$output[t] == VBX\$Q2[t], IB\$Q2[t] == I\$BC\$Q2[t] +
    I\$BE\$Q2[t] - CBC\$Q2[t] VBC\$Q2′[t] - CBE\$Q2[t] VBE\$Q2′[t] - CJX\$Q2[t] VBX\$Q2′[t],
IC\$Q2[t] == -I\$BC\$Q2[t] + CJX\$Q2[t] VBX\$Q2′[t] - CCS\$Q2[t] VCS\$Q2′[t],
ICC\$Q2[t] == $1. \times 10^{-16}$ ($-1 + \text{E}^{38.6473\ \text{VBE\$Q2[t]}}$),
3. IFX\$Q2[t] == 3. ICC\$Q2[t], IFXS\$Q2[t] == IFX\$Q2′[t],
0 == -qb\$Q2[t] RBB\$Q2[t], z\$Q2[t] == 0, qb\$Q2[t] == 1., IC\$Q2[t] qb\$Q2[t] ==
    $1. \times 10^{-16}$ ($-\text{E}^{38.6473\ \text{VBC\$Q2[t]}} + \text{E}^{38.6473\ \text{VBE\$Q2[t]}} - 1.\ (-1. + \text{E}^{38.6473\ \text{VBC\$Q2[t]}})\ \text{qb\$Q2[t]}$) +
    $1. \times 10^{-12}$ ($-(1. + 1.\ \text{qb\$Q2[t]})\ \text{VBC\$Q2[t]} + \text{VBE\$Q2[t]}$),
IB\$Q2[t] == $1. \times 10^{-16}$ (1. ($-1. + \text{E}^{38.6473\ \text{VBC\$Q2[t]}}$) + 0.01 ($-1. + \text{E}^{38.6473\ \text{VBE\$Q2[t]}}$)) +
    $1. \times 10^{-12}$ (1. VBC\$Q2[t] + 0.01 VBE\$Q2[t]), CBE\$Q2[t] == 0,
CBC\$Q2[t] == 0, CCS\$Q2[t] == 0, CJX\$Q2[t] == 0}

Fig. 4. Equations of the original DAE system

corresponding values of the simplified system. To see the difference of the output in both systems the error $|y_i - \tilde{y}_i|$ is plotted in Fig. 7.

$$\{-1.96065 \times 10^{60}\ \text{E}^{-\frac{38.6473\ \text{RB2 RC1 IC\$Q1[t]}}{\text{RB2+RC1}} + 38.6473\ \text{VBC\$Q1[t]}} + 1.\ \text{IC\$Q1[t]} == 0,$$

$$-1. \times 10^{-16}\ \text{E}^{38.6473\ \text{VBC\$Q1[t]}} - 1.96065 \times 10^{58}\ \text{E}^{-\frac{38.6473\ \text{RB2 RC1 IC\$Q1[t]}}{\text{RB2+RC1}} + 38.6473\ \text{VBC\$Q1[t]}} -$$
$$\frac{4.54545}{\text{RB1}} + \frac{\text{VIN}}{\text{RB1}} + \frac{1.\ \text{RB2 RC1 IC\$Q1[t]}}{\text{RB1 (RB2 + RC1)}} - \frac{1.\ \text{VBC\$Q1[t]}}{\text{RB1}} == 0,$$

$$0.005 - 1. \times 10^{-16}\ \text{E}^{38.6473\ \text{VBC\$Q2[t]} + 38.6473\ \text{V\$output[t]}} - \frac{1.\ \text{V\$output[t]}}{\text{RC2}} == 0,$$

$$0.000454545 - 1. \times 10^{-16}\ \text{E}^{38.6473\ \text{VBC\$Q2[t]}} -$$
$$1. \times 10^{-18}\ \text{E}^{38.6473\ \text{VBC\$Q2[t]} + 38.6473\ \text{V\$output[t]}} - \frac{\text{RC1 IC\$Q1[t]}}{\text{RB2 + RC1}} - \frac{\text{VBC\$Q2[t]}}{\text{RB2 + RC1}} - \frac{\text{V\$output[t]}}{\text{RB2 + RC1}} == 0\}$$

Fig. 5. Equations of the simplified DAE system

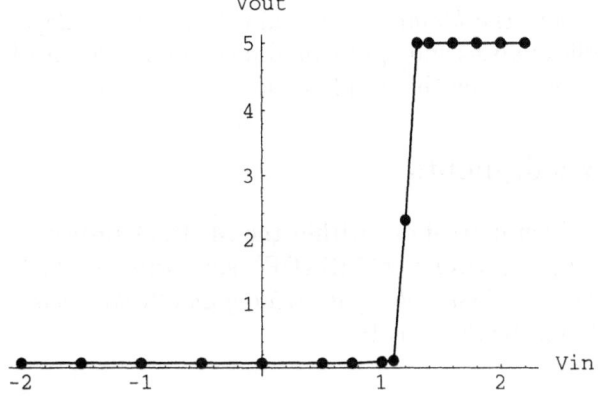

Fig. 6. DC-transfer plot of the original (solid) and the simplified system (dots)

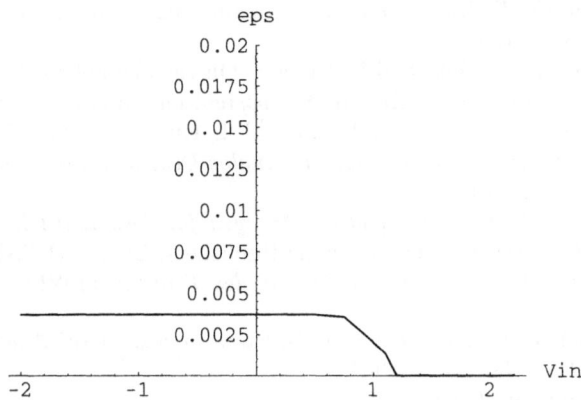

Fig. 7. Plot of the error $|y_i - \widetilde{y}_i|$

6   Conclusions

We presented a symbolic simplification algorithm for nonlinear DAE systems describing analog circuits. Based on several error controlled simplification techniques an approximated DAE system is generated which is accurate within the given error bound. The size of the resulting system is very small compared to the original one: in the presented example the system is decreased by one order of magnitude. The algorithm has practical applications in design, analysis, and modeling of analog electronic circuits.

The simplification algorithm has been implemented at IMS [8] within the Computer Algebra system *Maple V.*

ITWM develops the *Mathematica* Add-on package *Analog Insydes*, a toolbox for symbolic analysis and approximation of analog circuits [1]. The extension of *Analog Insydes* by the simplification algorithm is under construction.

7   Acknowledgments

This work has been carried out within the MEDEA project A409 "Systematic Analog Design Environment" (SADE), supported by the German *Ministerium für Bildung, Wissenschaft, Forschung und Technologie* under contract no. 01M3037F and by Siemens HL.

References

1. Analog Insydes Homepage. http://www.itwm.uni-kl.de/as/products/ai/
2. C. Borchers. The symbolic behavioral model generation of nonlinear analog circuits. In *IEEE Transactions on Circuits and Systems*, volume 45, pages 1362–1371, Oct. 1998.
3. C. Borchers, R. Sommer, and E. Hennig. On the symbolic calculation of nonlinear circuits. In *Proc. IEEE Int. Symposium on Circuits and Systems*, 1996.
4. F. V. Fernández, A. Rodríguez Vázquez, J. L. Huertas, and G. Gielen. *Symbolic Analysis Techniques – Applications to Analog Design Automation*. IEEE Press, New York (USA), 1998.
5. G. Gielen and W. Sansen. *Symbolic Analysis for Automated Design of Analog Integrated Circuits*. Kluwer Academic Publishers, Boston (USA), 1991.
6. E. Hennig and T. Halfmann. *Analog Insydes Tutorial*. ITWM, Kaiserslautern, 1998.
7. A. S. Householder. *The Theory of Matrices in Numerical Analysis*. Blaisdell Publishing Co., New York, 1964.
8. IMS: Research and Contact.
   http://www.ims.uni-hannover.de/ims.public.eng/research/analog.html
9. G. Massobrio and P. Antognetti. *Semiconductor Device Modeling with SPICE*. McGraw-Hill, Inc., second edition, 1993.
10. R. Popp, W. Hartong, L. Hedrich, and E. Barke. Error estimation on symbolic behavioral models of nonlinear analog circuits. In *Proc. Fifth International Workshop on Symbolic Methods and Applications in Circuit Design (SMACD '98)*, Kaiserslautern, 1998.
11. R. Sommer, E. Hennig, G. Dröge, and E. H. Horneber. Equation-based symbolic approximation by matrix reduction with quantitative error prediction. *Alta Frequenza Rivista di Elektronica*, 1(6):29–37, Dec. 1993.
12. A. Vladimirescu, K. Zhang, A. R. Newton, D. O. Pederson, and A. Sangiovanni-Vincentelli. *SPICE Version 2G User's Guide*. Department of Electrical Engineering and Computer Sciences, University of California, Berkeley, August 1981.
13. S. Wolfram. *The Mathematica Book*. Wolfram Media/Cambridge University Press, 3rd edition, 1996.
14. G. Zielke. Inversion of modified symmetric matrices. *J. Assoc. Computing Machinery*, 15(3):402–408, July 1968.

Symbolic Analysis of Computational Algorithms with SYDNA

Radu Zapotinschi

"Babeş-Bolyai" University, Department of Applied Mathematics,
Kogălniceanu 1, RO-3400 Cluj-Napoca, Romania

Abstract. The paper presents SYDNA (SYmbolic-Driven Numerical Analysis), a computer algebra library dedicated to the analysis and synthesis of numerical algorithms. The system provides a framework for expressing different parts of complex problem solving procedures. Numerical algorithms are specified using a higher-order functor system, which maximizes code reusability. Efficient implementations are generated by fully instantiating the functors at compile-time, optimizing specifications through program transformations and code generation.

1 Introduction

Several aspects of the analysis and implementation of numerical algorithms can be automated or aided by using computer algebra systems (CAS). This paper presents a symbolic computation library built on top of the CAS MuPAD [8] and devoted to supporting the process of numerical modeling at all its stages.

Besides Computer Algebra (CA) routines, MuPAD has a powerful programming language based on an extendable hierarchy of higher-order modules. One particularly useful feature of this language is the fact that it allows manipulating all its elements (including statements and modules) as first-order objects.

This CA-programming environment permitted us to base the development of our library on advanced design strategies. Thus, the design solutions provided by SYDNA include:

- it builds a hierarchy of parameterized classes (functors) that encapsulate the main types of objects from the computational universe, (i.e., types of mathematical problems and classes of numerical algorithms), and most importantly, the relations between them,
- uses this hierarchy to specify a database of generic algorithms for differential and inverse problems (discretization methods, linearization procedure, matrix solvers),
- develops a code rewrite system and a set of program transformations that are able to combine and to optimize together the specifications,
- implements a code generator based on the transformational system, which converts the computer algebra specifications into high level programming language code, thus eliminating overheads,

– allows the users to introduce scenarios, specifying the overall structure of their program as well as the main module.

In the next section we describe the method of higher-order program specifications on which the whole system is based. In section 3 the problem of efficient implementation of the specifications is discussed. Programs that are in some respects similar to SYDNA are reviewed in section 4. A typical application of SYDNA is sketched in section 5.

2   The Hierarchy of Functors

The field of generic programming is divided as it concerns the names of its central concepts. A module that is parameterized by another module may be called functor, parameterized domain or generic package. The MuPAD language offers the possibility to implement functors through its library package Domains ([5]).

In this section we present the principles on which the design of our higher-order functor system stands. As mentioned above, we propose a hierarchy of MuPAD domains and categories that intends to provide a natural decomposition of the computational problem into partial tasks that can be addressed separately. These domains constitute the skeleton on which a database of numerical algorithms is built. Due to their generic nature, the domains are highly reusable (e.g., the same discretization method can be used to solve problems having different mathematical natures, such as differential equations and optimization problems).

Probably the most challenging problem in designing such a hierarchy is to correctly model the relationships between different classes of computational objects. The types of relations between the domains/categories of our hierarchy are inheritance, containment and functor-arguments relation. Thus, the design problem is which of these types of relations represents better the relation that exists between two classes of mathematical objects. Two trivial examples that illustrate this problem: the domain of systems of ordinary differential equations must contain the domains representing the equations; the domain of partial differential equations is a descendant of the category of differential equations.

Besides the other two relations, which are treated in the usual object-oriented manner, the relation functor-arguments or (Domain-arguments) has to be used to define a generic algorithm. A domain implements procedures that perform computations with objects whose nature is not known, but may be subjected to constraints. For instance SYDNA::FiniteDifference1 domain has an argument which can be any domain from SYDNA hierarchy that has the SYDNA::AxFunctionalProblem axiom.

The domain with the most important function is SYDNA::SolveProblem; it combines problems, dicrete geometries, discretization methods, matrix algorithms and for all valid combinations it is able to generate the program specification that will be used in code generation.

The class of mathematical problems has to be refined by this hierarchy, too. This thing is necessary because we have to introduce constraints on the functor-arguments relation. Indeed, not all algorithms fit all categories of problems. For instance, Runge-Kutta integrators cannot be used to advance an IBVP, although many discretization methods that can be applied to both IBVPs and IVPs.

The inconvenience of having a strict classification of equations is attenuated by the fact that SYDNA defines "intelligent" interface functions, such as `SYDNA::IDifEqProb` (general differential equation problem) or `SYDNA::IDifEigProb` (general differential eigenfunction problem) that are able to automatically classify problems, provided they are fed with data in the format they expect.

In the present version of the program the most elaborate part of the hierarchy is the part that refers to the discretization procedure.

From a mathematical perspective, a discretization is a method that approximates a problem defined on an infinite-dimensional space (i.e., a space of functions) with a similar problem defined on a finite-dimensional vector space. From a computational perspective, the discretization is a procedure that takes a problem whose unknown is a function and returns a sequence of equations whose unknowns are the values of the function on a finite sample of its domain. For each discretization method, the process of deriving the form of the discrete equations from the form of the functional equations is a matter of algebraic manipulation.

The specific implementation of the same discretization method may vary substantially with the nature of the problem it addresses. However, in SYDNA one is allowed and encouraged to specify algorithms in their most general setting and then to tailor optimized codes through program transformations. Therefore, we base the discretization system on a mathematical approach, considering these methods as abstract operators, which map a space of functions into a finite-dimensional space. Thus, these methods may be specified in an abstract manner, disregarding the nature of the problem they solve and even disregarding many specific aspects of their definition.

The discretizations that are actually implemented or in an advanced stage of development are finite-differences, spectral methods and spline function-based methods.

Differential and integral problems may be specified in MuPAD using two new operators, `Diff` and `Int`, the lazy-evaluated derivative and antiderivative/definite integral. They do not assume all identifiers are constants; furthermore `Diff` produces a prettier output than the standard library function `diff`.

3   Generating Implementations

It is important that the generic setting of our system does not imply any run-time overheads. This is possible because all functors are instantiated at compile-time and the implementations will be optimized by the transformational system, which takes into account both problem-specific and method-specific information.

SYDNA's tools used to generate an efficient implementation from the generic MuPAD specifications are TransPAD, the transformational system and CodePAD, the code generator.

3.1   TransPAD

TransPAD, the transformational system performs the following tasks:

- preprocessing, i.e., combining different parts of the program and performing static evaluation
- overall optimization of the code (e.g., sparse matrix solvers whose optimization depends on both the problem and the discretization method)
- constitutes the base of the code generator (which for the present status of the project can be targeted only to scalar architectures)

TransPAD is essentially an extended code rewrite system. Its central concept is the pattern; patterns have attributes that can specify actions to be performed when the pattern was matched, supplemental conditions, local variables, etc. Among these attributes the essential one is the transform, which specifies the replacement of the expression matched by the pattern. Patterns may be coupled to produce complex transformations.

An interesting feature of TransPAD is the fact that it works itself as a code generator. In contrast with usual rewrite systems, which compile a transform to a data-structure, the result of pattern compilation in TransPAD is a MuPAD procedure, tailored for the given pattern. This way, most of the overheads due to accessing the internal pattern structure are eliminated. Nevertheless, TransPAD transformations are not as fast as those produced by systems that have kernel support for the transformational system. This thing is evident especially when permutations have to be applied to orderless expressions.

3.2   CodePAD

At the final stage of the development, the specifications no longer contain symbolic manipulation procedures; they can be translated to a high level programming language. Since the overheads introduced by the CAS are usually unacceptable, code generation is required at this moment.

The main features of CodePAD are:

- a static evaluation capability, based on explicit declaration of variables that may by statically evaluated; by this, code-synthesis directives may coexist with run-time statements in the same specification,
- some knowledge on C standard library functions; especially mathematical functions and input routines are correctly translated from MuPAD to C,
- MuPAD - C - MuPAD double code generation for data output. A Mu-PAD specification of the form `syplot2d(y,"filename.mu",...)` will be translated into a complex C procedure that, at its turn, will generate at run-time a MuPAD source-file which displays the graphic of the vector y. By this facility, the numerical results produced by the generated code may return to MuPAD for postprocessing.

Static evaluation is an extremely important feature of CodePAD. In fact, the typical use of the system consists in writing a CodePAD specification that uses the SYDNA library function calls that are evaluated statically. Therefore, the general structure of the generated program can be specified independently from the structure of SYDNA-generated code. This allows users to clearly specify the goals of the computation and to address physical intricacies that cannot be included in SYDNA's hierarchy.

In the present status of the program, CodePAD can generate only C source code and only for sequential computer architectures. The code generation procedure consists in transforming the MuPAD specifications into a sequence of unevaluated MuPAD function calls. The evaluation of this sequence produces the target source code as a side effect.

3.3 Sparse Matrices

The typical example of code optimization is the derivation of the storage for sparse matrices resulting from the discretization of a boundary value problem (BVP). The structure of the matrix is determined by three factors: the discretization method, the discrete geometry and the actual problem (partial differential equation, eigenvalue problem or optimization). It is important to note that in solving BVPs the discretization matrix is a by-product of the problem-solving process. Indeed, the matrix is neither a part of the input, or of the output of the problem. Of course, at each linearization step, it is computed from the equation parameters and the previous approximation and it determines the improved solution of the problem. Therefore, the actual data-structure used to represent the matrix may be transformed to any other data-structure as long as the code operates the same computations on the new data. The actual data-structure used to store the non-zero elements of the matrix is called primary store.

For sequential computers, the optimal data type used as a primary store is, of course, the vector. The typical approach used to allow the matrix algorithms to work with the primary store is to create another data-structure called secondary store, which translates the references to matrix elements into references to the new structure. In simple cases, the role of the secondary store can be taken by a function.

For the cases when the sparsity structure of the matrix is fixed at compile-time, the approach used by SYDNA is different. In these cases, TransPAD is used to translate the whole matrix algorithm preserving its semantics but changing its data representation. The specific form of these transformations is derived at compile-time from the actual structure of the matrix. At the same time, the code that updates the matrix values at each linearization step is transformed too, in the same fashion.

4   Related Work

It is beyond the purpose of this paper to present a complete overview of recent work in the fields of computational science our system relies on. However, we intend to review a number of systems that inspired the work described in this paper and to present certain projects that address the same problems and share the same design principles with SYDNA.

4.1   Generic Programming in Computer Algebra and Computational Mathematics

The first widespread programming language that offered some generic facilities was Ada [2]; however, the language that had the most important impact on the field of generic programming is Standard ML [14]. As it concerns general-purpose computer algebra systems, the concept was adopted by Scratchpad II, the late version of the actual AXIOM [12] system. Another computer algebra system based on a domain hierarchy is MuPAD [5]. Although Maple is not built around this idea, it also implements the package Domains [10], which allows users to build generic domains.

In the field of Computational Science generic programming has not penetrated especially to the fact that genericity usually implies run-time overheads. However, this inefficiency can be eliminated if the functors used in a specification language can be fully instantiated at compile-time. This is the case of code-generators as SYDNA. A promising framework for generic programming in Computational Mathematics is provided by the HPGP [15] project.

4.2   Problem Solving Environments

Being a "system that provides all the computational facilities necessary to solve a target class of problems" [9], SYDNA can be regarded as a Problem Solving Environment (PSE). Indeed, there exist several PSEs that are in many respects similar to SYDNA.

An interesting system dedicated to solving partial differential equations (PDEs) through code generation is CTADEL [11]. It has been successfully applied to compute dynamic three-dimensional atmospheric models. The efficiency of the code seems to be the main concern of this project; the system is able to include non-trivial problem-dependent information in the process of code generation.

Another fine PDE solver based on a flexible design is UG [3]. It is devoted to the implementation of multigrid methods on unstructured meshes. The system allows the code to be targeted to different hardware platforms. Furthermore, the discretization method can be changed without affecting the functionality of the system.

There are important design differences between SYDNA and these computational environments devoted to solving PDEs. Unlike the majority of PSEs, our system is oriented to the algorithm developers in the same measure as it is addressed to the end-users. SYDNA provides a framework that is capable to integrate the actions at all the levels of a problem-solving task, while for the majority of PSEs, the specification of new algorithms and implementations is restricted to the original development team. Therefore, generic programming and other reuse techniques were not considered, as it is the case with SYDNA.

One particular PSE that excels through its object-oriented structure, its integration with a Computer Algebra System and its openness is SciNapse [1]. Developed in Mathematica, SciNapse enables the code generation process with a wide range of algebraic and symbolic manipulation techniques. The template system conjugated with the possibility to express constraints creates a generic programming environment that is equivalent to the functor system of SYDNA, except for the possibility to express higher-order algorithms. SYDNA's discretization management is more elaborate than SciNapse's. However, the algorithm database of SciNapse is more consistent and it is enhanced by a decision-support system that is not implemented in SYDNA.

At the same time, we have to mention that, compared to all mentioned PSEs, SYDNA is in a preliminary status. The most important features the SYDNA misses yet are a graphical input interface and the possibility to generate code for parallel architectures.

4.3 Transformational Systems and Code Generators

The design of TransPAD was influenced by the design of the following transformational systems:

- Mathematica transformation rules [17],
- the TAMPR transformational system as described by Fitzpatrick [7],
- the transforms of the POLYA programming language [6].

There exists a variety of C source code generators developed in different computer algebra systems (e.g., the Maple libraries MacroC [4], and Mascotte [16]). MuPAD itself implements in its standard library a procedure that offers the possibility to generate C source code. However, this procedure offers little control on the resulted code, and no static evaluation facilities.

5   Using SYDNA: A Case Study

A complex physical application in Stellar Astrophysics is under development with SYDNA. The application involves computing equilibrium models for solar and stellar interiors, determining their small oscillations around the equilibrium states, and solving several inverse vibration problems for these systems. The aims of these calculations are to determine the most adequate computational methods for modeling stellar interiors and to extract as much information as possible from the inverse problems.

In the development of this application SYDNA proves its value: most of the derivations require computer algebraic manipulations, the derived problems have to be solved numerically, from one problem to the other many of the methods can be reused.

We do not intend to detail here the discussion of the structure of this application. As a matter of fact, many of the physical complications involved by modeling these systems are not yet taken into account. However, we will use a small part of its MuPAD/SYDNA implementation to sketch the way a specific SYDNA program should look like.

The equations governing the structure and evolution of spherically symmetric stars [13] can be put in the form:

$$\frac{\partial f}{\partial x} = \mathrm{N}(f, \mathrm{D}_{it}(f), p(x, f)), \tag{1}$$

where N is a nonlinear operator and D_{it} is a multiple derivative operator w.r.t. the temporal variable; the unknown functions f are physical parameters of the stellar interior,while p are state parameters of the stellar material (e.g., density, opacity).

We note that the specific form of these equations constitutes the central information for all the direct and inverse modeling steps. Except for some physical intricacies, the form of the problems that have to be solved can be derived automatically using simple Computer Algebra techniques.

The first step of the process implies building an equilibrium model, then deriving and solving a set of linear oscillation equations for the given system. The final step of this application consists in formulating an inverse problem that uses the differences between the computed eigenvalues and those obtained from observations to improve the values of the parameters p.

The MuPAD program that performs the symbolic and numerical procedures required for the first stage of the application should have the following structure:

```
Equilibrium:=proc()
.... # derives the equilibrium equation #
```

```
LWE:=proc()
... # derives the linear wave equations #

loadlib("SYDNA"):
# ... setting SYDNA variables ... #

Sample:=proc
( eqs, # general problem - list of for equations#
  unkf, # list of unknown functions #
  unkf0, # list of unknown functions for the equilibrium problem #
  bc0, # list of boundary conditions for the equilibrium problem #
  unkf1, # unknown functions for the problem of small prturbations #
  bc1, # list of boundary conditions for the oscillation problem #
  x, # spatial variable #
  t, # time variable #
  omega # eigenvalue variable #
)
local eqs0, # equilibrium equations #
      eqs1, # oscillation equations #
      prob0, prob1, geometry, dgeometry,
      epsilon, ndiv, y0_list, dy_list, omega_i, i;
begin
    STATIC_EVALUATION(eqs, unkf, unkf0, bc0, unkf1, bc1,
        eqs0,eqs1,prob0,prob1, geometry, dgeomtry);

    EVALUATE(y0_list:=[y0.i $i=1..nops(eqs)]);
    EVALUATE(dy_list:=[dy.i $i=1..nops(eqs)]); # forces evaluation #

    TYPE(y0_list, ARRAY[DOUBLE], 1000); # type declarations #
    TYPE(omega_i, ARRAY[DOUBLE], 100);
    TYPE(dy_list, ARRAY[DOUBLE], 1000, 100);

  # equilibrium problem #
    eqs0:=Equilibrium(eqs, unkf, unkf0, x, t);

    prob0:=SYDNA::IDiffEqProb(eqs0,bc0);
    geometry:=SYDNA::GetGeomtry(prob);
    dgeometry:=SYDNA::EqualSpaced(geomtry); # discrete geometry #
    dmethod:=SYDNA::FiniteDifferences1(prob);
    lmethod:=SYDNA::GaussSeidel();
    prog0:=SYDNA::ProblemSolve(prob, dgeometry, dmethod, lmethod);
                                            # program skeleton #

    # ------------------------------------------------------------------- #
    # these lines will not be statically evaluated, they will produce code #
    user_print("EQUILIBRIUM PROBLEM");
    user_read("Introduce the number of intermediate points ", ndiv);
    user_read("Introduce the convergence ratio ", eps);
    EVALUATE(prog0::generate(prog0(y0_list,[ndiv],[eps])));
                                            # forces static evaluation #
    syplot2D(y0_list,"PLOT0.MU");
    # ------------------------------------------------------------------- #

  # Small oscillation problem #
    eqs1:=LWE(eqs,eqs0,unkf0,unkf1);
    prob1:=SYDNA::IDiffEigProb(eqs1,bc1);

    # .................................. #

end_proc:

# ... CodePAD settings ... #
CodePAD::generate(Sample,"SAMPLE.C"):

# -- after compiling and running SAMPLE.C, postprocessing: -- #
read("PLOT0.MU"); # plots the equilibrium solution #
```

For the sake of mathematical simplicity, we considered that the equilibrium model could be derived by solving a BVP. In the real physical case however, the equilibrium model can be directly obtained only for the "zero-age" star and then the slow evolution of this model during the star's life should be computed.

We have to observe that the concrete equations (1) are given as parameters of the function Sample. They are specified only once in the whole program. Thus, adjusting the program for a completely different set of equations would be immediate.

6   Conclusions, Status of the Project and Further Work

We have presented the structure of a system that combines computer algebra capabilities, generic programming, transformational refinement techniques and code generation. The aims of the design were:

- to allow the specification of mathematical problems in a natural notation
- to implement mathematical algorithms in their most general perspective
- to increase the reusability of the code
- to provide a set of protocols (functor interfaces) on which cooperative software development can be based
- to eliminate run-time overheads determined by the generic setting
- to globally optimize the programs by incorporating problem-specific and method-specific information.

Although the design of the system is founded on a clear separation of different stages of code design and implementation (such as algebraic computations, symbolic manipulation or numerical algorithms), its strength is shown especially in those applications that heavily rely on all these steps. An important example of this kind is given by the B-spline discretizations, a library that is under development at the moment.

The hard constraints imposed by the functor hierarchy are susceptible to discourage a part of its prospective users. The only chance to surpass this disadvantage is to have a structure and interface that are as close as possible to the vision and requirements of their users.

At the present time the system is tested, documented and prepared for its first public release, which is expected for the end of April 1999. SYDNA will be available for download from http://members.xoom.com/raduz/SYDNA.

Although SYDNA is already a complex program package, we consider that it is only in its infancy. Significant developments are expected in both its interface and the algorithm library. The discretization system is based on solid concepts, but a significant extension is required. The structure of the algorithm database allows a decision support system to be implemented; this is another step that is intended to be taken in the near future.

Acknowledgements. This paper was partially supported by Romanian National University Research Council (CNCSU) under the grant 176-16/1998. The author wishes to thank the referee for pointing out a valuable source of information for this project.

References

1. Akers, R. L., Baffes, P., Kant, E., Randall, C., Steinberg, S., Young, R. L., Authomatic synthesis of numerical codes for solving partial differential equations, Math. Comp. Simulation, **45** (1998) 3–22
2. Programming in Ada, 4th edition, Addison-Wesley, Reading, MA, 1994.
3. Bastion, P., Birken, K., Johansen, K., Lang, S., Neuss, N., Rentz-Reichert, H., Wieners, C., UG - A Flexible Software Toolbox for Solving Partial Differential Equations. Computing and Visualization in Science, **1** (1997) 27–40
4. Capolsini, P., MacroC, C code generation within Maple, INRIA Research Report (1992)
5. Drescher, K., Axioms, Categories and Domains, Automath technical report 1, (1997)
6. Efremidis, S., On Program Transformations, Ph.D. thesis, Cornell U. (1994)
7. Fitzpatrick, S., Harmer, T. J., Steward, A., Clint, M., Boyle, J. M., The automated transformation of abstract specifications of numerical algorithms into efficient array processor implementations, Sci. Comput. Programming, **28** (1997) 1–41
8. Fuchssteiner, B., Drescher, K., Kemper, A., Kluge, O., Morisse, K., Naundorf, H., Oevel, G., Postel, F., Schulze, T., Siek, G., Sorgatz, A., Wiwianka, W., Zimmermann, P., Hillebrand, R., MuPAD User' Manual - MuPAD Version 1.2.2, John Wiley and Sons , New York, 1996
9. Gallopoulos, E., Houstis, E., Rice, J., Computer as thinker/doer: Problem-solving environments for Computational science, IEEE Computational Sci. and Eng., **1** (1994), 11–23
10. Grunz, D., Monagan, M., Introduction to Gauss, MapleTech **9**, (1993), 23–35
11. van Engelen, R., Heitlager, I., Wolters, L., Cats, G., Incorporating Application Dependent Information in an Automatic Code Generating Environment, Proceedings of the 11th ACM International Conference on Supercomputing, 1997, Vienna, 180–187
12. Jenks, R.D., Sutor, R.S., AXIOM: The Scientific Computation System, Springer-Verlag, New-York, 1992.
13. Kippenhahn, R., Weigert, A.: Stellar Structure and Evolution, Springer-Verlag (1989)
14. Milner, R., Tofte, M., Harper, R., The Definition of Standard ML, MIT Press, Cambridge, MA, 1990
15. Schreider, W., A Generic Programming Environment for High-Performance Mathematical Libraries, (1998) http://www.risc.uni-linz.ac.at/projects/basic/hpgp/papers/overview/paper.ps.gz
16. Vieville, T., Mascotte: A few Maple Routines for Real-Time Code Generation, INRIA Research Report, (1996)
17. Wolfram, S., Mathematica - A System for Doing Mathematics by Computer, Addison-Wesley, 1988

Author Index